Intermediate GNVQ Business

Helen Turner and Francis Nicholson

MACMILLAN

© Helen Turner & Francis Nicholson 1996

All rights reserved. No reproduction, copy or transmission of this publication may be made without written permission.

No paragraph of this publication may be reproduced, copied or transmitted save with written permission or in accordance with the provisions of the Copyright, Designs and Patents Act 1988, or under the terms of any licence permitting limited copying issued by the Copyright Licensing Agency, 90 Tottenham Court Road, London W1P 9HE.

Any person who does any unauthorised act in relation to this publication may be liable to criminal prosecution and civil claims for damages.

First published 1996 by
MACMILLAN PRESS LTD
Houndmills, Basingstoke, Hampshire RG21 6XS
and London
Companies and representatives
throughout the world

ISBN 0–333–62491–2

A catalogue record for this book is available from the British Library.

10　9　8　7　6　5　4　3　2　1
05　04　03　02　01　00　99　98　97　96

Printed in Hong Kong

Acknowledgements

The authors and publishers wish to thank the following for permission to use copyright material: Advertising Standards Authority for their logo; Amtrack Express Parcels Ltd for the reproduction of an advertisement; Bank of Scotland for the Centrebank Division's 'Declaration of Service'; British Railways Board for an adaptation of their 'Citizen's Charter', Customer Care Service; Cereal Partners UK for their Shreddies guarantee panel; CIPFA, The Chartered Institute of Public Finance and Accountancy for data concerning UK Government Expenditure for 1990/91; Creda Ltd for their CredaCare guarantee; Department of Employment for the Job Centre logo; The Guardian for 'Credit card users tighten up or drop out', *Guardian*, 2.4.94, Ian Wylie, 'Helping hand for beleaguered charities trying to make the most of their money', *Guardian*, 2.4.94, and 'Complaints' graphic by Steve Villiers, *Guardian*, 24.5.94; Hilton National for their guest questionnaire; Ewan MacNaughton Associates on behalf of the Telegraph PLC for graphic from 'Many decide that plastic's not so fantastic', *Daily Telegraph*, 9.4.94, an extract from Robert Reid and Peter Almond, 'Pregnancy major awarded £300,000', *Daily Telegraph*, 9.4.94, adapted material from 'Tribunal finds in favour of employee who closed door', *Daily Telegraph*, 9.4.94, and 'Licence to increase chances of success', *Daily Telegraph*, 13.4.92, copyright © The Telegraph PLC, London, 1994, 1992; The Controller of Her Majesty's Stationery Office for data from Department of Employment figures, and tables and data from *Social Trends 1992* and *Regional Trends 1992*, Crown copyright; National Council for Vocational Qualifications for their logo; New Scientist for material from Charles Arthur, 'The future of work', *New Scientist*, 16.6.94; Newspaper Publishing PLC for 'Job bar on headteacher "was racist"', *Independent on Sunday*, 17.4.94, and 'Small is beautiful at UK's new theme park', and accompanying photo by Glynn Griffiths, *Independent*, 7.4.94; Solo Syndication and Literary Agency Ltd for 'Big smiles for a better service', *Evening Standard*, 19.4.94, 'Computer firm's ideal programme', *Evening Standard*, 19.4.94, 'Lorraine is pretty generous', *Evening Standard*, 19.4.94, 'Keeping Parents Happy', *Evening Standard*, 19.4.94, and 'Daisy in control', *Evening Standard*, 19.4.94; Times Newspapers Ltd for Kirstie Hamilton and Sean Ryan, 'Persil soap war hits 11m homes', *The Sunday Times*, 12.6.94, graphic from 'Who's who in the Virgin Empire', *The Sunday Times*, 5.6.94, caption on photo of Lego theme park in Windsor, *The Times*, 7.4.94, Tim Jones, 'Underground faces huge claims after 100,000 left stranded', *The Times*, 7.4.94, 'Notebook newcomer ups stakes' from Bits and Bytes section of *The Sunday Times*, 13.2.94, and Christopher Lloyd, 'BT television link to offer video shopping', *The Sunday Times*, 29.5.94, copyright © 1994 Times Newspapers Ltd; Uniglobe Travel (UK) for their advertisement.

The following photograph sources are acknowledged: Aerofilms Limited p. 1; Alton Towers p. 37 right; British Coal p. 44 bottom left; British Telecommunications plc p. 37 top left; John Cocks p. 156; Peter Dare-Bryson p. 95 middle; Dept of Employment pp. 51, 113; Ford Motor Company Limited pp. 18, 37 middle, 44 top middle, 53; the *Independent*/G. Griffiths p. 62; Michael Jolly p. 227; Sarah Lindsey pp. 2, 9, 25, 27, 35, 37 middle and right, 44 all except top left, bottom left and bottom middle, 50, 53, 95 left and right, 137, 138, 150, 167, 171, 194, 209, 223, 227, 231, 234, 244; Lionel Photo p. 242; Yvonne Locker pp. 44 bottom middle, 79, 224; Marks & Spencer pp. 171, 231; Tesco Creative Services pp. 44 top left, 151; Andrew Wiard pp. 99, 100.

Every effort has been made to trace all the copyright holders but if any have been inadvertently overlooked the publishers will be pleased to make the necessary arrangement at the first opportunity.

Contents

The aims of this book *v*
Preface *vi*
Introduction *vii*
    What is a GNVQ? *vii*
    Why take a GVNQ? *vii*
    Terminology *vii*
    Assessment *viii*

Unit 1: Business organisations and employment *1*
    1.1   Explain the purposes and types of business organisations *1*
           Industrial sectors *18*
           Types of business activity *20*
           Multiple choice *24*
           Short answer *24*
    1.2   Examine business location, environment, markets and products *25*
           The scale and scope of organisations *29*
           The product of business organisations *33*
           Types of market *35*
           New products that meet identified markets *36*
           Multiple choice *38*
           Short answer *39*
    1.3   Present results of investigation into employment *39*
           Types of employment *40*
           Features of employment *44*
           Levels of employment locally and in another region *50*
           Effects of technology on physical conditions and levels of employment *56*
           Employment findings *57*
           Unit activity: Woodentops Incorporated *64*
           Multiple choice *65*
           Short answer *66*
    Unit test *67*
    Key terms *69*

Unit 2: People in business organisations *71*
    2.1   Examine and compare structures and working arrangements in organisations *71*
           Organisational structures *72*
           Working arrangements *75*
           Differences in working arrangements *77*
           The influence of different structures on working arrangements *78*
           Departments within organisations *80*
           Different structures and departments within business organisations *94*
           Changes in working arrangements *96*
           Multiple choice *98*
           Short answer *99*
    2.2   Investigate employee and employer responsibilities and rights *99*
           Employee rights and responsibilities *100*
           Employer rights and responsibilities *105*
           Legislation governing employee and employer rights *109*
           Multiple choice *112*
    2.3   Present results of investigation into job roles *113*
           Job roles in business organisations *114*
           The functions of different job roles *117*
           Tasks undertaken by different role holders *123*
    2.4   Prepare for employment or self-employment *126*
           Employment and self-employment *126*
           Opportunities for employment and self-employment and sources of information *127*
           Skills, abilities, strengths and weaknesses *128*
           Unit activity *130*

        Multiple choice *132*
　　Unit test *133*
　　Key terms *135*
Unit 3: Consumers and customers *137*
　　3.1　Explain the importance of consumers and customers *137*
　　　　Characteristics of consumers *138*
　　　　Trends in consumer demand for goods and services *145*
　　　　Causes of change in consumer demand for goods and services *147*
　　　　Multiple choice *149*
　　　　Short answer *150*
　　3.2　Plan, design and produce promotional material *150*
　　　　Objectives of promotional materials *150*
　　　　Constraints on the content of promotional materials *153*
　　　　Type of promotion *156*
　　　　Resources required to produce materials *161*
　　　　The potential of different media to produce promotional materials *165*
　　　　Multiple choice *169*
　　　　Short answer *169*
　　3.3　Providing customer service *170*
　　　　Customer needs *172*
　　　　Reasons to meet customer needs *180*
　　　　Business communication which meets customers' needs *181*
　　　　Dealing with customer complaints *191*
　　　　Legislation to protect customers *193*
　　　　Informing customers of their rights *202*
　　　　Multiple choice *205*
　　　　Short answer *205*
　　3.4　Present proposals for improvements to customer service *206*
　　　　Importance of customer service *206*
　　　　Monitoring customer satisfaction *209*
　　　　Improvements to customer services *214*
　　　　Unit activities *216*
　　　　Multiple choice *217*
　　　　Short answer *218*
　　Unit test *218*
　　Key terms *221*
Unit 4: Financial and administrative support *223*
　　4.1　Identify and explain financial transactions and documents *223*
　　　　Reasons for financial recording in business organisations *224*
　　　　Purchase transactions and documents *227*
　　　　Sales transactions and documents *230*
　　　　Payment transactions and documents *233*
　　　　Receipt transactions and documents *242*
　　　　Security checks *244*
　　　　Multiple choice *245*
　　　　Short answer *247*
　　4.2　Complete financial documents and explain financial recording *247*
　　　　Purchase documents *247*
　　　　Sales documents *250*
　　　　Payment documents *252*
　　　　Receipt documents *255*
　　　　Reasons for the correct completion of documents *257*
　　4.3　Produce, evaluate and store business documents *258*
　　　　Business documents *258*
　　　　Multiple choice *262*
　　　　Unit activity *263*
Guidance to students on portfolios *264*
Integrated activities *268*
Glossary of terms *286*
Solutions *288*
Index *289*

The Aims of this Book

The piloting of GNVQ programmes in some colleges in September 1992 marked the beginning of a major new initiative in education and training. It soon became clear that students and practitioners would need a radical re-think in terms of patterns of learning and modes of delivery.

It was perceived by the authors, themselves involved in piloting the new programmes, that it would not be viable to repackage old materials in the guise of GNVQ. Instead it has been necessary to start from scratch, allowing the internal structure inherent to GNVQs to dictate the format for this text.

GNVQ programmes are outcome-specific, so that accreditation is based upon a learner's ability to evidence understanding of the knowledge that underpins the competences of the GNVQ programme for the respective vocational area. It is the learner's responsibility to collect evidence relating to the performance criteria and the deliverer's responsibility to provide opportunities to the learner to demonstrate competence. It is vital, therefore, that supporting materials and activities relate directly to particular elements and performance criteria.

In this text the material is organised so as to correspond directly to GNVQ performance criteria. A system of numbering has been used such that *1.2.3*, for example, refers to Unit 1, Element 2, Performance criterion 3.

Preface

This book has been written to provide both students and tutors with a useful resource for an Intermediate GNVQ Business programme. Its content has been carefully organised to reflect the specific requirements of the award and reflects the need to develop and apply understanding against performance criteria. It offers all the essential underpinning knowledge for the Mandatory units as well as a wide range of assessment activities set within a realistic context. The content also includes a guide to GNVQs, a range of practise multiple choice papers and a glossary of terms. At the end of the book is a series of integrated assessment activities to be incorporated within learning programmes in the most appropriate manner.

The book may be read and studied in sequence or may be accessed and employed to reflect particular learning programmes. The content and activities for particular performance criteria and elements are readily identifiable. Where there are connections with related knowledge from other sections of the book, reference has been made.

The authors would like to acknowledge their gratitude to the following: the immeasurable help received from colleagues at Amersham & Wycombe College; the enduring patience of John Jackman and everyone at Macmillan; and most particularly the benevolent wisdom bestowed in large quantities throughout this endeavour by Peter Turner, to whom this book is dedicated.

Introduction

What is a GNVQ?

GNVQs are General National Vocational Qualifications.

They are *General* since they have wide application and are not specific to one particular job. A Business GNVQ is useful for working in a wide range of jobs, including accountancy, personnel, marketing, business, law, retail and production.

They are *National* because they have been written to national standards common across England and Wales.

They are *Vocational* because they relate to an area of employment, in our case Business. The knowledge and skills are those used by people at work.

They are *Qualifications* because they lead to a recognised and valued certificate.

Why take a GNVQ?

GNVQs allow students a lot of freedom.

Unlike more traditional qualifications there is no fixed limit on the time taken for completion. Individuals may work at their own pace.

There are levels to suit everyone – Foundation, Intermediate or Advanced. There are plans to introduce a higher level to replace HNDs.

There are no formal entry requirements. Any student with a reasonable chance of success may work towards the qualification.

There is the opportunity to choose the options which suit you best.

Students may progress from GNVQs to more training, further or higher education or into employment. The qualification is recognised by schools, colleges, universities and employers.

Terminology

There is some terminology or jargon used which it is important for you to understand. Getting to grips with this now will make it easier in the long run.

The Intermediate GNVQ Business is made up as follows:
    4 Mandatory (i.e. compulsory) units:
        Unit 1 Business organisations and employment
        Unit 2 People in business organisations
        Unit 3 Consumers and customers
        Unit 4 Financial and administrative support
    3 Mandatory core skills units:
        Communication
        Application of Number
        Information Technology
    2 Option units (students may choose from those available)

The content of the units has been written in a very precise manner. Each unit has a title which describes its content. The unit is then broken down into *elements*. The elements are the main topics within the unit. For example unit 1 is broken down as follows:

Unit 1   Business organisations and employment
    Element 1.1   Explain the purposes and types of business organisations
    Element 1.2   Examine business location, environment, markets and products
    Element 1.3   Present results of investigation into employment

Notice how the elements are numbered: 1.1, 1.2, 1.3. The elements of Unit 2 are numbered 2.1, 2.2, 2.3 and so on. Notice too that the elements are written as things which you must do, using words like 'investigate', 'explain', 'produce' and 'identify'.

The elements are broken down into *performance criteria*. These spell out in detail the requirements of the element. For example, Element 1.1 is broken down as follows:

Element 1.1
Explain the purposes and types of business organisations

Performance criteria:

- (PC) 1.1.1 Describe developments in industrial sectors
- (PC) 1.1.2 Explain the purposes of business organisations
- (PC) 1.1.3 Explain the differences between types of business ownership
- (PC) 1.1.4 Explain the operation of one business organisation

The performance criteria are often identified as 1.1.1, 1.1.2, 1.1.3 and so on, so that 1.1.3 is unit 1, element 1, performance criterion 3.

Finally, there are *range statements*, which indicate the breadth or the scope of the knowledge which must be demonstrated. For example, under Element 1.1 one finds:

range: industrial sectors: primary, secondary, tertiary

Introduction

Hence when explaining the purposes of different types of business organisations it is necessary to consider profit-making, public service and charitable purposes.

Assessment

It is vital that assessment covers all the criteria specified within the units. The complete performance criteria should be made available to you by your school or college. They will be a vital part of your programme of learning and collection of appropriate evidence. The evidence will be collected by carrying out the activities included in this book as well as those set by your tutor.

There are several key aspects to assessment:
- Portfolio of evidence
- Assessment activities
- External tests
- Action planning

Portfolio of evidence

The most important part of assessment is the student portfolio of evidence. In order to complete your programme of learning successfully you must compile evidence of competence for each performance criterion in the units of achievement. The portfolio is simply a large file in which to keep your work. Your tutor will help you with the process of collating appropriate evidence as you progress, including giving you a file and tracking documentation.

The evidence included in the portfolio may be:
- Written reports
- Letters
- Graphs
- Records of role play exercises
- Audio recordings
- Video tapes
- Pictures
- Diagrams
- Photos
- Records of oral presentations

Assessment activities

The activities in this book have been devised to include all the evidence you need for your Mandatory units and Core skills. Wherever a piece of work is set it should be clear which criteria are being assessed.

In each section of the book activities relate to the criteria of a particular unit. There are a number of small activities which relate to only one performance criterion. At the end of each element there is a larger activity which covers all the criteria from the element. Lastly, at the end of the unit there is a large activity assessing all the criteria from the whole unit.

In addition to these activities there are *integrated activities*, which assess criteria from a number of different units. The purpose of these is to demonstrate that aspects of business are interlinked. Your tutor should advise you which activities should be attempted.

The activities may take a number of forms, including:
- Assignments
- Case studies
- Role play exercises
- Time-constrained activities
- Continuous observation
- Projects
- Formal reports
- Simulations
- Group work

External Tests

Units 1, 2 and 3 are examined externally by a short one-hour multiple choice test. The object of these tests is to examine your understanding of the content of each unit. There are a number of opportunities throughout each year to sit these tests and your tutor will discuss with you appropriate dates. If you are unsuccessful on the first sitting you may have as many repeated opportunities as you need to re-sit. This will not affect your overall grade.

Practice questions have been included to help you with your revision.

Grading

At the end of your programme of learning your portfolio will be submitted to your school or college for grading. The three grades are:
- Pass
- Merit
- Distinction

The *minimum requirement* for a **Pass** is:
- Portfolio complete for all performance criteria across the whole range for:
  - 4 Mandatory units
  - 2 Option units
  - 3 compulsory core skills (communication, application of number, information technology) at the level of the award
- All external tests successfully completed

You may exceed the minimum requirement in a number of ways:
- Completing additional units
- Completing core skills to a level in excess of the award
- Providing evidence of action planning

Grades of **Merit** and **Distinction** are awarded on the basis of the quality of action planning shown in the Mandatory and Option units.

Action planning and grading

The *content* of your assessed work is judged either to show competence or not, by comparison with the requirements of the performance criteria and range statements.

Introduction

To secure a final grade of Merit or Distinction you must demonstrate higher levels of planning skills as well as greater skills in applying the knowledge and the terminology and concepts of business. For a **Merit** grade at least *one third* of your portfolio must show work of a Merit standard. Likewise, for a **Distinction** at least *one third* of your portfolio must show work of a Distinction standard.

For grading purposes at Intermediate level there are a number of *grading themes* and *grading criteria*, as follows:
- *Theme 1: Planning*
  1. Drawing up plans of action
  2. Monitoring courses of action
- *Theme 2: Information-seeking and information-handling*
  3. Identifying information needs
  4. Identifying and using sources to obtain information
- *Theme 3: Evaluation*
  5. Evaluating outcomes and justifying approaches
- *Theme 4: Quality of outcomes*
  6. Synthesis
  7. Command of 'language'

The requirements for a Merit are that these skills are consistently shown independently by the student in dealing with a series of discrete tasks.

The requirements for a Distinction are that these skills are consistently shown independently by the student in dealing with complex activities.

A record should be made by your tutor on each piece of your assessed work indicating your performance against each of these grading criteria, where appropriate, at either Merit or Distinction.

Advice for achieving Merit and Distinction grades

Theme 1: Planning
You will need to be able to demonstrate that you can plan and prioritise tasks. This means that you need to determine exactly what you need to do to meet the requirements of the activity and decide the order in which those targets should be met. Part of the planning must involve checking the performance criteria and range statements (otherwise how else will you know how much to do?). You should then set yourself realistic dates and times by which you expect to meet your deadlines. The action plan should read like a set of instructions to yourself about how you intend to complete the activity. The more detail you can include the more effective your planning will be. You may choose to use the following format:

Activities to be carried out to meet the requirements of the assignment	Date/time to be achieved	Date/time actually achieved
1.		
2.		
etc.		

Your action plan might show the following things:

- What you are expecting to produce at the end (a formal report, a questionnaire, a three-minute radio play, a film, a computer program etc.).
- Information sources you think may be useful and what you hope to learn from them.
- People and organisations you may need to write to, telephone, visit etc., and what you hope to get from them.
- Equipment you may need to use (computer, printer, CD-ROM, video monitor, calculator, video camera, stencils, pair of compasses etc.) and why.
- Materials you may need (cardboard, paints, transfers, video or audio tape, clay, wood etc.) and for what purpose.
- Things you may need to check up on (how to write a report, draw a graph, use a computer, work out a percentage etc.).
- How you plan to put the project together.
- The methods you will use to check that you are doing the right thing.
- What you may do if things do not go according to plan (alternative courses of action).

The action plan should be forward-looking. It should be done before you start the activity. It is **not** a record of what you did, but a plan of what you think you will have to do.

You will also need to show that you can **monitor** what you do as you progress. The best way to do this is to record underneath each of your own targets and deadlines what happened as you tried to carry out your action plan. Sometimes things will go according to plan. Sometimes things will go better than planned. And sometimes there will be problems. For the purposes of monitoring it doesn't matter, as long as you record what happens. In some cases this may mean that the rest of your plan needs changing. You can record things like:

- The places you visit
- The information sources you use and what use (if any) they are
- The experts you talk to
- The steps you go through piecing the information together
- The help (if any) you ask for
- The help (if any) you get
- The class notes you find useful and those you do not
- How well you are progressing
- How easy or difficult the tasks are
- How well or how badly you are meeting the performance criteria and range statements
- Reasons why things are not going according to plan (for better or for worse)

Theme 2: Information-seeking and information-handling
This can be broken down into three stages:
- Identifying the information sources you might need
- Using information
- Establishing the validity of information

Introduction

Firstly, then, you should list all the sources of information you think may be of use:
- Books
- Leaflets
- Brochures
- Posters
- Videos
- TV and radio programmes
- Tapes
- CD-ROM files
- Journals
- Newspapers
- Experts
- Organisations

There is a clear overlap with *Theme 1: Planning* here. It is perfectly acceptable to include all the likely sources of information in your plan of action. Remember that it is not only what you know that is important. Knowing where to find information is equally important, and it is this that you are trying to show.

Secondly, you need to show that you can make proper use of the information. You need to record what information you have used and how you used it. This will probably require a *bibliography*, which is a detailed list of all sources used, including authors, dates, and even chapters and pages of interest. If, for example, you use a newspaper article there is no need to include the whole article. You should simply record the name of the article, the name of the newspaper and the date of publication. To show how you used the information you might record that you:
- Read through completely making notes
- Skim-read for points of interest
- Used the index to find the useful facts
- Took sections of information and wrote a summary
- Used direct quotes from the information
- Read through and asked for assistance on pieces you did not understand
- Took figures from a book and draw graphs, tables, diagrams etc.
- Took a definition from a dictionary

You can record all of these things as part of your ongoing monitoring.

Above all, it is important that you are able to use information with some measure of judgment. You do not simply include every piece of information you happen to research. You do not copy out long sections of text books. You do not include leaflets, brochures, articles etc. in your work just for the sake of it.

For each piece of information you must ask yourself:
- Is it relevant to what I am doing?
- Is it reliable?
- Is it up-to-date?
- Can it be supported by other sources?
- Is it less detailed than I need?
- Is it more detailed than I need?

You need to record the steps you went through to check all these things. This too can be part of the ongoing monitoring.

You should then, when using the information:
- Express things in your own words
- Use quotation marks where you borrow directly from other sources
- Quote all your sources
- Refer to any diagram, table, article, appendix etc. (otherwise there is no point in including them)

Theme 3: Evaluation

There are two parts to this: **evaluating** outcomes and **justifying** particular approaches to tasks.

The best way to evaluate your work is against the measures by which it will be assessed: the performance criteria. Does the work meet the performance criteria? You must check. The best way to show that you have checked is to show in the work the places where particular criteria are met. In the margin you can write 1.2.4, for example, to show that that section relates to Unit 1, Element 2, performance criterion 4. When you have done this you can record that you have done it in your monitoring.

You must also evaluate alternatives. This means considering other ways in which you might have met the criteria. You should suggest improvements which could be made to your work in terms of layout, content, style, presentation, format, and so on (although by this stage you should be convinced that all the criteria have been met – if they have not then the work will be less than satisfactory, requiring further work).

Lastly, you need to reflect on your approach to the work. You can ask yourself questions like:
- Was my time management weak, okay, excellent?
- Was my planning realistic?
- Should I have used other information sources?
- Did I try to stick to my deadlines?
- What things caused me to change my action plan?
- How can my approach be improved?
- If I was doing this again what would I do differently?

Theme 4: Quality of outcomes

The grading criteria refer to **synthesis**. This means that you need to show that you are capable of linking knowledge, skills and understanding together in your work. It is a way of saying that you can complete the tasks to a professional standard. To put it simply: you know what to do, you know how to do it and you demonstrate that you have successfully completed everything to the required standard. You can apply your knowledge and skills to realistic situations.

Finally you are also required to demonstrate a **command of 'language'**. It is one thing to know the dictionary definition of 'private sector' or 'profit'. It is even more important to be able to use them in the correct context. It is again a question of being able to use the terminology of business to a professional standard. It is important therefore that you check that you fully understand all the key terms in the performance criteria and range statements. It may help to list them separately to be extra sure that you know them and that you include them in your work.

UNIT 1

Business Organisations and Employment

UNIT SUMMARY

This unit contains much that is introductory to the way business works, including important classifications of businesses which make it easier to understand their behaviour. It examines the reasons behind business activities and decision-making, including choice of location, type of product or service provided, and the influence of the market on business operations. Investigation of business activities covers the full range from local to multinational organisations. Employment is an important feature of business, and this unit examines employment in the United Kingdom, the different types of employment, working conditions, legal aspects, and so on, as well as the impact of new technology on working conditions.

ELEMENT 1.1
Explain the purposes and types of business organisations

Performance criteria

- (PC) 1.1.1 Describe developments in industrial sectors
- (PC) 1.1.2 Explain the purposes of business organisations
- (PC) 1.1.3 Explain the differences between types of business ownership
- (PC) 1.1.4 Explain the operation of one business organisation

Introduction
When you study a foreign language you must start by learning the basic words – the vocabulary of that language. It is the same in business studies. There are

Business Organisations and Employment

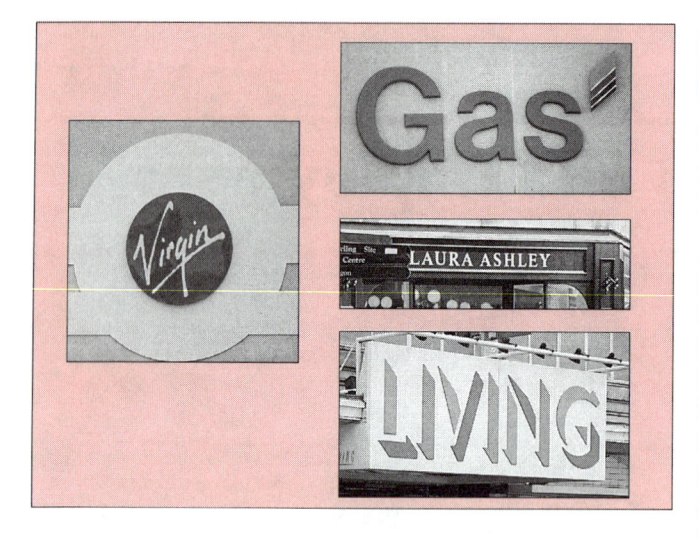

some terms and phrases that make up part of the basic language used when discussing business topics. It would be hard to make any progress unless these fundamental concepts are investigated at the start. For example, if we are talking about *business organisations* it is natural to ask, 'What is business?' and 'what is an organisation?'. For this reason we shall begin by looking at some of the most important concepts in business, beginning by looking at 'business' itself.

What is business?

The term 'business' is frequently applied to a large number of very different activities and organisations. It covers activities from simple exchanges between two parties to highly complex international transactions. It can be used to refer to organisations from elementary one-person firms to multinational corporations employing hundreds of thousands of people.

But what is it that links all of these affairs? What is it that they all have in common that allows us to call them all 'businesses'?

The simplest definition of business is this:

the buying and selling of goods and services

Therefore, any activity that includes the exchange of goods or services for financial return may be called *business*, and any organisation that involves itself in these activities may be called *a business*.

By *goods* we mean items that are made from a number of materials, such as clothes, newspapers and TV sets, as well as things that are grown or dug up, like vegetables or coal. *Services* are things that people ask other people to do for them, either because they cannot do them themselves or choose not to. Services include banking, health care, education and restaurants.

Examples of business activity include:

- Washing a car for spending money
- Importing cars to sell in this country
- Buying parts for construction of cars

Examples of business organisations include:

- A corner shop
- A supermarket
- A university

ACTIVITY

Below is a list of business activities. For each one identify an organisation which is involved in that business:

Activity	Organisation
Selling clothes	e.g. Top Shop
Health care	
Financial services	
Selling groceries	
Providing legal advice	
Extracting coal	
Manufacturing cars	
Producing records	
Selling environmentally friendly products	
Entertainment	
Selling goods to promote a cause	
Household cleaning	
Pest control	
Pharmaceuticals	
Security	
Dentist	
Film and video production	
Fast food	

What is an organisation?

It is not only in the world of business that we find organisations. We are all born into one, namely a *family*. Our birth may actually take place in one, a *hospital*. We receive our education in other organisations, *schools* and *colleges*, and spend our working lives in others. We cannot escape *organisations*, but what are they?

An organisation may be described as follows:

an individual or group of individuals joined together with a set of common objectives which they hope to achieve

An organisation has the following features:

- A set of rules
- A clear internal structure
- Roles and responsibilities for its members
- Common objectives

Organisations come in all shapes and sizes. They are not only found in the world of business, and examples of organisations include:

- Mosque
- Church
- Shop
- Night club
- Supermarket
- Taxi business
- Public house
- Publisher
- Pizza parlour

Business Organisations and Employment

ACTIVITY

Using the organisation of your school or college as an example, identify its main features under the headings of:
- Rules
- Structure
- Roles and responsibilities of members
- Objectives

Choose another organisation with which you are familiar (it may be a business you have worked for) and under the same headings compare it with your original findings.

Business organisations, therefore, are those groups of people involved in the buying and selling of goods and services

Why go into business?

People who go into business do so for a number of reasons. They may do so for the chance to be their own boss. They may wish to earn a lot of money or they may be content with simply being able to make ends meet. It might serve as a hobby or lead from a desire to provide a public service, for which money is not important.

It is not just people who go into business. The government also operates in the world of business, usually with the aim of providing a public service.

Other organisations are set up with the intention of raising awareness for a particular cause. Their aim is to collect money in order to improve the conditions for some under-privileged group of people.

There are then three main reasons for going into business:
- Profit-making
- Public service
- Charitable

Profit-making

For many organisations the main objective is to make a profit.

What is a profit?

On a day-to-day basis a business will make money through sales. By providing its product or service the business will earn an income from its customers.

However, a business will also incur a number of expenses through normal activities. These include:
- Wages
- Heating
- Rent
- Petrol
- Telephone
- Insurance

For a business to make a profit its sales must be bigger than its expenses:

Profit = Sales *minus* Expenses

If expenses are bigger than sales then the business will make a loss. Therefore if a business plans to make the largest profit possible, it must try to achieve the highest level of sales for the smallest amount of expense.

The reason that profit is regarded as important is because it belongs to the owners of the business. The bigger the profit the better. The owners may pay themselves out of the profits.

Private sector

Businesses whose main aim is to make a profit make up what is known as the *private sector*.

A private sector organisation is one which is owned by private individuals

This means that they are private business enterprises, run by individuals with an aim to make a profit.

This is not to say that profit is their only objective. Although the principal aim is to survive by making a profit, it is likely that the organisation will have many other objectives, including:
- Maximising profits
- Maximising sales
- Establishing a reputation
- Moving into new markets
- Providing customer care and service
- Adhering to health and safety regulations
- Adhering to legal requirements
- Respecting environmental factors
- Beating the competition

Examples of private sector organisations include:
- Marks & Spencer
- Virgin Atlantic
- ICI
- Eddie Stobart Ltd
- News International (publishers of the *Sun* and the *Times* newspapers)
- A local corner shop

Note: there may be one owner, or two or three or a hundred or a thousand, but unless it is owned by everyone equally then the organisation is in the private sector.

Accountability

Those who own the business have invested money in it and are entitled to a return on that money. Those who run the business (who may (or may not) also be the owners) are accountable to the owners to employ their capital wisely and to inform them of the state of the business. However, all organisations also have a wider responsibility to society and the environment.

ACTIVITY

1 What is the main objective of private sector organisations?
2 What other objectives do private sector organisations have?
3 Who are private organisations accountable to?
(1.1.2)

Business Organisations and Employment

Public service
Some organisations are set up in order to provide a public service.

What is a public service?
A public service is a benefit provided normally to improve the quality of life for the general public. Public services include:
- Local transport
- Health care
- Treatment of sewage
- Protection of civil rights

Public sector
Organisations whose main aim is to provide a public service are normally found in the *public sector*.

> *A public sector organisation is one which is managed by the government on behalf of the general public*

While they may need to make a profit in order to survive, this is not as important as providing the public with a service. Services offered by the public sector include:
- Health care by the National Health Service
- Education by schools, colleges and universities
- Sewage treatment by local authorities
- Protection of civil rights by the police force

These organisations are funded, at least in part, by the government using public money. Therefore they do not have to worry so much about making a profit. Their main concern is to provide the best possible service.

Examples of public sector organisations include:
- National Health Service
- Local councils
- Post Office
- Social services
- Education
- Fire brigade

ACTIVITY

From the list of organisations given below, state whether they are from the private sector or the public sector:

	Type of organisation	Chief aim	Public or private sector	Main source of finance
ICI	Large, located in more than one country	Profit	Private	Shareholders
British Coal				
British Rail				
NHS				
BUPA				
Boots				
Tesco				
British Telecom				
Abbey National				
British Gas				
Halifax				
BBC				
Window cleaner				
Johnson & Johnson				
ITV				
NatWest				

(1.1.2) (1.1.3)

Business Organisations and Employment

It is important to appreciate that organisations can move from the public sector to the private, or in the other direction. A lot of the thinking behind such changes is political and depends upon the government of the day. When an organisation moves from the public sector to the private sector the process is known as *privatisation*. Recent examples of organisations which have made this change include British Gas, the water authorities and National Power. The process of an organisation moving from the private sector to the public sector is known as *nationalisation*.

The process of privatisation is described in more detail later.

ACTIVITY

From the list of occupations given below decide whether they fall in the public sector or the private sector or both:
- Nurse
- Bus driver
- Miner
- School teacher
- Civil Servant

(1.1.2)

Charitable

There is a third group of organisations, whose main purpose is to act as a charity. Charities are set up to increase awareness of a particular cause, and then to raise funds from donations to improve the situation. They may carry out a number of business activities, such as running a shop or selling flags and badges. These activities in themselves aim to make a profit, but this is only to fund the charity's main activities.

Charities include:
- Greenpeace
- National Society for the Prevention of Cruelty to Children (NSPCC)
- Royal Society for the Prevention of Cruelty to Animals (RSPCA)
- Oxfam
- Cancer Research

In order to be recognised as a charity the organisation must apply for charitable status with the Charities Commission, operated by the government. Once officially recognised as a charity the organisation is no longer obliged to pay tax on its profits, so that its cause may receive maximum benefit.

For each of the three main purposes of businesses – profit-making, public service and charitable – there are a number of different types of organisation.

Private sector organisations

Individuals who risk their own money to set up new businesses in the private sector are known as *entrepreneurs*. They are an important provider of jobs. Before they make the decision to go ahead with their business ideas they must think carefully about what is involved.

ACTIVITY

Identify all the relevant factors that an entrepreneur should consider before going into business. Display this information on a flip chart and discuss your findings with other members of your group. *(1.1.4)*

Despite the wide variety of motives for going into business, it is very soon necessary to face harsh economic truths. In particular, if the business is going to survive in the long term it needs a regular source of finance. Borrowing from the bank, investors or personal reserves can only be a short-term solution. Hence for many businesses the main objective becomes that of making at least enough money to continue in business. The funds generated from trading can be put back into the organisation. Any extra profits can be kept by the owner or owners of the business.

Types of private sector organisation

Under the heading of 'Private sector organisations' there are a variety of different legal forms that a business may take. They differ according to the following important characteristics:
- The number of people who own the business
- The people who invest capital in the business
- The way in which the profits are distributed
- The liability of the owners
- The legal restrictions and requirements

There are five legal forms of private sector organisation:
- Sole trader
- Partnership
- Private limited company
- Public limited company
- Cooperative

The first four of these will be illustrated through a case study, Acorn Hi-Fi.

ACORN HI-FI: EPISODE 1
When Sanjar withdrew his savings and secured a bank loan he was finally able to realise a lifetime's ambition: to go into business as his own boss. A traditional 9–5 job had never suited him. Nor was he happy taking instructions from people who did not always know any more than he did. This was an opportunity to pursue his favourite pastime – music – because Sanjar's business was going to be a hi-fi retailer under the name 'Acorn Hi-Fi'.

He chose the name 'Acorn' because he knew that small acorns grew into large and mighty oak trees. He wanted his business to grow into a thriving organisation. He was worried that his business might be confused with a much more famous com-

Business Organisations and Employment

puting organisation. The small business adviser at the bank, however, told him that 'Acorn Hi-Fi' was distinctive, and he would have no problems using it as a trade name.

The business was a success. At times Sanjar felt a little lonely, having no one to really share ideas with. One thing he had not taken into account was how difficult it would be to find time to take a holiday. He also had the worry that if the business collapsed he might be left with nothing. However, it gave him great satisfaction to see his plans grow and flourish, and within two years he was keen to expand by opening a new store in a neighbouring town. The problem was that he did not have enough money. He also worried that even if he employed more staff he would be twice as busy with double the responsibility.

ACTIVITY

1 Why did Sanjar decide to go into business?
2 What factors did he need to take into account before going into business?
3 What are the main characteristics of a one-person business?
4 What problems did Sanjar face as a one-person business? How could he overcome these problems?
5 What external organisations exist to help small-business people like Sanjar?

(1.1.2) (1.1.3)

Sole trader

As the name suggests, a sole trader is a business owned and run by one person, although it is quite likely that others will be employed to assist in the day-to-day business. The sole trader provides personal capital (i.e. money) to set up the business, in addition to which extra funds may be borrowed from the bank or other sources. All profits generated by the business belong to the sole trader, but by the same token the losses are also that person's responsibility alone. A sole trader has *unlimited liability*, which means that, should the business fail and be unable to pay its debts, the sole trader's personal assets are at risk and may be sold to meet amounts owing by the business.

The benefits of being a sole trader include being able to run the business just as one chooses. There is no one else to say what to do or when or how – the sole trader is his or her own boss. There is also the satisfaction of achievement, of personal success in building a business from an original idea.

This does not suit all people, however, and the position of the sole trader may seem rather lonely. There is no one with whom to share responsibility, discuss ideas or (often significantly) to invest capital. Frequently, if a sole trader prospers and is looking for extra funds in order to expand, the individual will look to find a partner.

ACTIVITY

List the advantages and disadvantages of being a sole-trader.
(1.1.3)

ACORN HI-FI: EPISODE 2

The solution to Sanjar's problems came in the form of his friend, Sandra. Sandra had recently been made redundant and was looking for work. Her firm had given her a generous redundancy settlement and she was keen to invest it wisely. Sanjar suggested that they become partners and that Sandra should put her money into the business so that they could purchase the new premises. Through a solicitor they made the appropriate arrangements and Acorn Hi-Fi quickly expanded.

Sanjar was very pleased with the situation. Sandra had many good ideas about the running of the business and took responsibility for promotion and advertising, allowing Sanjar to concentrate on what he enjoyed most, buying hi-fi equipment from the suppliers. Sandra also had a head for figures and rapidly improved Sanjar's makeshift accounting system. They also worked out a holiday rota and Sanjar took his first long break in years.

Over the next five years the business continued to expand and Sanjar and Sandra took on two more business partners. It is true that occasionally they had disagreements, and compromises had to be reached, but by and large all the partners managed to bring new ideas and expertise to the business to strengthen it and enable it to grow further.

Unexpectedly, however, Acorn Hi-Fi had a bad year. They did not actually make a loss, but profits fell dramatically. Although things improved in the following year it made Sanjar think about the business. If the business failed completely then all of them would be in a very vulnerable position, standing to lose their cars and maybe even their homes. Sanjar wanted a way around this and thought about it for a long time.

ACTIVITY

1 When Sanjar and Sandra teamed up together what kind of a business had they formed?
2 What are the main features of this type of organisation?
3 How does Sanjar benefit from this new arrangement? In what ways does he lose out?

4 When forming such a joint business, what details should Sanjar and Sandra agree in advance?
(1.1.3)

Partnership

A partnership describes a business where two or more people have joined together with a view to making a profit. Their activities are regulated by the Partnership Act of 1890. Normally a partnership may not include more than 20 people, but some partnerships, such as accountants, surveyors and estate agents, may have more than 20 partners.

A partnership may choose a trading name, such as 'Wycombe Washers', or use the names of the partners, like 'Smith and Jones'. It is also common to see partnerships use '& Co.' and, for a family business, '& Sons'. It is important to remember that '& Co.' does *not* signify a limited company.

ACTIVITY

If you were going into business with other people as partners, what details would you want to agree before you started? List as many as you can with the reasons for their importance.
(1.1.3)

Partnership agreement

Partnerships usually commence with the drafting of a *partnership agreement*. This will normally cover the following matters:
- How much capital each partner will contribute
- How much interest (if any) each partner will receive on their capital
- How much interest (if any) each partner will pay on monies drawn from the business (known as 'drawings')
- How much salary (if any) partners will receive
- What share of the profits or losses each partner will receive

The Partnership Act rules that in the absence of a partnership agreement profits will be shared equally and no interest is receivable on capital or payable on drawings. However, amounts left in the business as a loan may receive 5% interest.

One of the advantages of forming a partnership is the increased capital available to fund the business. It also gives the partners a chance to specialise in their own areas of interest, swap ideas and share responsibility.

Like a sole trader, a partnership has unlimited liability, which means that the partners risk their personal assets should the business fail. The partners' liability for losses is in the same ratio as their share of the profits. If any partner is unable to meet his or her liabilities, the debts become the responsibility of the other partners.

ACTIVITY

List the main advantages and disadvantages of a partnership.
(1.1.3)

ACORN HI-FI: EPISODE 3
Eventually Sanjar came up with a solution to the problem of unlimited liability. His idea was to turn Acorn Hi-Fi into Acorn Hi-Fi Ltd. The partners could form a limited company and become company directors. Their personal belongings would no longer be at risk. There would be other advantages too. Being able to call themselves 'Limited' would have a certain amount of prestige attached to it and would be likely to attract bigger sales and allow more generous terms from suppliers. Also, if they needed to, they could invite other friends or family members to buy shares in the company and enable the business to grow further.

The partners readily agreed to Sanjar's suggestion and, after a lot of paperwork, Acorn Hi-Fi Ltd was born. This brought new responsibilities with it. Sandra was no longer free to prepare the accounts in any way she chose, but had to follow stringent guidelines and allow the books to be checked by an external accountant. When the accounts were prepared they had to be submitted for inspection to the Registrar of Companies and the public. Other records had to be maintained and the directors, as they now were, were obliged to have an Annual General Meeting.

Despite the restrictions it was generally felt that it had been a good move. Some relatives did invest in Acorn Hi-Fi Ltd, and over the next 15 years they were able to open branches in many towns and cities. At times, Sanjar felt that the organisation he had created was bigger than he was and he was no longer able to control it exactly as he would wish. But this did not stop him from taking the next and greatest step.

ACTIVITY

1 What reasons did Sanjar have for changing the organisation again?
2 What factors would he need to consider and discuss at the start?
3 How did Sanjar and the other partners gain by the new arrangement? How did they lose out?
(1.1.2) (1.1.3)

Business Organisations and Employment

Limited liability company

The chief problem with the two types of business organisation already mentioned is their *unlimited liability*. Businesses can overcome this by forming a limited company. The word 'limited' here refers to the limited liability. This means that those who have invested money in the company, the shareholders, do not risk losing their personal belongings – house, car, yacht. The most they stand to lose is the amount they originally invested. This is possible because, in law, the company is regarded as a separate entity from the people who form and manage the company, and therefore it is the company itself which is liable for the debts rather than the investors.

It is a common practice to talk about any business as a 'company', but this is confusing and should be avoided. The word 'company' should only be used to refer to a limited liability company.

There are two kinds of limited liability company, both of which are regulated by the Companies Act 1985–91: a Private Limited Company (abbreviation Ltd), which is normally a small affair consisting of family and friends, and the larger Public Limited Company (abbreviation plc), which is a company that may advertise its shares for sale to the public. Most, but not all, public limited companies are 'quoted' on the Stock Exchange, where their shares may then be bought or sold at any time.

Companies are financed by shareholders and managed by directors on their behalf. The *shareholders* are the people who invest their money in the company in exchange for which they receive a share certificate, which is a piece of paper recording the interest in a fraction (or 'share') of the company. The *directors*, who may also be shareholders, are employed by the company to manage its affairs. They are appointed by the shareholders and may be voted out by a majority decision.

To be incorporated (i.e. to become a company), a business must prepare several documents, the most important of which are known as the *Memorandum of Association* and the *Articles of Association*. The Memorandum records the name of the company, its chief objectives, the address of its registered office, the amount of authorised share capital it will have and the number of shares this will be broken down into. The Articles are more mundane, recording the day-to-day rules and regulations for running the company. These documents are sent, together with an application form, to the Registrar of Companies, who will, if properly convinced by the Memorandum and Articles, issue a Certificate of Incorporation and a registered company number.

All companies must abide by the following regulations:

- The directors must hold an Annual General Meeting for all members (i.e. shareholders).
- Annual financial accounts must be produced in the specified format and be submitted no later than nine months after the end of the accounting year to the Registrar and then be available for public inspection.
- A register of all shareholders must be maintained.
- The accounts must be approved by an external auditor.

Private limited company (Ltd)

The kind of organisation that Sanjar has now formed is a private limited company (Ltd). The main difference between this and a public limited company (plc) is that there is no minimum requirement for the amount of start-up capital needed. Theoretically, a private limited company may be started with only £1 capital, although this is unlikely to be enough for any business. A private limited company is formed in the way described above and has the benefit of unlimited liability for its investors. However, the formal requirements of necessary paperwork and administrative procedures, plus the set-up costs, may deter partnerships from taking this step.

ACTIVITY

List the main advantages and disadvantages of forming a private limited company.
(1.1.3)

ACORN HI-FI: EPISODE 4

Acorn Hi-Fi was regarded by the business media as something of a phenomenon, a success story of epic proportions, and many investors were thought to be keen to get in on the action. As a private limited company, Acorn Hi-Fi Ltd could not advertise externally for investors, nor could they quote their share price or trade their shares on the Stock Exchange. And this is what Sanjar wanted to do. This, for him, would be the big time.

Hence, following a massive publicity campaign, Acorn Hi-Fi plc emerged on the Stock Exchange as one of the newest and most exciting public limited companies, as the chairman Sanjar reflected how from tiny acorns mighty oaks can grow.

ACTIVITY

1. What type of organisation had been formed?
2. How does this differ from a private limited company?
3. What benefits are there for Sanjar and the other company directors? In what ways might they lose out?

(1.1.3)

Business Organisations and Employment

Public limited company (plc)

The final form of Sanjar's business is a public limited company. It has the same benefits and weaknesses of companies already mentioned above. Furthermore, there is a minimum requirement for start-up capital. Currently this means that at least £50,000 must be made available by the organisation before it can become a public limited company. (This figure is subject to regular review by the Chancellor and may change from time to time.)

Public limited companies do have an additional benefit: their shares may be advertised to external investors, including quoting their share prices on the Stock Exchange.

It is very important to realise that, despite its name, a public limited company is not in the public sector. Like a private limited company, a public limited company is financed by individuals for profit. Sometimes thousands of individuals will buy shares in a plc, but this is not the same as *everyone* having an equal interest in the organisation, as is the case in the public sector. Therefore public limited companies fall within the *private sector*. It is called a 'Public' limited company because a plc, unlike a Ltd, may invite members of the public to buy shares in it.

	Private limited company	Public limited company
Abbreviation	Ltd	plc
Private or public sector	private	private
Minimum issued share capital	no minimum	£50,000[1]
Minimum number of shareholders	two	two
Minimum number of directors	one	two
May be quoted on the Stock Exchange	no	yes
Advertise externally for investors	no	yes

[1]Note: this figure changes from time to time according to the Chancellor's budget

ACTIVITY

From the lists of advantages and disadvantages that you have drawn up for sole traders, partnerships, and private and public limited companies, prepare a table that compares and contrasts the relative merits of all of these organisation types.
(1.1.3)

Comparison of principal types of private sector business organisation

ACTIVITY

Copy out and complete the following table:

	Sole trader	Partnership	Ltd	plc
Minimum number of members				
Maximum number of members				
Method of formation				
Liability – limited or unlimited?				
Who has control?				
Who provides the capital?				
Example				

(1.1.3)

Other private sector organisations

Cooperative

A cooperative is another form of business enterprise which can be categorised under the private sector. Cooperative trading is essentially a self-help system in which the members of the cooperative collectively contribute skills, resources, finance and labour with the aim of making and sharing the rewards of their efforts.

There are two kinds of cooperative, since the members may be either the producers or the consumers. Hence, in a *producer cooperative* those responsible for production set up an organisation for the direct marketing of products they make themselves. They share the risks and benefits of their endeavours in the form of wages and bonuses.

Business Organisations and Employment

Consumer cooperative organisations are those that have been established by the customers for the supply to themselves of the commodities they wish to consume. The profits are distributed to the consumers in the form of lower prices or tokens, such as dividend stamps, which may be exchanged for gifts or money.

Cooperatives share many of the same advantages as limited companies. Legally, workers' cooperatives may exist as partnerships (in which case liability is unlimited) or as companies (in which case liability is limited). Similarly, a cooperative elects a representative committee with responsibility for the day-to-day running of the business in much the same way as a board of directors. The members also keep close control over the activities of the organisation, with relatively little bureaucracy and administrative procedure.

There are many examples of cooperatives in existence and a range of activities in which they operate. Insurance services, housing associations and funeral services are examples where cooperatives are common. More recently, cooperatives have been formed in the mining and steel industries as small groups of workers have joined together in order to safeguard their jobs and continue in business.

Cooperating to compete

The basic principles of cooperative organisations are:
- A member's share of profit is based upon effort rather than money invested.
- Members are responsible for controlling and making decisions within the organisation.
- Membership is open to anyone on payment of the membership fee.

The advantages of a cooperative as a form of business are:
- A cooperative provides an opportunity to pool together skills, resources and investment, thereby maximising the contribution of all those concerned – *the whole is greater than the sum of its parts*.
- Membership is open to anyone – i.e. it is not restricted, as in a limited company.
- All members have the opportunity to participate in the management of the organisation.
- A return based on effort rather than financial investment helps to increase motivation and commitment to the organisation and the work undertaken.
- An organisation based upon a cooperative approach may result in greater loyalty to the organisation.

Cooperatives also have some disadvantages as business organisations:
- Members often lack the necessary management experience, and this can result in ineffective strategic planning and direction of the organisation.
- The raising of capital may be limited as it is restricted to the amount the members can raise – it is often difficult for cooperatives to attract the large professional investments that public limited companies do.
- For cooperatives to run effectively the members must all support the aims and objectives of the organisation. Disagreements and arguments may occur, which disrupt the smooth operation of the organisation.
- Lack of awareness by the public at large about cooperatives and the benefits they can bring to members means that the public are often unwilling to join cooperatives.

ACTIVITY

Review questions
1. List the basic principles on which all cooperatives are based.
2. What are the main difficulties facing cooperatives?
3. Outline the ways in which cooperatives differ from limited companies.
4. Why do cooperatives find difficulty raising finance?

(1.1.2) (1.1.3)

ACTIVITY

Undertake further research to identify examples of new cooperatives that have been established in the last five years.

Present your findings using a variety of visual methods, such as flip-charts, posters, handouts etc. You should also include a written summary for your portfolio.

The cooperative movement has a strong historical origin, beginning in the middle of the 19th century in Rochdale. Using the learning resource centre or library, research the story of the so-called Rochdale Pioneers who started the cooperative movement and the basis on which the first cooperative was formed.

(1.1.3)

Franchise

Organisations in the private sector may have the legal forms already discussed:
- Sole trader
- Partnership
- Private limited company
- Public limited company
- Cooperative

These organisations usually trade under their own names. Alternatively, an organisation may buy the right to use the name of an already-established business. This is known as a *franchise*. A franchise is where a business idea is shared and people rent the use of that idea. This means the business acquires the right to sell or produce a well-established product or

Business Organisations and Employment

service under a nationally, and sometimes internationally, known name. Examples of franchises include:

Body Shop
Dyno-Rod
Prontaprint
British School of Motoring (BSM)
Wimpy Bars

A distinction should be made between the *franchisor* and the *franchisee*. The *franchisor* is the person providing the right to trade using the brand name for that product or service.

The major advantage of the franchise system is that the entrepreneur has a tried and tested product or service to offer.

In return for a start-up fee and royalties the *franchisee* receives:
- Training
- Help with premises and fittings
- The right to use well-known logos and trade names
- Stock
- The exclusive right to trade in the franchise name over a certain territory
- Assistance with national advertising campaigns
- The benefits of belonging to a large organisation

The franchisor retains certain rights of control and supervision which may result in a franchisee being constrained in its activities.

The cost of a franchise can range from £3,000 to £200,000 or more, depending upon the size and the nature of the business. The franchisor may also demand a proportion of the sales or profits.

The advantages and disadvantages, to both the franchisee and the franchisor, are listed in the table below.

	Franchisee	Franchisor
Advantages	• Tried and tested product/service • Help with training • Business advice about location, premises, advertising, promotion, staffing, hours • Clearly defined location taking into account competition • Stock is supplied • Competitive rates of finance	• Less risk than expanding on one's own • More capital • Shared responsibility
Disadvantages	• Loss of control as the franchisor keeps control of some of business • Lack of flexibility – must use franchisor's trade name, stock, business practices, training etc. • Levy on profits or sales	• Loss of profits • Need for constant support to franchisee • Possible bad publicity for entire organisation if franchisee proves unsuitable

STRIPTREES

Saul had been employed by a local furniture manufacturer for 10 years as a craftsman joiner. As a result of the recent recession, sales of specialist furniture have fallen and all employees have received notice of a voluntary redundancy scheme. In return for taking voluntary redundancy the firm are willing to pay an enhanced redundancy pay of £6,000. Saul signed up immediately.

Scanning the local newspapers in an attempt to find alternative employment Saul saw an advertisement inviting people to buy a franchise in a pine-stripping organisation called Striptrees, at a price of £10,000. In return for this sum the organisation guaranteed help and advice in establishing the business, supply of equipment and stocks, support with advertising and marketing, including the right to use the corporation logo and trade name and a guaranteed regional market of 20 miles. In return Saul had to buy stock exclusively from Striptrees, operating in accordance with their codes of practice, and in addition pay an annual charge of £500 plus 10% of profits in the form of royalties to the franchisor.

Saul was keen to become self-employed, and felt that a franchise arrangement would provide the specialist business skills that he was lacking.

As a small business advisor for the local bank, you have been consulted by Saul for advice about the franchise and a possible business loan.

ACTIVITY

1. Referring to the Striptrees case study, identify the arguments for and against Saul going ahead with the franchise arrangement.
2. What would be the advantages and disadvantages to the franchisor?
3. In what ways, if any, would Saul benefit as a sole trader? In what ways might he be disadvantaged?
4. Based upon the facts, would you advise Saul to go ahead with the idea? Give reasons for your decision.

(1.1.3)

Business Organisations and Employment

✎ ACTIVITY

Read the article below on franchising and answer the following questions.
1. What examples of the services provided by franchise outlets are mentioned in the article?
2. Do franchises have lower costs than other businesses?
3. What are the major advantages to the franchisee of buying the franchise license?
4. Many people buying franchises are not experienced in business. What help do they receive?
5. What advice do the National Westminster and Barclays banks give to would-be franchisees?
6. How do the figures for the survival of franchises compare with other new businesses?
7. List some of the many trade names that are used under a franchise arrangement

(1.1.3)

✎ ACTIVITY

1. Why do you think that franchising has become a popular form of business activity in recent years?
2. Make a list of as many types of business organisation as you can, with examples, that currently run under a franchise arrangement.
3. What other kinds of business activity might lend themselves to becoming a franchise?

(1.1.3)

Licence to increase chances of success

LUCK keeps companies afloat. What distinguishes the companies still with us after a long period of recession is that they are lucky – they do not seem to have been hit by the unexpected.

Luck is a rare commodity but the harder a manager works the more he has of it. Napoleon demanded to have lucky generals around him, and with good reason. It is the mark of good management: a surprise-free environment, prepared or braced for the unexpected.

Franchise operations seem to provide a surprisingly large amount of luck to judge by their substantially better survival rates.

There is after all not a lot that sets franchise outlets apart from other businesses. They are just service outlets providing anything from hire cars to hair dressing, hamburgers to hotels.

They do not even have lower costs. Often they are in relatively expensive sites on high streets with costly business rates.

On top of that they have an extra cost other shops are spared – the royalty payable to the franchise provider. They must therefore have something extra to compensate and yet survive.

The people who grant the franchise licences would say that, offsetting the extra costs of royalties, there is the benefit of wholesale buying. With the greater buying power and distribution for many items, the franchisor can often get a better price for supplies than an individual shopkeeper could manage.

In addition to providing supplies of 'consumables', the franchisor also normally provides the outlet with advice and frequently accountancy help, plus guidance on publicity and efficient management.

Indeed, there is little point in paying out good money from hard-earned income merely for a name. The businessman might as well go off and start his own photographic processor, print shop, or plumbing company but for the initial advice on how to run the organisation. Brands bring luck as well.

Certainly some of the largest companies think so – those such as Forte, Allied Lyons, Grand Metropolitan, McDonalds and Kentucky Fried Chicken spend much time and money developing brands which they are now franchising.

But although brands may be valuable aids for getting market share, they are not indispensable.

What the dealer buys is experience and assistance. This is vital because most people taking up franchises are not experienced in running their own businesses.

They may be former bankers or miners, students, nurses or printers but there is nothing in their previous experience that is much help in running your own show.

National Westminster Bank, in its 10 points to remember for would-be choosers of a franchise operation, says: 'Make a personal assessment of the franchiser's management skills and track record. Be sure his management structure is sufficient to support his existing and future plans.'

It also advises talking to a number of franchisees in the proposed franchise. 'In particular, ask them about the accuracy of sales forecasts, cost projections and the quality of the back-up he provides.'

Barclays Bank, which has a six-point plan, also suggests talking to existing franchisees about the product or service to be offered. This is good advice because even franchises are no guarantee of success.

In general, the failure rate of franchises is dramatically lower than the equivalents outside – though that sort of statistic is highly affected by definitions. Company liquidation figures have been more than double the level of a year before, with about half the companies dying within the first five years.

By contrast, according to the British Franchise Association fewer than 10 p.c. of franchise operators go under.

Moshe Gerstenhaber, chairman of Kall-Kwik Printing, has been using this as a promotional feature. 'If ever evidence was needed to prove the merits of franchising, the present difficult trading conditions have to be an example.'

Its rival Prontaprint, which has 258 outlets and won the franchiser of the year prize, reckons to have kept the failure rate to less than 3 p.c. a year.

When the financial conditions turn hostile it takes all the luck in the world for businesses to stay alive, much less prosper.

It seems franchising has a garland of white heather and four-leaved clover but some of the operations have rabbits feet wearing horeshoes as well. It is worth searching them out.

Source: Daily Telegraph, 13 April 1992

Business Organisations and Employment

Charitable organisations

Finally, there is a third category of organisation, namely *charities*. These are publicly or privately funded organisations that are set up in response to a perceived need, and aim at producing publicity and raising finance to alleviate a particular problem. They rely upon donations from individuals and sometimes from governments.

Many charities have historical origins. For example Dr Barnardo and Lord Shaftesbury formed charitable organisations in the 19th century, and although the nature of the work undertaken by these two charities has changed they still exist and thrive today.

ACTIVITY

Carry on reading about charitable organisations on page 14 and then copy out and complete the following table:

Name of charity	Aims & objectives	Methods of raising finance	Promotional methods
Unicef			
Cancer Research			
Band Aid			
Oxfam			
Save the Children Fund			
Samaritans			
Barnado's			
Red Cross			
Greenpeace			
RSPCA			
Age Concern			
Anthony Nolan Trust			
Arthritis Research Council			
Royal National Institute for the Blind			
Terrence Higgins Trust			
Macmillan Fund			
Guide Dogs for the Blind			
Breakthrough			
Mencap			

Choose one of the organisations listed, or one of your own if you prefer, and write for further information about their aims and activities. From the literature you receive produce a 10 minute oral and visual presentation outlining the aims of the organisation, its historical origins, location, methods adopted for raising finance and promotional methods employed.

Include your notes for your presentation as evidence in your portfolio.

(1.1.2)

Business Organisations and Employment

Charities and relief agencies may be temporary in nature, in that they are established to provide funds for particular causes and once they have achieved their objective they disband. Examples include fund-raising for victims of disasters, such as relatives of the victims of the Lockerbie plane crash, and families of those who died in the Penlee lifeboat disaster.

Other charities have a long-term commitment to providing funds for a particular range of causes, e.g. the International Red Cross and the NSPCC.

Charities and relief agencies exist to support and extend the work carried out by the state, but in some areas if the funds were not provided by charitable organisations the work would not be carried out at all. Specialist staff are employed by many agencies and much of the research undertaken into particular issues provides governments with information about worldwide problems, which might otherwise go unnoticed. For example, the media publicity surrounding the African famine of 1985 made all governments aware of the problems of starvation and malnutrition in Ethiopia. Similarly, the political problems in war-torn Yugoslavia, as it was then called, and the need to care for the victims of that war, resulted in many world bodies becoming involved. These include the Red Cross, the NSPCC and the Office of the United Nations High Commission for Refugees (UNHCR). This is a specialised division of the United Nations which distributes relief supplies, including food, clothes and medicines, to people who have been displaced from their homes due to military threat or natural disasters.

The United Nations Children's Fund (Unicef) aims to help children in underdeveloped countries and/or those facing emergency situations. All of the United Nations agencies raise their funds by voluntary donations by member governments and from funds donated by other fund-raising organisations.

Methods for raising funds for all charitable organisations have changed considerably in recent years. Mass appeals using television and radio raise public awareness as well as large amounts of money. Many viewers and listeners are so deeply affected by reports of starvation, cruelty, environmental abuse and loss of life that they contribute large donations. The introduction of paying by credit card during mass appeals has also helped this process. Bob Geldof established the Band Aid trust with the aim of helping famine victims in Africa. Worldwide TV coverage resulted in over $70,000,000 (about £45 million) being raised. Other regular TV appeals include Telethon, Children in Need and Comic Relief.

Other methods of raising finance include private donations and the selling of merchandise such as Christmas cards, books and clothing.

The public sector

There are businesses whose main objective is to provide a service and which are operated by the government to do so. The areas in which the government funds businesses to provide a service fall into three main categories.

Capital investment Often these are industries that require heavy capital investment, which only the government can provide, such as coal and steel and the railways. This led to the formation of British Coal, British Steel and British Rail. However, in the 1980s British Steel was *privatised*. This means that it was sold by the government to private investors, turning it into a public limited company in the private sector. There are also plans to privatise British Coal and British Rail.

National security Then there are those services that, in the interests of national security, cannot be left to private individuals, such as the armed forces, nuclear power and the emergency services. By keeping them in the public sector the government maintains a close control over them

Essential services Finally there are services that are regarded as essential and should not be operated in the interests of profit. This last category includes sewerage, health service and education.

These industries and services belong to the nation as a whole and are operated on everyone's behalf by the government. Together they make up the *public sector*.

State-owned industries and services often charge for their services, but may be *subsidised* by the government. This means that the government provides finance, so that the prices may be set at a lower rate than would be the case in the private sector. In some cases, such as the National Health Service, there is no charge at all to the public.

The money for subsidies and funding public sector organisations comes from taxation. Because the public effectively finances these operations they are accountable for their actions to the public. They must endeavour to operate as efficiently as possible as well as providing the best possible service.

The public sector incorporates:
- Government departments
- State-owned industry or service
- Local government (municipal)

Major government departments

Department	Main responsibilities
Defence	Defence policy Armed forces
Agriculture, Fisheries and Food	Agriculture, horticulture, food and fishing industries, safety and quality of animals and foods
Education	Promotion of education in schools Monitoring the implementation of educational initiatives, such as the National Curriculum and GNVQs
Trade and Industry	Commercial policy Industrial policy Domestic and foreign trade
Employment	Employment policy and benefits

Business Organisations and Employment

Environment	Protection of physical environment Environmental planning Maintenance of public and government buildings
Health	Monitoring the National Health Service
Foreign and Commonwealth	External affairs, foreign policy, negotiations with other countries
Home Office	Internal affairs Administration of justice Law and order Immigration

ACTIVITY

1 Identify a recent copy of the government's current public expenditure plans
2 Produce a bar chart to reflect the total expenditure planned for each major area, as listed above
3 Write a summary underneath stating whether you agree with the allocation of money or whether there are areas which you feel should be allocated a larger proportion from the total budget. Remember: if this is the case you need to identify where you would reallocate the money from.
   Share your views with the other group members.
4 Your tutor will allocate you to one of the following groups:
   Defence
   Education
   Employment
   Health
In your group identify a list of arguments and points as to why you feel that the proposed budget should be increased for your area of expenditure.
   For the debate to be effective, you should also identify where the reallocation should come from and how you are going to counter the presentations from the other groups effectively.
   Remember that the total budget is fixed, and any adjustments have to be made within the given total.
   Present your views to the group and debate the issues.
   Summarise your position at the end of the debate.
   Your tutor will decide the final allocations based on how effective the issues were presented and debated.
(1.1.2) (1.1.3)

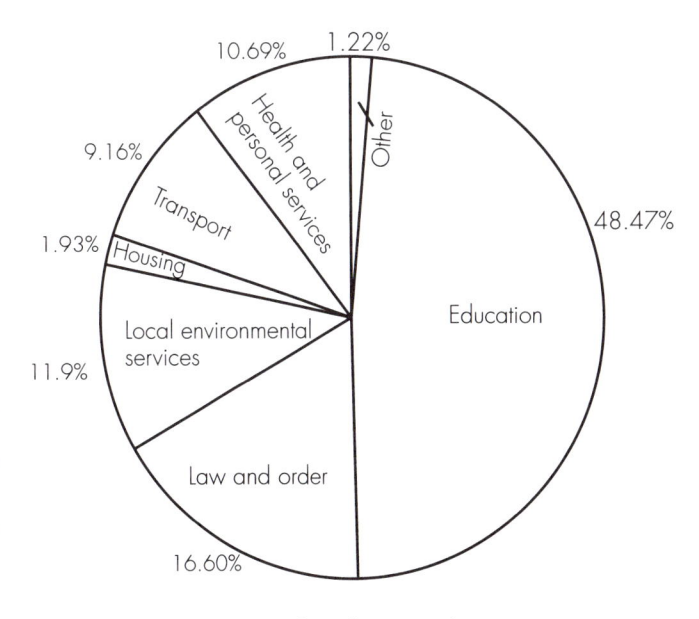

Total UK Government Expenditure for 1990/91
(*Source*: CIPFA, The Chartered Institute of Public Finance and Accountancy)

Pie chart values:
- Education 48.47%
- Law and order 16.60%
- Local environmental services 11.9%
- Health and personal services 10.69%
- Transport 9.16%
- Housing 1.93%
- Other 1.22%

Local government

Local government or local authorities also provide a range of services for the locality. The structure of local government and the provision of services varies from one region to another. In metropolitan districts and the London boroughs all the services are provided by one authority. Thus the authorities are responsible for:
- Planning
- Roads and traffic
- Housing
- Building regulation
- Checking safety in public places
- Refuse collection and disposal
- Education
- Social services
- Libraries
- Leisure and recreation

Metropolitan district councils exist in the urban areas of:
- Birmingham
- Manchester
- Liverpool
- Newcastle-upon-Tyne
- Sheffield
- Leeds
- Bradford

In non-metropolitan areas local authority services are provided at two levels. *County councils* are responsible for major services. These may include:
- Planning
- Roads and traffic
- Refuse disposal
- Police force
- Fire brigade
- Education
- Social services
- Libraries

District councils are responsible for:
- Housing
- Local planning
- Refuse collection
- Leisure and recreation

Business Organisations and Employment

ACTIVITY

Refer to a quality newspaper and identify three examples of different local and national business organisations operating within the wider economy.
1. Using the articles, produce a flip chart or poster displaying the information and highlight the key points.
2. Produce a brief summary beneath each article identifying:
   - The name of the organisation
   - The type of organisation (i.e. sole trader, partnership etc., private sector or public sector)
   - The types of external factors that have influenced the business activity
   - The reasons why the organisation has made the headlines

(1.1.2) (1.1.3)

ACTIVITY

Investigate local businesses by drawing a map of the high street of your nearest town, or a section of the high street, to include around 15–20 businesses. For the businesses included on the map determine what type of organisation they are (sole trader, partnership etc.). You should indicate these findings on your map using a suitable key (such as colour).

(1.1.4)

ACTIVITY

Visit your local district council and from leaflets and/or discussions with personnel determine the full range of services that they provide in the community. Design a poster that could be used by the council to inform the public of the variety of services available.

(1.1.1)

State-owned industry or service

Instead of a government ministry undertaking commercial work itself, the responsibility is sometimes given to specifically created public corporations. These are usually formed by the government passing a special law, which sets out the objects, powers, duties and responsibilities of the corporation. Examples include the Post Office and the British Broadcasting Corporation.

One of the main reasons for a government handing over some of its work to a public corporation is to put the activity under the control of a free and independent board of governors and managers who are not concerned with purely political issues.

ACTIVITY

1. Identify the services provided by the Post Office.
2. List, with reasons, why you think the Post Office should – or should not – provide the services. Would a privatised organisation provide a more efficient service?
3. Are there any services that the Post Office provides which now face competition from other organisations?

(1.1.2) (1.1.4)

ACTIVITY

The BBC is a public corporation, ultimately answerable to the Government. Independent Television operates as several public limited companies.

Compare the two services and answer the following questions:
1. Identify the sources of finance for the BBC and Independent Television.
2. Produce a list of key roles in the management of the two types of organisations.
3. To whom are they accountable?
4. Outline the similarities and difference in the provision of service offered by the two organisations.
5. Of the two types of organisation, which one, in your opinion, provides the best service and why?

(1.1.2) (1.1.3) (1.1.4)

Privatisation

The degree of mix between public and private sector enterprises reflects the political views of the government in power.

Since 1979, with the Thatcher and Major governments, we have seen many organisations transfer from public to private sector enterprises. For example, with what has become popularly known as the 'privatisation campaign' we have seen many nationalised industries that were in the public sector transfer to become public limited companies in the private sector.

The government's aim was to reduce the size of the public sector, expand the private sector and increase the number of shareholders by encouraging private investors to buy shares in the new companies.

In a famous budget speech the Chancellor of the Exchequer said in March 1986:

It is the long term ambition of this government to make the British people a nation of shareholders, to create popular capitalism in which more men and women have a direct personal stake in British business and industry.

Business Organisations and Employment

Examples of public sector industries that have been privatised and transferred to the private sector include:
- British Airways
- British Telecom
- British Steel
- The Rover Group
- British Gas
- British Water
- British Petroleum

More organisations are planned to be privatised in the near future.

ACTIVITY

Identify the dates on which the companies listed above were privatised.

How much were the shares when they were initially sold on the stock market? How much revenue was raised in total for the government after the initial sale?

How much are the shares quoted at today?
(1.1.3)

To the government, privatisation has many benefits.

1. When organisations are privatised it is no longer the responsibility of the government to ensure that they are well managed. The responsibility rests with the directors, who will be expected to run the company in an efficient and cost-effective manner.
2. Similarly, once in the private sector the company ceases to be a financial burden on the government, which no longer has to pay subsidies or suffer any deficits.
3. Privatisation and the selling of shares raises large sums of revenue for the Treasury.

However, it should be noted that once the organisation has been privatised the profits will go to the shareholders and not the government. Hence immediate gains for the government by selling publicly owned assets also means loss of revenue for future governments. This inspired a famous quote by Sir Harold Macmillan, a Conservative Prime Minister, to the effect that privatisation was the same as the government 'selling off the family silver'.

Methods of privatisation include:

1. *Denationalisation*: the transfer of ownership of the assets of an organisation from the public sector to the private sector, normally by the flotation of the company and an issue of shares. Sometimes the government will keep a proportion of the shares to maintain a controlling interest. These shares can then be sold off at a later date once the government is satisfied that competition exists and the service is operating effectively and fairly.

   Examples of corporations that have been denationalised include:
   - British Gas
   - British Telecom
   - British Petroleum

2. *Deregulation*: the removal of statutory monopoly rights, usually by abolishing restrictions and creating competition within a given industry.

   Examples of services that have been deregulated include:
   - Bus services
   - Telecommunications

3. *Contracting out*: allows private firms to bid for public services. The contract will be awarded to the organisation that submits the strongest bid.

   Examples of services which have been contracted out include:
   - Hospital cleaning
   - Refuse collection
   - Educational catering and cleaning

4. *Substitution of tax financing* of some services with a customer fee. Examples include:
   - Eye tests
   - Dental treatment
   - NHS prescriptions

5. *Cooperative buy-out*: worker ownership is achieved through the sale of shares to individuals or to bodies representing the employees. Examples are to be found in the coal industry, where employees have organised themselves into a cooperative to keep individual pits open and maintain their livelihoods.

The following table summarises the three industrial sectors.

Type of business	Main purpose	Main source of finance
Private sector	Profit-making	Profits from trading Money from investors
Public sector	Public service	Government funding and subsidies May also use profits from trading
Charitable organisations	Raise funds & awareness	Donations from public

ACTIVITY

Of the organisations recently privatised, are there any which you feel should be returned to the public sector? Give reasons to support your views.

Are there any enterprises in the public sector which you feel would benefit by being privatised? Give reasons to support your views.

Choose three examples of privatised organisations. Outline the nature of their business and their major competitors. State with reasons

Business Organisations and Employment

Primary *Secondary* *Tertiary*

whether you feel the quality of service has improved since privatisation.

Outline the advantages and disadvantages of privatisation to:
1 the government
2 the shareholders
3 the employees
4 the consumer
5 the general public

(1.1.3)

ACTIVITY

1 What changes have occurred in recent years in the balance between private and public sector activities?
2 What do you suppose are the main reasons for these changes?
3 Identify the main arguments for and against privatisation of public sector organisations.

(1.1.1)

Discussion points

1 'Privatisation of the health service would lead to a more efficient service.'

2 'If British Coal cannot operate effectively without government subsidies it should close down.'

3 'Privatisation of British Telecom has led to a better service for the customer.'

Industrial sectors: primary, secondary and tertiary

Introduction

We have already seen that organisations may be classified as being private sector, public sector or charitable. This is determined by looking at the way in which the business is owned and its main purpose.

Another way of grouping organisations together is by looking at the kind of activities in which the business engages. This is done by dividing organisations into three *industrial sectors*. These are:
- Primary sector (extractive)
- Secondary sector (manufacturing)
- Tertiary sector (service)

These simply mean first, second and third sectors, and are explained below.

Business Organisations and Employment

Primary sector

Primary sector organisations extract natural resources from the planet. *Natural resources* covers anything that is dug out of the ground, grown or taken from the sea. This includes agriculture, fishing, oil and gas extraction, and mining.

There are primary sector organisations in both the private and the public sectors:

Private sector	*Public sector*
Farmers	Forestry Commission
Fishermen	British Coal (at present)
British Gas	
British Petroleum (BP)	

Secondary sector

Secondary sector organisations manufacture the raw materials into a finished, or semi-finished, product. This includes processing raw materials and other parts from other industries, construction, building and assembly. Although oil *extraction* (taking oil out of the ground) is in the primary sector, oil *refineries* (which process crude oil into petrol, paraffin, plastics, and so on) belong to the secondary sector.

Following the privatisation of industries such as British Steel and British Leyland, there are very few public sector organisations operating in the secondary industrial sector.

Private sector	*Public sector*
Ford Motor Company	Atomic Energy Commission
Wimpey Homes	
British Gas	
British Petroleum (BP)	

Tertiary sector

Finally, the tertiary sector provides a service, either for other business organisations such as an advertising company, or for the general public, e.g. a dentist. Other examples of tertiary sector organisations include banks, hairdressers and estate agents.

Services may be classified as *direct* (or personal) services, which go to people, such as law enforcement and hairdressing, and *commercial* services, which go to other businesses, such as insurance and commercial banking. However, most services are used by both people and businesses.

There are tertiary organisations in both the public and private sectors. In fact, most public sector organisations are a kind of service. All charitable organisations are also in the tertiary sector.

Private sector	*Public sector*	*Charitable*
Midland Bank plc	British Rail (at present)	Greenpeace
W H Smith	Police	RSPCA
John Lewis	Fire brigade	Age Concern
British Telecom plc	National Health Service	Cancer Research

ACTIVITY

Classify the following types of organisation under the correct industrial sector:

Organisation *Sector*
Banking
Mining
Police
Teaching
Textile weaving
Oil extraction
Health care
Bus company
TV company
Farm
Marketing
Construction
Acting
Fishing
Pottery
Solicitor
(1.1.1)

The production and distribution of a product or service may involve contributions from all three industrial sectors. Consider, for example, the last plate of chips that you bought from the canteen.

The potatoes that went to produce the chips were planted by a farmer who then employed labourers to harvest them. Once weighed and sacked the potatoes were sold to a large frozen food catering organisation, who manufactured them into frozen chips. Boxes of the chips were then distributed by a transport fleet, hired by the frozen food company, to wholesalers throughout the country. One of the local wholesalers used a promotional campaign which attracted the attention of the catering organisation, who are always keen to buy food which is of high quality and value for money. The chips were prepared and sold as part of a sumptuous range of meals. The money raised from selling the food was counted at the end of the day and subsequently banked.

ACTIVITY

1. Identify the different stages and people involved in making and selling the product described above.
2. Classify the stages according to the appropriate sector
3. Think of your own examples and produce a storyboard outlining the processes involved.

(1.1.1)

Business Organisations and Employment

Developments in the industrial sectors

One country's business environment seldom remains the same for very long. The composition of its industrial sectors experiences constant change. This is due mainly to economic, political and social influences. As economies develop and become more advanced, there is often a decline in the primary sector and a growth in the tertiary sector.

This can be seen by observing economies in different stages of development in the world. The less developed economies are heavily dependent upon their primary sector (such as fishing, mining and farming). As these economies develop so too do their secondary sectors (especially manufacturing and heavy industry). Finally the more advanced economies develop their tertiary sector through the growth of service industries (like financial services, computing and consultancy).

Employment trends in industrial sectors

Social Trends provides useful information about employment trends by industrial sectors. In Great Britain there has been a gradual increase in the numbers of people employed in the service sector and a decrease in the numbers employed in the manufacturing sector. For example, figures show that one in four employees were employed in manufacturing in 1986. By 1993 this figure had fallen to one in five. In comparison the service sector employed two in three people in 1986. This increased to almost three in four in 1993.

ACTIVITY

Using *Social Trends* identify the total numbers employed in each of the three industrial sectors over the last 10 years. Choose the most appropriate graphical method to illustrate the changing trends in employment in the manufacturing and service sector for the dates mentioned. Remember to label your graph accurately. What interesting trends emerge?
(1.1.1)

Gross domestic product by sector

Another way of looking at the changes in industrial sectors is to compare the gross domestic product by sector over a period of time. Gross domestic product is an economic term which refers to the total output or economic activity within the United Kingdom. A useful way to understand what gross domestic product means is by remembering that:

gross	means	total
domestic	means	home
product	means	goods and services

i.e. the total amount of goods and services produced in the United Kingdom.

The *Annual Abstract of Statistics* provides useful information about changes in gross domestic product or output by industrial sectors. In 1980 the total GDP or output for the United Kingdom comprised 11% from the primary sector, 32% from the secondary sector and 57% from the tertiary sector. By 1990 this has changed to 7% for the primary sector, 28% for the secondary sector and 63% for the tertiary sector.

Clearly output in the primary and secondary sectors is declining and therefore their contribution to the total UK output is declining too. In contrast output in the service sector is increasing and it therefore contributes significantly to total UK output.

ACTIVITY

Choose the most appropriate graphical method to illustrate the changing trends in gross domestic product for the United Kingdom by sector for the dates mentioned. Remember to label your graph accurately. What interesting trends emerge?
(1.1.1)

ACTIVITY

Obtain a copy of the *Annual Abstract of Statistics*. Look for the table titled 'Gross domestic product by industry'. Make a list of the main industries listed and their total output in £m over a period of time – ideally 1984 to 1994. Present this information in table format and briefly describe and illustrate the trends using the most suitable methods. Present the information in a format suitable for a wall display.
(1.1.1)

Types of business activity

There are many different types of business activity that operate within the local and national economies. Examples include:
- Transport and distribution
- Retail and wholesale
- Manufacturing industries
- Service industries

In the previous activity, where we identified the key stages followed before the plate of chips reached its destination, i.e. the final consumer, a cycle of production and distribution had taken place which incorporated a range of business activities. This can be illustrated as follows.

Transport and distribution

Transport and distribution firms clearly have a major role in ensuring effective distribution at all stages of the production and retail process. Transport methods could include air transport, shipping, rail, lorry, cars and even motor cycle couriers. Effective communication links are vital for successful and efficient business activity.

Retail and wholesale

Wholesalers

The chips activity also referred to the role of wholesalers and retailers in the production process. The main purpose of the wholesaler is to act as an intermediary between the producer, who wants to sell in large quantities, and the retailer, who wishes to buy in smaller quantities. The wholesaler will therefore buy either a wide range of goods or specialist merchandise in bulk and will then sell these items in smaller quantities to the retailer.

Because the wholesaler buys such large amounts, extensive premises and accommodation are required to stock and store the goods. Most wholesalers offer extensive credit and transport facilities to the retailer.

The functions of the wholesaler include:
- Bulk breaking – buy in large quantities and sell in smaller amounts.
- Provision of credit – by providing credit facilities to the retailers (which are not available from the producer), the wholesaler is assisting the process of production and consumption.
- Storage facilities – wholesalers are able to store goods in specialised warehousing facilities, which enables retailers to buy the quantity of goods that they are able to manage.
- Transport facilities provided by the wholesaler assist retailers in receiving their goods.
- Removal of fluctuations.

By buying and storing goods in large quantities the wholesaler ensures a steady supply of goods to the retailer. This in turn helps to keep prices stable.

Retailers

A retail firm liaises directly with the customer. The size of retail firms varies considerably. Small retail organisations have the advantage of being able to locate their premises close to the customer and are able to make changes to product ranges very quickly. Larger retailers are able to offer greater discounts on prices and a wider range of merchandise.

There are many different types of retailer. They include:
- Market stall trader
- Corner shops
- Department stores
- Chain stores
- Supermarkets
- Mail order firms

Business Organisations and Employment

ACTIVITY

1. What are the functions of wholesalers?
2. Identify the advantages and disadvantages that a wholesaler would experience if it was to supply directly to the retail trade instead of using a wholesaler.
3. What role does a retailer have in the economy?
4. Distinguish between the different types of retailer.

(1.1.4)

Manufacturing industries

Manufacturing industries are classified under the secondary sector and contribute to the system of production and consumption by processing and combining raw materials into finished products. Certain areas of the United Kingdom are famous for their history of manufacturing.

ACTIVITY

Identify which manufacturing industries have been traditionally located in the following areas:
- Bradford
- Sheffield
- High Wycombe
- Staffordshire
- Scotland
- Nottingham
- The Clyde
- Cowley, Oxford

and give possible explanations why this may be the case.

(1.1.4)

Service industries

Not all businesses have a product or items to sell. Instead, they raise revenue by offering skills, advice, expertise, information or amenities to prospective customers. All service industries are classified under the tertiary sector, and they are the most common form of business enterprise in the United Kingdom today.

Examples include marketing organisations, local window cleaners and refuse collection.

ACTIVITY

Identify as many other examples of service industries as you can under the headings public and private sector.

(1.1.2)

Business Organisations and Employment

So far we have identified the purposes of different types of business organisations and classified them according to type and industrial sector. It is now necessary to apply this information by looking at different examples of organisations operating on a local and national basis.

ACTIVITY

Who are they and what do they do?

The purpose of this assessment is to familiarise you with a variety of locally and nationally based organisations and for you to undertake a study of the characteristics of those organisations.

Survey at least seven local and national organisations. They must range in size and should include:
1 a sole trader
2 a partnership
3 a private limited company
4 a public limited company
5 a public sector organisation
6 a cooperative
7 a charity

from a range of business activities, including:
1 transport and distribution
2 wholesale organisations
3 retailing
4 manufacturing
5 service industries

From your research identify:
1 the types of business organisation
2 their purpose, i.e. profit- or non-profit-making
3 the industrial sector, i.e. primary, secondary or tertiary
4 the type of business activity

You will be expected to gather information to enable you to present your work. Complete the task sheet below for each organisation and prepare a visual display of your findings.
(1.1.2) (1.1.3)

ACTIVITY

Simply a franchise

Look at the advertisements opposite for franchises which appeared in a national paper.
1 Identify the types of product or service that are available within a franchise arrangement
2 How much is each company charging for the franchise and what benefits do you receive?
3 Can you identify any problems that might occur if you were to become a franchisee? What support would be available from the franchisor?
4 If you had £10,000 in savings and you were considering becoming a franchisee, which one would you join and why?

(1.1.3) (1.1.4)

The Abbey goes public

A change in the law has recently meant that building societies can now transfer from being a Friendly Society (another name for Building Society, as the customers benefit from the profits) to becoming a public limited company, like the banks. At present only the Abbey National has 'gone public', having gained the support from the majority of their investors in 1989. The Halifax Building Society, the biggest in this country, has decided to remain a Friendly Society for the time being.

The Abbey National put forward many reasons as to why they wanted to become a public limited company. These can be summarised as follows:
1 As a plc they would be more able to meet their customer needs and be able to respond more quickly and flexibly to changing market conditions.
2 Additional capital, raised by floating the organisation, would provide its members with better services and facilities, and larger branches.

	Organisation checklist			
Type of organisation	Public ☐	Private ☐	Nationalised ☐	Sole trader ☐
	Central government ☐	Local authority ☐	Public limited co. ☐	Private limited co. ☐
Activity	Product ☐	Service ☐		
Legal status	Limited liability ☐	Unlimited liability ☐	Other ☐	
Size of operations	Large scale ☐	Small scale ☐		
Organisational objectives	Profit-making ☐	Non-profit-making ☐	Product diversification ☐	
Sources of finance	Owner capital ☐	Share capital ☐	Loan capital ☐	
Market	Local ☐	National ☐	International ☐	
Industrial sector	Primary ☐	Secondary ☐	Tertiary ☐	

Business Organisations and Employment

AMTRAK Express Parcels Limited
Create your own Business by Joining this World-Wide Success

Amtrak
▲ is a leading World-Wide Express Parcel Company
▲ has grown from zero to £20m in just 5 years
▲ has 125 depots nationwide operating 40 trunking vehicles

The benefits to you are:
- Existing Business within your area
- No invoicing or bad debts
- No cash flow problems
- No premises or employees

To learn more about this exciting business opportunity send off the coupon to:
David Hadley,
Franchise Development Manager
Amtrak Express Parcels Ltd
FREEPOST BS7220
Company House
Tower Hill, Bristol BS2 0BR

BRITISH FRANCHISE ASSOCIATION FULL MEMBER
The Franchise Licence Fees are £12,500
Please forward an Amtrak Franchise information pack

Name ....
Address ....
....
Postcode DML21

Looking to develop into a major market?

- Seeking maximum exposure for minimum investment?
- Wishing to leave behind the negative aspects of working for someone else?

It's time to . . .
. . . focus on **SunnySnaps**

We are an established high street retailer with an excellent reputation in the photography market.

Holiday snaps, professional portraits, wedding photos, family celebrations – all form part of our album!

SunnySnaps as a franchise has been established for five years. In that time the national photography market has grown by 15%, while profits have risen by 4%.

We are seeking to expand further in your area. Franchises are available for a minimum amount of £15,000, for which you receive help and advice with establishing the business, equipment, training and an exclusive geographical market.

Remember: we have the image if you have the profile.

Call now on **01921 376453**

Thinking of starting up your own business?

Uncertain of the future? Wouldn't it be nice to know that you had fifty years of experience to back you up, with an established product to sell?

MacTucky Chicken invite you to join an internationally respected chain of quality fast-food outlets. We offer you expertise, guidance, advice, training and above all exclusive rights to trade under the familiar brand name and sell the famous MacTucky products in your area.

This is an exceptional offer. Initial size of investment depends upon the location of the store.

Call now on freefone 0800 1234567 for more information or write to us FREEPOST at:

MacTucky Chicken UK
FREEPOST
27 Cambridge Road
Maidenhead
Bucks

The travel franchise for business people

To run a successful franchise, you have to stay close to the business, which means you have to really like what you are doing.

As someone with a professional business background, can you see yourself "hands on" operating a fast food restaurant, a cleaning service or print shop? We can't either.

Consider joining UNIGLOBE Travel. For around just £50,000, we can get your agency open as part of the largest travel agency franchise network in the world, working in the exciting and growing business travel market.

Ring 071 418 0150 today.

UNIGLOBE Travel

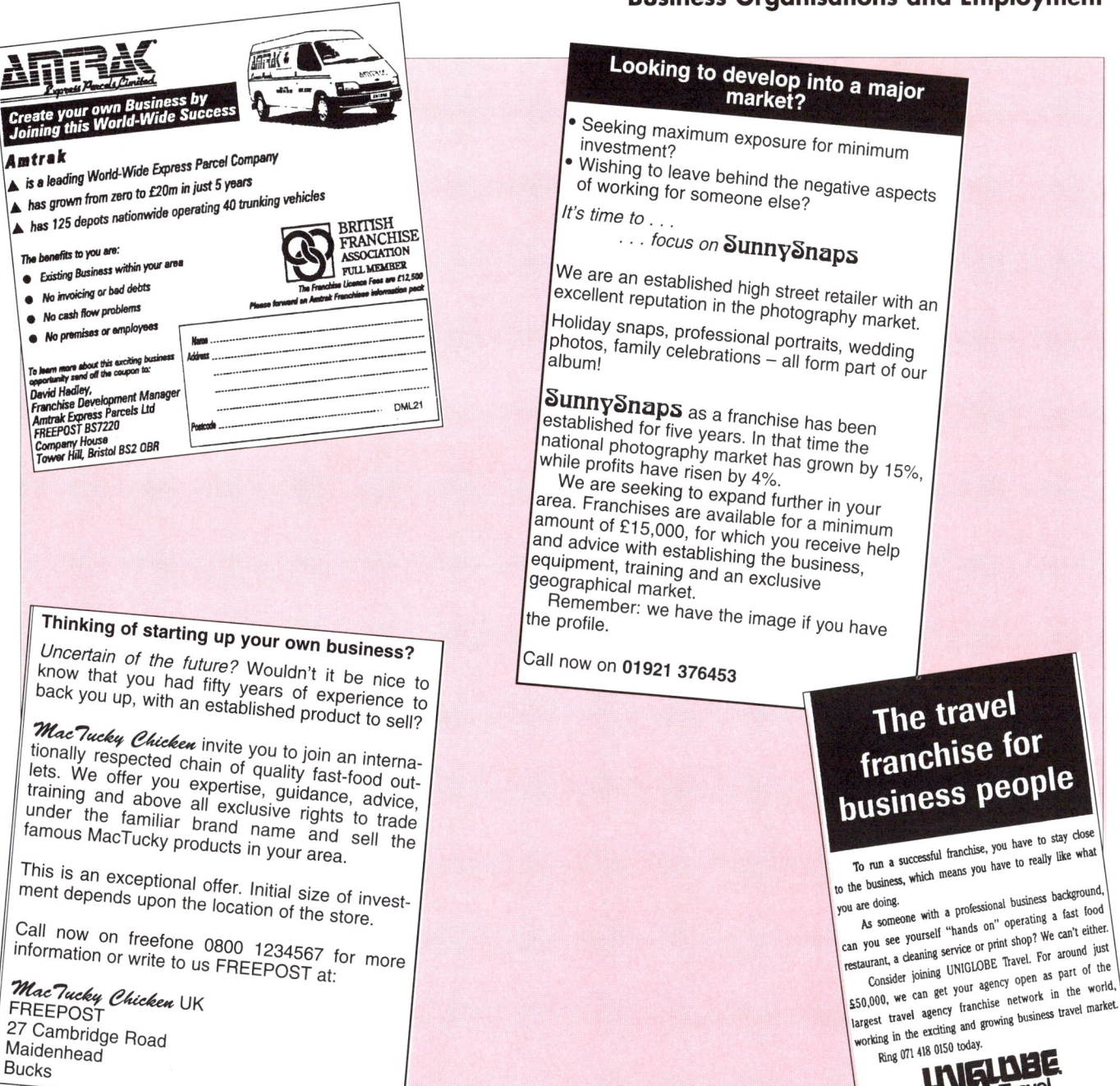

3   The organisation would be more able to offer mortgages at competitive rates if it were a plc.
4   As a plc the organisation would be better able to meet increasing competition from abroad and within Europe.

However, many of the Abbey's original investors were opposed to the transfer to plc status. They argued that, as a Friendly Society, the Abbey had to operate in the interests of its members; any surplus funds had to be used to benefit the members. As a plc, however, dividends for shareholders have to be taken from those same funds. Members could only suffer.

✎ ACTIVITY

1   Using this information and further research contrast the role of a Friendly Society, such as the Skipton, with a building society with plc status, e.g. the Abbey National, looking particularly at:
  (i)   objectives
  (ii) funding and
  (iii) accountability
2   Compare the service offered by the Skipton and the Abbey National. Which do you feel offers the best service in terms of:
  (i)   range
  (ii) price
  (iii) facilities
3   Compare the service offered by the Abbey National with a large high street bank. What are the similarities and how do they differ? Which do you feel offers the most effective service? Give reasons for your decisions.
4   Do you feel that a building society which decides to 'go public' does offer a better service? Give reasons for your decision.

(1.1.2) (1.1.3) (1.1.4)

Business Organisations and Employment

MULTIPLE CHOICE

1. Which of the following organisations is in the private sector?
   A Police force
   B National Health Service
   C British Telecom
   D HM Customs and Excise

2. Which of the following types of organisation is in the public sector?
   A Public limited company
   B Private limited company
   C Sole trader
   D Public corporation

3. The *main* aim of a private sector organisation is likely to be:
   A To make a profit
   B To provide a service
   C To employ the maximum number of people
   D To produce an accurate accounting record of its activities

4. The *main* aim of public sector organisations is to:
   A Beat the competition
   B Diversify into new markets
   C Maximise profits
   D Provide a service

5. The best description of an entrepreneur is:
   A Someone who is often in the news
   B A person who risks personal capital in setting up and running a business
   C An organisation that lends money to new businesses
   D A wealthy individual who no longer needs to work

6. The main function of a charity is to:
   A Make a profit
   B Sell shares
   C Sell flags and badges
   D Raise funds for a particular cause

7. Which of the following organisations is a charity?
   A NHS
   B RSPCA
   C RAF
   D BT

8. Which of the following organisations is in the secondary sector?
   A Primary school
   B Secondary school
   C Tertiary college
   D Steel works

9. The activities of a bank would be classified as:
   A Transport and distribution
   B Retail and wholesale
   C Manufacturing industry
   D Service industry

10. A sole trader, who is a builder, seeks information from the bank for investment advice for private savings. This activity would be described as:
    A Extractive
    B Manufacturing
    C Commercial services
    D Personal services

SHORT ANSWER

1. Explain what is meant by the term 'unlimited liability'.
   What groups of people in business have unlimited liability?

2. Explain what is meant by the term 'limited liability'.
   What groups of people in business have limited liability?

3. What is the purpose of a partnership agreement?
   Outline the main details that are likely to be agreed in the agreement.
   What provision does the law make for these issues in the absence of any formal partnership agreement?

4. What are the differences between a public limited company and a private limited company?
   Give three examples of each.

5. Explain the workings of a cooperative as a business.

6. What are the chief advantages of a franchise to the franchisee and the franchisor?
   Outline any disadvantages.

7. What reasons have there been for some services and industries being included in the public sector?

8. What services are commonly provided by local government?

9. Give three examples of the following kinds of organisations and state whether they operate on a local or a national basis:

Type of organisation	Examples	Local or national?
Transport & distribution	1. 2. 3.	
Retail & wholesale	1. 2. 3.	
Manufacturing industry	1. 2. 3.	
Service industry	1. 2. 3.	

10 What is meant by 'privatisation'?
    Discuss the different ways in which public services and organisations may be privatised.

11 State two advantages of being a sole trader rather than a partnership or limited company.
    State two disadvantages.

Business Organisations and Employment

ELEMENT 1.2
Examine business location, environment, markets and products

Performance criteria

- **PC** 1.2.1 Explain the reasons for location of businesses
- **PC** 1.2.2 Explain influences of the business environment on business organisations
- **PC** 1.2.3 Describe markets for businesses' products based on demand
- **PC** 1.2.4 Identify products provided by business organisations
- **PC** 1.2.5 Explain activities undertaken by businesses to improve their market position
- **PC** 1.2.6 Propose products which would meet market demand

Manufactured goods

Services

Business Organisations and Employment

Introduction

The location of industry is concerned with the factors that are taken into account when choosing the site for a particular firm. success or failure may well depend upon the choice. Sometimes, firms have 'just developed' in certain areas for no apparent reason, or because the owners were living there at the time. More often, the site was chosen after careful consideration of several factors.

ACTIVITY

Identify the factors that the following businesses would need to take into account when deciding where to locate:
1 a haulage firm
2 British Rail
3 a fish wholesaler
4 a shoe shop
5 a Chinese restaurant
6 a paper mill
(1.2.1)

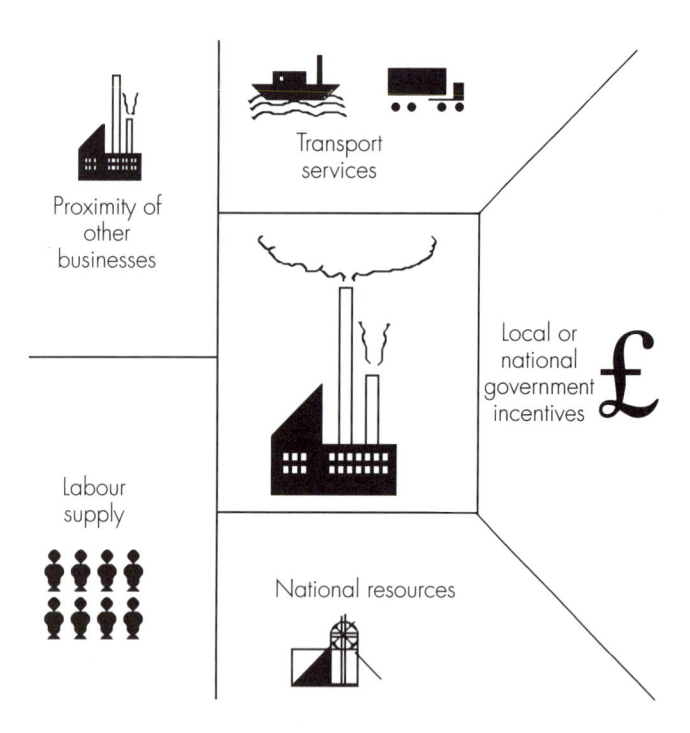

Reasons for location of industry

Natural resources

One of the most important factors in the siting of an extractive industry is the presence of raw materials. It is also an important consideration for manufacturing firms, as it is cheaper to transport finished products than it is raw materials if the item is *bulk reducing*. This means that the inputs that go to make the product are heavier and bigger than the final product that is produced. In such cases the firm will tend to locate close to the raw materials.

Likely location for a business which is bulk-reducing

An example of a bulk-reducing business is the production of sugar. The raw sugar (sugar cane) is very bulky and must be processed to refine it into sugar, which is less bulky. Hence sugar producers tend to locate near to places where sugar cane is grown, such as Africa and Jamaica. A paper mill would also locate close to a supply of wood for similar reasons, and a flour mill will locate near to the supply of wheat.

At the other end of operations, a business must also consider its market. Being near to the market is very important when the production process is *bulk-increasing*, that is, the finished product is much bulkier than the raw materials that are used for its production. It is more manageable for the producer to bring the raw materials to the production plant located near the customers than it is to transport the finished goods over long distances.

Likely location for a business which is bulk-increasing

An extreme example of bulk-increasing is in the construction of a house. It is much easier to bring the raw materials to the building site than it is to bring a ready-made house to the customer!

It is also important to locate near the market if the item is fragile in nature, such as glass, or likely to deteriorate rapidly, such as fresh-cut flowers and vegetables. Similarly, businesses offering direct or personal services to customers must be located near the customers concerned, e.g. a retail shop. Finally, an organisation that needs to sell in large quantities to get a small return also needs to be located close to the market, e.g. a bakery.

ACTIVITY

Think of three examples of organisations that have located close to their sources of raw materials. Name the organisations, the regions in which they are located and the type of natural resources that they use.
(1.2.1)

Labour supply

The availability of a workforce with the relevant skills is another factor that influences the location of many organisations. If workers are not available, then firms have to recruit them from elsewhere, and

Business Organisations and Employment

this can prove to be very expensive. Certain regions are well known for having workers with certain specialised skills, and firms will often locate there if they require those skills, e.g. ship-building on the River Clyde (although this industry has rapidly declined) or technological skills in Milton Keynes.

Wage rates are also a relevant factor. In areas of high unemployment, labour is available in large quantities and therefore the wage rates tend to be lower. In areas where there is very little unemployment, labour is in much shorter supply and this is often reflected in higher wages paid.

ACTIVITY

Think of three examples of organisations that have located in a region because of the availability of labour with specialised skills. Name the organisations, the regions in which they are located and the specialist skills employed.
(1.2.1)

ACTIVITY

Think of three examples of organisations that have located in a region in order to be close to the market. Name the organisations, the regions in which they are located and the type of customer that they are trying to attract.
(1.2.1)

Local, national or international incentives

The advantages of locating in a particular region can be very strong and industrialists tend to be more concerned with the benefits than with broader social issues. This means that certain regions may have too many organisations located there, while other areas have too few. Therefore local and national governments will often intervene in order to try to maintain some control over location and thereby ensure a fair distribution of industry throughout the country.

This can be tackled in two ways, by 'stick and carrot' methods:

1. *Control of the siting of new business*
   This involves restricting the location of businesses within certain areas by excessive taxes or by refusing planning permission. This is a 'stick' method, since it aims to stop businesses locating in protected areas, such as those of outstanding natural beauty, or in densely populated regions.
2. *Offering financial incentives in areas of high unemployment*
   Many regions of Britain qualify for financial support from local and national government and/or from the European Union. This money is then used to attract firms to that area by:

(i) providing organisations with available space and accommodation
(ii) reducing rents and local business tax for a specified period of time
(iii) providing help in employing staff with the relevant skills and expertise

These areas are known as development or intermediate areas, which are collectively known as assisted areas. In addition, some areas have enterprise zones which receive further support. These are 'carrot' methods, since they entice businesses to locate in some regions, especially where areas are deprived and are in need of capital investment.

Proximity of other organisations

When deciding where to locate, an entrepreneur will often consider where the major competitors are located in order to avoid competing for the same market. In fact one of the advantages of being a franchise is that the franchisee is given a geographical area to operate within, in the knowledge that no one else will operate the same franchise in that area. In addition, the siting of an organisation often attracts other subsidiary firms to provide a service for that organisation. This is particularly true for the car industry. Many suppliers of car materials are located close to large car manufacturers. Subsidiary firms may also locate close to a large organisation to take advantage of the benefits of established resources and/or markets.

Footloose organisations

A footloose organisation is one that can locate in any area and is not influenced by the factors described above.

Business Organisations and Employment

ACTIVITY

Working in groups undertake a survey of the organisations in your locality. Identify the types of organisation and the products or services produced. Using a large sheet of paper, map out the roads and communication links for the area and locate the organisations on your map. Photographs can be an effective method of illustrating your information if you cannot draw. Give a short written explanation that accounts for any interesting features that emerge from your diagram.

From your research identify what factors led to those firms being located in those areas.

Do you consider that any one of the firms would find it advantageous to move to another area? What difficulties would arise in making such a move?

Do you think there are any areas in your region where there is already too much industry? If so, what problems do you think have arisen from this and what should be done about it?

Remember: both the diagram and your written account can be used as evidence within your portfolio. Presentation is therefore very important. A photocopy or photograph of the finished diagrams can be used as evidence by group members.

(1.1.4) (1.2.1)

Transport services

Unless a business is lucky enough to find its suppliers and customers in the same place it is likely to need transport services. Some of the large organisations are able to afford to run their own transport fleets. Smaller organisations have to buy in the services of a transport firm. Good transport routes are of particular importance for organisations that operate on a national or international basis. They are necessary in order to move raw materials to the production site and to transport finished products to their destinations, as shown by this diagram:

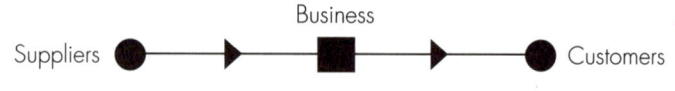

Suppliers ● ▶ ■ Business ▶ ● Customers

ACTIVITY

Think of three examples of organisations that have located in a region close to good transport and communication links. Name the organisations, the regions in which they are located and identify the influencing transport/communication links.
(1.2.1)

ACTIVITY

1. List the principal factors that determine the location of industry.
2. In what ways is it possible to control the location of industry?
3. What factors influence the location of organisations that have branches in many countries?
4. How has the European market influenced the location of business?

(1.2.1, 1.2.2)

MICHA SIMONE LTD

Micha Simone Ltd is a small organisation located in an industrialised area in the South of England. The company produces a range of specialised cotton fabrics used in the making of ladies' clothing. The demand for the product has been increasing steadily and is likely to rise further. The present premises, which are old fashioned and located in a densely populated area, cannot cope with any increase in production. The options facing the firm are:

(a) to expand the present site
(b) to build a second factory on the edge of the town
(c) to relocate completely in modern premises in a new area that qualifies for regional aid.

ACTIVITY

Prepare a short report for management, listing the considerations that they should bear in mind when reviewing each option.
(1.2.1) (1.2.2)

Business Organisations and Employment

The scale and scope of organisations

Growing pains

If a business is successful, if it manages to survive the trials and tribulations of the first few years, then sooner or later it is likely that it will have to face a big decision: to grow or not to grow?

On the one hand, it may be easier to keep things going in the same way as before. You know where you stand and you feel secure. You have found a successful formula. Why fix it if it isn't broken? The business is already 'grown up'.

On the other hand, you may argue that a business is a living thing – if it doesn't grow it will die. Businesses cannot always stay the same and remain profitable. The world is changing all the time, presenting new opportunities, which should be taken. Larger scale operations enable more to be done for lower unit costs.

Growing up

Two factors help to determine the size of an organisation:
- *Capital required*: small organisations tend to need small amounts of capital. An organisation that requires a large amount of capital will almost always operate on a large scale in order to gain the turnover and profit needed to justify the original investment.
- *Size of the market*: if the market potential is small and local then a small organisation will operate. In situations where there is a large demand for a product or service on a national or international scale, a larger organisation will exist.

To put it simply, growth costs money. Somehow the business must raise capital and one of the best ways of doing this is by encouraging investment in it by individuals or other businesses. For many small businesses this may involve the decision to become a private or public limited company.

Scale of organisations

The scale of a business organisation refers to the size of the firm. This can range from a small market trader to a large company. There are two different ways of measuring the scale of business operations: the number of employees and the market share.

Number of employees

One simple measure of the scale of a business organisation is by counting the number of employees. A sole trader employing no one else will have zero employees, while the National Health Service has a quarter of a million employees.

The significance of employees for organisations is enormous. For most organisations the item of salaries and wages is the single largest expense, especially if they are *labour-intensive*, meaning that their activities require a high number of personnel. This is true of service industries. Even *capital-* (or *machine-*) *intensive* businesses, which rely more on equipment, usually have a high labour bill. Mass production techniques, although highly automated, still require workers. Increased automation and advances in technology do reduce the dependence on people. The Fiat plant in Turin is virtually fully automated, leading to the publicity slogan: *Fiat, built by robots*.

Other activities are highly labour-intensive. This means that there is a high concentration of people in the process. This is true of manufacturing processes that require skilled workers in assembly and finishing, and particularly true of service industries.

Therefore it is sometimes difficult to use the number of employees as an indicator of the scale of a business, because a large-scale capital-intensive manufacturing plant may employ very few people. On the other hand, an organisation providing very expensive hand-crafted products may employ many staff but operate on a relatively small scale.

Market share

Another way of showing the relative size of an organisation is by looking at its market share. The market is the total number of sales or customers for a given product or service. The market share, therefore, is the fraction of the total market that is provided by one organisation.

The record industry is a good example, where the market is dominated by a few giants. PolyGram, Thorn EMI, Warner Brothers, CBS/Sony and RCA/BMG between them occupy over 80% of the total market. PolyGram, for example, has a world market share of 18% (according to *The Observer*, 8 August 1993). Large organisations benefit from economies of scale. In the record industry the giants

Business Organisations and Employment

buy up other labels, increasing their market share. For example, in 1990 PolyGram bought A&M and Island records, while Thorn EMI bought Virgin records in 1992 and PolyGram purchased Motown in 1993.

This picture of a few giants taking most of the market share is repeated for many industries and products. In 1977 doorstep deliveries of milk represented 90% of the total sales of milk. However, cut-price competition from supermarkets, and the use of cartons, rather than glass bottles, has led to a sharp increase of the market share held by supermarkets.

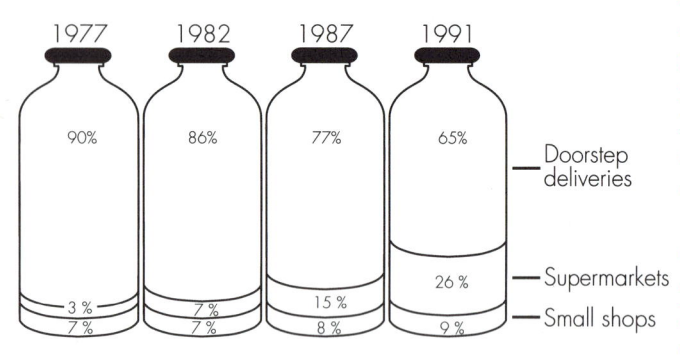

	1977	1982	1987	1991
Doorstep deliveries	90%	86%	77%	65%
Supermarkets	3%	7%	15%	26%
Small shops	7%	7%	8%	9%

Estimated market share of milk sales
(*Source*: Auditors of Great Britain)

ACTIVITY

Carry out a local survey of business organisations. From statistics held by the local authority or the local library draw a pie chart that illustrates the division of the local labour market by the large employers.
(1.2.3)

ACTIVITY

Select an industry that interests you – computer games, sportswear, record industry, garden furniture etc. – and conduct research into the market share of the leading organisations in that business. Using the most up to date information available to you present your findings in diagrammatic form.

You may choose an industry or a particular type of product or service. For example, you may wish to examine how the confectionery market is supplied by the leading manufacturers, or look at soft drinks, especially Pepsi and Coca-Cola.
(1.2.3) (1.2.4)

Persil soap war hits 11m homes

The war of the soaps took a new turn this weekend with the deployment of the first of 11m free samples of Persil Power, the controversial powder alleged to rot underwear.

Unilever, the maker, is to deliver 120 g packs to virtually every home in Britain with a washing machine in an effort to counter accusations made by its market rival, Procter & Gamble, about the effect the new soap has on clothes.

The counter-strike, believed to be Britain's biggest direct marketing exercise, is part of a campaign costing Unilever £25m. The first samples were delivered yesterday in the Newcastle upon Tyne area, the operational heartland of P&G, which has paraded shredded underwear before the press to support its allegations.

Unilever's incursion into P&G territory intensifies a dispute of startling ferocity between the world's two largest purveyors of soap powder.

It will take until the end of August for the 11m homes, half the households in Britain, to receive their Persil Power samples. Unilever believes it will end reports of the destructive power of its new brand, said by P&G to have rendered cotton cloth ragged after fewer than 30 washes under extreme laboratory conditions.

Yesterday the exercise provoked mixed reactions in the northeast, seen by both sides as an important battleground in the struggle for Europe's £6 billion detergent market.

To Unilever's satisfaction, a steady stream of shoppers queued at its 'Persil roadshow' at the Gateshead MetroCentre, near Newcastle, to hear how the brand is made with a manganese compound to speed the cleaning process.

'I'm giving the stuff a try,' said Sandra Clarke from Walker, Newcastle. 'After all, they are giving it away.' Joan Garrick, 54, from Sunderland, was unconcerned by the risk that her husband's underpants might disintegrate. 'They don't last very long anyway,' she said.

P&G will take consolation, however, from the comments of several women who clearly believed what they had read in the newspapers. Karen Roche, a mother of four from Cramlington, Northumberland, summed up their suspicion: 'Persil wouldn't be giving it away if they weren't worried. If any is posted through my letterbox I'll probably chuck it in the bin.'

The dispute between Unilever, the Anglo-Dutch company, and its American rival began in April when an unnamed P&G executive was quoted in an Amsterdam newspaper that carried the first reports of fabric damage.

Unilever has since displayed for the cameras cotton knickers said to have been washed hundreds of times without any ill-effects. It has taken out full-page advertisements to contradict what it regards as black propaganda to undermine its most important new product for years.

A senior Unilever source claimed this weekend that it had been like fighting an arsonist. 'They spend a minute starting a fire. We then have to spend hours putting each one out. P&G are keeping their fingerprints off this activity, but we know they have been planning this for six months.'

P&G has denied 'planting' hostile stories in the press but confirms that it commissioned research to test whether the 'Power' brand could harm clothes. The company claims that if Persil Power goes wrong, its own products could be blamed by consumers who switch between brands. It believes the whole industry may suffer.

Unilever, which dismisses such suggestions, admits in turn that it has studied plans to retaliate against other P&G products if the assault continues. For the moment, however, it is holding fire.

'They have terrific guerrilla tactics,' said a Unilever source. 'There is a real dilemma here. If we descend to that level we depart from the normal moral high ground we like to hold.'

Sainsbury, Britain's largest supermarket chain, has done tests and says it has no intention of embarking on more. 'Sales are in line with expectations,' said a spokeswoman.

Marks & Spencer says it will analyse Persil Power to see whether P&G's claims were accurate. 'We have 14m customers and some of them must be users of the powder. Therefore we have a responsibility to find out a little more,' said a spokesman.

Source: Sunday Times, 12 June 1994

ACTIVITY

Market share of European detergent market (*source*: Henderson Crosthwaite):

Proctor & Gamble (makers of Ariel)	£2.0 bn
Henkel	£1.5 bn
Unilever (makers of Persil)	£1.4 bn
Others	£1.1 bn

Market share of concentrated powder 1994 (*source*: Henderson Crosthwaite)

Date		Ariel Ultra (%)	Persil Ultra (%)
March	12	34.0	23.0
	19	35.0	19.0
	26	35.0	19.0
April	2	36.0	19.5
	9	37.5	19.5
	16	36.5	20.0
	23	36.0	20.0
	30	35.5	20.5
May	7[1]	34.5	21.0
	14	33.0	23.0
	21	29.5	31.5
	28	28.5	32.5

[1] Launch of Persil Power

Read the article on the left, study the figures and complete the following tasks:

1. Draw a pie chart to illustrate the European fabric detergent market share, clearly showing the percentage share held by each group.
2. Draw a line graph showing the changes in the market share of concentrated powder for Ariel Ultra and Persil Ultra (one line for each on the same graph).
3. Answer the following questions relating to the article:
   (i) What is said to be wrong with Persil Power, according to their rivals Proctor & Gamble (P&G)?
   (ii) What are Proctor & Gamble using as evidence for their claims?
   (iii) How is the maker of Persil, Unilever, fighting back?
   (iv) What region is regarded as being crucial in the battle for European supremacy?
   (v) What has been the public response to the 'Persil roadshow'?
   (vi) Unilever think that P&G have not been playing fair. In what ways might P&G have used the press to their advantage?
   (vii) How do P&G counter these claims?
   (viii) How have retail chains, like Marks & Spencer and Sainsbury, responded to the situation?

(1.2.2) (1.2.3)

Business Organisations and Employment

Scope

The scope of an organisation refers to the geographical size of the market for that organisation. It may range from a small local market for a sole trader to a large international market for a major company.

The scope of an organisation's activities can be measured in geographical terms, depending upon the spread of the market it supplies. The market for a product or service may be purely local or national, or it may even be international, depending on the nature of demand for that particular item or service and the extent of the competition from other suppliers.

Local

A purely local business only provides goods and services for the local community. Exactly how big the 'local community' is varies, depending upon the business. A market stall holder, for example, may only supply the people who visit the market, whereas a local garage can provide services for any motorists passing through the area.

National

National businesses, on the other hand, provide goods and services across the entire country. They usually grow out of small, local businesses, steadily increasing their scope. Many high street shops, for example, are part of national chains. WH Smith, Marks & Spencer and Boots fall into this category. The same is true of supermarkets such as Tesco, Sainsbury and Waitrose. High street banks like Midland, NatWest and Barclays also have a national scope.

Multinational

Multinationals are large organisations which locate and operate on an international basis. This may mean that production is split between more than one country. This is common in car manufacturing and the computer industry. Alternatively, a multinational may simply be one that has its headquarters in one country and subsidiary companies in other countries.

Multinationals include:
- Unilever
- IBM
- BP
- Shell
- Ford
- General Motors
- Apple
- Coca-Cola
- McDonald's

As multinationals are very large they can exert a powerful influence over the countries in which they are operating, especially if they are developing economies. A multinational may also use its power to take unfair advantage over competing rivals who lack the same influence.

Business Organisations and Employment

	Advantages	Disadvantages
To the multinational:	• Cheaper labour costs • Can avoid strong unions • Maximise investment grants • Minimise tax liability	• Difficult to control • Strained communication links • Diseconomies of scale
To the host country:	• Employment • Prestige • Attracts other industries • Technological know-how • Investment	• Possible exploitation of labour and environment • Limited financial return • Possible political manipulation

ACTIVITY

Select a multinational organisation and identify the type of product or service that it provides. List the markets in which the organisation operates. Using a copy of a map identify the countries in which these markets are located.
(1.2.4)

Large-scale operations

Advantages The larger the organisation, the greater the opportunities for large-scale or mass production. These can be described as *economies of scale*. Economies of scale may include the ability to:
- Have specialist departments to carry out specific roles, e.g. personnel, marketing
- Buy in bulk and therefore at a cheaper unit price
- Use up-to-date technology
- Produce items in large quantities using automated methods

Large firms can afford to employ staff with specialised skills to carry out specific roles. This is often called division of labour. In a smaller organisation one person may be responsible for a range of specialised functions.

Bulk purchasing Because a big organisation produces on such a large scale, it can afford to buy its raw materials in bulk and at a cheaper unit price. Small firms are not able to sell in such large quantities, as mass production would lead to expensive storage and wastage. They therefore have to buy materials in smaller quantities and at a higher unit price.

Mass production Large firms can afford to buy specialised machinery which produces products in much larger quantities in a quicker time. Smaller firms cannot justify the expenditure on expensive mass production machinery; nor could they sell all of the output.

Financial Larger organisations are able to negotiate large loans at competitive rates from financial organisations. They also have a range of other sources to secure investment from, e.g. shareholders.

Support services Large organisations can usually afford to employ specialised staff to provide an efficient support service to operational activities, e.g. marketing, distribution and personnel.

There are a number of disadvantages to large scale production. These are known as diseconomies of scale.

Coordination As organisations grow in size, problems often occur in ensuring effective communication and coordination of activities within the firm.

Less responsive Larger organisations often find it difficult to respond quickly to changes in the market. There is often a loss of personal service and attention to detail.

Inflexibility The larger the organisation, the greater the complexity of the internal structure. As such, it is often difficult to change policies, or to get people to make decisions and to move direction.

Alienation Mass production methods often make people feel that they are bored with their jobs and unimportant because their work is such a small part of the overall product or service. This can lead to a deterioration in the quality of items produced and high absenteeism from staff.

Lack of personal interest As an organisation grows in size, employees often feel that they have less of a personal interest and commitment to the organisation.

Storage If the organisation is not able to sell all the stock produced, money is wasted in expensive storage costs.

The survival of the small firm

Though the economies of large-scale production easily outweigh the diseconomies, many small firms continue to survive, and it is still the most popular form of business organisation. The reasons why small firms are successful and remain popular can be summarised as follows:
- Small markets do not attract large firms.
- Simpler organisations result in fewer managerial problems.
- Greater involvement and commitment from employees.
- Quicker decision-making and flexibility.
- A personalised service with attention to detail.
- Quicker response to changes in market conditions.

GIANNI AND DOMENICO

Gianni and Domenico have built up their own business making and selling quality denim trousers. They have their own workshop, employing 10 people to cut the material, stitch the trousers and pack them.

They have low overheads and very low distribution and advertising costs. Most of their customers are local retailers or market traders who benefit from Gianni and Domenico's low prices. Some of the local traders have asked for particular designs that have proven popular with young people seeking a distinctive designer look. Gianni and Domenico can meet individual requests with their small set-up, changing patterns at relatively short notice without making major and costly adjustments to the production process.

The originality of their designs recently gained national exposure by being reviewed on *The Clothes Show*. As a result orders from around the country have flooded in and Gianni and Domenico face a dilemma.

To meet the extra orders they need capital investment for larger premises, new machinery, computerised production systems, large quantities of material and more staff. They have no more money themselves and would therefore need to borrow substantial sums either from banks and building societies or from individual investors.

Either way they are concerned about becoming personally liable for greater debts should the business fail. They would lose control of business activities, since it would be necessary to appoint assistants and managers to oversee key production and marketing activities. They also worry that they would lose flexibility and originality, since their designs would need to be standardised in order to meet the increased demand. Distribution costs would increase significantly, since the new orders are scattered throughout the country as opposed to selling to the local markets and traders. It is also likely that larger quantities of stock would be held at any one time, thereby increasing costs and the risk of theft or damage.

On the other hand they would benefit in other ways. They would be able to make savings by buying denim in bulk. This would also lead to less wastage, with computerised production methods ensuring maximum efficiency and cost-effectiveness. Staff could specialise in the production process, with personnel responsible for cutting, sewing, putting in zips, attaching rivets, and packing the finished article. All of this would contribute to a cheaper product.

Gianni and Domenico are attracted to the higher national profile that accepting the orders would naturally bring. They are also aware of the potential that the European and international markets have to offer. However, their individual image may be lost as the organisation grows in size and they become answerable to other colleagues.

ACTIVITY

1 Outline the advantages and disadvantages of rejecting the new orders and concentrating on the local market.
2 If Gianni and Domenico make the decision to expand, what kind of organisation would you recommend, taking into account the raising of additional finance, responsibility, liability and control?
3 What are the advantages of expanding and accepting the new orders? Your answers should refer to division of labour and economies of scale.
4 What problems are Gianni and Domenico likely to encounter if they make the decision to expand and take up the new orders? How can these problems be overcome?

Recommend the most appropriate course of action to Gianni and Domenico based upon your answers. *(1.1.3) (1.2.3) (1.2.5)*

The product of business organisations

There is a very basic distinction that can be made between different organisations on the basis of the goods or services they are selling or providing. The distinction is usually made between goods that are manufactured and the provision of services.

Manufactured goods

Some organisations produce something from raw materials. For example, a furniture manufacturer buys glue, wood, nails, plastic, screws and polish, and produces chairs, tables and cupboards for sale to its customers. Manufacturing refers to any process that takes raw materials or other goods from other businesses and combines or processes them into a finished or semi-finished product. Semi-finished products include the components for computers and cars, which are made by many different organisations and put together by another.

Manufactured goods are therefore simply those things that are made. This involves processing and combining raw materials and other produced parts together into something new. It covers a vast range of items – from paper clips to jumbo jets, and motorways to aspirins.

Everyday life is filled with manufactured goods, things that someone has designed and produced. Just from looking around you it would not take long to produce a list of many hundreds of such items. You should remember that they are part of the world of business – they have been planned, marketed, manufactured, distributed and purchased. It is likely that many organisations have contributed to each one being where it is now – the providers of the raw materials, the producers, the wholesalers, the

Business Organisations and Employment

retailers and the distributors. All of this activity has been aimed at meeting a particular market.

Services

Other organisations offer their services directly to the customer. There is no tangible product. For example, a bank offers guidance and assistance, and even arranges overdrafts and loans, but the customer does not receive a manufactured product as such, only a service. Other examples of service organisations include hairdressers, accountants, retail shops, travel agents and solicitors. As economies develop and become more advanced, the service sector increases, employing more people and providing a range of facilities. However, as the service sector grows there is usually a corresponding fall in the size of the manufacturing sector.

Many businesses sometimes provide both a manufactured product and a service. A garage may sell a new car with a warranty. The customer then receives the vehicle as well as receiving the service of repairs for a period of time.

Consumables and durables

Another distinction made between the products provided by businesses refers to use made by the consumer.

Some are classified as *consumables*, because they are short-lived and are used up by or 'consumed' by the consumer. Examples include food, electricity, petrol and all other services.

Others are classified as *durables*, since they last longer. The consumer purchases these items to keep them for a period of time. These include furniture, stereo systems and cars.

ACTIVITY

Below is a list of organisations. For each one, identify the product the organisation produces or the service that it provides.

Organisation	Product or Service	Consumable or durable
Marks & Spencer	Sells clothing, food and furniture to suit most tastes	
Ford Motor Co.		
Estate agents		
Building society		
BP		
BBC		
Oxfam		
Levis		
College		

(1.2.4)

Business Organisations and Employment

Market research

Types of market

The term 'market' can mean several different things. First, it may refer to a certain geographical area, such as the British market, European market or world market.

Second, it may be used to identify a particular group of people who are likely to buy the product or service, such as the female market, the student market or teenage market.

Third, the term may refer to an actual location where buying and selling takes place, such as the town market, stock exchange, or Petticoat Lane market in London.

Fourth, 'market' may be used to indicate the demand or otherwise for a particular product or service, for example the market for bread, CDs or houses. Finally, it may be used to classify the market according to business activity. This is illustrated by the following table:

Market	Type of business activity
Wholesale market	Buying from producers and selling to retailers
Retail or consumer market	Selling directly to the consumer
Commodities market	Buying and selling of raw materials, often importing and exporting
Industrial market	Trading in manufactured goods
Agricultural market produce	Buying and selling of cultivated
Money market	Trading in currency

In each of these senses – geographical, groups of people, location, demand or business activity – the word 'market' obviously means something slightly different, but in all cases they are related to one thing: namely the buying and selling of products and services.

In whatever sense the word 'market' is used there are three basic economic activities involved (producing, consuming and trading), and all are dependent upon each other. Since the main aim of producing goods and services is to sell them, the consumer plays a vital role in helping to determine what is to be produced. The really successful business person is the one who can accurately forecast what consumers need and want now, and what they might need and want in the future. Of course, consumers can only buy goods and service if they have been produce. However, goods will only be produced if there is a likelihood of them being used. To determine this requires market research.

The purpose of production, therefore, is to satisfy the needs and wants of consumers. Some organisations cater to meet *needs*, while others provide for people's *wants*.

Needs

Many public sector organisations service the *needs* of individuals, for example by providing essential services like bread, water, street lighting and sewage. Needs are defined as essential items that consumers cannot do without. If a person has an increase in salary it is unlikely that their expenditure on these items will increase. Consumers buy sufficient to satisfy their basic needs and no more.

Wants

Other organisations provide products or services to satisfy people's *wants*: for example, the music industry attempts to satisfy a range of musical tastes. Similarly, the clothing industry provides a range of garments of differing designs to satisfy varying styles of dress. Wants can be defined as products or services that consumers would like to own although they may not be regarded as essential.

Markets should always be classified according to what customers want or need, not on the basis of the products which are bought. Organisations should always concentrate their efforts on determining the ever-changing nature of customer needs and wants, rather than simply producing a product or service because 'they have always done so' and 'it has proved popular in the past'.

Wish to buy

Another feature of the demand by customers is their wish to buy. This is not the same as customers' needs. A customer may desire or need a product or service and yet be unwilling to buy it. New patterns of spending and saving affect people's desire to buy.

If asked to express a preference it is likely that people would rather spend their money on luxuries than necessities. Given the choice consumers would

Business Organisations and Employment

spend their money on new cars or new clothes rather than bread, milk, meat and heating. In this way the pattern of people's spending does not necessarily match their wishes.

For example, NHS prescriptions were free of charge when they were first introduced. When the government started to charge for this service consumers were not used to paying, since they were accustomed to receiving medicine free. They needed to find money which they previously used in other ways.

Another example is illustrated by the introduction of the CD player. When they first became available the public were not greatly interested. They were quite happy with their vinyl records. Why did they need this new technology, especially when there was a relatively small selection of CDs available? However, as fashions changed and the advantages of CDs became more widely known, people's wish to purchase a CD player increased.

Ability to buy

A final factor which influences demand is an individual's ability to pay. We all long to purchase products and services which we cannot afford to buy. What we can afford depends upon the amount of available earnings we have at our disposal. People on low incomes or on income support may wish to purchase items which other people take for granted. This may include heating, holidays and interesting food. For demand to be effective it must be matched by an ability to pay.

People are able to extend their ability to pay by taking advantage of credit deals or by borrowing money. However, this is only a short-term solution which must be supported by actual income over any period of time.

The popularity of the National Lottery reveals the hopes and aspirations of people to be able to buy things they cannot afford without a substantial win.

Four key areas are important in offering a total package to customers in meeting their needs and wants. The four areas, known as the *marketing mix*, are:

Price
lace
romotion
roduct

This involves identifying the nature of the *product* or service wanted by customers, selling it at an acceptable *price*, in the correct location or *place* and informing customers of this through the use of effective *promotion*. By following this process organisations are able to anticipate and fulfil customers' wants and needs.

ACTIVITY

Decide whether the following products or services are examples of needs or wants:
- Package holiday
- Loaf of bread
- Season ticket for the local football team
- Car
- Television
- Hospital facilities
- Water

What other factors influence consumers' spending?
(1.2.3)

ACTIVITY

In the rapidly changing area of sportswear, many companies have introduced a range of merchandise aimed at fulfilling specific needs and wants in this particular market.

Research two companies who sell sportswear and identify the nature and range of products produced. From this information try to assess the particular markets at which they are aiming.
(1.2.3) (1.2.4)

ACTIVITY

Decide the type of customer who would buy the following products or services and the specific needs or wants being catered for:
- Savings account
- Fast food
- Reliant Robin
- The *Sun* newspaper
- Theatre ticket
- The *Guardian* newspaper
- Leisure facilities
- Rave dance ticket
- Bus ticket

From the list, identify which items you would choose to buy if you could afford to. What factors influence your decision?
(1.2.3)

New products that meet identified markets

When developing new ideas the market may be divided in a number of useful ways. What the supplier supplies may be classified as:
- Manufactured goods
- Services

Also, what the customer requires from the supplier may be defined as:

36

Business Organisations and Employment

Innovative products

- Needs
- Wants

These distinctions make it easier for a supplier to understand the market and therefore to be more successful filling that niche.

Goods and services are provided by suppliers to satisfy the wants and needs of the market. A wise supplier will determine what people want *before* they start producing. Sometimes it happens by chance. The inventor of the board game *Monopoly*, for example, made the first set only to amuse himself during the depression of the 1930s in America. It was not until later, on the insistence of friends, that he decided to produce it for others. Now, of course, it is a classic game played all around the world.

Sometimes people will try to guess what the market requires. Sir Clive Sinclair is famous for his technological innovations. With the ZX80 computer he almost single-handedly revolutionised the industry. For the first time, the computer was available to a wide market. With his C5 electric car, however, the response was somewhat different. Although something of a novelty, it never truly caught on in the way that he had hoped.

The safest approach (which is not always the most interesting!) is to discover a niche in the market. A *niche* is a unique position that has not yet been filled and for which someone may be lucky enough to come up with something which will do the trick. Wash & Go shampoo is a good example. Its makers saw an opportunity, a very simple concept, to combine shampoo and conditioner in one bottle, and very quickly established a new brand. Other manufacturers soon copied the idea. Anita Roddick successfully found a market for her particular brand of product and service when she launched the Body Shop. Likewise Sophie Mirman located her niche when she started Sock Shop. Other projects are even more ambitious. Market research supported the building of Euro Disney. Sales to date have been disappointing, but time may change that, especially since another innovation, the Channel Tunnel, has opened.

All products or services can be identified as going through particular stages of development in their life cycle. The key stages are:

1 *Development*: the organisation researches and develops a new product or service in response to perceived market needs or wants
2 *Launch*: the product is launched onto the market with the appropriate promotional activity to bring it to the customers attention
3 *Growth*: as the product or service becomes established in the market place, sales increase and competitors begin to compete for market share
4 *Maturity*: as the product or service reaches its peak, the market begins to reach saturation point. There are now many new competitors in the market all fighting for a share of the sales.
5 *Decline*: as customers begin to look for alternative products or services in order to satisfy their ever-changing wants or needs, the demand for the original item begins to fall considerably and is often withdrawn from the market. It is essential that an organisation is able to launch a new product or service in order to re-establish itself in the market in order not to be affected in the long term by the decline of an outdated and outmoded product. This can be illustrated diagrammatically as follows:

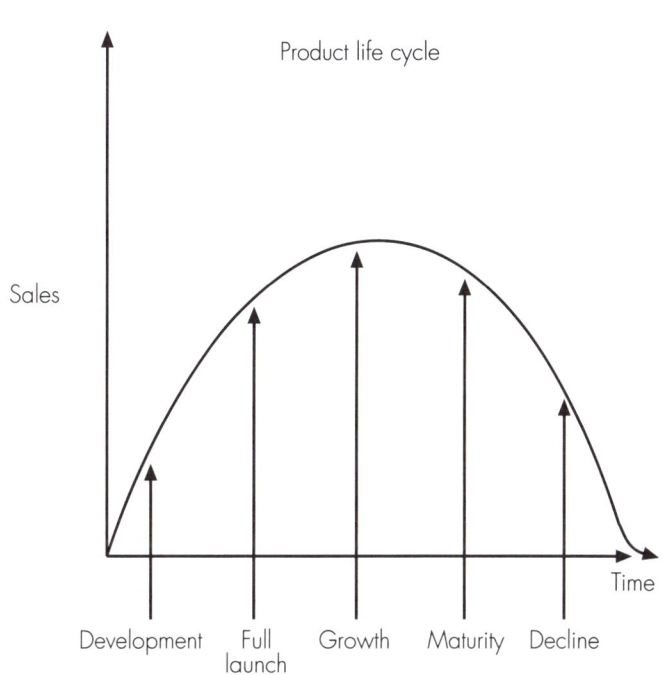

Product life cycle

Sales / Time

Development — Full launch — Growth — Maturity — Decline

Business Organisations and Employment

ACTIVITY

There are a lot of examples of products or services going through a product life cycle. Given the following examples, try to identify the stage they have reached:

Product or service	*Stage in product life cycle*
Interactive CD-ROM	Development stage
Reebok trainers	
Heinz ketchup	
House music	
Ink pen	
Video telephone	
Bell-bottom trousers	
Voice-activated computers	
LP records	

(1.2.5)

Market research

As no product lasts for ever it is important that organisations continue to monitor what the consumer is wanting. This is called *market research*. New or improved products or services will be developed based upon the results gained from the research. Although costly, market research can – if undertaken properly – take much of the risk out of production and avoid expensive mistakes being made. The actual research can be undertaken by the manufacturer's own staff or by independent agencies which specialise in doing this work on behalf of other firms.

ACTIVITY

The newspaper article below reports on a new notebook computer which is being introduced into the market. Read the article and answer the following questions:
1 What are the features of this new invention?
2 How does the product differ from those produced by rival companies?
3 What type of customer would be interested in buying the notebook and for what purpose would it be used?

(1.2.5) (1.2.6)

ACTIVITY

Identify three business organisations that differ in the product or service which they sell. Examples could include Heinz, Rowntree, Nike, EMI, Hanson, McDonald's, Virgin, Kellogg, ICI and British Rail.
1 Using the organisations as case studies, identify:
 • The scale and scope of the organisation
 • The products or services produced
 • Where the organisations are located
2 From your research identify how the organisation has addressed the 4Ps (product, price, promotion and place), looking particularly at the launch of new products or services that they have recently introduced onto the market.
3 Can you identify any gap in the market where there is a clear customer need or want and the organisations are not presently addressing it?

(1.2.3) (1.2.4) (1.2.5) (1.2.6)

MULTIPLE CHOICE

1 A 'footloose' organisation is one which:
 A Encourages its employees to wear open-toed sandals
 B Has a high staff turnover
 C Is free to locate where it chooses
 D Is labour-intensive

2 A bulk-reducing organisation is likely to locate:
 A Near to its customers
 B Near to its suppliers
 C Half-way between its suppliers and its customers
 D In any place it chooses with no special constraints

3 A bulk-increasing organisation is likely to locate:
 A Near to its customers
 B Near to its suppliers
 C Half-way between its suppliers and its customers
 D In any place it chooses with no special constraints

Bits & Bytes

Notebook newcomer ups stakes

CANON has upped the stakes in the competition to provide the most useful notebook computer with its Intel 486 SX-based BN100C with colour screen and built-in bubble-jet (mono) printer. The screen provides clear (256) colours and better than usual contrast (18:1 compared with 13:1 for most liquid-crystal display screens) by actually being two screens, each driven by its own microchip, so that refresh rates are higher than with most conventional systems.

Two Type-2 PCMCIA slots allow genuine portability. Those who need more disc capacity than the 120/210 megabytes on the built-in C-drive can slot in a £600 micro hard disc built into a PCMCIA card with capacities of 610–1005 megabytes. But for £2,349, excluding value-added tax, the machine is pricey.

The new machine is part of Canon's plan to secure 10% of the UK market for notebooks, 75% of which is now controlled by Toshiba and Compaq.

Source: Sunday Times, 13 February 1994

Business Organisations and Employment

4 A multinational organisation may be described as an organisation that:
  A Exports its products to more than one country
  B Employs people from more than one country
  C Is managed by the government
  D Is located in more than one country

5 In a typical product life cycle the *maturity* stage of a product is reached when:
  A The product is first introduced on the market
  B Sales of the product are becoming established
  C The product has reached its peak as an established item on the market
  D Sales of the product are falling due to loss of popularity

SHORT ANSWER

1 Factors influencing the location of business organisations include:
  (i) Natural resources
  (ii) Labour supply
  (iii) Local or national government incentives
  (iv) Proximity of other businesses
  (v) Transport services
  Which factor is likely to be the most significant for each of the following organisations moving to a new location?
  A A car-manufacturing plant requiring a large and skilled workforce
  B A firm of commercial cleaners
  C A fish wholesaler
  D A large supermarket
  E A footloose organisation

2 What is meant by 'economies of scale'? Give examples of economies of scale.

3 What is meant by 'diseconomies of scale'? Give examples of diseconomies of scale.

ELEMENT 1.3
Present results of investigation into employment

Performance criteria

- 1.3.1 Describe and give examples of types of employment
- 1.3.2 Collect, analyse and explain information about employment in different regions
- 1.3.3 Compare working conditions for employees in different organisations
- 1.3.4 Present results of investigation into employment or comparison of working conditions

Introduction

We have identified in the last two elements some key factors that are necessary for the effective process of production and consumption. These are:
- *land*: necessary for location
- *capital*: necessary for investment

These two inputs, together with *labour*, make up the three so-called *factors of production*. Element 1.3 focuses on this third and very important element, labour.

Business Organisations and Employment

APPOINTMENTS ❖ RECRUITMENT

LDR Recruitment
In line with the expansion plans of our sales team, LDR are actively seeking high calibre sales persons with proven technical abillity
If you are looking for a challenge then contact us at
0161-783 7831

MEADOW LANE NURSING HOME
SOUTH LYMPTON
REQUIRE **RGN'S**
Day duty / Night duty
Full and Part-time hours available
salary commensurate with experience
Please telephone Matron on 675934

Oldcastle College of Catering
Cook/chef
You should possess City and Guilds Certificates 706/1 and 2, and have a wide range of experience in the hotel, restaurant and volume catering sectors of the industry.
0191 874 0989   O.C.C

DRIVERS LGV Class 1 & 2 Multidrop, 7.5 Ton, etc.
Required urgently
Oldcastle OE4 8FT
078 67378

SECURI-SHUTTERS
ACCOUNTS CLERK
MUST BE FULLY CONVERSANT IN SAGE ACCOUNTS UP TO TRIAL BALANCE
TELEPHONE
4678000

STAFF VACANCIES
Mould's Garden Centre one of the largest garden centres in the area have vacancies for the following positions
Clerical staff
Head florist
Florists
remuneration subject to experience and qualifications.
09867444

A new career in driving instruction
could earn you up to £20,000 per annum
0164 89567

ARMY CAREERS
15,000 VACANCIES
There are 135 different jobs on offer, ranging from driver, chef, to electronics technician and infantry men.
contact Army Career Centre on
6789662

WELDER
The successful applicant must hold a C.I.T.B. forklift truck driving licence
Salary £8,200
Please write with fulll .C.V.

A.L.P.U
Qualified Teachers
Required as soon as possible for exciting new college setting in Oldcastle
Please reply in writing to

Types of employment

Consider the following case study.

SINGH AND ROBINSON – A PARTNERSHIP PRODUCING HAND-MADE CONFECTIONERY

In 1989 Satnam Singh and Sophie Robinson decided to establish a partnership making hand-made confectionery to sell to the local tourists in Haworth, Yorkshire. Haworth is famous for the Brontë sisters, who wrote many books, and visitors often come to the moorlands of Haworth to see where the sisters grew up.

Haworth has many cobbled streets with little craft shops. Sophie and Satnam realised that these shops offered a potential market for their individual biscuits and cakes. The confectionery proved to be very popular and the sales increased each day as more customers requested orders. As such, Sophie and Satnam decided to expand their operations in 1990 by working from bigger premises and employing additional staff.

The current staffing structure is as follows:
- *Sophie Robinson* and *Satnam Singh*: owners, working full-time within the organisation.
- *Charlotte Johnson*: has been working for the organisation since 1990. Her contract indicates that she is expected to work 37 hours a week, five days a week. This may include weekends should the need arise. She is employed as a 'product designer', developing and extending the range of provision available for sale.
- *Ben Nicholson*: is employed on a regular basis, working 12 hours a week. His contract details that he is expected to provide secretarial and administrative support for the organisation.
- *Peter Herbert*: has been employed during the summer, working 35 hours a week, to assist with the production process.
- *Sasha Voysey* and *Alice Crombie*: two members of staff who share a full-time job, working on the production line with *Martin Woods*, another full-time member of staff.

Demand has increased considerably in the 1990s and the partners are seriously considering implementing computerised production processes, which will increase production and reduce costs. However, this will mean that Peter, Sasha, Alice and Martin will no longer be required within the firm. This is a moral dilemma that Sophie and Satnam have to face. Do they move with the times and update their processes, or do they retain their hard-working and dedicated team?

The case study illustrates that within any organisation a range of personnel are normally required to help achieve the aims and objectives. Some organisations only require one individual to take responsibility for all aspects of business operations. In contrast, other organisations have a highly complex structure, employing specialised staff for key areas.

The case study also helps to illustrate that in recent years there has been a growing trend to employing people on a part-time or temporary basis. Computerised and automated working practices are also affecting working practices in all organisations, regardless of size.

Self-employed

The simplest type of organisation in the private sector is a sole trader, who is described as being *self-employed*. Literally, this means that the sole trader employs him- or herself, taking a wage out of the profits. Similarly, within a partnership the partners are self-employed, sharing the profits out between themselves.

Self-employed workers can also 'sell' their specialised skills to other organisations, but are not regarded as employees of that organisation. Examples would include joiners, builders, engineers and finance specialists. They operate on a freelance or consultative basis, offering their skills and expertise in return for a wage.

Business Organisations and Employment

> **ACTIVITY**
>
> Read the Singh and Robinson case study and identify which of the individuals are self-employed.
> Identify the advantages and disadvantages of being self-employed. What reasons can you think of to explain why there has been a considerable increase in the number of people becoming self-employed in recent years?
> *(1.3.1)*

Employed

Anyone who is hired by another person or organisation, providing their labour in exchange for a monetary reward, may be said to be *employed*. The party who employs and pays the wage or salary is known as the *employer* and the person who is employed and provides their labour, in exchange for a wage, is known as the *employee*.

Characteristics of the self-employed	Characteristics of employed workers
• Is responsible for getting regular work and negotiating the price to be charged	• Is given a specific role or duties to perform in return for a wage
• Has to maintain own records for tax and national insurance	• Has tax and national insurance records completed by employer
• Makes decisions about hours and holidays worked	• Hours and holidays are agreed within contract of employment
• Is responsible for providing own tools and equipment	• Uses the tools and equipment provided by employer
• Does not get sick pay and is not protected by the Employment Protection (Consolidation) Act	• Is entitled to sick pay and usually protected by the Employment Protection (Consolidation) Act
• Responsible for debts incurred by the organisation	• Not responsible for the debts of the organisation

> **ACTIVITY**
>
> 1 From the Singh and Robinson case study identify which of the individuals are self-employed and which are employees.
> 2 Produce a table outlining the advantages and disadvantages of being an employer and an employee.
> 3 You have just been offered a full-time job working for a local organisation. Make a list of the terms of employment that you would like to agree upon with the employer before you make a decision to accept the job.
> *(1.3.1)*

Within any organisation workers may be employed on a full- or part-time basis. Full-time employees are expected to be provided with a job description and a contract of employment.

Full-time

Full-time permanent staff may also receive protection from employment legislation, e.g. The Employment Protection (Consolidation) Act 1978, the Sex Discrimination Acts 1975 and 1986, the Race Relations Act 1976 and the Employment Act 1989. Protection is based upon length of service and numbers of hours worked.

Full-time staff may also be employed on a permanent or temporary basis. Workers who are employed on a full-time permanent basis are protected by the relevant employment legislation mentioned above.

Temporary staff are often employed, however, to cover short-term for full-time workers who are off work for sickness or holidays. Alternatively, full-time temporary staff may be employed to provide specialised skills for a particular task or activity.

For temporary full-time staff who are employed for a short period of time, in order to perform a specific job, there is usually no need to provide them with written particulars about their job. If the temporary position is for an extended period, e.g. usually for a period of three months or more, it is necessary to provide them with written details relating to their employment.

Clearly, for workers who are employed on a temporary full-time basis, the organisation is under no obligation to continue with their services once the period of time has been served. In some cases, temporary contracts are renewed if the organisation feels that it is appropriate and that there is a job still to be done. The length of service and the number of hours worked will determine whether a temporary member of staff is entitled to employment legislation protection.

> **ACTIVITY**
>
> Review the Singh and Robinson case study. Identify which staff are employed on a permanent and temporary full-time basis.
> How do their employment rights differ?
> Identify the advantages and disadvantages to both the employer and employee of working on a permanent and temporary basis.
> *(1.3.1)*

Part-time

Within any organisation there may be a variety of tasks that need a few hours of work to complete, and for these activities part-time staff are often employed, either on a temporary or permanent basis. Examples include caretakers, cleaners, catering staff and consultants.

Business Organisations and Employment

Part-time staff may also be employed to meet temporary increases in demand, e.g. an increase in the sale of confectionery during the tourist season. There is a legal requirement to provide employees who work eight hours or more with a written statement outlining the terms and conditions of their employment.

Increase in part-time staff

The number of staff who are employed part-time has increased considerably in recent years throughout a range of industries, including, clerical, retailing, hotel and catering. Part-time workers are cheaper to employ, provide greater flexibility and do not receive the same legal protection as workers employed full-time.

From the employee's point of view, part-time work can be combined with domestic responsibilities, leisure activities or studies.

ACTIVITY

1. Review the Singh and Robinson case study and identify which staff are employed on a part-time basis.
2. Produce a table outlining the advantages and disadvantages of part-time employment to both the employer and employee.
3. Using local and national newspapers identify how many job advertisements apply to full-time and part-time employment. Illustrate this information using appropriate numerical methods.
    Cut out a selection of advertisements for full-time and part-time positions from the papers. Are there any typical characteristics associated with the jobs advertised in the local paper in comparison with those advertised in the national paper?
    Now compare the full-time and part-time positions. What kinds of jobs are being advertised on a part-time and full-time basis? Do any interesting trends emerge?
4. As a group, identify which students work on a part-time basis and the characteristics of those jobs. Identify the companies involved and the terms and conditions offered. Which organisation appears to be the best employer, based upon your findings?

(1.3.1) (1.3.2) (1.3.4)

Job sharing

The process of job sharing is becoming more popular as individuals move towards combining a career with their personal lives, e.g. raising children. A full-time position is shared between two individuals who agree the distribution of work. Each individual would have a personalised contract of employment, outlining the particular details of their position, e.g. duties, hours and pay.

ACTIVITY

Review the case study and identify the individuals who are currently job sharing within the organisation.

Outline the advantages and disadvantages of job sharing to both the employer and the employee. *(1.3.1)*

Employment figures: Distribution of the workforce in the UK (all figures in thousands). *Source:* Department of Employment

	1981	1986	1991
Total workforce	26,697	27,877	28,340
Male	16,288	16,442	16,240
Female	10,409	11,435	12,100
Total unemployed	2,176	3,121	2,293
Male	1,605	2,154	1,739
Female	571	967	554
Workforce in employment	24,323	24,559	26,043
Male	14,569	14,173	14,498
Female	9,754	10,386	11,544
HM Forces	334	322	297
Male	317	305	278
Female	17	16	19
Self-employed	2,119	2,633	3,143
Male	1,694	1,993	2,396
Female	425	640	747
Employees in employment	21,870	21,379	22,259
Male	12,558	11,748	11,613
Female	9,312	9,631	10,646
of whom:			
Total production and construction industries	8,068	6,777	6,247
Total all manufacturing	6,230	5,242	4,846
Work-related government training programmes		226	343
Males		127	211
Females		99	132

Important terms
Workforce: refers to the workforce in employment plus the unemployed who are claiming benefit.
Workforce in employment: includes employees in employment, the self-employed, HM Forces and work-related government training programmes

ACTIVITY

Using the information listed above, identify the trends that emerge in relation to the distribution of the workforce in 1991, looking particularly at the breakdown of employment for particular years and comparisons between years. Present your findings using appropriate numerical and graphical methods.

Obtain comparable figures for the most recent year available to you.
(1.3.1) (1.3.2) (1.3.5)

Business Organisations and Employment

An employee's contract of employment may be *permanent* or *temporary*. Until recently, temporary employees did not enjoy the same rights and employment protection as full-time employees. Now, however, issues such as terms of notice, maternity leave, benefits, rates of pay and so on are virtually the same for all employees (see Unit 2).

Permanent
An employee on a permanent contract can reasonably expect to continue in their job until retirement. Their contract has no fixed expiry time included in it, and therefore the only closing date is likely to be when the employee reaches retirement age. However, they are still open to *redundancy* (that is, being made unemployed during times of organisational restructuring). Alternatively, they may be fairly dismissed for disciplinary reasons.

Temporary
An employee on a temporary contract has a fixed term of employment. The contract will specify the period of employment – one month, three months, a year, and so on. When this period has passed the contract may be renewed, although the employer has no obligation to do so.

Skilled employment
Employment may also be classified according to the activities carried out by the worker. *Skilled* employment requires the worker to have a level of expertise to perform complex tasks. Examples include:
- factory operator
- electrician
- lawyer
- nurse
- plumber
- accountant

To work in skilled employment it may be necessary to have particular qualifications and training. However, it may also be sufficient in some areas to demonstrate competence through experience. For example, while there are qualifications which actors may take, many famous and highly skilled performers have never been to drama school.

Unskilled employment
Unskilled employment includes those jobs which do not require particular expertise, previous experience or qualifications. Examples include labourers, waste disposal workers, window cleaners and road sweeps. These jobs tend also to be lower paid as there is a greater supply of people in a position to do them.

ACTIVITY

Examine the list of occupations below. From the list identify whether the jobs are:
- skilled or unskilled
- permanent or temporary
- a teacher on a fixed three-year contract
- an accountant who is a partner in a firm
- an administrative clerk on a government training scheme
- a labourer employed until the completion of a housing development
- a self-employed engineer involved in a project to widen the M25
- a doctor in a local practice
- a trainee nurse
- a medical student doing a cleaning job for the summer
- a potato-picker on a local farm

(1.3.1)

Labour mobility
Mobility means the 'ability' to change position. In the context of employment, labour mobility refers to the ease of changing jobs, either geographically or occupationally.

Geographical mobility This refers to the movement of workers from one town or region to another. The primary reason for this move is the need to search for work coupled with the shortages of jobs in the local area.

Occupational mobility This refers to the movement of workers from one job to another. If the job is unskilled or semi-skilled it is relatively easy to move occupations. However, if a worker wants to change jobs completely, possibly due to the lack of employment opportunities in the original job or because of a desire to find more interesting work, then further education and training maybe required.

ACTIVITY

Identify the factors that may limit the mobility of labour, both geographical and occupational.
How can these problems be minimised?
(1.3.3)

Division of labour
Many organisations have broken down jobs into specialist processes or tasks in order to maximise efficiency and productivity. Each task is performed by a separate person who in turn becomes highly skilled in performing that activity. This is called the division of labour and is very common in large scale production processes.

Advantages of the division of labour
- Increases in output.
- Improvements in quality, as each person performs a limited job repeatedly and therefore builds up a high level of skill.
- Time saving, as production follows an efficient process.

43

Business Organisations and Employment

Disadvantages of the division of labour
- Boredom of staff due to the increased monotony of work. This can lead to a reduction in quality and poor workmanship as workers become careless and frustrated.
- Alienation. This means that the worker has no pride in and cannot identify with the finished product.
- De-skilling of work as processes are broken down into simple tasks, with the corresponding loss of craftmanship.

ACTIVITY

Think of some examples of organisations which use the division of labour.
What are the advantages to the organisations in using this method? How can the problems be minimised?
(1.3.4)

Features of employment

Physical working conditions
It is generally regarded that good working conditions lead to an increase in motivation and commitment from workers, a higher level of morale and well being, greater efficiency and a positive company image.

However, the working conditions will vary according to the type of work undertaken. For example, the work undertaken in the primary sector is very different from the work undertaken in the tertiary sector, and as such the working conditions will be very different.

For example, the underground workings of a mine present coal miners with very different working conditions from those found in a college or school by a lecturer or teacher. The type of job and working conditions may also affect the type of clothes worn, the hours worked and the length of holidays given.

ACTIVITY

Try to identify from the brief description of working conditions given below the type of occupation and the industrial sector to which the occupation belongs. Then summarise the main features about the working conditions for each job.

Job 1
'I have to work regular shifts – mornings, afternoons or nights. My job involves me working underground in dirty working conditions, which are cramped and dusty. I have to say, though, the conditions have improved from when my father worked here. Today we have modern machinery to work with and there are strict health and safety checks. My father, on the other hand, had to work with a pick and a shovel, and the blaring out of the

Business Organisations and Employment

horn to the local village indicated yet another accident. It is important that we wear our safety helmets and bright orange overalls. This means that we can see and be seen in the dark, poorly ventilated hole in which we work. Clearly there are no toilet or washing facilities down here, although these are available once we have finished our shift and are back in the daylight again. I sometimes worry about my future. The conditions might not be ideal, but at least it is a job and the feeling of team spirit among the workers is excellent.'

Job 2
'I face a class of 30 seven-year-olds, five days a week. The building was built forty years ago, so it needs money spending on it to bring the canteen and sport facilities up to date. However, my base room has lots of visual materials on the walls and the furniture is well looked after. The staff have a recreational area where we can relax during breaks, although we eat with the students in the main canteen.'

Job 3
'I work on the land. The seasons and elements are my boss as they dictate when I do things and the hours I work. It is great to be outside, even in the cold, dark mornings of winter. Up-to-date equipment, fresh air and hard work. . . what else could anybody want?'

Job 4
'I have a regular job, 9.00 to 5.00, Monday to Friday. However, there are other workers on this production line who work on a shift basis. My job is to ensure that the exhaust pipes are put in the right place and sealed before they move down the conveyor belt to the next person. I have become quite an expert at my job and have perfected the art of performing the task efficiently while at the same time thinking about what I am going to do that evening. The working conditions are not too bad either. It is rather noisy in the factory and the work is quite dirty. However, we have modern machinery to work with and there are regular health and safety checks. The factory floor, or shop floor, as it is sometimes called, is well ventilated and we are allowed to play Radio 1 throughout the day. I have to wear overalls and flat shoes and tie my hair back. The canteen facilities and rest room are great. The food in the canteen is excellent and we are allowed to smoke in the rest room although it is banned on the shop floor and in the canteen.'

Job 5
'The staff here are allowed to work flexi-time, which means that as long as we work a 35 hour week and get our work done the organisation is prepared to be flexible in terms of allowing us to start between 8.00 and 10.00 and finish between 16.30 and 18.00. The layout within the office is open plan, so we are able to communicate across the filing cabinets and desks! We have a central typing pool, which all staff can use, and the photocopying is undertaken by the office junior. I am in charge of checking invoices and raising payments. The accommodation layout is modern, with lots of plants and good lighting. It is well ventilated, with an efficient heating system, which means when it is cold outside we can still dress smartly.'
(1.1.1) (1.3.3)

ACTIVITY

What type of job would you like to have? Give a brief description of the type of working conditions you would expect to find with this job.
(1.3.3) (1.3.4)

ACTIVITY

Copy out and complete the following table, identifying different jobs from the primary, secondary and tertiary sectors and describe the working conditions associated with that job and any key features, e.g. shift working or safety clothing. What interesting trends emerge?
(1.1.1) (1.3.1) (1.3.3)

Type of job	Sector	Typical working conditions	Special features
Miner	Primary	Underground, dirty and dangerous	Shift work Safety helmets

Business Organisations and Employment

NISSAN

The Japanese car manufacturer Nissan, located in Sunderland, has attempted to improve radically the working conditions of its employees working on the factory floor. All employees, directors and workers eat in the same canteen. Individuals are encouraged to present ideas and proposals to improve working conditions, and are then given the authority to see them through. On the shop floor the company is committed to encouraging team working and they expect all staff to take responsibility for good housekeeping and maintenance. All individuals have responsibility for quality by checking their work before passing it on to their neighbours. Quality controllers as a separate group of employees are a thing of the past. Finally, flexibility is the key to working at Nissan. Workers perform different tasks daily, which reduces boredom and increases productivity.

ACTIVITY

Identify the key features about a typical working day at the Nissan car plant.
(1.3.3) (1.3.4)

Although working conditions may vary, employers are responsible for providing good working conditions and protecting their employees by providing safe working methods. As part of their duties, employers should:
- Ensure that the working conditions are safe and healthy
- Make regular checks to establish the safety of machinery and equipment
- Train staff to follow health and safety guidelines
- Try to provide a quality working environment where employees want to work

Quality working environment
There are a range of factors that need to be addressed in order to create a quality working environment.

Space There should be sufficient space for individuals to work within. Overcrowding leads to inefficiency in working practices and arguments between staff. The minimum legal requirement is 40 square feet, although some studies indicate that 60 square feet is more appropriate.

Heating, lighting and ventilation Effective use of heating, lighting and ventilation contributes to increases in productivity and staff morale. The minimum temperature required in an organisation is 16 °C. Wherever possible, lighting should be natural, and where artificial lights are needed, strip lights should be used, not bulbs.

The air ventilation should filter out smoke and dust but not create a draught.

Furniture and equipment Furniture and equipment should be appropriately placed to encourage the flow of work by ensuring that those who work together are sitting in close proximity. Central resources and services, e.g. clerks, should be accessible to everyone. The furniture should be comfortable and supportive, with the emphasis being on what is functional as well as what is attractive.

Layout of departments The layout of departments is a relevant factor too. Areas that include heavy machinery should be kept at ground level, and dining and recreational areas should be separate from the working environment. Departments that involve design, drawing and planning need a lot of natural light, and conference facilities need to be located away from noise and interruptions.

Noise Interruptions in working practices due to noise can be reduced with effective carpeting, sound-absorbent walls and ceilings.

Decor The decor is also a relevant factor when planning the working environment. Blinds and curtains help to reduce unwanted light and help to provide privacy. Effective use of colours can also create the right atmosphere – brown, yellow and, magnolia are warm colours and will help to put workers at ease. White and cream give an impression of space, which is important if the organisation is operating within small premises. Green is a very restful colour, which is why it is often used for VDU screens.

ACTIVITY

1. Look at the diagram at the top of the next page. Plan the office to maximise efficiency and minimise disruption. Write some brief notes beneath your diagram explaining your choice of layout.
2. Interview three employees from a range of jobs and industries. Find out as much information as you can about their jobs and their working conditions. What interesting trends emerge? Present your findings using appropriate visual and written methods.

(1.3.2) (1.3.3) (1.3.4)

Business Organisations and Employment

Clerical Administrator
£10,000 a year
The Company: Transform Ltd
Based in Leeds
Market Leader in veneered/laminated doors

Are you:
- Calm and methodical?
- Numerate?
- Good at using the telephone?
- A neat writer?
- Able to use a VDU?
- Able to deal with customers?
- Experienced in dealing with business documents?

Do you have a GNVQ in Business?
The benefits:
25 days holiday a year
35 hour week
Contributory pension scheme
Profit-sharing scheme
FLEXI-TIME
Apply giving full personal details to Box Number 234

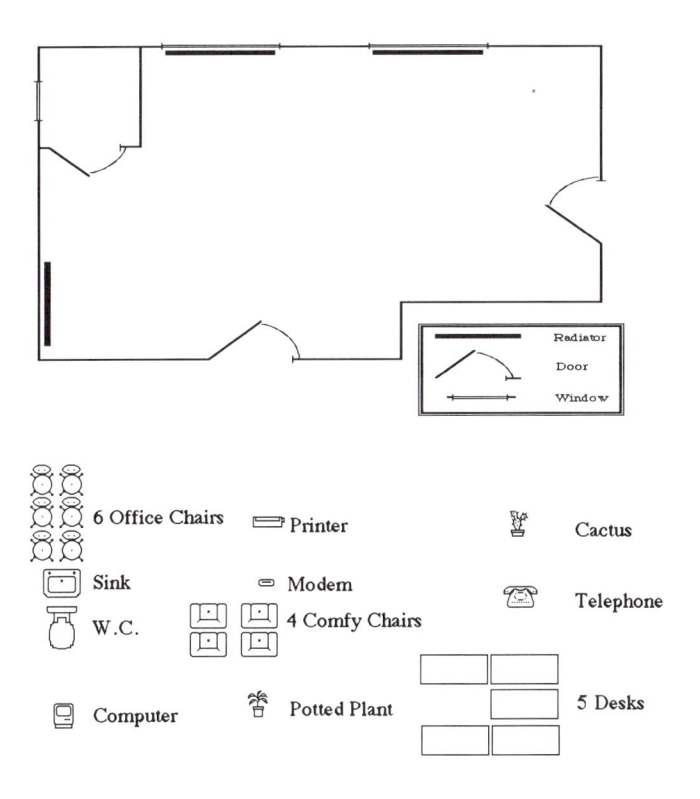

Employment contracts

A contract of employment is an agreement between two parties, usually an employer and an employee. It may be made orally or in writing and should provide a written statement of the main terms of employment given to most full-time and some part-time employees. The contract of employment would usually include:
- The names of the employer and the employee
- The date when the employment began
- Whether it is a new appointment or continuous service from a previous appointment
- The scale or rate of pay
- The hours to be worked
- The holiday entitlement and holiday pay
- Sick pay
- Details relating to pension schemes
- The length of notice required by both the employer and the employee
- The job title with a brief description of duties

ACTIVITY

Using the following advertisement, try to produce a contract of employment that includes all the relevant information.
(1.3.3)

Wages

An important part of any job is the wage or salary to be paid in return for the services received. There is an important distinction between the two terms.

A *wage* is defined as a payment in return for work or services that is usually paid to workers on a daily, hourly, weekly or sometimes a monthly basis. It is usually related to the number of hours worked or the number of units made by the worker.

A *salary*, on the other hand, is defined as a fixed regular payment made by an employer, usually a yearly sum divided into twelve equal monthly amounts, for professional or office staff as opposed to manual work.

Basic wage

The basic wage refers to the amount of money paid to an employer or employee before any additional payments are added. The basic wage may be supplemented by:

Overtime: paid for hours worked over and above the basic requirement.
Performance-related pay: share of the profits for meeting specified targets.
Commission: additional payments may be earned by the number of sales achieved.
Bonuses: Some organisations operate a bonus scheme as a method of thanking staff for their efforts.

ACTIVITY

Look at the wage slip at the top of the next page. Identify the basic wage, overtime and commission.
(1.3.3)

47

Business Organisations and Employment

PAY ADVICE							
Name of Employee	Paco Sanchez	Payroll No.		139/B			
National Insurance No.	NP 54 32 78 B	Date		August 31 1994			
Pay Period	month 6						
		Gross	**PAYE**	**NI**	**Other**	**Net Pay**	
Basic Pay for Period		2249.23	427.75	202.43	0.00	1619.05	
Overtime	5 hrs @ £12.25	61.25	24.50	5.51	0.00	31.24	
Expenses		125.66	0.00	0.00	0.00	125.66	
Bonus		500.00	200.00	45.00	0.00	255.00	
Union Subscriptions		0.00	0.00	0.00	12.25	−12.25	
TOTAL FOR PERIOD		2936.14	652.25	252.94	12.25	£2018.70	
TOTAL PAY TO DATE		17524.27	3827.25	1190.88	73.50	12506.14	

The wage slip clearly indicates the gross wage and the net wage. The gross wage refers to the amount paid before any deductions, and the net wage relates to the amount paid after deductions and is effectively the take-home pay for the individual.

Statutory deductions

Any wage or salary paid will be reduced by statutory deductions. A statutory deduction is a deduction that organisations are legally obliged to make. They include income tax and national insurance.

Taxation

Income tax is a compulsory deduction at source, taken from the salary and paid to the government. The amount paid is directly related to the amount that an individual earns and is usually calculated on a PAYE basis – pay as you earn. The only exceptions to this are those who do not earn enough to pay tax and the self-employed, who pay their tax in two instalments during the financial year.

Before deductions are taken, a calculation is made to identify the total amount of allowances that an individual is entitled to. The following criteria are used:
1. single person's allowance
2. married person's allowance
3. mortgage allowance
4. disability allowance
5. specialised clothing and equipment allowance

Taxation is used by the government for general public spending.

National insurance

National insurance contributions are also related to the amount that an individual earns, and are deducted from the gross salary (in the case of self-employed workers it can be paid in several instalments). The wage slip indicates the national insurance contribution paid by the employee. In addition, the employer is expected to make a national contribution on behalf of the employee too.

National insurance contributes towards a range of benefits and grants. Some of these are:
1. the state pension
2. unemployment benefit
3. statutory sick pay
4. statutory maternity pay
5. child benefit

ACTIVITY

Referring to the wage slip above, identify the amounts paid in taxation and national insurance. What percentage of the total salary has been deducted through statutory deductions?
(1.3.3)

The wage slip also indicates some voluntary deductions. These may include:
- Trade union subscriptions
- Charity donations
- Social club subscriptions

ACTIVITY

From the wage slip identify the voluntary deductions. How much of the total salary has now been deducted in both statutory and voluntary deductions?
(1.3.3)

Training

The government has recognised that a well-qualified and trained work force leads to greater productivity and efficiency, and they have produced National Training Targets that reflect this. The training targets aim to train individuals to NVQ and GNVQ standards.

In order to achieve the national training targets and in an attempt to improve the quality of the workforce, the government is encouraging individuals to maximise their educational opportunities and encouraging employers to support the training and education of all employees.

The overall aims are to:
- Make further education or training available for all 16- and 17-year-olds.
- Increase the all-round attainment of young people.
- Increase the proportion of young people acquiring higher levels of skill and expertise.

(*Source*: DES Education and Training for the 21st century)

It is hoped that GNVQ and NVQ qualifications will provide:
- Broader and more relevant programmes for students in preparing them for life and work.
- Employers with better qualified and well-prepared employees.
- Qualifications that are relevant to the world of work.

Education and training can be on a full- or part-time basis. For individuals who are in work, training can take place in a variety of ways:
- *Day release*: the employer recognises the need for training by providing employees with a day in college once a week.
- *Block release*: the employee attends college for a block period, e.g. once a month or three times a year, and returns to work for the periods when not in college.
- *Training on the job*: training is conducted within the workplace either by the training officer or by a college lecturer who will teach within the organisation for a period of time.

Education and training can continue throughout an individual's life. People can progress from full-time education to part-time when in work, and throughout their working lives employees can continue to study for relevant qualifications. The process of education and training is mutually beneficial to both the employer and the employee.

Qualifications

The final feature of employment that we must examine is qualifications.

Qualifications refers to formal recognition of skills and expertise that an employee may possess. When a job application form asks for qualifications the candidate should record details of those that they have achieved. It is not enough to *believe* that you are qualified – the employer will expect to see certificates and documents.

Starting work is not the end of obtaining qualifications. Many employees will continue to study and work for new qualifications to assist their work and increasing responsibilities.

Qualifications can be categorised as follows.

Academic qualifications   This covers certificates and awards received from schools, colleges and universities that are wholly knowledge-based. They do not relate specifically to any one job area and have no direct practical application. Examples include:
- GCSEs
- AS levels
- A levels
- Degrees
- PhDs

Vocational qualifications   Vocational qualifications, on the other hand, are practical awards that relate to an area of work. They may be very specific, relating to a narrow area of skills used in work. Alternatively they may be broad-based with a general application to a vocational area. Examples include:
- GNVQs
- NVQs

Occupational or professional qualifications   This covers examinations passed for professional bodies. These are normally specific to particular vocational areas and are available at a variety of levels. Professional bodies that have exams include:
- Association of Accounting Technicians (AAT)
- Institute of Management
- Institute of Marketing
- Institute of Personnel Management
- Institute of Purchasing and Supply
- Institute of Bankers
- Institute of Credit Management

Of course, qualifications have a close connection with training. It is becoming more common for training schemes to allow for *accreditation of prior learning and achievement*, often abbreviated to APA or APL. This means that a trainee may receive formal recognition of skills and expertise that they already have, especially if they do not possess certificates and records to show this.

ACTIVITY

1. Outline the advantages and disadvantages of providing educational and training opportunities to both the employer and the employee.
2. Undertake a study of your organisation. What educational and training opportunities are available for individuals? Interview a selection of people on a range of programmes and identify their reasons for studying and what their aspirations are.
3. Produce a life plan for yourself. Identify where you are now in terms of experience and qualifications and then identify what your plans are for the next 20 years in terms of career aspirations and education and training targets.

(1.3.3) (1.3.4)

Business Organisations and Employment

Levels of employment locally and in another region

Investment

Problems arise if people are unable to find alternative employment despite undertaking retraining. This results in areas of very high unemployment, poverty and deprivation, due to lack of investment in the area. The government and local authorities have to address this problem by providing funds to reinvest into the region in the hope of attracting new firms into the area. Assisted areas which are given financial help in this way are classified as development or intermediate areas.

ACTIVITY

Using relevant government publications, e.g. Department of Trade and Industry publications, *Social Trends* or *Economic Trends*, identify a map of the United Kingdom which details the assisted areas within the UK. Draw the map, including the assisted areas. What interesting trends emerge? Are you located in an assisted area?
(1.3.2)

Natural resources

Levels of employment and unemployment rates vary from region to region. This is because levels of employment reflect the availability of jobs in a particular region, which in turn reflect the resources of that area. It was the presence of coal and iron ore which helped to make England the leading industrial country in the 18th and 19th centuries – with a higher productivity at that time than any other country in the world.

Natural resources are located in particular regions, and exploitation of those resources therefore creates employment for people in those regions. For example, Wales has a natural supply of coal and therefore mining was a major occupation in that area. North Sea oil and gas provided employment for many people in the north.

Therefore if an area is dependent upon a particular industry for providing employment and that industry is in decline because the product or service is no longer wanted, then high levels of unemployment will result.

A lot of people were employed in the steel industry in Sheffield, for example, and had to retrain to find alternative employment when the steel works closed. Coal mining in Yorkshire and Nottinghamshire and tin mining in Cornwall are other examples. More recently, full-time jobs have tended to disappear in farming as the growing trend is to employ part-time staff.

ACTIVITY

Different regions are famous for the presence of various natural resources. These include:

coal	timber	sand and gravel
gas	limestone	chalk
water	clay	land suitable for farming
salt	water suitable for fishing	

Using *Social Trends*, identify the types of jobs and natural resources that are most commonly found in the following regions of England:

Region	Jobs and resources
North	
Yorkshire and Humberside	
East Midlands	
East Anglia	
South-East	
South-West	
West Midlands	
North-West	

Which famous towns and cities are found within these regions?
Produce a list of problems that may occur if an individual is made unemployed.
Why is it not always possible to find alternative employment despite retraining?
(1.3.2)

Business Organisations and Employment

Labour and skills supply

Areas of high unemployment may contrast markedly with other areas where there is considerable investment resulting in many jobs of different types. Clearly, the regional imbalance in investment creates regional inequalities in the availability of jobs, levels of income and spending.

Regional differences

The following points provide some important facts about regional differences in employment for the United Kingdom in 1992.

Self-employment   Self-employment is highest in the South-West, Wales and East Anglia, where around one in seven of the workforce are self-employed.

Employees
- The public administration sector is the biggest employer in Northern Ireland. Almost one third of all male employees and over half of all female employees are employed in this area. It is much higher than in any other region.
- The South-East employs more people in the financial sector than any other region. Almost one in six people work in this area.
- The West Midlands still employs a large proportion of people within manufacturing, despite recent decline in this industrial sector. Two out of five males and one out of five females are employed in manufacturing in the Midlands, which is double the rates in the South-East.

Qualifications of the workforce   The highest qualified workforce is in the South-East where eight out of every ten people have a qualification of some kind and one in seven are educated to degree level.

Unemployment   Long-term unemployment is much worse in Northern Ireland, where one in five unemployed men have been out of work for more than five years. In comparison, only one in forty men have been long-term unemployed in the South-East, the South-West and East Anglia. The average for the United Kingdom as a whole is one in twenty.

The recent trend in unemployment reflects that those areas with low levels of unemployment have seen the largest increases in unemployment rates and those regions that have had the highest levels have seen the smallest increase. For example, the South-East has seen an increase in unemployment rates between 1991 and 1992 of 55.1% and over. In comparison, the percentage increase for Northern Ireland, which has the highest rate of unemployment, was 10% and under for the same period.
(*Source*: *Social Trends 1992*.)

ACTIVITY

The tables on the next two pages illustrate unemployment rates by duration and sex and unemployment by age and sex for 1992. Look at the tables and identify the interesting trends that emerge. Which regions have the highest levels of unemployment for the longest periods of time? Which areas have the lowest levels of unemployment for the shortest periods of time? In what way does the age of an individual affect their chances of becoming unemployed?
(1.3.2)

Business Organisations and Employment

Unemployment[1]: by age and sex, 1992 (*Source*: Employment Department, *Social Trends* 1992)

	\multicolumn{6}{c	}{Percentage aged}	Total
	Under 20	20–29	30–39	40–49	50–59	60 and over	(= 100%) numbers
Males							
United Kingdom	7.1	38.2	22.6	15.8	13.7	2.6	2,045,371
North	7.9	38.9	22.4	15.2	13.8	1.7	123,461
Yorkshire & Humberside	7.9	39.5	21.4	15.0	14.0	2.2	180,725
East Midlands	7.7	37.7	21.4	15.9	14.3	3.1	128,208
East Anglia	7.8	36.1	21.0	16.7	14.5	3.8	54,899
South East	5.9	37.3	23.9	16.1	13.6	3.2	592,310
South West	7.0	36.2	21.6	17.5	14.6	3.2	152,408
West Midlands	7.5	37.5	21.6	15.5	14.5	3.4	197,400
North West	7.7	40.5	22.3	14.9	12.7	1.9	249,966
England	7.0	38.0	22.5	15.8	13.8	2.8	1,679,377
Wales	7.9	40.1	22.9	15.7	12.0	1.4	101,149
Scotland	7.4	39.5	22.4	15.3	13.8	1.7	184,108
Northern Ireland	6.6	35.8	25.1	18.1	12.9	1.4	80,737
Females							
United Kingdom	13.0	40.6	16.6	15.8	13.9	0.1	628,493
North	15.5	39.6	16.0	15.2	13.7	0.1	34,535
Yorkshire & Humberside	14.8	41.0	15.7	14.9	13.5	0.1	52,365
East Midlands	13.8	39.9	16.2	16.2	13.9	0.1	40,264
East Anglia	13.6	38.8	15.7	17.8	14.1	0.1	18,208
South East	10.7	41.6	18.0	16.1	13.5	0.1	191,914
South West	12.7	38.9	16.1	17.9	14.3	0.1	48,921
West Midlands	13.5	40.0	15.8	15.9	14.6	0.1	61,392
North West	14.8	41.6	15.2	14.5	13.8	0.1	71,990
England	12.8	40.7	16.6	15.9	13.8	0.1	519,589
Wales	15.3	40.1	16.0	15.8	12.7	0.0	27,606
Scotland	13.1	40.2	16.5	15.4	14.8	0.1	57,243
Northern Ireland	12.5	38.8	18.3	15.3	14.8	0.3	24,055

[1] Unadjusted figures

ACTIVITY

Identify the countries which make up the European Union (EU). Within your class group form small groups of about three and select one of these countries (excluding the UK).

Undertake research and identify the following:
1 Percentage of people in employment classified according to:
   male and female
   industrial sectors
   public and private sector
   employed and self-employed
   skilled and unskilled
   full-time and part-time
   permanent and temporary
2 Unemployment rates by duration, age and sex
3 Work conditions in the EU country in comparison with conditions in the UK
4 Employment opportunities in the EU country compared with the UK
5 A job or jobs in the EU country which you would choose to do

Present your findings to other members in your class using suitable visual aids.
(1.3.2) (1.3.3) (1.3.4)

Business Organisations and Employment

Unemployed claimants: by duration and sex, 1992[1] (*Source*: Employment Department *Regional Trends* 27, © Crown copyright 1992)

	2 weeks or less	Over 2 and up to 8 weeks	Over 8 and up to 13 weeks	Over 13 and up to 26 weeks	Over 26 weeks up to 1 year	Over 1 and up to 2 years	Over 2 and up to 3 years	Over 3 and up to 5 years	Over 5 years	Total (= 100%) (numbers)
Males										
United Kingdom	5.8	13.8	10.0	18.1	22.2	17.0	4.7	3.3	5.0	2,045,371
North	4.9	13.8	9.7	17.5	20.3	17.8	5.4	4.2	6.4	123,461
Yorkshire & Humberside	5.6	13.6	9.6	17.9	21.8	17.3	5.3	3.7	5.2	180,725
East Midlands	6.2	15.0	10.5	18.1	21.9	16.9	4.6	2.9	3.9	128,208
East Anglia	7.4	17.1	11.8	18.8	21.1	15.8	3.9	1.7	2.4	54,899
South East	6.4	13.8	10.5	19.2	24.6	17.0	3.8	2.1	2.5	592,310
South West	6.7	15.8	11.4	19.4	22.5	16.3	3.6	1.9	2.4	152,408
West Midlands	5.5	13.1	9.6	17.8	23.8	17.3	4.6	3.1	5.2	197,400
North West	5.5	13.1	9.5	17.2	20.9	17.6	5.6	4.3	6.3	249,966
England	6.0	14.0	10.2	18.4	22.8	17.1	4.5	2.9	4.1	1,679,377
Wales	5.5	13.6	10.4	18.5	21.7	18.5	4.7	3.1	3.9	101,149
Scotland	5.3	14.5	9.9	17.2	20.0	16.1	5.3	4.7	7.0	184,108
Northern Ireland	3.1	8.2	6.3	13.0	15.6	16.0	7.5	8.4	21.7	80,737
Females										
United Kingdom	9.2	15.8	11.3	21.0	21.6	12.1	3.1	2.5	3.4	628,493
North	8.7	15.5	10.6	20.8	20.7	12.8	3.7	2.8	4.4	34,535
Yorkshire & Humberside	8.9	16.3	10.5	20.3	21.5	12.2	3.3	2.9	4.0	52,365
East Midlands	9.7	16.0	11.0	20.7	22.1	11.7	3.0	2.3	3.5	40,264
East Anglia	11.6	18.0	12.9	20.6	20.3	10.9	2.3	1.4	2.1	18,208
South East	9.2	15.2	11.5	22.4	23.3	12.1	2.6	1.6	2.0	191,914
South West	10.5	16.8	13.2	21.5	20.4	11.1	2.4	1.8	2.3	48,921
West Midlands	8.7	15.0	10.4	20.8	23.0	12.6	3.1	2.4	4.0	61,392
North West	9.0	16.0	10.8	20.2	20.5	12.6	3.8	3.1	4.0	71,990
England	9.3	15.7	11.3	21.3	22.1	12.1	3.0	2.2	3.0	519,589
Wales	9.6	17.6	12.5	21.5	19.7	11.3	2.8	2.3	2.8	27,606
Scotland	9.3	17.0	12.1	18.7	20.0	11.7	3.5	3.4	4.3	57,243
Northern Ireland	6.7	11.4	8.0	19.2	18.3	13.4	5.6	6.5	10.8	24,055

[1] At January

A highly automated, high-tech production plant at Ford

Effects of technology on physical conditions and levels of employment

Technology

The nature of many jobs has changed in recent years because of the influence of new technology. Employers have decided to introduce new technology and methods of working because computerised technology tends to be reliable and efficient. Computers do not go on strike or suffer from ill health and they do not expect to be paid overtime for working longer hours. Entirely new occupations have also been created within the technological industry. It is important to look at these changes and the impact that they have on employment.

There are three main areas of technological innovation:
- Robotics
- Telecommunications
- Computers

Business Organisations and Employment

Robotics

Manufacturing industries

Manufacturing industries have been greatly influenced by the arrival of automated working practices. Production, orders and stock control are now the responsibility of computer operators within many factories. Computers are also used to support production planning, product design and actual production processes and manufacture.

For example, in the printing industry, the computer revolution has meant that the entire process of inputting and processing data and printing the material involves the use of computerised technology. Similarly, in car manufacturing, the design, production and sale of cars are also supported by technological systems and equipment. In fact one leading car manufacturer used the following advertising slogan as part of their marketing campaign:

Designed by computers, built by robots

The impact of computerised technology in manufacturing has resulted in the de-skilling of some jobs, as workers are trained to observe and check the production process as opposed to actually taking responsibility for technical design and production processes themselves. There has been an increase in the number of specialised computer technicians and engineers required to implement and monitor the new systems, but these new jobs do not compensate for the number of operatives who find themselves replaced by technology and computerisation.

Computers

Technology within the office

The electronic office exists within most organisations with a variety of machinery, equipment and systems. When looking at computer technology a distinction has to be made between hardware and software. *Hardware* can be described as the devices making up a piece of machinery or equipment. Computer hardware includes:

- VDU (visual display unit, also known as a monitor)
- Keyboard
- Mouse
- Central processing unit (the 'brains' of the computer, sometimes housed in the VDU, but more usually in the main system box)
- Disk drives (for hard disks and floppy disks)
- Modem (for connection with other systems along the telephone network)
- Printers (laser, dot matrix and bubble jet being the most popular kinds)
- Scanner (to enable print and graphics to be scanned into the computer)

Software, on the other hand, is the programs and data that are used with the equipment. The main applications commonly used are:

- Word processing (such as Word, WordPerfect)
- Desktop publishing (like PageMaker)
- Spreadsheets (including Excel, Lotus, SuperCalc)
- Graphics (CorelDraw, SuperPaint etc.)
- Databases (like dBASE or Access)

At work, the introduction of modern technology has resulted in major changes in how the office is operated. Computers can be used for electronic filing and retrieving documents and therefore the need for a paper-based system is becoming less important. Photocopying important documents onto microfiche also allows for a considerable reduction in paper storage.

The use of word processing, spreadsheet and database packages has virtually made the typewriter redundant. Fax machines allow the transfer of written and visual information from one organisation to another and have tended to replace telex machines, which can only transmit text.

Mobile telephones have become very popular and allow communication to take place while workers are on the move. More recently, some organisations are installing videophones, which enable you to receive a live picture of the person to whom you are talking. Effective communication is further made possible by telephone answering machines, which record messages from enquirers even when the organisation is closed. These can be promptly dealt with the following day.

The impact of the electronic office has meant that staff have had to update their skills and become accustomed to changing work practices. Typing skills have to be updated and applied to working a word processor. Operating a VDU is very different from sitting behind a typewriter, and not all staff can adjust to the changes. Keeping up to date with the latest computer software is also essential, and therefore staff training has to occur regularly.

In some organisations the introduction of computerised systems has led to a reduction in the number of staff needed to operate the office efficiently. There is also a growing tendency to employ part-time as opposed to full-time staff in the automated office.

Finance and commerce

The traditional world of the Stock Exchange has not escaped the technological revolution too. 'Big Bang', as it was called, marked the introduction of computerised systems for the buying and selling of stocks and shares on the Stock Exchange floor. It also resulted in the linking of worldwide markets, allowing buyers and sellers to buy and sell stocks and shares 24 hours a day through a computerised network system.

A customer walking into bank or building society will be surrounded by technology and its applications. All financial transactions are recorded on computer, and by a flick of a switch an operator can view the customer's account, detailing payments into and out of the account. Automated terminals allow customers access to banking services outside banking hours. Cheques can be paid in, cash taken out, statements and cheque books requested by the use of computer terminals located outside branches.

Computerised accounts have resulted in a greater need for computer operators to deal with customers' enquiries and input data and less need for accounts and ledger clerks. There is also a growing trend towards employing staff on part-time contracts.

Finally, wholesale and retail outlets have experienced major changes in their operations with the introduction of new technology. Computerised stock control and POS (point of sale) terminals have resulted in efficient, accurate and up-to-date records of goods in and out of the organisation. Staff have had to be trained to use the new equipment and understand its applications.

ACTIVITY

Using the offices within your college, school or organisation as a case study, identify the types of technological systems that have been introduced, including both hardware and software. What skills are required in order to use the equipment? Can you identify any areas where computerised systems could be introduced in the future?
(1.3.3)

Telecommunications

To communicate using technology it is necessary for the information to be in the right 'language', the language understood and spoken by computers. Computers speak in *binary digits*, or *bits* for short. In effect, microprocessors are a large array of switches that can be in two positions – off or on. Binary digits are simply the numbers 0 (for off) and 1 (for on). The information is translated into a number of ons and offs. Digital storage and transmission of information relies on the data being converted into bits.

Once it has been translated into a language that the technology can understand and speak, the information can be stored on magnetic tape or disk, or on optical disk, as in the case of CD-ROMs. It is also possible to send the information down a telephone wire or as a beam to a satellite dish and across the world.

Telephone

The simplest form of telecommunications (which literally means talking and listening at a distance) is using a telephone for a spoken conversation. The first telephone message was made in 1876 by its inventor, Alexander Graham Bell, in which he asked his assistant to come into the room. This was across a very short distance from one room to the next. Developments followed rapidly, and soon it was possible to communicate across the Atlantic. Now it almost seems commonplace to speak with people anywhere in the world.

The implications for business are enormous. Some businesses do most of their buying and selling over the phone. Externally, customers and suppliers can be contacted immediately. Internally, all personnel in the organisation are connected.

ACTIVITY

If you are at work, write down all the times that you, or your colleagues, use the phone in one day. If you do not work, then write down as many situations you can think of where the telephone might be used. In each case describe the benefits that using the telephone brings, and describe what would have to be done if the telephone did not work.

Are there any disadvantages of using the telephone? When would it not be appropriate to use it?
(1.3.3)

Pager

A pager is a device small enough to put into your pocket. When a message is received it makes an electronic beep. The display shows a short message on a liquid crystal display.

If someone wants to contact a person with a pager they must place a call with the telephone operator. Each pager has its own 'phone' number, which must be quoted, and a message can then be passed on to the operator. The operator sends the message electronically to the pager, which causes it to beep. The message must be kept short. Normally there is enough space to say something like: telephone Mr Smith on 0181 4536 785.

Videoconferencing

Imagine being able to meet a number of people from all around the world, holding face-to-face discussions – and none of you having to leave your own offices! This is possible with video conferencing. It is two-way verbal and visual communication between numbers of people. It requires that each person has a monitor, a video camera and a telephone line. The equipment is expensive, but it allows people to 'get together' without the cost of air fares and hotel bills.

Fax

The word fax is an abbreviation of facsimile, which means copy. A fax machine looks like a cross between a photocopier and a telephone, which is pretty much what it is. It allows documents to be transmitted between users. It works by converting the information on the document, which can be a combination of graphics and text, into a digital signal, which is carried by the telephone network to the receiver, who must also have a fax machine. It is a very rapid way of conveying very detailed information. The fax copy, however, is seldom of high quality, so while the information can be used, the printout itself could not be used as part of a professional document.

Business Organisations and Employment

Email
Electronic mail is an alternative to the conventional postal service. The messages are converted into electronic signals for transmission. There is no need for a paper copy, although printouts can be made.

Communication using email takes place via computers transmitting on a telecommunication network. Alternatively, email may be used within an organisation utilising computer networks. In both cases, the receivers have access to the messages when they log onto their terminals. If passwords are used this could ensure confidentiality of the information.

Modem
A modem allows a computer to link into a network of other computers and a whole system of information via the telephone line.

Information superhighway
The digital translation and storage of information coupled with vast networks of telephone cables and satellite links connecting computers, TV sets and video cameras makes up the so-called information superhighway. It is really only just beginning. The possibilities for the world of entertainment are staggering. Already, lawyers are being asked to join in complicated arguments over copyright.

For business it is likely to mean a whole new approach to the way we work. 'Going to work' will no longer be important, provided you have a workstation at home (or maybe in your briefcase).

Advantages and disadvantages of technology
The application of technology has several key advantages:

Speed Computers work much faster than human beings.

Accuracy Computers tend to be very accurate and when problems do occur they can usually be traced to human error.

Reliability Apart from rare faults, a computer will faithfully carry out any task that it is able to do. Problems tend to occur only if the system is overloaded, information inputted is inaccurate or if the system is asked to do something that it is not programmed to do.

Easy access Information can be stored and accessed easily without searching through mountains of paper.

However, those must be weighed against some disadvantages.

Cost Computer hardware and software can be very expensive and as technology advances there is a need to continually update and improve systems. This can result in major costs to the organisation on a long-term basis.

Maintenance Computer maintenance is essential to keep systems operating effectively and it is a further expense to the organisation.

Security A lot of information held on computer may be confidential, especially personnel records. Procedures will have to be adopted to limit access to these records and staff will also need to be aware of the Data Protection Act.

Training Staff will require training before they are able to use the computer systems. This takes time and costs money.

Error Despite being more reliable and accurate, computers can go wrong and when they do the errors might go unnoticed. There is a saying: 'To err is human; to really screw things up requires a computer'.

Redundancy Computerisation may mean that certain jobs are no longer required and staff may be made redundant. As a result many staff feel very insecure about the introduction of new technology.

ACTIVITY

Read the three case studies on this page and the next, which report on technological developments within three organisations. Identify the organisation, the technological developments that

---

A graduate sets up a business offering neck massages to City executives in their offices. The adverts don't mention that she doesn't have an office. All she needs is a fax machine, some printed letterheads, and – most important – a pager that can store up to 20 messages at a time.

An advert in *Nature* offers supplies of an enzyme used in DNA analysis, with a London phone number. Call it early in the day and you get an apologetic answering machine. Call it later, or in the evening, and your call is routed to the company head office – in Phoenix, Arizona. The company doesn't want to spend money on hiring a London office, but it can easily afford a London phone number.

A British consumer products company [Amstrad] has a research and development division in Hong Kong, with the division manager based at the head office in England. Every day the Hong Kong staff work on new developments; before going home they fax them to the manager's office, just at the start of the British day. The manager studies them, makes corrections and suggestions, and sends the revisions to Hong Kong in time for the next working day.

A journalist wants to interview the extremely busy head of a multinational. He decides that the best first approach would be via e-mail, and sends a message. A while later the executive e-mails a brief reply. The journalist poses more questions. The executive replies. The dialogue continues, electronically; eventually the journalist publishes the 'correspondence' as part of his article.

Source: New Scientist, 16 April 1994

Business Organisations and Employment

Notebook newcomer ups stakes

Canon has upped the stakes in the competition to provide the most useful notebook computer with its Intel 486SX-based BN100C with colour screen and built-in bubble-jet (mono) printer. The screen provides clear (256) colours and better than usual contrast (18:1 compared with 13:1 for most liquid-crystal display screens) by actually being two screens, each driven by its own microchip, so that refresh rates are higher than with most conventional systems.

Two Type-2 PCMCIA slots allow genuine portability. Those who need more disc capacity than the 120/210 megabytes on the built-in C-drive can slot in a £600 micro hard disc built into a PCMCIA card with capacities of 60–1005 megabytes. But for £2,349, excluding value-added tax, the machine is pricey.

The new machine is part of Canon's plan to secure 10% of the UK market for notebooks, 75% of which is now controlled by Toshiba and Compaq.

Source: *Sunday Times*, 13 February 1994

• Portable computer users will be able to dial straight into their office systems from a mobile phone with a new modem from BT specialist Communicate. Using credit-card sized PCMCIA technology, the modem slots into a portable PC for transmission over a cellular phone link.

Communicate has formed a consortium with Cellnet, IBM, Motorola and software house Lotus to market the product as a package called CLIC. This includes an IBM ThinkPad notebook computer, Motorola Micro TAC phone and Lotus Notes software. Communicate's 1440C PCMCIA modem costs £599.

Source: *Sunday Times*, 13 February 1994

Theme parks head for moon

Visitors to American theme parks such as Disneyland could soon be exploring the moon by operating a lunar rover. LunaCorp, an American company, plans to raise $110m to launch a 400kg lunar buggy, equipped with TV cameras, and land it at the site where Neil Armstrong first stepped on the moon 25 years ago.

The buggy would provide the ultimate theme-park attraction – the world's first interactive space-exploration centre, giving the public an opportunity to drive the rover on the moon using video commmunications, or 'telepresence'.

David Gump, LunarCorp's president, hopes to raise the money from theme-park operators, TV networks, corporate sponsors and advertising agencies.

The buggy would be launched in 1997 on a Russian Proton rocket at a cost of $50m. It would be designed by William Whittaker of Carnegie Mellon University and be based on his polar exploration robot and other Mars and moon-rover technology developed by Nasa. A quarter of its time would be spent on scientific experiments.

Source: *Sunday Times*, 20 February 1994

are reported and how the organisations are going to benefit from these developments.
(1.3.3)

Using government publications such as *Economic Trends*, *Social Trends* and the *Annual Abstract of Statistics*, find out as much information as you can about employment in your region. Look particularly at the types and features of employment for the area, where the jobs are located, the proportion of self-employed, the numbers unemployed etc. Compare the information you have collected with the information available for another region. What interesting trends emerge? What are the similarities and what are the differences?

To what extent has the introduction of new technology had an effect on the types of jobs available and the skills required in the two regions?

Present your findings in a visual display to other members in your group or in the form of a report.
(1.3.2) (1.3.3) (1.3.4)

Employment findings

One of the vital skills in studying business is the ability to handle and interpret numerical data. Employees within central and local government departments need the skills to present government statistics and administrators within organisations need to handle numerical data as a technique in the tasks of problem-solving and decision-making. In order to understand how to use and interpret data, employees must be familiar with the principal statistical and accounting techniques and procedures. There are three principal aspects to the handling of numerical information. The first is concerned with the problems associated with *obtaining* the data; the second is concerned with *processing* those data; and the third with *presenting* it to those who are to received it.

Business Organisations and Employment

Obtaining the data

If an employee or manager wants numerical information for a certain purpose, the first task is to obtain it. It may well be that the information concerned is readily available from within the organisation. Examples include data referring to labour turnover, profits over past years and sales forecasts for future years. Information is also available to the organisation from external sources, and this involves not only knowing what to look for, but also where to look. This requires a good knowledge of the principal sources from which relevant numeric and statistical information can be obtained.

Primary data is *new data*, generated from original sources. The data may have been collected by a questionnaire enquiry as part of a market research exercise or census project. Alternatively the data may be in published format. For example, government publications like the *Annual Abstract of Statistics*, *Social Trends* and *Economic Trends* provide very relevant facts and figures about employment, economic activity, social issues and regional comparisons. This sort of data is called *secondary data*.

The task is not limited simply to knowing where to look and what to look for. It may well be necessary to select from a mass of information the particular data that will be relevant to a particular job and to assemble it in convenient format so that it can be more easily handled, processed and understood.

Example

An employee working for the Department of Employment would be interested in analysing the levels of employment/unemployment for the country as a whole and then comparing data for particular regions. In addition, the employee may also be concerned with making national and international employment comparisons. The employee would therefore need to find the relevant facts and figures to support each area of study.

If a comparison of data is to be made with previous periods, then it is vitally important to check that the same definitions have been used. For example, the official definition of 'unemployed' has been changed on a number of occasions over the last few years. Therefore it is important when comparing sets of figures to check that the figures have been compiled using the same technique.

Processing the information

Once the relevant data have been obtained, it is usually necessary for the employee to work upon them and to calculate additional information from them. This may involve only a few simple additions and subtractions; alternatively, it may require the application of more sophisticated techniques such as percentages and averages.

Presenting the information

The data that the employee has obtained and the calculations made may be needed for internal purposes only. The findings may, however, have to be communicated to others. There are many different ways in which numerical data and conclusions can be communicated. One of the most common is by means of statistical tables which set out neatly and concisely the relevant figures. Another method is by use of graphs, bar charts, histograms, pie charts and other various forms of pictorial representation. This then raises the question of the possible use of colour, and whether any figures should be given prominence by the use of bold or italic type.

ACTIVITY

1 Using relevant government publications, list in a neat and concise table data for each of the last five years concerning the total numbers in the United Kingdom who:
   (a) make up the 'total working population'
   (b) were employed in manufacturing industries
   (c) were unemployed
2 As part of your research obtain and list definitions for:
   (a) working population
   (b) economically active
   (c) working age
   (d) unemployed
   Why do you think it is important to know exact definitions of these terms?
   (1.3.2)

Presenting information

Having established that one of the most important skills in business is that of being able to present numerical information – both financial and non-financial – we need to know the format in which it can best be understood by those who will be receiving it. One of the most common ways in which this is done is by means of tables.

Tables are very familiar forms of presentation. They are seen on television, in newspapers and magazines and in a range of documents at work. However, considerable time and careful attention has to be paid to presenting and interpreting the tables in the right manner.

The first essential in the preparation of a table is to ensure that it is set out within the structure of a proper framework.

Structure of gross domestic product and labour force 1992

(£000,000)	In value value	% of total force	Labour labour	% of force
Agriculture	9,309	1.8	577,000	2.1
Mining	9,842	1.9	—[1]	—[1]
Manufacturing	114,698	22.2	4,985,000[1]	18.0[1]
Construction	32,002	6.2	1,515,000	5.5
Public utilities	13,717	2.7	414,000	1.5
Transport & communication	41,613	8.1	1,497,000	5.4
Trade	72,549	14.1	5,351,000	19.3
Finance	121,704	23.6	3,086,000	11.1
Public administration				
Defence	89,114	17.3		
Services	32,892	6.4	10,314,000[2]	37.1[2]
Other	−22,846[3]	−4.4[3]		
TOTAL	514,594	100.0	27,739,000	100.0

Notes:
[1] Manufacturing includes mining
[2] Includes 2,732,000 unemployed not distributed by sector
[3] Plus rent less bank service charges

ACTIVITY

Look at the above example.
1 What are the important features which make up a table?
2 What important conclusions can you draw from interpreting the table?
(1.3.2)

The basic elements that all tables should possess are:
(a) A concise title that adequately describes what the table is all about
(b) Clear headings for each of the principal columns making up the table
(c) A note (if relevant) of the units used in each column
(d) A statement of the source from which the information was obtained

In addition, it may be necessary to add some footnotes to the table to provide additional explanation of some of the points.

Tables should, however, be regarded as something more than just so many columns of figures. The employee or manager should be able to understand the content and to draw from the figures valid conclusions to support the data. In addition, when interpreting a table it is often necessary to consider what the tables could have contained but did not, and what additional information might be required before an informed judgement can be made.

Tables often have to be prepared from jumbled information contained in a report, newspaper article or other source. In preparing a table from such material, it is essential to plan carefully the arrangement of the figures so that they will clearly and fairly indicate the important facts to be illustrated. It is also important to include a correct title, proper headings for the columns, a statement of units used, and of course, sources of information.

Business Organisations and Employment

ACTIVITY

The following staffing summary has been produced by the personnel manager of Kittle Ltd and has been forwarded to you with the request that you design a suitable table to show the staffing position over the past 12 months and comment on the figures.

'In looking at the staffing position over the last year, I am able to tell you that on 1 January 1993, the beginning of the last full financial year, the company employed 230 skilled workers, 400 unskilled staff and 47 clerical staff. During the course of the year, 24 new unskilled workers were signed on, and by the end of the year their total number had been reduced to 250 due to resignations. There was some turnover among skilled workers, with 23 leaving and 14 new staff being recruited. On the clerical side, 13 clerical staff left and were not replaced.'
(1.3.2)

Pie charts

An alternative form of presenting data is by means of pie charts. With a pie chart, a circle (the pie) is used to represent the whole and the pie is divided up into parts in the same ratio as the original information.

A pie chart is a suitable method for presenting information that divides a particular total into a number of categories or headings. It is not suitable, however, for showing trends in data over a period of time. When producing a pie chart, each category or heading has to be expressed as a fraction of the pie. This is achieved by dividing each category by the total figure and then multiplying by 360° in order to find the size of the angle of each sector. All angles are rounded to the nearest degree.

Example   Winter Woolies plc have six departments and employ 500 employees in total. The numbers of employees for each department are as follows:

Design and production	300
Finance	30
Sales and marketing	20
Personnel	25
Administration	75
Distribution	50

In order to present the information as a pie chart the following calculations have to take place:

Business Organisations and Employment

Heading	Calculation	Angle size to nearest degree
Design and production	(300 ÷ 500) × 360 =	216°
Finance	(30 ÷ 500) × 360 =	22°
Sales and marketing	(20 ÷ 500) × 360 =	14°
Personnel	(25 ÷ 500) × 360 =	18°
Administration	(75 ÷ 500) × 360 =	54°
Distribution	(50 ÷ 500) × 360 =	36°

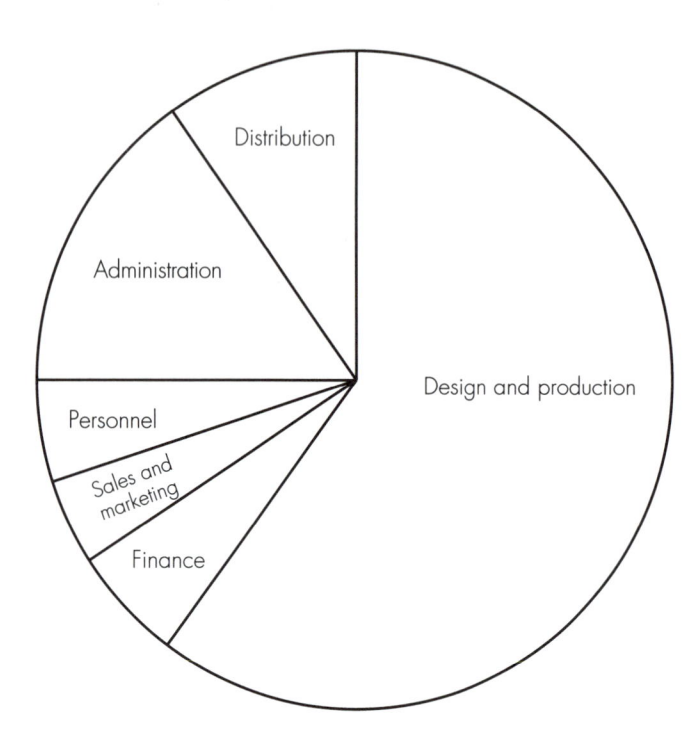

Bar charts

A further method of presenting data is by means of a bar chart. When comparing discrete data (that is, information which can be 'counted') a simple bar chart can be used. All bar charts have axes. These are two lines that are at right angles to each other and are used to record the number and type of data. Bar charts can be used to display the information horizontally or vertically. The height or length of each bar represents the data.

Example The information used to produce the pie chart for Winter Woolies plc could also be presented in bar chart format.

Winter Woolies plc have six departments and employ 500 employees in total. The number of employees for each department are as follows:

Design and production	300
Finance	30
Sales and marketing	20
Personnel	25
Administration	75
Distribution	50

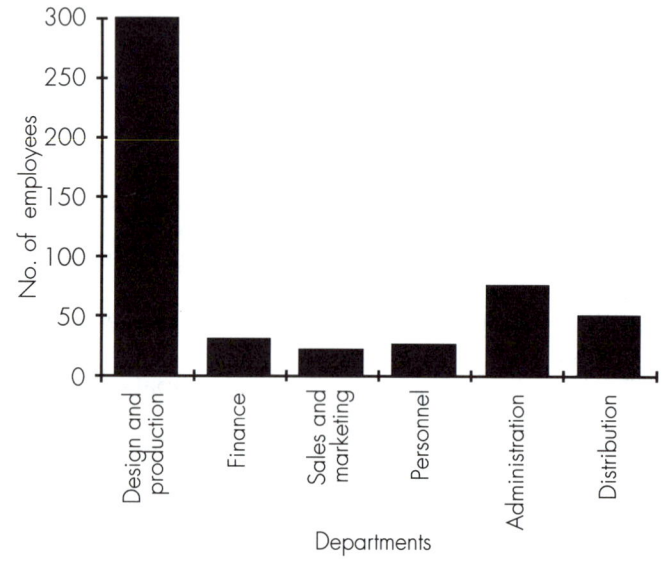

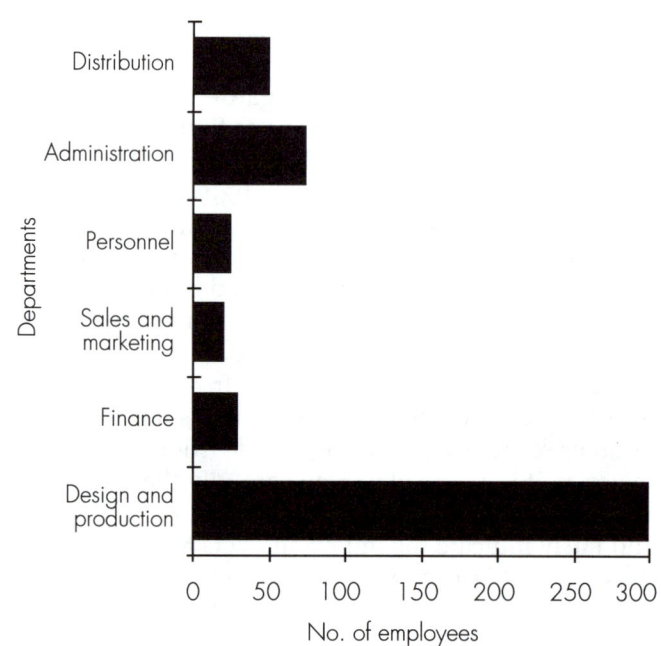

ACTIVITY

The following regional figures for unemployment were produced by the Department of Employment for December 1993. Undertake the necessary calculations and present your findings in a pie chart format.

Region	Total Unemployed
South-East	900,500
inc. Greater London	461,200
East Anglia	80,200
South-West	206,800
West Midlands	270,000
East Midlands	176,900
Yorkshire & Humberside	236,700
North-West	310,500
North	166,600
Wales	127,900
Scotland	236,600
Nothern Ireland	103,100

(1.3.2) (1.3.4)

If there is insufficient room in the chart to label each sector, it is necessary to shade the sectors and then to provide a key.

Bar charts, like other diagrams, need a title and a source. It is also important to label the axes clearly so that the reader understands the nature of the data and what they represent.

Line charts

Line charts are particularly useful for illustrating trends over a period of time. A variety of trends can be represented on the same chart by having more than one line. It is important, however, to label each line clearly so that the reader can distinguish one trend from another. A line chart is commonly used to illustrate the changing levels of employment/unemployment over a period of time.

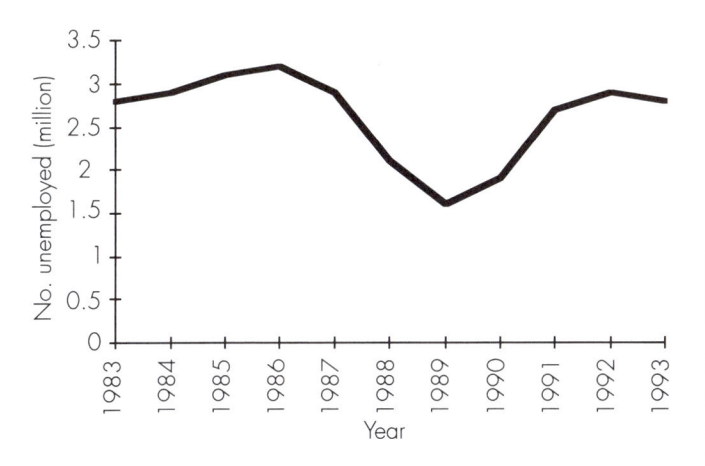

Pictograms

Pictograms display data through the use of pictures. The pictures usually reflect the data and therefore the diagrams have a major visual impact. They are not suitable for illustrating complicated information, but can show comparisons, trends and totals. They should include the actual figures, as it is not easy to read the results accurately from the pictures.

Business Organisations and Employment

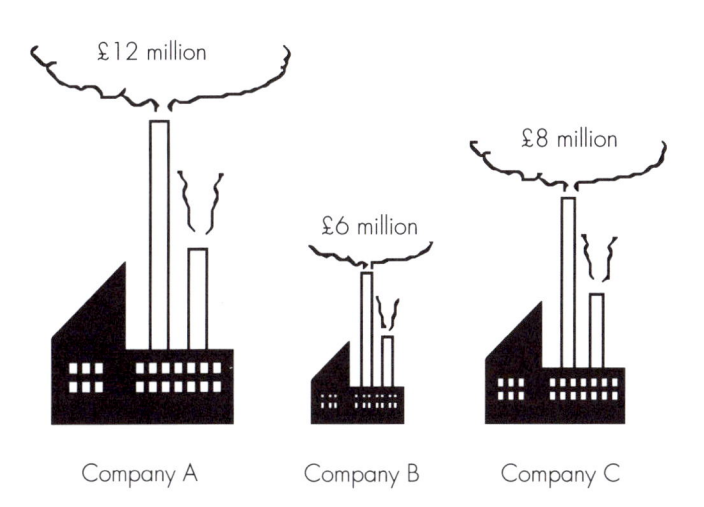

Example In the illustration below the picture of a factory is used to represent the level of turnover of the three companies. The pictogram is increased or decreased in proportion to the turnover. Note that the actual figures have been quoted for each company.

An alternative way of using pictograms is to repeat a picture which represents a given quantity. For example, in the diagram below the picture of a spanner is used to depict a turnover of £2 million:

Annual turnover 1994

Company A   £ 12 million
Company B   £ 6 million
Company B   £ 8 million

ACTIVITY

Read the following information about different regions in the United Kingdom and important characteristics associated with each. Identify the regional differences, looking at investment, resources, labour and skills supply. Present your findings using appropriate graphical, visual and written methods. (The information is based on findings within *Regional Trends*.)

Regional profile: Yorkshire and Humberside
The population of Yorkshire and Humberside has grown by 0.7% since 1981. The urban areas are heavily populated, in contrast to the rural areas, which are thinly populated. For example, the population density is over 1000 people per square kilometre in West Yorkshire but just 87 in North Yorkshire. There is a high percentage of unmarried mothers – the third highest in the country – with three in every ten births being to single mothers. While house prices in some regions have fallen during 1990 and 1991, they actually rose in Yorkshire and Humberside by 4%. During the 1980s this region was one of the worst affected by strike action with an unemployment rate of 10% (January 1992) which is above the national average for the United Kingdom as a whole.

Wages and salaries account for nearly two thirds of household income, slightly more than in any other region. Male wage earners are among the lowest paid in the United Kingdom, with an average income of £287 per week. However, they earn more from bonuses, commission and other incentive payments than workers in other parts of the country – over £16 a week on average in 1991.

More fish is eaten in this region than in any other

Business Organisations and Employment

and Yorkshire and Humberside has the heaviest drinkers in England and Wales – with men drinking 9 pints of beer on average a week and women 2.5 pints. Finally it has the third highest reported crime rates in England and Wales for 1990, with one offence recorded for every ten people.

Regional profile: Northern Ireland

The population in Northern Ireland is the youngest in the United Kingdom. In 1990 there were over one in four people under the age of 16. As a result birth rates are very high, with nearly 17 births per 1000 of the population in 1990. However, the region has the lowest number of births to unmarried mothers compared with other regions, with fewer than one in five in 1990. There has been a major increase in house building in Northern Ireland – an increase of 14% between 1981 and 1990.

Correspondingly, the price of houses also increased more in the region than in any English region, with an increase of 8% between 1990 and 1991. More pupils within Northern Ireland left school without a qualification than in any other region. In contrast, students studying for A levels in the region out-performed pupils studying elsewhere.

Northern Ireland has the highest unemployment rate in the country, currently about 13%; however it has one of the lowest rates of increase. Long-term unemployment is a major problem in the region, with one in five unemployed men out of work for more than five years. There are more police officers per head in Northern Ireland than in any other region – one for every 192 people – and the region has the youngest cars – less than four years old on average.

Regional profile: South-East

Of the total United Kingdom population, nearly one third is located within the South-East, although the density of population is greater in the North-West. The profile of the population reflects a high concentration of ethnic minorities – one in twelve of the population.

Within the suburban areas, there is a high number of people who own their own house. For example the rate for the area of the South-East outside Greater London is, at three-quarters, the highest in the country, and the rate for the whole of the South-East is close to the national average. The biggest employer in the South-East region is the financial services sector, with almost one employee in every six working in this field – the highest proportion in the county. The region also has the most qualified workforce, with eight out of ten workers having a qualification and one in seven having a degree. The South-East has the highest earnings, although the number of hours worked is slightly shorter than in any other region. Almost one in three people in this region owned shares in 1992. The area has the highest ratio of car ownership, with almost a third of households having two cars or more. Crime rates for drug offences are far higher in the South-East than in any other region, and the police force is the least successful at clearing up crime. Of all crimes committed in this area, only one in five were solved in 1990.

(1.3.2) (1.3.3) (1.3.4) (1.3.5)

ACTIVITY

Technology and change

The following articles clearly illustrate the development of new ideas, technology, products and services to meet the changing needs and wants of customers. Read the articles carefully and answer the questions that follow.

Work began yesterday on a £75 million Lego theme park in Windsor – the first to be built outside Denmark. About 600 jobs will be created by the project, which will create 30 tonnes of Lego models out of 55 million bricks. The park, on the site of the old Windsor safari park, will feature scale models of landmarks such as Stonehenge, Tower Bridge, Nelson's Column and St Paul's Cathedral – all made of Lego – as well as rides.

The main attraction will be Miniland, which will feature about 1,200 models. Many of the creations to be featured in the park have been built by Marianne Flodgaard, co-ordinator of shows and rides.

Two young boys helped to launch the project by planting an oak tree. Christopher Kerswell, nine, and Malcolm Jack, six, of Windsor, wearing hard hats and sporting their Lego Club badges, joined Kjeld Kirk Kristiansen, president of the Lego group, in the planting ceremony. The 30ft oak was lowered into the ground by crane before the boys helped shovel in earth around it using a spade made of Lego bricks. The tree is one of 10,000 being planted on the 147-acre site.

Lego was invented by a carpenter in Billund, Denmark. The word after which he named his toy is a shortened version of the Danish for 'play well'. About 1.4 million people a year are expected to visit the British park when it opens in two years' time.

Source: *The Times*, 7 April 1994

Business Organisations and Employment

Blood tested in minutes

A blood test that can detect the HIV virus in minutes has been developed by researchers at Cardif University.

At present it can take specialist laboratories many hours to discover whether blood samples contain traces of HIV or diseases such as hepatitis. But the new ultrasound method obtains results in minutes, according to Terry Coakley, professor of biophysics at Cardiff.

'Infectious diseases are normally detected by mixing samples of patients' body fluids with millions of minute polystyrene beads that have been chemically coated with antibodies to the disease in question,' he says. 'If a disease such as hepatitis is present it will stick to the beads and gradually form clumps. We have found that by applying ultrasound the process can be speeded up.'

Coakley and his team are developing a prototype portable ultrasound machine, about the size of a shoebox, that can be used for diagnostic purposes in GPs' surgeries – saving the expense and inconvenience of sending blood samples to specialist laboratories for analysis.

A blood sample in a test tube goes into the machine, an ultrasound wave is beamed into it and, using electronics developed by Industrial Developments Bangor (a spin-off company from Bangor University), the result can be obtained within minutes.

Cardiff University has patented the technology. With £130,000 from the venture-capital firm Venture Link Investments, it hopes to have the prototype ready for two-year clinical trials by the end of the year. It should become available commercially at a cost of about £200.

Coakley believes that it could make a significant contribution to healthcare in Third World countries, where doctors and aid agencies have problems diagnosing diseases because laboratory facilities are scarce. With this technology, healthcare workers could conduct tests without laboratory assitance.

Source: Sunday Times, 29 May 1994

Phone taps into on-line services

A telephone that incorporates a slide-in keyboard is promising to open up the world of on-line information for noncomputer users, *writes Mike Hewitt*.

The M.Phone looks like a conventional telephone, but slide out the keyboard and it becomes a computer which, according to the developer, M.Power of New York, makes access to the Internet and other on-line information services as easy as writing a note.

With a menu-driven interface, users can make an ordinary telephone call or dial through to on-line services such as home banking, CompuServe, and e-mail through the Internet. At the heart of the M.Phone lies a signal-processing chip with inbuilt software that can be updated over the phone line. It also includes facilities for adding peripherals such as disc drives and printers.

The M.Phone is scheduled to appear in American shops in September, initially costing $300 (£200), and will reach Britain next year.

Source: Sunday Times, 29 May 1994

BT television link to offer video shopping

The home shopping revolution is about to begin. BT is in advanced negotiations with some of Britain's biggest high street stores, including W H Smith, Argos and Thomas Cook, to offer video shopping services through its television system this autumn.

Commercial details have emerged from a team of BBC graphic artists that has been contracted by BT to work on its video-on-demand system. This uses conventional telephone lines to offer video services on television sets. Graphics already designed show that nine retailers – HMV, Mothercare, W H Smith, Olympus, Argos, Next, MFI, Thomas Cook and B&Q – are being lined up by BT to offer products using videoclips and interactive menus.

Home shoppers will be offered a box that connects their television set to the telephone line. They will use a remote-control handset to choose products after seeing video clips transmitted over the phone line. Transactions will be completed by entering a credit or debit card number and home deliveries are expected to arrive within a few days. Some special deliveries could be made the same day.

Paul Sharma, a BT spokesman, admitted that the company was talking to retailers. 'At this stage we are in serious negotiations with some of them. We do not expect all nine to be signed up by this autumn. But as we roll out the service we expect to sign up more,' he said.

BT's video-on-demand service, which has already begun technical trials for 70 of its employees in Suffolk, is due to begin in October with 2,500 subscribers in the Colchester area in Essex. The service is then set to move into Westminster, central London, where BT has a cable televison franchise. By operating there, BT believes it will be able to reach a key political and media audience.

The Department of National Heritage has confirmed there are no regulatory objections to BT's plans, despite objections from emerging cable television franchises.

BBC graphics, signed up in a £100,000 deal by BT more than six months ago, also revealed that BT is preparing home banking, personal finance and video games services.

The BBC, too, is preparing to offer 'on-demand' educational programmes using the BT system, particularly for A-level and university students. But it could face criticism for charging consumers extra for watching BBC programmes over the BT system when they are obliged to pay a licence fee.

Source: Sunday Times, 29 May 1994

---

1. How have the organisations identified different markets?
   (1.2.3)
2. Make a list of new products or services which have been produced to meet these new markets.
   (1.2.6)
3. Identify for each example whether or not you think the new products or services will be successful. Give reasons for your answers.
   (1.2.6)
4. To what extent have advances in new technology supported the developments of these new products or services?
   (1.2.6)
5. What effect will the introduction of these new products or services have on employment?
   (1.3.4)
6. Undertake some research of your own and see if you can find further examples of product development.
   (1.2.6)

Business Organisations and Employment

✎ UNIT ACTIVITY

(1.1.1–4) (1.2.1–6) (1.3.1–4)

Woodentops Incorporated

Background
Woodentops Incorporated is a multinational company based in the United States. They specialise in all areas of production and retail of wooden furniture and have three main divisions:
- Treetops – for handling production of timber
- Worktops – for the production of furniture
- Shoptops – for retail and distribution of Woodentops furniture

In addition there is also the Woodentops head office, based in New York.

The organisation has branches in many countries, but not yet in the United Kingdom. Expansion in all of the divisions has been considered and the managing director, Hazel Redwood, is considering locating some of the new sites in the UK.

Obviously, before such a major decision is taken, a lot of research and investigation needs to be carried out. Then, if it is decided to set up new sites in the UK, any personnel to transfer from the United States would need to be brought up to date on the economy and country into which they are moving.

Scenario
As a member of a UK-based research organisation you are asked to undertake relevant research and make appropriate recommendations. You are to report directly to Hazel Redwood.
(1.3.4)

Procedure
1 In what ways will the activities of Woodentops Incorporated be influenced by the business environment in the UK? You should consider the effects of competition, legislation, the environment and the general public.
(1.2.2)
    What factors determine the spending patterns by consumers and customers on a given product?
(1.2.3)
    How would you classify Woodentops' goods in terms of service or product, durable or consumable? Define these terms.
(1.2.4)
    What kinds of activities might a business organisation undertake in order to improve its market position?
(1.2.5)
2 Investigate the feasibility of Woodentops Incorporated setting up branches of all three major divisions in the UK. You should concentrate on three main topics:
- Geographical location
- Market for wooden furniture in the UK
- Employment market in the UK

Include your findings in a formal report and make appropriate recommendations. Your terms of reference are as follows:
- What factors should be taken into account when considering the location of a business? *(1.2.1)*
- Is your local area an appropriate place for Woodentops to locate any of its three divisions (Treetops, Worktops and Shoptops)? If so, why? If not, why not? *(1.2.1)*
- What gaps are there (if any) in the market for quality wooden furniture? *(1.2.3, 1.2.6)*
- What are the levels of employment in your local area? How does this compare to another area in the UK which might be considered for location? *(1.3.2)*

3 You are also required to produce an information leaflet or booklet for Woodentops for those employees who may be moving to the UK with the company, aimed primarily at executives unfamiliar with UK business practice. This should be informative but 'user-friendly' and should take the following points into consideration:
- The economy of the United States is quite different from that of the UK – for example, the USA does not really have a public sector – and therefore the differences between public sector and private sector organisations need to be explained *(1.1.2)* as well as other terminology used to describe industrial sectors. *(1.1.1)*
- The structure of businesses in the UK will be unfamiliar to Woodentops' executives, and they will need to understand the different organisation types with which they might be trading. *(1.1.2) (1.1.3)*
- It is important that the Woodentops executives understand the full range of business activities in the UK, at both the local and national levels, and an account of the types of business activity in the UK would be useful. You should use examples of major organisations to illustrate these points, giving an indication of the scale and scope of their activities *(1.1.2) (1.1.4)* and identifying their products *(1.1.4)*
- Lastly, Woodentops personnel need to familiarise themselves with UK employment practices, which again differ widely from those in the United States. You should describe the types of employment *(1.3.1)* and the principal features *(1.3.4)*, and explain how technology has had an impact on conditions and levels of employment. *(1.3.3)*

4 The future of Woodentops Incorporated has not yet been decided. The directors are seeking new ideas for product innovation and ways of moving into new markets.

Business Organisations and Employment

Suggest new products which Woodentops could launch in the UK. These may be developments of existing products or completely new lines of business.
(1.2.6)

What new employment opportunities may be created by the expansion of Woodentops Incorporated into the UK and perhaps into other EU regions?
(1.3.3)

Guidance

In all your assessment activities the first thing you should do is draw up a plan of action. This will help you to identify and prioritise your targets. The action plan should clearly show times and dates by which you expect each of your goals to be completed and the actual time and date it was achieved. Where targets took longer than you thought (as they often do) you should record the reasons. As you proceed you will need to add to and amend your action plan with new pieces of information and newly identified targets.

Your action plan will demonstrate to your assessors that you are able to arrange your time in a constructive and organised way and can be used as evidence in your portfolio on the basis of which higher grades may be awarded.

Detailed knowledge of the furniture industry is not required. You should concentrate on general business principles. You need to consider the problems of location that face any business. You will need to be familiar with your local area and investigate the feasibility of Woodentops locating there. You will not be downgraded for arriving at the conclusion that the local area is not suitable, provided that your report gives evidence of careful research and your recommendations are clearly justified. You will need detailed knowledge of employment levels in your local area and in another area in the UK for comparison. If possible, choose an area you already know something about and for which you can easily obtain information.

You should employ appropriate research techniques. This will involve you accessing your library and learning resource facilities, text references, especially *Annual Abstract of Statistics*, *Social Trends* and *Economic Trends*, and maybe a CD-ROM and/or videos. A local business contact would be useful for first-hand data. The local authorities will also have details on employment, industrial estates, business rates and so on. Market research may include questionnaires used on members of the general public. In designing questionnaires take care to ensure that the questions are clear, unambiguous, in good English and relevant to the purpose in hand. Ask yourself: 'What do I need to find out?'.

Your findings should take into account the information available to you about Woodentops Incorporated. In particular, you should remember that there are three main divisions, for growing timber, production of furniture, and retail and distribution.

Make sure that you use a formal report format and that you read through your work to check for spelling and grammatical errors. When you read it does it make sense? You may use diagrams and illustrations to support your findings. Remember also to avoid the trap of including information just because you have it. Only use it if it is relevant to your terms of reference.

The information booklet should be written in an appropriate style. There are no formal restrictions, and ideally it should be 'user-friendly'.

The numbers of the performance criteria have been included so that you know what is being assessed. Check with them and the range statements for further guidance. This will make it easier for you to determine whether your work meets the required standards.

MULTIPLE CHOICE

Select the answer which accurately and fully answers the question or completes the sentence.

Unit 1

1 Which of the following statements is *false* regarding private limited companies?
   A They may sell shares
   B Their shareholders have limited liability
   C They may quote their share prices on the Stock Exchange
   D The shareholders may also be directors

2 Who owns a public limited company?
   A The general public
   B The government
   C No one – it has a legal identity of its own
   D The shareholders

3 Which of the following organisations comes from the public sector?
   A NHS
   B BUPA
   C PowerGen
   D British Gas

4 Which of the following best describes a 'dividend'?
   A A sum of money invested in a company
   B A share of the profits paid to a shareholder
   C Profit that a company makes after tax
   D A pay rise received by directors of a company as a result of large profits

65

Business Organisations and Employment

5. In the absence of a partnership agreement, which of the following statements is true?
   A   Partners who invest the most capital receive the most profits
   B   The most senior partners receive more profits
   C   Partners receive 5% interest on all their capital
   D   Partners share profits equally

6. The word 'limited' in private limited company refers to the fact that:
   A   The number of shares that can be issued is limited
   B   The liability of the shareholders is limited
   C   The number of directors in the company is limited
   D   The activities of the company are limited according to their Articles of Association

7. Which of the following occupations is in the tertiary sector?
   A   Estate agent
   B   Coal miner
   C   Ship-builder
   D   Carpet weaver

8. The defining characteristic of a multinational organisation is that it is one which:
   A   Sells to countries overseas
   B   Buys raw materials from more than one country
   C   Employs a mix of nationalities
   D   Is based in one country and has branches in one or more other countries

9. A bulk-increasing industry is likely to:
   A   Locate near its customers
   B   Locate near its suppliers
   C   Rely on government subsidies
   D   Employ a high proportion of part-time staff

10. A 'footloose' industry is one which:
    A   Has a bad reputation for staff development
    B   Frequently issues new shares
    C   Is not restricted in its choice of location
    D   Is under scrutiny for malpractice

11. If people are described as part-time workers it means that they:
    A   Are temporary
    B   Are self-employed
    C   Do not have a contract of employment
    D   Work less than the standard number of hours per week

12. Which of the following types of organisation is in the public sector?
    A   Local council
    B   Private limited company
    C   Public limited company
    D   Cooperative

13. If a business has the name 'J. Smith & Co.' then it is most likely to be a:
    A   Sole trader
    B   Partnership
    C   Private limited company
    D   Public limited company

14. A 'sleeping partner' refers to a partner who:
    A   Does not receive a share of the profits
    B   Does not contribute capital
    C   Does not get involved in the day-to-day running of the business
    D   Starts work late each day due to extreme tiredness

15. One *difference* between a private limited company and a public limited company is that:
    A   A private limited company can raise capital by selling shares
    B   A public limited company must make its accounts public
    C   A director of a private limited company may not own shares in the same company
    D   A public limited company can quote its share prices on the Stock Exchange

16. Which of the following occupations is in the primary sector?
    A   A farmer
    B   A telephone hygenist
    C   A lathe operator
    D   A primary school teacher

SHORT ANSWER

1. A biscuit manufacturing organisation has a production department in which a number of people work. Details of the working practices of some of these people are given below. For each person you must decide whether they are self-employed or employed, full-time or part-time, and permanent or temporary. The normal working week is 35 hours.
   A   Timothy Cootes was taken on last summer on a 12 month contract. He works 35 hours a week.
   B   Mary Garvy has her own consultancy business. She provides advice for the organisation. She has been hired for a six-month period for 5 hours a week.
   C   Sue Savoury has been working for the organisation since she was recruited 15 years ago. She works 35 hours a week.
   D   Nicholas Bayley has a contract with no fixed finish date. He works mornings only.
   E   Christopher Paul is a specialised machine operator, trading under the name of 'Rainbow'. At present he works the whole week for the organisation, but this arrangement comes up for renewal in 3 months.

	Person	Self-employed or employed	Full-time or part-time	Permanent or temporary
A	Timothy Cootes			
B	Mary Garvy			
C	Sue Savoury			
D	Nicholas Bayley			
E	Christopher Paul			

UNIT TEST:
Business organisations and employment

1. The main purpose of an entrepreneur is to:
   A Benefit the community
   B Trade in order to make a profit
   C Create competition
   D Employ local workers

2. A company has certain characteristics. Decide whether each of these statements is true or false
   (i) a company has unlimited liability
   (ii) a company sells shares to its shareholders
   Which option best describes the two statements?
   A (i) T   (ii) T
   B (i) T   (ii) F
   C (i) F   (ii) T
   D (i) F   (ii) F

Questions 3–5 share answer options A–D:
   The following are examples of large businesses or organisations:
   A Woolworths
   B Department of Health
   C RSPCA
   D Market stall owner
   Which organisations fit into the categories below?

3. Charitable organisation
4. Central government
5. Public limited company

6. The purpose of a public sector organisation is to:
   A Offer a service only when it is profitable
   B Create competition for private sector organisations
   C Provide a service to the general public
   D Raise capital for the government by privatising the service

Questions 7–9 share answer options A–D.
   There are many stages involved in the production and distribution of breakfast cereal. Businesses fall into the following sectors:
   A Primary
   B Ancillary
   C Tertiary
   D Secondary
   Which sector involves the following:

7. The growing and harvesting of the cereal on the farm.

8. The production of the cereal in factories.
9. The selling of the cereal in shops.

10. Wholesalers and retailers are important forms of business organisation. Decide whether each of these statements is true or false:
    (i) A wholesaler buys in large quantities and sells in smaller quantities to the retailer
    (ii) A retailer sells to the general public
    Which option best describes the two statements?
    A (i) T   (ii) T
    B (i) T   (ii) F
    C (i) F   (ii) T
    D (i) F   (ii) F

11. A small retail shop is more likely to locate:
    A Near a densely populated town
    B In a city centre
    C In an out-of-town industrial estate
    D Next door to a supermarket

12. An organisation which produces products that are bulk-increasing is more likely to locate:
    A Near the raw materials
    B Near the customers
    C Near the competition
    D Near the suppliers

13. An organisation that produces products of a fragile nature is more likely to locate:
    A Near its suppliers
    B Near the customers
    C Near a subsidiary
    D Near the factory

14. An area of high unemployment has established an enterprise zone. The industrial units on the enterprise zone would be attractive to:
    A A small retail shop
    B A firm of solicitors
    C A firm of accountants
    D A warehouse firm

15. An organisation producing products which are bulk-reducing is more likely to locate:
    A Near the raw materials
    B Near the customers
    C Near the competition
    D Near the suppliers

16. The problem with areas of high unemployment is that the young mobile population leaves to find work and the older and less mobile population is left behind.
    Decide whether each of these statements is true or false
    (i) There will be a decline in the types of goods demanded by the 17–50 age group.
    (ii) The remaining population will find that the area becomes deprived as more firms leave due to lack of business.
    Which option best describes the two statements?
    A (i) T   (ii) T
    B (i) T   (ii) F
    C (i) F   (ii) T
    D (i) F   (ii) F

Business Organisations and Employment

17 An organisation's decision about what to sell will be based upon:
   A What the manager wants to produce
   B What the workers are able to produce
   C The needs and wants of the likely customers
   D The decision of the board of directors

18 A company selling electrical equipment is:
   A A manufacturer
   B A primary producer
   C A secondary sector organisation
   D A service provider

19 A new accountant is established within the area. Decide whether each of these statements is true or false:
   (i) This is an example of a tertiary sector organisation.
   (ii) A service sector organisation is classified under the public sector.
   Which option best describes the two statements?
   A (i) T   (ii) T
   B (i) T   (ii) F
   C (i) F   (ii) T
   D (i) F   (ii) F

20 An organisation will attract custom away from the competitors if the organisation:
   A Offers a similar product range
   B Extends the product range to meet the changing needs of customers
   C Raises the prices of the product range above those of the competitors
   D Promotes outdated products by expensive advertising

Questions 21–23 share answer options A–D
There are a number of different types of employment including:
   A Full-time work
   B Seasonal work
   C Temporary work
   D Part-time work
Which type of employment would best describe:

21 A student working at weekends in the local supermarket

22 A labourer employed on the farm during harvesting

23 A student working during the Christmas holiday for the Post Office

24 When an employee starts a full-time job she should be given:
   A A uniform
   B An itemised pay slip
   C A P45
   D A contract of employment

25 An employee's pay packet will show deductions for:
   A Corporation tax
   B Value added tax
   C Income tax
   D Capital gains tax

26 A new employees introduction to an organisation is called:
   A A professional training programme
   B An exist interview
   C On the job training
   D An induction programme

27 Employees may resist automation because they fear:
   A A deterioration in the quality of the product
   B Greater managerial control of the workers
   C Redundancies due to less work for employees
   D Decrease in production and sales

28 With the introduction of computerised systems some people are able to work from home. Decide whether each of these statements is true or false:
   (i) Working from home reduces congestion on the roads.
   (ii) Employees are able to communicate with their office by using sophisticated telecommunications.
   Which option best describes the two statements?
   A (i) T   (ii) T
   B (i) T   (ii) F
   C (i) F   (ii) T
   D (i) F   (ii) F

29 Decide whether each of these statements is true or false:
   (i) A computerised production system enables raw materials to be used more efficiently.
   (ii) The introduction of a computerised accounting system will mean that the company will have to retrain the accounting staff.
   Which option best describes the two statements?
   A (i) T   (ii) T
   B (i) T   (ii) F
   C (i) F   (ii) T
   D (i) F   (ii) F

30 The introduction of computerised stock control is likely to lead to:
   A Greater accuracy and efficiency of stock records
   B More paperwork and administration
   C New job vacancies
   D Increased sales

Business Organisations and Employment

🔑 Key terms

- Articles of association
- Authorised share capital
- Capital
- Central government
- Charities
- Command economy
- Companies act
- Consumable
- Cooperative
- Council
- Debentures
- Directors
- Diseconomies of scale
- Dividend
- Division of labour
- Domestic market
- Drawings
- Durable
- Economies of scale
- Employed
- Franchise
- Goods
- Government incentives
- International market
- Issued share capital
- Labour supply
- Limited liability
- Local government
- Market economy
- Market share
- Memorandum of association
- Mixed economy
- Municipal
- Nationalised industry
- Natural resources
- Needs
- Ordinary shares
- Partnership
- Partnership act
- Partnership agreement
- Preference shares
- Primary industrial sector
- Private limited company (Ltd)
- Private sector
- Privatisation
- Public limited company (plc)
- Public sector
- Secondary industrial sector
- Self-employed
- Services
- Share capital
- Shareholder
- Sleeping partner
- Sole trader
- State-owned
- Tertiary industrial sector
- Unlimited liability
- Wants

UNIT 2

People in Business Organisations

UNIT SUMMARY

This unit examines business organisations from the inside, looking at the ways in which they are organised, the roles and functions played by people within the organisation and the rights and responsibilities of both employers and employees. The structure of the organisation is broken down into key components and the relationships between these parts are described. Although no two organisations are exactly the same there are a lot of similarities in the way that they are organised internally. This unit is tested externally, and at the end of the chapter there are some practice test questions.

ELEMENT 2.1
Examine and compare structures and working arrangements in organisations

Performance criteria

- (PC) 2.1.1 Describe organisational structures
- (PC) 2.1.2 Produce organisational charts showing departments
- (PC) 2.1.3 Describe the work and explain the interdependence of departments within business organisations
- (PC) 2.1.4 Identify and explain differences in working arrangements
- (PC) 2.1.5 Explain and give examples of reasons for change in working arrangements in one business organisation

Introduction

Organisations have already been described as groups of people working towards a common goal (see Unit 1). For this to be possible the people within the organisation need to be *organised* in the following ways:

- The members of the organisation need to have clearly defined *roles* so that everyone knows what they are expected to do.
- There need to be effective lines of *communication* so that information within the organisation can be passed to the right people efficiently.
- There need to be clear lines of *authority* so that appropriate people in the organisation know who

People in Business Organisations

is responsible for each part of its operations, allowing decision-making to be directed and effective.

These three aspects:

- Roles
- Communication
- Authority

play a vital role in organisations. The larger an organisation is, the more important it becomes that they are understood by all concerned. Failure to have a clearly-defined system in place is likely to lead to disaster:

- Members of the organisation will not know what tasks they should be carrying out.
- Information will not be passed on to the people who need to know.
- When action has to be taken, either no one will take responsibility or several people will act at once, all pulling in different directions.

In short, the organisation will no longer act as an organisation and will fall apart like a badly made building.

An examination of *organisational structures* will help to develop an understanding of how people in an organisation work in relation to each other. An *organisational chart* is a diagram of the structure of a business, showing the relationships between individuals and departments. By breaking the organisation down into *functions*, the key areas of a business can be identified and clearly divided into different departments. Lastly, by spelling out in detail the *job roles* held by individuals in the organisation it is possible to determine exactly what tasks each person is responsible for carrying out.

Organisational structures

The internal structures of organisations can be described in different ways. Words and phrases can be used to explain how the people in the organisation relate to each other in carrying out their duties. It is commonly said that someone is 'under' their boss or manager and that they in turn have people 'under' them who they are in charge of. Alternatively, these relationships of being above or below other people can be readily shown in the form of a picture, known as an *organisational chart*.

This simple diagram shows that person A is 'above' person B, meaning that A is more senior than B. Similarly, person C is 'below' person B, meaning that B is more senior than C.

This is a very simple organisational chart. The vertical lines indicate *lines of authority*. So as well as being more senior, A is responsible for and in authority over B, and B is responsible for and in authority over C.

In most organisations it is common for several people to be 'on the same level' which means that they are equal in terms of seniority. They all have the same people above and below them.

In this diagram, persons 1, 2, 3, 4 and 5 are all on the same level. Person A is more senior than all of them, and likewise they are all more senior than the people on level C. The vertical lines of authority clearly show that although 3 and 5, for example, are on the same level, only 3 is in direct authority over the persons on level C. This can be expressed by saying that 3 is the *line manager* for the persons on level C. A member of an organisation is accountable first and foremost to their line manager, which is why it is important for every employee to be clear

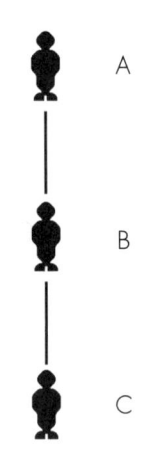

who their line manager is. Likewise, managers should know the employees for whom they are responsible.

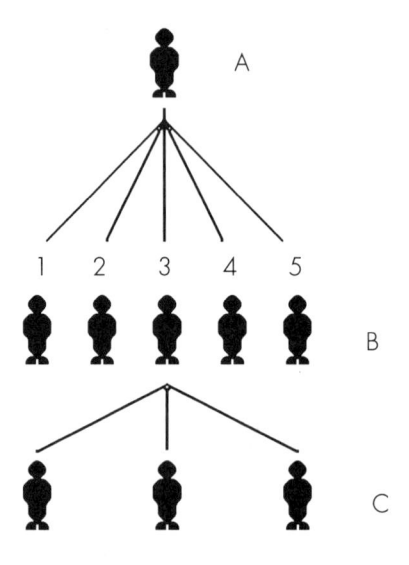

The *span of control* of each manager is determined by the number of people they are responsible for – the more people the greater the span of control. In the diagram above, person 3 has a span of control of 3. This is an important aspect of the organisational structure. If managers have a very narrow span of control they can spend more time with each person, but it may be that the managers are not being used to their fullest potential. If their span of control is very wide the quality of management is reduced, since the manager can spend less time with each person. They are in danger of becoming over-stretched and ineffective.

People in Business Organisations

A hierarchical structure

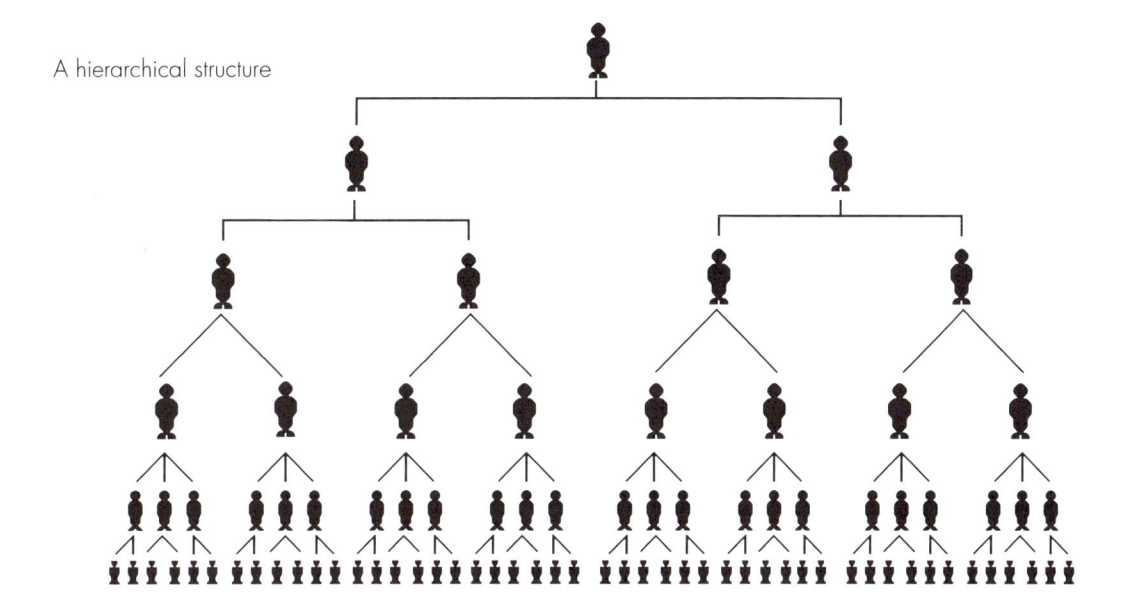

Despite the variety of possible organisational structures, they can be split into two broad categories. Where there are many layers of seniority the organisation is said to have a *hierarchical* structure. Where there are very few layers the organisation is said to have a *flat* structure.

Hierarchical structure

The features of a hierarchical structure are:
- There are many layers of seniority.
- At each higher level there are fewer individuals, producing a pyramid-shaped structure.
- At the top of the structure there is normally just one individual with supreme authority over the whole organisation – this is generally the managing director or equivalent.

This has been the traditional structure of many large organisations. Employees typically begin at the bottom and attempt to work their way up. One of the problems is that it is so far to the top, and from each level fewer and fewer people can progress, so that employees will often lose the motivation even to try. Another problem is that the complexity of the structure means that lines of communication are very long, which can lead to information being delayed and distorted. Anyone who has ever played the children's game of passing a whispered message from one person to the next will know how easy it is for the message to become unrecognisable after just a few repeats.

Middle managers is the term often used to refer to managers in a hierarchical structure who are below the senior managers and above the junior managers.

ACTIVITY

Can you think of any organisations that have a hierarchical structure? They tend to be large limited companies or public sector administrations. List as many as you can. Compare your list with a colleague and 'swap' any organisations that your lists do not share.

In discussion with your colleague examine the advantages and disadvantages of hierarchical structures.
(2.1.1)

Flat structure

In order to overcome the problems of a hierarchical structure, many businesses are turning to a more streamlined *flat* structure. In a flat structure the top management team has control over the whole organisation, which is split into a number of independent parts. The business may be divided according to geographical area, or different products or specialisms. This serves to increase the motivation of employees, since they have clearer prospects for promotion. However, the span of control of the upper management team becomes very wide, which may result in poor control of the whole organisation. Also,

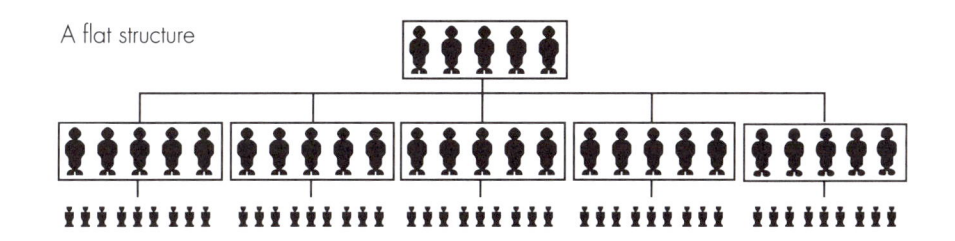

A flat structure

People in Business Organisations

the width of the structure can lead to poor communications between each section of the organisation. Separate branches may begin to work in isolation. Furthermore, it is quite common for branch managers to feel that they are in competition with each other. This is healthy to a degree, as it may promote increased productivity in an attempt to be the most efficient department. However, too much competition within the organisation can also lead to disharmony and resentment.

ACTIVITY

Can you think of any organisations that have a flat structure? They tend to be smaller businesses or very large companies broken up into smaller pieces. List as many as you can. Compare your list with a colleague and 'swap' any organisations that your lists do not share.

In discussion with your colleague, examine the advantages and disadvantages of flat structures. (2.1.1)

Comparison of organisational structures

	Flat	Hierarchical
Advantages	Less bureaucracy	Clear areas of responsibility
	Faster and more effective communication	Members may specialise in an area of expertise and interest
	Faster and more effective decision-making	Top management freed from operational activities to concentrate on policy decisions
	Easier to respond to customer needs	Organisation can have specialised departments leading to greater efficiency
	Easier to respond to external changes	Clear lines of authority
	Managers are close to the employees and customers promoting a caring image	
	Employees are motivated by possibility of promotion to the highest levels	
Disadvantages	Poor communication between departments and/or branches	Poor communication from top to bottom
	Branch managers may feel that they are in competition with each other	Likely to be bureaucratic
		Slow decision-making
		Difficult for employees to raise to highest levels
	Managers must be more generalised in areas of expertise	Higher levels of management are far removed from workers and customers
	Wide span of control leading to less effective management	Slow to respond to change

Circular

A *circular* structure is suited to simpler organisations which wish to support the independent work of specialists. It allows individuals to contribute their specialist skills independently of others. It emphasises the responsibility of individuals and their professional skills. Each individual may have some administrative, financial or personnel support, for example, but this forms a semi-independent unit within the organisation.

A typical example is a dentists' clinic. Each dentist acts quite independently of their colleagues, providing care and treatment according to their specialisms and skills. Each dentist may have their own receptionist, anaesthetist and assistant. Another example may be a firm of consultants who each specialise in providing consultancy advice on particular areas of expertise.

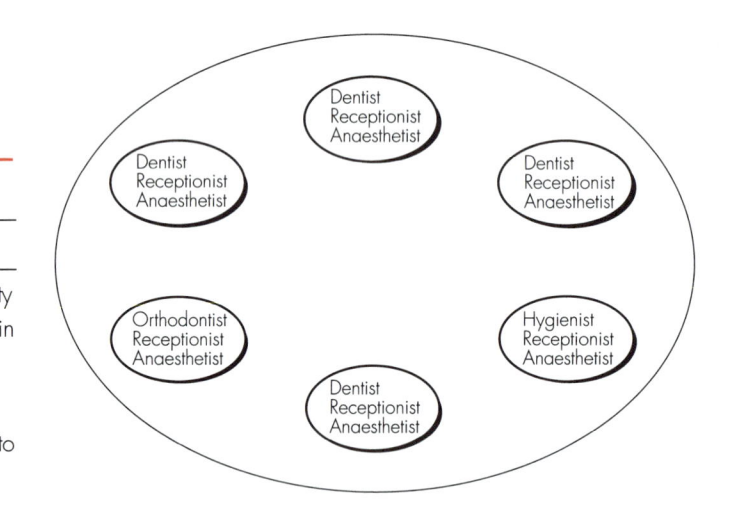

A circular structure

Matrix

A *matrix* structure is ideally suited to a complex organisation. It emphasises that people from different departments nevertheless work very closely with each other, particularly on large projects.

In a matrix structure work is focused into project groups combining people of different skills. The project manager has responsibility for overseeing the entire project, meeting deadlines and working within the agreed budget. Management have only to deal with one person to get an overview for the project. This cuts down on bureaucracy. The customer too can also check up on the progress of their order by dealing with one person.

By its nature a matrix structure is most commonly found in complex manufacturing organisations, where teams are formed to work together from the design stage to the marketing and distribution stage.

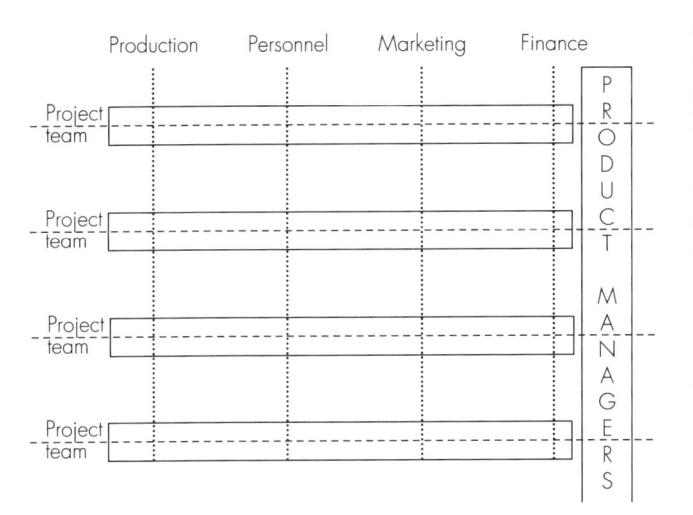

A matrix structure

Communication

Ideally communication should flow across the organisation as well as up and down. Regional managers of different branches should be able to swap information and ideas easily. Likewise, the person at the top should be able to communicate effectively with the workers at the bottom of the organisation, and they should be able to communicate their concerns up to the highest level.

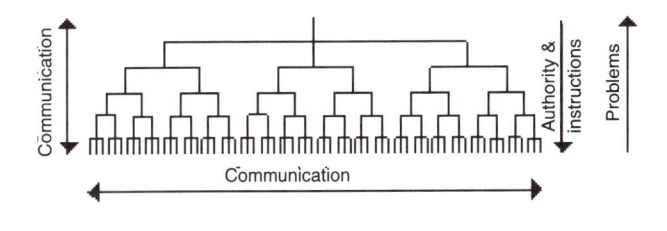

The diagram illustrates that problems and responsibility flow up the organisation. An American president (Harry S. Truman) once remarked, 'the buck stops here'. The person on top 'carries the can' – that person is ultimately responsible for the whole organisation. Authority and instructions flow downwards, requiring effective lines of communication. Those in authority need to be able to communicate their instructions to those who must carry them out.

Organisations with tall, hierarchical structures may experience a poor flow of communication up and down. This may lead to hostility and resentment from the persons lower down the structure.

Businesses with flat structures may have problems with communication horizontally between departments and regions. This may be made worse if the branch managers become more competitive.

ACTIVITY

Choose an organisation with which you are familiar. It may be your school or your college or may be an organisation in which you work. You may even choose your family. If possible, choose the largest and most complex organisation of those that you know.

Draw up an organisational chart for your chosen organisation, clearly showing the different levels of authority. In notes attached to your diagram consider the following points:
1 For everyone in the organisation describe the role that they play and state their span of control.
2 State whether the organisation has a flat, hierarchical, circular or matrix structure.
3 Suggest aspects of the structure which may give rise to problems and make recommendations as to how the structure may be improved.

(2.1.1)

Working arrangements

The working arrangements within an organisation depend upon its size, the nature of the work undertaken and its internal structure. Different ways of working suit different organisations.

Centralised

Centralised organisations tend to focus their management within one headquarters and manage the organisation from there. All major decisions about the operation of the branches will be taken by the senior management team at headquarters. Pricing, publicity posters, staff uniforms, even the layout of stores will be decided by head office and applied equally throughout all branches.

Centralised organisations often have a centralised purchasing system, so that the buying and re-ordering for all the stores is done at one point. There are savings to be made by buying in such large quantities, and it becomes possible to have centralised warehouses supplying a number of branches. It is also possible to have suppliers who make a product exclusively for the organisation.

You can walk into any branch of Boots the Chemist in the country, for example, and have a very similar experience. The range of products available, the notices on the wall and even the type of lettering used to price goods will be the same. This is only possible if all branches are managed centrally and operated according to the same policies.

ACTIVITY

Can you think of other organisations which are highly centralised in their management and operation? You should plan to visit at least two stores of the same organisation and make a note of

People in Business Organisations

all the things that are the same.

What are the advantages of a centralised organisation?
(2.1.2)

Decentralised

Decentralised organisations allow branch managers much more authority to operate their site as they choose. The directors and senior managers do issue instructions for the whole organisation, but there is much greater freedom for managers to choose for themselves.

An example of a highly decentralised organisation is illustrated by education in this country. The government passes laws which regulate how schools operate. Local authorities provide schools with finance. The headteachers, however, still have a very large degree of freedom in deciding how to manage their own schools.

ACTIVITY

Make a list of 20 large organisations which are located throughout the country. Ensure that you select at least five public sector organisations. Produce a table showing whether each organisation is (i) public or private sector and (ii) centralised or decentralised.
(2.1.4)

Centralised and decentralised organisations

	Centralised	Decentralised
Features	• Authority focused at head office • Most decisions made at the top • Centralised purchasing	• Authority devolved to branches • Many decisions made at branch level • Localised purchasing
Advantages	• Uniform service across the country • Savings made in bulk purchasing • Exclusive suppliers • Greater control over organisation	• Service tailored to meet local needs • Greater freedom for branch managers • Less bureaucracy • More personal service
Disadvantages	• Less flexibility to meet local needs • Less freedom for branch managers • Highly bureaucratic	• Variety of service across country • More expensive cost of buying • Less control of whole organisation

Flexible working hours

The traditional view of the working day is that it is fixed for all employees. Everyone is expected to 'clock on' at the start of the day at 8 a.m. or 9 a.m. If they do not then they are late and are likely to lose pay. Likewise, everyone 'clocks off' at 5 p.m., unless they are working overtime.

This traditional concept is certainly no longer applied in all organisations. Some organisations often have a system of *shift work*. On this basis some workers will be clocking on as others are finishing their shift. It might work like this:

shift 1   08.00–16.00
shift 2   16.00–00.00
shift 3   00.00–08.00

In this way, with workers starting and finishing shifts throughout the day, the organisation need never shut down.

ACTIVITY

What kind of organisations might operate shift work? List as many different kinds of organisations as you can. What are the advantages to the organisations for doing this?
(2.1.4)

There are a whole variety of reasons for operating shiftwork. Some organisations must stay open all hours because they provide an essential service. Examples include hospital trusts, the fire brigade and residential nursing homes. Other organisations will need as much working time as possible to meet targets. A road construction company, for example, is likely to have agreed dates to meet for completion. Often they will receive a bonus for early completion and incur a penalty for finishing behind schedule. Therefore the company will be willing to pay the crew more money to work through the night to ensure that they meet the deadlines. Lastly, there are organisations which continue operating 24 hours a day because it is cheaper than closing down. For blast furnaces, for example, the costs of shutting down and then starting up again are enormous. Therefore they remain operating around the clock tended by rotating shifts of workers.

Flexi-time

Another break with the traditional working day is the introduction in some organisations of *flexi-time*. As the name suggests, this refers to flexible working hours, and is particularly applicable to office work. If individuals are able to perform some or all of their duties on their own, then they do not need to wait for everyone else to arrive before they start working. Many offices open as early as 6 a.m. for cleaning, and where a system of flexi-time is in operation this would allow workers who wished to do so to start work. Alternatively they might work later into the evening. The advantage to the employees is that it allows them to plan their week more flexibly to allow for personal preferences and other commitments. For the employer there is little or no extra cost and the benefit is a more motivated work force.

People in Business Organisations

> **ACTIVITY**
>
> 1 Over the last 15 years there has been a sharp increase in the popularity of flexi-time. What changes in social lifestyles do you think are responsible for this increase?
> 2 For each of the following jobs state whether they would lend themselves to flexi-time arrangements. Give your reasons:
>   - teacher
>   - secretary
>   - nurse
>   - cleaner
>   - taxi driver
>   - filing clerk
>
> (2.1.4)

Contracts of employment

There is a distinction made between two different kinds of contract. *Fixed short-term* contracts, as the name suggests, run for a fixed period of time, such as six months, a year or three years. These are often given to new and less experienced workers, or for a promotion to a more senior post, where the person is 'on trial'. At the end of the period of their contract, if their performance has been satisfactory and there is sufficient work for them to do, they may well have their contract renewed or perhaps made permanent. *Permanent* contracts have no in-built time period. They are effective until retirement, or when the employee chooses to leave. However, even employees on permanent contracts can lawfully be made redundant or given the sack. In this way they have neither more nor less protection in law than employees on fixed-term contracts (see Element 2.2 for more detail on employee rights relating to contracts of employment).

In recent times many more people have been taken on fixed short-term contracts rather than permanent ones. This is a reflection of the economic uncertainties of the age. There is no such thing as a job for life any more. Employers are naturally more cautious when taking on new employees or in promoting people to more senior positions.

Working from home and mobile working

People have worked from home ever since the start of light manufacturing work. Outworkers could stitch, sew, glue, paint and assemble at their dining table rather than be brought into work. A worker would typically be paid *piece rate* for such work, according to the number of items completed.

However, this kind of home-working is in decline, as the economy in the UK continues to witness a decline of the secondary industrial sector and growth of the service sector. Where working from home is increasing it is largely due to improvements in information technology and telecommunications. Such work is often called *teleworking*, which literally means working from a distance (in the same way that *television* means pictures from a distance). The telephone, the home computer, the fax, the modem and the Internet all make it very easy for a large number of office-based workers to perform their tasks from home and at the same time communicate with other people instantaneously.

With the continuous improvement of these items as they get smaller and more effective, it becomes possible for executives to have a mobile office in their cars. This is sometimes referred to as *mobile working*. With a portable fax, a laptop computer and a mobile phone an employee can work very well from almost anywhere in the world.

Working from home may suit self-employed people, as well as members of much larger organisations. The employer can save money on office accommodation or factory space if their workers can do the job in their own front room. The employees benefit from the convenience of not travelling into work each day and of working in a relaxed and familiar environment around which they can accommodate their other commitments.

> **ACTIVITY**
>
> 1 What advantages are there to the (i) employee and (ii) to the employer of working from home? What disadvantages might there be?
> 2 What advantages are there to the (i) employee and (ii) to the employer of mobile working? What disadvantages might there be?
> 3 What minimum equipment would someone need to work from home or for mobile working effectively? Justify your choice.
>
> (2.1.4)

Differences in working arrangements

In different organisations of different sizes and different structures people work together in many different ways. It is even possible for people to work in different ways within the same organisation over a period of time, depending upon the kind of work they are undertaking.

Individual working

Most jobs involve a combination of working with others as part of a team as well as working alone for some of the time. A large amount of individual work is usually only possible if the person can offer a high degree of skill or expertise.

As a style of working it is particularly applicable to *flat* and *circular* organisational structures, where individuals have a high degree of autonomy and as specialists can work quite independently of other people in the organisation. Examples may include doctors in a clinic and teachers in a small school.

To succeed, individuals need to be highly motivated and be able to work a lot of the time

People in Business Organisations

without input, guidance and leadership from other people. It suits people who are independent and get a lot of satisfaction in working things out for themselves.

Team working

Working as part of a team for a large proportion of the time is common in many organisations, especially those with a *matrix* structure. Here the employees are organised into teams of a variety of skills to enable the same group of people to work on a project from its very beginning at the product design stage right through to its marketing and distribution. Good team workers are those people who are effective communicators with others, being able to express their ideas and contribute their opinions. They must also be good listeners, giving fair consideration to other points of view and accepting criticism. Most importantly, to be a good team member it is vital that each person recognises their role in the team and works effectively within that role. The expression 'a chain is only as strong as its weakest link' is very appropriate.

Level of independence

The level of independence which employees are given is a measure of how much they work in a team and how much on their own. Those who have a large amount of individual work are said to have a high level of independence. As has already been said, this depends on the nature of the organisation, its size and structure, and the kind of work being done. On an individual basis it also depends upon a person's seniority and experience. New employees are likely to be given less independence until they learn the skills needed for the job and can demonstrate their competence. They will need closer supervision during their first few months. As time progresses, however, and they are able to show their reliability and efficiency at the job, the employee will be given a higher level of independence.

ACTIVITY

1 Decide whether the following jobs are better performed mostly in teams or mostly individually:
- open-heart surgery
- police work
- violin making
- vehicle assembly on a production line
- GP
- plumbing
- mining

2 Make a comparative chart of the skills needed for (i) team working and (ii) individual working. Taking account of the skills you have and the kinds of jobs you would like, decide which style of working you are better suited to. Would you prefer a higher or a lower level of independence?
(2.1.4)

Chain of command

We have already noted the importance of clear lines of authority, particularly when working within a very tall, hierarchical structure. The lines of authority (who's in charge) are sometimes referred to as the *chain of command*.

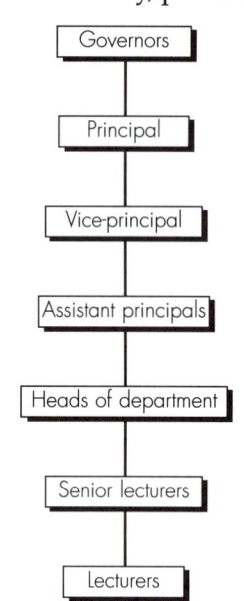

The figure illustrates the chain of command in a college. *Instructions* are passed down the chain of command and *accountability* (being answerable to someone for your actions) flows up the chain. For example, the senior lecturers will receive instructions from the heads of department, who in turn must respond to instructions from the assistant principals. Likewise the vice-principal is accountable for his or her actions to the principal, who is ultimately accountable to the board of governors.

Governors
│
Principal
│
Vice-principal
│
Assistant principals
│
Heads of department
│
Senior lecturers
│
Lecturers

ACTIVITY

For your school, college or place of work draw a diagram showing the chain of command.
(2.1.4)

The influence of different structures on working arrangements

Decision-making

One important difference between the flat and hierarchical structures is the way in which decision-making takes place.

Authority flows down the organisation, typically from managing director at the very top, through the

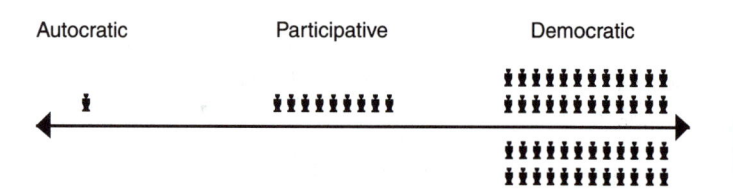

Autocratic   Participative   Democratic

Styles of leadership

People in Business Organisations

Tele-conferencing can help with discussion and decision-making

layers of managers and middle managers and finally down to staff. This means that decisions made at the top must be carried out by those underneath. There are a variety of different *leadership styles*, which affect the ways in which decision-making takes place.

Autocratic
As an extreme style of leadership, *autocratic* leaders are the only persons to make decisions. Everyone else is simply instructed to carry out their orders. This may be possible in a very small organisation. The smallest organisation, for example, is a sole trader with no other employees. In this case the sole trader would *have* to make all the decisions – because there is no one else! As an organisation grows it becomes virtually impossible for the person at the top to make all decisions at all levels – not only major policy decisions affecting the shape and the future of the organisation but also day-to-day decisions about what paper to use in the photocopier and dealing with customer queries. In a hierarchical organisation the people in the many layers take responsibility for different levels of decisions. However, leaders can still be highly autocratic in their style if they make all the high-level decisions with little or no consultation with anyone else.

An autocratic style can be very satisfying for managing directors. Their ideas are pursued by the organisation – because they say so! Sometimes this approach is necessary to make changes when not everyone agrees. However, it can lead to directors, managers, supervisors and staff feeling frustrated and powerless. At some level everyone needs to feel involved in decision-making so that they feel the decisions are their own. Then they are more likely to carry out instructions willingly.

Participative
If a leadership style is more *participative*, then the leader takes the advice of other people before making decisions. This too can work to different degrees. The managing director may only take the advice of the directors. This is participative but still fairly autocratic. Alternatively, the managing director may include managers, supervisors and even staff members in consultation before reaching a decision.

Democratic
A truly *democratic* business will give everybody in the organisation an equal say in decision-making. In its extreme form every decision would be put to the members of the organisation for a vote and the majority decision would be carried. This is impractical, since there are many tedious day-to-day decisions that need to be made immediately – you cannot find time to vote on who should answer the phone! However, in a highly democratic organisation the major policy decisions that affect the working practice of the majority of its members will be put to a vote.

A democratic approach is beneficial because it is seen as being fair. Everyone is involved in decision-making and they are therefore more willing to follow instructions. However, it cannot be used for all decisions because it simply takes too long. Furthermore, there are some decisions that involve very complex issues which it is fair to say that not everyone is able to understand. Even if they could understand it would take a long time to explain it to them. They may also be some top-level decisions that are too sensitive to tell everyone about before they are taken. In the worst possible scenario, the staff may vote for large wage increases that the organisation simply cannot afford.

People in Business Organisations

Virgin Organisational Chart

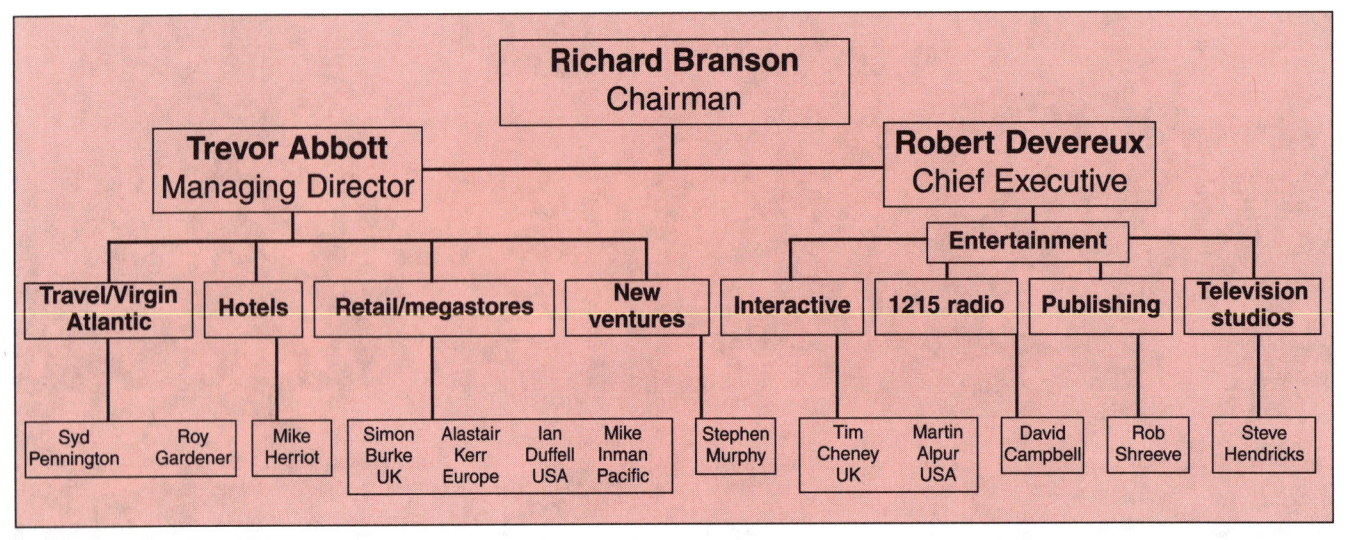

- **Richard Branson** — Chairman
  - **Trevor Abbott** — Managing Director
    - Travel/Virgin Atlantic
      - Syd Pennington
      - Roy Gardener
    - Hotels
      - Mike Herriot
    - Retail/megastores
      - Simon Burke (UK)
      - Alastair Kerr (Europe)
      - Ian Duffell (USA)
      - Mike Inman (Pacific)
    - New ventures
      - Stephen Murphy
  - **Robert Devereux** — Chief Executive
    - Entertainment
      - Interactive
        - Tim Cheney (UK)
        - Martin Alpur (USA)
      - 1215 radio
        - David Campbell
      - Publishing
        - Rob Shreeve
      - Television studios
        - Steve Hendricks

Source: Sunday Times, 5 June 1994

ACTIVITY

Study the organisational chart for Virgin and answer the following questions:

1. What are the main divisions within the Virgin organisation?
2. Who is the senior manager for the Virgin 1215 radio station?
3. Who is the line manager for Roy Gardner?
4. What position does Ian Duffell hold?
5. How would you describe the organisational structure?
6. What style of leadership do you think Richard Branson has?
7. What problems might be experienced in the process of communication?

(2.1.1) (2.1.3)

Departments within organisations

TRUFFLES: EPISODE 1

Ten friends have grouped together to form a new business, called Truffles. They aim to design new chocolate bars, produce them and sell them to local shops and, eventually, supermarkets across the country. They have had many meetings and know exactly what they need to do, but for some reason they never make any progress.

For example, when they try to agree a design for the chocolate bars everyone has an idea what shape they would like to see – square, oblong, chunky, flat, bubbly, smooth, even triangular or round. Mark and Ali have particularly strong ideas and some previous experience of design. The others tend to be rather fanciful and unrealistic in their suggestions.

Likewise, when the group of friends discuss the best ways of marketing their products they talk for hours with no agreement. Should they use newspapers, TV, radio or leaflets? What should be the content of any adverts? Orphée and David are both media studies students with experience of putting advertisements together, but no one will listen to anyone else.

What about production? Antonio worked in a small sweet shop for the summer and has suggestions to make about the best methods to use. But it seems that they can all think of ways of making chocolate, pouring the chocolate into shapes and wrapping them up. Why should anyone listen to Antonio?

Rashda has a love of figures, but no one will leave her to devise a suitable system for recording financial transactions. They all think that handling money is easy, but they cannot agree a system.

Mike and Joanne have lived in the area all their lives: they are well-known and know all the streets and shops better than anyone, but the whole group has ideas about the best shops to use as traders. Most of them are talking without experience and just mentioning shops that they know and like.

Jacob has been on a secretarial training programme and volunteers to keep records and write letters, but the group wants to decide on the best way of doing it first. They talk for hours about the benefits and problems of using a computer. No decision is made.

It seems that Robert wants to do everything himself. He has plenty of good ideas, but cannot work them through because he is always trying to work on everything at once. He does not believe that anyone else can do a better job than him. He says he has a vision, that he can see the whole picture, but he does not trust anyone else to get it right.

And so they go round and round in circles, each person feeling frustrated and disappointed at the lack of progress. At least they are agreed on something: they need to find a new way of working together.

People in Business Organisations

> ### ✎ ACTIVITY
>
> What advice would you give to the ten friends? Should they give up or is there a better way of working together? Make detailed suggestions for each person named in the case study. You may like to discuss your ideas with your group.
> *(2.1.3)*

Introduction

It should be obvious from the case study that there are times when it is better for a group to share out the tasks that they need to do. Everyone has a different specialism which they need time to concentrate on. If everyone pulls in a different direction then the group will go nowhere, but if in smaller groups they focus their efforts on one area each they will make progress. To do this, each person needs to trust the expertise of the others and allow them to come up with the answers. This may mean letting other people make mistakes at first, because this is one way of learning.

Mark and Ali should be left to design the products – they have experience and have some strong ideas. Orphée and David are media studies students, ready and able to produce advertising materials and run a suitable marketing campaign. Antonio has relevant experience for production and is the best person for the job. Rashda could keep the books, Mike and Joanne could use their local knowledge to find customers, and Jacob is just ideal for taking charge of administration. Robert may be a good manager, having ideas and discussing them with each specialist, but he needs to trust other people's capabilities.

To overcome similar problems, large organisations are usually divided into a number of *functions* or departments. The reason for this is economy and efficiency. Each section of the business can specialise in a different department, devoting their efforts towards one aspect of the organisation's activities.

This division of departments may not be needed for small organisations. Where there are only a few staff, tasks may be shared out on an informal basis, and it may be necessary for some people to take on two or three different areas. Hence there is less *specialisation* in smaller organisations. Individuals are expected to be more general in their skills.

Departments

Organisations are broken into departments in a number of different ways, according to what is most useful to the business. This will depend on features of the organisation such as size, type of business, main organisational goals, traditions and business ethos, as well the personal preferences of the management team.

Likely departments include:

- Research and development (often referred to simply as 'R and D')
- Production
- Purchasing
- Accounts/finance
- Human resources, or personnel
- Marketing
- Sales
- Administration
- Computer services
- Transport
- Distribution

These may be broken down further. Alternatively it is quite common for some functions to be combined into one department. This chapter will refer to six main departments, combining different functions as follows:

1. Design and production (including R and D)
2. Personnel
3. Finance (incorporating accounts and purchasing)
4. Administration (including computing and IT services)
5. Sales and marketing
6. Distribution (including transport)

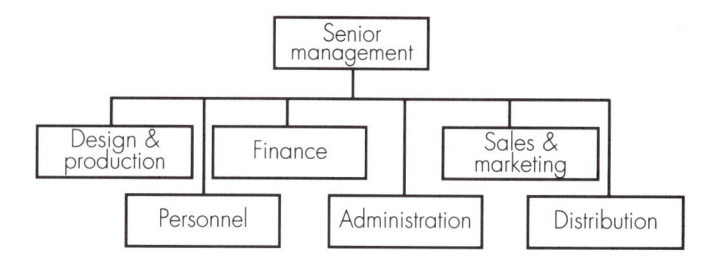

```
                    Senior
                  management
                      │
   ┌──────────┬───────┼───────┬──────────┐
Design &   Finance          Sales &
production                  marketing
   │          │               │
Personnel  Administration  Distribution
```

There is a horizontal or staff relationship between these functions. This means that no department is in charge of another. Instead, they cooperate with each other and advise and support each other's activities. None can exist on its own, nor can one act without affecting the others. The senior management team must issue appropriate instructions and give guidance to ensure that the departments work in harmony with one another.

Design and production

> **TRUFFLES: EPISODE 2**
>
> Having decided to divide operations to allow individuals to specialise, Mark and Ali come up with some designs. They show these to the whole group. They have a number of different suggestions:
>
> 1. 'Chocolate Cigars': cigar-shaped bars of chocolate
> 2. 'Stick-o-bars': chocolate covered in a gooey, sugary coating
> 3. 'Knife Bars': knife-shaped, hard chocolate with a sharp edge
> 4. 'Mini Bars': accurate scale models of the Mini Cooper car with doors that open

People in Business Organisations

> 5 'Incognito': plain chocolate in plain wrappers with no print on them to create a sense of mystery
> 6 'Stone Bars': a bar so hard it is virtually impossible to eat
>
> The group then discusses all of these possible designs.

ACTIVITY

Critically assess all the designs that have been put forward by Mark and Ali. What problems do you see with the designs? Suggest guidelines that Mark and Ali should follow in future which will help them design a more suitable product.
(2.1.3)

The Chocolate Cigars would be unappealing to many customers since it might be thought that they encourage children to smoke. The Stick-o-bars are impractical – consumers do not like to get messy fingers. The Knife Bars are dangerous and would break the law (under the Sale of Goods Act – see Unit 3). The Mini Bars sound wonderful but are likely to be very difficult to make and therefore very expensive. Incognito is an interesting idea, but the problem is that it could not be used to establish Truffles and build up its reputation, since no one would know who the manufacturer was. Stone Bars are also unattractive, since they are almost impossible to eat.

Design and production may be separated into two separate departments, but they are quite often combined as they are closely related.

Like all other functions, the design function has to work with the rest of the organisation. Designs should be made that the production function can readily make, the finance department can afford, the personnel department can find people to work on, the sales department can sell, and so on. The role of the design function, therefore, is to ensure that products:
- Are both functional and appealing to customers
- Comply with safety standards and other regulations
- Reflect a corporate style
- Can be produced within physical and budgeting constraints

Designs change for many reasons, including:
- Fashion
- New technology becomes available
- Changes in production techniques
- Environmental concerns
- Changes in law

From time to time businesses will redesign old products to meet new needs or even to create new demand for something that may have lost popularity. The Royal Mint often make changes to the coins and notes in circulation, making coins smaller, replacing notes with coins and changing the designs, often to keep ahead of would-be forgers. The car industry is always introducing new features as standard to improve safety and performance and to encourage people to replace their old cars for newer and better models. Clothes and shoes are always changing so that customers will feel unfashionable unless they buy the latest items.

Increasingly, computers are being used to assist designers in making better products. The latest roller-coaster 'white-knuckle' rides, for example, such as Nemesis at Alton Towers, have been designed with the help of CAD (computer-aided design) systems, bringing new features never previously considered by human brains alone. Computers can make very complex calculations very quickly and therefore can design and even 'test' many products in a short space of time, without going through the lengthy process of actually making anything.

ACTIVITY

Undertake research into a number of products. You may like to choose from:
- **Motor cars**
- **Calculators**
- **Fast food**
- **Computers**
- **Music systems**

Alternatively you may choose other items.

Your research should include a comparison of at least *five* different designs of the same kind of product. This should help you recognise the design features that have been included. Then you should carry out the following tasks:

1. **Explain what design features you have discovered in your products and give reasons why you think the features have been included in the product (such as fashion, legislation, usefulness, safety and corporate image).**
2. **From your research, decide which of the various designs you prefer, giving reasons for your answers.**
3. **By examining recent changes in design describe these changes and give the most likely reasons for them.**

(2.1.3)

ACTIVITY

Having given Mark and Ali some clear guidelines to consider when making designs, you should now suggest a few designs of your own. You may like to research this by investigating the chocolate bars that you enjoy and deciding which features you like about them. You could then try to combine these features in one design.
(2.1.3)

People in Business Organisations

Production

TRUFFLES: EPISODE 3

Mark and Ali have finally come up with a design that is perfect, and it is now up to Antonio to produce it. He suggests five stages:

Stage 1: Only the best (and therefore most expensive) ingredients (sugar, cocoa, milk solids etc.) shall be used, in huge quantities, mixed in a giant 50 gallon container and heated for 20 minutes by one person producing enough chocolate for 2000 bars – this involves working in extremely hot conditions.

Stage 2: The chocolate is poured into moulds, which will take 5 people 5 hours.

Stage 3: The chocolate has to cool for 3 hours.

Stage 4: The name of the bar is stamped on each bar, taking 2 highly skilled people 4 hours.

Stage 5: Lastly the bars will then be wrapped by a machine operated by one person taking 8 hours – a very repetitive and boring process.

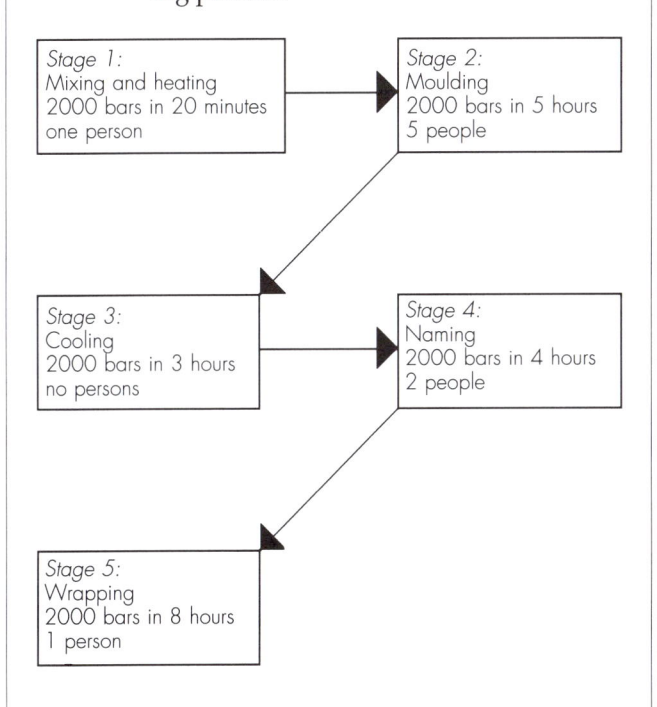

```
Stage 1:                    Stage 2:
Mixing and heating  ----->  Moulding
2000 bars in 20 minutes     2000 bars in 5 hours
one person                  5 people
       |
       v
Stage 3:                    Stage 4:
Cooling             ----->  Naming
2000 bars in 3 hours        2000 bars in 4 hours
no persons                  2 people
       |
       v
Stage 5:
Wrapping
2000 bars in 8 hours
1 person
```

The whole process lasts 20 hours and 20 minutes. Although some of the equipment is very expensive, savings can be made by using home-based workers to stamp the bars with the name.

Antonio presents his proposals to a meeting of the whole group for discussion.

ACTIVITY

Examine the process of production stage by stage. What problems do you think the production process would experience? How could it be improved? When you have identified as many potential problems as you can, compare your answers with a colleague. Together, draw up a set of guidelines that the production function should follow in future.
(2.1.3)

Antonio seems to have forgotten that the production function must work in cooperation with the other departments. The costs must be agreed by the finance department, which may not accept that buying such large quantities of ingredients all at once is such a good idea. Using only the best materials is a good idea, but it may also make the product too expensive to sell, which will upset the selling and marketing people. The personnel department will find it difficult to find anyone to work in the extreme heat for stage 1 or to undertake the long tedious wrapping process of stage 5. These jobs may even be in breach of employment protection legislation (see later). Asking home-based workers to work on the bars could save money, but it would be very difficult to ensure that proper hygienic procedures are followed, as required by law. Finally the whole process is seriously flawed – why produce enough chocolate for 2000 bars in stage 1, which only takes twenty minutes, if it is going to take five people five hours to mould it? The whole process immediately grinds to a halt at this and later stages. Better planning and use of workers would ensure that the whole production runs smoothly with no serious hold-ups.

From consideration of these problems it is possible to draw up some guidelines within which the production function should operate. Using the designs from the design department the role of the production function is to:

- Decide the raw materials, including quantities, to be used
- Plan the process of production including the labour needed
- Calculate the time needed for each stage in production
- Work within legal requirements
- Work within financial constraints

Some stages in the production process may be labour-intensive, because the operations are complex and require skilled workers to assemble or finish. Other stages may be machine-intensive, where the operations are simple and repetitive and readily automated. It is important to find a proper balance to avoid a bottleneck in production – there is no point in producing many items quickly by machine if there is a hold-up when it comes to assembly or finishing. Also, the production process must also take into account any legal requirements for the safety of the

People in Business Organisations

workers and the protection of the customers.

The production process must be organised to ensure that the finished product meets all the required standards. If poor quality goods are made and sold to the customer the organisation will suffer a loss of credibility and customers will be less likely to buy from the same organisation again. No production method is guaranteed 100%, and regular checks should be made of the quality of the finished goods. This is known as *quality control*. It is common for items to be taken at random from the production process at various stages and times of the day and tested. Where problems are discovered the process must be changed to prevent similar faults recurring. A method to improve quality is to make each person on the production line responsible for the quality of the goods they pass on to the next person.

Many businesses use a system known as *just-in-time* purchasing. This means that the materials needed for production are purchased only when they are needed. This avoids the costs involved of holding quantities of stock. This can only work if the organisation can arrange for the supplies to arrive almost immediately so that production is not halted. For this privilege suppliers will usually charge more for their goods. Only larger organisations are able to take advantage of the just-in-time system, since suppliers are unwilling to provide such a service to small customers.

There are three main kinds of production processes that may be used, depending on the type and number of items being produced. These are:
- Job production
- Batch production
- Flow production

Job production is suitable where the articles made are unique one-off jobs, tailor-made to suit the individual customer. Job production is usually found in smaller organisations. It is possible that one person will complete the job from start to finish, especially in the case of hand-crafted objects such as vases, sculptures and jewellery. Even if one person takes charge of the whole process, there are likely to be several stages – preparing material, cutting, shaping, polishing, finishing and so on. More often a different person will take charge for each process and the job will move around the factory. The workers will need to be skilled.

Batch production is used by businesses that make a range of different products that are fairly complex (they have several stages of production) and for which demand is variable. Rather than pass one item around the factory for each process, a batch of several identical items are made at once, taking advantage of economies of scale. For example, once a piece of machinery has been set up to cut one piece it is almost as quick to cut ten. Also, if the worker has to wait for paint or glue to dry before proceeding, they can be working on the rest of the batch. A fairly high level of skill is still necessary. Typically, books and clothes use this kind of production method.

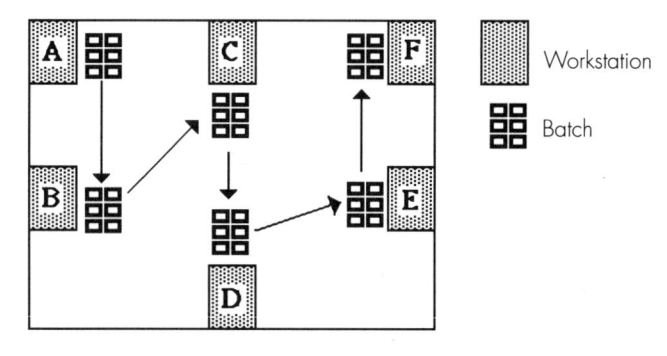

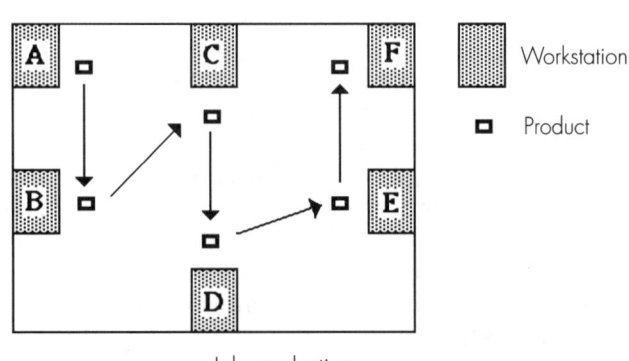

Flow production is suited to mass production, where many similar units are produced in high quantities. It is commonly used by large industrial organisations in the production of motor cars, electrical units, chemicals and oil. The products flow through the factory on a continuous basis while workers perform standard, repetitive tasks on them. Care is taken in designing the balance of labour and the design of the physical environment to ensure that there are no bottlenecks. Workers are less skilled since they undertake a very narrow task through a highly developed division of labour.

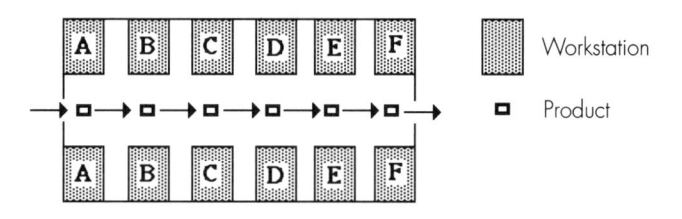

Batch production

Job production

Flow production

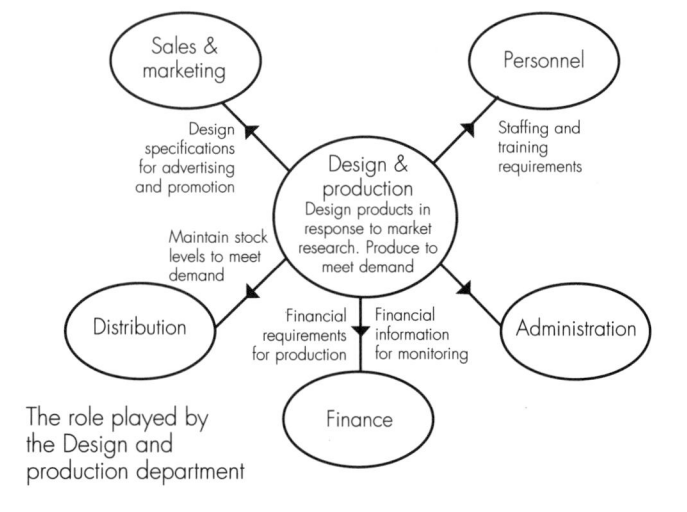

The role played by the Design and production department

People in Business Organisations

ACTIVITY

For each of the following businesses, state what production method or methods would be the most appropriate (job, batch or flow):
- TV sets
- Yachts
- Skis
- Pencils
- Newspapers
- Top designer clothes
- Shoes
- Customised cars

(2.1.4)

ACTIVITY

Having identified the problems with Antonio's production methods and produced some general guidelines, suggest a more appropriate production method that may be used. State whether you would use job, batch or flow production. Draw a diagram illustrating the different stages in the production of your chocolate bars. What advantages would just-in-time purchasing offer?

(2.1.3)

Personnel

TRUFFLES: EPISODE 4

Having finally settled on suitable production methods the business now needs to employ people to work in the factory. Robert decides that he would like to take responsibility for this.

First of all he places an advertisement in a national newspaper, at great expense. The advert reads:

> Chocolate factory seeks hard-working women for production. It's a good job with good pay near a large town. It's a great place to work with an international reputation for the finest chocolate in the world.

Robert is disappointed that no one replies, until he realises that he has forgotten to put the phone number in the advert. He places another advert in the same paper, which reads:

> Due to an error we forgot to give our phone number last week. Anyone wanting to apply for the chocolate factory jobs should telephone 01298 264185 – but be quick as replies are already flooding in.

Robert waits by the phone. When people ring about the job he asks them to send a letter to him enclosing a photo. When the letters come he makes a decision from the photos about which people he would like to interview.

When the applicants come for interview Robert is very disorganised. He has letters of application in untidy heaps in his office and he has to rummage through them to find the right one. As he is interviewing the telephone often rings and he has to interrupt the conversation. He discovers that he does not really know what to ask people and so he just makes polite conversation, deciding on appearances which people to employ. When they ask him questions about the rates of pay, the amount of holidays and the conditions of employment Robert has to make things up on the spot, which he cannot remember later on.

During the first few weeks several employees leave without warning. One says, 'This job is so boring. I am doing the same task for hours on end. And it is so hot and steamy in there that I am beginning to feel ill'. Another says, 'Why is it that other people doing the same job are getting paid more than me? It's not fair. Also some of them only seem to work half a day and then go home early. Well, why not if you can get away with it?'.

Robert is in a mess. Just when he thinks things can't get any worse he gets a phone call from the local tax office asking to see his employee records. He has not had time to do them yet because he has been too busy.

ACTIVITY

Where did Robert go wrong? Read through the steps that he has taken and record anything that you think is not right and which could be improved. Try to break the job up into a number of key points. From your findings make a list of recommendations to be followed by Robert in the future.

(2.1.3)

Where did Robert go wrong?
- When placing the advert he did not take care to choose an appropriate medium – a national newspaper is very expensive and does not necessarily target the right people.
- The advert contains fundamental flaws:
  - it is sexist ('hard-working women')
  - it is vague ('good job, good pay, great place')
  - it does not tell people how to apply
  - it does not say what skills or experience are needed
  - it makes false claims ('international reputation')
  - it does not even mention the name of the organisation
- Asking applicants to send photos and using that as a basis for interview is illegal and unlikely to get the best candidates.
- The interview was badly organised:

85

People in Business Organisations

- papers all over the place
- telephone kept ringing
- no questions planned
- no job details agreed in advance
- basis of selection (appearance) is unacceptable
- There are no records of employment.
- People are expected to do boring repetitive jobs.
- Employees feel discriminated against if others are getting better pay for the same job.

These aspects of employment are normally organised by the *personnel function*. The word 'personnel' is just another way of saying 'people', and more specifically the people employed by the organisation. The personnel function is also referred to as 'human resource management', which accurately sums up the central concern of personnel: how to make the best use of the resource of people within the organisation. The organisation regards its employees as a resource, in a similar way to money, machinery and the buildings. This means that in the interests of efficiency it is vital for employees to have the right skills and the right attitude, to be deployed in the right place and in the right way. Of course, from the employees' point of view, it is also very important that they get paid the right amount and at the right time as well, and it is one of the duties of the personnel function to see that this happens too.

The key functions of the department, therefore, are:
- Staff recruitment
- Employees' contracts
- Staff appraisal
- Staff training and development
- Personnel records (rates of pay, tax, national insurance etc.)
- Employee representation and consultation
- Staff grievances and disciplinary procedures
- Redundancies

Staff recruitment

All organisations will need to recruit staff from time to time. Vacancies arise not just when a business is new, but also as existing employees leave (for a new job, retirement or death) or are promoted within the organisation. Also, new positions can be created due to expansion or reorganisation.

The personnel department must be notified of any vacancies as they arise so that steps can be taken to recruit appropriate people. This normally follows several stages:
- Advertising
- Short-listing
- Interviewing
- Selection and appointment

In all aspects of the recruitment process care must be taken to comply with equal opportunities legislation. With a few exceptions it is not lawful to specify which sex or race the successful candidate will be in the job advertisement. Nor should people with disabilities be discriminated against. The process of selection must take into account only relevant details to determine whether someone is suited for a particular position.

Advertising   Advertising new positions should take a lot of thought. Many things have to be considered:
- *Likely sources of recruits*: schools, colleges, job centre, local community, nationwide etc. This will help in the decision of how and where to advertise and target the right people. Some candidates may be *internal candidates*, which means that they already work in the organisation.
- *Job description*: this is a detailed description of the roles and responsibilities to be undertaken as part of the job, including rates of pay, holiday entitlement and so on. The main duties should be included as part of the advertisement.
- *Person specification*: this is a description of the skills and qualities needed to undertake the job successfully, including qualifications, relevant experience, personal skills and so on. These details should also be included in the advertisement.
- *Where and how to advertise*: this depends on the likely source of recruits. Many trades have their own specialist publications and most newspapers have days for focusing on particular areas of employment. Alternatively, a postcard in a shop window might be enough. The job needs to advertised within the organisation to allow internal candidates to make an application.
- *Methods of application* – the would-be candidates need to know how to make an application, who they need to write to or telephone, what they need to send, when the deadline is etc.

Short-listing   Once candidates have made their applications it is not normally possible to interview every one. However, most businesses prefer to carry out a personal interview before appointing a new member of staff. Therefore it is necessary to draw up a short-list of candidates to interview on the basis of the *letters of application*, their *curriculum vitaes* and their *application forms*:
- A *letter of application* is a personal account of the candidate's reasons for applying for the job, outlining relevant experience and expertise.
- A *curriculum vitae* (or CV) is a written summary of a candidate's personal details, qualifications and work experience.
- Alternatively an organisation may require the candidate to complete an *application form*, which is a pre-printed form inviting the candidate to provide relevant details.

Those applications which reveal a lack of the desired qualifications and experience will be discarded. A number of the more promising candidates will be invited for interview.

Interviewing   The object of the interview is to get a more detailed picture of the candidate and to ask particular questions to determine their suitability for the job. An interview room should be set aside which is free from disruptions so that interviews can proceed smoothly. The candidates should be put at ease. The interviewer or interview panel should have an agreed strategy about what they are going to ask

People in Business Organisations

and what they are looking for. This format should be used for all candidates equally to ensure equal opportunities.

Selection and appointment A decision is then made based upon details relevant to the job, taking into account the original application and matters arising from the interview. All candidates should be notified of whether they have been successful or unsuccessful. This may take place immediately after the interview or after a short period. The successful candidate should receive formal notification of their appointment.

The organisation is not obliged to appoint any candidate if it feels that none is suitable for the position. This does happen occasionally, in which case the job is re-advertised and the process begins again.

ACTIVITY

You are employed by World Vacations Ltd, a large travel agent. As a member of the personnel department you are asked to help with recruitment for a new branch. The table below shows the positions that are available.

For each vacancy you are required to write a suitable advertisement. You should include as much of the job specification as you can along with a person specification based upon the qualities you consider essential for the job. For each vacancy state where you would use the advert (local radio, local or national paper, trade magazine, postcard in a shop window etc.).

You should also suggest the most appropriate selection techniques for each job – CVs, application forms, letters of application, interviews, questions to be asked at interviews etc.
(2.1.3)

ROLE PLAY

As a role play exercise with your colleagues, take it in turns to play the personnel manager at interview for each of these positions, while someone else plays the applicant. Remember to plan your questions in advance and keep the atmosphere friendly and business-like and above all fair.
(2.1.3)

Discussion point

Are there any kinds of people (young, old, male, female, able-bodied, disabled, white, coloured etc.) that you consider to be more suitable for particular positions than others? You may like to consider the following jobs:
- Soldier
- Fire officer
- Cleaner
- Bank clerk
- Waiter in a Chinese or Indian restaurant
- Nurse
- Doctor
- Nanny
- Gardener
- Lollipop person
- Hairdresser
- Police officer

Join in a group debate and make notes to write up for your portfolio.
(2.1.3)

Position	Duties	Hours	Pay	Perks
2 cleaners	Clean office	10 hours a week	£5 per hour	
1 clerical assistant	Basic office duties	35 hours a week	£6,500 per year	
5 experienced travel agents	Operate computers Provide customer information Sell holidays	35 hours a week plus some weekends	£13,000 per year	Cheap holidays 5 weeks' holiday
1 qualified accountant	Manage accounts of whole site	37.5 hours a week	£35,000 per year	Company car 6 weeks' holiday
1 senior director	Join senior management team to run company	30 hours a week Expected to work some evenings	£50,000 per year	Company car Private health care 7 weeks' holiday

People in Business Organisations

Employees' contracts
Most businesses give new members of staff a *contract of employment* signed by both the employee and the employer. According to the Employment Protection (Consolidation) Act 1978, any employee working more than eight hours a week must receive a *written statement of employment* within two months of starting work. The statement should include:
- The name and address of the employer and the employee
- The date of the start of employment
- The amount of pay and when it is to be paid (weekly, monthly etc.)
- Hours of work
- Holiday entitlement, including holiday pay
- Job title and job description
- Place of work

Information regarding sickness, injury, pension, disciplinary procedures and period of notice must also be made available.

Staff appraisal Many organisations have introduced a system of staff appraisal. Members of staff are interviewed on a regular basis by their line manager and assessed on their performance. It is also an opportunity to discuss any problems and to determine any training and/or development needs. Performance may be related to pay or bonuses. Care should be taken not to present staff appraisal as a hostile or intimidating ordeal.

Staff training and development It is not always possible to find someone who is perfectly suited to a job, with all the necessary skills and experience. They are likely to need some training. This is made even more likely by the fact that as working conditions change, due to new technology, reorganisation, expansion and so on, staff will need training to be able to meet the new challenges. Employers may also provide staff *development* to enable them to broaden their existing abilities and experiences and to help them achieve their potential for the organisation.

Personnel records (rates of pay, tax, national insurance etc.) The personnel department will keep records of all the employees on the payroll. This includes personal information (name, date of birth, address) as well as details of rates of pay, tax, national insurance and the like. These records are confidential and should not be accessible to unauthorised personnel. Under the Employment Protection (Consolidation) Act 1978, employees working more than eight hours a week are entitled to an itemised pay statement (or pay slip) showing:
- Gross amount of pay
- Amount of deductions
- Net amount of pay

Employee representation and consultation One of the roles of the personnel function is to negotiate with trade unions and their representatives regarding any issue relating to terms and conditions of work.

Staff grievances and disciplinary procedures It is important that an organisation has a clearly defined system allowing staff to voice their complaints and grievances. It should be conducted in a fair manner that does not intimidate employees nor make them feel in danger of losing their jobs just for voicing a complaint. Likewise, any disciplinary action should be carried out in accordance with agreed guidelines and administered fairly to all employees. There is plenty of legislation protecting people at work (see Section 2.2).

Redundancies Redundancy is the same as 'getting the sack'. It is normally an enforced exit from an organisation. It is often a means of saving money by an organisation threatened by falling sales and rising costs. The amount of redundancy pay an employee is entitled to is specified by employment legislation. The personnel department needs to handle redundancies sensitively.

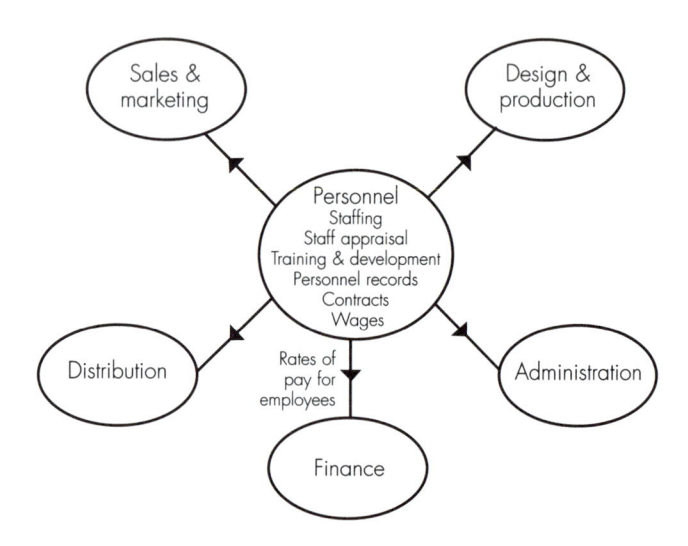

The role played by the Personnel department

ACTIVITY

You are to organise suitable procedures for recruiting employees for Truffles to work in production. Your tasks are to help Robert by:
1. Deciding where to place advertisements
2. Writing the job specification and the person specification
3. Writing an advert to be printed
4. Recording an advert to be played on the radio
5. Writing questions to be used at the interview
6. Stating the procedures to be followed once the staff have been to appointed

(2.1.3)

Finance

TRUFFLES: EPISODE 5

Rashda takes charge of finance. Production is running smoothly and Robert has sorted out his personnel problems. When it comes to pay-day there is a bit of a problem – Rashda is completely unprepared and it takes several trips to the bank to withdraw the right amount to pay everyone.

At the next big meeting of directors (as the group of ten friends now like to call themselves), Rashda is asked how well they are doing. 'All right, I guess', she says. She doesn't really know.

Back in her office her telephone is ringing. It is one of the suppliers wanting to know when they are going to be paid. The account is four weeks overdue, and they threaten to take legal action if the money is not sent straightaway, Rashda searches through a box full of invoices to sort it out.

Mark and Ali pop into her office. They want to know how much a bar of chocolate costs for them to make. Rashda stares in disbelief: 'Don't *you* know?', she asks. 'You work in production.' Mark then asks if they can buy a new piece of machinery that will improve productivity. 'Or at least I think it will', he says. In confusion Rashda agrees to the new equipment.

Robert comes to her office and asks if the personnel department can buy a new computerised system for employee records. Rashda says, 'You'd better wait. I've just agreed to production having some new equipment'. Robert is angry. 'They get to spend all the money. Personnel is desperately in need of a computer, but we never seem to get anything.'

A letter arrives from their financing company informing Rashda that the quarterly loan repayment and interest is due. They are concerned that the last repayment was not made and they want to see her records. Unfortunately Rashda hasn't yet had time to draw them up yet.

When Rashda phones the bank she is told that they have already gone overdrawn. This takes her completely by surprise. How will she pay all the bills coming in, not to mention next week's wages?

People in Business Organisations

All departments are related to each other, but with finance the links are very obvious. Design and production purchase equipment and materials, personnel organise the wages and salaries and arrange staff development and training, sales and marketing run advertising campaigns, and distribution gets the goods out of the organisation and out to the customers. At virtually every stage money is being spent and collected from customers, and this involves the finance department.

The main roles of the finance function are:
- Forecasting
- Budgeting
- Setting targets
- Monitoring performance
- Calculating costs and fixing prices
- Maintaining accounting records

The finance department should be doing a lot more than simply watching the money go in and out of the bank account.

Forecasting By using accurate estimates of likely future sales and costs a cash forecast can be prepared. This will show the availability of money over future months.

Budgeting Based on how much money the organisation thinks it will have, as shown by the forecast, cash budgets can be prepared. A budget is simply a plan showing the amount the organisation intends to spend on different items over a period of time. Budgets can be prepared for the organisation as a whole as well as for each individual department. This will show each manager the amounts they can spend on materials, equipment, advertising, wages etc.

Setting targets The budgets can be used as targets. Each departmental manager can see the limits on their expenditure and will be expected to keep within them. The targets will be set to encourage managers to improve performance by cutting costs and increasing productivity and sales.

Monitoring performance Once targets have been set it is easy to measure how well each department is doing. Actual costs and incomes can be compared to the planned costs and incomes. Then against each cost and income heading it will be clear whether the department is doing better than or worse than planned. Where there are problems improvements must be found. Where the department is doing well rewards should be offered as encouragement.

Calculating costs and fixing prices The finance department should be responsible for ensuring that there is a proper accounting system in place which provides up-to-date information on the costs incurred in each area. This is easy to see in the case of production. The business will want to know how much raw material, labour, electricity, packaging and

ACTIVITY

What exactly should Rashda be doing which she is not? You should provide details of the service that the finance department ought to be providing for the rest of the organisation. What problems will the business face if these duties are not carried out? *(2.1.3)*

People in Business Organisations

all the rest it takes to make one unit of production. Only when the unit costs are known can a selling price be calculated and the profit to be made on each item worked out.

Controlling expenditure Setting targets will help control expenditure. Another more direct way of doing this is to insist that all purchase orders over a certain limit are authorised by the finance department (see Unit 4). This means that large purchases, particularly of new equipment, must be agreed by the finance director.

Maintaining accounting records Unit 4 describes the financial documents that should be maintained by an organisation. Keeping records enables the finance department to do all the other things described above. The importance of keeping financial records is described in Unit 4, including these points:

- Records enable a business to monitor its performance so that it knows how well it is doing.
- Some records are required by law for tax and other reasons.
- They enable a business to predict its future performance and therefore to plan accordingly.
- They allow a business to keep track of the people they owe money to and the people who owe them money.

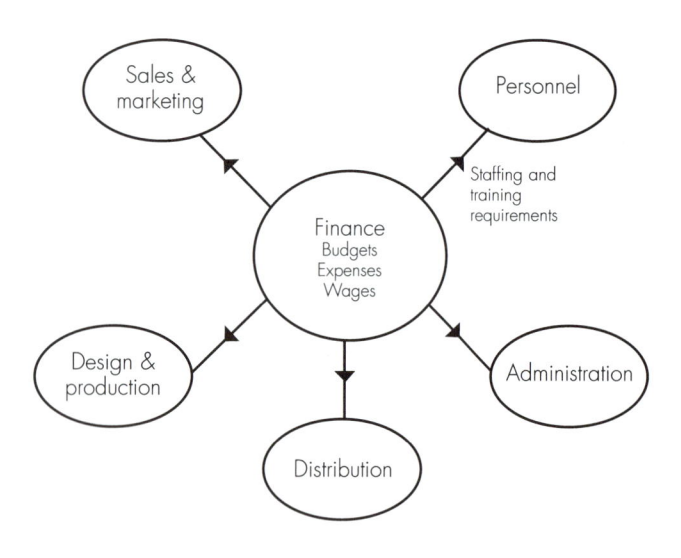

The role played by the Finance department

ACTIVITY

You are employed by an organisation that is experiencing the following problems:
- Managers are not motivated. They seem to have no direction and no plan. They certainly do not work together as a team. Each department does its own thing. There even seems to be rivalry and competition between managers. They all have to have the latest photocopier or computer to prove that their department is the most important. All this is costing the business a lot of money.
- Sales have fallen, despite a lot of money spent on advertising. The reason would seem to be that the selling prices are higher than their competitors'. But no one wants to lower the prices. They worry that they will not be able to make a profit. There is no evidence to support this.
- As a result costs are rising and productivity barely changes. Sometimes the business only just manages to pay its bills, especially when the large ones come in, like VAT and salaries.
- Customers know that they can delay payment for a long time because no one ever chases them up. The truth is that the business does not really know who owes them money, or when the money is due.

Your task is to review the business and make recommendations as to how the business can be improved. Consider each problem carefully, thinking hard about what is wrong. Decide how changes in the organisation could make it better. Present your findings in an informal report.
(2.1.3)

Administration

TRUFFLES: EPISODE 6

The organisation is growing. Confidence is increasing and new staff are being taken on in all departments. Mark and Ali are working on new designs and Antonio has production running efficiently. Robert has sorted out personnel and is involved in recruiting new staff. Rashda has a careful control on finance and each department has its own budget.

Jacob takes charge of administration. It sounds good, but he is not really sure what it means. So he has a look around the organisation to see what might be needed.

The first thing he notices is that departmental managers are doing a lot of complaining. He wonders why the managers never communicate with each other.

Robert, the personnel manager, says that he wastes a lot of time with little things when he would rather be 'getting on with it'. When asked to explain he says, 'It takes me three hours every day typing out letters to applicants. Then I have to go and buy stamps. Then I can post the letters. After that I start pulling my hair out because I can never find any documents that I want. Only then can I get some work done, that is if I haven't got to answer the phone or meet people at reception'.

The finance department has a particular worry. Rashda says, 'Every department needs to do photocopying and so everyone has hired a copier. Likewise they all need word processors and printers and so they've all bought them. Of course it comes out of their own budgets, but it does seem

People in Business Organisations

like a waste'.

The production department has its own worries. Antonio says, 'I am always chasing around after information. I make a batch of chocolate. I want to know how much the ingredients cost, and so I'm looking for invoices. I want to know how much the labour costs were, so I'm chasing after pay records. How much electricity? How much wastage? By the time I've got all the information it's either out of date or I've forgotten what I wanted to do'.

As Jacob walks around the building he notices how dirty it is and wonders whose job it is to make sure it is cleaned.

ACTIVITY

Assume that the problems that Jacob has discovered are his responsibility as administration manager. What systems could he introduce that would vastly improve the situation?
(2.1.3)

There are a number of key problems with the organisation, even though things are beginning to go well. These problems fall within the responsibility of the administration department:

- The managers fail to communicate with each other. This is probably because there is no organised internal communication system. The administration function should provide effective links between all parts of the business.
- There are no secretarial support or reception services. Managers are typing, answering the phone, posting letters and meeting guests when administration should provide a service to do all this, allowing the managers to get on with managing.
- There is no organised filing, which means records go missing and time is wasted – administration should provide a comprehensive filing system.
- Administration should also provide a photocopying and duplication service. It makes sense to *centralise* these services so that each department is not needlessly incurring costs that could be shared.
- The whole information system could be combined so that detailed information about all aspects of the business could be readily available.
- Cleaners should be employed to clean and tidy the premises and it is the responsibility of administration to make sure this happens.

Administration plays a vital role in any organisation in keeping it running and keeping it organised. It is not always represented at the director level, although in the case of a limited company the company secretary may oversee administration. It cannot really be seen as a separate department, although sections of it may be grouped together.

Administration offers service and support to all other departments. The services that it offers include:
- Secretarial support
- Reception service
- Photocopying
- Internal and external mail
- Management information system

Some organisations may have a highly centralised administration that takes responsibility for all these duties for all departments. Other organisations may be less centralised, so that individual departments may have their own secretaries, photocopying facilities and so on.

Management information systems (MIS) link together aspects of information from the whole organisation by computer. This can be a very powerful tool for managers. It provides up-to-the-minute information about staffing, material costs, levels of production, absenteeism etc. Decisions can then be taken in response to accurate and current information providing more effective control of operations.

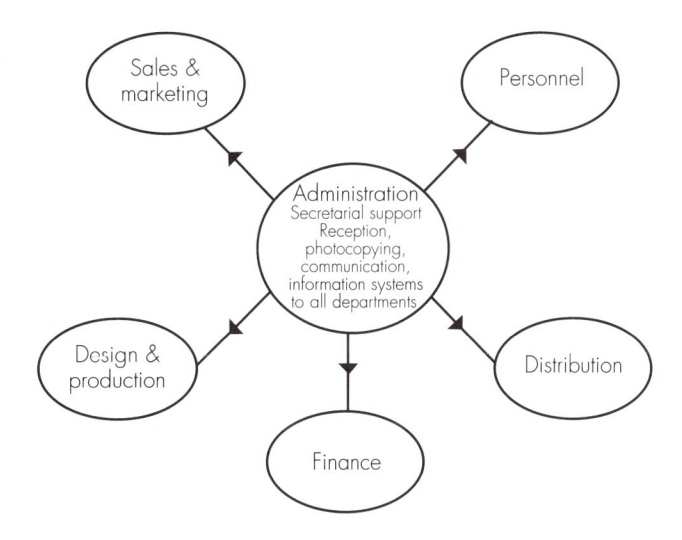

The role played by the Administration department

ACTIVITY

The administration function needs to ensure that all members of staff are kept up to date with events in the organisation. One of the most effective ways of communicating with the whole staff is by an in-house magazine. This could contain information on:
- The organisation's recent activities
- Plans for the future
- Changes in rules and regulations
- New employees
- Employees leaving and retiring
- Articles of general interest
- Forthcoming social events
- Cartoons, competitions
- Individual members of staff's personal achievements

The format should be informative but user-friendly.

People in Business Organisations

In small groups of 3 or 4, design an in-house magazine for your own organisation (school, college or place of work). For information to include in it you may like to run surveys, send out questionnaires, invite people to contribute ideas, interview members of the management, look at recent newspaper articles, take photographs, design crosswords, and virtually anything else to keep it interesting and informative.
(2.1.3)

Sales and marketing

TRUFFLES: EPISODE 7
Everything is ready. A meeting of all the directors is called. Orphée and David, the sales and marketing directors, have to start work. Orphée addresses the meeting:

'We have made a few sales to local shops, but that is just the beginning. We have perfected our production techniques, thanks to Antonio, and we have five new chocolate bars to sell. We know that people are interested. We know there is a market. It is important that we capture the imagination of people, make them believe that our product is better than anyone else's. We want every supermarket to stock our bars. We want the public to know we are here. And this is how we are going to do it....'.

ACTIVITY

How would you do it if you were Orphée and David, responsible for marketing and sales for Truffles? Make detailed suggestions which would meet the objectives of letting the public know, making them believe that Truffles are the best and generally selling as many bars of chocolate as possible.
How do they know that there is a market?
(2.1.3)

Some of the techniques that Truffles may use include:
- A public launch of the company, inviting important people from business, politics and the media to a ceremony, formal speeches and a meal.
- A high-profile advertising campaign using posters, leaflets, TV and radio advertisements, and articles in newspapers.
- A mail-shot to all the supermarket buyers with information about the new bars.
- A team of sales representatives to go to supermarkets and the public with samples.
- A promotion of the products, offering free samples in public places such as railway stations, or vouchers in magazines for free samples.
- Competitions.
- A special introductory low price to encourage people to try the products.

The sales and marketing function is committed to finding customers for the goods or services offered by the organisation. It is no good the organisation being highly efficient at producing goods or providing their service if there is no one to buy it.

Selling is the actual business of exchanging goods and services with customers for money. Many organisations employ sales representatives (or reps) to carry out the hard task of encouraging people to part with their cash by demonstrating the product and being available to answer questions and provide information. A lot of this may be done over the telephone to individual customers. Sales reps will also provide the link with corporate customers, that is, other organisations wishing to buy the product or service. The world of selling is highly competitive. Many sales reps work for commission – the more they sell the more they get paid.

Marketing is a much larger undertaking, which incorporates selling. It is the whole process of matching supply with demand. It is not just a question of making something and then trying to find someone to buy. Many products and services are designed in response to customer needs. This means providing what the customer wants. This can only be achieved if the organisation knows what the customer wants, and this requires market research. Then the right goods and services can be offered knowing that there is a market. To back this up the organisation must tell people that their goods and services are available. This will involve advertising. Finally, having recognised a need, responded to it and told everybody what the organisation has to offer, the sales reps need to encourage people to buy. This can be summarised as:

- Find out what the customer wants *(market research)*.
- Provide what the customer wants *(targeting)*.

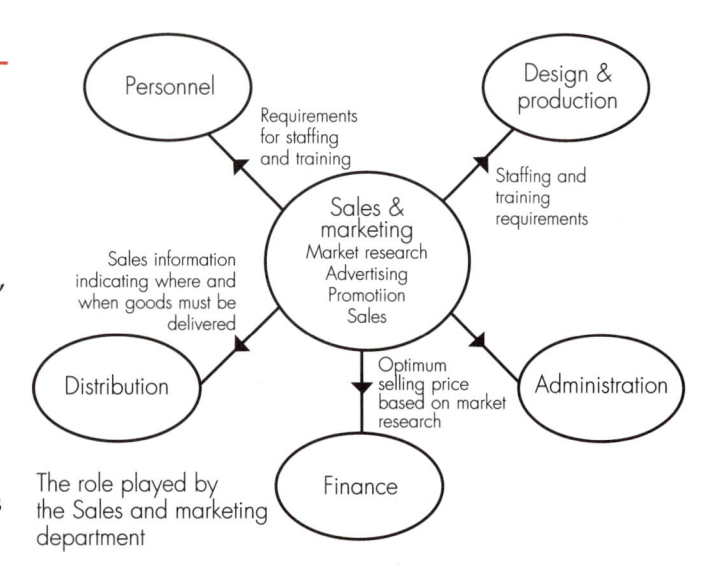

The role played by the Sales and marketing department

People in Business Organisations

- Tell the customer that you've got what they want *(advertising)*.
- Encourage the customer to buy it *(selling)*.

All of this requires careful planning.

ACTIVITY

Design publicity material for Truffles. The names of their five new products are:
- 'Flute': a sweet that can be played like a whistle
- 'Mud': a soft chocolate and caramel bar
- 'Bim Bams': very thin plain chocolate suitable for strict vegetarians
- 'Baggles': large, chewy sweets full of nuts and biscuit
- 'Seepee': bags of large, round mints with letters of the alphabet on

You should think of suitable advertising slogans which stress the unique selling points of each product. You may like to design posters or leaflets.
(2.1.3)

Distribution

TRUFFLES: EPISODE 8

Mike and Joanne are taking charge of distribution. Customers have been found. Truffles want to satisfy their customers in every way and so have run a survey asking them what they would expect from the distribution department – that is, what is important to them in terms of delivery, packing, quantities received, supporting documentation, and so on.

From the research undertaken, Mike and Joanne have drawn up a *statement of intent*, which is a detailed promise of the service that Truffles guarantees to provide to all its customers. This serves two purposes: first, it sets targets that Truffles has to live up to in terms of the quality of the distribution system, and second it gives customers a clear picture of the service it should be receiving, which they are free to use for complaints if the service is not good enough.

ACTIVITY

You are to draft a statement of intent for Truffles. It should clearly describe the service that every customer can expect, giving precise measures. It should also show exactly what Truffles will provide in compensation to its customers if the targets are not met.

It may help to think of similar statements like British Rail's Passenger's Charter. In that document British Rail, made precise promises to its customers. They promised that x% of its trains would be on time within so many minutes. If the trains were not on time then there were precise statements regarding how much refund the passengers could claim. There was also a description of the quality of the stations, the cleanliness of trains, the standard of other services (food, drink, assistance etc.) and so on.
(2.1.3)

The products have been designed, produced and effectively marketed. The sales reps have done their jobs and the customers have been found. To satisfy the customers they must receive their goods at the right time, in the right place and in good condition. This is the function of distribution. If the customers are retailers then they have to satisfy their customers, and problems with deliveries will mean lost sales for them. If the customers are the final consumer they are seeking satisfaction. Late deliveries, damaged goods, wrong goods and goods taken to the wrong premises all make it less likely that the customer will buy from the same organisation again.

Large organisations may have their own lorries for distribution. Supermarkets, for example, are able to take advantage of technology linked to the sales tills. All sales are recorded by computer. When stocks of an item fall to a certain level the goods are automatically re-ordered from centralised warehouses. Once the size of the order is sufficiently large the order will be made up, loaded on to a lorry and delivered. In this way the supermarket should never run out of stock. At any large supermarket deliveries are being made throughout the day, as shown by an endless stream of lorries.

Smaller organisations may use other haulage companies to transport their goods. There are many national and international firms, such as Eddie Stobart Ltd.

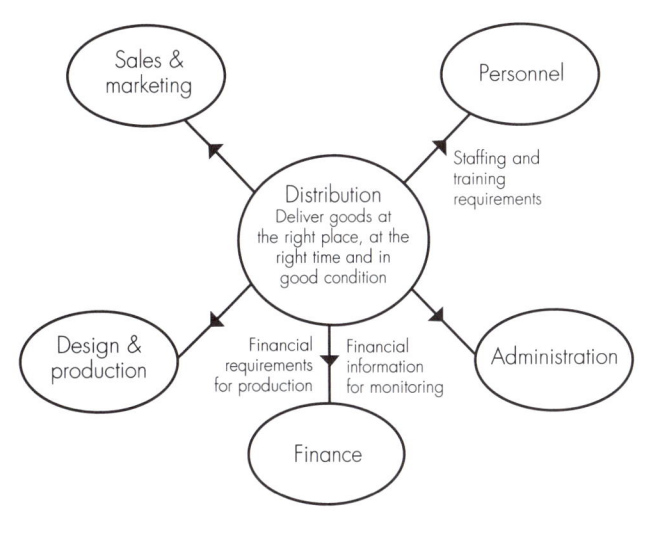

The role played by the Distribution department

93

People in Business Organisations

Summary of main responsibilities of departments

Department	Responsibilities
Design & production	Design and test new products Improve existing products Produce samples Produce goods to meet consumer demand Ensure production minimises wastage and maximises efficiency Quality control Order raw materials for production Stock control
Personnel	Ensure that human resources are sufficient for needs of the organisation Deploy human resources effectively Provide staff training and development Provide counselling and support Maintain personnel records Negotiate with trade unions Conduct staff appraisal Write job and personnel specifications Recruit new staff
Finance	Plan and control expenditure and income Maintain accounting records Monitor performance Set budgets Produce annual accounts Authorise purchase orders Pay wages and salaries
Administration	Provide administrative support for all departments including: • typing • postage • reprographics • word processing • desktop publishing • printing Centralised purchasing Internal communications
Sales & marketing	Prepare sales plan Monitor sales Undertake market research Produce marketing and publicity material Carry out marketing campaigns
Distribution	Deliver goods to customers on time Ensure products arrive undamaged Maintain fleet of lorries Design appropriate delivery routes Packing of goods Maintain appropriate records including delivery notes

Different structures and departments within business organisations

EAST ORCHARD COLLEGE
East Orchard College is a college of further education with an organisational structure as shown in the diagram opposite.

The college is controlled by a board of governors, but within the organisation the principal has the highest authority. The levels of the college can be compared to a limited company as follows:

Board of Governors	= shareholders
Principal	= managing director
Vice-Principal	= senior director
Assistant Principals	= directors
Programme Leaders	= managers
Senior Lecturers	= supervisors
Lecturers	= staff
Students	= customers

Each assistant principal has responsibility for a particular function: personnel, marketing, finance, estates (i.e. equipment and premises) and curriculum (i.e. subjects and courses). All assistant principals have support staff (administrative and clerical), who are not shown on the diagram.

The programme leaders are the heads of department. They have a responsibility for a subject area and for all the students and lecturers in their area. They are line-managed by one of the assistant principals, as shown.

The programme leaders have one or two senior lecturers, depending upon the size of their department. Finally, each department has a number of lecturers.

In addition there are two other managers, information systems and administration, who have a cross-college role, servicing all areas.

The Principal decides that the college needs to expand by 15% over the next two years. She knows that two of the college's nearest rivals are planning aggressive expansion in direct competition. She informs the assistant principals of her plan without telling them why and instructs them to move into action straight away.

ACTIVITY

Study the organisation chart for East Orchard College carefully and then answer the following questions:

1. **How would you describe the organisational structure of the college? What kinds of problems could such a structure lead to?**
2. **How would you describe the management style of the Principal? What problems is this likely to cause? How could her approach be improved?**

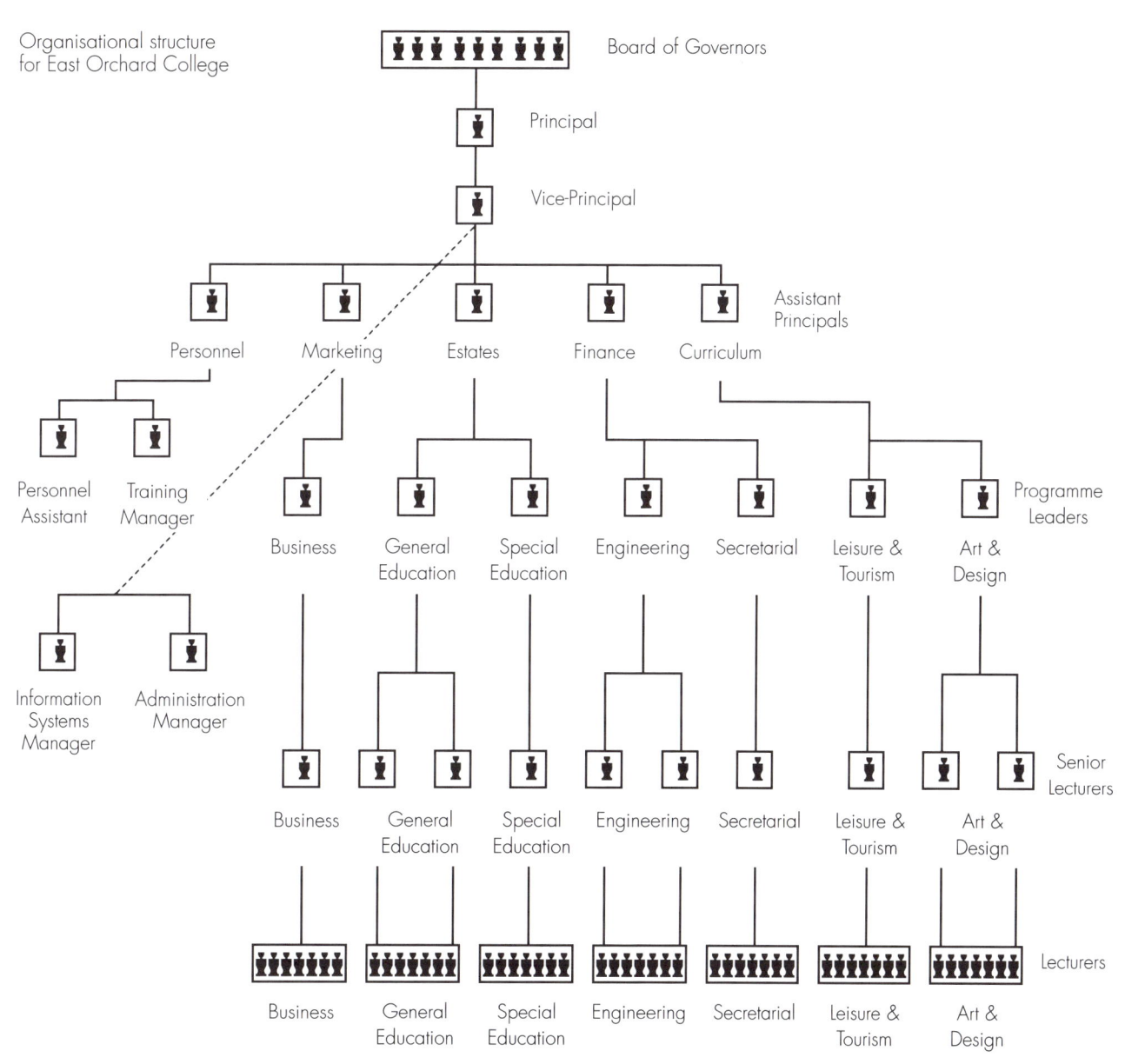

People in Business Organisations

Three different types and size of business

Organisational structure for East Orchard College

- Board of Governors
- Principal
- Vice-Principal
- Assistant Principals: Personnel, Marketing, Estates, Finance, Curriculum
- Personnel: Personnel Assistant, Training Manager
- Information Systems Manager, Administration Manager
- Programme Leaders: Business, General Education, Special Education, Engineering, Secretarial, Leisure & Tourism, Art & Design
- Senior Lecturers: Business, General Education, Special Education, Engineering, Secretarial, Leisure & Tourism, Art & Design
- Lecturers: Business, General Education, Special Education, Engineering, Secretarial, Leisure & Tourism, Art & Design

People in Business Organisations

3. As part of the new expansion it is proposed to offer new programmes in business for mature students. Whose responsibility is it to:
   - Produce advertising material?
   - Develop the new subject areas?
   - Recruit staff to teach the new groups?
   - Find rooms for the new classes?
4. The Principal receives the memos detailed on this page. You should advise the Principal on the best course of action. This will involve deciding which person or persons in the organisation should be notified of the problem and the best course of action to be taken. You might feel that the problem should be referred to someone else. In some cases you may even suggest a change to the organisational structure.

MEMO
to: The Principal
from: Secretarial lecturer
date: 20 June

Help! We are simply snowed under with the amount of work we have to do. Now that the new classes have started we cannot cope. We are all working overtime (voluntarily, I should point out, and at no extra pay). We simply can't do any more. We've tried cramming more students into the rooms but that doesn't help much since there are only so many machines. There is no point having two people on one typewriter.

There is another problem. The new appointment, John, quite frankly is not up to it. He doesn't seem to know what he is doing. The computers seem completely foreign to him. He is okay on the basics but he is having real problems with spreadsheets and word processing. I am worried that he feels under a lot of stress.

MEMO
to: The Principal
from: Personnel Assistant
date: 27 June

It may seem strange to complain that I have not got enough to do — but that is exactly my problem.

The Assistant Principal (Personnel) wants to do it all himself. We have had a lot of interviews this week and he did them all, although I know that he had to cancel a lot of meetings to be able to do it.

I took it on myself to send letters to all staff members to tell them about the changes in the pay system. The Assisant Principal (Personnel) was furious when he found out. "You should have asked me first!" There was nothing wrong with the letters: it was just that he wanted to do it.

Can't you do something?

MEMO
to: The Principal
from: Programme Leader (Business)
date: 17 July

I feel I must write to you about the lack of sectarial support that I am currently getting - or not getting. If I want a letter or memo typed or a fax sent or anything photocopied I have to do it myself. Occasionally I can "borrow" the secretary from Art & Design, but this is not satisfactory.

I have spoken to my line manager on several occasions about this but he is not interested and in desperation I am writing to you.

(2.1.1) (2.1.3)

Changes in working arrangements

Organisations are always changing. In this way they are like living organisms. This can be a helpful picture of an organisation. Like something which is alive, a business organisation may change its shape, grow larger or smaller, replace parts of its 'body' or lose parts altogether. It will need things to sustain it, to make it healthy. It will need to change when its environment changes. It may have predators and it may have prey of its own. It will fight for its survival, but may not always succeed.

People in Business Organisations

Looking at an organisation's working arrangements there are several good reasons why these may change. In the face of increased *competition*, for example, a company may need to find ways of being flexible enough to meet customers' needs. The greater the flexibility the better their chances of providing a good service. An organisation may be flexible in the way it makes its decisions and in the working arrangements for its employees. Different patterns of working may improve the *productivity* of the organisation. Likewise it may also benefit the *quality* of the product or service being provided. If staff are more involved in the decision-making process or have greater flexibility in planning their work, they are likely to be more highly motivated and loyal to the organisation. This could lead to improved productivity and higher quality work. Finally, an organisation always needs to be able to use new *technology* as it becomes available, if this will make it more productive or provide a competitive edge.

ACTIVITY

Pesto are a major manufacturer of motor vehicles in Italy. They grew from a small family firm into one of the largest producers of family cars in the country.

They have a very traditional management structure. Members of the original Pesto family make up the board of directors based at the company headquarters in Turin. There they make all the main decisions for the company, which has showrooms and car plants throughout Italy. At all of these places the day starts at 08.30 sharp and ends at 17.00. Everyone stops at 12.30 for an hour's lunch. Even the sales reps are required to check into their office at the start of each day and again in the evening. The directors say that this is the only way to ensure that they do an honest day's work. This is how it has always been done.

The business is facing a few problems.
1 The showroom managers feel frustrated that they cannot make decisions for themselves. They like to be able to reflect a bit of local character and respond to local needs. Market research shows that this is what the customers want.
2 Some of the office staff complain that the working hours do not suit them. As a result they do not feel loyal to the company and the quality of their work is affected. It is especially bad late in the afternoons and on a Friday.
3 Pesto is facing ever-increasing competition. Italian, German and Japanese car manufacturers are producing vehicles which directly compete with their range. The competitors, however, are cheaper and probably just as good. Pesto need to make more cars, more quickly and more cheaply.
4 The sales reps are unable to reach as big a geographical range of customers as they would like, since they are tied down to their local offices.
5 The directors see themselves as very fair employers. The factory workers very often come to Pesto straight from school and are given a permanent contract. It is a job for life. Unfortunately they often find that they are stuck with unreliable workers that they cannot easily ask to leave.
6 The firm uses traditional production techniques, which are highly labour-intensive. The directors have inherited these methods from the founders of the organisation. It is a good way to make a quality vehicle, but it is very expensive.

Task
Your task as an adviser to the company is to make recommendations to the directors. How should they change their working arrangements to meet the demands of the changing environment? Make your arrangements as detailed as possible, giving a clear justification for each proposal. Present your recommendations to the directors in the form of a formal report.
(2.1.5)

ACTIVITY

Select four different organisations for research. Alternatively you may like to work in a group and each member select one organisation. The more variety in the choice the better. Your four organisations must include at least:
- One local organisation
- One national organisation
- One small organisation
- One large organisation
- One public sector organisation
- One private sector organisation

You could for example choose a small local business from the private sector and a large national organisation in the public sector, plus two others. For each organisation you must:
1 Draw an organisational chart – where possible use the names of the people in the organisation as well as their positions. *(2.1.3)*
2 State whether the organisation is flat, hierarchical, circular or matrix. *(2.1.1)*
3 Describe the (likely) process of decision-making and state whether the style of leadership (as far as you can tell) is likely to be autocratic or participative. *(2.1.2)*
4 Describe the key roles played by each department within the organisation and describe how the work of the departments is related. *(2.1.3, 2.1.4)*
5 Describe any problems that the organisation may experience as a result of its structure. *(2.1.2)*
6 Suggest changes and improvements to the structure to overcome these problems. *(2.1.5)*

People in Business Organisations

MULTIPLE CHOICE

1. A hierarchical organisation structure is one which:
   A. Shows only line relationships
   B. Gives staff a wide span of control
   C. Has few middle managers
   D. Has many layers of authority

2. A wide span of control arises when:
   A. The organisation structure is hierarchical
   B. Decision-making is carried out at the lowest level of authority
   C. A large number of employees have the same line manager
   D. Each employee has many duties to carry out

3. Which of the following is a *true* statement about flat organisation structures?
   A. Members of staff have a narrow span of control
   B. Bureaucracy is likely to be lengthy and time-consuming
   C. All members of staff are likely to be involved in the process of decision-making
   D. There are many layers of middle managers

4. The relationship between the personnel director and the marketing assistant may be categorised as:
   A. Line
   B. Staff
   C. Strategic
   D. Supervisory

5. Placing adverts in local newspapers to recruit new members of the production department is one of the functions of:
   A. Administration
   B. Personnel
   C. Production
   D. Sales and marketing

6. Which of the following is most likely to be a *true* statement about a large public limited company?
   A. Key functions, such as sales and marketing, are likely to be centralised
   B. There will be no equal opportunities policy
   C. It will have a flat organisation structure
   D. The organisation structure will have line relationships only

7. Which of the following is a *true* statement about a personnel specification?
   A. It explains the roles and responsibilities to be undertaken
   B. It is a description of the terms and conditions of employment
   C. It outlines desirable and essential skills and attributes
   D. It is a list of all employees with their personal details

8. An 'internal candidate' for a vacant job describes someone who:
   A. Is already in a similar kind of organisation
   B. Is a member of the relevant professional body
   C. Works for the organisation that is advertising the job
   D. Is part of the interview panel

9. A flow production method is suitable for the production of:
   A. One-off items, such as sculptures
   B. Many identical items, such as cars
   C. A small batch of similar items like clothes or books
   D. Small complicated items such as watches

10. In a retail organisation which department is responsible for planning staffing levels?
    A. Production
    B. Administration
    C. Distribution
    D. Personnel

SHORT ANSWER

1. What are fringe benefits? Give examples.

2. Recruitment and selection of employees may involve the use of:
   (i) Letters of application
   (ii) CVs
   (iii) Application forms
   Describe each of these, assessing their usefulness.

3. What are the main functions of the administration department?

4. Describe the differences between the following styles of leadership and decision-making:
   (i) Autocratic
   (ii) Participative
   (iii) Democratic

5. Compare flat and hierarchical organisational structures, listing the important advantages and disadvantages of each.

People in Business Organisations

A picket line – see page 103

ELEMENT 2.2
Investigate employee and employer responsibilities and rights

Performance criteria

- (PC) 2.2.1 Explain the benefits of employer and employee cooperation
- (PC) 2.2.2 Describe ways to resolve disagreements
- (PC) 2.2.3 Explain employer rights and responsibilities
- (PC) 2.2.4 Explain employee rights and responsibilities to their employers

ACTIVITY

When employees start work they naturally have certain expectations about:
- Their pay
- The hours they will work
- Their treatment at work
- The written documents they expect to receive
- Things they are allowed to do
- Things they are not allowed to do
- The physical working conditions

Imagine that you are starting a new job (possibly your first job). Write down all the things which you would expect under the headings given above. *(2.2.4)*

Introduction

Employees and employers need each other. Except for sole traders, who only employ themselves, employers and employees have to work with each other. In an ideal world the employer and the employee would do whatever was best for all concerned. Unfortunately, people are liable to take advantage of others. In particular, employers are in a position to exploit their employees. Therefore the employees need protecting, and much work has been done to introduce laws that effectively protect the *rights* of the employee by putting *responsibilities* on the employer.

The employee can reasonably expect:
- To be paid fairly
- To be treated fairly
- To work in safe conditions
- To have reasonable breaks and holidays
- To be able to join a trade union and take industrial action
- To have a contract of employment
- To have the terms of the contract honoured by the employer

It works the other way too – employees have to fulfil certain responsibilities to protect the rights of the employer. Employers can expect that the employee will:
- Arrive on time
- Be honest in their time-keeping
- Notify the employer if sick
- Undertake normal duties
- Dress appropriately
- Be polite and courteous
- Fulfil the terms of their contract

The chief Acts of Parliament which relate to the rights and responsibilities of employees and employers are:

Health and Safety at Work etc. Act 1974
Employment Act 1990
Citizen's Charter 1991
Employment Protection (Consolidation) Act 1978
Wages Act 1986
Trade Union Reform and Employment Rights Act 1993
Trade Union and Labour Relations Act 1992
Sex Discrimination Act 1986
Race Relations Act 1976

According to the Health and Safety at Work etc. Act 1974, an *employee* is 'Someone who works under a contract of employment or contract of apprenticeship. The contract may be express or implied and if express, may be oral or in writing'. An *employer* is defined as 'Someone who has employees. Employers include not only individual people, but also corporate bodies, such as limited companies, nationalised industries, local authorities etc.'.

Industrial tribunals

If the rights of the employee are not honoured then they may take the matter to an industrial tribunal. If, for example, employees feel that they have been unfairly dismissed, or that their pay has been

People in Business Organisations

unfairly adjusted, the case can be heard by an independent body to decide the matter. Compensation may be paid to the injured parties if the tribunal finds in their favour.

Employee rights and responsibilities

Remuneration

Remuneration covers payment of salaries and wages for employed service.

Unless they are voluntary workers, employees earn a gross salary or wage made up as follows:
- Basic salary (normally a fixed monthly sum equal to $\frac{1}{12}$ of the annual salary)

or
- Basic wage (normally based upon the number of hours worked at an hourly rate or the number of items produced on a piece rate)

plus
- Overtime (for hours worked in excess of contracted hours)
- Bonuses (as a reward for meeting targets)
- Holiday pay (according to annual entitlement)
- Statutory Sick Pay (for days missed due to illness)
- Statutory Maternity Pay (for pregnant women on maternity leave)
- 'Golden handshakes' (a lump sum when leaving an organisation)
- 'Golden hellos' (a lump sum when joining an organisation)

Unfortunately the employee will never see all of this. The employer will make deductions from the gross pay on behalf of the employee. These deductions are either:
- Compulsory deductions (income tax (PAYE) and National Insurance)

or
- Voluntary deductions (private pension schemes, union subscriptions, saving schemes, charitable donations etc.)

The amount of basic pay normally depends upon the employee's age, experience, expertise and qualifications. Most jobs have *pay scales*. An employee will start at a certain level and is normally entitled to one increment (or step up) each year. It is possible to move up the pay scale more quickly in recognition of hard work.

In addition to paid wages and salaries some employees may receive *fringe benefits*. These are non-monetary rewards. They include company cars, subsidised travel, subsidised health schemes and paid holidays.

The guidelines given by the law relating to pay are the minimum requirements, and many businesses choose freely to exceed them.

Equal work, equal pay   Regardless of race, sex, or any other differences, everyone doing the same work in an organisation must be paid the same. This is covered by the Equal Pay Act 1970, the Race Relations Act 1976 and the Sex Discrimination Act 1986.

Therefore different rates of pay can only be applied on the basis of differences in jobs undertaken, years of experience and qualifications.

Itemised pay statement   By the Employment Protection (Consolidation) Act 1978, every employee who works more than eight hours a week is entitled to a written pay statement (or payslip). This must show:
- Gross amount of wages or salary
- Amount of deductions
- Net amount of wages or salaries

Members voting at a union meeting

Deductions According to the Wages Act 1986 deductions may only be taken from an employee's wage or salary if:
- They are required by law (National Insurance, PAYE)
- They have been agreed by the worker in the contract of employment or in writing (e.g. private pension fund, union subscriptions)

Maternity The Trade Union Reform and Employment Rights Act 1993 states that, regardless of the length of service, a female employee is entitled to 14 weeks maternity leave. The start of the leave may be any time during the 11 weeks before the expected birth. After this period she is entitled to go back to her job. During the period of maternity leave the employee is entitled to Statutory Maternity Pay (SMP) according to the Social Security Act 1986.

Redundancy payments Redundancy payments are covered by the Employment Protection (Consolidation) Act 1978. Generally, any full-time employee with at least two years' continuous service who is dismissed because of redundancy is entitled to a lump-sum payment. For each year of employment they should receive the following:

from age 41 to 64   1.5 weeks' pay
from age 22 to 40   1 weeks' pay
from age 18 to 21   0.5 weeks' pay

Enforced redundancy must be accompanied by a written notice to that effect.

ACTIVITY

You are employed by the Citizen's Advice Bureau promoting equal opportunities in employment.
Below is a list of enquiries you have received from local employers and employees. Give your response to their question and state your reasons:
1. An employer has recently taken on two new employees at work. They have roughly the same experience and qualifications and are about the same age. One is a married woman and the other is a single man. The employer wishes to pay the woman more on the basis that she is the sole breadwinner in her family and has a husband and two children to support. The employer wishes to know whether this is acceptable.
2. To save money in the personnel department, an employer is considering cutting down paperwork to a minimum. He has therefore telephoned to ask whether it is legal not to give his employees payslips.
3. An employee decided to have a baby and her employer is refusing to pay to cover the cost of her maternity leave. The woman phones to ask what support she is legally entitled to.
4. An employee is currently earning £120 a week. He has been working for the employer for the last 15 years. The employer is considering redundancies and because the employee is 59 years old it seems fair that he should be the first one to go. The employee wishes to know how much redundancy pay he is entitled to.
5. An employer has decided that the employees within the organisation should contribute to a company health scheme and wishes to start making deductions from their pay on their behalf. Is this legal?

(2.2.2) (2.2.3) (2.2.4)

Safe working conditions

An employee is protected at work by the Health and Safety at Work etc. Act 1974. Under its terms an employee is entitled to a safe working environment. This is spelt out in detail under five headings:
- Safe equipment and machinery
- Safe materials and substances
- Information, instruction, training and supervision necessary for health and safety
- Safe premises, including entrances, exits, floors, walls, ceilings
- Safe working environment regarding noise, lighting, ventilation, heating

ACTIVITY

Look out for hazards at home, at school or college and at work – dangerous equipment and machinery, high levels of noise or fumes, electrical fittings, things to trip over or into and things to cut yourself on. Look out for information (how to use equipment, fire exits clearly marked, fire procedure etc.), safety equipment (fire extinguishers, fire blankets, fire alarms etc.) and safety exits. Write a report on your findings, indicating where you think health and safety provisions are adequate and where perhaps improvements could be made.

(2.2.3) (2.2.4)

Contract of employment

According to the Employment Protection (Consolidation) Act 1978 an employee who works more than eight hours per week is entitled to a written statement of employment within two months of starting work. This is not exactly the same as a *contract*, since it does not include all the terms and conditions of employment, nor does it have to be signed. Many organisations do give employees a written contract, which is signed by both parties. However, in law, the written statement of employment is sufficient. It is accepted that, whether there is a written contract or not, a contract in fact exists between the employee and the employer.

The statement should include:
- The name and address of the employer and the employee
- The date of the start of employment

People in Business Organisations

- The amount of pay and when it is to be paid (weekly, monthly etc.)
- Hours of work
- Holiday entitlement, including holiday pay
- Job title and job description
- Place of work

Information regarding sickness, injury, pension, disciplinary procedures and period of notice must also be made available. The employee, therefore, must be informed about the procedures to be followed if they have a complaint (*grievance* procedures), or if the employer has a complaint against them (*disciplinary* procedures).

Periods of notice

Again, under the Employment Protection (Consolidation) Act 1978 an employee is entitled to statutory periods of notice. This means that if they are to be dismissed for any reason they cannot simply be told about it the day before. The amount of period an employee is entitled to depends upon their length of service. An employee is entitled to the following periods of notice:

- One week after one month's continuous employment
- One week for each year of continuous employment between 2 and 12 years, up to a maximum of 12 weeks

During the period of notice employees are entitled to normal pay. The law has recently been changed to give part-timers the same protection after two years of service.

Unfair dismissal

Under the Employment Protection (Consolidation) Act 1978, an employee, full-time or part-time, may not be unfairly dismissed after continuous employment of two years or more. This means that during the first two years of employment, the employer may decide to sack an employee. Provided that proper notice is served no reason has to be given. After two years an employer may sack an employee for the following reasons only:

- Lack of capability or qualifications
- Misconduct
- Redundancy
- Breach of contract
- Some other substantial reason

If an employee is dismissed for any other reason after two years of continuous employment they may take their employer to an industrial tribunal. In particular an employee may not be fairly dismissed on the following grounds:

- Belonging to a trade union
- Refusing to join a trade union
- Being pregnant
- Refusing to undertake dangerous or hazardous tasks
- On the basis of race or sex

ACTIVITY

You are a member of an industrial tribunal. You are required to hear the following cases and decide whether the employer or the employee is in the right. In each case state your findings and describe what should be done as defined by the law. You may like to prepare your answers and then join in a group debate.

1. Victor Chang is from the Chinese community in this country. He is employed as an office clerk and is paid £125 a week. He discovers that his colleague, who carries out the same duties, is being paid £140 a week. He thinks that he has been unfairly discriminated against.

   The employer says that Victor is slightly less experienced than his colleague. Victor has only just started his job whereas his colleague has been doing it for six weeks. However Victor also discovers that while this is true, his colleague has *always* been on the higher wage of £140, from the very start.

2. Sandra Dee tells her employer that she is pregnant. She has been working part-time for her employer for five years. She asks for maternity leave. Instead her employer says, 'I am sorry, but we are going to have to let you go. We can't manage without you and so you are being replaced. You leave at the end of this week'. Sandra thinks she has been unfairly dismissed. Her employer maintains that it is purely a matter of economics.

3. Selina Miles is a factory supervisor. A new machining technique means that the factory is frequently filled with dust. Selina reports this to her boss. Her boss says that her contract requires her to work in the factory. It is her job to make sure that production is carried out properly. Selina refuses to work under those conditions. The employer says that if she does she will be in breach of contract and therefore could be fairly dismissed.

4. Charles Johnson has been with his employer for four months, working full-time. He is a member of the union. The union has a dispute with the employer over pay. No agreement has been reached and so the union members, including Charles, go out on an official strike.

   Charles is given the sack. He claims that it is unfair dismissal. The employers say that his conduct was 'unsatisfactory'. When Charles threatens to take them to a tribunal they point out that he has no contract of employment. His boss says, 'You never signed anything. We never signed anything. You're not protected'.

(2.2.2) (2.2.3) (2.2.4)

People in Business Organisations

Trade union membership

Trade unions are independent organisations set up with the intention of regulating relations between the members and their employers. Unions elect officials known as *shop stewards* to represent the interests of the workers at negotiations with the employers. The strength of a union is that the interests of the workers are given a common voice. Rather than individuals seeking to improve their conditions of service and taking their own grievances to the employers, the union speaks for all its members. This is known as *collective bargaining*.

Unions can use a number of techniques to put pressure on the employers in a dispute:
- *Working to rule*: each union member undertakes only to do exactly what their job description says. This can be effective, since most organisations only run smoothly by employees doing more than they are contracted to do. It is the little things, like answering the telephone, working during breaks or working late that can be quite damaging if they are not done. Working to rule is also known as a withdrawal of goodwill.
- *Demarcation*: union members refuse to do any work that is someone else's responsibility. This is similar to working to rule and has the same effect of slowing everything down.
- *Overtime ban*: workers refuse to do any overtime, 'clocking off' exactly at the end of the normal day.
- *Go slow*: workers carry out their normal duties but at a deliberately slower rate.
- *Strike*: the most severe action a union can take is to withdraw the labour of its members. Strikes may be for half days or whole days, or may even last for weeks or months.

When an official strike is called union members have the right to form a *picket* at the entrances to the organisation. The purpose of the pickets is to inform people that there is a strike on and to encourage others not to go into work.

An employee has a right to join any trade union (except where restricted from the union by trade). As such they cannot be victimised for being a member of a union.

Similarly, an employee has a right to choose *not* to join a trade union if they so wish. Up until the Trade Union Reform and Employment Rights Act 1993, membership of a particular union could be a requirement of the job. This situation was known as a *closed shop*. Closed shops had been common in the industrial sector, but had declined in popularity. They have now been outlawed.

An employee may not be disciplined by their union for any of the following reasons:
- Failing to take part in or support industrial action
- Refusing to break the terms of their contract of employment
- Resigning from the union
- Working with non-union members

Discussion point

Are there some circumstances when it would be wrong to strike? Should people in the following professions be allowed to go on strike?
- Police force
- Nursing – National Health Service, private health care
- Army
- Politician
- Teacher
- Fire service

Under what circumstances might industrial action be acceptable? What kinds of industrial action, other than striking, might members of these organisations take?

(2.2.1) (2.2.2) (2.2.3) (2.2.4)

Employee responsibilities

Compliance with terms of contract

When an employee accepts a job, he or she agrees to be bound by the terms of the contract. This does not apply if any of the terms deny the employee statutory rights, including all those rights already described relating to remuneration, contracts, health and safety, and trade unions. Otherwise the terms of the contract are binding on the employee (and the employer – see below). Being in breach of contract is one of the grounds for fair dismissal.

Most organisations will have a clearly laid-out system for disciplinary action. Copies of the procedures should be made available to every employee at the start of their employment. Instant dismissal is very unlikely, and there are usually several stages of action:
- *Caution*: for simple faults an employee is likely to be spoken to rather than sacked on the spot. For example, if an employee is late for work their supervisor may call them in 'for a word'.
- *Verbal warning*: if the behaviour is repeated, or perhaps is more serious in the first instance, then an employee may receive a formal warning. For example, if an employee is repeatedly late a rather more severe verbal warning could be given, a record of which will be kept in the personnel file. Other offences may be considered serious enough to justify a verbal warning on the first occasion. Rudeness to one's line manager might fall into this category.
- *Written warning*: for more serious errors or continued repetition of the same fault. If after a verbal warning the employee continues to be late, the individual may receive a written warning, which is also put on the file. Extreme rudeness to a member or the organisation or a customer might warrant a written warning.
- *Disciplinary hearing*: for the more serious breaches of contract. After a number of written warnings an employee may be taken before a disciplinary

103

People in Business Organisations

board. Alternatively for some activities an employee may be disciplined in this way immediately. Misdemeanours considered to be professional misconduct are likely to result in such a hearing. It is common for trade union members to be represented by union officials at such hearings.

- *Suspended*: employees may be suspended while awaiting a disciplinary hearing. This is because the employer considers the alleged offence to be too serious to allow the person to continue until the matter is resolved.
- *Dismissal*: as a final resort, for the most serious breaches of contract employees may be dismissed.

Compliance with health and safety regulations

Not only do employees have a right to expect employers to provide a safe, working environment, they also have a responsibility to contribute to health and safety. The Health and Safety at Work etc. Act 1974 requires that employees:

- Take reasonable care for the health and safety of themselves and others who may be affected by what they do and what they fail to do
- Cooperate with employers in fulfilling their duties for health and safety

Employees who fail to comply with health and safety regulations may be prosecuted.

The requirements basically mean that employees must not act recklessly at work. They must follow safety procedures. They must take reasonable care in carrying out their duties.

Tribunal finds in favour of employee who closed door

A SOLICITOR sacked for refusing his employer's instruction to work with his office door open was vindicated yesterday when he won his claim of unfair dismissal. 'Dismissal was not within the reasonable range of responses,' ruled a tribunal in Holburn, central London.

It heard that 36-year-old Mr Roland Taylor's troubles started when he was subjected to an 'appalling campaign of pique and spite' after his employer's wife discovered the office secretaries had been invited to his wedding before she was.

Mr Taylor was finally dismissed by Mr Joseph Aaron, owner of the solicitors Joseph Aaron and Co, of Gants Hill, east London, in August 1992, because he refused to keep his door open.

Ruling the dismissal to be unfair, Mr Christopher Carstairs, industrial tribunal chairman, said Mr Aaron's complaints against Mr Taylor had 'started at about the time wedding invitations were sent out'.

During Mr Taylor's honeymoon, the invitations had caused 'a great deal of fuss, poisoning the atmosphere in the firm,' which Mr Aaron should have dealt with.

Mr Carstairs dismissed Mr Aaron's claims that Mr Taylor was rude and abrasive. 'It was Mr Aaron's practice to belittle his employees and Mr Taylor stood up to him.'

As regards the argument as to whether the office door should be shut or not, the tribunal ruled: 'Mr Taylor was simply trying to get on with his work in peace.'

Source: Daily Telegraph, April 9 1994

Pregnancy major awarded £300,000

AN ARMY major who was forced to give up her career when she became pregnant won record compensation of at least £300,000 yesterday.

Mrs Helen Homewood, now 44, whose award could eventually rise to £500,000, was a high flier with ambitions to become a brigadier when she became pregnant in 1981, an industrial tribunal heard in Glasgow.

At that time Army regulations gave pregnant women no choice but to resign. But Mrs Homewood wrote to her superiors: 'Old-fashioned as it may be, I believe that my family must come first and I do not feel I could do justice to either family or work by attempting to do both.'

Questioned at the tribunal about the wording, she said she had 'wished to be gracious when resigning' and had been making a 'virtue out of necessity'. Mrs Homewood left the Army early in 1982 after 10 years' service.

In an unusual move, the tribunal did not order the Ministry of Defence to pay out the £300,000 immediately, saying that there might be more to come.

Its figure of £299,951 – almost double the previous highest award in the present spate of similar sex discrimination cases – is based on loss of earnings, prospective earnings and fringe benefits as well as hurt feelings. That does not take account of pension and other rights. They could bring the award close to £500,000.

Army officials indicated that the ministry would almost certainly appeal, describing the size of the award as 'ridiculous' ... Yesterday's ruling that Mrs Homewood had suffered sexual discrimination followed a hearing in February.

The panel of two men and one woman said it was abundantly clear that she had been devoted to the Army. She had had a 'promising and exceptional' career and could have become a colonel by the year 2000. She had hoped to become a brigadier ... The tribunal heard that she had been well aware of the regulations requiring pregnant soldiers to quit, and had several times discharged other pregnant women, including a fellow officer ... Until it was ruled in the late 1980s that the services were not excepted from the 1976 Equal Employment Opportunity Act, the Government had assumed that the special demands of military life meant that women had to be as available for duty as men...

THE LOST CASH

THIS is how the tribunal assessed the award (figures include interest):

1. Loss of earnings: £214,458.
2. Prospective loss of earnings: £64,328.
3. Loss of fringe benefits: £15,752.
4. Solatium consolation damages: £5,413.

Source: Daily Telegraph, April 9 1994

✎ ACTIVITY

Read the article above and answer the following questions.
1. Why was Mr Taylor given the sack?
2. What was the ruling of the industrial tribunal?
3. Do you agree with the tribunal? Give reasons.
4. Under what circumstances can an employee be dismissed fairly?
5. What are the benefits of employer and employee cooperation?

(2.2.1) (2.2.2) (2.2.3) (2.2.4)

People in Business Organisations

ACTIVITY

Read the article opposite and answer the following questions:
1. Why was Mrs Homewood forced to resign?
2. Why was it not until the late 1980s that the armed services were ruled to be legally bound by the Equal Employment Opportunity Act of 1976?
3. On what grounds is Mrs Homewood entitled to compensation, i.e. what is her claim against the army?
4. Do you think she should be entitled to compensation?
5. Look at the calculation of the lost cash. How do you think the figures have been worked out? What assumptions have been made in calculating:
   (a) loss of earnings
   (b) prospective loss of earnings (i.e. possible extra earnings)
   (c) loss of fringe benefits
   (d) solatium consolation (i.e. for hurt feelings)?
6. Do you think these figures are fair? Remember that they have been guessed at, which involves a number of assumptions.
7. What do you understand by 'fringe benefits'?

(2.2.1) (2.2.2) (2.2.3) (2.2.4)

Employer rights and responsibilities

Employer rights

Many employer rights mirror the responsibilities of the employee. As has been mentioned before, where there is a *right* to something there must be a *responsibility* on someone else to provide or allow that right. Therefore an examination of employer rights involves some repetition. Details of legal requirements will not be covered in as much detail if already described above.

ACTIVITY

When an employer appoints new employees they will have certain expectations of them regarding:
- Their behaviour
- The hours they work
- The way they treat the employer
- Their respect of the working environment
- The way they treat customers
- Their appearance
- The way they talk about the organisation to other people

Imagine that you are are employing some new members of staff. Write down all the things which you would expect of them under the headings given above.

(2.2.2)

In the same way that the employee expects certain things of their employer so the employer will have expectations of their employees.

Disciplinary action

An employer has the right to discipline employees and even to dismiss them under some circumstances. The disciplinary procedures should be clearly presented and made available to every employee at the start of their employment. If employees do not comply with the terms of their contract an employer may take disciplinary action against them.

Disciplinary action should be fair. It would not be a suitable punishment to sack someone simply for not addressing their employer as 'sir'. There are normally several stages in the disciplinary process, from cautions to dismissal. Before action as severe as dismissal can be taken there ought to be a formal hearing where the facts of the case can be settled and the employee can have a chance to explain his or her actions.

Where possible it is preferable for line managers to deal with disciplinary issues. They will be more familiar with the requirements and difficulties of employees' tasks as well as their normal attitude and behaviour and any previous disciplinary action taken.

People in Business Organisations

💬 Discussion point

What action, if any, do you consider should be taken against the following employees?

1. A production worker who swears at their supervisor
2. A supervisor who swears at a production worker
3. An employee who is repeatedly late because of 'domestic problems'
4. A typist who is drunk in the office
5. A teacher who is drunk in the classroom
6. A doctor who is drunk in surgery
7. A factory worker who is drunk in charge of a fork-lift truck
8. A shop assistant who tells a customer, 'Well, actually, you can buy this cheaper down the road'
9. A machine operator who damages some expensive equipment through improper usage
10. A secretary who uses the office photocopier to make invitations for a private party
11. A shop assistant who takes items off the shelf for friends
12. A finance director who puts a computer for himself through the books of the company
13. A director who takes money from the cash box
14. An office clerk who is banned from driving for drink-driving (out of office hours)
15. A nurse fined for shoplifting (out of work hours)
16. A teacher awaiting trial for a sex abuse offence alleged to have happened in class
17. An accounts clerk guilty of sexist comments in the office
18. A manager guilty of racist comments in the boardroom
19. A sales rep guilty of fiddling a travel expenses claim by £2.50
20. A receptionist who is HIV positive

Unless otherwise stated assume that these are 'first offences'. Would it make any difference if they were not?

(2.2.2) (2.2.3) (2.2.4)

Working to terms of contract

The terms of a contract of employment may be *implicit* or *explicit*. The *explicit* terms are those that are spelt out in writing. An employer has the right to expect employees to fulfil their responsibilities regarding hours of work, holidays and duties and responsibilities.

There are also a number of *implicit* terms, which, although not actually included in the contract, are taken as obvious and too lengthy to write down. These require the employee:

- To be available to work
- To exercise reasonable care
- To carry out tasks to a reasonable degree of accuracy and skill
- To follow instructions
- To protect the property of the employer
- To be courteous to all members of staff
- To dress appropriately
- To act in good faith
- To avoid any action which diminishes the reputation of the organisation

These obligations do not extend to any requests by the employer that are unreasonable, dangerous, hazardous to health and safety or unlawful.

✏️ ACTIVITY

Consider each of the following requests by an employer and decide whether you think it is reasonable or unreasonable. Give your reasons.

1. An employer asks one of his employees who works in a kitchen to shave off his beard for reasons of hygiene. The employee claims that his beard is part of his identity and refuses.
2. A male employee works in a firm of chartered accountants. His employers ask him to remove his earring. The employee claims that this is unfair since he is always very smartly dressed and the earring is very small, besides which his female colleagues wear earrings. The employers say that they have some very traditional clients who would regard his appearance as a fall in standards.
3. An owner of a nightclub employs female bar staff. One of the bar staff complains that the uniform, which includes a miniskirt, is too revealing. The employer demands that she wears the skirt saying that the club has a certain image, and the bar staff are meant to be pleasing on the eye.
4. A worker on a building site is a Sikh. His employer demands that he wears a hard hat for his own safety. The Sikh refuses, because he cannot wear it without removing his turban, which, he says, a Sikh should never do. The employer says that they will both get into trouble with the health and safety executive if he refuses.
5. An employee working on the reception desk of a sports centre is confined to a wheelchair. One day a week children from the local school come to the centre to do games. The employer tells the receptionist that some of the children are distressed when they see someone in a wheelchair. The school is thinking about taking their pupils somewhere else. The receptionist is asked to work in another part of the office on the day the children come to the centre. The

People in Business Organisations

receptionist refuses, saying that there is no way of working without the wheelchair. If the children are distressed it is because people in wheelchairs have been hidden away for too long.

6 A shop assistant has a dental appointment during working hours. The employer refuses to let the assistant go, saying that such things should be arranged outside working hours. The employee says that it was the only time available for six weeks, especially as the shop is open six days a week. An appointment is needed fairly quickly as a filling has fallen out. The employer insists that any time taken off for appointments will be in breach of contract.

(2.2.2) (2.2.3) (2.2.4)

Employer responsibilities

ACTIVITY

Employers have a number of responsibilities to their employees. These cover areas such as:
- Their behaviour towards the employee
- The records they must keep and the documents they must provide
- The condition of the working environment
- The hours they expect the employees to work

Imagine that you are are an employer in an organisation. Write down all the things that you would expect to have to do for the employees under the headings given above.

(2.2.3) (2.2.4)

Equal opportunities and employment law place detailed *responsibilities* on the employer. Much of these have already been examined as part of the employee's rights (see above). These include:
- Written documentation
  - statement of employment
  - pay statement
- Equal pay for equal work
- No discrimination on grounds of sex or race
- Allowing membership of trade unions
- Ensuring health and safety
- Periods of notice
- Grounds for dismissal
- Redundancy
- Sick pay
- Maternity leave
- Consultation

In addition there are specific requirements about the number of hours employees may work and the breaks and rests to which they are entitled.

Not only do employers have the right to expect employees to fulfil the terms and conditions of the contract of employment, they also have an obligation to carry out their end of the deal. Hence they must allow employees to take the holidays, breaks and any other benefits and generally work within the framework described in their contracts.

Health and safety at work

The Health and Safety at Work etc. Act 1974 requires that an employer prepares a written statement of their safety policy. The purpose of the safety policy is to ensure that employers think carefully about the nature of the hazards at the workplace. The employer must find the best means of reducing those hazards and making the workplace safe and healthy for their employees. The policy statement should set out the employer's aims for improving health and safety in accordance with the requirements of the Act.

The policy also serves to increase the employees' awareness of health and safety issues. The employer has a duty to bring the policy statement to the attention of every employee. This should be done when employees join the organisation. The policy statement may also be posted on noticeboards.

The policy statement must also be kept up to date. New rules are introduced by law and organisations also change their own arrangements for safety.

Employers have a duty not just to ensure the health and safety of their employees but also anyone else who may be affected by the actions of their organisation. This includes customers, suppliers, visitors and ordinary members of the public. This means that an employer has a responsibility to limit the likely effects of fire, explosions, falls from scaffolding and releases of harmful substances into the environment.

ACTIVITY

As an employer it is your duty to ensure that you inform your employees of safe ways of using equipment. For each of the following you are expected to produce a safety notice which shows:
- 'Dos': things a user of the equipment should do
- 'Don'ts': things a user should not do

In the office
1 Computer: monitor, keyboard, mouse, printer, disk drive
2 Paper shredder
3 Photocopier
4 Electric heater

In the factory
1 Electric saw
2 Fork-lift truck
3 Motorised floor polisher

(2.2.3) (2.2.4)

Remuneration

Employers are bound by law to give their employees pay that is:
- *fair* for the work they are doing
- *equal* for all workers doing equal work or work of equal value

People in Business Organisations

They are also bound to provide employees with a written statement of pay outlining the deductions that have been made. Voluntary deductions (private pension scheme, donations to charity, savings scheme etc.) cannot be made without authorisation from the employee.

Employee consultation

An employer is under obligation to consult and/or notify their employees before doing any of the following:
- Change terms and conditions of employment
- Make employees redundant
- Selling the business to another owner
- Making voluntary deductions from the employees' earnings

If employees feel that they have not been treated fairly they may take their complaints to their employer. This is known technically as a *grievance*. The procedures for grievances should be made available to all employees. Trade union representatives may be present at grievance proceedings to represent their members.

Another way of employees presenting their views to their employers is through their trade unions. Employers notify the union representatives of proposed changes to the organisation. The representatives convey this information to the union members for discussion. If it is considered appropriate, union members may vote on the most appropriate action and the representative will go back to the employers to inform them of the members' views. The aim is to find a solution that both sides agree to.

In normal circumstances neither the employers nor the employees will want this process to break down. However, sometimes the two sides reach deadlock, which is likely to result in industrial action. Even with the threat of strikes an agreement is not always reached. This is when extra help can be gained from ACAS.

ACAS stands for the Advisory, Conciliation and Arbitration Service. It is an independent body set up in 1974 and its chief goals can be found in its name:
- *Advisory*: to give advice to employers and employees who are in an industrial dispute.
- *Conciliation*: to bring the opposite sides in an industrial dispute together so that they might find a solution between them.
- *Arbitration*: to find appropriate solutions to industrial disputes when conciliation has failed.

Its general duty, therefore, is to promote the improvement of industrial relations.

Equal opportunities

If you look in any newspaper at the job appointments you will notice that many adverts end with the phrase, 'We are an equal opportunities employer'. What does this mean? If employers do not promote equal opportunities they are breaking the law.

There are several aspects to equal opportunities:

- Race
- Sex
- Disability
- Religion
- Age

It is not possible for every person equally to do any job. For one thing, qualifications, expertise, skill and experience vary from person to person. These are acceptable grounds for discrimination. However, an employer cannot use race, sex, disability, religion or age as the basis for deciding suitability for a job, or promotion, except in a few instances. For example, it is acceptable to request *Indian* waiters only for an Indian restaurant. Similarly, some work is more suitably carried out by male or female workers – working in boys' or girls' hostels, acting and modelling fall in this category. But these are exceptions, and in all other cases appointments, promotion, training, dismissal, benefits and general treatment at work must be decided only on *relevant* differences between candidates. It may be that a candidate's inability to climb a ladder (for a builder) discriminates against people in wheelchairs, or to lift heavy loads (for a fire officer) discriminates against women and older people.

There is specific legislation relating to the employment of disabled people. Under the Disabled Persons (Employment) Acts 1944/58 any organisation that employs 20 or more people must employ a quota of disabled people. If it fails to do so it must provide acceptable grounds for its failure or face a fine.

ACTIVITY

Which people are discriminated against by the requirements of the following jobs? Do you consider the discrimination to be acceptable or unacceptable?
1. Professional footballer
2. Bouncer at a nightclub
3. PE teacher at a Roman Catholic girls' school
4. Leader of a Mosque
5. Sales assistant in a four-storey department store (with no lifts)
6. Waiter in a Chinese restaurant
7. Fire officer
8. RAF pilot

(2.2.4)

People in Business Organisations

EOC hails 'stunning victory' for part-timers

The Lords ruling means 640,000 part-time workers can now enjoy the same protection as full-time staff

A LANDMARK judgment in the House of Lords has given part-time workers the same employment protection as full-timers, and could open the way for thousands of unfair dismissal and redundancy claims.

Under the 1978 Employment Protection (Consolidation) Act, those who worked between eight and 16 hours a week had to hold a job for five years before they became eligible for redundancy pay or could claim for unfair dismissal. Those working more than 16 hours a week were defined as full-timers and won these rights after two years.

The Equal Opportunities Commission (EOC) has spent four years fighting those provisions in the courts. After losing in the High Court and the Court of Appeal, the EOC won its case when four out of five law lords supported its argument that the act breached European Union laws.

Article 119 of the Treaty of Rome recognises the principle of equal pay and rights for men and women in equal work. The EOC argued that since Britain's full-time workforce is more than 60% male, and its part-time workforce over 80% female, to give lesser rights to part-timers is to discriminate against women. The case was brought on behalf of a part-time school cleaner who was sacked just before acquiring employment protection rights after five years.

The Lords ruled that part-time workers should receive full employment protection after two years. Those who work less than eight hours a week will win the same protection. The EOC's chairwoman, Kamlesh Bahl, said the commission had scored a 'stunning victory'.

'Given that most of the new jobs being created in the next decade will be part-time and will be taken by women, equal treatment for part-timers is now an essential aspect of equal opportunities, and must be seen as such by the government,' she said.

The Department of Employment acknowledged it would have to alter the existing legislation to comply with the ruling, but the decision has immediate force.

The EOC calculates that 640,000 people will now be protected. Lawyers are still studying the implications of the judgment, but it is likely the ruling will grant rights to those made redundant or unfairly dismissed in the past. It seems certain that those still within the time limit for a complaint – three months in the case of unfair dismissals and six months for redundancy claims – will be able to claim.

A similar situation arose over pregnant servicewomen, whose dismissals were adjudged to have breached EU law. In that case backdated claims were allowed and now appear likely to cost the taxpayer tens of millions of pounds. If the same logic is applied to the part-timers ruling, claims could be launched dating back to 1987, when the Employment Protection (Consolidation) Act was passed.

Employers warned that companies would be reluctant to take on part-timers in future because of extra liabilities. The Institute of Directors said the judgment would 'harm the interests of the very people it is supposed to help'.

Other developments in employment rights can be expected as pressure groups use European law to overrule British statutes. The EOC is currently backing the industrial tribunal case of a part-time teacher, whose pension calculated from her earnings in the last 365 working days was lower than those of her full-time colleagues.

Another European Union-inspired change to working conditions looks likely after the issue of an opinion by the advocate-general of the European Court of Justice nine days ago. The case centres on whether unrecognised trade unions, staff associations and ad hoc staff committees should have the same rights to be consulted on redundancies as recognised independent trade unions currently have under British Law.

The opinion of the advocate-general is that they should have this right; in theory the judgment of the full European Court, expected in two to three months, may differ from the opinion, but in practice it rarely does.

Source: Sunday Times, March 13 1994

ACTIVITY

Read the article above and answer the following questions:
1. What is the 'stunning victory' for part-timers mentioned in the headline?
2. What was previously the law under the 1978 Employment Protection (Consolidation) Act? How has this now changed?
3. What was the basis of the argument made by the Equal Opportunities Commission, and the basis on which the case was won?
4. What is the likely outcome of the ruling?
5. What is a possible negative outcome of the ruling?
6. What future changes in employment legislation are likely on the basis of current European Union activities?

(2.2.2) (2.2.3) (2.2.4)

Legislation governing employee and employer rights

Introduction
Much has already been said of various laws and regulations, which impose responsibilities and confer rights on employers and employees. In this section the chief pieces of legislation are outlined to summarise the points discussed in detail in the previous two sections.

Health and Safety at Work etc. Act
Health and safety at work is the responsibility of both the employee and the employer. The Act is aimed at:
- Securing the health, safety and welfare of people at work
- Protecting members of the public against the dangers of activities carried out at work
- Controlling the storage and use of dangerous substances
- Controlling the release of noxious substances into the atmosphere

People in Business Organisations

Employers must provide machinery and equipment that is safe in a safe environment, making safety equipment (face-masks, clothing, goggles etc.) available if needed. They must ensure the safe handling and use of materials. They must give their employees the information, instruction, training and supervision that may be needed to guarantee health and safety, including emergency procedures, fire drills, first-aid and the routine checking of equipment. Requirements for heating, lighting, ventilation, noise, washing facilities, seating etc. are also covered.

Employers are required to produce a written statement of their safety policy to be made freely available to all employees. This increases both the employer's and the employees' awareness of health and safety issues.

Trade Unions have a right to appoint a safety representative to investigate health and safety issues and to consult the employers on behalf of their members.

Employers have similar responsibilities to members of the public who may visit their premises, or may be affected by the activities carried out by the organisation.

Employees are required to take all reasonable care and precautions for the health and safety of themselves and of any other persons who may be affected by what they do or fail to do. They must avoid reckless behaviour and be aware of all the potential hazards. The employee must cooperate with the employer in their efforts to ensure health and safety.

The Health and Safety Commission and the Health and Safety Executive have been set up to promote and enforce the requirements of the Act. The commission provides information and training relating to health and safety issues. The executive has powers to enforce the law by carrying out inspections and, where necessary, initiate proceedings against an employer or employee for failing to comply.

Failure to comply with the terms and conditions of the Act may result in heavy fines or even imprisonment.

Equal opportunities

It is a common mistake to assume that there is an Equal Opportunities Act. There is no single act. Equal opportunities legislation is made up of a number of very important acts, including:
- Race Relations Act 1976
- Sex Discrimination Act 1986
- Equal Pay Act 1970
- Equal Pay (Amendment) Act 1983
- Employment Act 1989
- Disabled Persons (Employment) Acts 1944, 1958

Between them these laws require employers to discriminate between employees on *relevant grounds only*. In nearly all cases sex, marital status, colour, race, nationality, criminal records and ethnic or national origins are not relevant. They may *not* be used as the basis for employing or not employing someone, for offering them different terms and conditions, or for promotion, training or benefits. They may not be included in job advertisements or contracts of employment. Organisations of a certain size must employ a specified number of disabled employees – if they fall below the required number they must endeavour to engage disabled persons when suitable posts arise. Any employee who is treated differently on these grounds may justly argue that they are being *victimised* and bring charges against their employer.

There are few exceptions. The most common are referred to as a genuine *occupational qualifications*. That means that discrimination may be made on the basis of sex, race, age and so on only if it is a requirement of the job. The need for physical strength may exclude female applicants, as in the case of a fire officer, for example. Modelling or acting parts may specify male or female only. Indian restaurants may favour Indian applicants.

In some instances employers exercise what is known as *positive discrimination*. The object of this is to favour minority groups in an attempt to improve the balance. Generally this is unlawful since it is discrimination. For example, if an employer refuses to employ someone who is white because they are white, the employer is guilty of racial discrimination and liable for prosecution. However, employers may take *positive action* to overcome the effects of past discrimination. This can be done by encouraging minority groups to take up jobs that have a poor balance of racial groups, or a biased male/female ratio. Provided the employer can prove that it has very good reasons for favouring one particular group then this type of action is allowed. Sometimes advertisements may read, 'We would welcome applications from female candidates' (or other groups). Here it is clear that while favouring one group of people the employer is not excluding anyone else.

In law there is a distinction between direct and indirect discrimination. *Direct* discrimination occurs when employees are treated less favourably on grounds of race, religion, sex, colour, and so on. *Indirect* discrimination occurs when other conditions of the job unfairly count against a minority group.

Various commissions have been set up to ensure that the requirements of these acts are fulfilled. These include:
- The Manpower Services Commission (for disabled employees)
- The Commission for Racial Equality
- The Equal Opportunities Commission

In addition, the European Commission on Human Rights acts to enforce the requirements of European Human Rights legislation.

People in Business Organisations

💬 Discussion point

In each of the following cases, based upon real-life examples, decide whether the discrimination is lawful or unlawful. Join in a group discussion highlighting the arguments on both sides.

1. A woman was refused a job at a youth centre. The employers argued that because she was pregnant she would shortly be unavailable for work. They appointed someone else. The woman claimed that taking pregnancy into account was direct sex discrimination.

2. In a security firm that employed women a man applied for a job. He was refused. The employers argued that during the 12 hour shifts the workers were given a long rest period. Beds were provided for this purpose. The female employees would undress to their underwear. In the interests of decency the man could not be employed.

3. A men's tailor advertised for a new shop assistant stating that a 'male' worker was needed. A woman who applied for this job but was refused claimed she was unfairly discriminated against. The employers claimed that as a gentleman's tailor the assistant was required to measure the inside leg of male customers, and so the job was 'unsuitable' for women.

4. A Sikh applied for a job in a chocolate factory but was refused. The employers demanded strict adherence to hygienic regulations specifying that beards and long hair were unacceptable. The Sikh claimed this was indirect discrimination against Sikhs, who never cut their hair on religious grounds.

5. An overseas graduate applied for a job at a legal firm. UK students were required by the firm to undertake a one-year course of study. Students with overseas degrees were required to take a 21-month course. The overseas student argued that this was indirect discrimination against non-British employees. The firm argued that it was necessary to ensure an equal academic standard.

(2.2.1) (2.2.2)

Equal pay
The Wages Act 1986 and the Equal Pay Act 1970 stipulate that employees are entitled to equal pay for equal work or work of equal value.

Employment law
The chief components of employment law are:
- Employment Protection (Consolidation) Act 1978
- Trade Union and Labour Relations (Consolidation) Act 1992
- Trade Union Reform and Employment Rights Act 1993

The main provisions of these laws are:
- The right not to be unfairly dismissed
- The right to have suitable rest breaks, holidays, and fair conditions of service
- The right to return to work after having a baby
- The right to a written statement of employment
- The right to a written pay statement
- The right to choose or refuse to join a trade union and take part in official action

✏️ ACTIVITY

Read the article on the following page and answer the following questions:
1. What two reasons did Berkshire County Council give for rejecting Dr Vigneswaren's appointment?
2. What were the stages in the original appointment and the reversal by the Council?
3. What arguments did the County use to deny the charges of racism?
4. What phrase is used to described discrimination that is acceptable?
5. What must be proved to show that this is a case of racial discrimination?
6. John Patten has agreed to try to settle the debate. How would you go about it if you were asked to investigate? Think about the questions you would have to find answers to and how you might get those answers.

(2.2.2)

People in Business Organisations

Job bar on headteacher 'was racist'

CHARGES of racism have been levelled at a county council after it blocked the appointment of an Asian headteacher at one of its schools.

John Patten, the Secretary of State for Education, has agreed to intervene in a bitter dispute between Lea First School, in Slough, and Berkshire County Council.

The Commission for Racial Equality is also investigating the case and has launched industrial tribunal proceedings on behalf of Dr Kanagarajah Vigneswaren, who was offered the headship of the school by its governors – only to have it withdrawn weeks later.

The council objected to Dr Vigneswaren's appointment because it claimed recruitment of the head involved irregular procedures. It also said that he lacked primary school experience, although Dr Vigneswaren had been deputy director of a primary school in the United States before working as head of year in a Slough secondary school.

Dr Vigneswaren and several of the Lea First School governors say racism is at the root of the matter. 'I am bitter,' Dr Vigneswaren said. 'I am from Sri Lanka and I am an idealist so I don't like to think negatively about anyone, but I am forced to feel there is a lot of racism in Berkshire.'

Mr Ram Kumar Kaushal, chairman of the school's governors, echoed this view. 'At first we were told it was about primary school experience, now it is a procedural matter. It all boils down to the fact that the person we have appointed is Asian,' he said....

Dr Vigneswaren was selected, although he was not a unanimous choice, and the governors ratified the decision. Mr Kaushal made the offer in writing, and normally the council's endorsement would have been a formality. However, councillors voted to block the appointment, and put the school's governors under pressure to reverse their appointment. This they eventually did, and instead renewed the contract of the acting headteacher, a retired secondary head, for another term.

Mr Goodchild [chief education officer of Berkshire] denied that there had been any racism by the authority, and said that it had acted properly throughout the whole process. Several local schools, including the nursery and middle schools attached to Lea First School, had black teachers, he said.

'We have been very proud of some of the black heads we have appointed in recent times. Our racial policies have national recognition and we take that aspect of our work very seriously indeed.

'We like to feel we support governing bodies fully in the appointment process.'

The Department for Education confirmed that Mr Patten would decide whether or not Berkshire has acted properly in blocking the appointment.

Source: Independent on Sunday, April 17 1994

MULTIPLE CHOICE

1. The Health and Safety at Work etc. Act:
   A Guarantees a minimum wage to all employees
   B Forces employers to recruit a number of disabled workers
   C Ensures safe working conditions
   D Restricts the ways in which a product may be advertised

2. 'Remuneration' in a contract of employment refers to:
   A Pay
   B Promotion
   C Working conditions
   D Roles and responsibilities

3. If employees are required to operate VDUs then they are entitled to:
   A Longer holidays
   B A pay rise
   C Regular rest periods
   D Free glasses

4. Regardless of their length of service or hours of work women are entitled to:
   A 10 weeks maternity leave
   B 12 weeks maternity leave
   C 14 weeks maternity leave
   D 16 weeks maternity leave

5. A staff relationship implies:
   A An advisory or service function
   B Control and supervision of staff
   C A junior position in the organisation
   D A permanent and pensionable post

6. Individuals have a legal right to:
   A Join a trade union
   B Go on strike
   C Have a pay rise
   D Refuse to undertake duties outlined in their job description

7. Line organisation refers to a:
   A Vertical structure of authority
   B Lateral structure of authority
   C Horizontal structure of authority
   D Functional structure of authority

8. The personnel function does not include:
   A Organising induction courses for new employees
   B Ensuring proper welfare facilities exist
   C Dealing with complaints from customers
   D Maintaining personal history sheets for each member of the staff

9. Horizontal communication exists between the:
   A Production director and the personnel manager
   B Company secretary and office supervisor

C Chief accountant and the ledger clerk
D Personnel director and the senior training officer

10 In a rigid, authoritarian, management structure, communication flow will tend to be:
A Vertical and upwards
B Vertically upwards and downwards
C Vertical and downwards
D Vertical and horizontal

11 Health and safety in a firm is a responsibility of:
A Line managers
B Functional managers
C Specialist managers
D All managers

12 The person responsible for the correct conduct of meetings is the:
A Director
B Secretary
C Organiser
D Chairman

13 A person who is denied a job due to their sex may seek redress under:
A The Race Relations Act
B The Health and Safety at Work Act
C Trade Union and Labour Relations Act
D The Sex Discrimination Act

14 When employees begin work they are entitled to a written statement of terms of employment within:
A 1 week
B 1 month
C 2 weeks
D 2 months

People in Business Organisations

ELEMENT 2.3
Present results of investigation into job roles

Performance criteria

PC 2.3.1 Identify and describe individuals' job roles at different levels within business organisations

PC 2.3.2 Explain the benefits of team membership in performing job roles

PC 2.3.3 Identify activities performed by individuals at different levels within organisations

PC 2.3.4 Identify tasks in job roles

PC 2.3.5 Present results of investigation into job roles

Introduction: organisational charts revisited

Organisational charts show very clearly the vertical line relationships, or lines of authority. Employees are accountable in the first instance to their *line manager*, the person most directly above them on the organisational chart.

An organisation also has *staff relationships*. Senior managers, for example, have personal assistants. Assistants have no authority of their own but may act only in the name of their senior manager. They may offer advice and support, but they may not insist that their advice is accepted. Hence when a personal assistant makes suggestions to other staff members they are not obliged to carry out their requests, since their relationship is a staff and not a line relationship. The personal assistant is likely to say, 'The managing director has asked me to tell you that...'.

People in Business Organisations

An organisational chart

Personal assistant

Staff relationships - - - - - - - - - -
Line relationships ─────────

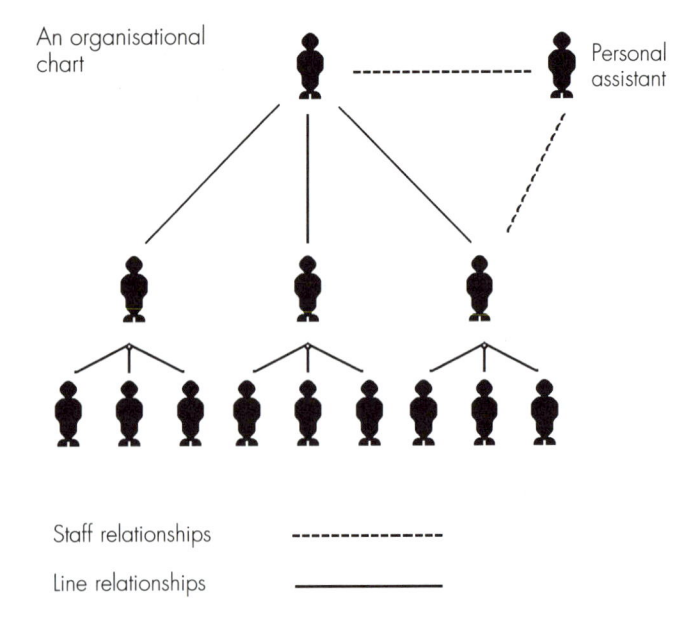

Finally there are also *functional relationships*. These relate to members of the organisation who have responsibilities across a number of different departments. For example, the training and development function of personnel will service all departments. The staff training officer has a functional responsibility to provide appropriate training and development for all employees in the organisation. Effectively the training officer is saying, 'I suggest you do this like this. . .'.

Job roles in business organisations

The terms *director*, *manager* and *supervisor* will probably be familiar to you. Indeed, these terms have already been used quite freely in this unit. It is now time to define them more precisely by investigating the roles and responsibilities they hold in an organisation.

Most large organisations have organisational structures with hierarchical layers as shown below.

Limited companies and incorporated organisations must have directors by law. The senior director is often referred to as the *managing director*, who has effective control over the whole organisation. In other businesses senior personnel may also be referred to as directors or simply as senior managers. The words used to describe each layer of authority vary widely, especially in the public sector. Colleges, for example, have heads of department, assistant principals and vice-principals.

ACTIVITY

Research into the following organisations in order to find out the typical layers of hierarchy. Try to determine the normal span of control for each managerial position. Display them in a simple diagrammatic form:
1. The fire service
2. An airline company
3. Local government
4. Your school, college or place of work
5. The police force

(2.3.1)

Proprietors

The *proprietors* are the owners of the business. These will vary according to the type of organisation (refer to Unit 1, Element 1.1). The role of the proprietor is quite straightforward – to provide sufficient funds to enable the business to operate effectively.

In many businesses the owners are also responsible for running the business and will therefore have a much larger role.

ACTIVITY

Identify five local businesses and name the proprietors. Arrange an interview with one of the proprietors and ask him or her to outline the roles and responsibilities of being the owner of the business.

(2.3.1)

Directors

The directors make up the board of directors, which effectively runs the organisation. They decide all important matters, including setting targets. However, the directors of limited companies are answerable to the shareholders who have the power to vote directors on or off the board. In the public sector the directors are appointed by the government. Once again, if they do not carry out their duties in an effective and appropriate manner they are likely to be removed from office.

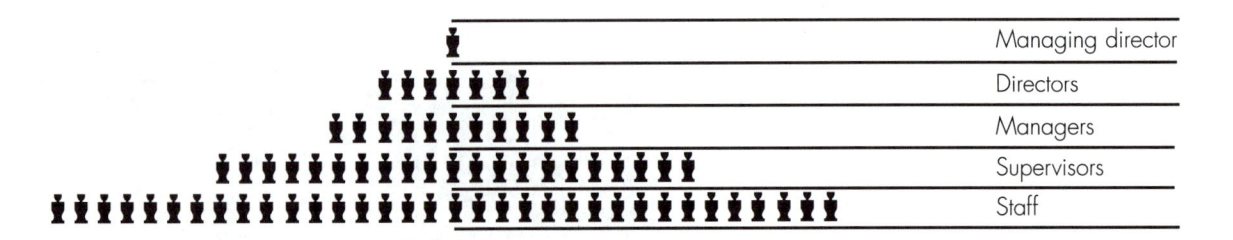

	Managing director
	Directors
	Managers
	Supervisors
	Staff

114

It is common for directors to have strategic responsibility for the key functions or departments of the organisation. *Strategic responsibility* refers to the fact that directors take a long-term view in their planning and setting goals. They are not normally involved in the day-to-day running of the departments.

Strategic issues include:
- Changes to the organisational structure
- The deployment of staff and physical resources
- Setting budgets and targets for the whole organisation and for each department
- Launching new products and advertising campaigns
- Deciding the objectives of the organisation
- Making plans for expansion or relocation

In all cases there are limiting factors, including financial, legal and physical constraints. Above all, the directors of private sector organisations must comply with the wishes of the shareholders, or else risk being voted off the board. Similarly public sector organisations must work within the guidelines set down by the government.

It follows that the board of directors may include:
- Managing director
- Finance director
- Marketing and sales director
- Design and production director
- Personnel director
- Distribution director

Where the organisation has several locations the directors take responsibility for their respective functions for the whole organisation. Answering directly to the directors will be managers for those departments at each branch.

As already mentioned the precise job titles may vary. The make-up of the board of directors also varies widely, depending upon the size and structure of the organisation and the nature of its business. Smaller organisations tend to have fewer directors, and managers in general, so that those in managerial positions must fulfil several different roles. Hence they become more *generalised* in their expertise. Distribution, for example, might become part of the job of the design and production director, while the managing director may also have to take on the role of finance director. Larger organisational structures allow for greater *specialisation*. Tasks and responsibilities can be broken down into narrower areas of expertise.

ACTIVITY

Obtain copies of company reports for *five* different companies. These may be available at your school or local library. Alternatively you may write to companies requesting copies of their latest annual report. From this information draw up a list of the members of the board of directors including their job titles for each company.
(2.3.1)

Managers
There may be several layers of managerial responsibility in an organisation. The most senior managers are responsible directly to the board of directors and normally have operational responsibility for a department and the employees in that department.

Operational responsibility means that they take charge of day-to-day decision-making related to running the department within the targets set by the directors. Senior managers may have other managers beneath them to take responsibility for particular aspects of their department.

So both the directors and all levels of management have decision-making as part of their job. What differs is the scale and scope of the decisions made. Directors make decisions that affect the whole organisation and have far-reaching implications. Managers have to focus on more specific issues relating to their department.

It is likely that thousands of operational decisions are made every day at every level of responsibility. Operational issues include:
- Credit control of customers' accounts
- The decision to buy or rent a new photocopier
- Maintenance of equipment
- Writing job advertisements
- Designing publicity materials
- Ensuring staff work efficiently

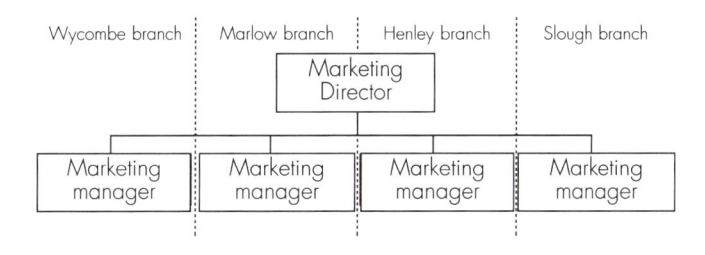

```
                    Wycombe branch  Marlow branch  Henley branch  Slough branch
                                       Marketing
                                       Director
                    ┌───────────────┬──────────────┬──────────────┐
              Marketing         Marketing      Marketing      Marketing
              manager           manager        manager        manager
```

People in Business Organisations

In general, managers ensure that the targets set by directors are achieved by the most effective and efficient use of human, financial and physical resources. They translate the targets into appropriate action that will meet the targets, and keep the directors informed of progress made and problems encountered.

For example the production director may wish to increase production by 5%. That is the target. The managers in the production department will then need to find ways of achieving that level of growth. Does it mean investing in new machinery? What can be done to existing production methods to maximise efficiency and productivity? Is there too much wastage at present? Can the materials used be improved by using different suppliers? The managers, then, are faced with solving the problems and finding practical solutions.

Supervisors

A lower level of management is represented by *supervisors*. They share many of the responsibilities of managers listed above, but in a more restricted capacity. Chiefly, their role is to ensure that the work is carried out according to instructions and report back to more senior managers. Supervisors are normally responsible for managing a team of workers.

In smaller organisations there may not be a distinction made between managers and supervisors.

ACTIVITY

At work or at school identify the day-to-day decisions made by managers and supervisors. Interview one manager and one supervisor to establish a clear idea of the duties involved in each of their jobs.
(2.3.1)

Operators

The term *operators* is often used to describe employees who are responsible for particular activities or roles. It is more commonly used when describing workers in a production team or manufacturing organisation. Operators may be highly skilled, such as lathe operators.

Operators may work individually or as part of a team as a team member.

Team members

The team members are the people that will ultimately carry out the day-to-day routine duties. While they may be called a team it does not always mean that they work together at all times. The production team almost certainly will, cooperating with each other in meeting deadlines and targets and ensuring that the instructions of the manager are carried out. The sales team, however, may have regular meetings together to discuss strategy and progress, but may work in much smaller groups or even individually, taking responsibility for geographical regions, perhaps.

Team members need to obey the instructions of their supervisors and cooperate with their fellow team members. Like a football team, it does not work if everyone wants to be a centre forward. The goalkeeper, the defenders and the midfield players are all equally important.

ACTIVITY

What are the attributes of a good team member? In groups of four or five discuss the essential features which make up a good team member. Use flip chart paper to draw up a list of the *six* most important features, in order of importance. As a group make a short presentation to the class based on your findings.
(2.3.1)

ACTIVITY

How well do you work as a team member? Think about the last activity. How did you make your contributions? How well did you listen to others? Did you take the beliefs of other people seriously? Did you compromise on any of your beliefs? Write a short appraisal of your contribution for your portfolio.
(2.3.1) (2.3.2)

Support and service staff

Employees of an organisation not directly involved in producing or delivering the main business may be classified as *support or service staff*. Organisations, whether large or small, usually require the assistance of support and service staff for effective operations. The chief roles include routine maintenance, administration, sales and marketing, the personnel function and finance.

For example, a large manufacturing organisation will require support and service staff such as a training manager, finance clerks, secretaries, caretakers, security guards and engineers.

ACTIVITY

For your school, college or place of work, identify the jobs which may be classified as support or service. In what ways do each of these people contribute to the effective running of the organisation?
(2.3.1)

People in Business Organisations

The functions of different job roles

For this section we are going to examine the job roles in a typical organisation. Unfortunately there is no such thing as a typical organisation. So much depends upon the size, the nature of business, the sector of industry and the unique aims and objectives of the business. Major differences exist between public sector and private sector organisations, and between those providing a service and those making a product.

However, there are some broad similarities. Organisations of any kind face similar kinds of problems and constraints and have similar ways of solving them. Hence the roles and responsibilities described below may not be an accurate description of any business in the world, but the kinds of tasks outlined will exist and are likely to be carried out by someone. Remember that the job titles will vary widely, and smaller organisations tend to have more generalised personnel taking on several roles.

Design and production

> There is more to design than *The International Design Yearbook*, which covers only furniture, lighting, tableware, textiles and products such as computers, telephones and cameras. It omits graphics, packaging, signage, illustration, fashion, vehicles, interiors, street furniture and information design....
>
> ... The future of design must not be one of restless innovation, but one where existing standards are refined. The public does not want to be mugged by successive novelties, but wants to enjoy more of what it already appreciates to be excellent.
>
> So what is the mission of the industrial designer? He or she should be applying creativity to the challenges of our age, namely designing information rather than twiddling about with the shape and colour of a desk lamp. The designer will be involved with experience, not just appearance.
>
> David Kelley, the Californian who created Apple Computer's first mouse, a design that changed the way the world thinks and works, put it this way: 'I used to think creativity was designing a product to solve a problem. Now I think it's deciding what problem to work on.'
>
> Source: *Daily Telegraph*, May 28 1994

A typical structure of the Design and production department

Design and production may be combined or may exist as separate functions. They are closely related and hence need to work closely together. The structure of the department may appear as in the following diagram.

It sometimes happens that someone, or a group of people, has a flash of inspiration for a new product or service. The inventors of the popular board game *Trivial Pursuit* thought the concept up in a few minutes and made a fortune. Usually it requires a period of research and development. The organisation has an idea of what it is trying to do, but getting it to work takes more time. This is particularly true of electronics and pharmaceutical companies, who spend significant sums on research and development, or R&D. Across the world thousands of scientists are trying to find a cure for the AIDS virus. They know what they are trying to produce, but no one is yet sure how to do it.

It is unlikely that the organisation will choose to design and produce something just because it has come up with an idea. Although business is about taking risks to some extent, it makes sense to minimise those risks where possible. Hence the likely starting point for design and production is market research. This idea for rocket-powered roller-skates, for example, must be investigated.

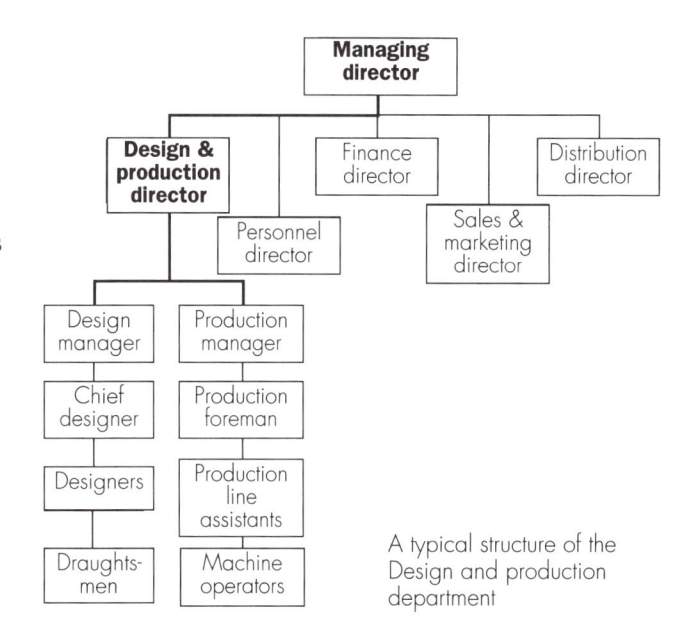

- Can we make it?
- How much will it cost?
- Will people want to buy it?

The main stages in design and production are:
- Original concept
- Prototype model – a one-off mock-up of the product, which may lead to changes in the design, use of materials, or even result in the project being scrapped as impractical
- Pilot – involving a production run and possibly product on the market
- Full-scale production

At all stages consideration must also be given to financial, legal, health and safety, environmental and ethical issues.

Design and production director   In consultation with the marketing department the design and production director will make the decision whether to pursue a particular product innovation.

Design manager   The design manager is responsible for overseeing the various stages of product design. This will involve close cooperation with the production department. There is no use in designing something which either cannot be made or else would prove too difficult.

Designers   Whether the original idea is a flash of inspiration or the result of intensive research and development, once the decision has been made to pursue the idea the designers will be instructed to produce the precise specifications of the product. The specifications will show:
- Precise measurements of all parts

People in Business Organisations

- The method of assembly
- The materials to be used
- The degree of *tolerance* (which shows just how precise production needs to be)

Draughtsmen The draughtsmen will be required to produce the *blueprints* of the product to the specifications of the designers. These are simply technical drawings detailing the layout and construction which the production department will use when setting up the production process.

Production manager In close cooperation with the design team the production manager is responsible for ensuring that production meets the design specifications. Once production is up and running the production manager oversees the production process to meet targets, maximise efficiency and productivity, maintain stock levels and guarantee the quality of the items produced. This involves setting up appropriate production methods and work patterns.

Production foreman The production foreman is usually found on the factory floor, directly taking responsibility for a production run, assisting the team in problems that may arise, and answering to the production manager.

Production line assistants and machine operators These people carry out the routine tasks of producing, according to the instructions of the foreman and manager.

ACTIVITY

The design and production director is approached with a new product concept. The idea is motorised roller skates. Describe all the likely stages from this initial idea to final full-scale production, outlining the possible problems and constraints.
(2.3.3)

Personnel

The personnel department has the responsibility for the most valuable resource of the organisation: its staff. This includes recruitment, training, welfare, health and safety, promotion and industrial relations.

Personnel director The personnel director has overall charge over the department, taking part as a member of the board of directors. All departmental directors will report to the personnel director about their staffing requirements for the forthcoming period. The personnel director will oversee the most effective deployment of human resources, ensuring that training programmes are initiated as appropriate.

Personnel manager Personnel managers take responsibility for staffing issues for their particular

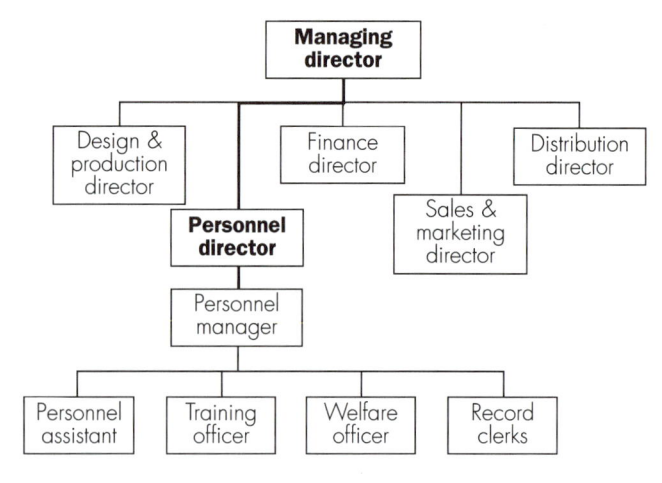

A typical structure of the Personnel department

site or branch. They report directly to the personnel director and their chief task is to implement policy relating to human resources.

Personnel assistant The personnel assistant works closely with the personnel manager, carrying out the manager's instructions and acting on his or her behalf when the manager is absent.

Training officer The training officer initiates training programmes, encouraging employees to take part and upgrade their skills and qualifications. This is necessary from time to time to keep personnel up to date with new laws, technology and systems. *In-house* training is provided by the organisation at work, so that participants do not need to book time off or make travel and hotel arrangements. Other training will involve workers attending sessions and workshops away from their normal place of work.

In times of recession staff development and training is one of the areas that usually suffers first. It is difficult to measure its immediate economic advantage. However, it is clear that an organisation needs a trained, highly skilled and well motivated workforce to be successful, all of which is provided by ongoing training.

Welfare officer The welfare, health and safety of all employees is coordinated by the welfare officer. The organisation must comply with health and safety regulations, and issues arising out of this as reported by staff representatives are investigated by the welfare officer. Welfare also includes all staff benefits such as canteen, social facilities, counselling service and information on pensions and other financial matters. Staff welfare, therefore, is essential for staff morale and well-being.

Record clerks The personnel department must keep the personal information on all employees up to date. This includes name, date of birth, address, National Insurance number, tax code, start date, qualifications, current rate of pay and so on. This is therefore highly confidential and must be kept secure.

People in Business Organisations

ACTIVITY

1. Allied Chandlers is a major manufacturer of soap, candles and oil paint. The organisation has many branches in the United Kingdom, including its head office in Basingstoke. The people listed below work in the personnel department at head office.

    Mike Taylor is the personnel director, a member of the board of directors, with overall responsibility for personnel at all branches and answerable to the managing director, *Kelly Kerrigan*.

    Bill Laswell is Mike Taylor's personal assistant.

    Sinead MacKenzie is personnel manager for the Basingstoke branch, answerable to the personnel director and taking charge of personnel issues relating to the branch.

    Hereward Free is Sinead MacKenzie's personal assistant.

    Dorothy Samuel is the departmental secretary, with a functional relationship with the personnel manager but line-managed by the administration manager, *Abid Hussain*.

    Neil Cooper is the personnel officer, line-managed by the personnel manager.

    Lucy Milligan is the personnel assistant, answerable to the personnel officer.

    The three clerical assistants, *Thomas Burgess*, *Marc Johnson* and *Brigitte Simpkins*, are line-managed by the personnel assistant.

    The welfare officer *Kirit Patel*, the health and safety officer *Bartholomew Nannery* and the training officer *Suki King*, are all answerable to the personnel officer.

    You are required to draw up an organisational chart for this department *(2.3.1) (2.3.3)*

2. Below is a list of roles and responsibilities which fall within the personnel function. For each one you are required to state the job title and the name of the person responsible for carrying out those tasks.

Role and responsibility	Job title and name
• Running training programmes • Deciding company policy on recruitment procedures • Completing personnel records • Acting on behalf of the personnel manager (Basingstoke) when the manager is absent • Listening to reports from staff regarding working conditions • Answering the telephone, distributing post in the department and typing letters	

(2.3.1) (2.3.3)

Finance

The finance department is interested in both the money coming into the organisation from customers and investors and the money going out to pay suppliers for goods and services received. There is a need to record the progress of money at all stages, so that the financial situation can be monitored and therefore controlled.

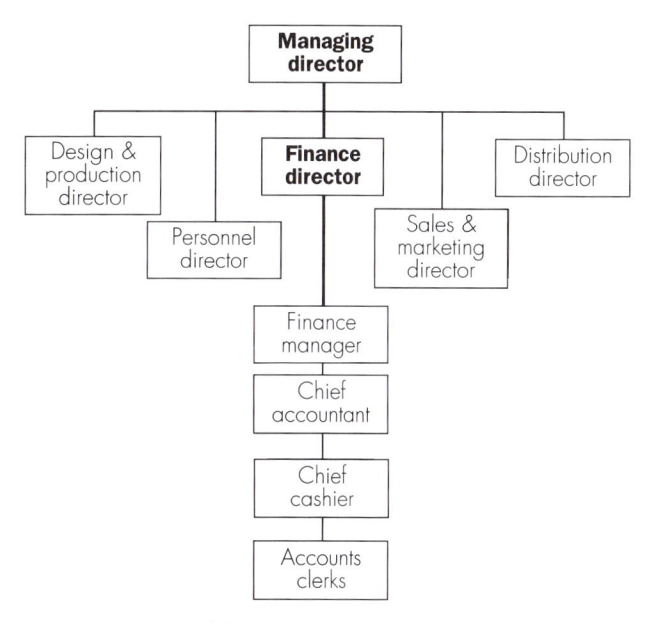

A typical structure of the Finance department

Finance director The finance director is a member of the board of directors and determines the financial policy for the whole organisation. In consultation with the other directors, the finance director determines the targets for growth and budget limits for expenditure. In some organisations each department has to bid for its budget, which means that they present detailed figures and arguments to the finance director, detailing how much money they think they will need for the forthcoming period. The finance director then has the final decision and fixes the departmental budgets.

Finance manager Finance managers normally have control over the budgets of their own branch or site of the organisation. They will report directly to the finance director.

Chief accountant The chief accountant will work closely with the finance manager and take charge of the administrative aspects of accounting. It is likely that the chief accountant will produce reports that can be analysed so that financial performance is monitored.

There are three main types of accounting reports:
- *Financial accounts* report on what has happened in the past, so that levels of spending and income can be compared with the budget to assess the performance of the business.
- *Management accounts*, which are forward-looking

People in Business Organisations

and based upon predictions, so that decisions can be made about future spending.
- *Cost accounting*, which breaks the information down so that it becomes clear how much individual units of production cost to make.

Chief cashier Chief cashiers are responsible for handling and recording the money. They will operate a cashbook which shows the money received from sales and the money spent on expenses and equipment. They will be authorised to refund staff for business expenses, and may also be one of the *authorised signatories* for cheques. The authorised signatories are those people in the organisation who may sign the cheques, and will be restricted to senior managers. Often business cheques require two signatures before they are valid.

Accounts clerks The accounts clerks will be responsible for all the clerical work, including:
- Preparing invoices
- Preparing customer statements
- Keeping records up to date
- Filing
- Checking invoices received from suppliers
- Preparing cheques for signature
- Reminding customers when payment is due

ACTIVITY

The finance department of Collins Ltd has the following personnel:
- *Finance manager*
- *Chief accountant*
- *Chief cashier*
- *Accounts clerks*, including:
  - *Wages clerk*, responsible for calculating staff pay and preparing payslips.
  - *Purchase ledger clerk*, responsible for keeping records of amounts owing to suppliers, checking invoices received and preparing cheques for payment of suppliers.
  - *Sales ledger clerk*, responsible for keeping customer accounts up to date and reminding customers when payment is due.

The board of directors have made a number of decisions about changes in the accounting system. For each decision (i) state which member or members of the finance department will be affected and (ii) how their job(s) will change as a result.

1. Financial and management accounts will be prepared each month for each department to allow more detailed monitoring of the business.
2. Customers will only be allowed one month's credit in future.
3. Expense claims will no longer be paid in cash, but will be included in wages.
4. Any expense claim from a member of staff over £50 must be checked by the finance manager before payment.
5. The overtime rate for all staff, currently different for different types of work, is to change to one standard rate of £14 per hour.

(2.3.1) (2.3.3)

Administration

A typical structure of the Administration department

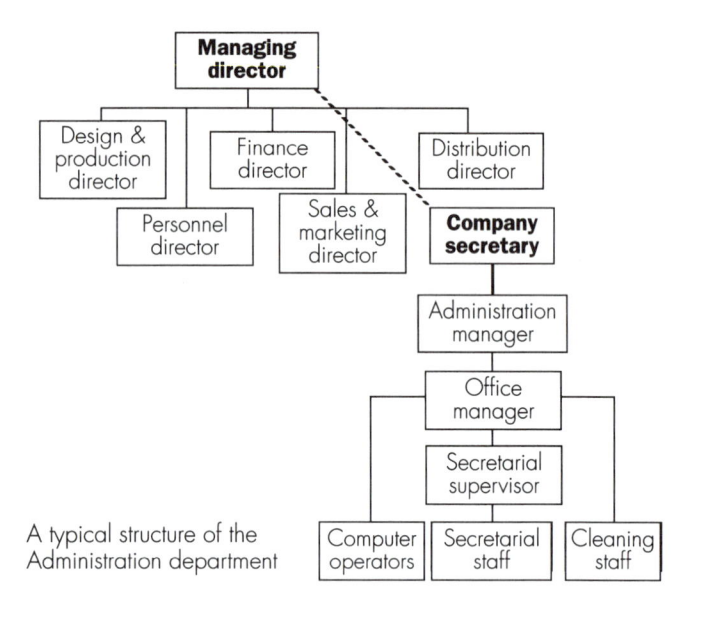

Company secretary It is unusual for the administration department to be represented on the board of directors with an administration director. If there is a senior person who takes responsibility for administration for the whole organisation it is likely to be the company secretary who reports directly to the managing director. All limited companies must have a company secretary by law. As well as keeping minutes of board meetings, the company secretary would oversee administrative affairs, such as pensions, legal matters and the register of shareholders.

Administration manager Each branch or site of the organisation will have an administration manager responsible for the smooth running of that branch. The administration manager should ensure that secretarial, reception, computer, clerical and cleaning staff and technicians are deployed efficiently. Collectively these staff are called *support staff*, since they support the activities of the organisation. The personnel manager discusses with other managers their needs for support staff.

It is often true that administration systems are not noticed unless they go wrong. Of course the administration staff should not be taken for granted, but their job is to make the organisation run as smoothly as possible and sometimes their role is not realised unless a problem arises. Maybe the post is not collected or delivered, or letters are not typed, or telephone messages are not passed on, or the floors are dirty.

The administration manager may also be the line manager of the *computer operators* and *cleaning staff*.

People in Business Organisations

Office manager Office managers take responsibility for the secretarial and clerical staff. They would ensure that work is evenly distributed, that deadlines are met and equipment is kept in working order. They would also check that stocks of stationery are maintained.

Secretarial supervisor and staff The secretarial team would take charge of the following administrative tasks:
- Typing or wordprocessing letters, reports, minutes of meetings etc.
- Collecting letters and parcels for posting, franking them and ensuring they are collected by the Post Office.
- Distributing incoming mail to appropriate departments.
- Photocopying.
- Reception duty.

ACTIVITY

Investigate your school or place of work and list all the tasks carried out by administration staff. What problems would arise if the administration staff all went on holiday at the same time?
(2.3.1) (2.3.3)

Sales and marketing

The sales and marketing department plays a key role in determining the direction of the activities of the entire organisation. Businesses cannot afford to design, produce and launch a new product without first deciding whether people want it. Market research will help to determine what the needs and wants of different groups of people are, and what is currently provided by existing suppliers.

Once the decision has been made to provide a particular service or make a particular product the sales and marketing team need to tell everybody about it. They need to find the customers. The market is likely to be highly competitive. The organisation will be trying to encourage the public to use its product or service instead of those of its competitors. Appropriate advertising and marketing strategies must be found to show why the organisation is the best, the cheapest, the most effective or the most convenient.

Public sector organisations have less need of sales and marketing. However, with increased competition from the private sector, and a growing need to demonstrate public accountability, local authorities and other public sector organisations are using marketing techniques.

Sales and marketing director The sales and marketing director will decide the focus of activity for the whole organisation. In consultation with the other directors, the sales and marketing director will plan the approach to launching new products and continuing promotion of existing ones, and the style in which the organisation will promote itself.

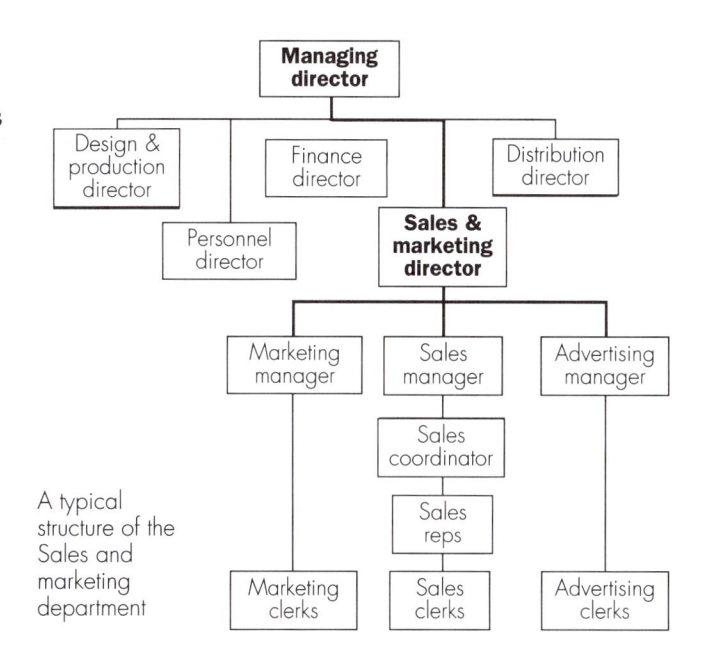

Almost every organisation has a *logo*. The logo is the recognised name and design by which the organisation is known. The logo is part of the corporate image. Its design will say something about the organisation. Occasionally, the business may choose to change its logo, but such a major decision would have to be agreed by the board of directors. The sales and marketing director would decide how the logo would be used in advertising and on the letters and memos of the organisation.

Sales, marketing and advertising managers The three main functions of sales and marketing may be divided between separate managers:
- *Sales* involves finding the customer and making the deal.
- *Marketing* is the more general function of finding out who the customers are likely to be and what they want. This information will be of great importance to the design and production department, providing guidelines for the types of products and prices that people are prepared to pay.
- *Advertising* requires getting the message across to the potential customer in the best possible way using the most appropriate medium (radio, TV, magazines etc.)

The managers will take responsibility for these respective areas within their branch or division. Alternatively the roles may be combined into one manager's job.

Sales teams One common way of finding customers and making sales is to employ a team of *sales representatives* (or reps for short). The sales reps will visit potential customers and, with samples and/or literature, demonstrate the product or service being offered. They may be able to give special discounts and free samples as a method of enticing the customer.

A typical structure of the Sales and marketing department

121

People in Business Organisations

Sales reps may call door-to-door within a geographical area, trying each house in turn for an opportunity to demonstrate and (hopefully) make a sale. Organisations sell encyclopaedias, tea-towels, floor mops and vacuum cleaners in this way. Alternatively, the sales team may work from the office, making telephone calls within a given area in an attempt to arrange to visit the potential customer. This is called *cold-calling*, as the person receiving the call has no prior warning or knowledge. The sales rep will then phone again or plan a visit. Double glazing and financial services are often sold in this manner. Sales reps may also operate in public places, inviting people to sample the goods and collect information.

Selling to other businesses is usually conducted in a different way. The sales reps will normally arrange a visit with someone from the purchasing department of possible buyers and then visit with samples and information.

Sales teams are likely to meet regularly to discuss progress and strategy. The *sales coordinator* will need to ensure that the team is working in a collective fashion. It is common for the coordinator to divide the target regions into geographical areas and assign the reps to a particular area. The rep will then concentrate their activities within that region. The sales coordinator can also report progress to the sales manager.

The *sales clerks* will need to keep an up-to-date record of places visited, telephone numbers rung, people who have been approached and the sales made by each rep. This is particularly important to the reps if they are paid a *commission*. A commission is a bonus based upon the number of sales made.

ACTIVITY

Sales and marketing is becoming increasingly important for public sector organisations. Your school or college and your local authority are likely to have a marketing function. You are required to investigate one of these in order to determine the following for your chosen organisation:
- The job roles in sales and marketing
- The logo it uses
- Methods and examples of advertising
- Examples of promotional material
- Its target market(s)
- New services or products that are being offered

(2.3.1) (2.3.3)

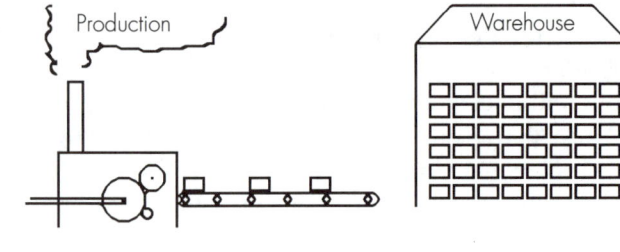

Distribution

Finally, the product has been designed and produced, the market has been identified and the sale has been made. All that remains is for the organisation to make sure that the product is in the right place at the right time. This is the role of the distribution department. Obviously they need to work closely with the production department when checking stock levels and with the sales and marketing team to know when and where the goods need to be delivered.

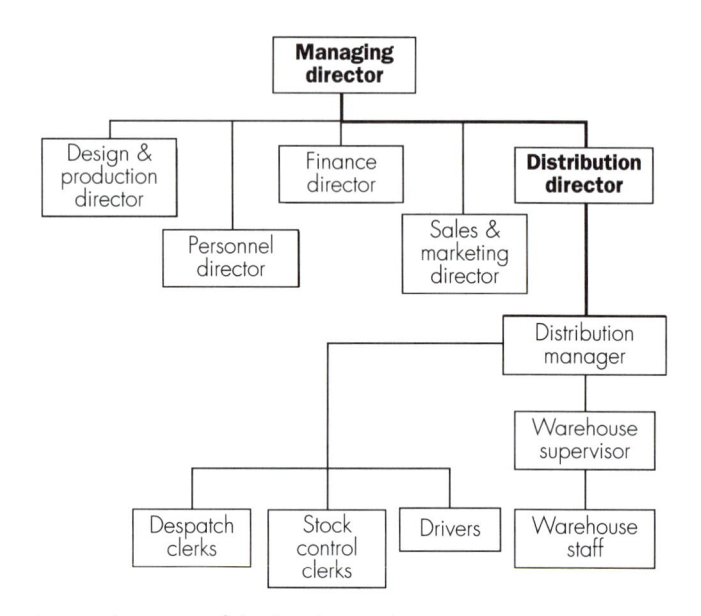

A typical structure of the Distribution department

Distribution director The distribution director is part of the board of directors. He or she decides the overall approach by the organisation to the problems of getting the product out to the customers.

Distribution manager Distribution managers take responsibility for the distribution of goods for a particular division or branch. They will have overall charge of scheduling the distribution of goods.

The role is divided up into two parts:
- Storage
- Transport and delivery

Warehouse team The organisation will normally maintain a level of stock in storage. This is to prevent the situation where the demand for goods cannot be matched by production. Orders can be taken and made up from the warehouse stock, which is

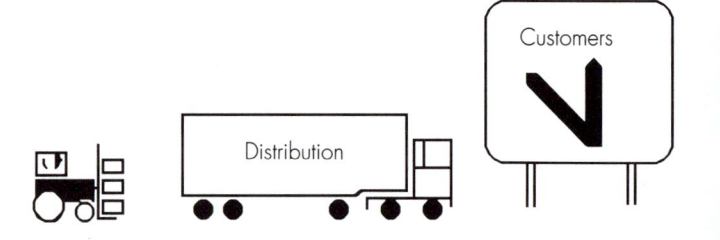

People in Business Organisations

replaced by further production. It is important to operate a suitable *stock control* system. This involves three key aspects:
- Recording stock as it is taken into the warehouse and again when it is despatched. This is necessary to monitor stock levels so that production can be stepped up if necessary to replace diminishing stock. This will be carried out by stock control and despatch clerks.
- *Stock rotation*, which means that old stock is sold first. This prevents stock being held in the warehouse for so long that it becomes outdated or unusable and therefore unsaleable.
- Careful storage so that stock is not damaged. A lot depends upon the nature of the product: food normally needs to be kept at low temperatures to prevent it going off; computer equipment must be handled carefully to prevent damage; and gases and chemicals need to be stored securely to prevent explosion, leakage or damage to the environment.

Distribution team The distribution team has the task of despatching the goods and transporting them to the customer. The same kind of care needs to be taken when transporting goods as when they are stored. No customer wants to receive damaged supplies. The *drivers* need clear instructions on where to take the goods, together with a date and time for delivery. They will normally take a delivery note, which the customer signs in acknowledgement of receipt of the goods (see Unit 4).

ACTIVITY

Distribution does not just take place by road. Some organisations still use canals and horse-drawn carts. Conduct a survey into local businesses to investigate the methods of distribution used. What factors are taken into consideration when deciding the most appropriate form of distribution?
(2.3.1) (2.3.3)

ACTIVITY

You are required investigate a large organisation, which has the following (or similar) departments:
- Personnel
- Administration
- Design and production (these may be separate departments)
- Finance
- Sales and marketing
- Distribution

Remember that organisations tend to be unique in their set-up and may use different titles for their departments.

From your research:
1 Draw an organisation chart.
2 Describe the functions carried out by each department, including an account of how each department relates to the others (how personnel provides training to other departments, how finance sets budgets etc.).
3 Describe the key job roles carried out in each department.
(2.1.3) (2.1.4) (2.3.3)

Tasks undertaken by different role holders

Planning

Planning is an essential part of all business management. To put it simply, it is a matter of deciding how to get to where you want to go. Lack of planning inevitably leads to failure to achieve. This is why action planning is a central feature of GNVQ grading.

Planning is carried out at all levels of the organisation, but at quite differing scales. Directors and senior managers will take a long-term view in their plans. Decisions to invest, for example, in particular projects may be based on a twenty-five year plan, or more. It is common for budgets and forecasting to be prepared for up to five years in the future. All individuals of the organisation must plan in order to be able to work effectively, on either a daily, weekly or monthly basis. For example, work supervisors must plan staffing rotas.

Decision-making

We have already seen one aspect of decision-making in large organisations. Decisions are made all the time and at all levels in the hierarchy. Generally, the senior management team, the directors, are responsible for long-term *strategic* decisions, while the day-to-day decision-making, or *operational* management, is left to the middle managers. But even team members need to make decisions all the time as part of their normal duties.

ACTIVITY

Hargreaves Fabric Ltd is a designer and producer of textiles based in Selby in the north of England. It has been suggested that they change their name to HFL, which is easier to remember.

They are thinking of launching a new kind of fabric, a mixture of elastic and cotton. If they do it will require sending out teams of sales representatives together with a series of advertisements to be run in the national press.

Decide whether each of the following decisions is strategic or operational. Also decide on the person or persons most likely to make that decision, e.g. managing director, board of directors, director of finance or production manager.

123

People in Business Organisations

Decision	Operational or strategic	Most likely decision-maker
To change the name of the organisation		
To launch a new product		
To order more paper for the photocopier		
To write an advertisement for a national newspaper		
To send samples to a particular customer in response to an enquiry		
To send sales reps to a particular town as part of the marketing campaign		

(2.3.4)

One practice which is common to any organisation beyond the smallest sole trader is the act of *delegation*. To delegate means to pass on. Line managers may delegate tasks to people underneath, which means that rather than trying to do everything they pass on some tasks to other people. For example, the marketing director may instruct the marketing manager to start a new marketing campaign. The marketing manager will not do it all – instead the manager will instruct the sales coordinators and the market researchers and the supervisors to do their bit. It is important to remember that *you can only delegate the task, not the responsibility*. As the American President Harry S. Truman once remarked, 'The buck stops here'. The managing director has the ultimate responsibility. If a task is delegated the person who delegates still has the responsibility to ensure that the task is carried out.

Problem-solving

Problem-solving is mostly undertaken by managers. The general problem for them is: how can the targets set by the directors be achieved?

The production manager may be required to increase productivity by 5% and cut the costs of materials by 10%; the personnel manager may be asked to increase staff motivation and reduce staff turnover; and the sales and marketing manager may be expected to raise the image of the organisation. How they are going to achieve these targets involves solving problems.

The process of problem-solving should be systematic. The method a manager adopts to solve a problem might include the following steps:
1. An analysis of the problem
   - What am I expected to achieve?
   - How can success be measured?
2. A consideration of possible solutions, taking into account the costs, time taken, practical problems, skills required etc.
3. Selecting the best possible solution (this involves making a decision!).
4. Monitor the progress and revise the plan if success does not look likely.

The more calm and calculating the problem-solving process is, the more likely the chances of success.

ACTIVITY

Think of some problems that you have to solve. They could involve schoolwork or problems at work, or they might relate to your social or home life. For these problems work through a systematic appraisal as shown above, recording the steps taken and the eventual outcome. If you select genuine problems you should discover that this systematic approach makes for a clearer and more effective decision.
(2.3.4)

Setting targets

The role of setting targets rests chiefly with the directors. This determines the direction the organisation will take. Targets include:
- Reducing costs (wages, salaries, materials, overheads)
- Increasing productivity
- Increasing volume of sales (that is, the number of units sold)
- Increasing value of sales
- Increasing market share
- Diversifying into new markets
- Increasing national or international profile and reputation
- Selling more shares
- Improving customer care

Targets are used in both the public and the private sector, for similar reasons. Failure to set targets can

result in stagnation and falling morale. The reasons for setting targets, therefore, are:
- To improve performance: managers will seek to meet the new targets.
- To measure performance: the targets provide a standard against which to measure actual performance.
- To improve motivation: especially if teams are rewarded for meeting new targets.
- To improve competitiveness: by being able to provide the best service, the best product, at the best prices.

Targets need to have the following features if they are to be of use:
- The targets need to be *precise*. There is no point in telling production managers simply to increase production. They can achieve this by making just one more unit. A 5% increase or an extra 10,000 units, for example, is a much more precise target.
- It follows also that the targets need to be *measurable*. This is not always easy or even possible. How, for example, can you measure an improvement in customer care? You might choose to count the number of complaints that have been successfully dealt with. How could you measure an increase in national reputation?
- The targets need to be *achievable*. There is no point setting targets that are so hard that they cannot realistically be met. The managers will realise this and will not even try. At the same time they should not be too easy, since this will not result in the best possible improvement.

Setting targets and monitoring performance requires up-to-date information. This is normally provided by each department for the finance department.

ACTIVITY

Consider the following targets and suggest a practical way in which they could be measured.

Target *Method of measurement*

Sales & marketing:
- Increase volume of sales
- Increase value of sales
- Increase market share
- Improve customer relations

Administration:
- Improve internal mail system
- Reduce delays in typing

Finance:
- Improve credit control
- Reduce bank charges

Distribution:
- Reduce number of damaged goods
- Improve delivery time

Personnel:
- Improve staff training & development
- Reduce absenteeism

Production:
- Reduce wastage of materials
- Increase productivity
- Improve quality control

(2.3.4)

Achieving targets
It falls mainly on the team members to work towards the targets and try to achieve them. Of course this is only possible if the targets fulfil the criteria outlined above. Some of the targets might be painful to achieve: reducing staff costs by reducing wages or making a number of employees redundant will always be a difficult decision.

People in Business Organisations

Manufacturing staff may be motivated to reach productivity targets by linking it with pay. This can be done in a number of ways:

- *Piecework* or *piece rate*: workers are paid according to the number of units they produce, and the more they make the more they get paid. This is usually applied when workers work from home, where they cannot clock on and off.
- *Productivity bonus*: employees are paid their normal wages plus a bonus if they reach the target.

Similar schemes can be introduced for other employees. Sales reps may receive a *commission*, which is normally a bonus based upon the number of items sold. Other staff may be put on a *performance-related pay* scheme, which means they receive bonuses for meeting targets, and may be penalised for failing to meet them.

ELEMENT 2.4
Prepare for employment or self-employment

Performance criteria

- **PC** 2.4.1 Identify types of employment and self-employment
- **PC** 2.4.2 Identify opportunities for employment or self-employment
- **PC** 2.4.3 Select information from relevant sources which applies to identified employment opportunities
- **PC** 2.4.4 Analyse skills for employment or self-employment
- **PC** 2.4.5 Discuss own strengths and weaknesses in relation to skills for employment or self-employment

Employment and self-employment

Introduction

Very few people are fortunate enough to choose not to work in order to earn their living. Even those who have the choice may recognise the personal advantages that employment offers. Some people will decide to work for someone or for an organisation, while others may prefer to work for themselves and set up their own business alone or in partnership with others. Others still may take the decision to work in order to help others for no reward. Many people will do some or even all of these at some time of their life.

A useful distinction is made between employment and self-employment. The term *employment* will be used to refer to work done by an employee for someone else (the employer). This is to be compared with *self-employment*, which is literally work done for oneself. A self-employed person is their own boss. Self-employed people may be:

- Sole traders
- Partners in a partnership
- Franchisees

The term *freelance* is used to describe a self-employed person who offers their work to other businesses for a fee. They are not employed by any one organisation, but are in effect a sole trader or (if in partnership with others) a partner. (Refer to Unit 1 for a full account of these different kinds of organisations.)

Whichever option you may decide you prefer, it is useful to consider what is involved. The first step is to recognise the types of employment and self-employment that are available to you.

Element 2.4 is aimed at drawing together many of the ideas of the whole GNVQ award and putting them to practical use. The purpose is to help you identify the range of work opportunities available to you so that you can make an informed choice about your future career aspirations. It is also designed to allow you to develop the necessary skills for work. To do this it will be important to identify your own particular strengths and weaknesses.

Some of the considerations which you may take into account when deciding the type of career you wish to follow are likely to include:

1. The rewards (pay, job satisfaction, chances of promotion, benefits)
2. Job security
3. To be employed or self-employed
4. To work in the UK or abroad
5. The nature of the tasks undertaken

When you prepare for work you must be aware of the range of organisations that you can work for. These cut across the public, private and voluntary sectors, as outlined in Unit 1.

Much of the work in this section is of a highly practical nature, inviting you to apply your knowledge in reviewing your own situation and your own employment prospects. You will need to conduct research into employment opportunities. This will involve interviewing other people, as well as collecting background information.

We begin first with an outline of different kinds of employment.

Paid employment

For a lot of people the most interesting parts of employment are when they get paid and how much. We hope to show that these are not the only features, nor even the most important. They might well be what attract you to working in the first place, but there should be more things to keep your interest than money.

In the public and private sectors, people are rewarded for their work by being paid. For employed workers, a *salary* is usually given to clerical and managerial staff, calculated as a fixed annual amount divided into twelve monthly instalments. Alternatively, a *wage* is offered, especially for manual work, normally paid weekly at an hourly rate (based on the number of hours worked) or a piece rate

People in Business Organisations

(based on the number of items completed). Payment may also come in the following forms:
- Holiday pay
- Sick pay
- Maternity pay
- Bonus (a lump-sum reward for meeting targets, for example)
- Commission (a kind of bonus usually based on the number of sales made)
- Golden handshake (as a reward on retirement)
- Golden hello (as an incentive to start work)
- Profit-sharing (in some organisations a portion of the profit is paid to the employees on a agreed basis)
- Expenses (to repay staff for expenses relating to work paid out of their own pocket)
- Benefits in kind (non-monetary reward, such as a company car)

Self-employment
Self-employed people may choose to pay themselves any way they like – wages, salary, bonuses and so on. In effect it makes no difference. As the owner or joint owner of their business they are entitled to the profits or a share of the profits. Any payments they make to themselves for personal use are referred to as *drawings*.

People often start their own business, alone or in partnership, by using their own money and borrowing from family or friends. They may also borrow from the bank. The government helps small businesses during the first most difficult months by offering self-employed people income under the *government enterprise scheme*.

ACTIVITY

As an adviser at a local careers centre you are employed to give advice to people getting jobs or setting up their own business for the first time. You are required to prepare an advice sheet which provides information on:
1. What it means to be employed or self-employment, including how payment might be received
2. The comparative advantages and disadvantages of being employed and self-employed
3. Possible sources of capital for self-employed people, including the government enterprise scheme

(2.4.1)

Voluntary work
In the voluntary sector, unlike the public and private sector, people work for no monetary reward. They offer their services free of charge, or at a rate sufficient only to cover their own expenses. This may involve collecting money for charities, offering help to the sick or elderly, or joining a Neighbourhood Watch scheme.

ACTIVITY

Carry out research into the voluntary sector to enable you to list 10 different such organisations. For two of these describe the job roles undertaken by people working in the organisation.
(2.4.1)

Opportunities for employment and self-employment and sources of information

Having identified the different types of employment it is important now to identify the opportunities that exist for work of any kind. We shall be considering local, national and international opportunities. In each case it is important to identify the appropriate sources of information for seeking details of these opportunities.

Sources of information for jobs can be found in a variety of places, including:
- Job Centres
- Career offices
- Local and national newspapers
- Local and national radio and television
- Training and Enterprise Councils (TEC)
- Charitable organisations
- Banks

Job Centres are usually located in the centre of a town. They are a public sector service provided by the government through the Department of Education and Employment. In a Job Centre you will find a range of jobs advertised with brief details about rates of pay and terms of conditions. The jobs are commonly displayed on postcards in the window and inside the centre, carrying a description of the job but not usually naming the organisation. People who are interested in applying for the posts may receive more information from the assistants, who can arrange interviews for applicants. General advice is also available to people who perhaps are not sure what kinds of jobs they are looking for.

Local authorities provide a careers service principally for school-leavers embarking on their first jobs. The *careers office* will offer general information on the kinds of employment available, helping candidates identify jobs for which they have suitable qualifications and skills. A range of methods may be used to help match the skills and interests of the candidate with possible job options. These include computer applications, psychometric tests and job search methods.

Both *local and national newspapers* advertise jobs for a range of occupations. Generally small local firms will use the local papers to inform people of vacancies for jobs. Larger organisations are likely to use the national papers, particularly when looking for qualified and skilled workers. Many national papers have designated days of the week for specialist occupations. For example, the *Guardian* on

People in Business Organisations

Tuesday is dedicated to jobs in education. In addition there are a range of specialist publications which promote available jobs in particular vocations. Examples include the *Times Educational Supplement*, *Computer Weekly* and *Campaign* (for sales and marketing posts).

Occasionally jobs are advertised on *local and national radio and television*. Because this kind of advertising is very expensive it is not used very often and is not likely to be a major source of information.

The *Training Enterprise Council* is a government initiative which seeks to promote and develop education and training on a regional basis for people in and out of employment. One current development aimed at supporting school-leavers is the Modern Apprenticeship Scheme. This scheme provides training on and off the job and helps young people develop the necessary skills and expertise for their chosen occupation.

A range of *charitable organisations* exist which provide opportunities and information for many people. For example, Voluntary Service Overseas (VSO) is an organisation established to provide training, education and support to Third World nations. Other voluntary organisations, such as the Prince's Youth Business Trust and the Federation for the Self-Employed, seek to promote enterprise skills with would-be entrepreneurs hoping to launch their own business initiatives.

Most high street banks provide a range of services for those who may be considering self-employment. All the leading commercial banks are very much in the business of lending money and many have special schemes to meet the needs of small businesses. Competition is intense and it is advisable to shop around to find the best services.

ACTIVITY

Identify possible reference sources which you could use and organisations to contact in order to find out information about:
1 Seasonal jobs in the tourist industry
2 Training schemes for school leavers
3 A job as a computer operator
4 Opportunities abroad
5 Advice about becoming self-employed
6 A career as a clerical officer with the Civil Service
7 Further opportunities in education
8 A career in finance
9 Joining the police force
10 Other career opportunities
(2.4.3)

Skills, abilities, strengths and weaknesses

Making a decision about your future career is not easy. There are many opportunities available and important decisions have to be made. Should you stay on at school and gain further qualifications? Should you get a job and continue your education on a part-time basis? What type of job do you want to apply for? Do you want to work for yourself or for someone else? These are the types of questions you need to be considering over the next few years. Many people will be able to help and advise you when making that decision – your parents, teachers, careers officers etc. – but the final decision is yours.

The following activities have been devised to try to help you find out about yourself in order that you can make an informed decision about your future career. By getting you to focus on the kinds of things that you are good at, your skills and experience and your weaknesses too, you will be better able to identify the types of jobs which you are most suited to.

ACTIVITY

Who am I?
Produce a table which lists all the things which you think represent your strengths or that you enjoy. The list should include:
- Subjects at school
- Qualifications
- Interests and hobbies
- Part-time work
- Sports and other activities

Using the same headings, identify the areas which you think represent your weaknesses or things which you don't particularly enjoy.

What are my skills?
An important part of your GNVQ Business course is helping you to develop a range of skills in preparation for employment or self-employment. This activity will provide you with an opportunity to reflect upon how well you have developed those skills and how useful they will be in your chosen occupation.

Copy out and complete the following table by identifying how confident you are about your ability to perform the skills listed. Put a tick in the column that represents how you feel about your ability to perform each one.

Use the completed table to identify your main strengths and weaknesses.

People in Business Organisations

Skill	Very confident	Confident	Need to improve
Action planning	☐	☐	☐
Working with others	☐	☐	☐
Working independently	☐	☐	☐
Managing my time	☐	☐	☐
Prioritising	☐	☐	☐
Making decisions	☐	☐	☐
Solving problems	☐	☐	☐
Taking responsibility	☐	☐	☐
Finding and using information	☐	☐	☐
Evaluating	☐	☐	☐

Communication

Writing in formal business style:

	Very confident	Confident	Need to improve
letters	☐	☐	☐
memos	☐	☐	☐
reports	☐	☐	☐

Participating in business meetings:

	Very confident	Confident	Need to improve
organising meetings	☐	☐	☐
taking minutes	☐	☐	☐
contributing ideas	☐	☐	☐
making decisions	☐	☐	☐

Oral presentations:

	Very confident	Confident	Need to improve
one to one	☐	☐	☐
to a small group	☐	☐	☐
to a large group	☐	☐	☐
Listening to others	☐	☐	☐
Telephone skills	☐	☐	☐

Application of number

Calculations:

	Very confident	Confident	Need to improve
mental arithmetic	☐	☐	☐
using a calculator	☐	☐	☐
Using formulae	☐	☐	☐
Interpreting data	☐	☐	☐

Information technology

	Very confident	Confident	Need to improve
Word processing	☐	☐	☐
Spreadsheets	☐	☐	☐
Graphics	☐	☐	☐
Databases	☐	☐	☐

The perfect post
This activity will enable you to identify the key features and characteristics that you would like to find in your ideal job.

Task 1
Rate each of the aspects of work given below on the following basis:
1 Highly desirable aspect of the job
2 Desirable aspect of the job
3 No strong preference or dislike
4 Undesirable aspect of the job
5 Highly undesirable aspect of the job

The organisation	1	2	3	4	5

How do I feel about a job working:

	1	2	3	4	5
in a large organisation	☐	☐	☐	☐	☐
in a medium size organisation	☐	☐	☐	☐	☐
in a small organisation	☐	☐	☐	☐	☐
from home	☐	☐	☐	☐	☐
for the private sector	☐	☐	☐	☐	☐
for the public sector	☐	☐	☐	☐	☐
outside	☐	☐	☐	☐	☐
inside	☐	☐	☐	☐	☐
in an office	☐	☐	☐	☐	☐
in a shop	☐	☐	☐	☐	☐
in a bank	☐	☐	☐	☐	☐
locally	☐	☐	☐	☐	☐
nationally	☐	☐	☐	☐	☐
internationally	☐	☐	☐	☐	☐
other places of work:					

Working arrangements	1	2	3	4	5

How do I feel about a job which involves working:

	1	2	3	4	5
full-time	☐	☐	☐	☐	☐
part-time	☐	☐	☐	☐	☐
on a fixed-term contract	☐	☐	☐	☐	☐
on a permanent contract	☐	☐	☐	☐	☐
flexi-hours	☐	☐	☐	☐	☐
in a team	☐	☐	☐	☐	☐
independently	☐	☐	☐	☐	☐
for myself	☐	☐	☐	☐	☐
for others	☐	☐	☐	☐	☐
with people of my own age	☐	☐	☐	☐	☐
with people of all ages	☐	☐	☐	☐	☐
mostly with males	☐	☐	☐	☐	☐
mostly with females	☐	☐	☐	☐	☐
with males and females	☐	☐	☐	☐	☐

Nature of the job	1	2	3	4	5

How important to me is:

	1	2	3	4	5
working with animals	☐	☐	☐	☐	☐
working with children	☐	☐	☐	☐	☐
working with old people	☐	☐	☐	☐	☐
working with the general public	☐	☐	☐	☐	☐
working with business people	☐	☐	☐	☐	☐
making decisions on my own	☐	☐	☐	☐	☐
working with supervision	☐	☐	☐	☐	☐
manual work	☐	☐	☐	☐	☐
clerical work	☐	☐	☐	☐	☐
simple, routine tasks	☐	☐	☐	☐	☐
complicated, demanding tasks	☐	☐	☐	☐	☐
working with computers	☐	☐	☐	☐	☐
working with figures	☐	☐	☐	☐	☐
working with documents	☐	☐	☐	☐	☐
communicating with customers	☐	☐	☐	☐	☐

People in Business Organisations

Task 2
Summarise those aspects of the job which you have awarded a 1 or 2.

Task 3
Using the analysis and research you have carried out as part of this and the previous activities, produce a master checklist outlining your main strengths, skills, characteristics and preferences.

Task 4
Undertake research into job opportunities at a local, national and international level using the sources suggested, and match them against your own criteria from task 3.
(2.4.1) (2.4.2) (2.4.3) (2.4.4) (2.4.5)

ELEMENT ACTIVITY

(2.4.1–5)

'All our working lives'

Task 1
Identify three different jobs which you might be interested in pursuing for a future career. If there are many jobs which you are interested in, choose three which are very different in nature.

Make contact with people currently working in those jobs. This may involve you making telephone calls, writing letters or using personal contacts. Organise an interview with each person to determine:
1 How they came to be in their current employment
2 The tasks undertaken as part of the job
3 A summary of the skills needed to undertake the job effectively
4 Opportunities for promotion and progression
5 Details of the organisation they work for (including name, size, nature of business, type of organisation, chain of command, structure)
6 Working arrangements (part-time, full-time, flexi-time, working from home, temporary, permanent, team work, individual work etc.)

If you have an interest in working for yourself make sure that one of your interviewees is self-employed.

Task 2
Having carried out these interviews, analyse whether you have the appropriate skills, qualifications and experience to gain employment in the jobs. Produce a chart showing the skills needed for the three jobs and match against your own achievements, strengths and weaknesses. Identify which skills need to be improved and developed and how you can achieve this.

Task 3
Produce an action plan setting targets and goals which you must accomplish in order to pursue a career in the areas chosen.

Task 4
Identify a range of job opportunities in these careers at a local, national and international level. Your research may include job advertisements, media articles and careers information.

Task 5
Produce a checklist of the 10 most important things you should research about an organisation and the job before going for an interview.

Task 6
Produce a CV (curriculum vitae) and letter of application which could be used when applying for one of the positions you have researched.

UNIT ACTIVITY

(2.1.1–5, 2.2.1–4, 2.3.1–5, 2.4.1–5)

You are employed by Fiery Eye Ltd, a medium-sized manufacturer of kaleidoscopes, telescopes and binoculars. They have a number of branches in the Midlands.

You are employed as the personnel assistant for the Wolverhampton division. The organisational structure for the Wolverhampton branch is shown opposite.

The organisation is currently undertaking a major recruitment drive to employ new employees in all departments to cope with increased demand. As the personnel assistant you are expected to help in every way with this.

1 The interviews are being conducted over a period of several weeks. Groups of candidates arrive at the start of the day to look around and learn about the organisation. It is part of your job to describe the way the organisation is structured in a five-minute presentation to a group of interviewees. *(2.3.5)*

Your first task, therefore, is to prepare a five-minute presentation as an introduction to the organisation that addresses the following issues:
(a) The organisational structure is described and illustrated. *(2.1.1) (2.1.2)*
(b) Different working arrangements are described. *(2.1.4)*
(c) The different departments are identified and described, with a brief outline of the functions played by each department. *(2.1.3)*

2 The interviews have proved successful and this has led to a large number of new members of staff. Many of the new employees have recently graduated from university and have never been in full-time employment before. The personnel manager suggests that it would be useful to prepare an employees' handbook that describes

People in Business Organisations

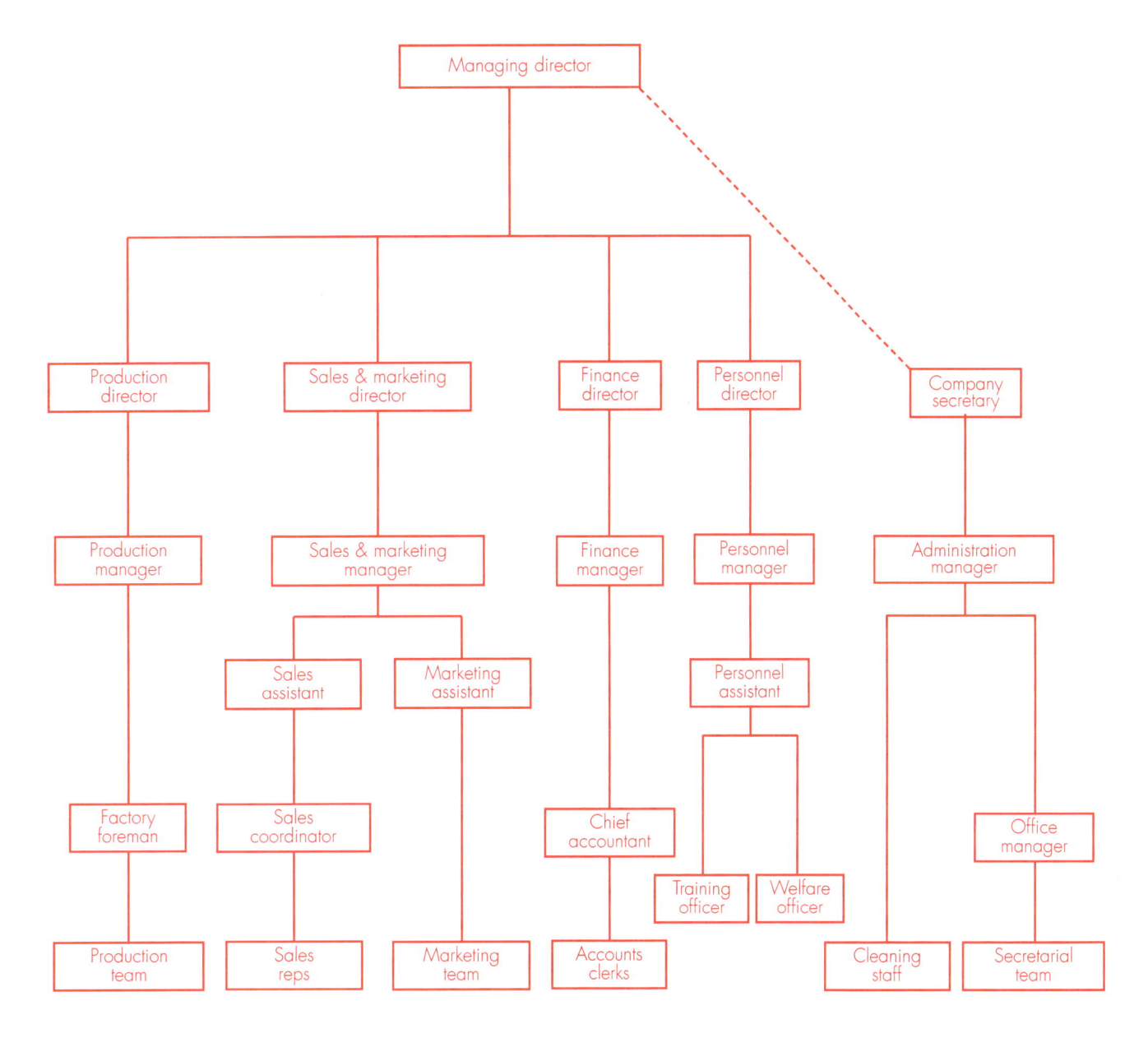

```
                        Managing director
     ┌──────────┬──────────────┬──────────┬──────────┐
  Production  Sales &       Finance   Personnel   Company
  director    marketing     director  director    secretary
              director
     │          │              │          │          │
  Production  Sales &       Finance   Personnel   Administration
  manager     marketing     manager   manager     manager
              manager
     │          ├────┬─────┐    │         │          │
              Sales  Marketing            Personnel
              assistant assistant         assistant
     │          │                │         │          │
  Factory    Sales                      Chief                    Office
  foreman    coordinator                accountant               manager
                                          ├──────┬─────┐
                                        Training  Welfare
                                        officer   officer
     │          │         │              │                │          │
  Production  Sales    Marketing      Accounts         Cleaning   Secretarial
  team        reps     team           clerks           staff      team
```

the roles and responsibilities of employers and employees, with an outline of appropriate employment legislation.

Your second task, therefore, is to prepare an employees' handbook which clearly describes the following issues:

(a) Employee rights and responsibilities. *(2.2.4)*
(b) Employer rights and responsibilities. *(2.2.3)*
(c) Relevant employment legislation. *(2.2.4)*
(d) The benefits of employer/employee cooperation. *(2.2.1)*
(e) Ways to resolve disagreements. *(2.2.2)*

3 The final stage in the reorganisation and growth of the division is to set up a whole new department: distribution. This will involve appointing people at all levels, from a director for distribution right down to lorry drivers. You are required to help with writing job descriptions for three positions:
- Distribution director
- Middle manager in distribution (for Wolverhampton branch)
- Distribution team members (warehouse clerks)

Your third and final task, therefore, is to write job descriptions for these posts, concentrating on the following issues:

(a) The job roles. *(2.3.1) (2.3.4)*
(b) The functions of the job roles. *(2.3.3) (2.3.4)*
(c) The tasks undertaken by the different roles. *(2.3.2)*

4 The reorganisation has caused some anxiety among existing employees who are concerned about job security. They think that changes in working arrangements can only mean loss of jobs.

Your next task is to draft a newsletter which explains to the employees that changes have been necessary to working arrangements in order to improve *productivity*, maintain *quality*, remain *competitive* and introduce new *technology*. There is no threat to the security of jobs. *(2.1.5)*

5 Gretl, a friend of yours, has come up with an idea for a computerised comic book. She developed

People in Business Organisations

this at home for her children and thinks it has great potential as a new toy. She wants to know whether the directors of Fiery Eye will be interested in buying the idea. However, you realise that it is not within their usual product range.

Gretl has come to you for advice. One option she is thinking about is to resign from her existing job and set up business on her own, manufacturing and marketing her new product. She asks you whether you would like to join her business as a partner, given your experience of working with children's toys. Alternatively she might try to sell the idea to a business like Fiery Eye Ltd.

You have to decide what you and Gretl should do.

(a) What do you think are the opportunities for marketing the product, in this country and abroad? *(2.4.2)*

(b) If you decide to go self-employed, what are the types of organisations which you could form with Gretl? List the advantages and disadvantages of employment and self-employment. *(2.4.1)*

(c) Produce a table which describes the main features and skills of employment and self-employment. *(2.4.4)*

(d) Make a list of your own strengths and weaknesses in relation to the skills needed for (i) employment and (ii) self-employment. *(2.4.5)*

(e) What sources of information might help you in deciding whether to remain employed or go self-employed? *(2.4.3)*

Based on your research state whether you decide to remain with Fiery Eye Ltd or take the plunge with Gretl.

Remember to check with the unit specifications and the range statements to ensure that the evidence you produce is sufficient across the whole range.

MULTIPLE CHOICE

1. Which of the following is the role of a manager?
   A Make policy statements
   B Translate policy statements into working practice
   C Ensure activities are carried out
   D Carry out routine tasks according to instructions

2. Setting targets is principally the role of:
   A Directors
   B Managers
   C Supervisors
   D Team members

3. The manager of a marketing department is responsible for:
   A Credit control
   B Ensuring customers receive their goods on time
   C Advertising the organisation's product
   D Providing support staff for clerical duties

4. Recruitment and training are the responsibility of which department?
   A Personnel
   B Finance
   C Administration
   D Distribution

5. The responsibility for running a department is normally given to a:
   A Director
   B Shop steward
   C Supervisor
   D Manager

6. A good team leader should:
   A Make all the decisions on behalf of the team
   B Take no part in making decisions
   C Put all decisions to a vote and go with the majority
   D Involve the team in decision-making but take final responsibility

7. The best approach to problem-solving is:
   A A systematic and calm approach
   B Trusting intuition
   C Change your mind many times
   D Ignore the problem and hope it will solve itself

8. One reason for setting targets is to:
   A Reduce tax liability
   B Fulfil legal obligations
   C Improve performance
   D Increase the use of raw materials in production

9. If someone 'delegates' a task it means that they:
   A Pass the responsibility on to someone else
   B Inform their line manager that the task is too difficult
   C Instruct someone below them in the organisational structure to carry out the task
   D Only carry out the task when they have finished what they are doing

10. An organisation produces industrial steel girders for construction of large buildings. An appropriate method for the sales reps to adopt would be:
    A Door-to-door calls in the town centre
    B Mailshot to major construction companies followed by a personal telephone call
    C Display of samples in the local shopping centre
    D Adverts on local radio and in local daily newspaper

UNIT TEST: People in business organisations

1. Decide whether each of these statements is True (T) or False (F):
   (i) In a hierarchical organisational structure there are many layers of authority.
   (ii) In a flat organisational structure each employee has more than one line manager.
   Which option best describes the two statements?
   - A (i) T (ii) T
   - B (i) T (ii) F
   - C (i) F (ii) T
   - D (i) F (ii) F

2. One common problem for large organisations with flat organisational structures is:
   - A Poor communication from top to bottom
   - B Difficult for staff to achieve promotion
   - C A very high cost of middle managers' salaries
   - D Slow movement of information between departments

Questions 3–5 share answer options A–D:
Decision-making in organisations can be carried out in a number of different ways. Four different styles of decision-making are described below:
- A The managing director alone makes all the decisions
- B Employees are sometimes consulted on some decisions
- C Important decisions are decided by a majority vote of the employees
- D Decisions for the whole organisation are made by individual managers in rotation

What styles of decision-making do the following terms refer to?

3. Participative
4. Autocratic
5. Democratic

Questions 6–8 share answer options A–D:
An organisation is expanding. It has new products to sell and is taking on new staff. This will involve a lot of new activities by different departments. Some of the departments involved in the expansion include:
- A Personnel
- B Sales and marketing
- C Finance
- D Distribution

Which department will be responsible for the following activities?

6. Recruiting new staff
7. Advertising the new products
8. Providing training for the new staff

9. A manufacturing organisation has made the decision to launch a new product. Decide whether each of these statements is True (T) or False (F):
   (i) The sales department will be responsible for taking the product to the customers
   (ii) The production department will be responsible for ensuring that stocks of the new product are large enough
   Which option best describes the two statements?
   - A (i) T (ii) T
   - B (i) T (ii) F
   - C (i) F (ii) T
   - D (i) F (ii) F

10. Decide whether each of these statements is True (T) or False (F):
    (i) Deciding company policy is the main role of the managers
    (ii) Carrying out routine tasks is the role of team members
    Which option best describes the two statements?
    - A (i) T (ii) T
    - B (i) T (ii) F
    - C (i) F (ii) T
    - D (i) F (ii) F

11. Staff training is one of the roles of:
    - A Personnel manager
    - B Staff welfare officer
    - C Staff development officer
    - D Recruitment assistant

12. An advertising manager would work in the:
    - A Finance department
    - B Sales and marketing department
    - C Administration department
    - D Personnel department

13. An organisation has six main departments, as shown in the diagram:

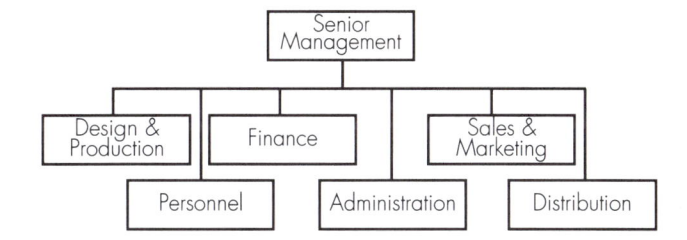

    Senior Management
    ├── Design & Production
    │   └── Personnel
    ├── Finance
    │   └── Administration
    └── Sales & Marketing
        └── Distribution

    Decide whether each of these statements is True (T) or False (F):
    (i) If the sales manager is experiencing difficulties with the departmental secretary the matter should first of all be reported to the marketing and sales director
    (ii) Each department will work independently of the others
    Which option best describes the two statements?
    - A (i) T (ii) T
    - B (i) T (ii) F
    - C (i) F (ii) T
    - D (i) F (ii) F

14. The main task of directors is:
    - A Decision-making
    - B Problem solving
    - C Setting targets
    - D Achieving targets

15. A company has decided to change its logo (the design of its name as it will appear on headed notepaper, advertising material, packaging,

133

People in Business Organisations

documents etc.). Decide whether each of these statements is True (T) or False (F):
(i) The decision to change the logo will be made by the sales and marketing manager
(ii) All departments will need to use the new logo when it has been designed and agreed
Which option best describes the two statements?
A (i) T   (ii) T
B (i) T   (ii) F
C (i) F   (ii) T
D (i) F   (ii) F

16 One of the tasks of the finance director in a large organisation is to:
A Prepare wage slips for the employees
B Authorise petty cash payments
C Send reminders to customers whose accounts are overdue
D Fix budgets for all departments

17 One of the tasks of the office manager in the personnel function is to:
A Type routine letters and memos
B Plan the use of administrative staff throughout the organisation
C Organise the jobs to be carried out by the office secretaries
D Authorise orders for new office equipment

18 Meeting visitors at the entrance of the building is one of the jobs of the:
A Personnel assistant
B Receptionist
C Marketing manager
D Managing director

19 Ensuring that customers receive goods on time is the responsibility of:
A Sales manager
B Accounts clerk
C Distribution manager
D Marketing director

20 Decide whether each of these statements is True (T) or False (F):
(i) A strategic manager is involved in planning the activities of individual departments
(ii) An operational manager is responsible for organising teams of people
Which option best describes the two statements?
A (i) T   (ii) T
B (i) T   (ii) F
C (i) F   (ii) T
D (i) F   (ii) F

21 Decide whether each of these statements is True (T) or False (F):
(i) An organisation that provides a service will not need a sales and marketing department
(ii) An organisation in the public sector will not need a finance department
Which option best describes the two statements?
A (i) T   (ii) T
B (i) T   (ii) F
C (i) F   (ii) T
D (i) F   (ii) F

22 Decide whether each of these statements is True (T) or False (F):
(i) An employee may be fairly dismissed if they take part in unofficial strike action
(ii) An employee who works part-time is not entitled to any maternity leave
Which option best describes the two statements?
A (i) T   (ii) T
B (i) T   (ii) F
C (i) F   (ii) T
D (i) F   (ii) F

Questions 23–25 share answer options A–D:
Below are some of the important pieces of legislation protecting employees' rights:
A Sex Discrimination Act
B Health and Safety at Work etc. Act
C Race Relations Act
D Trade Union Reform and Employment Rights Act
Which law gives employees the following rights?

23 All employees working more than eight hours a week are entitled to a written statement of employment

24 Employees must be provided with protective clothing if their job requires it

25 The possibility of having a baby in the future cannot be used as a basis for withholding promotion

26 Decide whether each of these statements is True (T) or False (F):
(i) An employee is entitled to refuse to carry out routine tasks on the grounds that they are not included in their contract of employment
(ii) If duties which are dangerous to health are included in a contract of employment, an employee may legally refuse to carry them out
Which option best describes the two statements?
A (i) T   (ii) T
B (i) T   (ii) F
C (i) F   (ii) T
D (i) F   (ii) F

27 Repetitive strain injury (RSI) is likely to be caused by:
A Sitting too close to a computer screen
B Long periods of typing without a break
C Working in a badly lit office
D Returning to work after a long holiday

28 Decide whether each of these statements is True (T) or False (F):
(i) An employer is entitled to make deductions from an employee's wages without prior agreement
(ii) An employee working more than eight hours per week is entitled to a printed wage slip showing the deductions which have been made
Which option best describes the two statements?
A (i) T   (ii) T
B (i) T   (ii) F
C (i) F   (ii) T
D (i) F   (ii) F

People in Business Organisations

29 The health and safety of the working environment is the responsibility of:
   A The employers only
   B The employees only
   C The employers and the employees
   D The safety representatives only

30 A new employee starts work at a large industrial plant.
   Decide whether each of these statements is True (T) or False (F):
   (i) The employee can be dismissed by the employers for refusing to join the trade union
   (ii) After joining the trade union the employee can be disciplined by the union for refusing to take part in industrial action
   Which option best describes the two statements?
   A (i) T   (ii) T
   B (i) T   (ii) F
   C (i) F   (ii) T
   D (i) F   (ii) F

31 One of the implied conditions of a contract of employment is that the employee will:
   A Carry out any order they are asked to do
   B Break the law on behalf of their employer if necessary
   C Dress appropriately
   D Pay for safety equipment needed to carry out the job

32 A new finance director takes over at an organisation and wants to make a few changes.
   Decide whether each of these statements is True (T) or False (F):
   (i) The finance director can pay employees who carry out the same tasks different rates of pay in order to save money
   (ii) The finance director can insist that employees contribute to a private pension scheme
   Which option best describes the two statements?
   A (i) T   (ii) T
   B (i) T   (ii) F
   C (i) F   (ii) T
   D (i) F   (ii) F

33 An employer can take disciplinary action against an employee if the employee
   A Joins a trade union
   B Refuses to work overtime
   C Requires training to cope with new technology
   D Does not work to the terms and conditions of their contract

Questions 34–36 share answer options A–D:
Remuneration to employees can take a number of forms including:
   A SMP
   B Piecework payments
   C Holiday pay
   D Productivity bonus
Which of these would be paid to an employee:

34 Taking time off to have a baby?
35 As basic wages according to the number of units made?
36 Producing more units in a given period of time?

37 Which of the following may be deducted from an employee's pay without their permission?
   A Charitable donations
   B Contributions to a company pension scheme
   C PAYE
   D Union subscriptions

🔑 Key terms

ACAS
Achieving targets
Administration function (or department)
Autocratic leadership style
Batch production
Centralised
Chain of command
Circular
Citizen's Charter 1991
Collective bargaining
Compulsory deductions from wages
Computer-aided design (CAD)
Contract of employment
Curriculum vitae (CV)
Decentralised
Deductions at source
Delegation of duties
Democratic leadership style
Design and production function (or department)
Director
Disciplinary action and procedures
Distribution function (or department)
Employment Act 1990
Employment Protection (Consolidation) Act 1978
Equal opportunities
Finance function (or department)
Flat organisation structure
Flow production
Fringe benefits
Grievance procedures
Health and Safety at Work etc. Act 1974
Hierarchical organisation structure
Human resource management
Job description
Job production
Job roles

Just-in-time purchasing
Letters of application
Line manager
Lines of authority
Management information system (MIS)
Managers
Marketing function (or department)
Matrix
National Insurance
Operators
Organisational chart
Organisational structure
Participative leadership style
Pay scales
PAYE
Person specification
Personnel function (or department)
Problem solving
Proprietor
Quality control
Race Relations Act 1976
Recruitment
Remuneration
Service staff
Setting targets
Sex Discrimination Act 1986
Span of control
Staff appraisal
Staff development
Statutory maternity pay (SMP)
Statutory sick pay (SSP)
Supervisors
Support staff
Team members
Trade Union and Labour Relations Act 1992
Trade Union Reform and Employment Rights Act 1994
Voluntary deductions from wages
Wages Act 1986

UNIT 3

Consumers and Customers

UNIT SUMMARY

Organisations in both the public and the private sectors need to meet the demands of their customers. If they do not they can never be successful. In the public sector the general public will complain to the government about the poor service being offered and the government will take steps to make sure that the situation improves. After all, public sector organisations are spending public money, so it is important to provide a service that meets their needs and wants. In the private sector, if a business cannot satisfy customer requirements then someone else will. The customer will go elsewhere and the business will lose the sale. It is vital then that businesses focus on their customers and their needs and wants. This unit investigates ways of identifying customer needs and the best ways to satisfy them. This unit is tested externally, and example test questions are provided at the end of the unit.

ELEMENT 3.1
Explain the importance of consumers and customers

Performance criteria

- **PC** 3.1.1 Describe the effect of consumers on sales of goods and services
- **PC** 3.1.2 Identify and explain the buying habits of consumers with different characteristics
- **PC** 3.1.3 Identify trends in consumer demand
- **PC** 3.1.4 Produce graphics to illustrate the trends
- **PC** 3.1.5 Explain causes of change in consumer demand for consumer goods and services
- **PC** 3.1.6 Explain and give examples of the importance of customers to business organisations

Consumers and Customers

Characteristics of consumers

Introduction

'The customer is always right' is a famous expression which helps to explain how important it is for the organisation to be aware of who their customers are and what their customers want. A *customer* or *consumer* is 'the person who is going to buy and/or use the product or service that is being designed, produced and marketed by an organisation'. An organisation needs to be aware of the changing needs, wants and ability to purchase of a consumer or customer in order to satisfy that consumer or customer profitably.

Society is always changing, and so are the habits and needs of consumers. Organisations are increasingly aware of the need to continually research, market and analyse consumers' perceptions and demands in order to provide products and services that will be bought and used. If an organisation wants to be successful it cannot assume that it knows better than the consumer. An organisation would not be able to survive if it did not respond to the needs of its customers. It is therefore important that an organisation is able to identify:

- Who its customers are
- The changing trends in consumer demand for goods and services

The importance of consumers and customers

A useful distinction is made between customers and consumers.

The *customer* is the person or organisation that pays for the goods or services. The *consumer*, who is often the same person as the customer but not always, is the person or organisation which actually uses (or 'consumes') the goods or services.

For example, for children's sweets the customers (very often the parents) are not the same as the consumers (children). This distinction becomes important when thinking of marketing the product. Sweets have to appeal to children, but must also be acceptable to parents.

Consumers, therefore, play a key role. They are responsible firstly for *creating demand* – an organisation will only provide goods and services which meet the demands of the consumer. Secondly, consumers are responsible for causing *change in demand*. As the tastes of consumers change demand for goods and services changes. An organisation needs to anticipate those changes where possible and respond to them by supplying what the consumer wants. Hence, consumers are also responsible for *stimulating supply* of goods and services to meet demand.

Weak and strong demand

Demand can be defined as being either weak or strong. *Weak demand* is demand for goods or services which is not matched by an ability to pay at the market price. Consumers may demand a new car every year, but find themselves unable to afford it. Their demand, therefore, is only weak demand. *Strong demand* is for goods and services that consumers are both able and willing to purchase at the price set by suppliers.

There are a number of factors which affect the level of demand for goods and services. The *level of income* of customers affects their ability to make purchases. Therefore, the higher the income, the greater the potential to demand goods and services of different types and demonstrate strong demand. People on low incomes are less able to purchase and therefore their demand is weaker.

Social or religious convention also affects the strength of demand. For example, there will be weak demand for alcoholic drinks in a Muslim community and a stronger demand in communities where drink is freely permitted.

Consumers and Customers

The strength of demand may also be affected by changes in *taste* or *fashion*. Demand for CD records is growing as consumer preferences change and vinyl records decline in popularity. Organisations need to be sensitive to changes in consumer tastes and fashion in order that they can anticipate and respond to customer needs and wants.

You should remember that demand is customer led. Organisations respond by supplying what customers want. Customer demand creates the supply, not the other way round.

ACTIVITY

It is often said that the customer is always right. This is because the consumer and customer play such an important role in any organisation.

Imagine that you are employed in an organisation which seems to have forgotten the importance of its customers. The organisation designs and manufactures computer components. It is more interested in productivity targets, efficient administration, working conditions, pay rises and long holidays.

One employee has been quoted as saying: 'We haven't got time to worry about the needs of the customer – we've got more important problems of our own!'. Another employee has said: 'We know what our customers want, we've been in this business for years. It is just a matter of telling the customer what they want!'.

Your task is to produce a newsletter to all employees which outlines the importance of the customer to the business and the effect that the consumer has on demand for goods and services. (3.1.1) (3.1.6)

Who are our customers?

'Who are our customers?' is a quotation that you might hear discussed at many board meetings. All organisations, large and small, are faced with the task of identifying who their customers are.

ACTIVITY

Individually identify four products or services that you have bought in the last week. Write down the name of the product or service, your reason for buying it and why you chose the particular organisation from which you made your purchase. Compare your findings with other individuals in your group and with your partners, relatives and friends. Using the information copy out and complete the following table:

Age and background of the customer:
Product or service bought:
Price paid:
Organisation:
Reason for purchase:

What interesting trends emerge and what does it tell you about customers and who they are? (3.1.2)

Customers can be characterised using a variety of headings. These may include:
- Age
- Sex
- Socioeconomic group
- Tastes and trends
- Income
- Lifestyle

Every individual is different, but by classifying according to these headings organisations are able to research consumer behaviour and purchasing patterns and draw some general conclusions about buying habits.

Age

Organisations need to be aware of the age group to which their product or service appeals so that they can cater to the needs and wants of their customers. For example, a customer who purchases an item of clothing from Marks & Spencer may well be older than the customer who regularly shops at Wallis or Next.

Similarly, Radio 1 tends to attract a younger listener than Radio 2. The larger organisations tend to have a range of merchandise that caters for all different age groups. On walking into the music department of WH Smith you will find CDs and cassettes for all generations, appealing from the very young right up to the very old.

ACTIVITY

1. Think of six different products or services which appeal to different age groups. Make a note of the products or services and the age group to which they appeal with possible reasons. Share your ideas with other students in the group.
2. Look at the following table. Identify the age group of the likely customer for each product or service, and note any other features that might characterise them (*do you think they are male or female, 'brainy', trendy, square, with a family, single, left-wing, conservative, or what . . .?*)

139

Consumers and Customers

Product or service	Age group	Other features
Heinz baked beans		
U2 CD		
Window cleaning		
MOT service		
Mortgage services		
Avon cosmetics		
Nappies		
Pint of lager		
Public transport		
Football season ticket		
Almay cosmetics		
Classical music CD		

3 Some products or services are produced for the younger age group but very often it is the parents or adults who actually buy them. Can you think of examples where this is the case? How should organisations market or advertise products or services where the purchaser may be different from the user?

4 Organisations are very often criticised for advertising toys and games during children's television time. Identify the reasons why organisations can be criticised for this and suggest recommendations that you would put forward to solve the problems.
(3.1.2)

Sex
In addition to catering for different age groups, organisations often design, produce and advertise products or services for either the male or female market. For example the sale of perfume and aftershave is aimed at specific *sex* groupings.

ACTIVITY

Think of five products or services that are aimed at either the male or female market, giving reasons why. Share your ideas with others in your group.
(3.1.2)

In segmenting the market in this way the organisations need to be aware that in many cases it is the opposite sex who actually buys the product or service and therefore it needs to appeal to both parties. In addition, it is becoming increasingly fashionable for women to buy and use men's products (e.g. men's jeans and jumpers are often bought and worn by women) and organisations need to respect these trends if they are to maximise sales.

ACTIVITY

Can you think of five examples of products or services that were initially introduced to meet the needs of either men or women but which have now become popular or fashionable for both sexes?
(3.1.2)

In these modern days of equality it is important that organisations do not appear sexist in the way they portray their product or service.

There is increasing criticism of washing powder adverts, for example, which show women in the kitchen. Advertising companies are careful to show a more balanced view.

The advertising of cars on television also now reflects the fact that both men and women have their own cars. Car promotions are aimed at attracting both sexes and no longer rely on showing the car as a sex symbol.

Adverts for aftershaves and perfumes usually show the reactions of the opposite sex: men buying flowers impulsively for a woman wearing a new perfume, women becoming powerless at the smell of a man's aftershave. The reason for this is that these are items usually bought as presents for a loved one by their partners.

ACTIVITY

Referring to promotions within magazines or on television, identify three examples of products or services that have been aimed at the male market and three promotions aimed at the female market. In what ways do the adverts differ? Has the organisation also attempted to appeal to the opposite sex in order to attract both parties? Explain your findings.
(3.1.2)

Socioeconomic group
Organisations are often interested in the social background of the customers who purchase their products or services and the disposable income that they have to spend. This provides important information about the pricing strategies that the organisation should adopt to ensure that the product or service is made available at an affordable price for those who will be purchasing it.

For example, the selling of expensive unusual foods in Harrods attracts a different type of customer from the items available in large high street supermarkets, and this is reflected in the prices charged.

A great deal of relevant and useful information about social backgrounds and class is available through the census results, published by the government. The scale used by the government to classify people in the census returns is often called the *Registrar-General's scale*. The scale uses the following headings:

I   Professional occupations
II Intermediate occupations (including most managerial and senior administrative occupations)
IIIA Skilled occupations (Non-manual)
IIIB Skilled ccupations (Manual)
IV Partly skilled occupations
V   Unskilled occupations

It is important to note that although this system may be used to classify people, including customers, the divisions between the groupings are very narrow. In recent years there has been less of a divide in the wages and salaries paid to different occupations. This reflects itself in the types of products and services demanded by people. Things that were once regarded as luxuries are now seen by many as essential items. Most homes now have a car, a video, a telephone and probably two or three television sets.

ACTIVITY

1 Using an organisation of your choice, identify how the range of products or services provided aims to attract customers or consumers from different backgrounds with different incomes. Give reasons for your choice of examples.
2 This time choose one product or service and identify how it is offered by a range of organisations, each targeting a different client group. One organisation might sell very expensive designer jeans, for example, while another organisation may sell jeans at rock bottom prices. List your examples, name the organisations and identify the type of customer that they are attracting.

(3.1.2)

ACTIVITY

Identify a group of people of different ages, sex and backgrounds and ask them the relevant questions in order to complete the following table:

Buying habit	Person 1	Person 2	Person 3	Person 4
Drink				
TV programme				
Sport				
Music				
Radio station				
Type of car				
Author				
Holiday				

What interesting results emerged? Were there any similarities in the answers given or were they very different?

(3.1.2)

Taste

People are individuals. They each have their own interests, hobbies, aspirations and goals. People have different tastes in fashion, music, cars, food, entertainment etc., as you will have found out from the little piece of research that you have just completed. It is important that organisations are aware of these differing tastes in order to ensure that they are catered for profitably.

People's differing tastes in life are a reflection of their personality, interests, ambitions and education. Tastes may change over a period of time, as fashions change or as people get older. They also change as people's circumstances change. It is unlikely that a person will go out to buy furniture until they have a place of their own for example. People rarely buy cars before the age of 17, when they are taking driving lessons.

Promotions, advertising and the latest trends clearly influence people's tastes and therefore their buying behaviour. Television advertising is a very powerful form of medium and sales often increase after a major promotional drive. Organisations are keen to identify different tastes and trends and market their products accordingly. People are attracted to products or services, having been informed through various advertising campaigns that cater for differing customer needs.

ACTIVITY

Using a copy of the prospectus of your school, college or place of work, identify a small sample of the range of provision available to customers. What tastes are being catered for and to whom might the provision appeal?

(3.1.2)

Income

People's incomes, and more importantly their disposable incomes, influence their purchasing ability and the types of products and services that they buy. *Disposable income* refers to the income that an individual has to spend once tax, National Insurance and any essential commitments, like mortgage repayments etc. have been paid. The greater people's disposable incomes, the greater the likelihood that they will buy a wider range of goods and services, especially consumer durables. Consumer durables include items such as washing machines, cars, music systems and televisions.

ACTIVITY

If you had recently gained promotion at work and/or won a sum of money, how might the increase in salary reflect itself in the items that you buy regularly? Would you change the make or types? Would you buy these items more frequently than

Consumers and Customers

before? Also identify, with reasons, purchases that you would make for items or services that you do not currently buy. Are there any products or services that perhaps you would *not* buy now that you are better off?
(3.1.2) (3.1.5)

Lifestyle
The final influence on purchasing or buying behaviour is a person's lifestyle. Lifestyle refers to people's attitudes, beliefs and opinions, and clearly affects what people do and do not buy and the way they live their lives. You would not buy meat if you were a vegetarian for example, but you may well buy vege-burgers, lentils and beans. The newspapers that people buy and read are also a good indicator of the views they hold, both socially and politically.

Lifestyles may change as society and fashion change. The increase in women returning to work has led to an increase in the demand for child care, and reflects how a change in society affects the demand for goods or services. Similarly, as individuals and society become increasingly aware of the importance of environmental issues and protecting the planet, we have seen a corresponding increase in the demand for environmental friendly products that do not harm animals or the planet. The way we dress can be a reflection of what is fashionable as are the cars we drive and the music we listen to.

ACTIVITY

Look at the products and services listed in the table in the next column. Identify how they might in some way reflect the lifestyle of the customer who would purchase the item. Remember that in such an exercise we are making general assumptions, and they might not always apply to all customers. The first example has been done for you.
(3.1.2)

ACTIVITY 2

Identify the type of lifestyle that the following people are likely to lead and the products or services that they would buy.
- A famous pop star
- A student
- A marketing manager
- A teacher
- A pensioner
- A redundant factory worker

(3.1.2)

Item	Possible lifestyle
Cars	
Volvo Estate	An individual probably with a family who wants safety and reliability from a car
Mini Cooper	
BMW Convertible	
Newspapers	
The *Sun*	
The *Independent*	
The *Times*	
The *Guardian*	
The *Daily Mirror*	
Eating	
A burger and chips	
A vegetarian meal	
Caviar	
Clothing	
501 Jeans and a sweatshirt	
Pinstripe suit	
Tracksuit and Reebok trainers	
Music	
Classical	
Rock	
Reggae	
Opera	

Consumers and Customers

Using all this information about the characteristics of customers, including age, sex, class, tastes, income and lifestyles, organisations are able to improve existing products and services or introduce new ones. In the process they are meeting the varied and changing needs of customers or consumers.

Local, national and international factors

The goods and services that people buy very often reflect the area which they live, locally, nationally and internationally. This is because the area, region or country and the people who live there have their own characteristics, lifestyles, tastes and fashions. Within Britain there are areas that are more prosperous than other areas and this is reflected in the purchases people make and the way they live their lives. When you go on holiday, whether in the United Kingdom or abroad, you will notice that the area you are visiting is different from the area in which you live. It is therefore important to be aware of these differences when looking at consumer and customer demand.

Locally

The locality in which someone lives is distinctive and has its own identity. The type of people who live there, their different cultures and beliefs, the work they do and the available amenities and leisure activities help to characterise the area. These factors are then reflected in the lifestyles of people who live in that locality and the goods and services that they demand.

For example, if an area has a large proportion of people who are unemployed because the availability of jobs is low, the locals are unlikely to have the money to spend on fast cars and an expensive lifestyle. In contrast, the way of life for someone living in a prosperous area, where there are many available jobs, will be very different.

ACTIVITY

Identify the characteristics of the region in which you live. Look particularly at the geographical location of the area, the types of jobs that are available, levels of unemployment, the cultural mix of the population, the age of the population and whether the area is prosperous or not. Then look at the types of organisations that are offering goods and services for sale within the locality. What information does this study give you about consumer lifestyles and customer demand for your area?
(3.1.1) (3.1.2)

Nationally

Having established that each locality is different and unique it is possible to look at the country as a whole in order to identify the characteristics and features of regions nationally.

Government publications, such as *Economic Trends*, *Regional Trends*, *Social Trends* and *The Family Expenditure Survey* all provide valuable information about regional differences in employment, earnings and expenditure. This information is very useful for organisations in helping to establish consumer demand on a national scale.

ACTIVITY

Market research can be time-consuming and expensive. When an organisation needs information about its potential customers, it can often use data that has already been prepared. It is important, therefore, to know where to find different kinds of information.

Below is a list of government publications:
1. *Annual Abstract of Statistics*
2. *Family Household Survey*
3. *General Household Survey*
4. *Household Food Consumption and Expenditure*
5. *Monthly Digest of Statistics*
6. *Regional Trends*
7. *Social Trends*

Indicate which of the publications above you could use to research into the following areas:

A Information about different regions, including population, housing, education, health, employment, income and spending, crime and justice, transport and the environment.
B Information about the buying of food and drink, published by the Ministry of Agriculture, Fisheries and Food.
C Information about individual and family expenditure and the types of goods purchased and in what quantities.
D Information from the Central Statistical Office on areas such as population, education, social services, defence, transport, national income and expenditure etc. over several years.
E Information about people, households and families.
F Information about a range of social issues.
G Monthly information about expenditure, prices and wages.
(3.1.2)

As we have seen, government publications can provide a range of information to organisations in identifying consumer demand. For example, *Regional Trends* 1992 provides some useful information about income and spending powers for different regions in the United Kingdom.

- People employed in the South East earn higher rates of income than other regions. The average gross weekly income for the South East was

Consumers and Customers

£272.40 for 1991. This compares with £245.30 for Yorkshire and Humberside, £243.00 for the West Midlands and £214.80 for Northern Ireland.
- In 1990 people in the South East owned more luxury goods than in any other region, especially for items such as dishwashers, telephones and video recorders. For example 92% of the population in the South East owned a telephone compared to 79% in the North. 65% owned a video recorder in the South East compared to 59% for Yorkshire and Humberside, and 54% for East Anglia.
- The South East also spends more on leisure activities, with 14% of the population engaging in such activities. This compares to 11.7% for the North, 13% for East Anglia, 13.5% for the South West and 11.6 for the West Midlands.

ACTIVITY

How might information relating to regional trends help an organisation in the production and distribution of its product or service?

What sources of information would be useful for the following organisations?
- (a) Clothing manufacturer
- (b) Toy manufacturer
- (c) A bank or building society
- (d) A further education college or school
- (e) A leisure centre

Refer to an up to date copy of *Regional Trends*. Identify the average weekly earnings for your region. Compare these earnings with three other regions and present your findings using tables and graphs.

Now identify what percentage of households in your region own:

1. A microwave oven
2. A washing machine
3. A tumble drier
4. A dishwasher
5. A refrigerator
6. A deep freezer
7. A telephone
8. A black and white television only
9. A colour television
10. A video
11. A home computer

What interesting conclusions can you identify about purchasing patterns in your region? How do they compare with purchasing patterns for other regions? Use a variety of graphs and pie charts to illustrate your findings. *(3.1.1) (3.1.3) (3.1.4)*

Look at the table at the foot of this page.

Tasks

1. Draw a pie chart for each region, outlining the percentage of average weekly household expenditure spent on commodities and services.
2. Draw a bar chart for each commodity or service illustrating how much each region spends on that particular item or service.
3. What interesting trends emerge?
4. What general conclusions can you come to about the characteristics of consumer demand nationally? How might this help an organisation? *(3.1.3) (3.1.4) (3.1.5)*

Internationally

A market for a product or service is not just limited to the country itself. Very often organisations are looking increasingly to European and international markets. The organisation might want to export abroad in order to grow in size, increase sales and

Household expenditure by commodity and service 1989–1990. Percentage of average weekly expenditure

	North	Yorkshire & Humberside	East Midlands	East Anglia	South East	South West	West Midlands	North West
Housing	16.7	15.7	18.2	20.0	19.2	18.8	19.1	17.0
Fuel, light & power	5.1	5.1	4.5	4.6	4.0	4.6	4.5	4.7
Food	19.6	18.9	17.9	18.9	17.6	17.7	18.3	18.0
Alcohol & tobacco	7.5	7.2	6.4	5.1	5.3	5.5	5.8	7.3
Clothing & footwear	6.8	7.1	6.6	5.5	6.5	5.8	6.4	6.6
Household goods and services	13.1	13.2	12.2	13.0	13.7	12.8	13.0	12.9
Motoring and fares	15.6	15.4	17.2	15.6	15.4	17.0	17.5	16.8
Leisure goods and services	11.7	12.8	12.6	13.0	14.0	13.5	11.6	12.6
Miscellaneous	4.0	4.6	4.3	4.2	4.5	4.3	3.8	4.1

Consumers and Customers

profit or to avoid the risk of relying on only one market. Developing economies often provide major new markets for organisations. McDonald's have successfully established themselves in the USSR, for example. Therefore information relating to the buying behaviour and income and expenditure patterns for other countries is used and applied by organisations when seeking new markets internationally.

Similarly, many international organisations are seeking to sell their products in the United Kingdom. The Nissan Group located itself in Washington, near Newcastle upon Tyne, in order to expand into the European market. The Japanese also have a major share of the electrical goods market in this country. Therefore statistical data and government publications help to provide foreign companies with an understanding of UK income and expenditure patterns and consumer demand too.

ACTIVITY

1 Which chocolate bar recently changed its name because the company wanted to sell it internationally under one name?
2 Undertake a study of 10 people and find out if they own any of the following items and if so which organisation made the product:
   Car or motor bike
   Hi-fi system
   Video
   Television
   Computer
Which organisation/s proved to be the most popular and why? What is the country of origin for these organisations?
   Of your survey, how many people 'buy British'?
(3.1.2)

Any organisation that wishes to export abroad must be sensitive to the varied cultures, values and beliefs of different countries. Language barriers can cause problems too, in that product names may have a completely different meaning in another country. The following organisations and publications provide valuable background information about trading internationally:

- Custom and Excise records provide information on imports
- The Department of Trade and Industry provides information on industrial production
- The British Overseas Trade Board has detailed information relating to all major overseas markets
- Trade directories give information about the location and numbers of firms for particular sectors in major overseas markets
- Trade magazines give background information on overseas markets
- A number of firms specialise in providing statistical information about markets and market shares.

ACTIVITY

A major source of information for organisations wishing to trade abroad is the Economist Intelligence Unit, which produces analytical and statistical surveys about a range of countries. The surveys review purchasing patterns for a range of goods and services by country and therefore provide a detailed picture about other countries' economies.

Look in your learning resource centre for a copy of the report entitled *Business Comparisons*. Identify three countries that you want to research in detail. Using the report, find out as much information as you can about the background to the country and the types of products and services that the population buys. Present your findings using a range of visual and written methods.

If you are working as part of a group, it might be useful for each group member to choose one country to research in detail. You will then be able to present your findings to each other and to get a detailed picture of a whole range of different countries.
(3.1.2) (3.1.4)

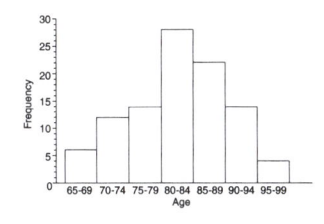

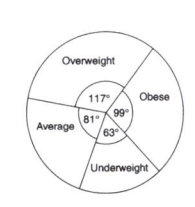

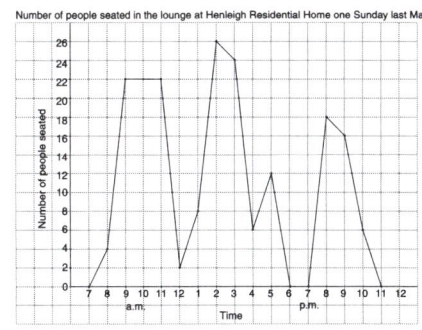

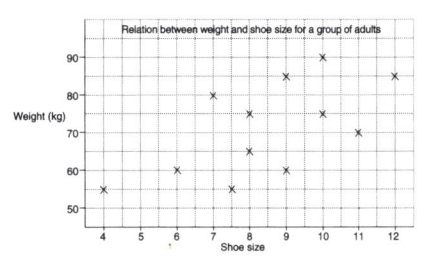

Consumers and Customers

Trends in consumer demand for goods and services

Buyer behaviour can be defined as:

the acts and decisions of individuals and groups leading to the purchase of products and services (Marketing, Howard Dunton)

It is important for an organisation to continually review consumer buying behaviour, i.e. what the customers want and what they are buying. Customers' needs are always changing, and this, together with changing fashions, trends and lifestyles, results in a dynamic market that needs monitoring. Products that were popular yesterday will not necessarily sell today.

For example, nylon shirts were fashionable in the 1970s. The non-crease, easy to care for fabric made them a popular choice for busy people who didn't want to spend their spare time ironing. However, with the greater interest in environmental issues and the desire to wear natural fabrics only, cotton has once again become popular. Likewise, consumer interest in vinyl records has steadily declined since the mid-1980s. The two main reasons for this are that, firstly, consumers would rather buy CDs for their greater durability and quality, and secondly, other products, especially computer games, are becoming more popular and are attracting money that would otherwise have been spent on music.

Advances in new technology also affect consumer demand. Computers have rapidly reduced in size in recent years as organisations advance with modern technology, leaving large, old fashioned and out of date machines behind. This results in changing demand for computers, stereos, CD players and cassette decks as children and adults continually feel the need to update their computerised appliances in keeping with the latest trends and fashions.

It is therefore very important for a company to try to appreciate the effects of consumer trends upon the possible demand for its product or service. Market forces, such as marketing and price, will affect buying behaviour, and consumer characteristics, such as interests and attitudes, are also important. The need to analyse consumer trends is further complicated by the fact that no two consumers are alike. Each customer will have different interests, hobbies, incomes and attitudes which influence what that person buys.

ACTIVITY

All businesses need to be able to identify who their customers are and how they may change over a period of time. This information enables the organisation to adapt to meet customer trends and ensure that what is being provided is what the customer wants.

Copy out and complete the table below by identifying how products or services may change in order to meet changes in consumer trends. Clearly there is no right or wrong answer as such. They are your views and assumptions. Share your answers with other group members to see whether or not they agree. The first one has been done for you.

Product or service changes	Current description	Possible future
Telephones	Two-way verbal communication	Video telephones
Petrol cars		
Leisure centres		
Schools and colleges		
Books		
Records		
Computer games		
Health care		
Entertainment		
Supermarkets		
Prisons		
Banking		
Hotels		
Travel agents		

(3.1.1) (3.1.3)

Government publications, such as *Social Trends* and *The Family Expenditure Survey*, provide organisations with useful information about buying behaviour and consumer trends. In addition, an organisation can gain further information by undertaking its own research into the market. Various methods can be used to undertake market research. These include:

- *Questionnaires:* A questionnaire is a list of statements or questions designed to obtain information about buyer behaviour. The reply from the interviewee (the person being interviewed) is recorded by the interviewer (the person asking the questions. The questions might be open questions, where a long detailed answer is recorded. Alternatively the questions might be closed, where boxes have to be completed and the answer is recorded in brief.
- *Interviewing:* An interviewer attempts to gain information directly from the interviewee by

asking questions and encouraging detailed responses. The interviewees can be interviewed individually or in groups.
- *Telephoning:* A group of customers are selected, telephoned and asked their opinions on certain issues. Their answers are recorded and analysed.
- *Prototype:* This involves producing a model of the product and asking prospective customers what they think about it. The views and comments of the customers will be used by the organisations in deciding how to proceed in launching the product.

ACTIVITY

When undertaking market research into consumer trends the organisation will choose the method that is most appropriate for the type of research it wants to undertake.
 Which method would be most appropriate for researching public opinion on:
 1 A new type of computer
 2 Attitudes towards television programmes
 3 Types of soup bought and reasons why
 4 The after-sales service received from a car salesperson
 5 Double glazing
 6 The effect of an advertising campaign
 7 A new brand of pet food
 8 Services offered by the local authority
 9 A new type of chocolate bar
 10 A Caribbean nightclub
(3.1.2) (3.1.3)

ACTIVITY

Each method used in market research has its own advantages and disadvantages. Working in groups copy and complete the following table:

Method	Advantages	Disadvantages
Questionnaires	Detailed answers	Time-consuming
Interviews		
Telephone		
Prototype		

(3.1.2)

Causes of change in consumer demand for goods and services

Since the sole aim of producing goods and services is to sell them, the consumer plays a vital role in planning production. The really successful producer is the one who can forecast accurately what the consumers will be willing to spend their money on in the future.
 Many factors affect the sort of goods that consumers are prepared to buy and in what quantities. These include:
 1 Level of income
 2 Confidence to spend
 3 Cost of living
 4 Changing needs and wants

Money to spend
A consumer's ability to spend is directly related to the level of income earned. The tendency is to spend more as you earn more. When undertaking market research, an organisation is interested in the consumer's disposable income. Disposable income is the amount a consumer has available after paying compulsory and essential bills, such as tax, national insurance, mortgage, living expenses etc.
 For example, a consumer may benefit from a wage rise, but if income tax, national insurance or mortgage payments rise too, there will be no additional income to spend on goods and services. On the other hand, if a consumer's disposable income rises, i.e. the wage rises without a corresponding increase in essential expenses, then the consumer will have more disposable income to spend.
 In addition the more a person earns the greater the likelihood that they will buy expensive luxury items and have savings in the bank. Consumers on lower incomes will tend to purchase essential items only. Therefore an organisation needs to identify who its customers are and what their levels of disposable income are before they market their products or services.

ACTIVITY

1 Assume you have a part time job that pays £30 per week. Construct a weekly budget that records how much money you receive and what you would spend that money on.
2 You have just been given a £10 per week rise to £40. Produce a second budget that illustrates income and expenditure now. What items are you now purchasing that you did not buy before?
3 Problems have occurred at work and they have reduced all part-time hours. Your income has fallen to £20. How would you cut your spending to meet this?
(3.1.5)

Consumers and Customers

Confidence to spend

In addition to a consumer's ability to spend, demand is related to a consumer's confidence in wanting to spend. If people are feeling insecure about the future, unsure whether or not they will still have a job and worried about likely increases in essential expenses such as tax, mortgages and VAT on heating, they are less likely to spend money on luxury items. On the other hand, when people feel confident about their jobs and secure about the future, levels of spending will increase.

For example, in the mid-80s the economy experienced a major boom in customer demand. The high incomes being earned and the wide number of jobs that were available at that time resulted in people buying houses, furniture, garden products, expensive cars etc. The price of these items rose considerably in relation to the high demand. Consumers had confidence in the market. However, gradually interest rates started to creep upwards, which resulted in people having less disposable income to spend. Unemployment rose as firms made employees redundant. The confidence in the market that had caused the increase in demand disappeared as people felt insecure about the future.

ACTIVITY

Make a list of products or services that you regard as essential and which you would continue to purchase despite losing confidence to spend. Produce a second list of items that you regard as luxuries and which you are prepared to stop buying if the need arose.
(3.1.5)

Cost of living

The cost of living refers to the value of money and what it is possible to buy with it. As prices increase the value of the pound falls. This means, for example, that a consumer is unable to buy as much with a pound today as was possible 20 years ago. If consumers' incomes do not increase to reflect the increase in prices the value of their disposable incomes will fall. They will be earning the same amount of money but will be unable to buy as much with it. Therefore the cost of living is an important factor when looking at consumer trends.

The cost of living is measured by the Retail Price Index, or RPI. This calculation attempts to price a typical basket of goods bought by consumers and then monitor any changes in the price of these goods month by month. An organisation can use the RPI to predict changes in consumer trends and buying behaviour.

ACTIVITY

Identify at least five different products or services that you buy regularly and which have changed in price over the last year. Try to estimate the original price roughly 12 months ago and compare it with the price today. If possible try to refer to an old price list and then compare it with an up-to-date price list for a more accurate picture of changes in prices. From these figures calculate the percentage increase (or decrease) of the price.
Remember:

$$\text{percentage increase (or decrease)} = \frac{\text{new price} - \text{old price}}{\text{original price}} \times 100$$

If this number is negative then it is a percentage decrease. Record your findings in a copy of the table below.

| Product | Original price | Current price | Percentage change |

What interesting trends emerge?
(3.1.5)

Changing needs and changing wants

There are are a number of other factors that affect the level of demand for a product or service as reflected in consumer trends. One is social or religious convention. The demand for alcoholic drink in a Muslim community will, for example, be considerably less than in a community where such drink is freely permitted. Other factors are the changing needs and wants of consumers.

Needs and wants in a less developed society will be very different from those in an advanced economy. The range of goods purchased in the United Kingdom for example would be of a different type from those demanded in the poorest regions of Eastern Europe. As societies develop customers begin to purchase luxury items in addition to the basic essentials of life.

Within the United Kingdom customer needs and wants change over a period of time. As living standards rise, people's expectations change too. An increase in income will result in people enjoying a higher standard of living, which reflects itself in the demand for a wider range of luxury items. What were once luxuries will now become regarded as essentials.

For example, computers have only become widely available in schools in the last 10 years, and the trend towards each family having one in the home has become popular in the last five years. Prior to this, computers were regarded as luxury items that only large organisations could afford to own. Another good example is music systems. In the early 1980s most homes had one, but the family shared the use of it. Now it is quite common for family members to have a music system of their own, playing their own type of music in the privacy of their bedrooms. A final example would be car ownership. The last ten years have witnessed a move from families owning one car to owning two or more. This is in stark contrast to the late 1960s, when car ownership was generally regarded as a luxury.

ACTIVITY

Can you think of other examples where products that were once luxuries have now become regarded as essential items? Can you identify reasons why this might be the case?
(3.1.1) (3.1.5)

ACTIVITY (3.1.1–6)

The caring community

The late 1980s and early 1990s have witnessed a major change in consumer demand as customers have become more socially and environmentally aware. Consumers have become very vocal in their demands for goods that are not tested on animals and which do not spoil the environment. The fur trade, which had proved to be big business in the 1970s, found that not only were consumers not buying their goods but they were campaigning against other people buying them too. Cosmetics were promoted on the basis that they had not been tested on animals, and detergents that were biodegradable were very successful.

Tasks:
1. Identify as many examples of products or services that are promoted on the basis of being environmentally kind as you can. Produce a second list of products or services that are no longer popular because they are not environmentally kind.
2. Identify the characteristics of the customers who would buy the environmentally kind products, looking at age, sex, taste and lifestyle.
3. Referring to government publications such as *Social Trends* and the *Family Expenditure Survey* try to identify the relevant facts and statistics that support the claim that there has been an increase in demand for these types of products or services. Produce graphics to illustrate your findings.
4. Identify possible reasons as to why consumer demand has changed in this way. Remember to focus on disposable income, cost of living and changing needs and changing wants.
5. To what extent have the trends towards environmentally friendly products and the decline of products such as furs, leather goods and veal been 'customer-led'?
6. Why have organisations been keen to reflect their customers' wishes? What is the importance of customers to business organisations?

MULTIPLE CHOICE

1. An organisation that produces fashion clothing is *most* likely to be interested in identifying its customers according to:
   A Social background
   B Taste and trends
   C Marital status
   D Birth sign

2. An organisation wishing to export goods to another country would benefit most from being aware of that country's:
   A Level of production
   B Gross domestic product
   C Export laws
   D Culture, values and beliefs

3. An organisation which produces children's toys is most likely to be interested in identifying its customers according to:
   A Name
   B Age
   C Qualifications
   D Car ownership

4. Which of the following government publications provides organisations with useful information about buying behaviour and consumer trends?
   A Gallup surveys
   B *Which?* magazine
   C *Family Expenditure Survey*
   D Kays' catalogue

5. The scale used by market research organisations to record social class is called the:
   A Registration General Scale
   B General Register's Scale
   C Registrar's General Scale
   D General Registrar's Scale

6. 'Disposable income' refers to:
   A Available income after tax, national insurance and essential commitments have been accounted for
   B Income earned before tax and national insurance
   C Extra income earned in the form of overtime, sick pay, holiday pay and bonuses
   D The amount of income spent on essentials every week

Consumers and Customers

7 The term 'lifestyles' refers to:
  A The growing popularity of leisure activities
  B Attitudes, beliefs and opinions that affect what people do
  C A classification of consumers according to age
  D The marital status of the individual

8 One advantage of questionnaires as a method of market research is that they:
  A Are time-consuming
  B Provide detailed answers
  C Provide information very cheaply
  D Are 100% reliable

9 One advantage of telephones as a method of market research is that they:
  A Lead to an immediate response
  B Are intrusive
  C Are very cheap to use
  D Provide access to all households

10 A customer's decision to buy a new car is *most* likely to be influenced by:
  A The sale of cars nationally
  B The cost of living
  C The exchange rate
  D The price of in-car stereos

SHORT ANSWER

1 When identifying its customers, in what ways may an organisation characterise them?

2 How might a person's lifestyle influence that person's choice of goods or services purchased?

3 Why is it important for organisations to be aware of the cultures, values and beliefs of a country with which they hope to trade?

4 (a) When might an organisation use questionnaires?
  (b) What advantages do they have over other methods?
  (c) What disadvantages do they have?

5 What are the differences between local, national and international markets?

6 Define 'buyer behaviour' and explain why it is important for organisations to continually review it.

7 List the main government publications that may provide useful information to organisations about their customers. Briefly explain the nature of the information found in each publication.

8 What is a 'prototype' and why is it useful to an organisation?

ELEMENT 3.2
Plan, design and produce promotional material

Performance criteria

(PC) 3.2.1 Identify and give examples of types of promotions used in marketing goods and services

(PC) 3.2.2 Describe constraints on the content of promotional materials

(PC) 3.2.3 Plan to produce promotional materials to promote particular goods or services

(PC) 3.2.4 Explain the purpose of the planned promotional materials

(PC) 3.2.5 Design and produce promotional materials and use them to promote goods or services

(PC) 3.2.6 Evaluate how successful the promotional materials were in achieving the stated purpose

Objectives of promotional materials

Advertising promotions can be seen as a process of communication between the producer and the consumer or the buyer and the seller. In promoting a product, service or issue (in the case of charities) the producer is informing the consumer about the product's benefits and in the process encouraging the consumer to purchase it. In order to promote the product effectively, the producer must be able to understand the consumer in terms of interests, language, imagery, attitudes and lifestyle.

Consumers and Customers

The aim when undertaking a promotion is to:
(a) Make customers aware that the product exists by getting their *attention*
(b) Ensure that the initial attention develops into *interest*
(c) Enable them to *recognise* the item in retail outlets
(d) Persuade the customer to *want* and therefore *buy* the product
(e) Encourage the customer to *continue* to purchase the item in the future. This is often called *brand loyalty*.

The following examples illustrate how effective promotions can be in raising public awareness. However, it is interesting to see how the consumers' reactions to the promotions were very different.

GUINNESS
During the 1980s Guinness wanted to increase the sales of their famous stout. They began a range of promotions which focused on a blond-haired actor dressed in black, supposedly representing a pint of Guinness. The actor was filmed in futuristic and imaginative locations, giving the image of an unusual and individualistic drink. The result was that Guinness was no longer seen as a drink for older people, but one that was fashionable and distinctive. Sales increased considerably.

WISPA
A whisper... something's happening... spread the word...
This was the type of promotion that preceded the launch of the Wispa chocolate bar. A new type of confectionery had been developed that had all the characteristics of the traditional Aero bar but developed into a countline bar (i.e. a snack for customers on the move). The advertisement raised public interest without telling the customer what was actually to be launched. The result was that when the product was brought onto the market sales exceeded supplies. Cadbury's had to review their total production process and during that time Nestlé Rowntree responded with their own countline Aero bar.

RATNERS
Gerald Ratner, director of the large jewellery retail outlets made a humorous reference at an after-dinner speech to the range of poor quality and cheap products sold by his shops. The comment was not intended to be widely broadcast nor did he intend it to be used as a method to promote awareness of the Ratner group. However, the resulting publicity affected sales so badly that it cost Gerald Ratner his job.

ACTIVITY

Read the case studies on this page and answer the following questions.
1. Identify how the promotions affected sales.
2. Identify the reasons why the promotions affected sales in this way.
3. Can you think of any other examples where promotions have either increased or decreased sales?
4. Look at Aero and Wispa chocolate bars. Compare the promotional techniques used, looking particularly at logos, packaging, style and colour of packaging and advertisements.
    Which do you think is most effectively marketed and why?
5. Open up the packaging. What are the similarities and what are the differences in the look of the chocolate?
6. Break the chocolate bars in half. How does the texture of the inside of the two bars compare?
7. Now for what you have all been waiting for! Bite into each bar. Which chocolate bar do you prefer and why?

(3.2.1) (3.2.6)

Consumers and Customers

Each of the case studies clearly illustrates the effect that a promotion, intentional or not, may have on an organisation. It is as easy for sales to increase as a result of a successful promotion as it is for sales to fall as a result of poor publicity. It is important that an organisation promotes the right image and message at all times.

Promotion methods have three main objectives:
(a) To create *demand*
(b) To create *sales*
(c) To give *information*

To create demand
An organisation will organise a promotional activity with the aim of increasing demand for the product or service or generating support for a particular cause. Demand will increase by:
1. Informing customers about the benefits and qualities of the product or service
2. Illustrating how the product or service will satisfy a particular need

Demand is further encouraged by using a range of promotional techniques, such as free offers or two for the price of one. The intention is to create brand loyalty, where the consumer will continue to purchase the item again and again.

To create sales
If promotional campaigns are to be successful they must have an impact upon consumers which will motivate them to purchase the product. The ability to motivate the customer reflects how effective the promotion was in:
- Identifying the needs and wants of the customer
- Reinforcing the message through the campaign
- Ensuring the customer was able to recall the message effectively

Sales are created by informing and persuading customers to buy a product or service which will satisfy their wants and needs. There are a number of stages involved in this:
1. Arousal of interest – the promotion should be aimed at getting the attention of the potential customer
2. Increase of knowledge – as a result of the promotion the customer should want to find out further information about the product or service
3. Desire to possess – as a result of finding out further information the customer should want to make a purchase
4. Consideration of price – the promotion should be aimed at those who can afford to buy the item so that price should not be a distraction
5. Decision to buy – if all the processes have been followed through effectively the customer should proceed with the purchase

To give information
A promotional campaign can be used to give information and create an impression with the consumer. In order to achieve this the company must use the promotional campaign to try to get the customers to focus on the favourable aspects of the organisation's business. If the organisation is able to promote a positive image effectively through its campaigns the customer is more likely to purchase the product or service.

The promotion should also convince the customer that there is something special about the product or service. A common device is to appeal to the customer's motives. These may include:
- Ambition and success
- Romance
- Hero worship
- Increased leisure
- The higher opinion of others

Ambition and success   The theme of the presentation could focus on how successful the customer would be if they bought the product or service.

Romance   The focus here would be how attractive other people would find the customer if she or he bought this product or service.

Hero worship   Customers will be attracted to the product or service because a famous person is involved in its promotion.

Increased leisure   The promotion focuses on how much additional time customers would have for leisure if they bought this labour-saving device.

The higher opinion of others   People are very often affected by what other people think. Therefore the theme of the presentation could focus on how envious other people would be of the product or service.

Effectiveness of promotional materials
When organisations design promotional materials they need to be able to evaluate how effective they are.

There are several key features to look for:
1. *Effectiveness in communicating to the audience*
   The business will want to judge whether the promotional materials have succeeded in getting the message across. For example, because there are tight restrictions on the advertisement of cigarettes, tobacco companies are not allowed to show smoking as being sophisticated, grown-up, healthy, attractive or fashionable. Instead they have to use quite abstract or obscure designs to sell their product. It becomes very difficult to establish whether they do get the message across. Take a look at some magazine adverts for cigarettes and you will be able to judge for yourself.
2. *Suitability for creating sales*
   It is important that the method used in promoting a product or service reaches the right people. Hence, TV adverts for toys will appear most frequently on a Saturday between children's programmes. Likewise sportswear is often advertised around the pitch at football grounds.

Consumers and Customers

3 *Influencing customers*

If a promotional campaign is successful it must influence customers and in the right way. Ultimately you are hoping to change spending habits to encourage customers to buy your product. For example, the adverts for Benetton have caused major controversy because of the outrageous images used to sell their clothes. This may have attracted some customers to the products. At the same time other customers may have been offended.

4 *Giving information*

Advertising is very expensive. A few minutes on national TV or a page in a national newspaper costs thousands of pounds. Therefore it is vital that the important facts are conveyed effectively. Key items, such as the name of the product or telephone numbers, may be repeated several times for added emphasis. If there is too much information people quickly 'turn off'. Information must be accurate, clearly presented and brief. It must also be presented in an interesting way.

ACTIVITY

Choose a product or service with which you are familiar and which you would like to promote. It might be an item of clothing, type of sweet or favourite car. Alternatively you may want to promote a particular service, like your local leisure centre, or a cause, like Greenpeace.

1 Produce a promotional activity that you feel will stimulate interest in the product or service. You may want to produce a storyboard showing a sequence of events that could form the basis of a television advertisement. Alternatively, if you have access to a video camera you may actually want to role-play an advertisement instead. Other methods may include producing a radio jingle, a poster or an information booklet. The choice is yours.

2 Having produced the promotion answer the following questions:
   (a) How would the promotion help to create a demand for your product or service?
   (b) How would it stimulate sales or support?
   (c) How would it help to influence consumer perceptions of the product or service?

3 Present your promotional activities to other members in the group, explaining why you chose the particular methods. As a group evaluate which of the promotional materials would be the most successful in achieving their purpose, giving reasons.

(3.2.3) (3.2.4) (3.2.5) (3.2.6) (3.2.6)

ACTIVITY

A range of different types of organisations use various methods of promotions to achieve particular objectives. Copy out and try to complete the following table by identifying the type of promotion used by organisations and what they hope to achieve. The first one has been done for you.

Organisation	Type of promotion	Aim
Small sole trader	Local advertisements Mail drops	Stimulate local sales
Partnerships		
Medium-sized companies		
Multinationals		
Charities		
Local authority		
Interest group, e.g. RSPCA		
Central Government		
College or school		
Football club		
Political party		
Bank or building society		
Police		
The BBC		
European Union		

Constraints on the content of promotional materials

'Smoke these cigarettes as they make you look more attractive to the opposite sex.'
'If you buy this slimming food you will look like Miss World by next week.'
'Definitely the best lager in the whole world.'
'A washing powder that all women should use to produce the cleanest washing for their husbands.'

These statements would not be allowed to be printed or broadcast by an organisation seeking to make a promotion. Why?

Marketing and advertising is a very powerful means of influencing the way people think. It is

153

Consumers and Customers

important that what is said, printed or broadcast is accurate and that it does not offend or make wild claims which cannot be proven.

'Smoke these cigarettes as they make you look more attractive to the opposite sex' would not be allowed because advertising cigarettes as promoting sex appeal is illegal. Cigarettes can only be advertised in magazines or on billboards and the style of promotion used is usually abstract, sometimes in the form of puzzles. All advertisements for cigarettes have to carry a government health warning.

'If you buy this slimming food you will look like Miss World by next week', and 'Definitely the best lager in the whole world' are statements that make wild exaggerated claims which would be difficult to prove, and an organisation would be unable to use them as part of a promotional campaign.

'A washing powder that all women should use to produce the cleanest washing for their husbands' is a clearly sexist statement in that it implies that only women do the washing and always for their husbands. A statement like this is regarded as unacceptable and the organisation risks offending many of its customers.

It is important therefore that any promotional campaign undertaken by an organisation is legal and ethical. A number of laws have been passed in order to protect the consumer against unfair practices by organisations. In addition organisations are expected to ensure that all their publicity is ethical. Ethical means conforming to a recognised standard of morals and principles. Any promotion that is sexist, racist or immoral would be seen as unethical.

Legal

Important consumer legislation that regulates the activities of organisations in selling their products or services includes:
- The Sale and supply of Goods and Services Act
- The Trade Descriptions Act
- Food Labelling Regulations
- The Consumer Protection Act
- The Consumer Credit Act

The Sale and Supply Of Goods and Services Act 1994

The Sale of Goods Act ensures that goods which are sold are of 'satisfactory quality'. This means that the goods are fit for their normal purpose, taking into account their price. Therefore a pair of jeans, advertised as fashionable and hard-wearing, should not fall apart after a couple of weeks. Similarly, DIY furniture should resemble the picture on the packet and be of reasonable quality.

The Sale and Supply of Goods and Services Act also states that goods should be as described. For example, a holiday hotel which is advertised as being close to the sea should not require a person to run a 4 minute mile to get there! Likewise, a customer responding to an advertisement for an 'almost brand new' car should not find a broken-down wreck on arrival.

The Trade Descriptions Act

The Trade Descriptions Act regulates the use of false statements and claims in advertisements. It is illegal for an organisation to make claims about products or services which are either untrue or cannot be proved. When Nanette Newman states that Fairy washing-up liquid washes more dishes than most other washing-up liquid, pound for pound, the statement would have to be proven to be accurate.

Food Labelling Regulations

Similarly the Food Labelling Regulations compel all organisations to accurately label the ingredients, weight, name and address of the manufactuer and the country of origin. In addition the picture on the front of the packet must be an accurate indicator of the goods inside. A tin showing sliced peaches in syrup should not contain whole peaches in juice for example.

The Consumer Protection Act

The Consumer Protection Act makes it illegal to sell, market or promote goods that are unsafe or to claim that goods are reduced or in the sale unless the reductions are genuine. Therefore it would be an offence for an organisation to claim that a three-piece suite was in the sale if in fact the price had not changed at all.

The Consumer Credit Act

The Consumer Credit Act requires all organisations to advertise their Annual Percentage Rate (APR) when advertising credit terms and loans. Consumers also have a period of time to cancel any agreement should they change their mind. Therefore if a consumer decides to buy a television on credit, for example, he or she is legally entitled to know the Annual Percentage Rate of interest being charged and the total interest paid.

ACTIVITY

Undertake further research to supplement the information given to you and produce a small handbook that could be given to consumers. The handbook should contain a brief summary of the different types of consumer legislation and protection offered. Remember to write the handbook in such a way that people who have very little knowledge about law can understand it. Illustrations would make it look more attractive and case studies would grab the reader's attention. (3.2.2)

ACTIVITY

Look at the following situations and identify the relevant consumer legislation which would protect the consumer. The first one has been done for you.

Consumers and Customers

Situation	Relevant consumer legislation
Purchase a car on credit.	Consumer Credit Act
A three-piece suite which has been ordered is of poorer quality than the one on sale in the showroom.	
A holiday booked from a holiday brochure shows a five-star hotel. On arrival the guests are booked into a two-star hotel.	
A customer orders a glass of diet coke. She is actually given normal coke.	
A customer buys a second-hand car described as a nearly new Ford Fiesta. The customer finds out later that it is 'ringed', i.e. a car made up from two wrecks.	
A wallpaper glue described as sticking anything actually sticks nothing.	
A DIY piece of furniture falls apart despite expert assembly.	
A packet of biscuits shown as fancies on the front picture actually turns out to be plain inside.	
Purchase of a computer using a credit card.	

(3.2.2)

Ethical

In addition to legal constraints organisations are governed by an agreed code of practice when promoting and advertising. This is to ensure that all promotions are ethical, meeting a required standard.

The agreed codes of practice for printed and cinema advertising are outlined in:
- The British Code of Advertising Practice
- The British Code of Sales Promotion Practice
  Codes of practice relating to advertising on commercial television and radio are laid down in:
- The Independent Television Commission Code of Advertising Standards and Practice
- Radio Authority Code of Advertising Standards and Practice

The codes of practice have been produced by people employed in the advertising industries and reflect a general standard that all organisations agree to operate within. The codes lay down basic principles, which state that all advertisement should be 'legal, decent, honest and truthful'.

ACTIVITY

Look at the following advertisements. Try to identify how they might break the relevant code of practice listed above. Remember to identify which code of practice applies. You may also find that some of the advertisements could be regarded as illegal by a particular piece of consumer legislation: see if you can identify which advertisements and the relevant legislation. (3.2.2)

Example 1: Radio jingle
   Buy these toys;
dolls for the girls
   and cars for the boys;
Tell your parents
   you want one now;
Ring this number
   and
we will tell you how. . .
on 0898 34521

Example 2: Dog food

Ultradog!
all dogs will love it
much better than anything else
on the market
dogs who eat it say they prefer it
do your dog a service
buy a can today
Once again at the low sale price
of 40 pence a can

minimum purchase 6 cans

Example 3: Old MusicMail magazine advertisements
Be cool, be in, be hip
Get to where it's all happening
Turn your dial to FM321
The number one pirate
radio show. . . Radio Jake

Example 4: Computer
Latest technological Laptop
Compatible with all software
Only £87 per month credit terms
Phone James or Asif on 01726 456211

Example 5: TV advertisement
A television advertisement for Sing Lager shows groups of young men and women drinking and smoking at the bar, singing pop songs as they gradually get drunk. The theme of the advertisement is that the lager is the strongest available on the market and the best type of beer if you want to become drunk quickly. The advertisement continues by stating that the lager might be expensive but is of the highest quality.

Consumers and Customers

The advertisement concludes with teenagers leaving the bar and driving home.

While most codes are not usually legally binding, they could influence court decisions if action was taken against an organisation. In addition, however, the codes of practice relating to advertising are further reinforced by the Control of Misleading Advertising Regulations.

The Advertising Standards Authority

This body is a voluntary, independent organisation which ensures that organisations who are involved in advertising and marketing operate according to the British Code of Advertising Practice. They encourage the general public to write and inform them of any advertisements that are not legal, decent, honest and truthful. An organisation which operates outside the code may be asked to change or withdraw their advertisement, as the media will not accept an advertisement if it breaks the code of practice. To avoid any controversy in the first place, some organisations will send sample advertisements to the ASA for approval before publication.

Independent Television Commission and Radio Authority

These organisations monitor all advertising on television and radio by ensuring that organisations operate within the Code of Advertising Standards and Practice. There are very strict guidelines that organisations need to be aware of and certain products are banned from television promotion altogether, e.g. cigarettes. All advertisements that appear on television and radio are checked and approved to ensure that they do not break any aspect of the code before they are broadcast.

ACTIVITY

Record a sample of television and radio advertisements. Watch and listen to them and see if you think the advertisements are *legal, decent, honest and truthful*. Produce your findings in an appropriate written format. Remember to note the reasoning behind your conclusions. Having reviewed radio and television, try to find a variety of advertisements within newspapers and magazines. Again identify whether you think the advertisements are legal, decent, honest and truthful, with reasons. Present your findings this time using an appropriate visual display.
(3.2.2)

Type of promotion

Advertisement

When an organisation decides to undertake a promotion a major decision has to be made about the type of advertising to use. A wide variety of methods are available and each one has its own corresponding advantages and disadvantages. The final decision about the most appropriate method will focus on what is being promoted, to whom, the budget involved and where the prospective customers are located.

The aims of all forms of advertising are to:
1. Provide information to customers about the availability of goods and their characteristics
2. Persuade customers to buy the product or service and so create brand loyalty.

The following methods can be used:
1. Newspapers and magazines
2. Television
3. Cinemas
4. Commercial radio
5. Posters
6. Catalogues and leaflets

Newspapers and magazines

Newspapers are printed on a daily or weekly basis and are aimed at a particular type of reader. Magazines are available weekly or monthly and may have a general appeal or may be subject-specific, e.g. gardening or cookery. Both forms of media publish their circulation figures, so it is possible for an organisation to assess the size of the potential market. As particular newspapers and magazines appeal to readers of a certain age, with particular interests, it is possible to place an advertisement where it is most likely to attract the reader.

Advantages
- The advertisement can be aimed at a local or national market.

Footballers carry advertising on their shirts – see page 160

- Circulation figures are known in advance.
- The market is segmented: therefore the advert, if correctly placed, is likely to reach the intended audience.
- Tear-off slips can be included for an easy response.
- A wide variety of methods can be used in placing the advertisement, e.g. the scent of a particular perfume can be included within a magazine.

Disadvantages
- Many adverts may appear on one page, especially within newspapers. This may result in a specific promotion going unnoticed.
- The quality of newsprint can sometimes be quite poor, and therefore the advertisement will not necessarily been seen to its best advantage.
- Newspapers and magazines are quickly thrown away, resulting in the advertisement going unnoticed and a poor response rate.
- If a reader is flicking through a paper or magazine quickly the advert may not be seen.

ACTIVITY

In which newspaper or magazine would you place the following advertisements:
(a) A special offer for summer plants and hanging baskets
(b) Launch of new perfume or brand of cosmetics
(c) Chatline
(d) New motor car
(e) A local craft fair
(f) Loans at at low interest rate
(3.2.1)

Television
Television advertising can only take place on the independent channels as no advertising is allowed on the BBC channels. It is regarded as one of the most powerful and effective methods in advertising. It is possible to reach a large national audience and is often used by organisations who sell their product or service throughout the country and abroad. The target audience can be chosen by deciding the time of day to advertise. For example, an advertisement for a new toy will usually be seen on children's television on a Saturday morning.

Organisations interested in advertising on television will buy time in a similar way to purchasing space in a newspaper or magazine. Television companies provide would-be advertisers with details of the numbers of viewers for particular programmes, which are like circulation figures for newspapers. At peak viewing time, e.g. 7.30 p.m., just before *Coronation Street*, an organisation is expected to pay a much higher rate than at off-peak time, e.g. 10.30 a.m.

Advantages
- Imagery can be used to promote the product effectively. Think about the powerful messages being presented by the woman in the Flake advertisement, the man climbing hills and skiing down mountains with a box of Milk Tray or the varied Levi jeans advertisements where Motown music is used to convey the message. All these advertisement are easily remembered because of the effective use of colour, images, music and mood.
- A national or local audience can be reached, and as the advertisements are often repeated regularly the target audience can very quickly identify with them.
- The quality of the advertisement and style of presentation are usually of a much higher standard than for any other type of advertising.
- The organisation can choose when it wants to advertise and between which programmes in order to reach the target audience. For example an advertisement for a new car may be shown during a review of a motor race.

Disadvantages
- Television advertising is very expensive and many organisations cannot afford to pay for it out of their marketing budget.
- The audience is so great that for many people the advertisement has no relevance.
- Viewers often switch channels when advertisements come on.
- The organisation has a very short period of time in which to present the information.
- If an advertisement becomes stale and boring, or if the message is perceived in the wrong way by the viewer, the advertisement may result in a fall in sales rather than a rise.
- Organisations must ensure that they operate according to the appropriate codes of practice and have their advertisement approved before broadcast.

ACTIVITY

At what time of day and on which day of the week would you buy viewing time for the following advertisements? Give reasons for your response.
1. Computer games
2. New chocolate bar
3. New leisure complex
4. Aftershave
5. Holiday in the Maldives
6. Guinness stout
7. A gardening magazine
8. New movie
9. Baked beans
10. A department store

Recall your favourite television advertisements. Why did you enjoy them? What factors, in your mind, made them effective? Did they encourage

Consumers and Customers

you to go and buy the product or service having seen the advertisement? Give reasons for your answers.
(3.2.1)

Cinema

Advertisements are screened prior to a film being shown at an cinema by both local and national advertisers. Very often the advertisements focus on sweets and drinks which can be bought to accompany the film, or alternatively they promote local eating establishments which the viewers can go to once the film is complete.

Advantages
- The audience is seated and generally watching the screen. Therefore the advertiser can guarantee that the advert will be seen by the audience.
- It is cheaper than television and therefore used by local organisations who cannot afford the cost of television advertising.
- It is usually possible to identify the type of audience who will watch a particular film. For instance a screen showing *Aladdin* will attract a different type of audience from a screen showing *Schindler's List*. In this way, an advertiser can usually choose the target audience for the advertisement.

Disadvantages
- The advertisements, especially local ones, tend to be of a poorer quality compared with television advertisements.
- It is sometimes difficult to present a message when the audience is waiting impatiently for the film to start.
- People do not go to the cinema as often as they watch television. Therefore the advertiser does not benefit from repeat showings in the same way.

ACTIVITY

List 10 films with which you are familiar. Identify the type of audience who would be interested in seeing each film, looking particularly at age, background, interests etc. Using this information identify the types of products or services which could be advertised on the screen before each film, matching the product with the target audience.
(3.2.1)

Commercial radio

Advertising is permitted on local commercial radio and more recently on national commercial radio. There are networks of local radio stations throughout the country. Advertising time is used by both local and national organisations and slots of time can be identified with a particular type of listener.

Advantages
- It is used by local organisations because it is much cheaper than television.
- Target audiences can be identified by placing advertisements at particular times of the day.
- The advertisement (or jingle as it is often called) can be repeated over a period of time for maximum effect.
- A large target audience can be reached.

Disadvantages
- Repeated jingles can become boring and monotonous.
- With local radio the organisation is limited to advertising in a local area.
- Jingles do not have the same impact as television advertisements, which combine colour, sound and imagery.
- Local radio stations do not command the same number of listeners as the national commercial or BBC radio stations.
- Listeners may become frustrated because the advertisements continue to interrupt their listening.

ACTIVITY

Choose a product or service with which you are familiar and identify the target audience. Prepare a radio jingle which will promote the product or service and appeal to the target audience. Remember to write down why you have chosen a particular style of advertisement and how it will appeal. Record a copy of the jingle on a tape. Play it to a group of friends or classmates. Write down their responses to the advertisement and how effective they thought it was.
(3.2.1) (3.2.5)

Posters

Posters are one of the oldest forms of advertising, yet one of the most effective. Unlike television and radio advertisements, posters may be displayed for 24 hours a day, seven days a week and for as many weeks as the advertiser can afford.

Most posters are displayed alongside busy roads and high streets for maximum effect. Motorists will see them as they drive past and in some cases have been known to have had accidents because they were busy reading the poster rather than watching the road!

Advantages
- A cheap and effective method of advertising.
- An excellent method for communicating visual and graphical illustrations with simple messages.
- Local firms can display posters in local areas.
- The posters are usually displayed for a period of time and therefore the messages are reinforced.

Consumers and Customers

Disadvantages
- Detailed statements and messages cannot be included.
- Their impact may be so great that they cause drivers to be distracted from their driving.
- They become soiled quite quickly and make the area in which they are displayed look shabby too.
- People may ignore them once they have been on show for a period of time.

✎ ACTIVITY

Produce a sample poster which could be used to advertise Green Fingers, a gardening shop located in your town centre. The shop stocks the whole range of gardening products from compost to garden furniture. Remember the rules about an effective poster: keep it simple and make it eye-catching.
(3.2.1) (3.2.5)

Catalogues and leaflets

These may be included within newspapers and magazines, especially Sunday editions. Alternatively they may come through the post or be pushed through the letter box. Catalogues are usually used for displaying a range of merchandise. Leaflets, on the other hand, are used to promote special offers or the opening of a store.

Advantages
- The literature is cheap to produce and easy to distribute.
- Using the postal service in the distribution ensures that geographical areas can be targeted.
- It is a relatively cheap method to use and appropriate for communicating simple messages.
- The use of photographs and diagrams within catalogues may capture the interest of the audience.

Disadvantages
- People may throw the literature away without even reading it.
- Messages have to be brief as space is limited.
- It is not always possible to guarantee that the person you want to read the material will be the one to receive it.
- Many organisations use this method to promote their product or service, so it is easy for a particular advertisement to lose itself in a pile of others.

✎ ACTIVITY

Look at the leaflets on this page, which have been produced to promote a particular product or service.
What is being promoted within each leaflet?
Which leaflet is most effective in presenting its message and why?
What do you think is wrong with the other leaflets and how could they be improved?
(3.2.6)

Example 1

> One Day Sale
> All Pine Furniture Half Price.
> Free gift for orders over £150
> Open all day Bank Holiday Monday
> Don't miss it ....
> Virdee's Pine Factory
> Just off the Ring Road
> Junction 23

Example 2

> Special Offer
> The Maldives
> From £599 for 14 nights
>
> Robinson Crusoe Islands in the Indian Ocean lie 400 miles southwest of India. Of some 1000 islands in all, around 200 are inhabited. Less than 50 are for tourists with one hotel on each island.
> The holiday is for those who enjoy the simple life; swimming, snorkelling, sunbathing and relaxing.
> Interested?
> Contact your local travel agent.

Example 3

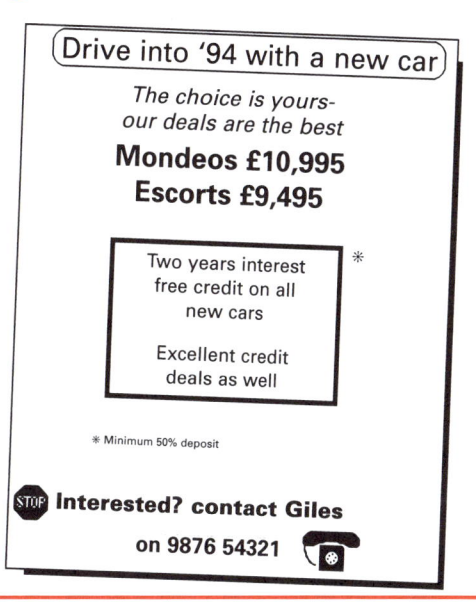

> Drive into '94 with a new car
>
> The choice is yours-
> our deals are the best
>
> **Mondeos £10,995**
> **Escorts £9,495**
>
> Two years interest free credit on all new cars
>
> Excellent credit deals as well
>
> * Minimum 50% deposit
>
> 🛑 Interested? contact Giles
> on 9876 54321 ☎

Consumers and Customers

Sponsorship

Another form of advertising and promotion is sponsorship. Two types of sponsorship exist:

1 The first form of sponsorship is when an organisation agrees to fund an event, team or person in return for advertising their product or service. For example, each major football team is sponsored by a leading organisation. In return, the players advertise the product or service on their shirts.
2 The second type of sponsorship is when an organisation pays a famous person to advertise its product or service for them. For example, Lucozade has been associated with the famous athlete Daley Thompson and Holsten Pils lager was advertised by Jeff Goldblum.

The aim of sponsorship is to heighten awareness of the product and increase sales by having the endorsement of a famous person, who customers want to associate themselves with.

Advantages

- Sponsorship at large events will be seen by thousands of people, locally, nationally or internationally.
- Customers may buy the product because they want to be associated with famous people, e.g. beautiful models sponsoring cosmetics.
- It is an indirect route to television coverage. By sponsoring a team or an event the company will be seen by viewers watching television, in addition to the crowd watching the event.
- The company will be associated with a particular event, team or person and this will raise the image and profile of the organisation.
- The organisation can benefit from the high profile that a particular team, event or person may be experiencing at certain times in the year. For example, when Linford Christie won the 100 metres in the Olympic Games the Milk Marketing Board, with which Christie is associated, also benefited from his success.
- Particular causes and charities can ask famous people to sponsor an event at no charge to the organisation in order to raise the profile of the issue being promoted. For example, Elizabeth Taylor gives a lot of time and money to organising events for AIDS awareness.

Disadvantages

- The cost of sponsorship is very high.
- If a famous star is associated with a controversy, the organisation's reputation may also be affected. For example, Pepsi Cola withdrew from a contract with Michael Jackson because of the adverse publicity that he recently received internationally.
- It is difficult to measure the success of sponsoring a particular event, person or team.
- When choosing a sponsor the organisation is assuming that people attend the events, know the people or support the team.

ACTIVITY

1 Find out who sponsors the following famous football teams:
 (a) Leeds United
 (b) Liverpool
 (c) Manchester United
 (d) Chelsea
2 Who would you choose to sponsor:
 (a) Vegetarian meals
 (b) Holidays in the Far East
 (c) Cosmetics
 (d) Aftershave
 (e) Greenpeace
3 Which large organisations sponsor the following events:
 (a) Tennis at Wimbledon
 (b) Premiership football
 (c) Inspector Morse (the television series)
 (d) The Olympic Games
4 With which product, service or charity to you associate the following sponsors:
 (a) Tom Conti
 (b) Jimmy Saville
 (c) Dudley Moore
 (d) Joanna Lumley
 (e) Jerry Hall

(3.2.1)

Restrictions There are restrictions that an organisation needs to be aware of when looking at sponsorship. Many cosmetic companies would love to have Princess Diana sponsoring their products, but unfortunately the Royal family is not allowed to sponsor anything other than charities and social causes. Restrictions also apply to Members of Parliament. Similarly, current newsreaders are not allowed to sponsor products or services, as it is felt that because of their high public profile, anything they say would be interpreted as fact rather than recommendation.

Competitions

Many organisations create competitions for customers to enter in an attempt to promote their products or services. Legally a customer does not need to actually buy the product to enter, which is why the promotion is often followed by the statement 'no purchase necessary'. Competitions can take many forms and may include:

1 Money inside crisp packets
2 Free draws
3 Crosswords
4 Slogans and catch-phrases
5 Games of skill, e.g. writing, drawing, designing

Consumers and Customers

Advantages
- Consumers may buy the product because they like the challenge of entering the competition.
- The entries will provide the organisation with valuable research data about the type of customers who buy the product and where they are located.
- Additional publicity can be gained for the organisation by organising a big promotion to announce the winner.

Disadvantages
- Time-consuming and difficult to administer.
- It may require minor adjustments to production processes, e.g. printing and including the competition details.
- It is necessary to be aware of and abide by the rules relating to running competitions.

ACTIVITY

Identify the types of competition used by the following organisations:
1. Walker's Crisps
2. Hoover
3. McDonald's
4. The *Times* Newspaper
5. Littlewoods

(3.2.1)

ACTIVITY

Design a competition that could be used by your organisation, school, college or work. You may want to design it for the people who work within the organisation or alternatively you may want to focus on your customers instead. Remember that the objective of the competition is to raise the profile of your organisation.

Note: Nationwide Building Society recently ran a competition for all its staff to produce an advertisement to promote the organisation. The winning entries were actually filmed and shown on television.

(3.2.5)

Other methods
Organisations use a variety of other methods to promote their products too. These can include:
- Free demonstrations
- Special displays
- Price reductions
- Bargain packs
- Free samples
- Money back coupons

ACTIVITY

Can you associate any of the other methods just listed with particular organisations?
(3.2.1)

Resources required to produce materials

Any promotion undertaken by an organisation involves four key resources. These include:
- Time
- People
- Materials and equipment
- Finance

Before a decision is made to go ahead with a promotion an organisation must assess the cost of these resources to ensure that they can afford to proceed.

Time
There is a clear process which any promotion follows from beginning to end and each stage takes time. The following diagram illustrates these stages clearly:

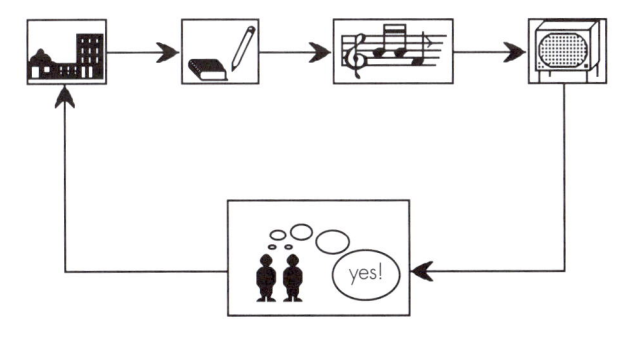

The key stages involved in devising a promotion campaign

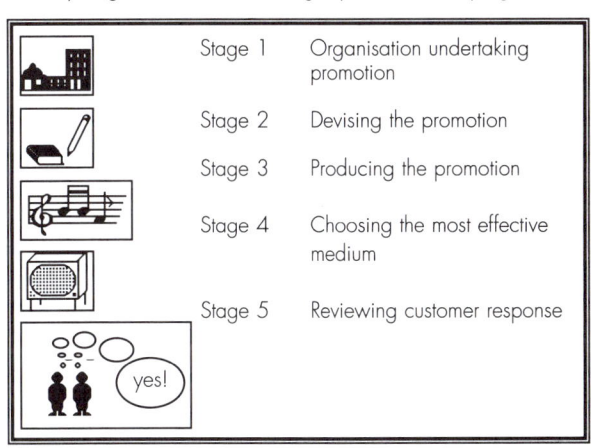

	Stage 1	Organisation undertaking promotion
	Stage 2	Devising the promotion
	Stage 3	Producing the promotion
	Stage 4	Choosing the most effective medium
	Stage 5	Reviewing customer response

161

Consumers and Customers

Stage 1 Identifies the organisation which is organising the promotional campaign. The organisation may decide to develop the campaign itself or to use an advertising agency to do it for them. This will depend upon the size of the budget allocated for the promotion and whether there are any qualified personnel within the organisation.

Stage 2 Involves the sharing of ideas about the best form of promotion to use and how the message is to be presented. A number of questions have to be asked at this stage:
- Who are our customers?
- What type of promotion would appeal?
- Should it include words, music or pictures?
- Who should the promotion be aimed at?
- What form of medium do they use?
- When should the promotion be launched?
- Which staff need to be involved?
- What resources are needed?
- How much has been allocated to the budget?

All these factors will be discussed in the planning stage and decisions reached before progression onto Stage 3.

Stage 3 Having agreed about the type of promotion, stage 3 involves the actual production of the advertisement. Qualified staff will be involved in a whole range of activities including:
- Designing story boards
- Creating slogans
- Drawing diagrams
- Choosing appropriate materials
- Taping voice overs
- Liaising with sponsors
- Dealing with printers
- Organising film productions

Stage 4 This stage involves the actual launch of the promotion and may include:
- Television
- Radio
- Magazines
- Newspapers
- Journals
- Cinemas
- Coupons
- Competitions

The choice of medium will depend upon who the organisation is aiming the promotion at, what form of media they refer to and the budget involved.

Stage 5 This is the final but very important stage, and involves evaluating the success of the promotion. The organisation will have to identify the total cost of the operation in terms of time, money, and physical and human resources. This then needs to be measured against customer attitudes and responses in order to assess the success or failure of the promotion. The time-scale involved in all five stages will depend upon the size and type of promotion undertaken.

People

An organisation which wants to undertake a marketing or promotional launch has to decide whether to organise the activity within the organisation or ask an external agency to organise the launch on its behalf. The decision will depend upon whether the organisation is large enough to employ specialised marketing staff. If not, the work is usually contracted out to an advertising agency.

An organisation which is able to undertake its own marketing will usually employ the following specialists:

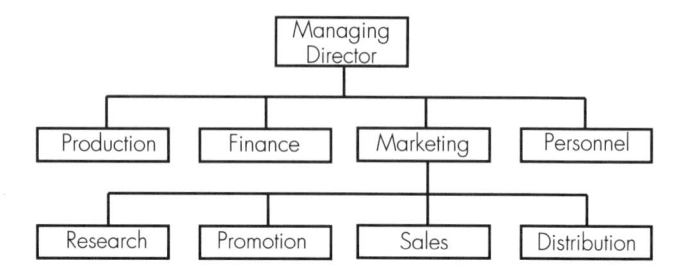

```
                    Managing
                    Director
        ┌──────────┬────┴────┬──────────┐
   Production   Finance   Marketing   Personnel
        ┌──────────┬─────────┬──────────┐
    Research   Promotion    Sales    Distribution
```

The *Marketing Director* will be responsible for planning the overall marketing strategy, including market research, promotion, sales and distribution.

The *Market Researcher* will be responsible for research market trends, suggesting ideas for product innovation, undertaking research and development and providing statistical data to support findings.

Staff responsible for *Promotions* will be involved in producing advertising materials, organising sales promotions and promoting good public relations. They will have to be creatively minded and highly skilled at graphics, computer design, artwork and lettering. They will also work as part of a team.

Sales Representatives are in charge of dealing with customers, finding new customers and providing an after-sales service.

Distribution staff oversee the warehousing, distribution, packaging and despatching of stock.

There are many advantages of employing specialised marketing staff within an organisation:
1. They have a detailed understanding of the workings of the organisation.
2. The customer is confident in dealing with the organisation because the employees have specialised knowledge about the product or service being promoted.
3. The promotions may be more effective because the marketing department knows its customers.
4. The organisation has greater control over the role of marketing and promotions within the firm.
5. When marketing is an integral part of an organisation, the organisation becomes much more customer-focused and responds to changing customer needs quickly.

In smaller organisations one person may be responsible for more than one function or the firm may employ specialised external organisations to undertake key roles. The distribution function is very often contracted out to transport firms: for example,

Eddie Stobart lorries are seen throughout Britain transporting goods for a variety of organisations. In addition, the promotional role may be undertaken by an advertising agency.

Advertising agency

An advertising agency will provide a range of specialised services to an organisation. These include market research, information about competitors, support with preparing a marketing plan and providing advice about the most suitable form of medium to use to promote a product or service into a particular market.

The advertising agency will also employ specialised staff who provide the creative services for the client. These include:
- Preparing television and press advertisements
- Advertising posters
- Mail shots
- Catalogues and leaflets
- Displays and stands

In addition, the agency will help to design company logos, letterheads, packaging and the overall image of the organisation.

Employing an advertising agency is not cheap. However, the cost is usually cheaper than employing staff to undertake the specialised functions needed. The advertising agency provides a comprehensive service with highly skilled personnel and an organisation can pay for these services as and when they are required.

> **ACTIVITY**
>
> Produce a job advertisement and job description for the post of a promotional assistant working within a large advertising agency, called Rufus Mancini Ltd. Remember to identify the types of skills needed and the duties to be undertaken. If you are not sure, look in the job advertisement section of the quality newspapers for ideas and refer to the earlier text of this book.
> (3.2.3) (3.2.5)

Materials and equipment

A range of physical resources may be used in the preparation of a promotional display and the final choice will depend upon the type of display to be produced and the skills of the team producing the display. The following materials are available for use by a promotional team wishing to create an original and eye-catching advertisement:

Resource and type	Advantages	Disadvantages
Paper and card		
Newsprint	Cheap to buy Good to practice on and jot down ideas	Poor quality Easily tears Short life span
Sugar paper	Cheap to buy Variety of colours Useful for backing designs	Poor quality Easily tears
Tracing paper	Effective tool for copying pictures and logos	Expensive Can smudge
Bond or cartridge paper	Good quality Various sizes Various colours Easy to cut to size Easy to paste	Quite expensive Not as sturdy as card Difficult to cover with adhesive film
Card	Sturdy Variety of sizes Variety of colours More professional finish Can be covered with adhesive film	Difficult to cut More expensive than paper Harder to stick onto display
Pencils		
Plain	Useful for planning Easy to rub out Cheap Different types are available: hard (H) for precise sketches and soft (B) for shading	Limited visual appeal Can smudge
Coloured	Effective for shading Wide variety of shades	Cannot rub out Not visible from long distance
Felt tip pens	Wide variety of colours, sizes, types Effective visual impact Useful for lettering	Permanent Can leak through paper Not suitable for extensive shading
Stencils and transfers	Effective presentation Wide variety of styles available	Expensive Difficult to keep in a straight line
Paints		
Water colours, oils, poster, acrylic, aerosol	Extensive coverage possible Wide variety of colours and types Effective visual presentation Wide variety of techniques can be used	Messy Need for specialist equipment and brushes Drying time makes production process longer Paints can run together if not mixed properly
Acetate film	Most suitable for use with an OHP Can use overlays Can be used with special pens or with the photocopier Coloured pens help produce a creative display	Expensive Print has to be of certain size to be seen Non-permanent pens can smudge Needs an oral presentation to support the message

Consumers and Customers

Resource and type	Advantages	Disadvantages
Videos	Moving pictures Mix of sound and visual impact Wider scope for style of presentation Can be used with other displays	Specialised equipment needed Specialised skills needed Expensive Needs monitor to present results Expensive
Audio tapes	Can be used for recording speeches Can be used with other types of display Cheap	Quality of taping music or needs to be good for the presentation to be effective Needs a recorder for the presentation Music might not appeal to all customers
Computer packages paper	Wide variety of packages available Varied applications Professional finish Lettering and graphics available Different size prints Colour and black and white print available	Expensive Specialised skills and machinery needed Software licences Printer can usually only take A4 Photocopier is needed to enlarge Colour copier is very expensive

When producing a display it is important that the following suggestions are taken into consideration:

1 The presentation must be eye-catching and should grab the reader's attention. A common trick is to begin the presentation with an intriguing question, e.g.:

Where will you be in ten years' time?

2 Using company logos as part of the promotion will help to project the company image, e.g.

3 Signs can be more effective than words in certain displays. If used correctly they will succeed in getting the customer's attention. They are also used for informing people of what they can and cannot do. For example:

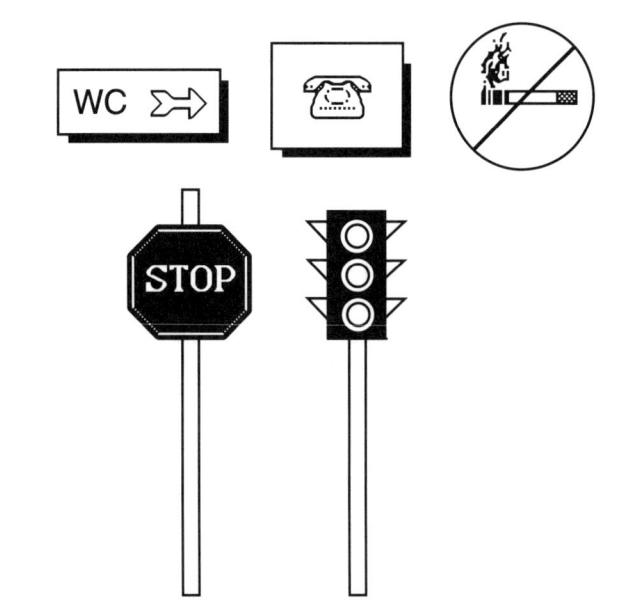

4 It is important not to put to much information on the display because it will look confused. On the other hand not enough information can make the presentation look bare. For example:

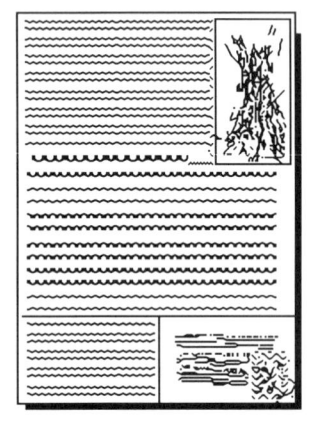

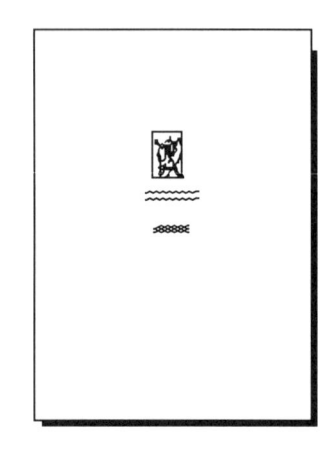

5 The display should contain all the relevant information and who to contact if further information is needed. For example

Interested?
For further details contact Dominic on 2341 43523

6 Key terms should be highlighted in bold print in order for them to stand out from the rest of the display, e.g.:

Downtown Nightclub
presents
a 24 hour dance sensation
Places limited
Tickets only £15.00
Saturday 12th May
Be there or be square
From 9pm onwards

7 The use of alliteration may help to present a message. This is when similar letters and sounds are used to reinforce a point, e.g.

Consumers and Customers

sweet smelling, sensuously scented Secret Perfume

8   A range of fonts and different size print can be used to display written information, e.g.

A A **A** A A A A **A** A A
A A A A A A A **A** A A

It is important that the font chosen is used to enhance the message not confuse it.

9   Colour can be used to highlight key areas, attract the reader's attention and to create an atmosphere.
    - Black, red and blue are bold colours which stand out from the display.
    - Green and cream are regarded as having a gentle calming effect.
    - Yellow and orange are bright, vivid colours which portray warmth.

10 Borders should be used to mount the display and provide a framework for the information within it.

11 It is important that the display can be seen from a distance. If the customer is not initially attracted to the promotion, he or she may never actually spend time looking at the promotion in detail.

12 It is important to be creative, imaginative and original.

ACTIVITY

Practise your creative skills by producing a suitable promotion to advertise the GNVQ courses within your college or school. You may just want to focus on business, or alternatively, if your institution delivers a range of GNVQ programmes, you may want to promote them all. Remember to identify the key features about the courses and your institution and emphasise them. Your promotion may include posters and leaflets, you may produce a video or tape or you may want to organise a GNVQ event day, for example. The choice is yours.
(3.2.3) (3.2.5)

Finance

All projects have to be costed at the start to ensure that the actual promotion does not exceed the planned budget. The costs are then monitored throughout the production of the project and if any additional funds are needed for unexpected expenses agreement would have to be obtained from management. At the end of the project it is important to produce an overall financial summary, indicating total costs involved and revenue received from increased sales.

For example, Hoover's free gifts of holidays abroad proved to be more expensive than the revenue received from increased sales, and caused the company very great difficulties.

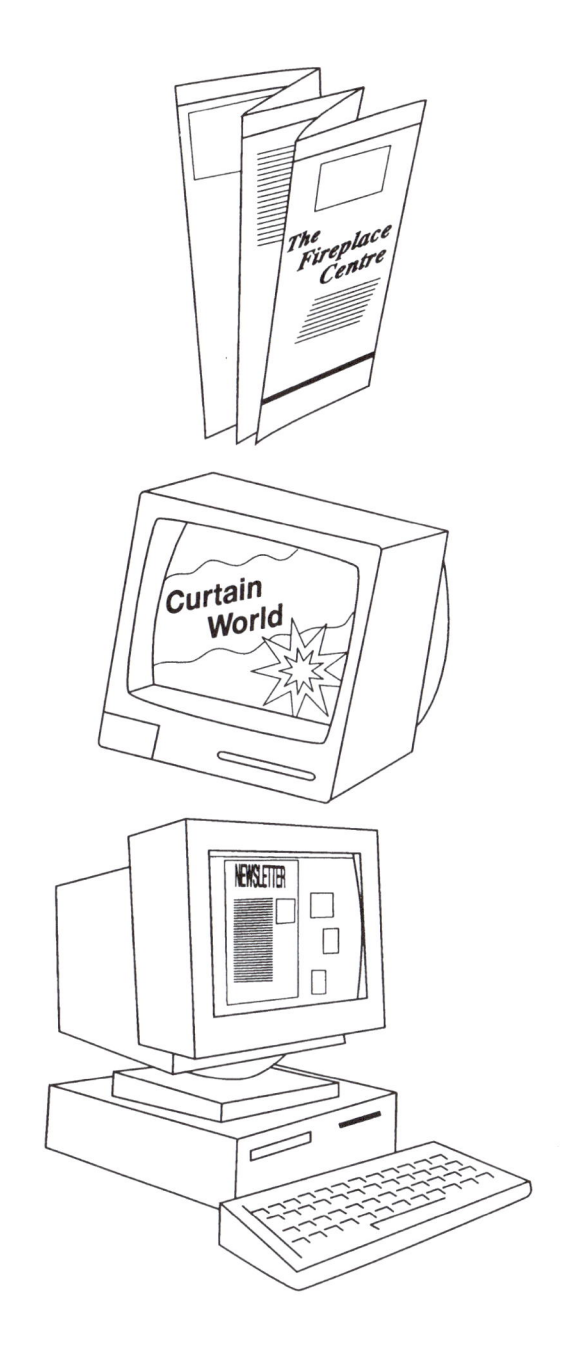

The potential of different media to produce promotional materials

A range of different media is available to assist organisations in the production of promotional materials. These fall neatly into three categories:
- Paper-based media
- Lens-based media and
- Computer-based media

Paper-based media

Paper-based media include sales letters, newspaper and magazine advertisements, posters, leaflets, house magazines, notices, circulars, hand-outs and visual displays. The methods are useful for both informing the customer of a product or service and persuading the customer to buy. Detailed information may be included within house magazines and circulars, whereas posters and leaflets are excellent methods

Consumers and Customers

for highlighting key issues. It is also possible to combine more than one method. A visual display for example may be comprised of posters and eye-catching signs. However, the customer may also pick up a detailed information booklet from the stand as he or she leaves.

The emphasis for paper-based media is placed on communicating facts to customers through words and diagrams. The materials may be distributed at random, door to door, circulated to key customers or displayed publicly for all to see. Larger organisations may employ specialist marketing staff to create the literature or enlist an advertising agency to do it for them. In smaller organisations one person may produce all the materials without having any specialist training at all.

The main advantages of paper-based media are that they are relatively cheap to produce, visual and written communication can be combined to create an eye-catching display and the resources are usually available within all organisations. The disadvantages are that the materials usually have a short life span and it is necessary to update ideas on a regular basis.

ACTIVITY

Produce an appropriate example of a paper-based medium to promote a new restaurant which is to open in your town next week. The restaurant is called Toppers and sells a range of pizzas and Italian dishes. It will be open 7 days a week for both lunches and dinners.
(3.2.5)

Lens-based media

Lens-based media include photography, slides, films and video production. Photography and slide-making are excellent methods of recording, as still life, an actual event which has taken place. Slides clearly need a projector to display the work, but photographs can be mounted and left for people to refer to. The advantage of photography is that it is possible to choose from both black and white or colour prints. Black and white photographs have a dramatic impact and promote a sombre and mellow mood. They are also cheaper than colour photographs. Colour film, on the other hand, effectively communicates warmth and realism.

Film and, more recently, video production, have become popular methods of promoting products and services. Both methods provide the opportunity to communicate through moving pictures and sound. The advances in technology have resulted in video production being relatively simple to use and a range of moods and messages can be conveyed through a short production. Recently, interactive videos have become popular. They incorporate sound, moving pictures and graphics and allow the user to make choices about the sequence and content of information. The technology is still being refined, but in a few years' time interactive videos will be commonplace.

If an organisation decides to produce a video or film to promote a product or service it is usual for the following important job roles to be filled.

The writer or producer The writer or producer will need to decide upon the idea and possible script. It is usual to produce a storyboard, which simply outlines the main theme of the promotion, people involved, their roles and what is said. The storyboard is referred to during production to ensure the sequencing of events is correctly applied.

The director The director has the responsibility for taking charge in the making of the film. The director will select the participants, rehearse the performance and liaise with the camera person to check the quality of the filming.

The camera crew The camera crew oversees the lighting and the filming of the production and will also be responsible for ensuring the quality of sound.

The editor Finally, the editor is responsible for editing the film if required and ensuring that the finished version is of the highest possible quality.

Lens-based media have the advantage of recording 'true life' either on stills or on moving pictures. They encourage creativity and can be very effective in presenting what would otherwise be detailed written information. People very often respond to pictures far more than to a written script, which demands a higher level of concentration. Remember the famous quotation: 'a picture speaks a thousand words'.

The disadvantages of lens-based media are that they are expensive, time-consuming and demand technical skills and equipment. The art of presenting information in a short video is also difficult, and some promotions fail to achieve the desired effect because the production has not clearly presented the facts. Some organisations therefore request advertising agencies to produce the promotions for them because of the high level of technical skill required.

ACTIVITY

Produce a storyboard which could be used to promote a new aftershave or perfume. You will need to decide upon a name for the product and the theme to the promotion. Record the promotion step by step on the storyboard and write out the script. Don't worry if you cannot draw: stick people will do – alternatively, use a computer.
(3.2.5)

Consumers and Customers

Computer-based media

Computer-based media include a range of computer packages, including word processing, desktop publishing, spreadsheets, databases and graphics. Each of these packages offers a range of functions which could be used within the production of promotional material.

Word processing packages provide a much more professional finish to typescript than written or typed versions. The variety of fonts and formats ensure a creative finish to the document. *Desktop publishing* enables the user to produce very professional publications combining text and graphics. *Spreadsheets* and *databases* allow the manipulation and storage of numerical and textual data. The results can be printed using a variety of tables and layouts. Finally, *graphics* enable the user to draw using the computer (and clip art actually provides a range of pre-drawn diagrams and illustrations, which is useful if the user cannot draw and lacks creative flair).

The advantages of computer-based media are that they provide a professional finish to the work being produced and a wide variety of techniques are available. The disadvantages are that the equipment and packages can be expensive and the technology is not always available within an organisation.

ACTIVITY

Undertake an audit of the range of computer technology within your organisation and the types of functions which are available. Look at both hardware and software. Remember to get hard copy evidence of the functions (e.g. a copy of a word-processed document or a spreadsheet) to use as evidence within your portfolio.
(3.2.5)

ACTIVITY

Which methods would you use for producing promotions for the following events?
1 The launch of a new product
2 The opening of a new superstore
3 A price reduction on an existing product
4 A college or school open day
5 A drama performance
6 A coffee morning
7 A rock concert
8 Raising funds for famine in Africa
9 The launch of a new GNVQ textbook
10 The Olympic Games
11 Blood donation
(3.2.1)

ACTIVITY

Geared up for sport

Identify an organisation that produces and sells sportswear, e.g. Reebok or Nike. From your research provide evidence for the following tasks:
1 Name the organisation and identify the characteristics of the consumers who purchase their product or service. *(3.1.2)*
2 Identify the recent trends in consumer demand for sportswear, using appropriate graphical methods. *(3.1.3) (3.1.4)*
3 Identify the factors that affect a change in demand for sportswear. *(3.1.1) (3.1.5)*
4 Produce a display that illustrates the promotional material produced within a range of media to promote the sportswear of your chosen organisation. You could include examples of advertisements in magazines, a picture board illustrating an advertisement on television or at the cinema, a tape of an advertisement on a local radio station etc. Highlight how the promotional material influences consumer behaviour and assess how successful the advertising campaign is. *(3.2.1) (3.2.6)*
5 Produce your own promotional material to market an item of sportswear and identify the type of consumer you hope to attract. *(3.2.5)*
6 Why have you chosen that particular method? *(3.2.4)*
7 What are the constraints in designing promotional materials? *(3.2.2)*
8 Identify the cost of placing your promotional idea in an appropriate form of medium. *(3.2.1)*
9 Why are customers important to a business organisation? *(3.1.6)*

You can undertake this activity individually or as part of a group. However, if the promotional materials are produced by a group your action plan must clearly illustrate the part you played in the process.

Consumers and Customers

Helping hand for beleaguered charities trying to make the most of their money

Britain's charities are handing out money faster than it is coming in, according to a report published last month, but a number of charitable banks and building societies are helping smaller voluntary organisations make the most of their funds.

The survey of 2,000 charities carried out by Hemmington Scott also suggests that small charities are being overlooked by the kind-hearted: the smallest 25% of charitable organisations saw their incomes fall by 5% last year, whilst the largest 25% enjoyed a 20% boost in funds.

The squeeze on charity balance-sheets is further compounded by current interest rates, but several building societies have improved the returns they offer on charity deposit accounts...

ACTIVITY

The article above was printed in The *Guardian* on 2 April 1994:

Tasks

The article clearly outlines that the large charities are successful in gaining financial support, whereas the smaller charities are losing out. One possible reason for this is that the large charities can afford to spend a lot of money on extensive, effective promotions, using a variety of media, and have famous stars to sponsor their cause.

Identify a small charity that you would like to promote. Find out the aims of the charity and the methods it uses to collect funds.

1. Using this information record:
   (a) The objectives behind your promotional campaign. *(3.2.4)*
   (b) The range of methods that could be used, listing the associated advantages and disadvantages, including constraints. *(3.2.1) (3.2.2)*
   (c) The type of promotion actually chosen and reasons for choice. Make a list of the resources needed beforehand to ensure that the materials are in stock. *(3.2.3) (3.2.4)*
2. Produce the promotion and evaluate how successful it has been. *(3.2.5) (3.2.6)*

ACTIVITY *(3.1.2–5) (3.2.1–6)*

Marketing the college or school

The objective of the unit activity is to apply all the concepts and ideas that you have learnt as a result of completing Elements 4.1 and 4.2 to producing a marketing activity for the college or school in which you are studying. We have seen that public sector organisations are as much focused on consumers and customers as are private sector organisations. The work that you produce either individually or as a team may be used by your organisation, and therefore it is important only to produce work of the highest quality.

The marketing activity will involve you in:
1. Undertaking research into the types of students who study at the institution.
2. Producing a marketing plan outlining the planned promotion and methods to be used.
3. Producing promotional material to help advertise the available programmes of study.

Tasks

1. In groups or individually undertake market research to identify the range of courses available, the numbers of students choosing to study these programmes and whether the students are full-time or part time. Present your findings using suitable computer- or manually generated graphics and a written account. *(3.1.2) (3.1.3) (3.1.4)*
2. Identify whether these results have changed in recent years. Have students' choices of courses changed over the last few years and if so how? What possible reasons could help to explain these changes? Present your findings using suitable computer- or manually generated graphics and a written account. *(3.1.3) (3.1.4) (3.1.5)*
3. Having established who your customers are you are now expected to produce a marketing plan and promotional materials that will inform new students about the range of courses available. Your marketing plan should identify the objective of the promotion and the legal and ethical constraints which you need to be aware of. *(3.2.2) (3.2.3) (3.2.4)*

    It should also identify the advantages and disadvantages of different forms of media and the reason for choosing a particular type. *(3.2.1)*

    Finally, the marketing plan should include the planned promotion that you want to produce plus the materials needed in order to carry out the activity. *(3.2.3)*
4. Produce the promotional materials to promote the college or school. *(3.2.5)*
5. Evaluate how successful the promotion has been. *(3.2.6)*

Consumers and Customers

MULTIPLE CHOICE

1 One of the objectives of promotional material is to:
   A Create demand
   B Stimulate the competition
   C Increase production costs
   D Maximise overheads

2 When producing promotional material the *most* important feature to be aware of is:
   A The organisational structure
   B Channels of communication
   C Legal constraints
   D Personnel problems

3 Sponsorship is a form of promotion. An example of promotional sponsorship is:
   A A famous slogan used on a television advertisement
   B A request to a local bank for funding
   C Endorsement of a product by a famous personality
   D A display stand at a national exhibition centre

4 Which of the following would be the best form of advertising for a manufacturer of clocks and watches wishing to launch an expensive new wristwatch across the country?
   A Local radio advert
   B TV advert
   C Competition run in schools
   D Free samples delivered in the post

5 The code of practice relating to advertising on commercial television is laid down by the:
   A Television Commission Code of Advertising Procedures
   B Independent Television Code of Advertising Campaigns
   C Code of Independent Television Commission
   D Independent Television Commission Code of Advertising Standards and Practice

6 One of the *main* advantages of advertising in newspapers and magazines is that:
   A Circulation figures are known in advance
   B Newspapers tend to be thrown away after one day
   C Striking imagery may be used to promote the product or service
   D Many adverts may appear on the same page

7 One of the *disadvantages* of advertising on television is that:
   A A national or local audience can be reached
   B Television is very expensive
   C The quality of production is usually poor
   D Advertising is restricted to a local area

8 One advantage of competitions as a form of promotion is that:
   A The entries may provide the organisation with valuable data about the customers
   B The activity is time-consuming and difficult to administer
   C The organisation is not obliged to inspect the competition entries or give away any prizes
   D The organisation can be sure that every customer will take part

9 One of the *main* advantages of employing specialist marketing staff within an organisation is that:
   A All aspects of the market can be targeted
   B The organisation should become more customer-focused
   C The organisation will secure a larger market share from its competitors
   D It is cheaper than using marketing agencies

10 The marketing director will be mainly responsible for:
   A Collecting market research data from primary and secondary sources
   B Producing advertising videos and radio jingles
   C Planning the overall marketing strategy, including market research, promotion, sales and distribution
   D Advertising for and interviewing marketing staff

SHORT ANSWER

1 Identify the roles and responsibilities of the following staff:
   Marketing director
   Market researcher
   Promotional staff
   Sales representatives
   Distribution staff

2 Distinguish between lens-based, paper-based and computer-based media.

3 What is the role of an advertising agency?

4 What physical resources are required to produce a promotional display stand?

5 What are the key stages involved in devising a promotional campaign?

6 Identify the relevant consumer legislation which would protect the consumer in the following situations:
   (a) Buying a hi-fi on credit
   (b) Purchasing a three-piece suite which has faulty springs
   (c) Buying a bag of biscuits which are described as mixed variety but which, when opened, are all of the same type

Consumers and Customers

7 What are the three main objectives of any promotional campaign?

8 What does the word alliteration mean and how might it be used when producing a promotion?

9 What is meant by the word medium? Make a list of different types of medium that an organisation may use when producing a promotion.

10 Distinguish between advertisements, sponsorship and competition as forms of promotion.

11 What are the legal and ethical constraints on an organisation when producing a promotion?

(PC) 3.3.5 Describe procedures in one business organisation for dealing with customer complaints

(PC) 3.3.6 Identify relevant legislation to protect customers

Providing customer service

A customer may be defined as:

'a person or organisation who requires or needs the product or service which another can provide.'

A customer may be *internal* to the organisation or *external*.

An *internal customer* is an employer or employee within the organisation who provides a service to another person also working within the firm. A receptionist, for example, provides a service to the secretary, who provides a service to the sales assistant who provides a service to the external customer. The receptionist, secretary and sales assistant are all internal customers providing a quality service which ultimately the external customer benefits from.

The idea of having internal customers means that everyone who is employed within the organisation understands that they must provide a quality service for each other in order to provide a quality service for their external customers. An *external customer* is an organisation or person who buys the final product or service offered for sale by the firm. The external customers may be local, national or even internationally based. Each one is an individual, with individual needs and wants.

Despite the move towards the importance of both internal and external customers, many organisations still have a traditional view of looking at customers. This is illustrated in the organisation chart at the top of the next page. You can clearly see the order of importance which the organisation places on its customers. In this situation it is the customers who appear to be providing a service to the staff who provide a service to the supervisors, and so on. The highest level of importance is given to the Managing Director (or in some organisations the Chairperson), who probably rarely meets a customer on a day-to-day basis.

A radical alternative to this view, and one which clearly shows the customer as providing the most important contribution to the organisation, is illustrated in the second diagram. The diagram clearly illustrates that the organisation is 'customer-focused' in that it places the customer at the top of the pyramid, thereby indicating how important and valued the customer is to the organisation. The importance of both internal and external customers to an organisation is very nicely illustrated by Jan Carlzon, who works for SAS Airlines and is quoted as saying:

'If you are not serving a customer – you'd better be serving someone who is.'

ELEMENT 3.3
Providing customer service

Performance criteria

(PC) 3.3.1 Identify an organisation's customers and its customer needs

(PC) 3.3.2 Identify and describe customer service in an organisation

(PC) 3.3.3 Identify business communications which meet customer needs

(PC) 3.3.4 Demonstrate business communications which meet customer needs

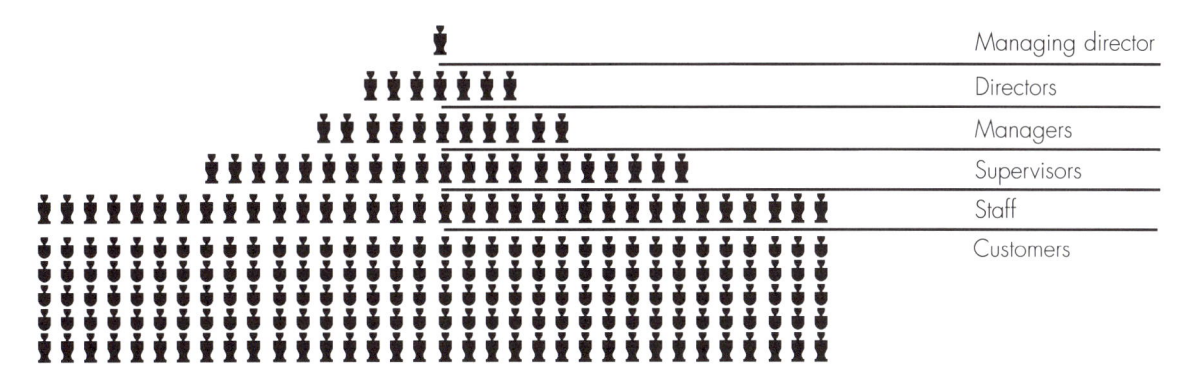

Consumers and Customers

Traditional view of customers

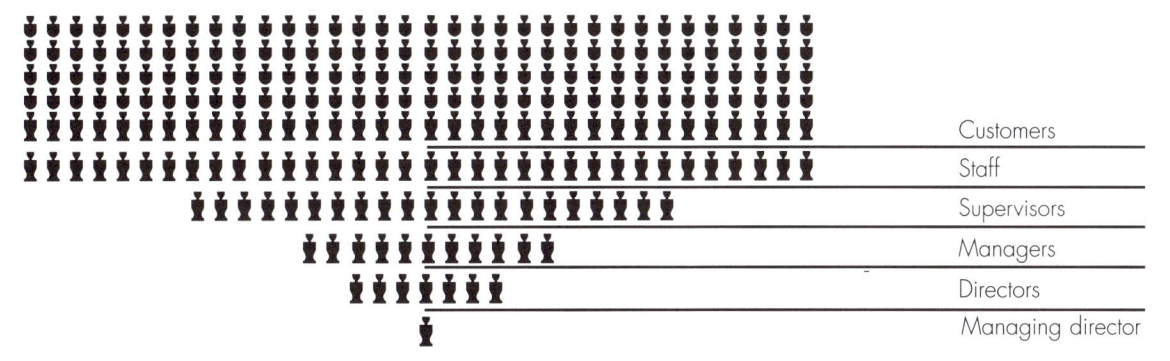

A customer-focused organisation

ACTIVITY

Look at your college or school. Who are its customers? Are they students, parents, employers or other individuals or organisations? To what extent is the organisation customer-focused? What facilities are available within the organisation for the customers and how does the school or college try to keep the customers informed?
(3.3.1)

Satisfied customers

ACTIVITY

Why is it important that all organisations try to satisfy their customers?
 Once the customers have left the store having made their purchases, does it really matter if they are not altogether happy with their goods?
 If a customer returns an item, why should the organisation be happy to give a refund? Doesn't this mean just another lost sale?
(3.3.1) (3.3.2)

A satisfied customer is the most effective advertisement an organisation could hope for. Satisfied customers mean repeat business. Satisfied customers also inform their friends, who in turn become satisfied customers. The multiplier effect takes over, and very soon the reputation and image of the company is known throughout the area. An improved company image and positive feedback from customers results in increased job satisfaction and individual commitment from every member of the organisation. Everybody benefits from a commitment to customer care and customer satisfaction.

Consumers and Customers

Dissatisfied customers

Similarly, the reverse is true. A dissatisfied customer is the worst possible advertisement for an organisation. In the same way that the company image is enhanced through positive feedback from customers, negative feedback can quickly damage the reputation of an organisation. It is important, therefore, that an organisation has a system for dealing with dissatisfied customers, identifying the nature of that dissatisfaction and taking action to rectify the matter.

ACTIVITY

Identify what an organisation can do to change a dissatisfied customer into a satisfied one.

Produce a poster or a leaflet that an organisation could use to promote their commitment to customer care and customer satisfaction.
(3.3.1) (3.3.2)

Customer needs

Serving the customer is clearly essential for any organisation to survive. Each customer is an individual with individual needs. In order that an organisation can provide the prospective customer with the service they expect, it is important that the organisation knows its customers and what their requirements are. By understanding who its customers are, the organisation will be able to anticipate some of its customers' needs.

Customer needs can be identified as:
1. Wishing to make a purchase
2. Seeking/requiring information
3. Asking for help
4. Needing customer care
5. Needing special service to meet special needs
6. Wanting a refund or to exchange goods
7. Making a complaint
8. Ethical standards

Wishing to make a purchase

A principal aim of any private sector organisation is to encourage customers to make a purchase. Therefore it is essential that this is made as easy as possible for the customer. If the customer is visiting the store the goods should be readily available for inspection. If the customer is making an enquiry, information should be made available effectively and efficiently, causing as little inconvenience to the customer as possible. It should be easy for the customer to get basic information about the product, in particular how much it costs and how it is possible to pay. Sales assistants should be on hand to provide additional information and assistance if required, but should avoid being too pushy. If the customer wishes to try the product this should be made possible, if appropriate. Lastly, the process of payment should be straightforward and friendly, so that the customer is not dissuaded or embarrassed.

ACTIVITY

The fast food chain McDonald's have worked very hard to ensure that it is as easy as possible for customers to make a purchase when they enter the store. Make a list of the ways in which McDonald's, or other fast food outlets, encourage customers to enter and make a purchase.
(3.3.1)

Information

The objectives of all organisations are to attract customers, provide them with a product or service which meets their needs and encourage them to return. The more detailed and varied the information that the organisation can provide the potential customer, the more informed the customer will be about the benefits and qualities of the product or service being offered. Advertising campaigns are just one form of promotion aimed at attracting and informing the customers. However, more detailed information also needs to be available to provide further information and help answer possible questions.

The following list outlines the possible methods that could be used to help inform a potential customer:

- A *catalogue or prospectus* providing information about the product or service, order codes and price. The information can be supported by photographs and a brief description for each item. The whole product range is available for customers to look at, either in the organisation or at ease in their own homes. It is important that the catalogue or prospectus provides the customers with details about how to proceed with the sale, e.g. telephone ordering, application form, names of relevant staff and methods of payment. Catalogues can be used both for mail order shopping and as a method of providing further information about product ranges within an organisation.

- *Leaflets* provide more detailed information about a particular product or service. Having seen something of interest, very often the customer requires further facts before proceeding with the sale. A leaflet or hand-out serves this purpose and should contain a detailed description of the product or service and a person to contact (with their telephone number) if further information is required. Very often organisations design leaflets in a question and answer format. The questions relate to common queries that customers have and the answers help to clarify details about the product or service.
- *Statements* should be sent out regularly to customers who are paying by credit or hire purchase arrangements. The statements should detail amounts paid by the customer and balances outstanding, with appropriate dates. If a customer has paid in full it is important that a *receipt* is issued with the amount paid and the date that the transaction was made. This ensures that there are no complications if the product or service has to be returned at a later date.

  If an organisation is providing *credit terms* as part of the service a leaflet or hand-out can be used to summarise the main features of the finance scheme. The annual percentage rate (APR) should always be quoted in the leaflet, as it is a legal requirement that customers are aware of the total interest charged. It is also important, however, that this information is further supported by a one-to-one interview in order to identify the particular needs of each individual customer.
- *Displays with notices* provide the customers with information about the location of products and services within the organisation. They are usually located at a level that can been seen from a distance. Supermarkets use the method to help the customer identify where products are located. They also serve as a useful reminder for customers who may forget to buy a purchase that they need.
- *Labelling* must be clear in order that the customer can see the price, size, quality or other features of the product or service. Further information required by law includes weight and details of ingredients.

  Layout of goods must be clear and orderly. Related products should be within close proximity so that the customers can find what they want easily. For example, a shop selling jeans may well display the belts close by. Similarly, a college or school will display prospectuses under key subject headings within the reception area, where customers can also get details about course costs and methods of payment.
- *Telephone enquiries* need to be dealt with efficiently and professionally. Telephonists need to be fully informed about the services offered by the organisation, so that the caller is informed and the call is transferred to the appropriate member of staff. A delay in answering the phone can mean a lost customer. Similarly, if the lines are always engaged, customers become frustrated and may seek advice elsewhere. Good telephone technique is crucial to the success of any organisation.
- *Open days and promotions* provide an opportunity to invite customers into the organisation and review what is available at their leisure. It is important that a range of display material and hand-outs are provided so that customers can refer to the information as they wander round. The supporting literature also provides a reminder to prospective customers when they read it at home after the event.
- *Face to face* communication is a very important method of providing customer information and should be used to support all the other methods listed above. Assistants should always ensure that they are fully informed about all aspects of the product range so that they can provide the answers to the questions raised by customers. Training days within the organisation should be used to inform all new staff of likely questions that customers may ask and the responses that should be given. In addition staff should be polite and courteous at all times.

ACTIVITY

Which method would you suggest is the most appropriate in providing customers with the information they require in the following situations?

1. Buying a car on credit
2. Recording the cash sale for a new handbag
3. Explaining the range of courses available in a college or school
4. Providing detailed information on a new type of video
5. Informing customers of a new layout within a shop
6. Enquiry about available bicycles, key features and prices
7. Information about money paid for mail order purchases and balance outstanding
8. Launch of a new book or magazine
9. Opening of a new leisure centre
10. New type of vegetarian dish

(3.3.3)

Consumers and Customers

Help

Customers have certain expectations when they enter an organisation. One of the expectations is that help and advice will be available from staff about the products and services that are for sale. Possible questions that customers may ask include:

- What do I get for my money?
- What is this and how does it work?
- Does the product come with any warranty or guarantee?
- How does the price compare with competitors?
- Is the product harmful to the environment?
- Is this compatible with the equipment I have at home?
- Have you got one of these that will fit me?

ACTIVITY

Can you think of any more questions that customers might ask when seeking help to be added to this list? (3.3.1)

It is important that an organisation is sensitive to customers who are seeking help and provides them with the answers that they require. The assistant who is dealing with the customer must be both able and willing to respond positively to the needs of the customer and provide them with the answers to their questions. If the subject is of a very technical nature, it is important that the assistant apologises to the customer, explaining that while they may not have the answers they will try to find someone who has. The assistant should then contact a member of staff who can provide that level of information for the customer, preferably immediately or by telephone later the same day.

There is nothing more annoying for a customer who is seeking information and assistance to get the following types of response:

'It's not my section, ask someone over there somewhere.'
'The answers to your questions are on the back of the box.'
'Can you come back later, I'm busy at the moment.'
'Sorry can't stop, it's my lunch break.'
'That's not my job and the person you want isn't in today.'

Some customers are passed from one assistant to another, asking the same questions and never getting the answers. There are a number of steps that can be followed to ensure that a customer does not receive this kind of treatment and that they leave the organisation as a satisfied customer.

- *Step 1: Acknowledge the customer*
  This involves greeting the customer who is seeking further information and support. Some organisations have a standard greeting. For example, staff who work in McDonald's greet their customers with the standard:

'Hello – can I help you?'

It is important that a standard greeting sounds natural and not monotonous or forced. In other organisations the greeting is left to the discretion of the assistant. Possible examples include:

'Good morning. Do you need further information?'
'Good afternoon. What exactly were you looking for?'
'Hello. Can I be of any assistance?'

Clearly some customers like to browse around on their own and do not feel the need to ask for advice. This is fine. However, others want assistance, but do not always like to ask. It is important therefore that the assistant is able to distinguish between the two types and offer assistance as required.

- *Step 2: Request for information*
  The customer, if seeking information, will communicate their request at this stage. It is important that the assistant listens very carefully to what is being asked in order that the correct response can be provided. Whoever the customer talks to initially is responsible for making sure that the customer's needs are met. Remember: first impressions count!

- *Step 3: Front line accountability*
  To achieve quality of customer service it is important that all staff feel confident to deal with customer enquiries, including the ability to identify the skilled personnel to pass the message on to. Each member of staff has clear areas of responsibility to ensure that this is achieved.

  Telephonists are responsible for checking that the call is passed on to the relevant person. *Receptionists* should ensure that waiting customers feel that their needs are being dealt with and that they are made to feel comfortable and at ease. *Sales assistants* should be competent at handling customer enquiries, and assistants on the customer service desk should provide an efficient and courteous service.

  Departments need to work together in order to provide a 'corporate approach'. This involves all staff having sufficient knowledge and information about the workings of the whole organisation in order that customers feel that they are informed. All staff are responsible for achieving customer satisfaction.

ACTIVITY

Read the following case study and identify how the organisation can become more customer focused.

Roles

Manager:	Kate Robinson
Sales Assistant:	Micho Allen
Sales Assistant:	Peter Frances
Cashier:	Hannah Clarke
Customer:	Charlotte Johnson

Consumers and Customers

Scene: Bookshop
Charlotte is wandering around a large bookshop looking for a copy of a new law publication which has recently been printed.

Charlotte	'Can you help me I'm…'
Micho	'Hang on, I'll be with you in a minute.'
Charlotte	'Well, can you point me in the right direction? I'm looking…'
Micho	'Look madam, I'm a little busy right now. These books need to go back on the shelves. If I don't do it now I'll be late for my lunch.'
Charlotte	'Well who else can help me?'
Micho	'Pete! Over 'ere – this woman needs some help.'
Peter	'Now what?'
Charlotte	'Yes, it *is* me that needs some help. I'm looking for a law publication…'
Peter	'Law? No, no, no, law's not my area. You need to speak to Helena and she's at lunch.'
Charlotte	'Well, can you tell me which area it is in at least please?'
Peter	'Oh yes, I can do that, why didn't you say that was all you needed? It's over there on the left.'
Charlotte	'Is it possible to use these book tokens for publications?'
Peter	'Oh no, I don't think so. You will have to check with the cashier.'

Charlotte wanders over to the law section and is approached by the manager.

Kate	'Good morning, do you need some help?'
Charlotte	'Oh, yes please. I'm looking for the latest publication on Consumer Rights.'
Kate	'Yes Madam, it's right here. I think this is what you are looking for.'
Charlotte	'Excellent. Oh, and by the way, can I use my book tokens for this?'
Kate	'No problem.'

Charlotte wanders over to the cashier, hands over the publication and the book tokens

Hannah	'You can't use tokens for publications – sorry love.'
Charlotte	'But the manager said I could.'
Hannah	'Well I wish someone would tell me what's what. I'll have to go and check. Typical!'

Charlotte eventually leaves with purchase paid for with book tokens. She had been in the shop over half an hour and was now late for her next appointment.
(3.3.1) (3.3.2)

Care
All customers expect to receive a certain standard of service when deciding to make a purchase. The following chart highlights the important points which an organisation should consider when providing excellent customer service and care. This can be referred to as the *five-point plan*.

The Five Point Plan in Customer Care

> ✔ 1. Live up to expectations
> ☎ 2. Prompt, effective and professional front line
> ✍ 3. Attention to detail
> ⌚ 4. Fast and effective response
> 📖 5. Be fully informed

✔ *Live up to expectations*   It is important that an organisation can honour any promises made to customers and in so doing live up to what the customer has come to expect. Expectations include:
- Polite and well-informed staff
- Meeting delivery dates and times
- Providing information and returning calls
- Replacing products that are faulty
- Ensuring an excellent after sales service

☎ *Prompt, effective and professional front line*
Customer enquiries must be dealt with efficiently and professionally.
- Telephone calls should be answered within five seconds of the call coming through. First impressions count and the receptionist is very often the first impression that a customer has of an organisation. If it is not handed professionally it may be the last impression that the organisation has of the customer!
- Receptionists should make customers feel welcome and at ease.
- Sufficient sales staff should be available to deal with customers at all times during the day. Increasingly, organisations are opening during evenings, at weekends and bank holidays to meet the needs of their customers.

✍ *Attention to detail*   Little things count when caring for the customer:
- When a customer pays by cheque or credit card, identify the name of the person and thank them in person when you finish the sale.
- Ensure the staff wear name badges.
- Listen to your customers and identify their needs.
- Make customer feedback sheets available.
- Ensure the environment is pleasant for customers.
- Provide an after-sales service – carrying bags to the car, replacing goods that customers are not happy with even if they are not faulty etc.

175

Consumers and Customers

Fast and efficient response
- Requests for information should be sent out first class so that the customer receives it within two days, when the idea is still fresh in his or her mind.
- Customers should not have to wait any longer than five minutes for help and advice. Long queues and insufficient staff at the front line simply mean that customers go elsewhere.

Be fully informed
It is important that all staff:
- Know the needs of their customers.
- Know about the product or service being sold.
- Know the aims and objectives of the organisation.
- Know the procedure to be followed.
- Know how to solve problems that occur.

Sales can be lost if the assistant doesn't know about the product or service, the price charged and the features offered. Training is essential to ensure that everyone is in the know.

Special service for special needs
All customers share a common goal in being able to reach a decision and make a purchase, feeling confident and uninhibited in the process. Some customers, however, require special attention in order to make this possible. The term *speical needs* covers a range of particular requirements which must be met if the customer is to receive an effective service. Special needs include disabilities as well as less obvious needs such as those of parents with young children.

Individual with special needs
An important part of an organisation's customer care policy must be to provide for handicapped customers. Lifts and ramps should be available to make all parts of the organisation accessible. In addition, staff need to be trained to understand the importance of meeting the needs of the handicapped without feeling embarrassed or patronising the customer.

The term 'special needs' covers many different types of customer.

The disabled
The disabled often find access to an organisation difficult. Ramps provide an alternative to steps. However, within the organisation, a lift should always be available, appropriately staffed, so that the problem of accessing different parts of the organisation is reduced. The width of aisles is also important. They should be wide enough to allow wheelchairs and prams to pass through comfortably. Staff should be observant and volunteer help and assistance if required. Holding open doors seems a very small gesture, but is one which benefits handicapped people greatly.

The deaf If a customer is deaf it may not be immediately noticeable. The important skill when communicating with a customer who is deaf is to speak face to face, slowly and clearly. If the need arises, a customer may prefer to write a request down in order to clarify exactly what is wanted.

The blind A blind customer will normally approach using a white stick, accompanied by a guide dog or with assistance from a friend or partner. If the blind customer is choosing something to buy or wishes to communicate with someone within the organisation, it is important that the member of staff does not communicate via the friend or partner. The customer may be blind, but this does not affect the person's ability to think for themself, make a decision or ask for advice. A blind customer may ask the member of staff to describe a product in order that he or she can visualise what it looks like. In addition, the person may want to hold and feel the object to get a better impression for themselves.

The mentally handicapped It is important to be patient with customers who are mentally handicapped because they may find it difficult to communicate what they want. It is important to listen carefully, not to interrupt and give them the time they need to express their needs. They may require assistance in counting out the money needed to pay for the purchase and it may be necessary to explain that they are entitled to some change if appropriate. At all times explain what you are doing and the purpose for which it is intended.

The elderly In the same way as it is important to deal with the needs of the handicapped, it is important to recognise the needs of the elderly. Many old people do not look handicapped, but may be suffering from failing sight, deafness and difficulty in walking. Staff need to be sensitive to these needs and provide help and support if required.

Getting it right Like customers who are handicapped, many elderly people are fiercely independent. The member of staff must learn to identify when assistance is needed and how to offer it. No customer likes to feel different, patronised or a nuisance. However, they maybe very grateful for help and assistance presented in the right way. Appropriate training will help staff to identify and assess the needs of each individual in each situation.

ACTIVITY

Review the range of customer care facilities available to customers with special needs in your area. Which organisation provides the best facilities? You may want to use the following table to help you.

Facilities	Available or not (✓, ✗)?
Ramps	
Lifts	
Assistance with goods to the car	
Supportive staff	
Wide aisles	
Enlarged signs for the partially sighted	
Parking for the disabled	
Wide doors	
Disabled toilets	
Any other facilities	

As a group, write to the manager of the organisation explaining the nature of the project undertaken and congratulate him or her for coming top. The manager may show the letter to all staff working within the organisation, thanking them for their contribution towards good customer care.
(3.3.1) (3.3.2)

Children

Children may be customers in their own right or they may be with parents or guardians who are customers to the organisation. It is important to ensure that the facilities that the organisation offers and the customer care training are sensitive to the particular needs of children.

Children as customers

Staff need to have very special skills when dealing with children as potential customers. It is quite common for children to change their minds on numerous occasions before making a decision about what they want to buy. Staff need to be patient to and encourage the child to come to a decision in a pleasant and friendly manner. The layout of goods for children needs special attention too. Toys need to be at a level that children can focus on. High shelves mean that the child is dependent upon adults to make the initial decision about what might be interesting to look at, rather than the children finding out for themselves.

Customers with children

Facilities need to be provided to ensure that customers with children have all the required services that they need. Most organisations now provide a mother and baby room, so that children can be fed and changed. In addition, staff need to be trained to deal with children who are upset or who have been separated from their parents. This involves reassuring the child while at the same time publicly announcing a message for the parents to meet the child at a specified area.

The layout of shops has sometimes been redesigned at the request of parents with children. Sainsbury's, the large supermarket chain, for example, placed large posters in its stores advertising the fact that they have removed sweets and chocolates from the checkout counters at the request of parents. Children used the time waiting to pay for goods to constantly ask parents for sweets, and many parents felt forced to agree rather than have a scene in public. This is a good example of an organisation responding positively to feedback gained from customers. Another good example is Boots, with the opening of their Children's World stores.

ACTIVITY

Children's World: a case study in meeting children's needs

Children's World – the large toy shop – is an excellent example of how an organisation has been designed to meet the specific needs of parents and children. Boots undertook market research in 1985 and identified that shopping with children was often very difficult. Crowded car parks, insufficient space between aisles and a lack of lifts made life very difficult when shopping with a pram or pushchair. In addition, shops that were designed for adults did not necessarily stimulate the interest of children. Therefore children became bored while their parents were shopping, and the whole experience became tedious for all involved.

Children's World was therefore planned and designed and brought a new era in children's shopping. The design focused on the needs of parents and children, and the stores were purpose-built to meet those needs. They sold everything that a child could possibly want up to the age of 12 and stocked clothes, books, furniture and toys. The aim was to make shopping a pleasure, not a chore, for parents and children.

The shop locations were out of town, in large warehouse-type outlets. This ensured that there was plenty of space for parking and the aisles within the stores were designed to allow two pushchairs to pass at the same time. Lifts were installed so that parents with prams could easily shop on numerous floors without having to drag the pram up difficult stairs.

The environment focused on the needs of children too. Brightly coloured building bricks made an archway entrance to the store and children could choose to enter the store either by going through the archway doors or down a brightly coloured slide. Inside the store the decor was exciting, distinctive and visually stimulating. The corporate colours were yellow, blue, beige, green and orange, which made the shop look bright and interesting.

The play area was full of toys for children to play with. Books weren't stacked up on high shelves. They were at floor level, in big piles so that children could sit and read them. Parents were also provided with chairs in the play area so that they could sit and rest while the children played with the toys. Looking upwards, children would see kites and banners hanging from the ceiling and if they wanted a rest from play, large television sets played cartoons all day.

Consumers and Customers

A range of other facilities were available for all the customers – tall and small. Restaurants traditionally offer adult menus with children's portions. Not in Children's World. Children's menus were available offering dishes that were not only smaller than adult portions but also more appetising to the younger appetite. The tables and chairs in the restaurant were the right height for little legs and a big clock with hands that went backwards helped to keep the children entertained as they ate their meals. Other important facilities included a children's hairdressing salon and a mother and baby room, which meant that children could be fed and changed easily.

Boots were keen to meet the differing needs of all their customers and Children's World illustrates beautifully how a whole new store system was created with that aim in mind.

Task
Make a list of all the features that Children's World offered
(a) Parents
(b) Children
as part of their commitment to customer care.
(3.3.1) (3.3.2)

ACTIVITY

These boots are made for scoring
Craig Johnston, a former Liverpool footballer, had a dream. He wanted to design a cheap football boot for children, who were just beginning the art of learning how to play the sport. The boot would be designed to make it easier for young players to learn basic skills. His aim was to develop a boot whose curve matched the curve of the ball, thus giving the shot more swerve and more velocity. In trials the boots proved to have 23% more swerve and 7% more velocity.

After months of research and developing prototypes Craig designed a boot made from rubber with special features of fins and jets. He took the prototype to Adidas, who agreed to manufacture and market the product under the name 'The Predator'. However, rather than marketing the boots at the cheap end of the market for children, Adidas decided to market the product at the top end and the boots were priced at about £40 per pair. Finally, as part of a promotional drive, Adidas asked Manchester United strikers to wear the new boots during games.

Questions
Why did Craig Johnston want to produce a new type of boot for children?

What made the boot different from other boots on the market?

Why did Adidas decide to sell the product at a different customer group?

To what extent were the sporting needs of children met by Adidas's decision?

Do you think children and their parents can afford to pay £40 for a pair of football boots? What problems may occur as a result?

In this case study, were children seen as the customers or are parents of children the customers?
(3.3.1) (3.3.2)

Refunds or replacements

All customers need to feel confident that if a product or service is not quite right they have the opportunity to change their mind. It may mean that they want to replace the item with another or it may result in them asking for a full refund. Customers are less likely to purchase an item from an organisation that has a reputation for quibbling about refunds or replacements.

Each organisation has its own policy with regard to refunds or replacements and staff need to be familiar with it. Richards fashion stores, for example, advertise that they will refund fully any product that does not match their high criteria for quality. If the product has gone out of shape, shrunk, or the colours have faded the company is prepared to fully refund the customer. Similarly, Marks & Spencer and John Lewis stores promote a similar assurance to customers. The companies hope that more customers will feel confident to buy, which will result in additional sales. The increased sales will clearly exceed any returns made. It also illustrates that the organisations are confident that what they are selling is of the highest quality.

This after-sales care is crucial to the success of an organisation and extends beyond refunds and replacements. After-sales care includes providing spare parts, maintaining a product and supporting a customer who has a query or a concern about the purchase made. Customer care does not end when the customer walks out of the door, having made a purchase. It is an ongoing process of support and attention to detail, provided by the organisation for the consumer.

In addition to the after-sales policy adopted by a company, customers have certain legal rights. Consumer legislation states that customers have an automatic right to a refund if the product is faulty in anyway. They do not have to settle for an exchange or a credit note. In addition, the customer may be entitled to additional money to compensate for damage done because of the faulty item. For example, if an iron's thermostat fails and the iron burns a hole in some clothes, a customer could expect a refund for the cost of the iron and the damaged clothes too.

ACTIVITY

Identify three organisations that promote a customer care and after-sales policy. Name the organisations and note down the important features of each policy. How effective do you think the policy is in meeting the needs of the customers? *(3.3.1) (3.3.2)*

ACTIVITY

The following extract is taken from Bank of Scotland's Centrebank Division's Declaration of Service. Read the statement and answer the questions which follow:

1. All completed mortgage applications will be given a decision, in principle within 48 hours of receipt.
2. All correspondence will be replied to within 24 hours of receipt.
3. All incoming calls will be answered within three rings.
4. If unable to be resolved immediately, all telephone enquiries will be responded to within 24 hours.
5. All requests for additional borrowing will be referred to the original introducer in order that the appropriate life cover can be arranged.
6. All mortgage customers will be contacted by letter on an annual basis with details of additional mortgage-related services which are available.

(a) Identify the different types of services offered to customers.
(b) Identify how the organisation is meeting customer needs.
(c) What evidence is there that the Bank Of Scotland is customer-focused?
(d) Are there other areas that the Bank of Scotland could include in their declaration?

(3.3.1) (3.3.2)

Making a complaint

Customers need to feel confident in their purchase. If they know that they can come back to the supplier with any queries or complaints then they will be much happier making the purchase in the first place. Organisations should view complaints as a free way of identifying action which can be taken to improve their service. As such the following checklist should be observed when dealing with customer complaints:

1. Customers should feel able to complain if they are unhappy with the service – it is the only way the organisation will learn how to improve.
2. Complaints can provide useful information about the reliability of the product or service.
3. Every complaint should be treated professionally – remember, the customer is always right!
4. Satisfied customers are much more likely to return – a dissatisfied customer is likely to warn other potential customers.

ACTIVITY

In a small group or singly, identify an organisation where you have experienced bad customer care and an organisation where you have received good customer care. What factors led you to form your judgement? Analyse how these experiences have affected your attitudes towards these organisations. *(3.3.1) (3.3.2)*

Ethical standards

Customers may reasonably expect business organisations which they deal with to act honestly and decently. The customer buys in good faith and will naturally assume that the seller acts likewise. When buying a used car, for example, the customer should be able to accept what is presented at face value: the odometer reading is accurate, the log book is up to date, the paint does not hide large holes in the bodywork. Similarly, when eating in a restaurant the customer can expect the food to be as described in the menu.

Customers should not be pressurised into buying something they are not sure of. Nor should they be deliberately misled.

A measure of an organisation's ethical standards is their honesty and approach to confidentiality when dealing with customers.

Confidentiality

It is important that employees are aware of the importance of confidentiality when dealing with customers. This is particularly relevant when the employee is dealing with customers about matters relating to financial, legal, health and personal issues. Confidential issues should be discussed in a private place so that the customer feels comfortable to talk. It also ensures that other customers do not hear the details under discussion. However, it is also important that once the customer has left, the employee does not discuss the details of the conversation in public. Employees who work for solicitors, accountants, doctors and banks are very often asked to sign a statement of confidentiality and can be sacked if they are found to be discussing customers' personal details with other people not related to the case.

Honesty

Honesty is the best policy, and customers will ultimately discover organisations who deliberately try to mislead or deceive them. Customers prefer an honest answer, even if it means admitting that the organisation has made an error. Honesty and openness should be central to any customer care policy, and should an organisation be found to have deliberately given the wrong information to customers it is likely that the organisation will be legally liable for its actions.

Consumers and Customers

✏️ ACTIVITY

Identify an example when, as a customer, you have bought a product or a service and at a later date found that the purchase did not live up to your expectations because the organisation had not been completely honest with you.

In what way had the organisation deceived you?
How did you feel about being deceived?
What action did you take and how did the organisation respond?
Would you buy from the same organisation again?
Share your answers with your other group members.
(3.3.1) (3.3.2)

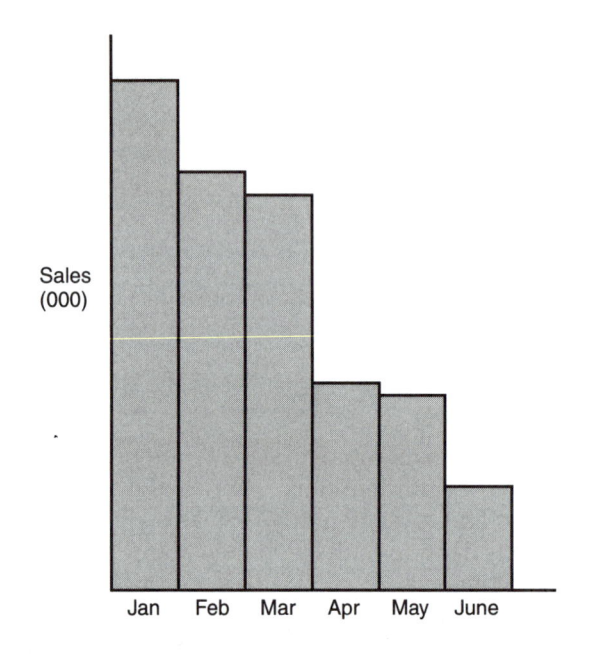

Reasons to meet customer needs

Meeting the needs of customers is important. We are all customers and we all expect certain standards as a customer. Therefore it is surprising that so many organisations still get it wrong. Rudeness of staff, poor delivery times and insufficient information about products or services are all characteristics of organisations who present an uninterested and unprofessional attitude to their customers.

Customer care and meeting customer needs are essential for the survival and success of any organisation. Companies like British Airways, the Bank of Scotland and Marks & Spencer are examples of organisations that have recognised this and have ultimately benefited from the quality service that they offer their internal and external customers. These organisations and others recognise that meeting customer needs is essential for:
1 Improving the service offered.
2 Improving business performance.
3 Improving morale of staff.
4 Improving the morale of the customers.

Improving service

Meeting customer needs will result in an improvement in the quality of service offered by the organisation. By dealing with customers efficiently and providing a a unified and informed approach from all staff, the image of the organisation will be enhanced. By enhancing the service provided to customers, the organisation will also benefit from reduced waste and fewer problems, improved communications between the customer and the organisation and greater customer loyalty. This means that customers will continue to return.

Improving business performance

Clear guidelines for staff about how to deal with customers will result in an improvement in business performance for the whole organisation. The following checklist can be used as a guideline for staff to improve the service for customers, but you can also see how, by following the checklist, the performance of the business will also improve.

Customer care checklist performance	Effect on business
Answer telephone within 3 rings	Improved communications
Reply to letters within 2 days	More informed customers
Meet delivery dates and times	Greater efficiency
Return telephone calls	Improved communications
Efficient, courteous staff	Increased customer loyalty
Sufficient, qualified staff	Reduced queues, greater productivity
Deal with customer complaints	Increased customer loyalty
Provide a good after-sales service	Increased sales, more repeat business

Improving morale of staff and customers

Staff

Employees are customers in the same way that customers are customers. We have already looked at the idea of employees being viewed as internal customers. By improving the quality of service internally and making all internal staff feel valued, the quality of service offered to external customers will also improve.

Staff who feel valued will want to belong to the organisation and will want to provide a quality service to the external customer. There will be greater cooperation between staff and increased efficiency. If staff feel that they are part of a team who are all aiming to provide a quality service for customers, there will be greater job satisfaction for all involved.

Customers

Better quality and more efficient service will result in customers feeling valued and cared for. This will reflect itself in greater customer loyalty towards the organisation. It is likely that the satisfied customers will inform other potential customers about the excellent service they received. Therefore sales will increase as the reputation of the organisation becomes well known.

Consumers and Customers

> **ACTIVITY**
>
> Prepare some form of promotional material that can be used within an organisation to advertise and inform staff of the importance of good customer care. The promotional material should refer to:
> 1 The different needs of customers
> 2 How the staff can satisfy those needs
> 3 The benefits of good customer care to all involved
>
> You may want to produce a staff handbook, a poster, a video or a tape. The choice is yours. Remember to refer back to the section on producing promotional materials if you want help and advice.
> (3.3.1) (3.3.2)

Business communication which meets customers' needs

Communication is the key to effective customer care and can be defined as:

'the imparting or exchanging of information.'

It may include:
- *Verbal communication*, which refers to speaking, including tone and pitch and which may be *face to face* or on the *telephone*.
- *Non-verbal communication*, which refers to body language, posture and general demeanour.

Oral communication

Oral communication is an important aspect of customer care. Staff need to focus both on what they say and the way they say it. Pleasant greetings, correct grammar and a pleasant tone are essential requirements of good oral communication. These skills are important methods of achieving effective communication, both between employees and in communication with customers.

Verbal communication is a powerful medium and is more likely to get an immediate response from the listener than written communication. However, it is also easier to misunderstand what is said as opposed to what is written down. Once spoken there is very often little record of what was discussed. Therefore if an important issue is under discussion it is important to support the verbal findings with a short written summary so as to avoid any confusion at a later date.

> **ACTIVITY**
>
> Ask a friend or a colleague to discuss with you their hobbies, interests and career aspirations. When you have both exchanged thoughts and ideas, write a short summary of what was discussed. Having written up the account, share your written findings with your friend or colleague and decide whether both parties agree that what was said has been recorded accurately within the written summary.
> (3.3.4)

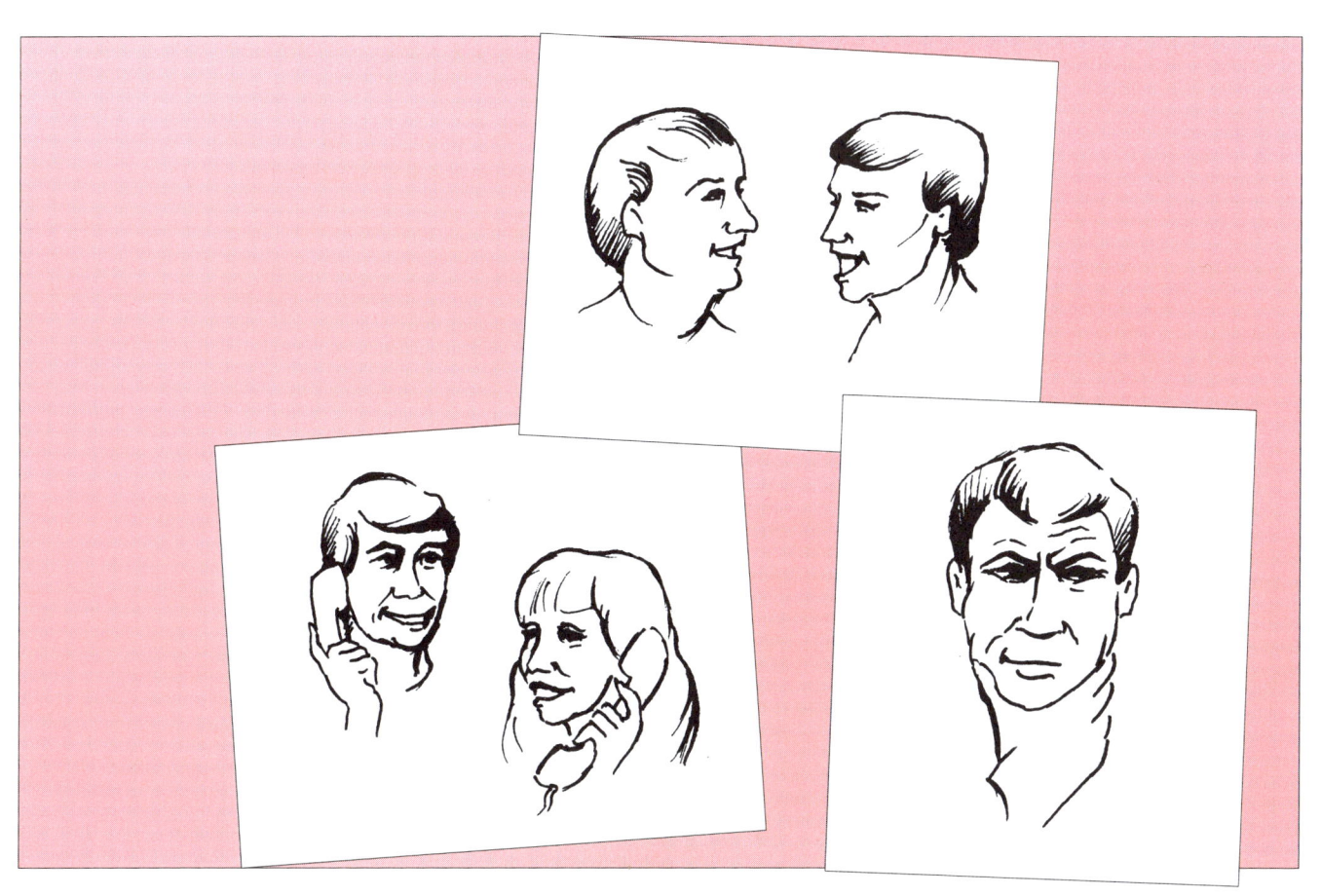

Consumers and Customers

The verbal skills used as part of effective customer care should include:
1. General greeting
2. Questioning
3. Appropriate phrases
4. Good listening skills
5. The ability to summarise
6. Pleasant tone and manner

General greetings

Opening and closing responses are important to put the customer at ease. The most commonly used opening statements include:

'Hello. How can I help you?'
'Good morning, Madam. Can I be of service?'
'Good afternoon, Sir. Do you need any assistance?'

Immediately the customer feels welcomed into the organisation and has the opportunity to ask for the help and assistance required.

It is also important that staff choose the correct closing statements as the customer is leaving as this will form the lasting impression of the organisation:

'Thank you for calling and please come again.'
'If you have any problems, don't hesitate to contact us.'
'Look forward to seeing you again soon.'

These mean that the customer leaves the organisation with a positive impression of the company.

ACTIVITY

Visit two or three organisations and make a note of their opening and closing greetings. To what extent did you feel that the greetings enhanced the image of the organisation? As a customer, did it make you feel valued?
(3.3.4)

Questioning technique

Questions are used to:
- Stimulate conversation
- Obtain information and get a decision
- Clarify points and check understanding
- To show interest in the customer

There are two types of question that can be used in oral communication: closed and open questions. A *closed question* requires a yes/no answer only. As such it is difficult to obtain additional information with closed questions and therefore developing a conversation is difficult. Examples of closed questions include: 'Would you like some help?', or 'Have you any problems?'.

Open questions, on the other hand, require a more detailed answer, which will provide staff with a more detailed understanding of what the customer wants and needs from a product or service. Open questions usually begin with words like how, why, describe, which, who, what and when.

ACTIVITY

Look at the following closed questions that may be used within an organisation. Rewrite them as open questions in order to develop two-way conversation with the customer:
1. Would you like some help?
2. Do you like this new product?
3. Have you shopped here before?
4. Would you like the item delivered?
5. Are you buying it as a present for somebody?
6. Your appointment is with the finance director isn't it?

(3.3.4)

Remember that each customer has different needs and different wants. These will only be identified if the member of staff talks to and develops a conversation with the customer. By asking the right questions the customer will willingly communicate those needs and wants. It is important therefore that the assistant listens carefully to what is being said and takes the appropriate action.

Appropriate phrases

When entering into conversation it is important to use the appropriate words and correct grammar. If in doubt the best policy is to always keep the sentences simple by avoiding technical words or jargon. Long complicated words do nothing to enhance the image of the organisation if they are used in the wrong context.

It is also important that the sentences used in conversations are positive statements rather than negative ones. 'You can't pay for that here Madam' could be changed from a negative statement to a positive one by saying, 'The cash till for your purchases is on the left Madam'.

ACTIVITY

Change the following negative statements into positive ones:
1. Sorry, those items are out of stock.
2. No, I can't help you: it's not my section.
3. Sorry, the line's engaged: please call back later.
4. No bankers card, no cheque. Sorry.
5. You can't pay with this. Your card is out of date.

(3.3.4)

Listening skills

Good listening skills are the key to effectively interpreting what is actually said. Very often people interpret conversation in terms of what they think was said as opposed to what was actually said. This can result in some very frustrated customers.

To be a good listener it is important to:

- Face the person and maintain good eye contact during the conversation.
- Nod positively to reassure the speaker that what is being said is understood.
- Clarify any points which are not clearly expressed.
- Restate what was said at the end of the conversation. This helps to clarify the conversation further and shows that the listener has both understood and has taken an interest in what the person has been saying.
- Summarise the position and, if appropriate, outline the action to be taken.

To be a good listener it is important to smile, repeat important points and seek out additional information. It is also important not to interrupt.

ACTIVITY

As a group or individually watch or tape a variety of interviewers on television. These could include:
1. An interviewer on the national news
2. Oprah Winfrey
3. Clive Anderson
4. Brian Walden
5. Jonathan Dimbleby
6. Robert Kilroy Silk

Compare their styles of interviewing.
- Do they use open or closed questions?
- Do they use positive or negative statements?
- Do they keep the language simple?
- Are they effective listeners?

Produce a short report or checklist to record your views. If possible, share your results with others in the group to see whether there is a consensus of opinion.
(3.3.4)

The ability to summarise

The ability to summarise is an important skill in checking that what the customer has asked for has been understood. The summary should include a brief recap about what was said, emphasising the important points. It could also include the action to be taken as a result of the conversation.

ACTIVITY

Summarise the key points from the following conversation

Receptionist	'Hello, how can I help you?'
Customer	'I wanted to see Ms Voysey, the Marketing Director.'
Receptionist	'Have you got an appointment?'
Customer	'Well no, not exactly.'
Receptionist	'Would you like to make an appointment or can I help in any way?'
Customer	'Well, I did speak to Ms Voysey on the telephone and she said if I was passing by to drop by. I have designed a new type of children's game which she is interested in looking at. I was hoping that today might be convenient, but if she is busy I suppose I could come back later. I'm only in town for today you see.'
Receptionist	'Well I'm afraid Ms Voysey is with the Managing Director at the moment, but if she said she would see you sometime today then I'm sure she will. I'll. . .'
Customer	'Well, she didn't exactly say today. You see she didn't realise that I was only in town today. Maybe you could tell her that I called and that I can send her a sample of the new toy through the post if she is interested. You must stress that I need an urgent response as there are a lot of other companies that are interested in buying the idea. I just wanted to give your company first refusal, because I like the way you produce things here. Everything is of the highest quality, don't you find?'
Receptionist	'Well, yes, as a company we do take pride in our work.'
Customer	'Yes, I know, which is why I want to do business with you. Could you tell Ms Voysey I called? She can contact me on 2345 12321. As I said, it is quite urgent.'
Receptionist	'May I take your name?'
Customer	'Oh yes, sorry, it's Judith Crombie.'
Receptionist	'Thank you. I'll make sure she contacts you either today or first thing tomorrow.'
Customer	'That's great. Goodbye and thank you.'
Receptionist	'My pleasure. Goodbye.'

(3.3.4)

Tone and manner

Very often it is not what is said that offends customers but the way it is said. A pleasant tone and manner are essential when liaising with customers and clients. The way a person is feeling and their attitude to the person they are talking to is very often expressed in the tone of the voice. We all know when someone is angry, annoyed or upset by the way they speak. Therefore, when communicating with customers it is important to sound pleasant, helpful and interested.

The pace of conversation is important too. People who speak too slowly sound bored and uninterested. Speaking fast gives the impression that a person is

Consumers and Customers

nervous and ill at ease. The pace should be relaxed and key words within the conversation should be stressed to highlight their importance.

ACTIVITY

Working with a partner, role play the following situations:
1. Customer and sales representative: enquiring about the price, features and delivery dates of new car.
2. Business manager and hotel receptionist: booking overnight accommodation.
3. Customer and assistant: returning a faulty hairdryer which gives the user an electric shock.
4. Customer and assistant: statement doesn't show the last payment.

Remember to apply all the techniques learnt about effective oral communication:
- Speak clearly
- Welcome the customer
- Use open questions and positive statements
- Summarise
- Be friendly and welcoming
- Show interest in the customer

(3.3.4)

Non-verbal communication

Body language refers to non-verbal communication. People can communicate with others using facial expressions, posture and gestures and this communication can display both positive and negative messages.

Positive gestures	Negative gestures
Smiling	Frowning
Nodding of the head	Shaking of the head
Eye contact	Averted eyes
Standing or sitting attentively	Fidgeting or being distracted
Open gestures	Closed gestures
Neat appearance	Untidy appearance

Facial expressions

Facial expressions can communicate messages from one person to another. Nodding of the head, smiling and good eye contact are all positive messages. However, frowning, yawning, shaking of the head and averted eye contact are all negative messages. When dealing with customers it is important to use positive not negative messages.

Posture

If a person stands or sits upright when talking to a customer and looks at them face to face, positive messages are being communicated. This type of posture should be used when talking with colleagues and customers. It makes the customer feel that the assistant is interested and encourages two way communication. It is important to avoid slouching, turning your back or refusing to communicate with somebody face to face, as these are clearly negative messages. It will give the customer the impression that the assistant is either uninterested or plain rude.

Gestures

Gestures can be both positive and negative. Positive gestures include firm handshakes, expressing statements with hand movements and leaning forward towards the client. It is important, however, not to invade the personal space of the customer – being too close to somebody can be as off-putting as being too far away. Other negative gestures include biting nails, folding arms and looking out the window rather than looking at the customer.

Appearance

Smart appearance of the staff and accommodation is essential in gaining the respect and loyalty of the customer. An untidy office reflects a disorganised and badly managed organisation. A customer once said that she could tell the quality of accommodation in hotels by the colour of the net curtains hanging at the windows! Similarly, within public sector organisations appearance is important. It should always be possible to tell what is taught in a classroom by the nature of displays on the walls. The displays should be well presented and free from graffiti.

Staff who dress in a scruffy manner appear to have a 'couldn't care less' attitude towards the organisation. Company codes of dress or uniforms help to present a corporate approach to the appearance and style of the organisation. The clothes worn should be appropriate for the job to be done and employees should feel both smart and comfortable.

ACTIVITY

Look at the following situations, identify the message being presented and identify how you would respond:

Body language	Possible message	Possible response
A customer complains about a faulty product – no eye contact and talking from behind her hand	Unhappy about item but embarrassed to return it	Reassure and exchange item
Interviewer leans back and looks out of the window while interviewing you for a job		
You show a promotional idea to your boss and he looks attentively at the idea, smiles and nods his head		
A salesperson arrives, biting his lip and playing with the cuffs of his shirt		

Consumers and Customers

Your boss calls you into the office. She has a copy of your report in front of her. She is frowning and looking stern.

A customer is tapping his fingers on the counter

Your assistant is in tears, bits of paper are all around her desk and the waste bin is overflowing

The manager calls you into the office, shakes your hand firmly and pats you on the back

(3.3.4)

Face to face
When dealing with customers face to face it is possible to interact verbally and non-verbally. There are a number of important points that must be observed when liaising with customers in person in order that a positive encounter is achieved.

The dos
- Smile and welcome them to the organisation
- Refer to them by name if they are a regular customer
- Take an interest in them as individuals
- Try to identify and satisfy their needs
- Treat them with respect and put them at their ease
- Use positive non-verbal gestures
- Thank them as they leave

The don'ts
- Avoid negative body language and negative statements
- Avoid chewing or eating when talking to customers
- Avoid taking to other people at the same time as dealing with the customer
- Never swear or curse either at or in the presence of the customer

Face to face communication is the most personal form of communicating with customers and if it is not handled in a professional manner, customers can easily become annoyed and frustrated. Remember: it is not just what is said, but the way it is said. Many employees may feel that they are presenting themselves in a professional and courteous manner, but their gestures, posture and facial expressions can present quite a different image to the customer.

Telephone
In addition to face to face situations, oral communication can also take place via the telephone. The telephone is a convenient and useful medium that allows you to communicate with customers worldwide. It is much faster to telephone a customer and get instant feedback than it is by writing a letter. Is is also easier to end a telephone conversation politely than it is to leave a customer you are dealing with personally. Telephone skills are very important to perfect and it takes time and practice to deal with business calls both professionally and efficiently.

Preparation   When making calls identify a time that will be convenient for both yourself and the person you are trying to contact. Identify what you want to say and to whom before making the call. If receiving a call make sure you have a telephone pad ready to record the message and a list of up-to-date extensions with relevant staff names so that you know who to pass the message on to.

Response time   It is generally regarded that telephone enquiries should be answered within three rings or five seconds. Customers do not like having to hold on for long periods of time. Time costs money and if the call is not answered within a reasonable period of time, the customer may take the custom elsewhere. Once the call has been answered it is important that the query is forwarded to the relevant member of staff. There is nothing more frustrating for a customer than waiting on the end of a line when he or she is paying for the call.

Speak clearly   When answering a call it is important to speak clearly by naming the company you are working for and asking what type of assistance is required, for example: 'Good morning, Hughes Ltd. How may I help you?'.

Similarly, if you are making a call it is essential that you introduce your organisation and state clearly the person or department you wish to be transferred to. For example: 'Good morning. I am telephoning on behalf of Hughes Ltd. May I speak to your Finance Director please?'.

Name the customer   If possible, ask for and use the customer's name. This makes the customer feel valued and important. It also makes the conversation less formal and more personable. When making and receiving all telephone calls it is important to be pleasant but concise.

Record the call   It is important that a record of the call is made. This should identify:
- The name of the caller and the organisation that they represent
- Who they wanted to contact
- The date and time the message was taken
- A brief summary of the caller wanted
- The action to be taken, together with contact number

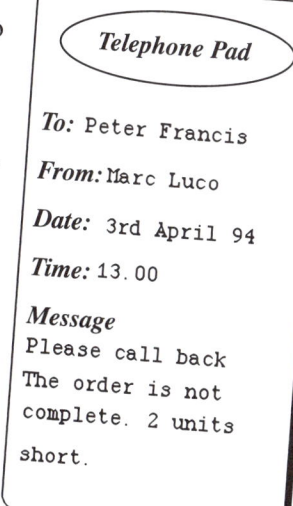

Telephone Pad

To: Peter Francis
From: Marc Luco
Date: 3rd April 94
Time: 13.00
Message
Please call back. The order is not complete. 2 units short.

185

Consumers and Customers

✏️ ACTIVITY

What important information is missing from the telephone pad on the previous page?
(3.3.4)

Thank the caller Summarise the main points of the telephone call and the action to be taken. It is important always to thank the caller for calling and to promise a return call if the relevant member of staff is not available to deal with the query.

Telephone technique – points to ponder
Remember that good telephone technique involves:
- Being prepared
- Answering promptly
- Speaking clearly
- Asking who the caller wishes to speak to and the caller's name
- Using expressions like 'one moment please'
- Not using expressions like 'hang on'
- Taking accurate messages when the person is not available
- Offering to ring back if the person is busy
- Never talking with your hand over the receiver – you can still be heard
- Making sure, that if you promise to return a call, the call is returned

✏️ ACTIVITY

The following checklist could be completed during work experience. Copy out and complete the following:

Effective telephone technique
- Do you answer calls promptly? ☐
- Are you always prepared? ☐
- Do you announce who you are and ask for staff clearly? ☐
- Do you listen attentively? ☐
- Do you ask the right questions? ☐
- Do you record all messages accurately? ☐
- Do you clarify points that you are unsure about? ☐
- Do you interrupt? ☐
- Do you make promises you cannot keep? ☐
- Do you summarise the main points of the conversation? ☐
- Do you clarify the action to be taken? ☐
- Do you thank the caller for calling? ☐

Remember: be polite, be positive, be pleasant
(3.3.4)

Written communication
In addition to verbal and non verbal communication, organisations used written communication as a method of communicating with both internal and external customers. The three main methods of written communication within an organisation are:
- Memoranda
- Letters
- Reports

The memorandum
The memorandum, or memo as it is usually known, is used to communicate with staff within the organisation. It is designed to record relatively short messages and therefore is an efficient and speedy method for informing other colleagues of important facts and issues. When producing a memo the following principles should be followed:

- The *name* of the person to whom you are *sending* the memo and their *position* should appear on the document. If the document is to be copied to more than one member of staff, then all the names should appear. The memo will then be duplicated and the respective copy sent to the relevant member of staff. A tick alongside each name is usually recorded to indicate which copy goes to whom.
- The *name* and *position* of *sender* is then recorded underneath.
- The third item to appear is the *date*.
- The date is followed by the *title* or *heading*. This indicates to the reader the nature and contents of the memorandum.
- The *main message* is written immediately beneath the title or heading. A memo is usually concise and to the point. Correct grammar and a professional style should be used throughout.

```
From:  Programme Leader - Leisure
To:    The Marketing Manager
Date:  30 April 1994

RE: Advertising and promotional
    campaign

Please can you confirm that your
budget will pay for the press and
radio advertising for the forthcoming
GNVQ regional colleges/schools
athletics meeting. The total cost for
planned advertising will not exceed
£500.

Thank you in anticipation.
```

Letters
Letters can be used for both internal and external communication. As a form of medium, they are less intrusive than telephone calls. They provide a written account that can be referred back to at a later date if a

query arises. Letters need careful phrasing so that the recipient fully understands the message. With a telephone call it is very easy to identify whether a person is confused by what is being said and the opportunity is there to clarify the situation immediately. It is not possible to use verbal or non-verbal communication to help clarify points with a letter, however, and it is therefore essential that the letter is clearly written.

Letters may be used for the following purposes:
- Giving and requesting information
- Responding to enquiries
- Making or answering complaints
- As circulars to sell or promote a product or service
- Requesting and acknowledging payment for accounts
- Providing references
- Applying for jobs
- Thanking customers and clients

The following guidelines should be observed when producing letters for either internal or external correspondence:
- The accepted format within organisations is to *left justify* all information. This is often called a *blocked* format. This means that all the information to be included within the letter should start from the left-hand side and indented paragraphs should not be used at all.
- The first item to be included in the letter is a *reference code*. This helps to identify who originated the letter and who typed it. If the letter is a response to a specific issue where previous correspondence has been filed, there will be two references – the organisation's reference number and the reference code, which relates to the receiver's file.
- The *date* of the letter follows the reference.
- If the *sender's* address is not printed on an official letterhead it would be included at this stage, followed by the *receiver's* address. If the letter has been typed on official paper, with the business address already printed, the receiver's address would follow the date.
- The address is followed by the *salutation*. This may be '*Dear Sir or Dear Madam*', in which case the letter should be completed by '*Yours faithfully*'. Alternatively, the letter may be addressed in person: '*Dear Mr Turner*' or '*Dear Ms Right*', in which case the letter should be completed by '*Yours sincerely*'.
- A main *heading*, identifying the contents of the letter, is printed beneath the salutation. Again it is blocked to the left-hand side and should not be underlined.
- The *opening paragraph* should outline the purpose of the letter and should refer to any previous correspondence by date. It may be appropriate to thank a person for previous correspondence in this opening paragraph. Alternatively, if you are making an enquiry a useful introductory sentence is: 'I should be grateful if you would identify whether it is possible for me to...'.

A letter of complaint could begin: 'With reference to the enclosed product, which I bought last week, I should like to complain about...'.
- The *following paragraphs* should develop the main body of the letter. It is important that the message is clearly expressed. The aims must be clarified and the facts should be written in a clear and concise manner. Throughout the letter the language should be professional and reasonably formal.
- The *final paragraph* should summarise the intended action expected by the sender. For example: 'I look forward to hearing from you...' or 'I will be in contact when further information is available...'. Clearly state what the next step will be. Alternatively, if no further action is to be taken a professional close to the letter may take the format of 'Thank you for your interest in the company...'. or 'I hope this answers your queries...'.
- The correct *complimentary close* should conclude the letter: '*Yours faithfully*' or '*Yours sincerely*'. This is dependent on which salutation has been used.
- The *name* of the writer and his or her *status* should come beneath the complimentary close, with a space for a signature.
- If the letter includes further documents, the reference *Enc* should follow the status. This clearly indicates both for reference purposes and for the benefit of the receiver that further documents are included with the letter.

An example of a typical letter is shown on the next page.

Reports

Reports are another form of communication within a business and may be used to inform employees within the organisation. Alternatively, they may be used by one business organisation to inform another. The ability to write reports using the correct headings is an important business skill.

The presentation of reports will vary from one organisation to another, as each organisation has its preferred style. However, the following format is a suggested structure that is recognised as acceptable by most organisations.
- *Terms of reference*
  This refers to the main purpose of the report. What was requested, by whom and to whom would be included within the terms of reference.
- *Procedure*
  The procedure relates to the process followed in order to get the information. It usually distinguishes between primary and secondary data.
- *Findings*
  This forms the main body of the report and includes the main results of the project, review, experiment etc.
- *Conclusions*
  This section provides a summary of the main findings. For people who do not have time to read through the main body of the report, the

Consumers and Customers

```
Ms F Hurt                                          East Orchard College
23 Littlemead Drive                                Fontwell Magna
Hartgrove                                          Hartgrove
Dorset                                             Shaftesbury
DN12 4JK                                           Dorset
                                                   DN12 4SD


                                                   Our ref: WE/TR
                                                   Your ref: YT/RE
Dear Ms Hurt

Re: GNVQ Enquiry                                   28 April 1995

Thank you for attending our open day on 12 April and for expressing an interest
in the GNVQ programmes delivered within the College.

The College is currently offering GNVQ programmes in three areas:
    Business
    Health and Social Care
    Leisure and Tourism.

As your enquiry related to GNVQs in general I have enclosed course details for
each area in order that you can identify which one is most appropriate for your
needs. If you would like to attend a taster day planned for 12 June, please
write and let me know. The taster day enables you to meet both staff and
students and gives you a more detailed insight into a typical day at College.

I have also enclosed an application form should you wish to apply for a place
within the College. The completed application form should be marked for the
attention of Central Admission and posted to the College using the enclosed
pre-paid envelope. You will then be invited for interview and further course
details will be made available at that time.

Please let me know if you require any further details. I look forward to
hearing from you. Best wishes for your future studies.

Yours sincerely


Helena Iwuji
Marketing Assistant

Encs
```

conclusions should provide them with the relevant important points.

- *Recommendations*
Finally, the recommendations provide an outline of recommended future action. For some reports it is not necessary to include recommendations: much depends upon the nature of the project.

The following document is an illustration of what a report might look like. Remember that this is only an example and proper reports have many more points listed under all the headings.

Circulation List:

The Principal

From:
Helena Iwuji – Marketing

Date:
28 April 1995

1.0 Terms of Reference
1.1 To report on the feasibility of opening a high street shop to promote vocational programmes.

2.0 Procedure
2.1 Visit estate agents to look at potential premises.

2.2 Distribute questionnaires to local residents to determine potential demand.

2.3 Meet finance director to look at costings.

3.0 Findings
3.1 Reviewed three shops in the High Street – details included. Two were too small. One shop in the High Street met criteria for accessibility, price and length of lease.

3.2 Liaised with finance to agree that project costings did not exceed projected target.

3.3 Finance also provided additional budget for furniture and promotional materials.

3.4 Analysis of market research supported the view that prospective customers would like a drop-in High Street location to review courses at their leisure.

4.0 Conclusions
4.1 The research undertaken indicated that the High Street location was most suitable and costings for project agreed by finance.

4.2 Market research supported the need for the shop.

5.0 Recommendations
5.1 To proceed with the plan and agree the lease immediately.

Consumers and Customers

ACTIVITY

Identify the advantages and disadvantages of using a telephone or writing a letter in each of the following situations:

1. A customer has written to complain about a faulty electric hair dryer which gave her an electric shock each time she used it. She has already returned it to the shop and been given a full refund, but wanted to put the matter in writing in order that the organisation could raise the issue with the manufacturer. Your supervisor has asked you to thank the customer for her time and trouble.
2. Your existing suppliers have just raised their prices by 8%. You have been asked to collect the price lists for as many alternative suppliers as soon as possible.
3. Your company has recently promoted a new range of leisure equipment and has received numerous enquiries. The organisation is planning to follow up the advertisement by running a sports show where visitors will be invited to watch the demonstrations and have a go at using the equipment. The only problem is that the show is planned to take place in three days' time.
4. Your boss wants to research customers' opinions about the quality of after-sales care that customers receive from the organisation. He has asked you to contact as many customers as possible to ask them their views.

(3.3.3) (3.3.4)

ACTIVITY

1. Write a memo to the transport department requesting assurance that deliveries to customers will arrive on time and that the backlog of orders will be dealt with immediately.
2. Write a letter to Mr J. Keeps, of 45 Wood Street, High Wycombe, apologising for the delay in the delivery of his order for a dining room suite and assuring him that it will be with him on Monday 23 April at 2.00 p.m.
3. Produce a short report reviewing the quality of customer care offered by organisations in your local town or city. The report should focus on four or five organisations and should review all aspects of customer care that you have looked at to date. For example, you may want to include:
   - Their opening greetings
   - How efficient they were at responding to your needs
   - Their attention to detail
   - Their verbal and non verbal communication
   - How much information they provided in response to your questions
   - Their after-sales service

Consumers and Customers

Your conclusion should summarise whether you felt the standard of customer care was satisfactory or not and your recommendations should identify possible areas for improvement.
(3.3.4)

Dealing with customer queries

> **✎ ACTIVITY 1**
>
> Dealing with customer queries is an important job in many organisations. Make a list of the types of customer queries an organisation may receive.
> *(3.3.3)*

If an organisation is going to meet the needs of its customers it is important that customers are encouraged to ask questions and give feedback about the quality of products or services bought and the customer care received. By encouraging customers to make enquiries and obtaining genuine, objective feedback, an organisation can strive to implement the improvements that the customers want to see.

An organisation may receive queries about a whole range of issues. These may include:
- A query about a customer account
- A query about methods of payment
- A letter of complaint about a faulty product
- Items returned because they don't fit
- A request to order a product that isn't in stock
- A request for a member of staff to assist a customer with special needs
- A customer seeking a member of staff's opinion, advice or expertise

Customer queries should not always be seen as a situation in which a customer wants to complain. As the list above illustrates, a customer is often wanting to seek an opinion or expertise from the member of staff. A lot of customers have queries they need answering, and staff should be able to provide advice and support to all customers. This may involve assisting a customer with special needs or offering an opinion about the best choice of product or service. All employees should be equipped to provide this type of customer care.

Dealing with complaints is slightly different, however, and each organisation will have its own policy as to who should deal with verbal and written complaints. It may be that all staff are trained to deal with complaints. Alternatively, many organisations will have designated members of staff who are specifically trained to deal with customer problems. These may be supervisors or they may work within a customer service department. Large stores, like Marks & Spencer for example, have an area which is allocated to customer services, and the staff who work within that department deal with customer problems and queries all day.

Staff training should equip employees to deal with the differing needs of customers in order that customer queries are answered to the customer's satisfaction. The training should also teach the employee the organisation's policy for customer complaints, so that staff are familiar with the procedure to be followed, including the respective member of staff who has the authority to deal with customer complaints. It is important that customer complaints are always referred to the correct person, who has the authority to make a decision.

> **✎ ACTIVITY 2**
>
> How would you deal with the following customer queries? Remember to identify which situations you could deal with and which you would need to refer to a higher authority. If you need to refer the problem, try to identify who you would contact to deal with the problem.
> 1. A woman wants to buy a very expensive dress that doesn't suit her and who asks for your opinion.
> 2. A disabled customer wants to look at items on the second floor, but can't find the lift attendant.
> 3. Your supervisor, who deals with all customer complaints, is talking to the manager on the telephone. A customer comes into the shop wanting to return an item of clothing because her husband doesn't like it. She hasn't got a receipt with the purchase.
> 4. A customer wants to know her balance on her customer account
> 5. A young man asks your advice about a possible Valentine's Day present for his girlfriend.
> 6. An elderly gentleman wants to buy a packet of cigars. He is clearly having difficulty recognising different types of coins to pay for his purchase.
> 7. Your organisation has a policy of no animals in the organisation. A customer enquires at your desk whether her blind mother can come in with her guide dog.
> 8. Your organisation has a customer service department on the second floor. A customer comes to you asking to return a faulty product. She states that she is unable to go to the second floor because she has difficulty managing the stairs.
> 9. A customer comes to tell you that he has just seen a shoplifter on the other side of the shop floor.
> 10. A customer has been in to complain that his furniture, which should have been delivered yesterday, has still not arrived.
>
> *(3.3.3) (3.3.5)*

Consumers and Customers

Dealing with customer complaints

An organisation that truly believes in customer care should support customers who are making complaints. Nobody likes making a nuisance or a scene, and customers very often accept inferior products or services rather than return them to the organisation and go through the ordeal of complaining. However, it is only through feedback from customers and listening and responding to their complaints that an organisation can truly improve the service it offers. It also helps to make an unsatisfied customer into a satisfied customer, with all the benefits that a satisfied customer brings.

A survey in the 1980s, which looked at customer care, identified that the most common causes of customer complaints are:
- Not enough staff when the organisation is busy
- Long queues
- Badly trained staff who appear to have little knowledge about the types of product that they are selling
- Staff who watch and crowd customers as they shop
- Staff who are totally uninterested in their customers
- Staff who make customers feel guilty about returning goods
- Lack of support and help when needed, e.g. packers at the supermarket
- Staff who speak and deal with customers in a rude and patronising manner
- Products that do not include additional extras, e.g. batteries and plugs

ACTIVITY 3

Can you think of any more complaints that you would like to add to the list?
(3.3.5)

Procedure for dealing with complaints

Each organisation will have its own procedure, which all employees should follow when dealing with customer complaints. The following guidelines provide a suggested process which could be followed.

- *Stage 1*
  Welcome the customer and ask the nature of the problem.
- *Stage 2*
  Listen to the customer, without interrupting, but using positive body language to encourage the customer to talk. It is important that the customer feels relaxed enough to communicate to the member of staff dealing with the problem.
- *Stage 3*
  Apologise that the customer has experienced a problem and for any inconvenience caused. Check any facts that you are unsure about and make sure you have got all the information.
- *Stage 4*
  Agree the action to be taken with the customer. Make sure that the customer is happy with what you are suggesting. If not, identify alternative strategies that are agreeable to both parties.
- *Stage 5*
  Organise the necessary action and thank the customer for bringing it to the organisation's attention.
- *Stage 6*
  Record the nature of the complaint for future reference. Implement procedures to ensure that the problem doesn't occur again.

Avoid confrontations

It is important to remember that a confrontation results in both parties becoming upset. Arguing, accusing, or not believing the customer will mean that a dissatisfied customer becomes an angry customer. This will do nothing to improve the image of the organisation, nor will the customer return to the organisation again. Dissatisfied customers do not want poor excuses. They want action and results. It is the employee's job to ensure that is what they get.

Written complaints

Customers do not always complain in person. Very often they will write a letter as a method of expressing their dissatisfaction. All letters of complaints must be replied to, and the style of the reply should be polite, professional and factual. It should never be offensive or imply that the customer is in the wrong. The letter must include an apology to the customer and an outline of action to be taken. A copy of the customer's letter and the reply from the organisation should be kept on file for future reference.

ACTIVITY 4

Draft replies to the letters of complaint on page 192.

Consumers and Customers

H. Gordon
The Mount
Hebdon Bridge
Kensington
KJ2 34P

The Manager
The Customer Service Department
The Regional Water Board
Hebdon Bridge
Kensington

14 May 1994

Dear Sir
Re: Limescale

I am writing to express my dissatisfaction with the quality of water that I am currently receiving.

The limescale is so bad that I am having to descale my kettle every week. I am also extremely concerned about the state of my washing machine, which has broken down three times in the last month. The engineer who came out to mend it said the faults had occurred as a result of the very hard water in the area.

The quality of drinking water is appalling too. I am having to buy bottled water every day, as I cannot bring myself to drink the water fresh from the tap. The floating limescale in the glass is enough to put anybody off drinking it.

I thought privatisation was expected to bring an improvement in service due to competition. Well, privatisation has been and gone and there's no improvement in service and certainly no competition. Rest assured: if I could change to a different supplier I would.

The final straw came this morning when I noticed that my bill had increased by 58%. How can this be? I am not using any more water and the increased price has certainly not resulted in an improvement in service.

I want action and I want it now.
Please advise.

Yours sincerely,

Mr H. Gordon

Green Gables
The Willow Bank
Oxfordshire

The Customer Services Department
The Car Dealer
Edinburgh
Scotland

4 September 1994

Dear Sir
Re: Customer Care

I am writing to express how unhappy I was with the quality of after-sales service I received having bought a new car from your company.

The car cost me in excess of £10,000, and in the first week let me down 3 times. Each time your firm promised that they would get a mechanic to me immediately. However on each occasion I was waiting in excess of three hours, thus making me very late for work.

The car seems to be nothing but trouble. As soon as one fault is mended another one occurs. However, nobody in your organisation seems to want to know. Not once have you asked me to bring the car in so that you can check it. It just seems that I have to wait until another problem occurs until you will do something.

As a customer who has bought from your organisation for a number of years, I feel very let down. Please let me know of your intended action.

Yours sincerely,

Roger Thorpe

(3.3.4) (3.3.5)

ACTIVITY 5

In pairs, role play the following situations and develop your skills of handling customer complaints.
1. A customer complaining to her bank that, despite having sufficient funds in her account, a cheque for a new television costing £499 has

Consumers and Customers

bounced. She complains of feeling humiliated and embarrassed.
2 A customer has booked a table for two, but the booking has not been recorded. The restaurant is now full. The customer is very angry because she was entertaining a business client whom she wanted to impress.
3 A customer returns an item of clothing, which appears to have been worn. He claims it is the wrong size and wants a refund. He has produced a receipt as proof of purchase.
4 A customer returns an item of clothing to the dry cleaner, claiming that the shoulder pads have moved and the buttons been tarnished as a result of the dry cleaning. The customer wants the dry cleaner to pay for a replacement.
5 A customer telephones an organisation to complain about the quality of a three-piece suite that has just been delivered to her home. She states that the fabric is of a poorer quality than that on display in the shop, the cushions seem hollow and the structure lacks support.
(3.3.4) (3.3.5)

Legislation to protect customers

In the provision of customer services it is important that organisations operate within the law. The Health and Safety at Work Act governs the rights and responsibilities of employers, employees and customers at work.

Health and safety
The Health and Safety at Work Act 1974 and the additional six health and safety regulations that came into force in 1993 have relevant sections that aim to protect the consumer. The legislation clearly states that the environment within an organisation must be free from health and safety hazards and that people who come onto the premises should not face any risk of injury. The legislation covers a wide variety of people, including visitors, customers, contractors and the general public, both within and outside the workplace if it is affected by work activities.

The standard of protection required for customers is similar to that which is expected for employees. However, it is important that people who are not employees have their attention drawn to potential hazards with notices and barriers. Clearly, employees will have an understanding of dangerous areas in a workplace. In comparison, a customer or member of the general public might not. Therefore by erecting fences and danger notices they are kept informed about areas to avoid and activities that are dangerous.

Many organisations take out insurance to protect themselves against legal action. The main type of policy that an organisation can have to protect itself against claims of personal injury caused by negligence or health and safety problems is public liability insurance. Protection against claims for injury because of faulty or dangerous products is covered by product liability insurance. There are a wide range of other insurance schemes that an organisation can use to protect itself from legal action, and the choice of policy is very much dependent upon the nature of the work undertaken by the organisation and the level of risk involved.

ACTIVITY

1 Identify as many different examples as you can of warning labels that you come across in your day-to-day activities which are aimed at protecting customers. Typical examples might include:
   • Warning labels on packaging
   • Warning signs informing customers of wet floors
   • Labels situated near hot objects warning customers not to burn themselves
   and many more.
   Draw the signs, notices or labels and write a short paragraph alongside each example, identifying the customer and the hazard from which they are being protected.
2 Think of different products, their usage and how they are sold. Identify a possible health and safety hazard that the consumer needs to be informed about. Examples include:
   • A step as the customer enters a shop
   • Peanuts should not be sold to young children
   • Plugs should be wired correctly
   Produce your own warning label aimed at protecting the consumer from the health and safety hazard.
(3.3.6)

In the purchasing of goods and services, customers are protected from products that are sub-standard or dangerous, guarantees that are misleading or inaccurate and services that are inefficient or badly run. The forms of protection include:
• Legislation:
  – The law of contract
  – Unfair Contract Terms Act
  – Sale and Supply of Goods and Services Act 1994
  – Consumer Protection Act 1987
  – Trade Descriptions Act
  – The Consumer Credit Act
  – The Data Protection Act
• Guarantees and warranties
• The Citizen's Charter
• Ombudsmen
• Consumer associations and trade associations
• The influence of the media and its controls

Contract of sale
In the buying of goods and services, consumers' rights and duties are outlined within the law of

Consumers and Customers

contract. A contract is a legally binding agreement between two or more parties. This means that those people who are involved in the making of the contract agree to 'honour' or 'abide by' the details within the contract. A contract can be made in a whole variety of situations, including the buying of goods, the booking of a holiday or agreeing to work for an organisation.

There are many misconceptions about what constitutes a legal contract. Some people think that a contract has to be a formal document signed in the presence of a solicitor. This is not the case. Contracts are made in our day-to-day activities. Paying the bus driver, the hairdresser or the shopkeeper are all examples of contracts being made, but no formal documents necessarily exist.

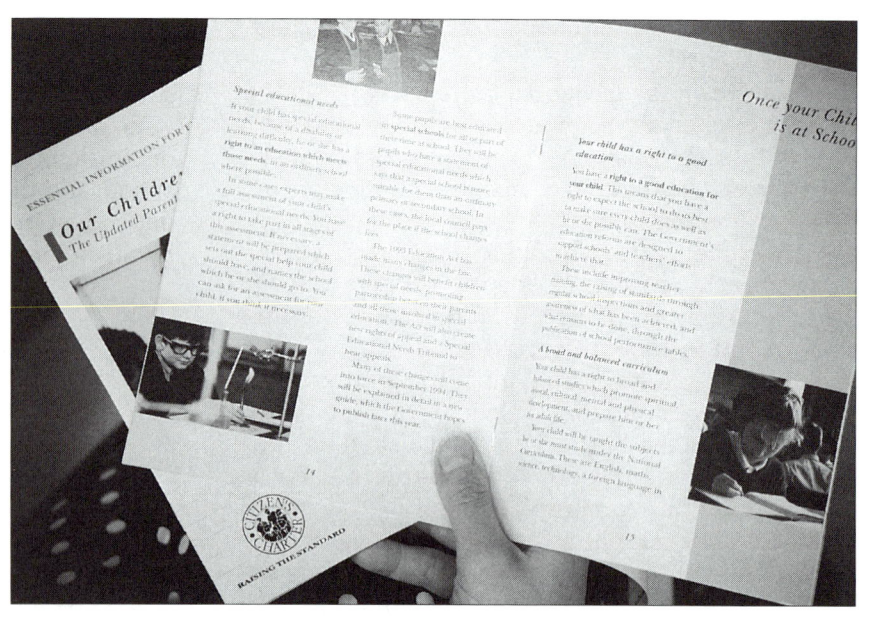

It is often thought that contracts have to be in writing. This is not the case either. A verbal contract between two or more parties, in most cases, is as legally binding as a contract made in writing. However, in some situations, where the details are very technical or there are large sums of money involved, it is in the interests of the parties to write down the precise details of the contract to avoid confusion later.

In the buying of goods or services a customer may be entitled to damages if a breach of contract has occurred. A breach of contract refers to a situation where one of the parties involved in the contract has failed to do what they promised or agreed to do. Examples include the failure to deliver goods or services on time or goods delivered in the wrong quantity or of the wrong type. It is important to remember that customers may also be in breach of contract if they fail to pay for their goods on time. The courts will decide whether there has been a breach of contract, how much compensation, if any, to award and whether the contract is to be cancelled or not.

Part of the Citizen's Charter

ACTIVITY

1. Identify as many examples as you can of written or verbal contracts that you have entered into this week. Write them down in the form of a short list.
2. What did the contracts require you and the other party to do in each situation?
3. Identify which of the contracts have been fulfilled and which are ongoing.
4. What would constitute a breach of contract by either party?

(3.3.6)

Exclusion clauses

Some organisations often try to avoid their responsibilities by using exclusion clauses. An exclusion clause is an attempt by one party to exclude or limit their liability to another party, usually the consumer. Examples of exclusion clauses that organisations may try to use include:

> *The Company will take no responsibility for poor quality products or badly manufactured items.*
>
> *Customers must check goods carefully before purchase.*

> No Refunds or Exchanges Buyer Beware!

Under the Unfair Contract Terms Act 1977 an organisation must be able to prove that the exclusion clause was fair and reasonable. If the court feels that an exclusion clause is unfair to the customer or is trying to exclude the organisation from its legal obligations it will ensure that it has no legal force. Generally, the courts do not like exclusion clauses and would not allow the examples above to be used.

If positioned correctly, exclusion clauses warning customers about leaving goods or parked cars at their own risk are usually acceptable:

> **Warning**
> Customers are advised that cars and personal possessions are left at the owner's own risk

Organisations that try to exclude liability for death or injury as a result of a faulty product or poor service will find that the exclusion clause will always fail.

ACTIVITY

Identify as many examples of different exclusion clauses as you can find. Produce a poster or a brochure to present your findings. Remember to include where you saw the exclusion clauses and whether you think they are fair or not.
(3.3.6)

ACTIVITY

The Sale and Supply of Goods and Services Act 1994
Read the following situations and identify what advice you would give the customer in each case.
1. A customer bought a very expensive Porsche for £30,000. However, he found that the car failed to start in the rain and the gearstick would not remain in place. After a few weeks he returned it to the dealer who exchanged the car for a new one. Unfortunately, the second car proved to be more unreliable than the first. The customer returned it to the garage stating that he wanted a full refund. The garage refused the refund but offered to repair the car again. The customer refused, stating that he wanted a full refund or he would take the matter to Court.
   Do you think the customer is entitled to a full refund?
2. A customer bought some woollen underwear, which contained a chemical used in the manufacturing process. Having worn the underwear all day the customer developed a skin rash which eventually resulted in dermatitis. The customer has asked for a full refund, but because the item has been worn the shop is arguing that he will have to exchange the goods for something else. Do you think the customer is entitled to a full refund?
3. A customer ordered 20 rolls of wallpaper having looked at a sample roll in the shop. When the customer picked up the order she found that the ordered rolls were of a much poorer quality than the sample roll in the shop. The shopkeeper is refusing to provide a refund, claiming that the customer had ordered the rolls having seen the sample and price. Do you think the customer is entitled to a full refund?

The Sale and Supply of Goods and Services Act 1994 includes some basic legal principles which aim to protect the consumer when buying goods. The Act covers goods bought from a street trader, shop, mail order catalogue or from door-to-door salespeople. The main features of the Act are described below.

1. Goods must be of *satisfactory quality*, which means that they must be fit for the purpose for which they are used. The obligation is on the seller to ensure that the quality of the product is what is expected, and if the buyer finds that the product is in any way faulty, he or she is entitled to a full refund. Therefore, relating this to the case study with the Porsche car, under the Sale and Supply of Goods and Services Act the customer would be entitled to a full refund or a new car because the car was not of merchantable quality.
2. If the goods have been bought for a particular purpose and the buyer made this clear when purchasing the goods the Sale and Supply of Goods and Services Act states that the goods should be *fit for that purpose*. Therefore, when buying food there is an understanding that the food will be edible. Similarly, when buying a hairdryer it is implied that it will operate safely. In relation to the case study the customer would be entitled to a full refund for the underwear, because despite the fact that he wore them, they were not fit for the purpose for which they were bought.
3. When goods are sold by *sample*, the Sale and Supply of Goods and Services Act states that the sample should be representative of the normal stock in terms of merchantable quality and purpose for which it is intended. Relating this to the case study, it is clear that the customer would be entitled to a full refund if she could prove that the quality of the wallpaper rolls was inferior to that of the one on display.

ACTIVITY

Actual cases which went to court and which illustrate the above legal points are:
   Rogers v Parish (Scarborough) Ltd 1987
   Shine v General Guarantee Corp Ltd 1988
   Grant v Australian Knitting Mills Ltd 1936
   Griffiths v Peter Conway Ltd 1939
   Godley v Perry 1960
If you refer to an up to date business law book the cases should be quoted. You can then include the information within your portfolio as evidence.
(3.3.6)

Goods bought in a sale are also covered by the Sale and Supply of Goods and Services Act. However, customers cannot expect to buy goods of perfect quality if they are either secondhand or seconds. In addition to the legal protection offered to customers under the Sale and Supply of Goods and Services Act, some organisations provide additional guarantees to their customers in an attempt to provide customer service of the highest quality. Examples may include exchanging goods that are the wrong size or which have lost their shape after washing.

The Act also covers goods supplied as part of a service, on hire or in part exchange. The Act also

Consumers and Customers

covers the provision of services by electricians, builders, plumbers etc. It states that these services should be provided at a reasonable price, completed in a reasonable length of time and care, and skill should be used by the worker in providing the service.

The Consumer Protection Act 1987

A producer's liability does not end when the goods are sold. Any harm caused to a consumer as a result of a defective product is the responsibility of the producer. For the producer to be liable the customer must prove that:

1. He or she has suffered injury or damage
2. The product was faulty or defective
3. The injury or damage was caused by the faulty or defective product

Compensation is available if death, personal injury or damage to property has occurred as a result of the faulty product.

There are a number of defences that a producer may be able to use to avoid being liable, and it is important that a customer who is considering taking legal action is aware of these before proceeding further. It is important to note that the consumer is only protected if he or she has used the product safely and for its normal use.

ACTIVITY

Look at the following situations. Identify whether the producer is liable or not. Give reasons for your answers.

1. Douglas Fairburn buys a new stereo player from the local electrical store. Using an extension lead, he plugs the stereo into a socket in the bedroom and takes the stereo into the bathroom as he has a bath. The stereo falls into the bath, there is a massive explosion and Douglas suffers first-degree burns and scalds.
2. Jacob Levy buys a new toaster and wires the plug incorrectly. As a result the toaster is set on fire and the kitchen is badly damaged. Jacob rushes in and throws water on the toaster to put out the fire. The toaster explodes and Jacob faints with shock. He hits his head on the kitchen units as he falls and needs hospital treatment for five stitches to the forehead.
3. Vera Conlon buys a new car from a large dealer. As she drives the car away and gathers speed down the motorway, the front wheel blows and the car veers into the central reservation. As a result of the accident Vera suffers severe cuts to the face and broken legs and arms.

(3.3.6)

The Consumer Protection Act and the Trade Descriptions Act

The Consumer Protection Act 1987 makes it a criminal offence for organisations to mislead customers about the prices charged for their products or services. This is particularly true for goods that are sold as sale items. It is illegal for an organisation to claim that an item has been reduced if the item was never sold at the original price. Consumers are further protected by the Trade Descriptions Act, which states that any trader who says or writes something which is untrue about goods (or in some circumstances services) is guilty of a criminal offence.

The Consumer Credit Act

For many consumers, the only way to afford expensive items like cars or three-piece suites is to buy them on credit. Some traders offer interest-free credit, but in situations where this is not the case it is important to check the rate of interest being charged. What might seem to be a small monthly repayment can work out to be much more than the original asking price when the total payments have been paid. Consumers have the right to change their mind about a credit deal if:

- The deal was agreed within the last few days
- The agreement was made in person and not over the phone
- The agreement was signed at home or away from the business premises

When consumers enter into a credit agreement they are entitled to a copy of the agreement clearly stating the cost of the item plus the interest to be charged. It should also state the procedure for cancellation.

ACTIVITY

Look in local and national newspapers for different examples of credit offers. Your examples may include:

- Credit offers for cash
- Credit offers to support the purchase of items like cars or furniture
- Consumer durables

Which organisations appear to provide the best offers?

Which organisations appear to offer the worst deals?

Remember to base your decision on the level of interest charged and the period of time available to repay the loan.

(3.3.6)

The Data Protection Act 1984

The Data Protection Act was passed in an attempt to control the misuse of personal information held on computers and sophisticated information technology. The Act lays down very strict guidelines about how personal information is stored and handled. The purpose is to protect information held about people on computers and to ensure that agreed standards are applied in the way the information is used. The objective of the Act is to reassure people that they can

Consumers and Customers

have access to any information or data that is stored about them in order to check its accuracy and protect against misuse of information.

The Act applies to any organisation that holds personal records on file. Such organisations have to register with the Data Protection Registrar and give details on:
- The nature of the data
- The sources of the data
- The purpose for which it is intended
- Who is likely to have access to the information

A person may be entitled to damages if the information kept on file is inaccurate or there is unauthorised access to that information. In order to check the accuracy of data a person is entitled to obtain access to their own personal file.

ACTIVITY

Identify as many examples as you can of different organisations who have requested personal information about you to keep on file. Your examples might include enrolling at your local college, joining a bank or building society or subscribing to a newspaper or magazine.

What sort of information did they ask for?
What purpose would the information be used for?
How might the information be misused if the Data Protection Act was not in existence?

(3.3.6)

ACTIVITY

The purpose of this activity is to consolidate your knowledge to date about the different forms of consumer legislation. Look at the situations below and identify which particular act applies and what the likely outcome will be. Remember you have studied the following acts within this chapter:
- The Law of Contract
- Unfair Contract Terms Act
- Sale and Supply of Goods and Services Act 1994
- Consumer Protection Act 1987
- Trade Descriptions Act
- The Consumer Credit Act
- The Data Protection Act

Situation	Relevant legislation and likely outcome
A retailer tries to exclude liability for damage caused to items of clothing during dry cleaning	
A retailer claims that a range of garden furniture is on sale at half price. In actual fact the garden furniture has never been sold at any higher price	
A travel agent forgets to book a holiday for a customer, despite taking the booking form, agreeing that a place is available and accepting the money from the customer. The holiday is now full and the customer is unable to get a place	
A secondhand car salesman claims that the car he is selling has only 24,000 miles on the clock. In actual fact the car has done in excess of 50,000 miles	
A customer buys a pair of jeans and when she tries them on at home she finds the zip is faulty and the button missing	
A customer agrees to take out a loan with a finance company that was selling its policies door to door. Later, when reading the information, the customer realises that the interest rate is very high and decides to change his mind	
A young child dies as a result of playing with a toy that has been manufactured in a dangerous way	
A customer has been refused credit by a large retail store and is demanding access to the computer where the information relating to his creditworthiness is stored	
A customer orders 150 wedding invitations and order of service sheets. When the invitations arrive the customer finds that the company has printed 350 copies and is insisting on payment for the additional copies.	
A customer has her hair bleached and it all falls out. The hairdresser tries to charge the customer £80	

(3.3.6)

Guarantees and warrantees

A guarantee or warranty is an assurance of quality by an organisation which usually covers the first few years of a product. The organisation states that goods or services will be of a certain standard and if the purchase does not live up to expectations the organisation will replace it or repair it free of charge.

The following example of a guarantee appears on a box of Shreddies cereal:

Consumers and Customers

> **Guarantee**
> We take every care to ensure this product reaches you in perfect condition. However if the contents are unsatisfactory, please send the whole of the top flap and a sample of the product, stating where and when it was bought, and we will be pleased to reimburse you. Your statutory rights are not affected.

The reference to 'your statutory rights are not affected' simply means that the guarantee is in addition to your normal legal rights as a consumer.

Credacare, who produce Creda Cookers, provide the following guarantee for all their customers:

> **CredaCare – Your Guarantee**
>
> All equipment manufactured by Creda is guaranteed for one year against faulty material or workmanship. If your appliance is found to be defective within twelve months of the date of purchase we, or our authorised service agent, will replace or repair the faulty component. There will be no charge for the materials, labour or transportation.

Guarantees and warranties are seen as additional rights for the customer and are part of an organisation's commitment to customer care and service. They are usually clear, easy to understand and are available for the customer to read prior to making the purchase. With some guarantees a registration card has to be completed and sent to the manufacturer detailing when the purchase was made and where. If the registration card is not completed the guarantee will not be valid.

ACTIVITY

Try to identify three examples of guarantees or warranties that apply to products and three examples that apply to services. For example, many of the newly privatised public services have recently introduced guarantees as part of their commitment to improving the quality of service for the customer. Similarly, brand new cars usually have a warranty, which can last from one year to about three. Outline the main features of the guarantees and identify how the customer benefits. (3.3.6)

The Citizen's Charter

In an attempt to improve the quality of public services and make them more answerable to the customers, the Government introduce the Citizen's Charter in 1991. The Charter attempts to provide a framework for:

- Setting standards of service
- Ensuring quality in the provision of services
- Auditing and inspecting services
- Complaints and redress

The Charter is very broad and applies to all public services. These include government departments, nationalised industries, local authorities, the NHS, the courts, police and emergency services. It also covers the newly privatised key utilities in the private sector, such as gas, water and electricity.

The aim is to make institutions in the public sector more accountable for their actions. The Government claims that it will provide a mechanism for improving choice, quality, value and accountability. The intention is to raise the standard of public services, improve quality and seek efficiencies.

The following table provides a summary of the main features of the Citizen's Charter for some key areas.

Area	Summary of main features
Education	School progress reports at least annually Clear publication of results achieved in school League tables to be produced Regular and independent inspection of all schools with the results reported to parents A Parent's Charter
Transport	Clearer information about service targets, timetables and performance Simple and effective complaints procedure Production of a charter outlining targets for performance, rights of redress and levels of compensation
The NHS	Clear information about available options about health care Choice of GP Access to patient records Published comparative information on the performance of health services Maximum waiting time for treatment
London Underground	98% of scheduled mileage will run No more than 7% of passengers will wait more than one and a half times the scheduled interval Trains will be cleaned inside every day and outside three times a day No more than 2% of passengers will wait more than 3 minutes for their tickets

ACTIVITY

The article on the next page appeared in the The Times on 7 April 1994. Read it very carefully and answer the questions.
1. Why is the London Underground facing large claims for compensation?
2. Who was to blame for the incident?
3. Who is allowed to claim compensation and why?
4. Why did the London Underground official appeal to customers not to claim compensation?
5. Do you think compensation should be paid and why?

(3.3.6)

Consumers and Customers

Underground faces huge claims after 100,000 left stranded

London Underground faces the largest claim ever lodged for a single incident under the Citizen's Charter following a power failure which affected 100,000 commuters on 300 trains yesterday.

However, passengers who were stranded on trains for up to 75 minutes during the morning rush hour may have to wait for months before claiming compensation of up to £250,000 due to a backlog of previous claims. The delay follows the admission by British Gas that it was to blame for the malfunction of a gas regulator which supplies power to generate electricity at the Underground's power station in Chelsea.

British Gas said it was still investigating the fault, but claimed supplies were restored within ten minutes. A spokeswoman said: 'We understand London Underground had subsequent difficulties in restoring electricity power.'

In contrast to last November's week-long closure of the Central Line, which began with 20,000 commuters being walked through tunnels to safety, London Underground yesterday decided it was safer to keep passengers in the carriages.

At that time, one LU official appealed to customers not to claim compensation so the money could be used instead to modernise the network. Under the terms of the Charter, passengers can claim compensation if they are delayed for more than 15 minutes.

While some passengers, such as Geoff Archard of Wanstead, east London, who was more than an hour late for work, vowed to reclaim his fare, others adopted a more world-weary attitude.

Mr Archard said 'I pay out £880 a year for my ticket and I am now an hour late for work. This will be the first time I feel angry enough to reclaim my fare. This sort of delay has happened before and I am sick and tired of it.'

But Colin Spence, 44, from Milton Keynes, said he would not be trying to get his fare back. 'It seems to be becoming a frequent occurrence. It happened to me seven or eight weeks ago and all the underfunding can't have helped.

'I pay £2,500 for an annual season ticket but I can't be bothered to claim any money back. It's just too much hassle.'

Andrew Gray, 31, a Lloyds insurance broker from Clapham, south London, also said he would not be claiming compensation. 'Most people put on a smile and just accept this happens. If I didn't think that, I would go barking mad. It has taken me an hour and 20 minutes to do a 45 minute journey.'

The power failure hit parts of the District, Piccadilly, Central and Northern lines, and completely closed the Victoria Line for a time.

A London Underground spokesman said passengers were kept on trains as it had been confident of regaining power quickly. 'Evacuation would have taken hours.'

Ombudsman

An ombudsman is an official, appointed by central or local government or a business organisation to investigate complaints and resolve problems. The term ombudsman means 'representative' or 'agent', and although an ombudsman appointed to office, the appointing authority cannot control the ombudsman's actions.

Ombudsmen have been appointed in a range of areas including:

- *Central government*   To investigate complaints about the service offered and decisions made by central government departments
- *Local government*   To investigate complaints about the way the local authority is operating and the decisions which they have made
- *Health service*   To review complaints made by both patients and staff about the way the hospital is managed, decisions made about health care and the quality of service received
- *Banking*   To study complaints about bank charges, accuracy of information and issues relating to the Data Protection Act
- *Building societies*   To analyse complaints relating to the purchasing and selling of houses, including valuations and mortgage decisions
- *Legal services*   To review complaints about the practices of barristers and solicitors and the costs of their services
- *Financial services*   To study complaints about investment and pension advice and estate agents to study complaints about fees, house prices and quality of service offered
- *Central government*   Responsible for checking that central government departments are operating fairly

The ombudsman usually investigates a complaint following a request from a member of the public or via an MP on behalf of a member of the MP's constituency. He or she will have access to official files and records, and although they have no power to make changes to the administration of the organisation that they are investigating, the ombudsman is permitted to make recommendations, which the organisation should act upon.

ACTIVITY

The purpose of this activity is to research the work of one ombudsman in detail. Choose an area that you are interested in researching. Remember you might want to look at:
- Central or local government
- The health service
- Financial services
- Estate agents
- Banking
- Building societies
- The legal profession

If you are working in groups it might be interesting to share out the areas so that you each research a different one.

Using the reference books in the library try to identify:
1 The name of the local ombudsman
2 The type of service offered
3 The procedure people have to follow in order to make a complaint

Present your findings using suitable visual and written methods.

(3.3.6)

Consumers and Customers

Consumer associations
There is a range of consumer and trade associations, which support customers in the making of a complaint or provide advice about the purchasing of goods and services.

Trading Standards/Consumer Protection Departments of local authorities
These provide advice and investigate complaints about the purchasing of goods and services. These might include:
- Inaccurate weights and measures
- Complaints about false or misleading descriptions
- Unsafe consumer goods
- Issues relating to consumer credit

Each authority appoints trading standards officers to investigate customers' complaints.

Trading Standards Departments sometimes run Consumer Advice Centres. These are usually situated near large shopping areas. Customers and traders can drop into the centres and get advice and information about a range of issues relating to the buying and selling of goods and services.

Environmental Health Departments
Environmental Health Officers are appointed to investigate matters relating to food and drink that are not suitable for consumption. They are also responsible for inspecting the cleanliness of shops and restaurants. If the environmental health officer is very concerned about a particular restaurant or shop he or she has the power to stop the owner trading until such time as the problems have been rectified.

ACTIVITY

As a group, contact your Environmental Health Officer and Trading Standards Officer at the local authority and ask them to come and talk to you about the work of their departments. It is important to ask useful questions, which may include:
1. How many officers work within each of the departments?
2. What are the departments responsible for?
3. What should customers do if they want to complain?
4. What happens to the complaint once it is made?

Remember to make notes that can be included in your portfolio at a later date and to thank the officers personally at the end of the talk and in writing the following day.

Trade associations
Many traders belong to trade associations who lay down codes of practice for their members. The code of practice, although not legally binding, can be used as a guide to determine whether the trader has operated outside the code that they claim to respect. If this is the case, the court or arbitrator may find in favour of the consumer. Not all organisations are members of trade associations, and it is therefore important that a customer checks this before employing the trader.

ACTIVITY

Using a copy of your local Yellow Pages identify how many traders advertise that they are members of trade associations for the following areas:
- Building
- Electrical
- Plumbing
- Travel agencies
- Removals and storage

For each area make a note of the name of the association that the traders are members of.
(3.3.6)

The Citizens Advice Bureau
The local Citizens Advice Bureau gives free advice and representation about a variety of problems, including:
- Housing issues
- Unfair trading activities
- Benefits
- Money problems

and a range of other issues.

ACTIVITY

Visit your local Citizen's Advice Bureau and collect a leaflet which outlines its role and function. Make a list of the different areas that they are able to provide advice about.
(3.3.6)

The Consumers' Association
The Consumers' Association is an independent organisation which tests and investigates goods and services offered for sale. The results of the research are printed in the magazine *Which?*. This magazine is extremely useful when purchasing goods or services as it produces tables comparing and contrasting the facilities, quality and prices of products produced by different manufactures.

ACTIVITY

You have decided to go into business and need to furnish an office with furniture and equipment. With a budget of £10,000, identify the items that you will need to buy. Your shopping list should at the very minimum include a computer, desk, chair and telephone. Look through as many *Which?* magazines as you can find to identify the types of equipment and furniture that they recommend.

Include your research and reasons for choice in your final proposal.
(3.3.6)

Utilities

Since the privatisation of utilities such as gas, water, electricity and telecommunications a number of utility watchdogs have been established to regulate the activities of the organisations and the prices charged. The regulatory bodies include Ofwat, which monitors the water suppliers and prices charged; the National Rivers Association, which monitors the quality of the waterways; Ofgas, which oversees the gas industry; Oftel, which is responsible for the telephone service; and Offer, the electricity industry watchdog.

ACTIVITY

Why do you think the government decided to establish utility watchdogs or regulatory bodies to monitor the newly privatised industries? How effective do you think they have been and why?
(3.3.6)

The National Consumer Council

This is an organisation that brings together government departments, traders, public sector organisations and consumers to discuss and agree policies on issues relating to consumer protection.

The British Standards Institution

The British Standards Institution is responsible for the setting of standards which manufacturers comply with. It was set up around the turn of the century and its stamp of approval is seen by customers as a mark of quality. The standards are agreed by representatives from industry, distributors, consumer groups and other interested parties. Goods which meet the standards laid down are awarded a kitemark, which informs the customer that the goods have been tested to the British Standard. The British Standards Institution is completely independent and is funded by government grants and subscriptions.

ACTIVITY

Next time you go shopping, carefully check the products that are being offered for sale.
   Which products carry a Kitemark?
   What does the Kitemark tell you about the product?
(3.3.6)

ACTIVITY

Read the article below, which appeared in the *Sunday Telegraph* on 15 August 1993.

Questions
1 Why is the British Standards Institution being criticised?
2 Who are the representatives who sit on the committees agreeing the standards for different products?
3 Identify the products where safety standards could be improved but where the manufacturers have resisted.

Doubts cast on safety standards

British Standards, the most widely-used guides to product reliability, are increasingly being influenced by manufacturers keen to cut costs, according to consumer safety experts.

Concern over the quality of British Standards follows last week's report in the Consumers' Association magazine Which? Way to Health that several brands of condom carrying the Kitemark – implying compliance with a British Standard – failed to perform well in rigorous tests.

Since the British Standards Institution was set up around the turn of the century, its stamp of approval has been widely regarded by the public as a guarantee of quality.

The technical specifications that lie behind the standards are arrived at during a long consultation process involving BSI committees on which sit representatives of manufacturing companies, distributors, consumer groups and other interested parties.

Insiders say much wrangling centres on establishing just how much the manufacturer can get away with. The result, say critics, is a 'lowest common denominator' approach to product safety and reliability.

'It suffers from having to reach compromises between often very different considerations,' said John Stubbs, head of research and materials testing at the Automobile Association. 'We try to introduce more consumer interest to the committees but they still tend to be heavily dominated by manufacturers.'

The Royal Society for the Prevention of Accidents is concerned about the effect of this domination.

According to the society's statistics, about 1,500 house fires each year are caused by washing machines that overheat. Safety experts say the answer is to fit a small electrical cut-out costing a few pence. Yet the British Standard still does not require it to be fitted.

According to RoSPA, each year about around 2,000 young children have to undergo hospital treatment after pulling appliances down on themselves after tugging at long electric cables. The simple solution is to have so called curly cables or cordless devices – but, according to Mr Jenkins, manufacturers are resisting making them compulsory. Instead they have agreed to cables being shortened from 39in to 27in.

'We are outnumbered five to one by manufacturers on the committees,' says Mr Jenkins. 'They are not going to introduce anything that cannot be easily achieved.'

The Association of Manufacturers of Domestic Electrical Appliances which represents product makers in the drafting of many British Standards, says compromises are often made by committees.

'At the end of the day, safety is down to cost; it's not nice to say, but it is,' said Stuart MacConnacher, senior product standards engineer at the association. He added, however, 'There is no mileage for us selling dangerous products.'

He defended the presence of manufacturers on the committees. 'We are talking technical subjects. The technical experts on products work for the companies that make them.'

Consumers and Customers

4. Why are the manufacturers concerned about raising the standards further?
5. What changes need to happen, according to John Stubbs, in order to reduce the influence of the manufacturers?

(3.3.6)

Media

The media are also highly influential in protecting consumers from unfair practices by traders. Television programmes such as *That's Life* and *Watchdog*, and radio programmes such as *You and Yours* attempt to raise public awareness about consumer issues and fight on behalf of customers who are in conflict with traders. The high profile that these programmes have and the national coverage that they achieve result in some very successful outcomes.

ACTIVITY

Make a list of the different types of consumer issues that have been raised, fought and won by the media on behalf of customers. Remember to note the organisations involved, the nature of the problem and how a successful outcome was achieved. If you are having difficulty in remembering issues that have occurred in the past, watch or listen to the programmes over the next few weeks and make a note of current issues.

(3.3.6)

Informing customers of their rights

Customers can be informed about their legal rights regarding consumer protection by a variety of methods. These methods can be divided into those used by trading organisations and those used by independent regulatory bodies.

Trading organisations

All organisations are beginning to recognise or have already responded to the importance of customer care. *Mission statements* and *customer charters* are often produced by the organisations to promote their commitment to customer service and to outline the procedure customers should follow if dissatisfied with the quality of service received. *Advertisements* and *promotions* may focus on guarantees and warranties that a customer may be entitled to when purchasing the product or service. *Catalogues* and *mail order magazines* outline in print the customers' rights, as do *consumer credit agreements* or *store card details*.

Independent regulatory bodies

Independent regulatory bodies like the Citizen's Advice Bureau, the Office of Fair Trading or the Trading Standards Association produce promotional literature aimed at informing customers about their legal rights. The promotional literature may include advertisements, booklets, posters or fact sheets, which the customer can take away and refer to. In addition, trained staff are always available to talk through particular issues with customers and advise on action to be taken.

ACTIVITY

Produce a promotional campaign which aims to inform customers about their legal rights. You may want to produce a poster, a booklet or even a video. The more creative and imaginative you can be the better. The Office of Fair Trading produce a booklet called 'A Buyers Guide' if you need some help with ideas.

(3.3.6)

ACTIVITY (3.3.1–6)

1. Levi's, the jeans maker
(Adapted from The *Independent*: Riveting aspirations, 17 April 94)

Levi Strauss & Co, the San Francisco-based jeans company, has recently produced the following mission or strategy:

to sustain responsible commercial success as a global marketing company of branded casual apparel.

The underlying theme to this statement is that the company and its products, e.g. Levi 501s, will set the standard for other clothing companies to follow. The reference to responsibility also implies that the company recognises the importance of customer care and responsibility to the wider community.

The mission statement continues by referring to the strategic needs of the business. These are identified as:

- Superior profitability and return on investment
- Market leadership
- Superior products and services

It continues

We will conduct our business ethically and demonstrate leadership in satisfying our responsibilities to our communities and to society. Our work environment will be safe and productive and characterised by fair treatment, teamwork, open communications, personal accountability, and opportunities for growth and development. We all want a company that our people are proud of and committed to, and where all employees have an opportunity to contribute, learn, grow and advance based on merit, not politics or background. We want our people to feel respected, treated fairly, listened to and involved. Above all, we want satisfaction from

Consumers and Customers

accomplishments and friendships, balanced personal and professional lives and to have fun in our endeavours.

The mission statement calls for leaders everywhere in the organisation to come forward and help bring the aspirations closer to reality.

The mission statement clearly illustrates that Levi's are attempting to improve the quality of service to both internal and external customers.

1. What is the difference between an internal customer and an external customer?
2. Make a list of the different types of merchandise produced and sold by Levi's and the prices at which they are sold.
3. The statement refers to 'responsible commercial success'. List the different ways that the company can be responsible to and meet the needs of its customers and the wider community. You might want to include things like environmentally friendly production techniques, hard-wearing good-quality jeans etc.
4. What does the company mean by 'we want to conduct our business ethically'?
5. Why is a safe working environment an important aspect of good customer care?
6. Levi's state that they want 'fair treatment, teamwork, open communications, personal accountability and opportunities for growth and development'. Identify and explain which aspects of this statement are important and relevant to a customer care policy.
7. Make a list of how the company is trying to improve the working conditions for its employees.
8. How will external customers benefit from the company's decision to improve conditions for internal customers?
9. Identify the different types of advertisement used by Levi's to promote their products. What messages and images are they trying to communicate to their customers?
10. Interview three customers who have recently purchased Levi's clothing. Ask them whether they are happy with the quality of the item and the price paid. What recommendations do they have, if any, for improving the quality of the product?

2. The article below appeared in the Sunday Times on 10 April 1994.

Tasks

1. What is meant by the term 'cashless society'?
2. How is the cash card or electronic purse meeting customers' needs?
3. How might an organisation use this system to improve the quality of service offered to its customers?
4. Produce an advertisement or promotion leaflet which an organisation who has introduced the system can use to promote the advantages of the new system to the customers.
5. What are the disadvantages of the new system?
6. If an organisation was to introduce the cash card, what types of systems and procedures would need to be in place to deal with possible customer queries and complaints?

(3.3.1) (3.3.2) (3.3.4) (3.3.5)

3. Grand National Printing Corporation

Grand National Printing Corporation is a medium-sized private limited company which specialises in producing and marketing quality printing merchandise for the retail market. It also has a small mail order service for selling directly to the general public. The product range of the company includes:

- Journals and magazines
- Letterheads and printed stationery
- Invitations and greeting cards

Card that is a step closer to a cashless society

EVER been in the embarrassing situation of not having enough money on you? Suddenly at the checkout you have left your cash at home?

Just imagine how easy life would be if all you needed was a plastic card that acted like cash and meant you could pay for any item, however small, in any shop, anywhere.

Visa Internaional, the payments group, says the technology for such a system will be in place within two years. The need to carry money will disappear altogether as shops, vending machines, petrol stations, fast food restaurants and pay phones become connected by the 'electronic purse'.

The purse is set to revolutionise the way we spend money and use banks. It is a plastic card containing a microchip that acts as a store of cash and, unlike credit or debit cards, reduces the value stored on it with each purchase. The card is swiped in the store and the value is instantly transferred. No signature or forms are necessary. A further advantage is that the user would not need a PIN (personal identification number) as the card could be electronically locked and unlocked using a personal code.

This cashless society came another step closer at the end of last month when Visa announced the formation of a technology group of international manufacturers to help make the electronic purse a reality throughout the world. The first companies to join the group were America's VeriFone, the world's leading provider of point-of-service payment systems, and Gemplus, the world's leading manufacturer of smart cards – plastic cards with computer chips inside them.

'We are trying to get everyone in the world on the level playing field of an open system conforming to a global standard of inter-operability and security,' said a spokesman for VeriFone.

Visa has already linked up with a number of bank-led groups around the world to work on common standards for the purse. The consortium includes groups based in Belgium, France, Portugal, Spain, Taiwan and America, all of which have been working independently on cards that incorporate microchips.

But the Visa-led consortium does not include groups in Australia and Singapore, which are developing their own smart payment cards, or a British venture launched last December by the National Westminster Bank, which is teaming up with the Midland and BT. NatWest will be testing its version of the electronic purse – the Mondex card – in Swindon next year and throughout the country by 1996.

Consumers and Customers

- Posters and advertisements
- Examination papers

The company employs the following staff:

Managing Director	Ellen Haversham
Managing Director's Secretary	Richard Makin
Chief Accountant	Heather O'Leary
Accountant's Secretary	Rachel Boyle
Personnel Manager	Duncan MacTavish
Personnel Secretary	Owen Matthews
Sales Manager	Rebecca Schelda
Sales Secretary	Imran Ramzan

You are employed as a receptionist and clerical assistant and are expected to deal with all general enquiries and correspondence. A typical day's activities are listed below. Deal with each enquiry separately and note down the procedure followed and the action taken. Specific problems relating to sales, personnel and finance should be referred to the relevant secretary. In such cases make a note of who you have referred the enquiry on to.

Enquiries

1. You have received a telephone call from Mr Roberts, a customer who has purchased stationery through the mail order catalogue. He is complaining that there is an imperfection in the paper and he is therefore unhappy about the quality of the product. He wants either a refund or a replacement.
2. Ms Jayne Simmons arrives at reception to be interviewed for a part-time job as a sales assistant.
3. A telephone call comes from Mr F. Thorpe, requesting a copy of the organisation's up-to-date price list. He had telephoned last week but the copy sent had last year's prices and was therefore out of date.
4. Hayley Miller telephoned wanting to know about the different types of wedding invitation available and the prices charged. The prospective buyer represents a very large stationery outlet which is looking to change from its existing supplier.
5. A sales representative arrives in reception. Apparently he has a meeting with the Sales Manager at 10.00. However, Rebecca said goodbye to you this morning, saying she had a meeting in town and would not be back until 13.00.
6. The Managing Director of your major competitor telephones sounding extremely annoyed. He demands to speak to your Managing Director immediately.
7. Frank Rogers, an accountant from a small retail outlet, telephones with a query about an outstanding balance on the company's account.
8. Ms Jones arrives at reception enquiring whether or not it is possible for the Company to design and print stationery for her newly formed business. She has brought some ideas with her, but unfortunately has not booked an appointment with the Sales Manager.
9. Mr Winters arrives at reception for a meeting with the accountant. You notice that he appears to have difficulty in walking and Accounts are based on the fourth floor, with no lift.
10. An advertisement has been placed in a printing magazine advertising the company and its products. As a result the switchboard is very busy and the Sales secretary is unable to deal with all enquiries quickly enough.

(3.3.1) (3.3.2) (3.3.3) (3.3.4) (3.3.5)

4. Providing customer service

This unit requires students to demonstrate that they can effectively provide a service to three different types of customer. The evidence may be collected from a part-time job, working in reception of the college or school, assisting at parents' evenings or similar functions, or through work experience.

A copy of the following profile can be signed by an employer or teacher to verify that the level of customer service was of the required standard. One form needs to be completed for each customer. This may then be included within the portfolio as evidence for the unit.

Performance criteria	Evidence	Date
Customer needs are identified: information help care refunds or replacements		
Communication: verbal non-verbal face to face telephone polite accurate		
Service: is provided promptly meets legal requirements is honest and confidential		
Customers include: children adults people with special needs		
Customer complaints are dealt with effectively		
Customer queries are dealt with effectively		

(3.3.1) (3.3.2) (3.3.3) (3.3.4) (3.3.6)

Consumers and Customers

MULTIPLE CHOICE

1. When a customer requests further information, the assistant should respond by:
   A. Asking him/her to telephone later when somebody will be available to help
   B. Apologising that the information is not available
   C. Listening very carefully to what is being asked in order that the correct response can be provided
   D. Providing a detailed handbook for the customer to find the information within

2. When seeking a refund a customer should be:
   A. Informed that it is not the organisation's policy to provide refunds
   B. Asked to wait until someone is available to deal with the problem
   C. Made to produce proof of purchase, give explanations as to why a refund is necessary and asked to consider a replacement instead
   D. Made to feel confident that a refund is available

3. After-sales care includes:
   A. Providing customers with literature about forthcoming sales
   B. Help and advice at the point of sale
   C. Providing spare parts, maintaining a product and supporting a customer with a query
   D. Undertaking market research to check whether a customer was happy with the service received

4. It is important to meet customer needs because it:
   A. Improves business and service performance
   B. Is what the managing director wants
   C. Is cost-effective in terms of both time and money
   D. Is a legal requirement within the Sale of Goods Act 1979

5. The morale of staff and customers increases when:
   A. Staff gain a pay rise
   B. Customer needs are met
   C. An organisation undertakes to promote a new product
   D. Goods are reduced in the summer sale

6. Which of the following situations is an example of non-verbal communication?
   A. Talking to a customer by telephone
   B. Shaking the customer's hand and saying good morning
   C. Smart appearance of the staff
   D. Tannoy message to customers informing them of sale items within the store

7. When dealing with children as customers it is important to:
   A. Be patient, supportive and helpful to the child
   B. Deal with the parent, as they usually pay for the product/service
   C. Check that the child does not spoil the display
   D. Encourage them to make a decision quickly as they tend to always change their mind

8. An organisation always wants satisfied customers because:
   A. They are easier to deal with
   B. They are the most effective advertisement for the organisation
   C. A great deal of money is lost in providing refunds
   D. It means the staff are doing their job properly

9. It is a legal requirement for an organisation to:
   A. Provide facilities for customers with special needs
   B. Comply with health and safety standards
   C. Provide customers with detailed information about products or services
   D. Ensure that all customers are satisfied customers

10. When dealing with a written complaint an organisation should immediately:
    A. File it for future reference
    B. Reply with a polite, professional and factual letter
    C. Deny liability and seek legal advice
    D. Telephone the customer and demand an explanation

SHORT ANSWER

1. Why is honesty always the best policy?

2. How should an organisation respond to customers with special needs?

3. How might an organisation convert a dissatisfied customer into a satisfied customer?

4. What is the difference between verbal and non-verbal communication?

5. Why is it important for an organisation to meet customer needs?

6. What procedure should an employee follow when dealing with customer complaints?

7. Why is it important for customer queries to be referred to the correct person and how might an organisation succeed in achieving this?

8. Make a list of customers with special needs and write a brief explanation as to how an organisation should respond to meet their needs

Consumers and Customers

9 What is the difference between internal and external customers and why are they both important to an organisation?

10 Make a list of the different methods which an organisation may use to keep their customers informed.

ELEMENT 3.4
Present proposals for improvement to customer service

Performance criteria

- 3.4.1 Explain the importance of customer service in business organisations
- 3.4.2 Identify how business organisations monitor customer satisfaction
- 3.4.3 Identify improvements to customer service
- 3.4.4 Present proposals for improvements to customer services in one organisation

The importance of customer service

We have already seen many ways in which an organisation may provide excellent customer care, and we have also noted some reasons why customer care is important. It is worth stating that business organisations need customers to operate at all, and therefore anything which increases the number of customers or improves their loyalty has to be a good thing. Organisations may be genuinely interested in their customers as human beings, and strive to keep them satisfied. However, in the final analysis the organisation needs to maintain good customer relations in order to survive.

We can identify four main reasons why customer care is important:
(a) to gain and keep customers
(b) to gain high customer satisfaction
(c) to gain customer loyalty
(d) to help the business survive

To gain and keep customers If an organisation can offer something more than its competitors by way of customer service then it is more likely to secure the business of that customer. If customers leave satisfied then they are more likely to return.

To gain high customer satisfaction Business organisations who care about their customers will be keen to ensure that there is a high level of customer satisfaction. The products or services provided genuinely meet the needs and expectations of their customers who are getting good value for money. High customer satisfaction is associated with high reputation and strong customer loyalty.

To gain customer loyalty Loyal customers are those who will return to the same organisation for the same product or service, because they were highly satisfied on previous occasions. It is easier to keep a customer by providing excellent customer care than it is to make a new customer through marketing techniques. Therefore businesses should be committed to holding on to their existing customers through providing excellent customer care.

To help the business survive A business needs customers. This is true of public and private sector organisations. Without the customer, an organisation cannot survive. The whole purpose of an organisation centres on its ability to provide a service or product which customers both want and are prepared to buy from that organisation. In many cases the quality of customer service received determines whether a customer will ever buy from that organisation.

OUR PROMISE TO CUSTOMERS

At **Super Shop** our aim is to give our customers the best possible service. If you have any problem at all with the product you purchase please do not hesitate to return the item with a receipt and we will do our best to replace it, or if this is not possible, we will happily provide a refund.

Guarantee

Importance of customer service

Many organisations in both the private and public sectors believe that customers are entitled to receive high-quality, cost-effective services which respond to their needs. In a highly competitive market, organisations which do not provide the quality of service that customers expect will find that they are losing business to those organisations that do. This is true of both the private and public sectors.

The types of customer services provided by business organisations in both the private and public sectors include:
1 Providing an efficient service:
- Meeting delivery dates
- Keeping appointments
- Replying to enquiries within the shortest time possible
- Fast, efficient and friendly service
- Goods and services that are reliable and cost-effective
- helping and assisting the customer

Consumers and Customers

2 Answering all telephone calls within five seconds and following the basic principles when communicating with customers by telephone.
3 Ensuring that replies to requests for information are with the customer within a reasonable period of time, e.g. three days:
   - Documentation should be up to date and accurate
   - Letters should be addressed personally, well typed and without spelling errors
4 Dealing with customers courteously and promptly
   - Queues to be kept to a minimum
   - Services to be provided on time
   - Available staff to assist and advice
5 Procedure for dealing with customer complaints and problems:
   - Establishing a customer services department
   - Appointing a member of staff to be in charge of customer services
   - Communicating effectively with customers
   - Ensuring that customer complaints are dealt with to the satisfaction of the customer
   - Providing refunds or replacing goods
   - Providing an efficient after-sales service
6 Reliable systems, facilities and procedures
   - Quick and efficient technology with good backup
   - Customer facilities in good working order
   - An understanding of procedures by all employees
7 Helpful staff who are fully informed about all aspects of the organisation, including:
   - The product or service
   - Prices and discounts
   - Procedures to be followed
   - How to resolve problems
8 Smart appearance of all staff: customers will often assess the quality of the organisation by the appearance of the staff.

Private sector

Private sector organisations have, for a long time, been aware of the importance of putting the customer first. In the private sector, customers are often free to buy products or services from a range of organisations, and their decisions will be based upon the organisation which they feel provides the best service. Marks & Spencer, for example, has been successful because it spends a great deal of time and money in providing quality merchandise and training staff to care for the customer.

Private sector organisations are aware, therefore, of the need to satisfy their customers if they are to prosper. High-quality services need to be provided which are responsive to the needs of the market and provided at affordable prices. Staff are aware of the need to deal with customers fairly, efficiently and courteously.

Public sector

Traditionally public sector organisations have not had to operate within a competitive environment. British Rail ran trains, British Coal mined and sold coal, and the NHS administered health care. However, since 1979 with the election of the Conservative government, many of the key industries in the public sector have been privatised. The aim was to create competition between providers and extended the range of choice to the consumer.

Competition within the public sector has raised the issue of the importance of providing and caring for the customer. The Government believes that the provision of public services should reflect:

- *Standards:* Customers should have access to explicit standards, published and displayed for all to see. The standards should include the organisation's commitment to courtesy and helpfulness from staff, accuracy of information, taking into account legal entitlements, and a commitment to action, including targets.
- *Openness:* Customers are entitled to be fully informed about all aspects of the organisation's business. This includes prices, profit, managers responsible for activities and published performance reviews.
- *Information:* Public sector organisations are expected to provide detailed and accurate information about the services provided. This enables a customer to compare the efficiency of one service provider with another.
- *Choice:* The views of customers should be listened to regularly by the staff who manage the public sector organisations. Where possible the public sector should also provide a choice of services to the consumer.
- *Non-discrimination:* Customers are entitled to receive the same quality of service regardless of race or sex. This includes the printing of leaflets in minority languages for customers for whom English is not their first language.
- *Accessibility:* The services provided should meet the needs of the customers, including flexible opening hours and a customer enquiry service.
- *Right of redress:* The organisation should have a customer complaints procedure to deal with problems when things go wrong. Customers may also be entitled to financial recompense for an inefficient service.

ACTIVITY

The examples on pages 208 and 209 illustrate the customer services provided by organisations in both the public and private sectors. Read the articles and identify:
1 The organisation quoted
2 Whether it is classified within the private or public sector
3 The main features of the customer services offered
4 Why do the organisations attach importance to customer care?
(3.4.1)

Consumers and Customers

Lorraine is pretty generous

WHEN Mary Campbell became confined to a wheelchair she couldn't go shopping and staff at Boots in The Moor, Sheffield, missed her. Beauty consultant Lorraine Bower heard the sad news and although she had never met Mary, she rang to offer help.

They chatted regularly over the phone and eventually Lorraine got to know Mrs Campbell well enough to choose cosmetics on her behalf and post them to her home.

One day, while out shopping in her lunch hour, Lorraine spotted a disabled persons' bus and immediately thought of Mary. After several persistent phone calls, she persuaded a dial-a-ride scheme to provide a door-to-door shopping service for her favourite customer.

For the first time in five years, Mrs Campbell was able to visit the store and choose her own cosmetics.

Manager Chris Neil says: 'Lorraine gave Mrs Campbell a new degree of independence and enabled her to meet people again in a happy and caring atmosphere.' The quality teams at all the 1,100 Boots stores try to make life easier for anyone who is disabled.

The installation of special 'scissor lifts' at Boots branches was the idea of a customer-care team in the store design department. Other staff-inspired innovations include mother and baby rooms already introduced into 150 stores, with more to follow, and the free Braille Christmas gift guide and audio tape launched last year.

'Many ideas for improving services develop through staff listening to what their customers says' says Public Relations Manager Val Evans.

(*Source*: *Evening Standard*, 19 April 1994)

Big smiles for a better service

For most of us, good customer care is the warm smile along with the common courtesies of please, thank you and sorry. People are being trained to provide these important responses, as companies strive to improve their quality of service, but it is not easy to know always what customers want, nor to find the right staff to maintain high standards.

Firms often promise more than they can provide. For example, it is hard to reconcile smiling TV commercials with the joyless congas that crawl slowly through banks and building societies at lunch time, particularly when half the counters are closed. In Britain we have been slow to recognise that satisfied customers bring many of the long-term benefits.

Tom Cole is a former Chairman of Granada UK Rental, which had more than two million customers. He is an independent consultant now and believes that too much attention has been placed on gaining new business.

He says: 'We all know it costs far less to keep a customer happy than to attract a new one, but too many people ignore this, because looking for new business is much more exciting. Out of 100 dissatisfied customers, only five actually complained. Ninety would never shop with us again, but virtually all would have stayed if we had tried harder.'

Britons tend to remain silent, but vote with their feet when faced with sub-standard service. More UK businesses should follow the example of Kwik-Fit Chairman Tom Farmer and do more to discover the public's opinion of their products.

Farmer, who regularly phones a random batch of customers, says: 'People are a bit surprised, but their comments can be very constructive. I always ask if they recommend us to their friends'. Phoning around for a performance response is common practice abroad. Richer Sounds sell hi-fi separates, and it, too, makes a point of ringing customers. Proprietor Julian Richer says: 'It is important to remain in touch with them as it is five times cheaper to keep a customer than find a new one'.

The policy has paid off – Richer's London Bridge store is in the Guinness Book of Records as the busiest retailer in the world.

Both Richer Sounds and Kwik-Fit use sale documents for service feedback. Richer's receipts even carry a free post questionnaire.

At Kwik-Fit a reply paid card is attached to every guarantee and Tom Farmer's staff are trained to draw the customer's attention to it when handing over the documentation. But the real key to customer care is to provide a quality service that is right first time, every

Education and the Rights of Parents

The chalk face of education has changed recently with the introduction of school performance records for parents' information. In particular parents are entitled to:
- school reports at least annually
- clear publication of results achieved in schools
- information on truancy
- regular and independent inspection of all schools with the results reported to parents
- fuller representation on the governing bodies of schools

The overall aim is to:
- raise standards in education
- promote parental influence and choice and increase accountability
- achieve better use of resources for pupils.

(Adapted from the *Citizen's Charter*)

Daisy in control

Arthritis victim Daisy Taylor, 81, from Croydon, still does her own cooking thanks to free control adaptors fitted to her stove under the GasCare Register. Through the scheme British Gas provides nearly a million disabled or elderly customers with free gas safety checks, priority servicing, advisers and a 'talking' bills facility.

'We are proud of the help we give to people, including those who are having difficulty paying bills,' says British Gas Customer Services Manager Helen Maunder.

(*Source*: *Evening Standard*, 19 April 1994)

British Rail Customer Care Service

British Rail are trying to raise standards by offering all customers the following guarantees:
- if trains are cancelled or unreasonably delayed passengers may apply for a refund
- if passengers decide not to travel because a train has been cancelled they will receive a full refund
- more and clearer information about service targets, timetables and performance
- key targets to include punctuality, reliability, clean trains, no queues at booking offices and value for money

(Adapted from the *Citizen's Charter*)

Keeping Parents Happy

A creche recently opened at Safeway's Enfield branch, full of mock groceries for children to play with. The Enfield branch was the fifth Safeway creche, all of which are run by Supercreche, a Grosvenor House Group subsidiary based in Harrogate.

Public relations Director Tony Combes stated that parents shopping without children spend more money because they have time to look and browse.

Despite this, most large stores are reluctant to follow suit. Sainsbury's recently asked their customers to list their preference out of 29 possible new facilities. Creche and play areas came in the bottom third.

Some organisations, like Selfridges, are afraid that they would be overrun with children and are concerned about ensuring that the child is correctly matched with the parent.

Ikea are committed to the idea, however. The branch on the North Circular Road in London has a ballroom where children can play in and on thousands of soft balls. In an area close by they can read and paint or watch a video. Alternatively they can play outside in the playground.

Facilities for changing babies' nappies are available in both the male and female toilets and the restaurant provides children's portions, play areas and facilities for heating baby food.

'Kids are welcome everywhere in the store. We don't mind them even climbing over the furniture' says a spokesman.

Almost all new Sainsbury supermarkets have baby rooms, as does Selfridges. You can change a baby on the fifth floor at Harvey Nicholls, the third at Dickens and Jones and on the fourth at Harrods, where there are special children's toilets with child-sized basins, loos and low hand driers.

In many organisations, the facilities are on the same floor as the children's department. However, with bags and buggies the ground floor would be more accessible.

(Adapted from the *Evening Standard*, 19 April 1994)

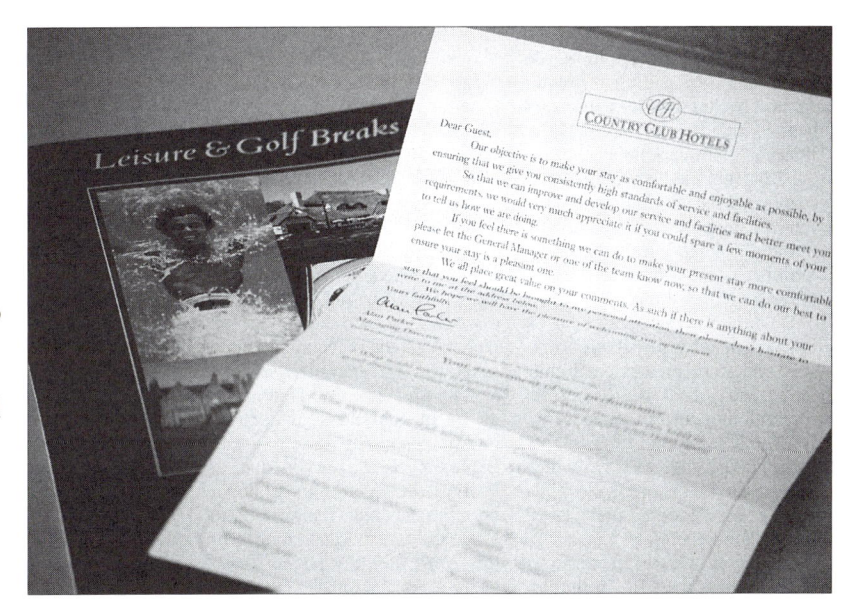

Monitoring customer satisfaction

Peter Drucker is quoted as saying:

The purpose of business is to create and keep a customer.

The term *customer loyalty* is often used to describe a customer who regularly buys from the same organisation. Loyalty is only achieved if the customer is satisfied with both the product or service purchased and the quality of customer care received. Customer satisfaction is sometimes referred to as the 'feel good factor'. Customers are so pleased with their latest purchase they regularly return to the same supplier to make a purchase again.

In order to assess and monitor customer satisfaction, performance targets have to be set and monitored. A performance target aims to measure a standard which the organisation is working towards. A variety of performance indicators may be used to measure customer satisfaction, including:
1 Sales performance
2 Feedback
3 Customer complaints
4 Market research

A customer questionnaire

Sales performance
In organisations a range of sales information is collected every day as part of the organisation's business. The data provides managers with important feedback about products or services that are currently in demand or where sales are falling. By analysing the statistical information in detail the organisation is able to draw conclusions about customers' attitudes and responses to a product or service, prices charged and the effect of competition. Sales information also enables an organisation to identify how many new customers have emerged and the number of repeat purchases made by existing customers.

Customer satisfaction can therefore ultimately be judged by the organisation's ability to sell its product or service. The level of sales is an important measure by which the organisation is able to measure whether or not it is customer-focused. If an organisation wants to maintain or even increase sales it has to be customer-orientated.

When reviewing sales performance the organisation may wish to look at different trends in order to monitor customer satisfaction. One important trend would be the level of overall sales for the organisation in comparison with previous years. In addition, valuable information can be gained by looking at the level of sales of a particular product or service within the product range and comparing the figures with previous years. Conclusions drawn from this research will provide useful indicators when analysing customer satisfaction.

To increase sales it is necessary to focus attention on the needs of the customers by identifying who the customers are and what they want. Researching into the needs and wants of existing and potential

Consumers and Customers

customers enables an organisation to widen the customer base and in the process achieve a higher level of sales.

ACTIVITY

Read the the following article and identify the factors that have led to the increase in sales for the company.

Computer firm's ideal programme

Computer distributor, Ideal Hardware, has built up a £45 million-plus turnover in seven years and Managing Director James Wickes believes this success is directly due to a scrupulous customer-care policy.

This includes monthly customer audits, a dedicated customer-care team of nine and a 90 minute, daily training programme – equivalent to 20% of the sales force's time.

Customer support offers a 24 hour, dedicated distribution service and an electronic catalogue, developed specifically from research into customer needs.

The investment in management time and money which these initiatives represent is high, but James Wickes believes it makes good economic sense.

He says: 'Our staff turnover has been less than 1% in the last four years. This is because our people know how we are developing their fullest potential, which leads to enhanced sales'.

Ideal's customer led policy means goods ordered at 7pm will be delivered the following morning, without the expense of a courier service. Warehouse personnel are trained to understand the fragile equipment they handle. The company receives 1,000 phone calls an hour, so each member of the office staff has an answerphone to ensure calls are returned without clients have to queue. Even the packing has removable labels to save retailers the expense of repackaging goods.

Ideal has invested in a 24 hour, modem-linked information service, which customers can access through their own PCs.

Wickes says 'Technical questions can be answered without using a phone or fax. That is easier for clients and frees our own internal resources'.

Ideal's latest brainwave is Profile, an electronic catalogue on compact disk, the first of its kind, and an idea that came from the firm's monthly phone survey of its 4,000 customers.

Wickes adds: 'Our approach makes financial sense because if you invest in customers, they will invest in you.' His clients agree – more than 8 out of 10 consider Ideal's service is the best in its sector.

(Source: *Evening Standard*, 19 April 1994)

(3.4.1) (3.4.2)

Feedback

A second method which can be used to monitor customer satisfaction is establishing a system of seeking feedback about the quality of service offered. Feedback about customer satisfaction can be derived from three main sources:
1. An employer quality review system
2. Customer feedback system
3. An employee feedback system

Quality review system

This is a structured system that enables an employer to determine the quality of service being offered to customers and the response of customers to that service. A check sheet or rating form can be used to identify the key areas to be audited. The manager will use the form to review at regular intervals the standard of service provided and customers' responses against the criteria.

For example, the following checklist could be used by a supermarket manager when undertaking a quality review audit of the standard of service provided by checkout assistants.

Quality Review Sheet

Quality indicator
2: More than satisfactory
1: Satisfactory
0: Less than satisfactory

Target group: _____
Name of assistant: _____

Attention to detail Grade 2 1 0
Friendly smile
General greeting
Good eye contact

Quality of service
Speed of checking goods
Accuracy of checking goods
Organised flow of goods
Goods handled carefully
Goods correctly packed

Assistance
Help provided in packing goods
Queries answered
Special offers and promotions explained
Supervisor contacted where necessary

Security
Cheques checked against cheque cards
Notes checked for forgery
Credit cards checked for signature and expiry date

ACTIVITY

Visit your local supermarket and on your return complete a copy of the quality review checklist. How would you rate the quality of service offered? Can you suggest any areas for improvement?
(3.4.2) (3.4.3)

An employer quality review system involves the manager being out where the customers are and seeing the activities taking place. The system involves the manager observing, examining and evaluating the quality of service offered by different employees in different sections or departments. The manager will also listen carefully to customers' questions, because the issues raised will form part of the evaluation of customer satisfaction.

ACTIVITY

Produce a quality audit checklist which can be used to review the quality of service offered by an organisation of your choice. Examples could include:
1 A bank or building society
2 Bus service
3 Leisure centre
4 Travel agent
5 Local council

Think about the activities and processes that the employer would want to review for your chosen organisation. Each quality audit checklist is unique in that it applies specifically to that particular organisation.
(3.4.2)

Customer feedback system
This is a structured and organised process of finding out what the customers think about the organisation, its products or services and the quality of customer care received. It can also be used to identify changes and improvements to the service offered based upon customer recommendations.

The information is collected in an organised and systematic manner and the results provide employers with important, up-to-date, first-hand information about what customers really think.

Different methods can be used to obtain feedback from customers. These may include:
1 Talking to your customers as they leave the organisation and encouraging them to share their thoughts about the service they have received.
2 Inviting selected customers to come into the organisation and discuss the quality of provision and service in an open forum. The group chosen should represent a cross-section of customers who regularly shop with the organisation.
3 Produce a feedback survey sheet and ask customers to complete the form, in person, over the telephone or by post.
4 Feedback forms and strategically placed suggestion boxes available for customers to complete at their leisure.

It is important that customer feedback is responded to and acted upon promptly, and customers should be informed of the action taken.

ACTIVITY

The following customer feedback sheet is used within a large Hilton National Hotel in order to seek customers' views about the quality of service offered.

Consumers and Customers

We are delighted that you have chosen to stay with us at the Hilton National and hope that you are pleased with our service and facilities.

We constantly seek to achieve and maintain a courteous and friendly atmosphere which you will recognise instantly and enjoy as typically Hilton. May we request your assistance in our efforts to keep the name Hilton synonymous with hospitality?

If you would like to leave this completed questionnaire at the reception desk, your comments will come to my personal attention.
General Manager

Reservations
How was your reservation handled?

☺ 😐 ☹

Source _____

Arrival
How was your registration handled?

☺ 😐 ☹

Guest room
Was your guest room:
Clean?   Comfortable?   Properly supplied?

☺ 😐 ☹

Restaurants and bars
Restaurant
Service   Quality

☺ 😐 ☹

Comments _____
_____

Bars
Service   Quality

☺ 😐 ☹

Comments _____
_____

Conference
How do you rate the quality of service?

☺ 😐 ☹

How do you rate the quality of facilities?

☺ 😐 ☹

Consumers and Customers

Guest services
How do you rate the following?
Telephone   Cashier   In-house TV
operator/messages

☺ 😐 ☹

Laundry/valet   Business centre   Health club
& pool

☺ 😐 ☹

Between us
Are you satisfied with your stay?

☺ 😐 ☹

Do you have any other suggestions or comment which would help us to make your next visit more enjoyable?
_____
_____
_____

Thank you for you cooperation.

Your name (please print) _____
Address _____
_____
_____
Date of your visit _____
Room number _____

Study the form and identify:
1 The type of information that the manager is trying to obtain from the customer.
2 How the information may help the manager to improve the standard of service offered.
3 Any questions which could be included but are missing from the form.
4 How the form might be improved.
(3.4.2)

Employee feedback system

An employee feedback system is a structured approach to recording employees' views and suggestions about the service provided and ways in which to improve that service. Employees deal with the customers daily and therefore are able to provide useful advice and information to the employer about the views of customers and whether the service provided meets the needs of the customers. Very often, the employees can make valuable suggestions about how to improve the quality of service offered.

Nissan, the Japanese car manufacturer, established in Washington, near Sunderland, have used this idea to great effect. Within the car plant, employees are organised into 'Kaizen' teams. These are groups of employees throughout the factory who meet together on a regular basis to share ideas and make suggestions to the managers about how the quality of service can be improved. As a result of the Kaizen teams, the company has improved the production process, increased sales and reduced the costs of manufacturing Nissan cars.

ACTIVITY

Nissan is prehaps one of the most successful organisations in applying employee feedback systems to the benefit of both the organisation and the customer. In groups or individually identify as much information as you can about the systems used within the company and how they benefit:
1 Customers
2 Employees
3 Employers
Information about the company can be found in learning resource centres and by writing to Nissan in Sunderland. Present your findings using suitable visual and written displays.
(3.4.2)

Customer complaints

A third way to monitor customer satisfaction is by recording customer complaints and implementing changes to ensure that the customer is not dissatisfied for the same reason again. Customers should be provided with a system where they feel comfortable about recording a complaint. Only by doing so can an organisation ensure that they are fully meeting the needs of all their customers.

An organisation that actively seeks and encourages complaints will be able to understand and meet the needs of the customers. If a customer is dissatisfied and is unable to express that dissatisfaction the organisation will never see that customer return. What is worse, the customer may also persuade potential customers not to shop within the organisation too.

A consumer affairs research study called TARP – Technical Assistance and Research Programmes – identified that:
1 The average business loses 10–15% of its customers through bad service each year.
2 Businesses do not hear from 96% of their dissatisfied customers.
3 For every complaint received, another 26 customers have problems and six have serious problems.

The report stated that customers with bad experiences were twice as likely to tell others about it as those with a positive story to recount. (*Source: Unisys Customer Care, Sunday Times*, 15 May 1994)

Customer complaints should be viewed as opportunities to improve a service offered rather than problems to be ignored. The causes of the complaints should be dealt with and lessons learnt. Customers making complaints should be seen as contributors to the process of improving customer services rather than awkward individuals who enjoy making life difficult for staff. By respecting customers and treating them accordingly the organisation will be able to monitor and improve the quality of service offered.

Tom Farmer, chairman and chief executive of Kwik Fit, states:

A complaining customer is the greatest opportunity we have to convert into a loyal – and delighted – customer. The strength of an organisation lies in constantly monitoring and evaluating its customer service, and when things go wrong, rectifying them quickly.
(*Source*: Unisys Customer Care, *Sunday Times*, 15 May 1994)

Goods that have been returned also provide useful information in the monitoring of customer satisfaction. Complaints about the quality, fit or design and effectiveness of the product or service can help organisations in planning and monitoring their stock in the future. Such complaints provide the organisation with important information about the quality of goods or services purchased from individual suppliers.

ACTIVITY

Read the article below and identify the key features of the customer care service provided by Virgin Airways, which has helped contribute to the success of the company. What lessons can other organisations learn from Virgin?
(3.4.1) (3.4.2)

Market research

The final method of monitoring customer satisfaction is through market research. Market research is a formalised method of obtained feedback and information from customers or potential customers about products or services that are available or soon to be made available. Obtaining feedback from customers is essential in learning how to improve the service offered. The process enables an organisation to understand:

1. The nature of the product or service from the point of view of the customer
2. What the customers are wanting
3. What the customer thinks of the organisation
4. What will make the customer feel valued
5. What sort of initiatives the customers would appreciate, e.g. special offers or discounts

If an organisation is to operate effectively it must be able to show that business decisions are supported by information and evidence gained through research. Therefore, through market research an organisation is able identify customers' opinions about:

1. Prices charged
2. New and existing products
3. Discounts and special offers
4. After-sales service
5. The quality of customer care provided by the organisation

Business decisions about these issues can then be made based upon the results of the research.

For example, the Royal Bank of Scotland sends out customer service questionnaires to 200,000 customers every six months, asking for their opinions on their branch. In addition 'mystery shoppers' posing as potential customers visit and phone the branches to ask for advice. Each quarter, every branch in the Royal Bank of Scotland network receives two visits and two phone calls from the mystery shopper, who then fills in a research form and marks the branch on

'We fly people, not planes'

Richard Branson's active involvement in his airline is of major benefit to his customers. His company Virgin has won many awards, mainly for its Upper Class service which offers a first class package at a business class fare. The airline carries 1.5m passengers a year and turnover is expected to top the £600m mark by the end of 1994.

Richard Branson was determined that his airline would not treat customers in a conveyor belt manner. Instead his aim was to provide travellers of all classes with the highest quality service at the lowest possible cost. They emphasise the fact that they fly people not planes.

The Managing Director Syd Pennington is quoted as saying:

'If someone has a bad flight we can't replace it – and that passenger is likely to tell 17 people. If he has a good experience he only tells 4. So we have to be in tune with what passengers want and deliver a consistent product that meets their aspirations. The skill is to treat everyone as an individual'.

'In promoting this culture we are absolutely open with all our staff. We run communication sessions to explain how we're developing the business and encourage staff to let us know their ideas and suggestions for improving the business. All 3,500 have Richard's telephone number at home and they do call him direct. We also encourage even the most junior staff to be pro-active in dealing with problems'.

In 1993, Virgin received 18,000 customer communications. Some contained suggestions for improvement, others were congratulatory. About half were core complaints reported by passengers on airport or in-flight forms, in the visitors books in Upper and Middle Class, by the supervisors on the aircraft or by letter.

The company aims to telephone everyone to discuss the complaint, its impact on the individual and what can be done to retrieve the situation. Virgin's customer service staff handle most of the calls. Branson and Pennington will also phone personally where possible.

'If you take the trouble to call customers you can win them back and keep them forever' says Branson.

Recruiting the right staff is critical to Virgin's operations. Only 1 out of every 50 applicants for cabin crew is accepted. Customer service features prominently in the cabin crew's initial training programme and thereafter staff undertake a refresher training programme which takes place once every eight weeks.

(Adapted from the Unisys Customer Care article, *Sunday Times*, 15 May 1994)

Consumers and Customers

factors such as courtesy, speed, selling skills and phone handling techniques. All the results are included into a customer service index for each branch. The findings are also published internally for all to see, with awards for those branches with the best achievements. (*Source*: Unisys Customer Care, *Sunday Times*, 15 May 1994)

It is essential that a manager acts upon any feedback gained through market research. Customers who provide feedback through market research need to be given recognition and thanks for their time and effort. This may be in the form of a card, letter or telephone call. In addition, it is vitally important that any action taken is also communicated to the customer.

ACTIVITY

A number of methods can be used to find out what the customer thinks of and wants from a product or service. These include:
1 Postal questionnaires
2 Personal interviews
3 Telephone interviews
4 Consumer panels
5 Customer feedback forms

Tasks
1 In your own words, define each method of market research listed above.
2 List examples of when each method might be used.
3 Produce a table listing the advantages and disadvantages for each method.
4 How might the organisation benefit from undertaking customer research using any of the methods listed above?

(3.4.2)

ACTIVITY

The Royal Bank Of Scotland
(Adapted from Unisys Customer Care, *Sunday Times*, 15 May 1994)

Market research undertaken by the Royal Bank of Scotland provided some interesting results recently. The bank decided to measure how much customer satisfaction dictated future buying intentions. The research divided the customers into one of three groups:
1 Those with a problem that had not been resolved
2 Those with a problem that had been efficiently dealt with
3 Those whose experience of the bank had only been positive

As was predictable, the customers who remained dissatisfied were the ones least likely to buy any more of the bank's services. However, surprisingly, those customers whose problem had been dealt with quickly and efficiently were more likely to use the bank's services again in the future than customers who had never experienced a problem. Customers responded positively to open, polite and helpful advice provided by the bank, even if the outcome was not what the customer was seeking, e.g. applying bank charges.

Findings similar to the Royal Bank of Scotland's have emerged from other customer attitude surveys undertaken across a range of businesses. On average, 40% of dissatisfied customers say they will repurchase from the same supplier, compared with 60% of satisfied customers and 80% of those who had a problem that was ultimately solved. The results of the surveys indicate that by keeping customers happy, the organisation will retain existing business and will increase future revenue from existing customers.

Tasks
1 Why did the Royal Bank of Scotland undertake a customer survey?
2 What did the results of the market research reveal?
3 How might the Bank of Scotland use this information to improve the quality of service offered?

(3.4.2) (3.4.3) (3.4.4)

Improvements to customer services

Excellent standards in customer service can only be achieved by having a system that enables you to constantly review and improve the service offered. What is an acceptable standard for a customer today will not necessarily be an acceptable standard tomorrow. Constant improvement is essential.

In a competitive environment, a business that fails to continually review and improve the service offered will find that it will lose customers to those organisations that do. Employees will also become uninterested as they see the standards and status of the organisation decline. They will become complacent and prepared 'to make do', rather than seeking to be the best by providing a service of the highest quality.

The desire to improve and be the best helps motivate staff by providing them with a challenge. It gives employees the opportunity to suggest ideas, use their initiative and participate in the development of the organisation. Excellent customer service provides a focus for all staff to work towards and results in increased job satisfaction for the employees, as well as increased customer satisfaction.

An organisation seeking to improve the quality of customer service offered must set quality service standards. The standards must be:
- Clearly explained
- Realistic for employees
- Easily measured

Consumers and Customers

Having clearly defined standards and a process to monitor those standards gives employees a goal to work towards.

Each organisation will have its own list of standards, but possible examples could include:
1. Time-scales for delivering to customers, ensuring that goods are ordered and despatched on time and delays and bottlenecks are avoided.
2. The flexibility of the organisation to meet the differing needs of customers and clients.
3. The effectiveness of communication within the organisation and externally to customers.
4. Opportunities for customers to feedback thoughts and ideas about available products and services and the quality of customer service received.
5. Effectiveness of staff training, development and appraisal.
6. The level of personal service, including appearance and manner of staff when dealing with customers.

ACTIVITY

Read the following case study and suggest improvements to the customer service offered. Use the standards listed above to guide you.

Matthew Marks Ltd is a small retail outlet which sells a range of fresh foods, vegetables and cakes. In addition to the shop, which opens from 9.00–12.00 and 13.00–17.00, the company runs a small delivery service for local people. Six members of staff are employed within the organisation:
- The manager, who remains in his office seeing to the paperwork
- Two warehouse boys, who are responsible for loading and unloading stock and delivering to the local residents
- Two assistants, who weigh the food for the customers and deal with the money
- A young trainee, who is responsible for stacking the shelves and replacing old stock

The shop has had many loyal customers because it has been open in the area for about ten years and the staff know most of the shoppers by name. However, the manager has recently noticed that sales have started to fall significantly, and realises that the opening of a new superstore next month could result in the closure of the shop altogether. In order to find out why sales have been falling he decides to spend some time in the shop, observing what is happening.

The warehouse boys were rushing around. A lorry had just arrived with a delivery of new stock which needed unloading and three urgent customer orders had yet to be despatched. The lorry driver was threatening to take the order away again unless it was unloaded in the next ten minutes. At the same time irate customers were phoning through asking whether their orders were on their way. The two boys were rowing with each other at the same time as tripping over other merchandise which had yet to be put away. Eventually the lorry was unloaded and the customer orders despatched, two hours later than planned. In the meantime, a backlog of other orders had developed as a result of the delay.

In the shop the manager noticed that the trainee had slipped outside for a cigarette, despite the fact that it wasn't her break. When challenged, the young girl said that she was not aware that she could only have time off for a cigarette during breaks. The manager also noticed that she was wearing jeans and a sweatshirt. He asked her where her uniform was and was told that she had yet to be issued with one. In the meantime she had decided to wear jeans because stacking goods onto dusty shelves was dirty work and she didn't want to spoil her better clothes.

Back in the shop the manager noticed that the trainee had a lovely manner with the customers. She would help them to their car with their bags and make friendly and polite conversation with them when they had time to stand and chat. She knew the customers by name, receiving them with a smile and a friendly greeting as they entered or left the shop.

Observing the two assistants, the manager noticed that they were very busy weighing goods, wrapping cakes, biscuits and bread, and dealing with the money. The cash till kept breaking down, resulting in a long delay for customers waiting to pay for their goods. Some customers left without buying because they were short of time. Another customer refused to buy a loaf of bread she had just ordered because the assistant had handled it without using gloves or tongs. The till was short of change, which resulted in a further delay as the assistant went to the shop next door to change a five pound note.

The manager called a staff meeting at the end of the day and raised his concerns. When he mentioned to the staff that he felt major changes were needed in order to improve the quality of service offered and the performance of the shop, all the staff nodded in agreement. Pleased with this response, the manger asked why the staff hadn't mentioned the problems and suggested improvements earlier. 'You never asked us', they replied.
(3.4.3)

ACTIVITY

Think of an organisation with which you are familiar. It might be somewhere you work part time, or it might be a service that you regularly use, like a bus or train. From your experience, identify:
1. The areas of customer services within the organisation that you feel need improving. You may want to include long queues at the cash till,

Consumers and Customers

not very friendly staff, a long wait before the telephone is answered etc. If possible, quote examples or your own experiences to help illustrate why you feel these areas are problems and need improving.
2 Methods which could be introduced to improve these areas and avoid the problems occuring in the future

(3.4.3)

✎ ACTIVITY (3.4.1–4)

Choose an organisation that will be happy for you to look at the customer services that they provide. It may be a small private sector firm, or you may want to look at a large public sector organisation. It may be somewhere you work part-time or a placement which you have had for work experience.

Visit the organisation and look at its customer service procedure. You may find the following table helps you to remember the areas to look for and the questions to ask.

Customer services provided	Notes
Information given to customers	
Help and assistance	
Customer care training	
Refunds policy	
After-sales service	
Process for monitoring customer care	
System for customers to feedback	
How complaints are dealt with	
Market research into customer needs	
Awareness of customer protection	
Communicating customer protection	

Write a short report of your visit and include:
1 The name of the business
2 The product or service that they sell
3 A description of the customer services provided
4 How the customer services are monitored
5 Examples of how the customer services have been improved as a result of feedback from the customers
6 A table listing the forms of consumer protection which the organisation has to be aware of
7 How the organisation communicates its customer protection policy to the customers
8 How important is customer care to the organisation and why?

✎ UNIT ACTIVITY

This Unit activity has been designed to assess your knowledge and understanding of Elements 4.3 and 4.4. Remember, when you are answering the questions, to use the performance criteria and range statements to guide you.

Keeping you posted (3.3.1–3) (3.3.5–6) (3.4.1–4)
The Post Office produce two very useful booklets for customers. One is entitled *Post Office Counters Code of Practice* and the other one is called *The Customer's Charter that keeps you posted*. As a group, obtain a few copies of the booklets and answer the following questions.
1 Identify the possible needs of customers who use the services of the Post Office.
2 What sort of services are provided by the Post Office and what standards do they hope to achieve?
3 How does the Post Office attempt to identify and meet customer needs?
4 What evidence is there within the Customer's Charter that staff within the Post Office are polite and friendly when dealing with customer needs?
5 What evidence is there within the Customer's Charter that customers are dealt with promptly and by the right person?
6 What advice does each booklet give for customers who want to make a complaint?
7 List the methods used by the Post Office to monitor customer satisfaction.
8 How might the service be improved?
9 What forms of protection does the customer have?
10 How effective are the booklets in presenting the information to customers? What improvements, if any, would you suggest?
11 Why is customer service important to the Post Office?

✎ UNIT ACTIVITY

The Dell Company
The article at the top of the next page appeared in a customer care document published by the *Sunday Times*, 15 May 1994. The report looks at a company called Dell who market personal computers direct to the consumer rather than through dealers. As a result they have had to introduce sophisticated telephone equipment and a help line to deal with customer problems as they arise. Read the article very carefully and answer the questions at the end.

Consumers and Customers

Calls that count

Nothing infuriates a customer with computer problems more than a telephone hotline that has gone cold. The other side of the coin, as Michael Dell discovered, is that strong customer support spells continued sales success.

Dell's computer corporation invented the idea of marketing PCs direct to the consumer instead of through dealers. No middlemen meant lower prices but it also removed the people who traditionally supported a computer installation. Dell soon found that helping people make sense of their PCs over the phone was as important as the original concept of direct selling itself.

Today Dell's European sales and customer support operations are based around a telephone operation in Bray, just outside Dublin. When a customer anywhere in Europe picks up the phone and makes a local call for help, it is in Bray that the call is answered by a member of a highly trained multi-lingual staff of 270.

The telephone management system at Dell, based on the company's American network, is an exercise in customer support which opened in January last year with two aims: to improve support services while reducing overall operating costs. It deals with 5,000 calls a day from UK customers alone and offers a 24 hour seven day support for Dell users across Europe.

Sophisticated computerised monitoring systems tell managers at a glance how quickly calls are being answered. The average response time for the system is less than 10 seconds and fewer than 1% of callers hang up while waiting to be dealt with. Improvements in the system are directly related to sales targets. As call queues were reduced by 25%, sales rose by 28% and fee based service contracts more than doubled.

Dell believes its place among the top five PC manufacturers and $2.9 billion (£1.9 billion) turnover are, in a large part, due to the loyalty of its customers. More than 80% of its custom is repeat business.

Questions (3.3.3) (3.3.5) (3.4.3) (3.4.4)
1 What product does the company produce?
2 What idea did the company invent which made it different from other companies in this area?
3 What was the advantage to the customer of this approach?
4 What was the disadvantage to the customer of this approach?
5 In order to overcome the problem the company introduced a telephone management system. What was special about this system?
6 What advice would you give the company in its training of telephonists, receptionists and sales staff?
7 What advice would you give the company when it is dealing with customer complaints?
8 The company also introduced a sophisticated computerised monitoring system. What does this mean and what does it do?
9 How might the results of the monitoring system be used to improve the quality of customer service further?
10 What happened to sales as a result of Dell's customer care policy?
11 What relevant consumer legislation would the company need to be aware of?
12 What methods could the company use to communicate the customer care policy to their customers?

MULTIPLE CHOICE

1 The term 'customer loyalty' can be used to describe a customer who:
   A Informs staff about the quality of a product or service
   B Informs other customers about the organisation
   C Buys the same product from a number of different stores
   D Regularly buys from the same organisation

2 Details about sales performance provide managers with important feedback about:
   A Customers attitudes and responses to a product/service, prices charged and the effect of competition
   B Organisational structures and lines of communication
   C The effectiveness of the marketing department
   D Internal customer satisfaction

3 A quality review system attempts to:
   A Inform customers about the quality of products and services on offer
   B Meet certain standards so that the organisation can be accredited with BS 5750
   C Check that products and services have passed the quality control standards
   D Review the quality of service being offered to customers and the response of customers to that service

4 An organisation may introduce the following method to obtain feedback from customers:
   A Exhibition stand and display promotions
   B Customer survey form and suggestion boxes
   C Sales representatives with promotional literature
   D In-house competitions and free gifts

5 Market research can be defined as:
   A A system for recording purchases and sales
   B An analysis of competitors and the nature of their business
   C A method of obtaining information and feedback from customers or potential customers about products and services
   D A process of recording customer queries and complaints

6 In the buying of goods and services, consumers' rights and duties are explained in the:
   A Law of contract
   B Law of abidement

Consumers and Customers

    C   Law of of partnership
    D   Law of purchasing and supply

7 In the sale of goods a guarantee:
    A   Replaces the customer's statutory rights
    B   Is not legally binding
    C   Is an assurance of quality
    D   Automatically entitles the customer to a full refund

8 The Sale of Goods Act states that the goods must be of 'merchantable quality'. This means that the goods must:
    A   Not fail during the lifetime of the product
    B   Be of the highest quality possible
    C   Be able to perform the task for which it was designed
    D   Be free from any defect or fault unless it has been drawn to the customer's attention

9 The types of customer services provided by organisations in both the public and the private sectors for external customers include:
    A   Meeting delivery dates and providing a fast and efficient service
    B   Informing staff of important dates, meetings and decisions
    C   Introducing performance related pay
    D   Providing recreational facilities and social events for staff

10 In the pursuit of improving customer services many public sector organisations have introduced:
    A   A Citizen's Charter
    B   Ombudsmen
    C   Citizen's Contracts
    D   Consumer associations

SHORT ANSWER

1 Outline the role of ombudsmen. In what kinds of organisations are they likely to operate?

2 Identify the different methods an organisation may use to obtain feedback from consumers. Which method (or methods) do you think is the most effective? Give reasons for your answer.

3 Why should an organisation actively seek complaints from customers? What negative effect may this create?

4 Why is market research important to an organisation? What are its main benefits?

5 Identify the different forms of protection for customers when purchasing goods and services.

6 What is an 'exclusion clause'? How does the *Unfair Contract Terms Act 1977* protect customers from exclusion clauses?

7 Identify the main features of the *Sale of Goods Act*.

8 Identify the role of consumer associations. Give as many examples as you can.

9 What are the main features of the Citizen's Charter?

10 Produce a list of after-sale services which an organisation can provide for its customers.

11 What are the main provisions of the *Consumer Protection Act 1987*?

12 Why is confidentiality important within an organisation?

UNIT TEST

1 The owner of a sports shop is selling more running trainers and less aerobic trainers. The reason for this is that:
    A   The popularity of sport is increasing
    B   The popularity of running is increasing and aerobics decreasing
    C   The popularity of aerobics is increasing and running is decreasing
    D   Consumers have less money to spend on sport

2 Many organisations develop products or services to meet the needs of certain lifestyles Decide whether each of these statements is True (T) or False (F).
    (i)   The lifestyle of customers influences what they buy
    (ii) The lifestyle of customers is influenced by what they earn
Which option best describes the two statements:
    A   (i) T   (ii) T
    B   (i) T   (ii) F
    C   (i) F   (ii) T
    D   (i) F   (ii) F

Questions 3–5 share answer options A–D
A customer's decision to buy a car is influenced by the following factors:
    A   The availability of a credit agreement
    B   The customer passing her driving test
    C   The status she feels that the car will give her
    D   The distance between the garage and the customer's home
Identify the influence above which applies to each of the factors below:

3 Social
4 Location
5 Financial

6 A company has just produced a new line in unisex fashion jeans. When planning their

Consumers and Customers

advertisement, what consumer characteristic will the company be most likely to take into account?
A Lifestyle
B Nationality
C Locality
D Sex

7 An organisation promotes a new type of chocolate by advertising at peak times on television. The purpose of such advertising is to:
A Increase prices
B Increase costs
C Increase demand
D Increase competition

8 The term sponsorship can be used to describe:
A Tokens issued by supermarkets to be cashed in for computers for schools
B A leading sports manufacturer supports a leading sportsman financially
C A spot the ball competition in a local newspaper
D A promotion within a department store – buy two and get a third one free

9 Demonstrations are often used as a form of promotion.
Decide whether each of these statements is True (T) or False (F).
(i) A demonstration usually takes place at the point of sale
(ii) A demonstration usually involves the demonstrator explaining the nature of the product to the customer
Which option best describes the two statements?
A (i) T   (ii) T
B (i) T   (ii) F
C (i) F   (ii) T
D (i) F   (ii) F

10 Many organisations use promotions as part of their marketing policy.
Decide whether each of these statements is True (T) or False (F).
(i) A promotion aims to increase awareness of the product among customer
(ii) A promotion may involve advertising on television, organising demonstrations or producing posters and leaflets
Which option best describes the two statements?
A (i) T   (ii) T
B (i) T   (ii) F
C (i) F   (ii) T
D (i) F   (ii) F

11 Advertising is expensive. Organisations are prepared to pay the price because:
A They like to keep their customers happy
B The increased sales usually more than cover the cost
C The extra costs are higher than the increased sales
D It is a way of avoiding paying tax

12 A small sole trader has just established a business stripping pine furniture in a small town. Which would be the most effective advertising method, based on cost and likely market?
A A television advertisement shown at peak time
B An advertisement placed in a national newspaper
C A leaflet distributed through letterboxes
D A demonstration within the workshop

13 Benetton advertisements have raised a great deal of controversy. Which organisation would monitor whether an advertisement breaks the advertising code of practice?
A The Advertising Standards Authority
B The Trading Standards Authority
C The Association of Advertisers
D The local ombudsman

14 An organisation will choose to advertise on television rather than on the radio because:
A It is cheaper
B It is more expensive
C It provides national coverage
D Listeners may change stations

15 When goods are sold on credit, the organisation must inform the customer about the conditions relating to the financial arrangement plus the total interest charged. This is an example of:
A A social constraint
B A legal constraint
C A moral constraint
D An ethical constraint

16 Which type of advertisement would be most likely to be used by a large retail store like Boots the Chemist?
A An advertisement in the local paper
B An advertisement in the local cinema
C A mail shot
D An advertisement on national television

17 A poster should be:
A Informative with a lot of detailed written information
B Printed in pale colours so as to be unobtrusive and in keeping with the area
C In picture form only
D Simple, striking and easy to understand

Questions 18–20 share answer options A–D
Customer needs can normally be identified as one or more of the following:
A Information
B Assistance
C After-sales service
D Care and attention
Which need is being met when you:

18 Explain the functions and specifications of a computer

19 Provide a fact sheet about the machine

20 Organise to fly in from the USA a particular computer package which the customer wants

21 A customer's image of a company is most likely to be influenced by:
A The after-sales service received
B Assistance provided within the organisation
C The first person to speak to the customer, either on the phone or face to face
D The colour of the interior of the building

Consumers and Customers

22 Decide whether each of these statements is True (T) or False (F).
   (i) When dealing with customers on the telephone it is important to greet them and write down their requests
   (ii) When dealing with a customer on the telephone it is important to ask the caller to 'hang on' as you try to find someone who knows the answers to the customer's questions
   Which option best describes the two statements?
   A (i) T   (ii) T
   B (i) T   (ii) F
   C (i) F   (ii) T
   D (i) F   (ii) F

23 Organisations are recognising the importance of customer care by offering a range of services to their customers.
   Decide whether each of these statements is True (T) or False (F).
   (i) Customer care services include information, help and advice, refunds and replacements and after-sales service
   (ii) Organisations who offer good customer care find that they keep their existing customers as well as attracting new ones by word of mouth
   Which option best describes the two statements?
   A (i) T   (ii) T
   B (i) T   (ii) F
   C (i) F   (ii) T
   D (i) F   (ii) F

24 Customer service can be improved by:
   A Training staff
   B Cutting costs
   C Reducing production
   D Increasing advertising

25 After-sales service refers to
   A Help and advice given prior to the sale
   B Help and advice given during the sale
   C Help and advice given when the customer purchases the item
   D Help and advice given at a later date

26 The effectiveness of customer service can be monitored using a range of methods.
   Decide whether each of these statements is True (T) or False (F).
   (i) One method of monitoring customer service is by analysing sales figures
   (ii) The number of customers making repeat purchases is an indicator of customer service success
   Which option best describes the two statements?
   A (i) T   (ii) T
   B (i) T   (ii) F
   C (i) F   (ii) T
   D (i) F   (ii) F

27 Many public sector organisations have produced charters as part of their commitment to customer care.
   Decide whether each of these statements is True (T) or False (F).
   (i) A charter is a legal document produced by solicitors on behalf of the government
   (ii) A customer charter aims to inform customers about the standards that an organisation is hoping to achieve and the procedure customers should follow if they are unhappy about the quality of service received
   Which option best describes the two statements?
   A (i) T   (ii) T
   B (i) T   (ii) F
   C (i) F   (ii) T
   D (i) F   (ii) F

28 Customer feedback is very useful in monitoring customer satisfaction.
   Decide whether each of these statements is True (T) or False (F).
   (i) Customer feedback can be achieved by on the spot questions from staff
   (ii) Customer feedback can be achieved by under-cover customers
   Which option best describes the two statements?
   A (i) T   (ii) T
   B (i) T   (ii) F
   C (i) F   (ii) T
   D (i) F   (ii) F

Questions 29–31 share answer options A–D
When trading it is important to be aware of relevant consumer legislation. The relevant Acts include:
A The Consumer Protection Act 1987
B The Trade Descriptions Act 1968
C The Sale of Goods Act 1979
D The Unfair Contract Terms Act 1977
Under which of these Acts is the trader prevented from:

29 Selling polyester shirts as silk?
30 Selling sub-standard merchandise?
31 A receipt with a clause excluding responsibility for damaged goods?

32 A hairdryer explodes as you are using it. The shop refuses to accept liability. The case should therefore be referred to:
   A The Citizen's Advice Bureau
   B Environmental Health Department
   C Trading Standards Department
   D The local ombudsman

33 Decide whether each of these statements is True (T) or False (F).
   (i) An ombudsman provides an independent and objective approach to resolving problems
   (ii) Ombudsmen cover a range of areas including local government, legal services, health service and building societies
   Which option best describes the two statements?
   A (i) T   (ii) T
   B (i) T   (ii) F
   C (i) F   (ii) T
   D (i) F   (ii) F

Consumers and Customers

Key terms

Advertisement
Advertising Standards Authority
Business communication
Buying habits
Competition
Confidence to spend
Consumers
Cost of living
Customer care
Customer loyalty
Customer service
Customer satisfaction
Demand
Health and Safety at Work Act
Needs
Point of sale
Promotions
Sale of Goods Act
Sponsorship
Strong demand
Supply
Trade Descriptions Act
Trading Standards Office
Trends
Wants
Weak demand

UNIT 4

Financial and Administrative Support

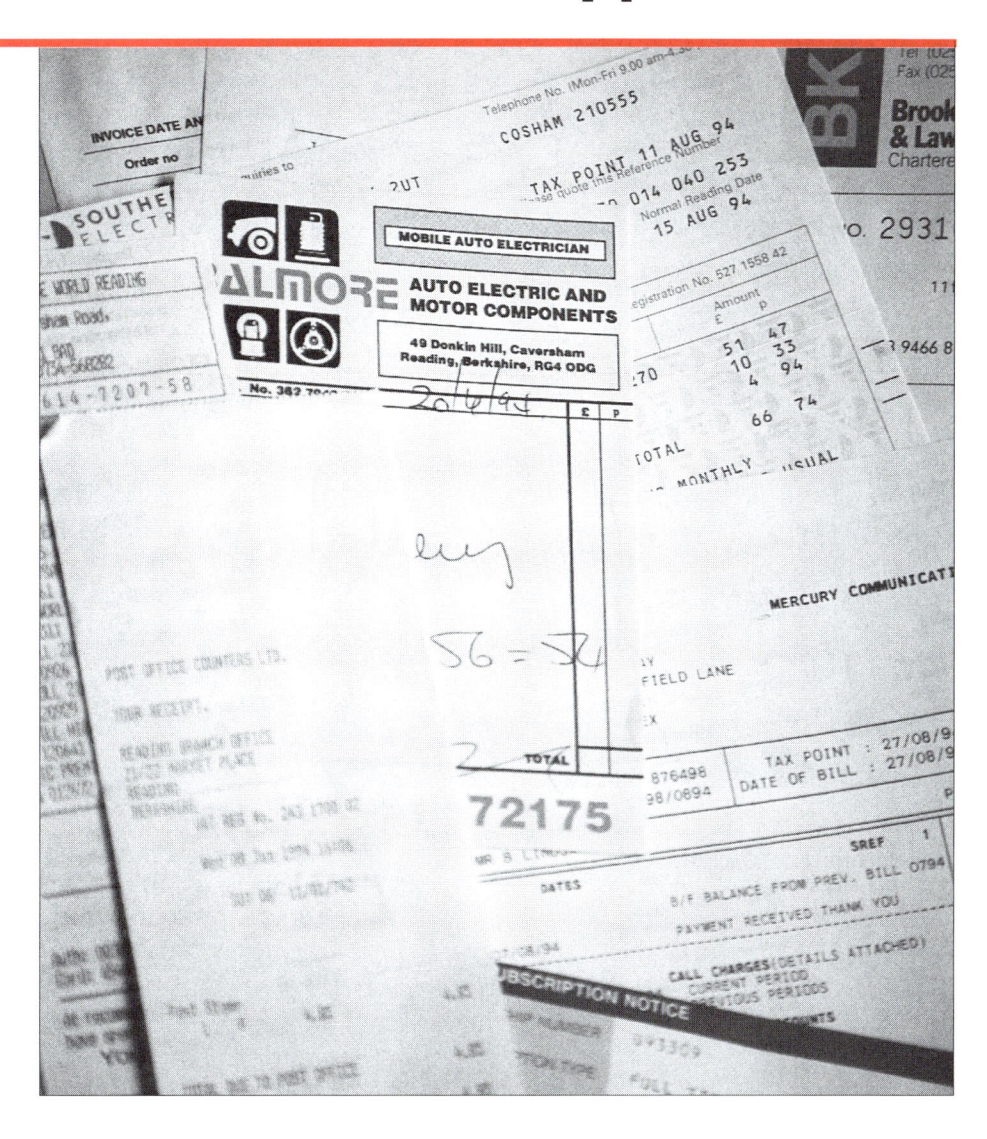

UNIT SUMMARY

This unit focuses on the business documentation used to record the buying and selling of goods and services, and the receipt and payment of money. It is necessary to be able to complete various standard documents as well as to explain their purpose. The security aspects of financial transactions and handling money are also examined. This unit is not tested externally.

ELEMENT 4.1
Identify and explain financial transactions and documents

Performance criteria

- PC 4.1.1 Explain financial transactions which take place regularly in an organisation and explain why records of transactions are kept

- PC 4.1.2 Explain and give examples of purchases and purchase documents

- PC 4.1.3 Explain and give examples of sales transactions and sales documents

- PC 4.1.4 Explain and give examples of payment methods and receipt documents

- PC 4.1.5 Explain the importance of security and security checks which are taken for receipts and payments

Financial and Administrative Support

also provide services – things like electricity, advice, banking facilities, repairs to the machinery and so on. The other main service that an organisation receives is *labour* from its employees. At the other end the business will give its goods or services to its *customers*, the people who will pay for these goods and services.

Money For private sector businesses, and even for many public sector organisations, the whole purpose of buying goods and services from suppliers and providing goods and services to customers is to generate an income. The suppliers and the employees need to be paid, and so money flows out of the organisation in that direction. However, money will also come in from the customers.

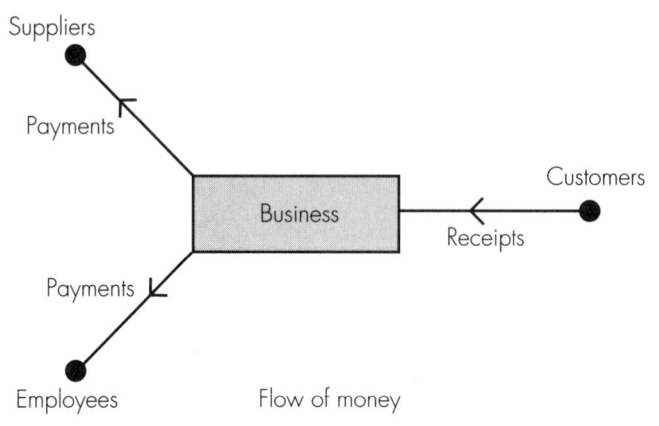

Flow of money

Reasons for financial recording in business organisations

Introduction
There are many things that pass through a business organisation as part of its normal activities:
- Goods and services
- Money
- Paperwork

Goods and services Paper for the photocopier, stock for resale, raw materials for production, petrol for the delivery van, oil for the machinery – these are some of the goods which a business receives all the time from its *suppliers*. The suppliers are those people and organisations that provide these goods. Suppliers

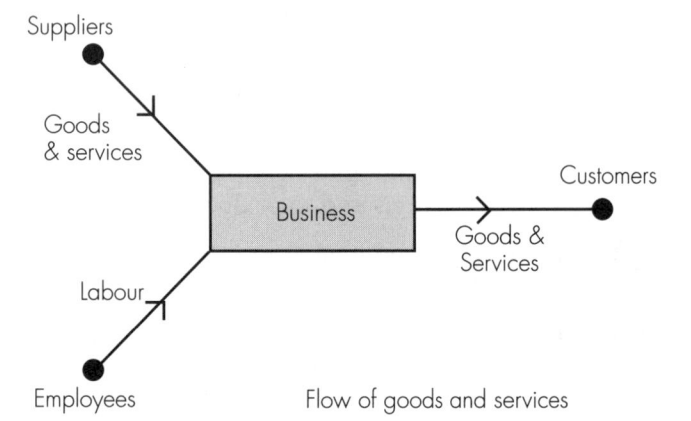

Paperwork As well as goods, services and money there is a third commodity that flows through the organisation, which some would say was the least important: bits of paper. Paperwork can be a businessperson's least favourite part of running the business, but it plays a key role in the success and profitability of the organisation.

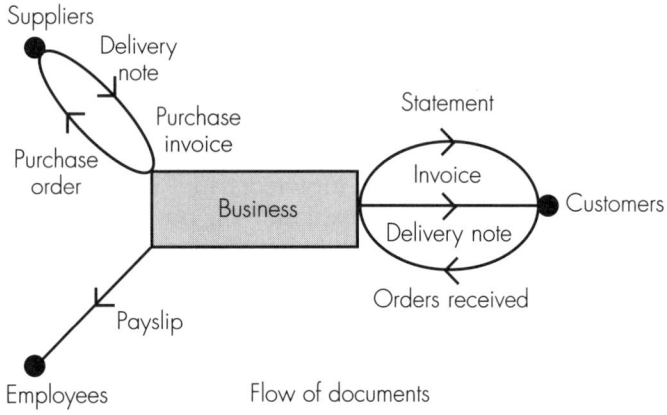

Flow of documents

Even though the use of computers reduces the amount of paperwork in the office, most transactions are still supported by a piece of paper, known as a *document*. A document is simply a formal record that a transaction has taken place, and may in some cases be used as evidence in law.

Flow of goods and services

Financial and Administrative Support

> ### ✏️ ACTIVITY
>
> Sogña is a brilliant businessperson. She has turned her hobby into a thriving enterprise in just a year. Orders are pouring in and the business is expanding rapidly. She knows little about accounts and so decides to employ a bookkeeper. The bookkeeper asks to see the records that Sogña has kept for the last twelve months. Sogña presents her with a box full of bits of paper. The bookkeeper is horrified, but Sogña says, 'Why do I need records? Just look at how well I am doing'.
>
> What answers would you give if you were Sogña's new bookkeeper?
> (4.1.1)

There are very many good reasons for financial recording in a business.

Keeping records
There are so many things that need to be remembered that it becomes vital to make a record of them. Here are a few details that need to be recorded:

Orders When customers place orders, they expect to receive the products or services that they require. It may also be necessary to notify them of how long it is likely to take. If they do not receive any reply then they will take their business elsewhere and their custom will be lost. Therefore a business must keep records of orders.

Stock It is no good ordering stock after the business has completely run out, because that will mean a halt in production. Therefore a record of stock levels should be maintained so that new orders can be made before it is too late.

Credit transactions A lot of business is done on the basis of *credit*, which means that goods and services are exchanged with the promise of payment later. Hence the business needs to know:
- Who owes the business money?
- How much do they owe?
- When should it be paid?
- Who does the business owe money to?
- How much does it owe?
- When should it be paid?

The opposite of a credit transaction is a *cash* transaction. A cash transaction is one where the goods and services are paid for at the time of exchange. This does not always mean that payment is made in coins and notes. Payment may be made in any way. In this context a cash transaction will include payment by cheques, debit cards and credit cards, as well as coins and notes.

Payroll The *payroll* is a record of all the employees, including:

- Personal details (name, address, date of birth and so on)
- Rates of pay
- Hours worked
- Tax code
- Amount of tax paid so far
- National Insurance details

It quickly becomes very complicated and really needs to be written down or set up on a computer.

Money For every business organisation it is essential to keep a record of how much money it has. If it does not then there is a danger that the business will be unable to pay what it owes. At the very least it may incur additional bank charges by exceeding agreed credit limits.

If a business is fortunate it will have a lot of money. Even so, it is important to know just how much is available so that any surplus can be invested wisely or used to help expand and improve the business.

Legal requirements There are certain records that any business is expected to keep by law. These include:
- Income tax
- National Insurance
- VAT (if the organisation is registered for VAT)

There are many more requirements for a limited company, including:
- Names of shareholders
- Names of directors
- Profits made
- Annual accounting statements

Producing annual accounts
Most businesses prepare at least two accounting statements each year:
- Trading and profit and loss account
- Balance sheet

The *trading and profit and loss account* indicates how well the business has performed. It shows how much profit or loss it has made in the last twelve months. The *balance sheet* shows how much the business is worth and how it has been financed. Therefore these two statements are of extreme importance to anyone who is interested in the business, including the managers, the investors, potential investors and possibly the public at large. The end of year accounts can only be accurately drawn up if regular and reliable record-keeping is maintained throughout the year.

Ensuring security
Some of the information that a business keeps may be confidential. This may include trade secrets about special production processes or ingredients. A business would not want this information to be available to its competitors and rivals. Other information, such as payroll details, is confidential and should not be accessible to all employees. Finally, in order to avoid cash and stock being 'lost' or 'borrowed', a business needs a record of how much cash or stock there should be.

Financial and Administrative Support

For all these reasons business information should be recorded and carefully retained.

Monitoring business performance

To *monitor* means to watch and record something as it happens. The problem with the annual accounts is that they show how well the business has done *over the last year*. They are in the past tense, since they look backwards. It may be too late to discover that the business made a huge loss. What is also needed is a constant up-to-date record of how well the business is doing *now*. Then it will be possible to change business activities before it is too late. Managers will be able to make decisions regarding pricing, production, spending, advertising, expansion, credit control, borrowing and everything else in response to present information.

ACTIVITY

Check your answers for the previous activity. How many of these reasons for keeping business records did you include in your list for Sogña? Add any that you have omitted.
(4.1.1)

Note: VAT

This is a good point at which to explain some basic facts about VAT. Most people have heard about it, but not everyone is clear what exactly it is. It is important for this unit because it affects the records that must be kept and the ways in which documents must be completed.

VAT stands for Value Added Tax. It is a tax levied by the government on non-essential or luxury goods and services. So, for example, food, books and children's clothing do not carry VAT, but petrol, TV sets and furniture do. The standard rate of VAT is currently 17.5%. Therefore the amount of VAT is calculated by finding 17.5% of the price of the goods or services being provided. The rate of VAT may change from time to time according to the Chancellor's budget. The selling price before VAT is added is known as the *net price*. The total price including VAT is known as the *gross price*. Therefore:

Net price + VAT = Gross price

VAT is added to the price of goods and services when they are sold. Items may be sold several times before they reach the final consumer. At each sale VAT may be charged. Consider the following diagram.

In this example, Business A cuts down trees. These trees are sold to Business B, which prepares the wood. This is sold to Business C, which makes furniture. The furniture is sold to Business D, a wholesaler. Business D sells the furniture to a retailer, Business E. Finally Business E sells the furniture to the final consumer.

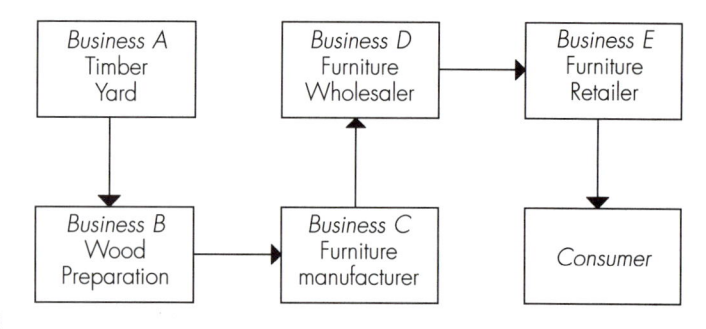

Transfer of goods from one business to another

VAT can be charged at every stage in this process. However, a business may only charge VAT *if it is registered to do so*. Small businesses do not have to register, but can if they choose to do so. Businesses of a certain size are required by law to register for VAT and must then charge VAT on their sales. Each year the Chancellor of the Exchequor decides in the budget what size businesses can be before they must register.

When a business registers for VAT it is given a unique VAT registration number, which should then appear at the bottom of all its sales invoices. This indicates to the customer that the business is registered and therefore has the right to charge VAT on top of the price of the goods and services.

Businesses cannot avoid paying VAT if their suppliers are registered. However, if the business itself is registered for VAT then it can deduct the amount of VAT it pays to its suppliers from the amount it hands over to Customs and Excise.

The VAT collected by a registered business must be passed on to the government, through HM Customs and Excise. This is normally done every three months. The business must complete a standard VAT document known as a *VAT return*. However, a business may deduct any VAT that it has paid to its suppliers. If this did not happen the government could effectively collect the same VAT several times. The calculation on the VAT return, therefore, is:

VAT owed to Customs and Excise = VAT collected from customers − VAT paid to suppliers

It is important to realise that if a business collects VAT from its customers this money does not belong to that business but to Customs and Excise. The business must keep careful records of all its sales and purchases to satisfy the authorities that the calculation shown above is correct. If the records are missing it is likely that Customs and Excise will make an estimate of the amount owing, which is usually in their favour.

ACTIVITY

VAT calculations can be a chore, but they are a fact of life for most businesses. If you are skilled at doing the calculations they become less of a

Financial and Administrative Support

burden – and may even be fun! With a calculator there should be no problem.

Laura Collins is the assistant in charge of pricing the goods in your DIY store – but she is off sick, leaving you to work out the prices. You have a list from head office giving the selling price for each item, but this does not include VAT. Your task, therefore, is to calculate VAT at 17.5% on each item and thereby work out the gross selling price. (Simply ignore any fractions of a penny: so £2.45789 becomes £2.45.)

Do It Now DIY

Item	Net price	VAT	Selling price
Aluminium ladder	25.00	4.37	29.37
Roll of wallpaper	4.99		
Plastic bucket	0.55		
Electric drill	12.50		
Spanner set	20.00		
Electric lawnmower	75.00		
Dustbin	3.25		

(4.1.1)

Purchase transactions and documents

Introduction

Most businesses need supplies of some kind. There are few exceptions. Maybe street entertainers need only their skills to bring in the money, but even they are likely to need some props and equipment.

ACTIVITY

Jamil is planning to set up his own business and is preparing a business plan. He is thinking of all the things that the business will do with its money and is becoming worried that there are many more ways of spending money than earning it.

To help Jamil in preparing his business plan list as many items as you can think of which a business will regularly need to buy. If you can see a good way of categorising them try grouping your items under three or four main headings.

(4.1.2)

Not only does a business spend its money on a lot of different items, it also needs to record how it has spent its money. For each transaction there will be a corresponding document.

The main items of expenditure may be grouped together as follows.

Materials

If a business is a *retailer* then it will buy a finished product from a *wholesaler* and then sell the same items directly to their customers. The materials, therefore, will be the business's stock in trade.

For example, a local corner shop will buy sweets in bulk at a discounted price from a wholesaler such as the Co-op. A Mars bar may cost the shopkeeper 18p. The sweets are then sold at their usual selling price for a profit.

If a business is a *manufacturer* then it will buy raw materials from which it will make a product. For example, a business which makes furniture will need glue, wood, plastic, nails, screws and so on.

Even a *service* organisation needs materials. For example, a bank offers a service to its customers, but its uses paper and staples, pens and paper clips.

Materials, therefore, can be the stock in trade as well as raw materials needed for production. In addition, a business will also need materials just to keep the business running: paper for the photocopier, staples, glue, Sellotape, oil for the machinery and ink ribbons for the typewriters and printers. This list is virtually endless and quite clearly will differ greatly from business to business.

Services

A business will also buy the services of other organisations to help it operate.

A service is something which somebody else does for you, either because you cannot do it your self or you choose not to. Services include:
- Electricity
- Repairs and maintenance of buildings, vehicles, machinery
- Gas
- Telephone
- Banking
- Insurance

Wages

The last major item for which the business will pay regularly is the cost of labour. The salaries and wages are very often a major expense for a business, especially in the service sector. As already

227

Financial and Administrative Support

mentioned, the *payroll* is a record of all the personal details of the employees and is part of the documentation required by law for income tax and National Insurance purposes.

Documentation

For all of these it is necessary for the business to make records using appropriate documents. For goods and services this may occur in three stages:

- *Orders*

  It may be possible to obtain materials and services immediately when they are required, but often they will have to be ordered. This is necessary to avoid costly delays waiting for materials to arrive. Careful monitoring of the business will enable managers to know when it is time to reorder stock.

  Orders are usually written, although they may be communicated over the telephone or by computer or by fax. The business can refer to its record of the order if there are any queries with the supplier.

- *Goods received*

  When a business receives the goods and services that it has requested it needs to make a record to this effect. It would normally check that the items received match up to the original order. The business can then update its stock records to include the new items. It can also make a record of any maintenance or repair jobs carried out.

- *Amount payable*

  A lot of business is carried out on a credit basis, which means that goods and services are exchanged between organisations with the *promise* of payment at a later date. It is very important that both the supplier and the customer know exactly how much is owing, what it is for and when payment is due. This is recorded on a document called an *invoice*.

From this it follows that there are three main purchase documents commonly used by business organisations:

- Purchase order
- Goods received note
- Purchase invoice

Note: at this stage it is enough that you are able to explain the purpose of these documents. For Element 4.2 you will also need to be able to complete them.

Purchase order

A *purchase order* is a document which is drawn up by the customer requesting goods or a service. Businesses often have their own name and address printed at the top.

A purchase order

Notice that there is space for the following items:
1. *Name and address of the customer* already printed – in this case Future Music
2. *Name and address of supplier*
3. *Delivery address* if the goods are to be delivered to an address other than the main address already printed
4. *Order number* as a unique reference
5. *Date* of the order
6. *Quantity, description and price* of goods being ordered
7. *VAT* (if applicable)
8. *Authorising name and signature* to prevent employees ordering goods that are not wanted

A copy of the purchase order is sent by the customer to the supplier. The *authorising signature* is very important. It is a security measure which prevents unauthorised persons from ordering goods on behalf of the business. It would normally be the budget-holder for the particular department who is a *designated signatory*, that is, the person who is authorised to sign the purchase order. In some cases, particularly in smaller organisations, there may be very few designated signatories, limited only to senior directors and/or the finance manager.

Financial and Administrative Support

Goods received note

A *goods received note* is a document that records receipt of the goods or services that have been provided. It is prepared by the customer as the goods are checked in. In this way it is genuinely a record of what is actually received. As the goods received note is prepared it is checked against the *advice note*, which is sent by the supplier to notify the customer what is being sent, and the *delivery note* (see below).

The goods received note is often confused with the delivery note. They do serve a similar purpose – namely providing a record of what has been received. However, there is an important difference: the goods received note is prepared by the *customer* based on what is actually received; the delivery note is prepared by the *supplier* and is normally carried by the transporter, who will require the customer to sign as proof and acknowledgement of delivery.

The goods received note includes the following information:

1 *Name of customer* – in this case Future Music
2 *Name and address of supplier*
3 *Date of goods received note*
4 *Description of goods*
5 *Quantity advised* which is the amount which the supplier said they were sending according to their *advice note*
6 *Quantity received*
7 *Signature* of person receiving goods and completing goods received note

Purchase invoice

The most important document in the buying and selling of goods and services is the *invoice*. This is prepared by the supplier and sent to the customer, sometimes with the goods, sometimes at a later date. The term *purchase invoice* is used to distinguish invoices received from suppliers from invoices which the business will prepare and send to its customers (*sales invoices*).

An invoice is necessary since most business transactions are on credit terms, which means that the payment is due at a later date. Both parties need to be fully aware of the amount owing and the due date. The

A goods received note

A purchase invoice

Financial and Administrative Support

invoice normally includes:
1. *Name and address of supplier* – in this case Sonic Boom Ltd
2. *Name and address of customer*
3. *Despatch address* if different from the customer's main address
4. *Invoice date*, known as the *tax point*, since the VAT falls due from this date
5. *Invoice number* (for reference)
6. *Quantity, description and price of goods*
7. *VAT and VAT registration number*
8. *Postage and packing*
9. *Any discounts*
10. *Terms and conditions*, which may include the period of credit and conditions of payment
11. *Total* amount owing in respect of items listed

The despatch address is for larger organisations where the goods and services are delivered to a different location from the finance department, which will deal with the invoice.

The *invoice date* is also known as the *tax point*. This means that from this date the VAT on the goods and services received is due. That is, from the point of view of HM Customs and Excise, who collect VAT, the amount of VAT stated on the invoice is now due for collection. Also, the period of credit which the customer has with the supplier will be counted from the invoice date.

As has already been mentioned, only if a business is registered for VAT can it charge this tax on goods and services that it sells. Every business which registers for VAT is given a unique registration number which it must quote on its invoices.

The *terms and conditions*, sometimes quoted on the back of the invoice, state any conditions which relate to the delivery and receipt of the goods and/or the payment of the amount owing. This includes the length of the credit period, the manner in which payment should be made, the penalties for late payment, and so on.

One common item found on an invoice under terms and conditions are the initials E&OE. This stands for Errors and Omissions Excepted. This means that, although the invoice is legally binding, the parties involved cannot be bound by any mistakes. For example, if the invoice records the selling price of a Jumbo Jet as £17,000 instead of £17,000,000, then the supplier is not obliged to accept the smaller amount.

Trade discount

Trade discount is offered to customers who are 'in the trade', that is, they are not the final consumer of the items purchased, but are buying the goods to sell to someone else. The goods can then be resold at the normal selling price (the recommended retail price) and still make a profit, equal to the original trade discount.

This situation will apply to retailers buying from wholesalers. It is also true of a business which provides a service which may include parts. For example, a garage will normally get trade discount from its suppliers when fitting parts as part of a repair job. The customer is charged the full selling price for the spares used.

Cash discount

Cash discount is a further discount offered as an incentive to the customer to pay quickly. Unlike trade discount there is a time limit in which the cash discount must be taken up. Once this time has passed the full price must be paid. The supplier is willing to accept less money in full settlement in order to get the money quickly.

ACTIVITY

Jon Munden works in the purchasing department of a large shoe shop. He is about to go away for a month's holiday. He has been asked to explain to the part-time assistant, who will replace him, the day-to-day duties that the job entails.

After Jon has finished speaking the assistant asks him the following questions, which you must answer:
1. Why does the business bother keeping financial records? *(4.1.1)*
2. What kinds of things does the business pay for on a regular basis? Give as many examples as you can think of and group them under appropriate headings. *(4.1.2)*
3. What is a 'credit' purchase? *(4.1.2)*
4. What documents need to be prepared to deal with:
   - Orders
   - Receipt of goods
   - Amounts owing? *(4.1.2)*

Sales transactions and documents

Introduction

Most business organisations have something to sell – this is how they make their money. There are some exceptions. Charities, although they often do sell things, are able to collect money simply by asking for it. Some public sector services are provided free of charge, such as street lighting and sewage. However, through taxation both local and central government are in effect charging their customers for the services they provide.

ACTIVITY

Jamil is still working on his business plan. You have already helped him in identifying the items of expenditure under the headings of services, goods and wages. The list seems almost endless. He is now concerned that by comparison the list of activities that raise money for the business is very short indeed.

Financial and Administrative Support

ACTIVITY

Are there any other examples of goods and services that organisations may sell that you can think of? What goods and services have you used in the last week?
(4.1.3)

Documentation

For all goods and services it is necessary to support the transactions with appropriate documentation and record-keeping. This occurs in several stages.

Orders When a business receives an order from a customer for goods or services then it must *process* it. This means one of two things:
1 The business may be in a position to prepare the goods for despatch immediately or to arrange for the service required to be provided.
2 Alternatively, the order may have to be set aside for a later date if the business is currently too busy to take it on.

Both of these require some kind of record to acknowledge the order and to decide when to carry it out.

Goods and/or service provided When the order is completed and the goods are despatched or the service is provided the business will require a record to this effect, including an acknowledgement from the customer that they have received their order.

Amount payable As a lot of business is carried out on a credit basis it is necessary to make a record of how much is owing. Both the customer and the supplier need a record of how much is owing, what it is for and when payment is due.

This is further extended to provide a regular update of the amount owing. The supplier will keep customers informed of the balance of their accounts, taking into account all the goods that have been provided and how much has so far been paid.

From this it follows that there are four main sales documents commonly used by business organisation:
- Advice note
- Delivery note
- Sales invoice
- Statement of account

> *Note:* at this stage it is enough that you are able to explain the purpose of these documents. for Element 4.2 you will also need to be able to complete them.

Quite often a business will save itself a lot of work by making duplicate copies of the sales invoice to use for different purposes. In particular, the top copy is usually the sales invoice, while three carbon copies can be used for:

To help Jamil in preparing his business plan list as many items as you can think of that a business can use to earn income regularly. Try grouping them under appropriate headings.
(4.1.3)

For classifying the sales of an organisation it is possible to use headings similar to those that are applied to purchases. Of course, every purchase is a sale from someone else's point of view. As a result, much of the accompanying documentation is also the same.

Goods

Wholesalers and retailers sell *goods*. This is simply another way of describing a *product*, a thing that has been made or excavated or extracted from nature. 'Goods' therefore include wood, iron, cars, newspapers, glass, vegetables, books, cigarettes, clothing, flowers and sportswear.

Services

Alternatively, businesses may provide *services*. This means that they offer skill, expertise, advice, information or an amenity. 'Services' therefore include dental operations, street lighting, consumer advice, teaching, police work and consultancy.

Financial and Administrative Support

- Advice note
- Despatch note
- Delivery note

This is possible because the information on all these documents is very similar.

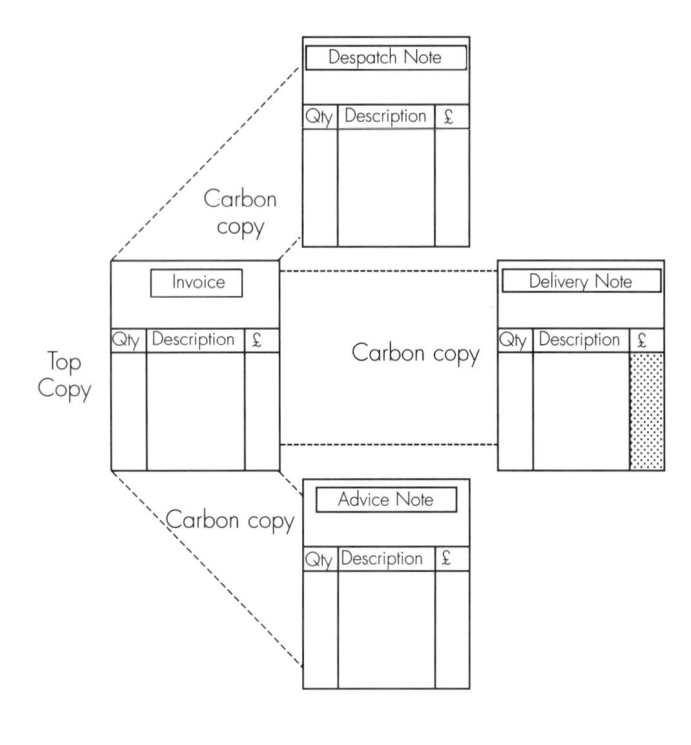

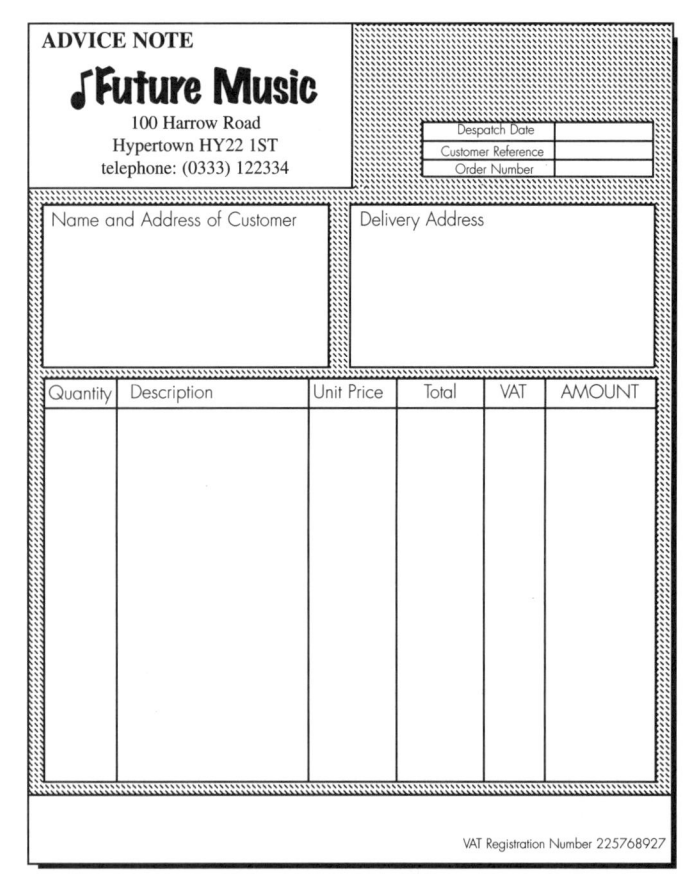

Advice note When a business receives an order from a customer it may issue an *advice note*, sometimes called an *acknowledgement note*. This is particularly useful if there is going to be a delay from the time the order is received to the time that the goods may be despatched or the services provided. The advice note is sent to the customer confirming that the order has been received and accepted and may give an estimate of the likely delay before supply of goods or service.

Despatch note If it is likely that the goods will take several days or weeks or possibly months to reach the customer, the supplier may send a *despatch note*. This informs the customer that the goods are on their way and may include an estimate of their arrival date.

Delivery note
When the goods are supplied the supplier will normally include a *delivery note*. This includes a description and quantity of the goods supplied. Customers can then check that they have received what they ordered.

The despatch note will often be carried by the transporter with the number and description of the packages included in the consignment. The customer will be expected to sign the delivery note and a copy will be kept by the customer, the supplier and the transporter.

The delivery note may be a copy of the sales invoice, but it will not show the prices. This is

An advice note

A delivery note

Financial and Administrative Support

because it is unnecessary for the person receiving the goods to know what the prices are. All they need to know is the number and description of items being delivered.

Sales invoice

As previously mentioned, a *purchase invoice* is received from the supplier and a *sales invoice* is sent to the customer. In every other respect they are identical documents. It is prepared by the supplier and a copy is sent to the customer as a record of the goods and services provided and the amount owing. It therefore includes exactly the same information as the purchase invoice.

Statement of account

Both the customer and the supplier will be interested to know the balance of any monies owing. This is determined by:
- Goods and service which have been supplied
- Amounts so far paid

This is only relevant if the customer is buying on credit. If the sales are cash sales (that is, where payment is made immediately) then there will be no amount owing. If the customer buys on credit the supplier will open an *account* in the name of the supplier. This simply means that the supplier will keep a record of all the amounts owing due to sale of goods and services and all the payments received so far. Periodically, usually at the end of the month, the supplier will send a copy of the account to the supplier. This copy of the account is known as a *statement*.

It is a common misconception that a statement is a demand for payment. Technically it is for information purposes only. It informs the customer of the balance remaining on the account at the month end. In practice, however, it may serve as a gentle reminder to customers that they still owe the supplier some money.

ACTIVITY

Jon Munden has been transferred from the purchasing department of a large shoe shop to the sales department. He asks you to explain to him the day-to-day duties that the job entails.

After Jon has finished speaking to you the following questions arise, which you must answer:

A sales invoice

1 **What kinds of things does the business receive money for on a regular basis? Give as many examples as you can think of and group them under appropriate headings.** *(4.1.3)*
2 **What is a 'credit' sale?** *(4.1.3)*
3 **What documents need to be prepared to deal with:**
   - **Orders received?**
   - **Delivery of goods?**
   - **Amounts owing by customers?**
   - **Monthly summaries of customers' accounts?**
   (4.1.3)

Payment transactions and documents

Introduction

If a business makes a *credit* transaction, then it undertakes to make payment at some later date for the goods and services it has received. Alternatively, it may make payment at the moment that the goods

233

Financial and Administrative Support

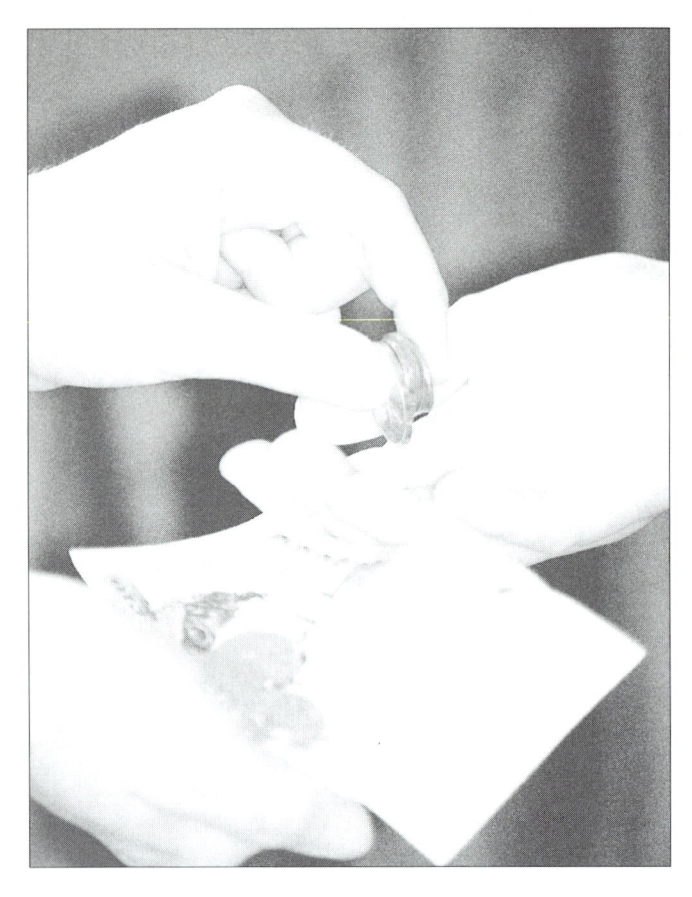

and services are exchanged, in which case it would be a *cash* transaction. Either way, a business will have to make payments to its suppliers and employees, and for these transactions it should make a record to that effect using an appropriate document.

ACTIVITY

1. List as many different methods of making payments that you can think of.
   (4.1.4)
2. For the methods you have listed, indicate the best way(s) that an individual may pay for the following items:
   - Newspaper
   - Pair of jeans
   - Personal computer
   - Squash racquet
   - Motorbike
   - Full trolley of groceries at the supermarket
   (4.1.4)
3. For each method of payment consider the relative advantages and disadvantages to complete a copy of the following table:

Method of payment	Advantages	Disadvantages

(4.1.4)

There a number of different ways in which a business may pay for the goods and services it receives. The most common methods include:
- Cheque
- Cash
- Credit card
- Debit card
- Credit
- Wages
- Petty cash

All of these methods must be recorded by the business and supported by appropriate documents.

Cheque

Making payment by cheque

When someone pays by cheque there are three parties involved:
- The *drawer*, who is the person who writes the cheque and signs it.
- The *payee*, who is the person receiving the cheque and who will be named on the cheque.
- The *drawer's bank*, which is the bank whose name is printed on the cheque who will make payment on behalf of the drawer to the payee.

A cheque may be defined as:

an unconditional order in writing instructing the bank to make payment of a certain sum of money to a named person on demand.

It is said that a cheque is an *unconditional order*, meaning that the person receiving it does so on the understanding that there are no conditions to accepting it. It is reasonable for the payee to expect to receive the money in due course from the bank.

Completing a cheque

A *valid* cheque is one that is correct in detail and can be presented for payment. An *invalid* cheque is one that includes errors and therefore is not acceptable by the bank. It is therefore important that proper procedures are followed when the cheque is completed. Guidelines will be given in Section 4.2, but the main points relating to the correct use of a cheque are described below.

Date Whenever a cheque is written the date will be put in the top right-hand corner. The cheque is then valid for up to six months after that date. After six months the bank will not accept it, although it can be used as proof that payment is owing for up to six years. Therefore if the cheque expires, the holder of the cheque may request the drawer to write a new one.

Cheques may be *post-dated*, which means that a future date is put on the cheque. The cheque is not valid until that date, and so payment is effectively delayed.

Amount The amount to be paid is written on the cheque by the drawer in both numbers and words. The date of payment is written on the cheque and then it is signed by the drawer.

Financial and Administrative Support

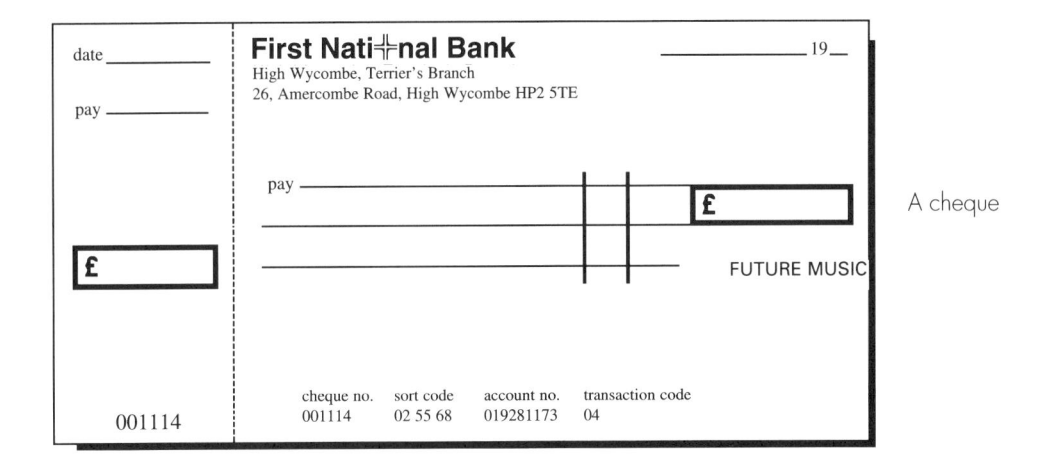

A cheque

Endorsements A cheque is made out to a named person, the payee. That person has the right to the cheque. However, the cheque may be *endorsed* by the payee. This means that the payee may write on the reverse of the cheque the name of another person and then sign it. The right to present the cheque for payment has now been transferred to the person named on the reverse of the cheque.

Crossings From the example shown above you can see that the cheque has two parallel lines running vertically across it:

Nearly all printed cheques have these lines, which are known as *crossings*. A cheque with these lines is a *crossed cheque*. This is an instruction to the banks that the cheque can only be paid into a bank account. It cannot simply be cashed, which means it cannot be presented at a bank in exchange for cash. The bearer of the cheque must pay it into his or her bank account.

There are some cheques which do not have these crossings. Banks will provide customers with cheque books with no crossings on request. These can then be used to pay people who do not have a bank account, who can then cash the cheques at the bank *where the cheque book was issued*.

Alternatively the crossings can effectively be cancelled by the drawer writing 'pay cash' or 'pay self' on the cheque. The cheque can then be cashed.

Special crossings Sometimes the drawer may write some further instructions to the bank between the crossings on the cheque. The most important of these are the words *'a/c payee only'*. This effectively prevents the payee from endorsing the cheque. The instruction means that only the person originally named as the payee can use the cheque. The right to present it for payment cannot be transferred.

How a cheque is processed
When the cheque is presented by the payee to the bank it will be sent to a *clearing house*, who then pass it on to the drawer's bank. The cheque is checked, and if it is valid the funds will be transferred from the drawer's account to the payee's account. Therefore, although payment is due *on demand*, in practice it takes about three days for a cheque to 'clear'.

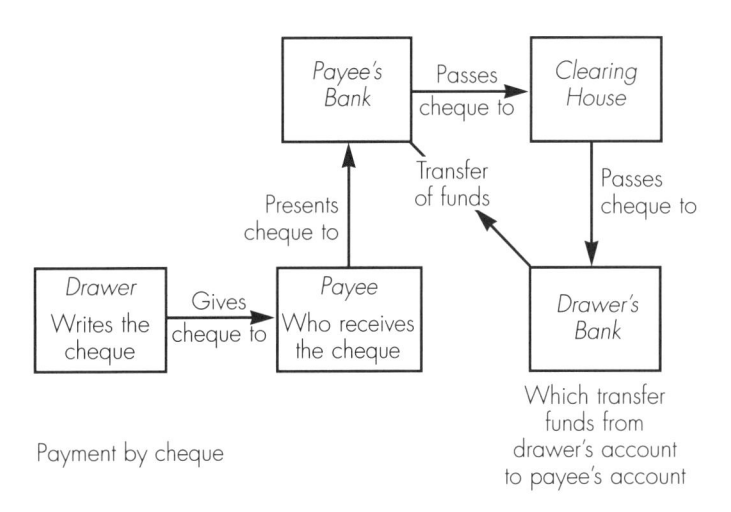

Payment by cheque

Cheque guarantee cards
When making payment by cheque it is normal for the payee to demand to see a *cheque guarantee card*. This is issued by the bank to the drawer with the cheque-book. It acts as a guarantee to the payee that, up to the limit on the card, payment will be made, regardless of the funds available in the drawer's bank account. Therefore the risk in accepting a cheque is minimised. The bank undertakes to honour the cheque, come what may.

Advantages of paying by cheque
Cheque payments are ideal for larger sums of money. They avoid the inconvenience and the security risk of carrying lots of cash for both the drawer and the payee. If cash is lost or stolen it can be used by anyone. A cheque-book cannot so easily be used by someone else, especially if the cheque guarantee card has not been lost. If a cheque-book is lost or stolen the drawer should telephone the bank to cancel all the cheques.

Financial and Administrative Support

Cheques are only payable to the person or organisation named on the cheque as the payee. If the cheque is lost, therefore, it cannot legitimately be cashed by someone else. The drawer can have confidence that the right person will get the money. Even so, if a completed cheque is lost the drawer should report it to their bank to avoid someone fraudulently trying to draw funds on it.

Because cheques normally take at least three working days to clear, purchasers effectively enjoy a short period of credit. In this time they may place additional funds into their account to cover the cheque amount. In addition, cheques may be *post-dated*, which means that the drawer may write any future date on it. The payee cannot pay in the cheque before the date on the cheque, and so the drawer can extend the delay before payment. However, most businesses will not accept post-dated cheques, as they require immediate payment.

Provided a cheque does not have a cheque card guarantee number written on the back (because, for example, it exceeds the value of the card or the number has simply been omitted), then it may be *stopped* by the drawer. This means that if the payee has not yet presented the cheque for payment the drawer can instruct the bank to cancel it, making it null and void. This puts drawers in the position of being able to change their mind about making the payment, although the bank will charge quite heavily for this service. On the other hand, anyone receiving payment by cheque without a gurantee number will be aware of this and is unlikely to allow the drawer to take expensive items away before the cheque has cleared without some other security. For example, if a customer is buying a car with a cheque for £4000, the garage would not usually let them drive it away before the cheque has cleared.

Disadvantages of paying by cheque

A cheque is not suitable for small sums of money. It is much more convenient for buyers to pull a few coins out of their pocket or notes out of their wallet or purse than it is to go through the process of writing a cheque. Many establishments will not accept a cheque for payment below a minimum amount, often £5, for this reason.

If someone is paying by cash it is physically impossible for them to spend more than they have. However, when making payment by cheque it is always possible to exceed the money in the bank account. The result will be that the drawer goes overdrawn or exceeds agreed credit limits, all of which increase the cost of bank charges. Therefore it is essential that accurate records are maintained to avoid this.

A cheque is not guaranteed above the limit of the guarantee card, usually £50 or sometimes £100. Therefore, for payments above these amounts a cheque will very often not be accepted.

Finally, a cheque is not *legal tender*. This means that no one is obliged to accept it in payment, and may insist on being paid in cash.

Cash

Making payment by cash

Making payment by cash is relatively straightforward. The person making payment may be able to give the correct amount or will require change.

From time to time the Royal Mint may issue new coins, but at present the currency has the following *denominations* (i.e. values) in circulation:

Coins	Notes
1p	£5
2p	£10
5p	£20
10p	£50
20p	
50p	
£1	

Advantages of paying by cash

The chief advantage is one of convenience. It is much easier to pull out coins and notes than it is to write a cheque.

Cash is therefore ideal for smaller payments. It can also be used for coin-operated machines selling stamps, drink, sweets, railway tickets and parking tickets, as well as in public telephones. Some of these machines also accept notes.

Cash is nearly always welcomed by businesses, even for large sums. A shopkeeper might be unwilling to accept £5 in 1p coins or a £50 note for a 25p purchase, but generally they will be happy to take the customer's money.

Disadvantages of paying by cash

Coins and notes are bulky and heavy. For large payments cash is inconvenient to carry around. Furthermore, cash in large quantities may not be *legal tender*. This means that a shopkeeper is not obliged to accept £5 in 5p coins, for example.

Anyone carrying large sums of cash with them is likely to feel vulnerable. Businesses hire security firms like Securicor to transport large amounts of cash. It is a dangerous occupation.

However, it is not just the danger of personal injury that makes people think twice before walking along the high street with £3000 in their pocket. If cash is lost it is difficult to recover it. It may be handed in to the police, but it is very easily used by others without detection.

Credit card

Making payment by credit card

A credit card is a means of short-term borrowing. The credit card company (Access, Visa, American Express, and so on) pays on behalf of the purchaser. The supplier of goods or services therefore receives payment, but the customer will enjoy a period of credit before paying their credit card company.

Financial and Administrative Support

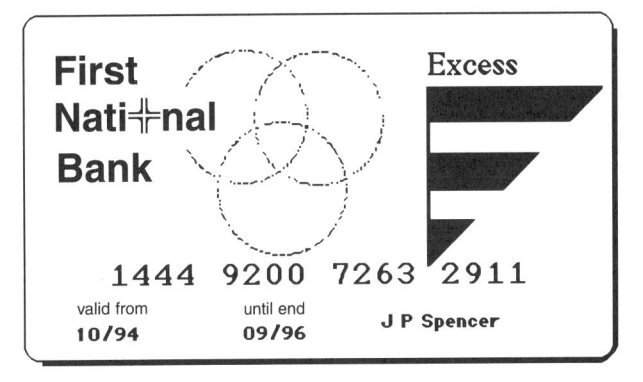

A credit card

Credit card payments may be processed using an electronic swipe machine or a manually operated system.

Electronic swipe The credit card has a magnetic strip in it which is passed through an electronic reading device. This links into a centralised computer system and accesses details of the customer's account. It can tell whether the card has been reported stolen or whether the customer is within their credit limit. The amount of the purchase is keyed in and, if it is accepted, the machine will print a credit slip. This is for the customer to sign in order to authorise the payment from the card. The person receiving payment should check the following details:
- The signature on the credit slip matches the signature on the back of the card.
- The card is valid for the date of the transaction by looking at the dates on the card that show the period in which the card may be used.

The storekeeper and the customer each keep a copy of the credit slip and the transaction is concluded.

Hand-operated machine For small transactions, normally below £50, a credit card is acceptable without the need to check with the credit card company. For larger payments it is usual for the person receiving payment to telephone the credit card company to receive an authorisation number for the transaction. This is to ensure that the card is valid and has not been reported stolen or lost and that the customer is within their credit limit. The credit card is then placed inside the hand-operated credit card machine with some carbon-backed slips. The lever of the machine causes the raised numbers and writing of the card to become inscribed on the credit slip. The amount of the transaction is written in by hand and the credit slip is signed. The same checks are then made as above and the transaction is concluded.

In addition to receiving a credit slip and receipt for each credit card payment, the card holder will also receive a regular update from the credit card company. This is called a *statement*. It is normally sent once a month. It lists all the transactions that have been made using the credit card, the value and the date of each item and any interest charged as well as any payments made by the card-holder to the credit card company. The balance at the date of the statement will also be shown together with the minimum that must be repaid.

Advantages of paying by credit card

The chief advantage to the buyer of using a credit card is the convenience. It avoids the need to carry large sums of bulky cash, with all the danger that that entails.

For large payments credit cards are one of the best ways to pay. Apart from the convenience it also usually grants buyers one month's interest-free credit. Therefore they can enjoy the goods or services straightaway and have at least a month to pay. They may choose to take longer than a month before paying the money, but they will then begin to incur interest charges, which can be fairly subtantial.

Some credit cards are acceptable all over the world and so may be used regardless of the currency of the country.

Credit card companies often give extra benefits as a reward for using the card. A purchase with a credit card may give the buyer insurance for transport of those goods. Sometimes Air Miles or other gifts and bonuses are given.

Disadvantages of paying by credit card

Credit cards are an attractive means of buying things that the buyer desires immediately, but it is easy to get into debt. People use credit cards because they do

Financial and Administrative Support

not have the money to pay immediately. But they should consider very carefully whether they will have the money in a month's time when the statement arrives.

It is an expensive way of borrowing. The amount of interest the card user must pay is usually significantly higher than bank interest. In addition, some card companies charge a user fee on top of any interest for the privilege of membership. The table below shows the costs of borrowing on popular credit cards:

Issuer	Monthly	Annual percentage rate
Robert Fleming/Save & Prosper (£12 annual fee)	0.95	13.9
**TSB Trustcard (£2,500+)	1.38	17.9
Leeds Permanent (£12 fee†)	1.42	19.9
*General Motors Visa (HFC Bank)	1.53	19.9
National Provincial	1.65	21.6
*Bank of Scotland (£10 fee)	1.57	21.7
*Barclaycard	1.58	21.9
Halifax (£10 fee†)	1.58	21.9
*Royal Bank of Scotland Visa (£10 annual fee)	1.45	22.0
Ford Barclaycard (£10 fee)	1.58	22.2
Ford Direct Visa (£10 fee)	1.60	22.2
*Midland Visa (£12 fee)	1.59	22.3
Girobank (£12 fee)	1.59	22.3
*NatWest Visa (£12 fee)	1.60	22.4
Co-op Bank (Robert Owen card)	1.70	22.4

*Issuers with a Mastercard version at same or similar rates
**Fees waived if you spend more than £1,500 on the same card in the year
†Different rates depending on card limit
Source: Daily Telegraph, April 9 1994

The table shows any annual fees, which are paid no matter how often the card is used, even if it is not used at all. The *annual percentage rate* (APR) is the cost of borrowing for a year. By law the credit companies must quote the APR. This enables customers to compare all forms of borrowing on the same basis.

The APR is slightly more than 12 times the monthly rate. This is because the interest over a year has a *cumulative* effect, which means that the card holder starts paying interest on the interest if the monthly bill is not settled.

If a credit card is lost or stolen it should be reported to the credit card company, who will cancel any future use of the card. Even so, credit card fraud does occur. A stolen card may be used before it is reported as missing and the signature may be forged. If a hand-operated machine is used there is no easy way of telling whether the card is legitimate.

Debit card

Making payment by debit card
When using a debit card the funds are deducted directly from the card-holder's account. Unlike a credit card, therefore, which is a form of short-term borrowing, a debit card involves an almost immediate payment: typically only 2–3 days passes between using the card and transferring the funds. It is very similar to writing a cheque – except there is much less hassle for both the customer and the person accepting payment.

Most banks will issue debit cards to their customers. Very often it is the same as the bank guarantee card. The card will carry a logo identifying that it is a debit card. The most common name for this is 'Switch'.

As more and more stores become equipped to accept debit card payments the cheque is slowly being replaced. Facilities are most commonly found at supermarkets, department stores and petrol stations. An electronic swipe machine reads the magnetic strip on the card. The cashier keys in the amount to be paid and a receipt slip is printed automatically, very similar to a credit slip for a credit card. The customer signs the slip to authorise payment, the cashier checks that the signature corresponds to the signature on the back of the card and the transaction is concluded. This system of payment is known as *EFTPOS*, which stands for electronic funds transfer at point of sale.

This is a very good description of what actually happens. At the point of sale, that is, at the place where the purchase is made, an instruction is issued and the funds from the customer's account are transferred electronically into the account of the seller. This is only possible because the system links into a centralised computer which processes all debit card transactions.

Advantages of paying by debit card
A debit card payment is very convenient. It is easier even than writing a cheque and may even be easier

Financial and Administrative Support

than a cash payment in some cases. Like cheque and credit card payments it avoids the security risk of carrying large sums of cash. If a debit card is lost the card-holder should telephone the bank so that it cannot be used by unauthorised persons.

The number of stores that accept debit card payments is increasing all the time. Therefore it is becoming a ready and even more convenient alternative to writing a cheque.

Disadvantages of paying by debit card
A debit card transaction takes place in about the same time as a cheque: about three days. However, by using a credit card the purchaser can enjoy up to a month's interest-free credit.

Again there is a possibility of fraud and misuse if the card goes missing. This can be minimised by keeping the card in a safe place and notifying the bank and police as soon as it is lost.

ACTIVITY

Read the article below and answer the questions.
1. What percentage of adult Britons held credit cards in 1993? How many in 1989? And in 1986?
2. In what way are credit card-holders using their credit cards differently?
3. What percentage of card-holders spread their repayments over a whole year? What percentage repay the full amount each month? How does this compare with 1989?
4. What two classes of people are least likely to spread their repayments?
5. What is the most likely reason for this change in the use of credit cards? What other reason is given?
6. What other form of payment have people switched to as an alternative to credit cards?
7. What is meant by the expression 'card closing' (paragraph 8)?
8. How have credit card companies changed their approach to issuing credit cards?
9. What is meant by the expression 'cherry-pick' (paragraph 10)?
10. How is Barclaycard attracting new customers?

(4.1.4)

Credit
The methods of payment so far examined:
- Cheque
- Cash
- Credit card
- Debit card

can all be classified as *cash* transactions. This can be confusing and should be understood carefully. Generally speaking, a *cash* transaction is one where payment is made straightaway. This is to be contrasted with a *credit* transaction, where the goods or services are supplied but payment is made at some later date, sometimes in instalments. A credit card payment falls into the category of a *cash* transaction because the supplier of the goods receives payment straightaway. The customer then settles up with the credit card company, not the supplier, at a later date. From the point of view of the supplier of goods, payment is received immediately.

Making purchases on credit
Frequently a customer arranges a period of credit with the supplier. In this way the customer can enjoy the goods and/or services without making full payment or any payment at all until later. This is essential to most businesses. For buyers it gives a useful breathing space in which to collect funds from their own customers in order to repay the supplier. For the supplier it is a way of attracting customers.

Credit card users tighten up or drop out

SHOPPERS are increasingly rejecting the 'buy now, pay later' mentality of the 1980s, according to a survey published today.

In 1993, the proportion of adult Britons holding credit cards fell to 31 per cent from a peak of 34 per cent in 1989 and 32 per cent in 1986, a study by the financial Research Survey and pollsters NOP have found.

While those with cards are using them more, most repay the full amount borrowed each month rather than in instalments.

The survey found only 20 per cent of card-holders spread their repayments last year, while 61 per cent paid back in full each month – compared with 24 per cent and 53 per cent respectively in 1989.

Pensioners, of whom 81 per cent repaid in full each month, were least likely to extend their credit, followed by professionals (71 per cent).

Amanda Watkins, of NOP, said it was likely that people were more uneasy about taking on debt after being hard hit in the 1980s credit boom.

This is reflected in increased use of debit cards, which take money out of a customer's account immediately after a transaction, among those who have surrendered their credit cards.

Ms Watkins said the decline in credit card holding was also due to the introduction of charges by most leading card companies, starting with Lloyds Bank in 1989. 'The peak in card closing coincides with the introduction of charges on cards.'

However, companies were also more selective than before in issuing cards, especially to the young. In 1993, 13 per cent of 18 to 24-year-olds had a credit card – down from 22 per cent in 1989.

'What makes the latest findings from the FRS of interest is that card-holding is now at pre-boom levels', said Ms Watkins. 'As new players in the card market cherry-pick existing active users, one has to wonder if there will be an expansion in the market again.'

However, Barclaycard – Britain's biggest credit card issuer with nearly 9 million card-holders – said that use of its card had never been higher, and that new card applications are now running at record levels.

A spokesman said: 'We have seen our market share increase to over 34 per cent in the last two years as a result of offering additional free benefits such as discounts on new Ford cars and purchase protection.

'Around half of Barclaycard holders pay off their account in full and therefore pay no interest, and card usage is at its highest level ever.'

Source: The Guardian, April 2 1994

Financial and Administrative Support

There are many different kinds of credit agreement, but they can be simplified into two categories:
1. In a straightforward credit transaction the goods or services are exchanged and the customer takes ownership of them immediately. Payment is normally due in one lump sum at some future date. Typically the period of credit is four weeks or a month. Taking ownership is important, since it means that customers can do what they like with the goods, including selling them to another party. It also means that customers are responsible for taking care of the goods so that they are not damaged or do not become a hazard to other people. The supplier may charge interest. Alternatively interest may be charged for late payment only. Cash discounts may be offered for early settlement of the amount owing.
2. Sometimes goods are bought on credit by *hire purchase*, often abbreviated to HP. A finance company provides the finance for the transaction, and details are normally arranged for the customer by the supplier. A deposit will be paid and a regular amount of repayment is agreed between the customer and the supplier, including some charge for interest. Typically hire purchase agreements run from one to five years. It will often be more expensive to buy goods on hire purchase, even before any interest is added.

Hire purchase is available to individuals as well as businesses. For both it is a means of buying expensive items without a major outlay of funds. Businesses may use hire purchase to buy machinery and vehicles. They may also use one of the many different kinds of *lease purchase* arrangements, which are similar to hire purchase. The significant feature of hire purchase is that ownership of the goods does not transfer to the customer until the last payment has been made.

Pay slip

Most businesses employ people and reward their labour by paying them a wage or a salary. A *wage* is normally the term used for pay received for manual labour and is usually calculated on an hourly rate or on a piece rate. An *hourly rate* is stated as so much per hour. For example, cashiers in a supermarket may receive £4.00 an hour. Therefore if they work 37 hours in one week their wage will be:

37 × £4.00 = £148

A *piece rate* on the other hand is stated as so much per item or volume produced or processed. For example, someone working at home for a manufacturer of leather goods may get paid £5.00 per briefcase and £2.00 per wallet. Therefore if they produce 8 briefcases and 7 wallets in one week their wage will be:

8 × £5.00 = £40
7 × £2.00 = £14
Total = £40 + £14 = £54

A *salary* is normally paid for non-manual work. It is usually a fixed annual sum paid in monthly or weekly instalments.

The employer is under a legal obligation to keep accurate records of how much the employees are paid and are required to give employees a written pay slip. The reason the government is concerned about employees' pay is that people are assessed for income tax and national insurance based upon how much they earn.

Study the pay slip opposite.

Sadly, employees do not receive all of their earnings. Usually before they even see the money a number of *deductions* have been made. These deductions are called deductions at source since the amounts are taken away by the employer on behalf on the employee.

The total amount that an employee earns is known as *gross pay*. This includes:
- Basic pay (salary or wage)
- Overtime
- Bonuses
- Sick pay/maternity pay
- Holiday pay

From the gross pay a number of deductions are made. The amount that the employee is left with, sometimes called the take-home pay, is known as *net pay*.

| Gross pay | minus | Deductions | = Net pay |

(basic pay   (compulsory:
overtime   National Insurance
sick pay   Income Tax
holiday pay   voluntary:
maternity pay   union subscriptions
bonuses)   charity donations)

The deductions fall into two main categories.

Compulsory deductions These deductions are required by law. They are:
- *National Insurance*
  This is collected by the Inland Revenue and passed on to the government to fund state pensions, sick pay, maternity pay, unemployment benefits and the National Health Service.
- *Income tax*
  This is also collected by the Inland Revenue and is used to fund general government expenditure. Most people pay income tax via the pay as you earn (PAYE) scheme. This simply means that an employee's tax is spread over the year as and when they earn money.

The compulsory deductions are calculated using a variety of formulae, which incorporate personal allowances so that the amount people pay is based upon the amount they earn, with adjustments for their personal circumstances. Allowance is made for:
- Marital status
- Physical disabilities
- Mortagage relief
- Specialist clothing needed for work

All of these details are reflected on the employee's pay slip.

Financial and Administrative Support

PAY ADVICE

Name of Employee	Paco Sanchez	Payroll no	139/B			
National Insurance no	NP 54 32 78 B	Date	August 31 1994			
Pay Period	month 6					

		Gross	PAYE	NI	Other	Net Pay
Basic Pay for Period		2249.23	427.75	202.43	0.00	1619.05
Overtime	5 hrs @ £12.25	61.25	24.50	5.51	0.00	31.24
Expenses		125.66	0.00	0.00	0.00	125.66
Bonus		500.00	200.00	45.00	0.00	255.00
Union Subscriptions		0.00	0.00	0.00	12.25	-12.25
TOTAL FOR PERIOD		2936.14	652.25	252.94	12.25	£2018.70
TOTAL PAY TO DATE		17524.27	3827.25	1190.88	73.50	12506.14

Voluntary deductions These deductions are not required by law but, as the name suggests, the employee may choose to pay. By law, the employer is not allowed to make these deductions from an employee's wages unless the employee authorises the employer to do so.

Why should anyone choose to make extra deductions from their pay which they are not required by law to make? They are usually made to the direct benefit of the employee. They may also include donations on matters of principle to charities or trade unions. Examples of voluntary deductions include:
- Charitable donations
- Union subscriptions
- Additional National Insurance contributions
- Private pension scheme
- Private health scheme
- SAYE (Save As You Earn)

Employees may receive their money in cash, especially if they are paid weekly. Businesses may also pay wages and salaries by cheque. Many salaries are paid directly into the employee's bank account via a system known as BACS, which stands for bankers' automated clearing system. This is an automated direct debit system. Funds are transferred automatically from the employer's bank account into each individual employee's account. The employer provides the bank with employee details, including the amounts to be paid. The chief advantage for both the employee and the employer is that payment is made promptly and with the minimum of fuss. BACS can also be used to pay suppliers.

Petty cash voucher
'Petty' comes from the French word *petit*, meaning small. Hence, petty cash payments relate to small amounts of cash.

ACTIVITY

Helen works in the finance department of a small business in charge of petty cash. Every time a small cash payment must be made, Helen is asked to open the cashbox and make the money available. She is surprised at how many different ways the business spends money on small items.

Although only small in value these goods and services are important for the running of the business on a day-to-day basis. Often they are expenses that the staff have to pay personally in carrying out their business. Afterwards the staff can claim their money back from Helen.

List as many different goods and services that the business might pay for in this way.
(4.1.4)

As well as the major costs, such as stocks and materials, salaries and wages, electricity and telephone bills, a business is also likely to incur many small costs for day-to-day goods and services. These include:
- Tea, coffee, milk, biscuits
- Petrol
- Train, bus and taxi fares
- Hotel accommodation
- Window cleaner
- Postage
- Light bulbs
- Computer disks
- Paper for photocopier and printers
- Envelopes, pencils, biros, paper clips, drawing pins

For convenience it is common for organisations to keep an amount of cash for these kinds of expense. There are three ways in which the petty cash made be used:
1. Sometimes the person in charge of the petty cash, the *petty cashier*, will make payments directly from the petty cash box. For example, the cleaner's wages may be paid in this way.
2. Occasionally the petty cashier may give an employee an *advance* from the petty cash box in anticipation of expenses that the employee will have to pay in the near future. For example, an employee who is going on a business trip by train

Financial and Administrative Support

may take an advance from petty cash to cover the cost of the fare.
3 More commonly, employees will make payments from their own pockets and claim the money back from petty cash. For example, an employee who has paid for computer disks to be used at work may be repaid by petty cash for this cost.

ACTIVITY

Helen now realises how many different kinds of payment may be made from petty cash. She is keen to work out a good system for operating petty cash.

What procedures would you recommend that Helen adopts for her petty cash? You should consider security, documentation, authorisation and rules for making payments.
(4.1.4)

There are several procedures that are usually followed when operating a petty cash system:
- The cash should be kept *secure* in a cash box. Only authorised people, including the petty cashier, will have access to the box. This is to prevent people helping themselves.
- Only *business expenses* should be paid for from petty cash. Employees cannot claim for private expenses.
- Petty cash should only be used for *small payments*. What counts as 'small' may vary from business to business. However, it is common for the business to set a maximum size for petty cash payments. Any payments over this size would normally be made by the main cashier by cheque.
- Petty cash payments should be supported by *proof of payment* where possible. Receipts, invoices and bus or train tickets are commonly used as supporting evidence that payment has been. This prevents employees making false claims for expenses that have not been incurred.
- A record of each petty payment should be made on a *petty cash voucher*.

A petty cash voucher

folio	The folio is simply the reference number given to the voucher so that it can be cross-referenced in the petty cash book.
date	The date the voucher is completed.
signature	The person receiving the petty cash should sign to acknowledge receipt.
passed by	The petty cashier should also sign to authorise the payment.

- Details from the petty cash vouchers are summarised in the *petty cash book*.
- Petty cash is often maintained on an *imprest system*, which means that at regular intervals the float (i.e. the amount of petty cash in the box) is topped-up to a fixed level.

Receipt transactions and documents

Receipt

When receiving payment it is common to provide a written confirmation. This is called a *receipt*. Most retailers give their customers a printed receipt from the till. Recipts may also be handwritten. Alternatively, an organisation may stamp the invoice with the word 'PAID', together with the date of payment.

It is unusual for a business to send a receipt acknowledging a postal payment unless the customer asks for one. This is partly to save money. It is also

Financial and Administrative Support

recognised that a cheque payment is recorded by the bank, which may be used as proof of payment.

A receipt normally identifies the following:
- The name of the organisation receiving payment
- The date of the transaction
- The items being paid for or the invoice being settled
- The amount of money paid

Individual receipts may also identify the name of the customer.

```
APHEX HI-FI

C90 cassette      .99
Cleaning fluid   1.25

TOTAL            2.24

Tendered         5.00

Change           2.76

12/03/94
```

A till receipt

Cheque

Receiving payment by cheque in person

When receiving payment by cheque, it is important to ensure that the cheque is valid. The payee should check the following details:

- The amount payable is the right amount.
- The amount payable written in words matches the amount given in numbers – if these amounts differ then the cheque will be invalid.
- The date is the date of payment, although sometimes a cheque may be *post-dated*, which means that a date some time in the future is written on the cheque before which the cheque cannot be paid. Once a cheque is six months old, according to the date written on it, it becomes invalid.
- The name of the payee as written on the cheque is correct.
- The cheque has been signed by the drawer in the presence of the payee.
- A valid cheque guarantee card is presented with the cheque and:
  - The cheque guarantee card expiry date has not yet passed
  - The account name, account number and sort code on the cheque guarantee card match those on the cheque
  - The signature on the back of the cheque card matches the signature on the cheque

Where payment is made by cheque, a receipt is not always necessary. This is because it is recognised that evidence of the cheque being paid can be used as proof of payment. Therefore when the cheque appears on a statement the customer may use that as proof that they have paid that amount to the supplier. If there are any disputes the drawer's bank may be contacted to provide further evidence that the cheque was indeed paid to the supplier.

Paying-in slip

At regular intervals any business which is collecting money will normally want to pay it into its bank account. This is chiefly for security reasons. The business will also be able to access the funds by use of their cheque book.

ACTIVITY

A business which collects payments from its customers will normally want to pay the money into its bank account. The payments from its customers may come in many different forms. List as many kinds of ways a business may receive payment which it will then want to pay into its bank account. (4.1.4)

Money paid into the bank can come in several forms, depending on the ways in which the customers make payment. These include:
- Cash
- Cheques
- Credit slips from credit card payments
- Postal orders

When paying money into the bank a document called a *paying-in slip* must be completed. This is sometimes

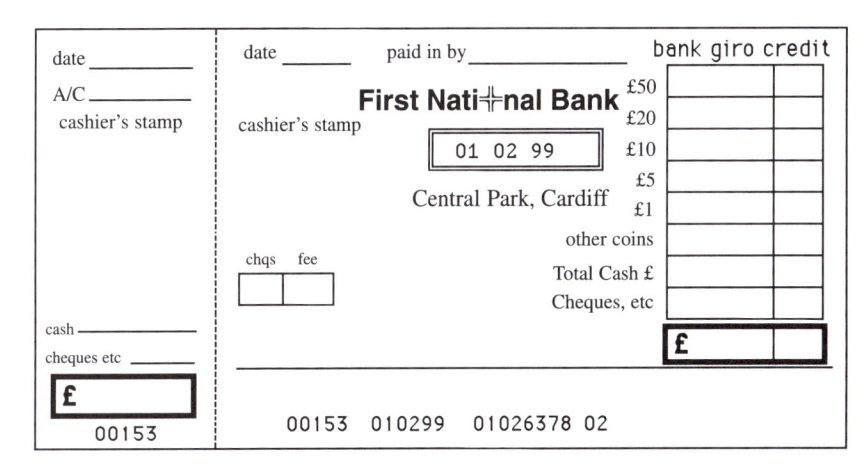

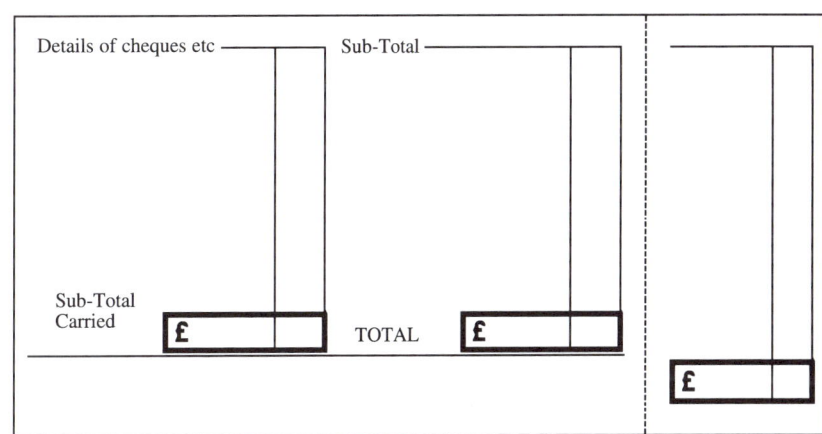

A paying-in slip; front side (above), reverse side (below)

Financial and Administrative Support

called a *bank giro credit* and details exactly what is being paid in, on what date and by whom. The cash is broken down into coins and notes on the front of the slip, while the cheques, postal orders, credit slips and others are detailed on the reverse side. The tear-off counterfoil on the left-hand side (indicated by the broken line) is kept by the business for its own records.

Bank statement

A bank statement is very similar to a statement of account, which a business would issue to its customers. The bank sends statements to its customers, normally at the end of each month, recording the following information:
- Customer details (name, address, account number)
- Date of statement
- Balance at the start of the month
- Receipts and payments made during the month
- Balance at the end of the month

The withdrawals, or payments, from a bank account may include:
- Cheques (the cheque number appears on the date the cheque is drawn)
- Direct debits (amounts taken directly by the bank from the account by order of the account-holder)
- Standing orders (similar to direct debits but a regular monthly amount)
- Bank charges and interest

Deposits, or receipts, into a bank account may include:
- Cash and/or cheques paid in using a paying-in slip (the paying-in slip number appears on the date the deposit(s) clear)
- Direct credits (direct transfer of funds from another person's account)

Security checks

Introduction

At the start of this chapter the importance of business documents was explained.
- Business documents serve as a record of transactions.
- From these records the financial statements are drawn up, which describe how well the business has performed.
- Performance should also be monitored on a regular basis, so that dangers may be avoided if

```
                 First National Bank      Confidential
26 Central Park        Account  CURRENT
Cardiff
CF1 2TT                John P Spencer

Telephone          Statement date        account no.
0222 142536        31 March 1994         01026378
```

date	details	withdrawals	deposits	balance
1 Mar	balance from February 28			211.87
3 Mar	001081	27.16		184.71
5 Mar	00191 CC		356.21	540.92
9 Mar	001084	32.98		507.94
15 Mar	001082	104.89		403.05
21 Mar	Bank Charges	15.23		387.82
29 Mar	Devon Union SO	117.90		269.92
31 Mar	001085	68.89		201.03
	Balance to April 1			**201.03**

```
Key  SO  Standing Order   CC  Cash &/or Cheques
     DD  Direct Debit     OD  Overdrawn

John P Spencer
18 French Hill
Cardiff
CF10 9HT
```

A bank statement

possible. At least the business will be able to prepare for possible dangers. Monitoring of business performance relies on the accuracy of documentation.
- Finally, business documents ensure security, so that confidential information is not accessible to unauthorised persons. Part of this information is required by law.

Financial and Administrative Support

For all these reasons, therefore, it is important that the documentation is accurate, reliable and up-to-date. Fundamental to all business activities is money. Even public sector organisations and charities, who are providing a service rather than chiefly trying to make a profit, are accountable for the money they use, and must keep proper documentation.

To ensure the accuracy of the records and to prevent money 'going astray' there are three security checks a business can include as part of it accounting systems:

- Authorisation of orders
- Checking invoices before payment
- Authorised cheque signatories

Authorisation of orders

A business needs to make sure that unauthorised orders are not being made. If the managers are not careful it may be possible for members of the organisation to place orders for goods and services without checking that the items are needed or whether there is sufficient money to pay for them. Even more seriously, someone may order items purely for private use.

Therefore it is recommended that purchase orders are always signed by selected authorised persons. For a small organisation this may be limited to one person, the manager in charge of finance. For larger organisations managers may be given responsibility for their own budget and may then be authorised to sign orders for their area. It is still likely that for large orders over a certain sum the director of finance will need to sign the purchase order.

Checking invoices

Before an invoice is paid a business should check certain details. Some businesses use a rubber stamp as a reminder that each of the following should be checked and signed off before the invoice is passed on for payment:

Goods Ordered	
Goods Received	
Prices	
Calculations	

- Were the goods ordered in the first place?
- Were the goods received?
- Are the prices charged correct?
- Are the calculations on the invoice correct?

ACTIVITY

You are employed in the accounts department of a large business. You have been asked to check invoice details before passing them on for payment.
1. What *four* pieces of information should you check?
2. For each of the above state where you would be able to find the information that you would need.
3. What problems could arise if this information was not checked?
4. What should you do if you discover that some of the details on the invoice do not match the other records?

(4.1.5)

The information for the four checks should be available as follows:

Check	Source
1 Were the goods ordered?	Copy of purchase order
2 Were the goods received?	Goods received note
3 Are the prices correct?	Price list or quotation
4 Are the calculations correct?	A calculator and the invoice!

These checks may reveal some errors in the invoice. Checks should be made internally with appropriate personnel to determine whether the invoice details are correct. If it seems that the invoice is wrong then the supplier should be contacted and a credit note may have to be issued.

If these checks are not made then it is possible for a business to pay for items it never ordered or never received. The business may pay more than the price that has been agreed or too much simply because of an error of calculation.

Authorised cheque signatories

In order to control payments from the bank account a business will normally limit the number of persons who are authorised to sign cheques for the organisation. This may be limited to one person in a small organisation. For larger organisations a number of persons may be authorised cheque signatories. Often a business cheque must have two signatures before it can be cleared for payment by the bank. This serves as an even better control of business payments.

MULTIPLE CHOICE

1. VAT is payable to:
   - A HM Customs and Excise
   - B Inland Revenue
   - C Local Authorities
   - D Registrar of Companies

Financial and Administrative Support

2 A goods received note is prepared by:
 A The customer as a record of goods received from the supplier
 B The supplier as a record of the goods received by the customer
 C The government as a record of the VAT on goods received by a business
 D The transport and distribution organisation as a record of goods delivered

3 The initials 'E & OE' are commonly found on an invoice. What do they stand for?
 A Envelope and Order Enclosed
 B Enquiries and Orders Expected
 C Errors and Omissions Excepted
 D Efficiency and Organisation Ensured

4 When a customer sends payment to a supplier it is common to include:
 A An advice note
 B A credit note
 C A receipt
 D A remittance advice

5 On a bank statement which of the following items would appear on the credit side?
 A Payment by cheque
 B Deposit
 C Bank charges
 D Standing order

6 The person to whom a cheque is made payable is known as the:
 A Drawer
 B Payer
 C Payee
 D Exchequer

7 Which of the cheques shown at the bottom of this page is valid? (Assume that today's date is 5 June 1994.)

8 The initials 'APR' are often used in connection with a credit agreement. What do they mean?
 A Annual percentage rate
 B Average payment rate
 C Actual percentage return
 D Average period of repayment

9 Petty cash is often operated according to the 'imprest' system. What does this mean?
 A The same amount is spent each month
 B The same amount is returned to the cash box each month
 C The balance of the cash box is restored to a fixed amount at regular intervals
 D Vouchers are used to record each payment

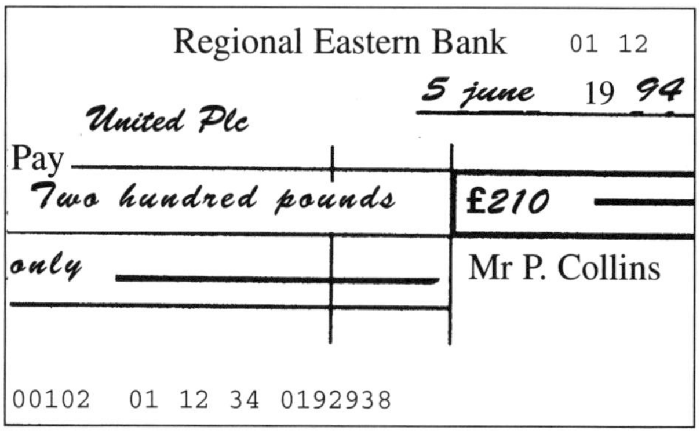

10 Before a customer pays an invoice they are likely to check that they goods have been received. Where might this information be found?
 A Purchase order
 B Catalogue
 C Despatch note
 D Goods received note

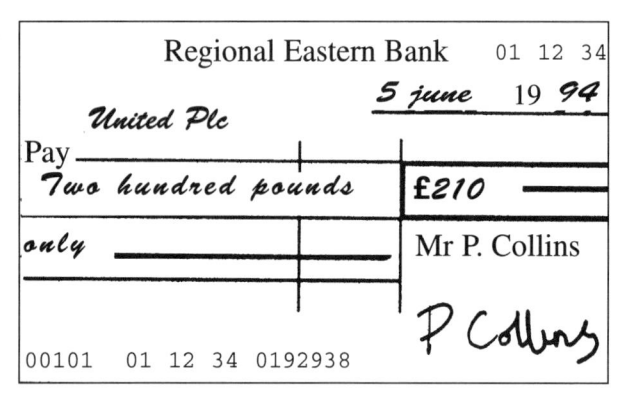

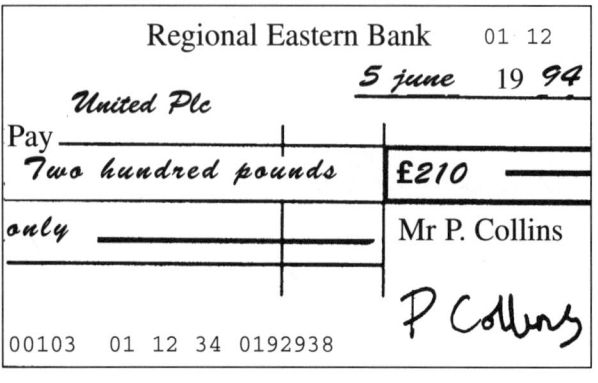

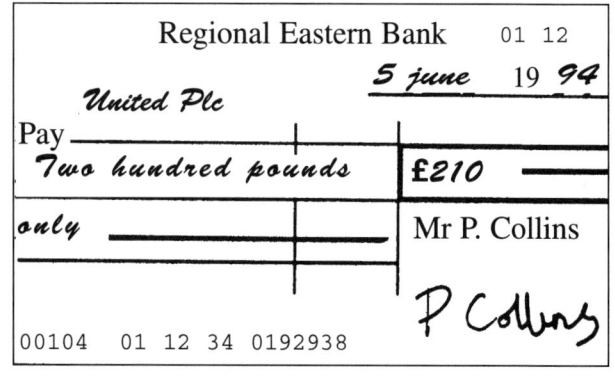

Financial and Administrative Support

SHORT ANSWER

1 What are the main reasons for keeping financial records and preparing documents?

2 A friend of yours who works in business is confused by VAT. Explain to your friend what you understand by VAT, including an account of what it is, how it is collected and how it is calculated.

3 What is a credit transaction? Give two examples.

4 What are the main advantages to the drawer of paying by cheque? Are there any disadvantages to the payee?

5 What purpose does a bank guarantee card serve? How should it be used?

6 Describe the main items that may be found on a payslip.

7 What are the main security checks for payment documents? Why are they necessary?

8 What is the difference between trade discount and cash discount?

9 What three situations might give rise to a credit note?

10 What information would one find on a customer statement? Describe the way in which the information is laid out, illustrating your answer.

ELEMENT 4.2
Complete financial documents and explain financial recording

Performance criteria

- 4.2.1 Complete purchase and sales documents clearly and correctly and calculate totals
- 4.2.2 Complete payment and receipt documents clearly and correctly and calculate totals
- 4.2.3 Record income and expenditure over time periods
- 4.2.4 Explain why financial information must be recorded
- 4.2.5 Identify and give examples of information technology which businesses use to record and monitor financial information

Purchase documents

Introduction

In this section it is necessary to return to the documents that have already been discussed and examine the procedures for completing them. The purposes of the documents will not be explained again, as these can be found by referring to the previous section.

The following sequence of documents relate to the following details.

Future Music is a large retailer of electronic instruments (100 Harrow Road, Hypertown, HY22 1ST, telephone (01333) 122334). One of the managers, Rose Clarke, is the finance manager responsible for authorising purchase orders.

Their main supplier is Sonic Boom Ltd (23 High Street, Amercombe, Bucks HP27 1TT, VAT Registration No. 2245 67 991 2). A section from their catalogue shows the following details:

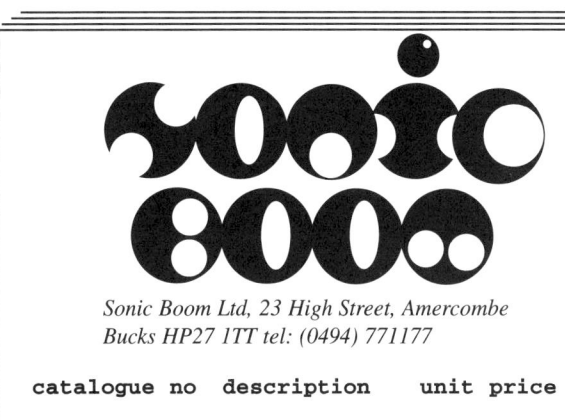

Sonic Boom Ltd, 23 High Street, Amercombe Bucks HP27 1TT tel: (0494) 771177

catalogue no	description	unit price
1002004	Akai S1000PB Digital Sampler	9000.00
1045569	Roland SH101 Analogue Synth	699.00
1122890	Casio CT400 Home keyboard	235.00
1356788	Emu Proteus Sound Module	589.00
1776044	Korg KMS30 Synchroniser	99.00

Orders placed

On 21 March 1994, Rose Clarke decides to order the following items from the Sonic Boom Ltd catalogue:
1 Digital sampler
4 Analogue synthesizers
1 Home keyboard
5 Sound modules
1 Synchroniser
Consequently she fills out the purchase order form as follows:

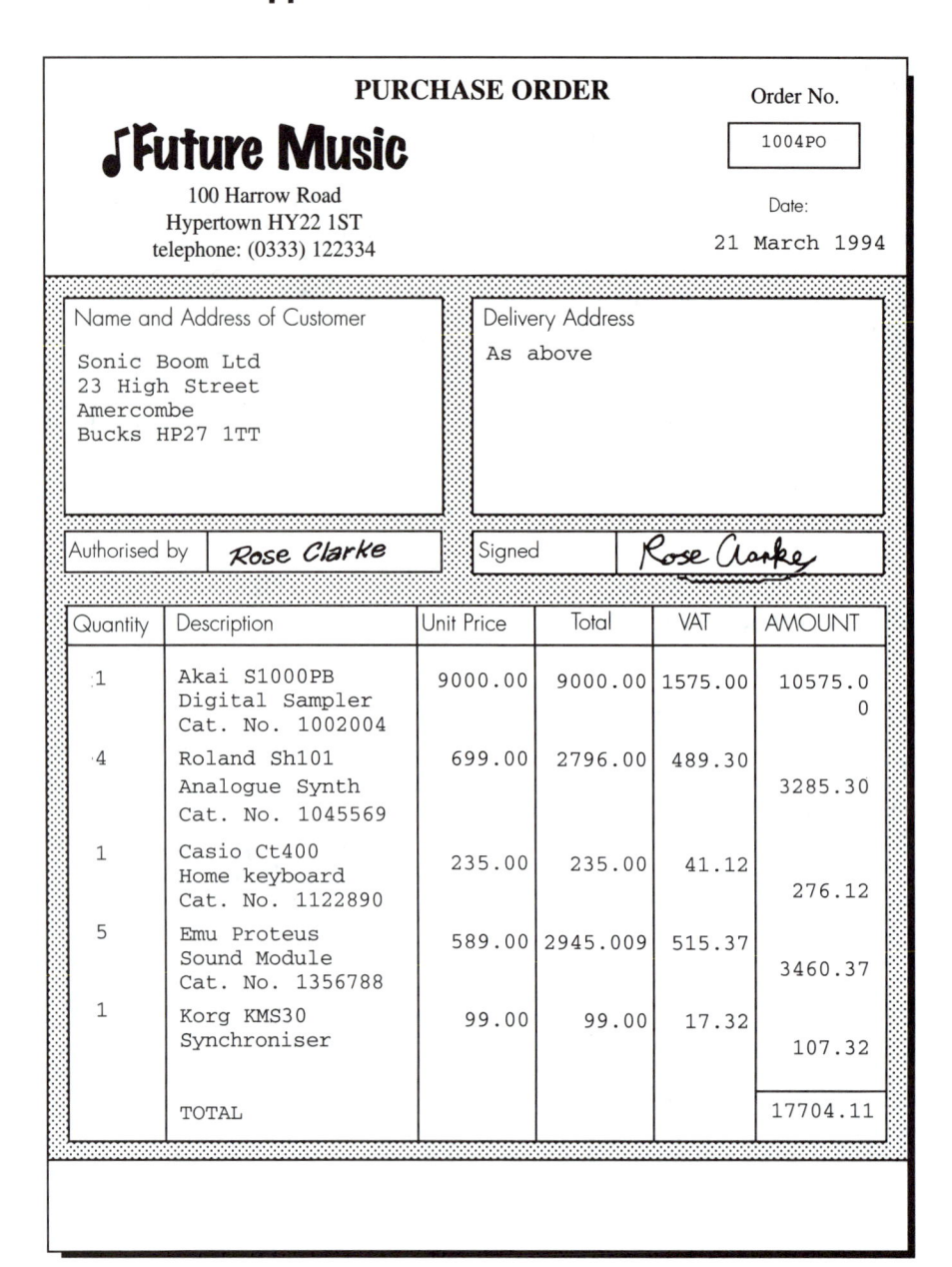

Financial and Administrative Support

A completed purchase order

PURCHASE ORDER

♪Future Music
100 Harrow Road
Hypertown HY22 1ST
telephone: (0333) 122334

Order No. 1004PO

Date: 21 March 1994

Name and Address of Customer	Delivery Address
Sonic Boom Ltd 23 High Street Amercombe Bucks HP27 1TT	As above

Authorised by *Rose Clarke* Signed *Rose Clarke*

Quantity	Description	Unit Price	Total	VAT	AMOUNT
1	Akai S1000PB Digital Sampler Cat. No. 1002004	9000.00	9000.00	1575.00	10575.00
4	Roland Sh101 Analogue Synth Cat. No. 1045569	699.00	2796.00	489.30	3285.30
1	Casio Ct400 Home keyboard Cat. No. 1122890	235.00	235.00	41.12	276.12
5	Emu Proteus Sound Module Cat. No. 1356788	589.00	2945.009	515.37	3460.37
1	Korg KMS30 Synchroniser	99.00	99.00	17.32	107.32
	TOTAL				17704.11

Notice how the *total* column is completed by multiplying the quantity of goods being ordered by the unit price. VAT is then calculated as 17.5% of the total. Check these calculations for yourself.

Rose Clarke keeps a copy of the order for her own records and sends it to the suppliers, Sonic Boom Ltd.

The suppliers process the order and send out an *advice note* which confirms that the goods will be despatched in due course.

ACTIVITY

Gianni Calvi is the purchasing manger of the Royal Inn (Crescent Hill, Tunbridge Wells, Kent TN12 3AB, Tel: 01476 242424). Their main supplier of towels and sheets is Cotton King (Tower Road, Brighton, Tel: 01296 80707). Gianni inspects the latest catalogue:

Catalogue No.	Description	Net price (£)
19978	hand towel	3.00
19979	bath towel	6.00
19980	face towel	2.00
20019	single sheet (fitted)	7.00
20020	double sheet (fitted)	10.00
20025	pillow case	4.00
20104	duvet cover – single	14.00
20105	duvet cover – double	18.00
20219	blanket – single	9.00
20200	blanket – double	12.00

VAT is charged on all items at 17.5%

For each of the following you are expected to draw up a purchase order:
1. On 12 September 1994 Gianni Calvi orders the following (purchase order number 18/GC):
   5 hand towels
   10 bath towels
   3 face towels
2. On 20 December 1994 Gianni Calvi orders the

Financial and Administrative Support

A completed goods received note

following (purchase order number 43/GC):
20 single duvet covers
20 double duvet covers
3 On 18 February 1995 Gianni Calvi orders the following (purchase order number 56/GC):
10 single sheets
15 single sheets
50 pillow cases
5 single blankets
2 double blankets
(4.2.1)

Goods received note
On 12 April 1994, the goods arrive from Sonic Boom Ltd. Asif Hussain works in the store room. He checks the goods that have been received and compares them with the advice note. He then completes a goods received note.

All the items that were requested have been received. Asif Hussain does not need to see the original order. He is only recording what is actually received. There is no need to record the prices either, only the number of items.

ACTIVITY

Refer to the previous questions regarding the Royal Inn. For each of the following deliveries you are required to draw up a goods received note:
1 Order 18/GC arrives complete on 30 September 1994
2 Order 43/GC arrives complete on 2 January 1995
3 Order 56/GC arrives complete on 3 March 1995
(4.2.1)

Purchase invoice
With the goods Sonic Boom Ltd include a copy of the invoice. This has a date of 7 April 1994, shortly after the order was received.

A completed purchase invoice

GOODS RECEIVED NOTE :   ♪Future Music
GOODS Received Note No: GRN 678
GOODS Received Note Date: 12 April 1994

Prepared By: Asif Hussain
Signed: A Hussain
Supplier   Sonic Boom Ltd
                23 High Street
                Amercombe
                Bucks HP27 1TT

Order Number	Catalogue Number/ Description	Quantity Advised	Quantity Received
1004PO	Akai S1000PB Digital Sampler Cat. No. 1002004	1	1
1004PO	Roland SH101 Analogue Synth. Cat. No. 1045569	4	4
1004PO	Casio CT400 Home keyboard Cat. No. 1122890	1	1
1004PO	Emu Proteus Sound Module Cat. No. 1356788	5	5
1004PO	Korg KMS30 Synchroniser	1	1

A completed goods received note

Sonic Boom

Sonic Boom Ltd, 23 High Street, Amercombe
Bucks HP27 1TT tel: (0494) 771177
Vat Registration No. 2245 67 9912

INVOICE

	65521
	1004PO
Date/Tax Point	7 Apr 1994

Customer:
Future Music
100 Harrow Road
Hypertown
HY22 1ST

Quantity	Cat. No	Description	Unit Price	TOTAL
1	1002004	Akai S1000PB Digital Sampler	9000.00	9000.00
4	1045569	Roland SH101 Analogue Synth.	699.00	2796.00
1	1122890	Casio CT400 Home keyboard	235.00	235.00
5	1356788	Emu Proteus Sound Module	589.00	2945.00
1	1776044	Korg KMS30 Synchroniser	99.00	99.00
				15075.00
		less: Trade Discount 7.5%		1130.62
				13944.38
		less: Cash Discount 4% for payment within 30 days		557.77
			Sub-Total	13386.61
			VAT 17.5%	2342.65
			TOTAL £	15729.26

Terms: Overdue accounts will be charged 2% interest per month

Financial and Administrative Support

It is important that the calculations on the invoice are carried out in the correct order. If this order is changed it is possible to get different totals, which are incorrect.

The order for calculations is:
- Catalogue price = total 1
- Minus trade discount (% × total 1) from total 1 = total 2
- Minus cash discount (% × total 2) from total 2 = total 3
- Plus postage and packing to total 3 = total 4
- Plus VAT (17.5% × total 4) to total 4 = total 5

If one or more of these items does not apply they can be left out of the calculation altogether.

In the example this works as follows:
- Total 1 = catalogue price: £15,075.00
- Trade discount = 7.5% × 15,075.00 = 1,130.62
  Total 2 = 15,075.00 − 1,130.62 = 13,944.38
- Cash discount = 4% × 13,944.38 = 557.77
  Total 3 = 13,944.38 − 557.77 = 13,386.61
- Postage and packing = 0.00
  Total 4 = 13,386.61
- VAT = 17.5% × 13,386.61 = 2,342.65
  Total 5 = 13,386.61 + 2,342.65 = £15,729.26

ACTIVITY

Refer to the previous activities regarding the Royal Inn. For each of the following purchases you are required to complete the purchase invoice that Cotton King would send to the Royal Inn. You should assume:

20% trade discount
3% cash discount for payment within 28 days
Terms and conditions: E & OE; 2 months' interest free credit, interest is charged at a rate of 1% per month on all outstanding balances
VAT is charged at 17.5% (VAT registration number 1 34 2625 132)

1. **Purchase Order 18/GC is received 14 September 1994. Purchase invoice number is CK196. Postage and packing is charged at £12.00.**
2. **Purchase order 43/GC is received 23 December 1994. Purchase invoice number is CK205. Postage and packing is charged at £7.00.**
3. **Purchase order 56/GC is received 20 February 1995. Purchase invoice number is CK218. Postage and packing is charged at £10.00.**
(4.2.1)

Sales documents

There is an obvious overlap between purchase and sales documents. After all, every purchase is, from the supplier's point of view, a sale. The difference then is only a matter of perspective. For this section documents that will be completed by the supplier are investigated.

This section will continue the previous example, except that now Future Music is the supplier, selling goods to a customer named Philip Kusmishko. He is setting up a music studio and is a regular customer, buying items on credit. Philip Kusmishko has sent the following letter:

```
Rock Cottage
Littlebrook
Uniton UN2 4TG

18 June 1994

Dear Sir/Madam

Further to our telephone call last week
I should like to order the following
items as agreed:

  Korg M1 Synthesiser @ £900.00
  Alesis Drum Machine @ £120.00
  Pack of 10 computer diskettes @ £9.99

Please confirm in writing.

Yours faithfully
Philip Kusmishko
```

Orders received
Future Music processes the order by producing a sales invoice with carbon copies. The first copy (see page 251) is sent as an advice note as confirmation that the order has been received and is being processed.

Delivery note
The goods are despatched two weeks later with the delivery note on page 251.

Sales invoice
Also included with the goods is the invoice on page 251.

ACTIVITY

The Royal Inn (Crescent Hill, Tunbridge Wells, Kent TN12 3AB, tel: 01476 242424) has the following charges:

Bed and breakfast:	
Single room – economy	**£30 per night**
Single room – deluxe	**£35 per night**
Double room – economy	**£45 per night**
Double room – deluxe	**£55 per night**
Evening meal (for one)	**£12**
Telephone	**£0.75 per minute**
Mini bar	**£2 per bottle**
Room service	**£5**

VAT is charged on all these prices at 17.5% (VAT registration number 4 18 1923 726)

During the month of June the hotel had the following guests. You are required to complete sales invoices for each customer:

Financial and Administrative Support

ADVICE NOTE

♪Future Music
100 Harrow Road
Hypertown HY22 1ST
telephone: (0333) 122334

Advice Note Date	22 June 1994
Despatch Date	14 days
Customer Reference	PK
Order Number	None

Name and Address of Customer
Philip Kusmishko
Rock Cottage
Littlebrook
Uniton
UN2 4TG

Delivery Address
Same

Quantity	Description	Unit Price	Total	VAT	AMOUNT
1	Korg M1 Synthesiser	900.00	900.00	157.00	1057.50
1	Alesis Drum Machine	120.00	120.00	21.00	141.00
1	Pack of 10 Disks	9.99	9.99	1.74	10.73
	Postage and Packing		24.50	4.28	28.78
	TOTAL				1238.01

E & OE
Terms:

VAT Registration Number. 22576927

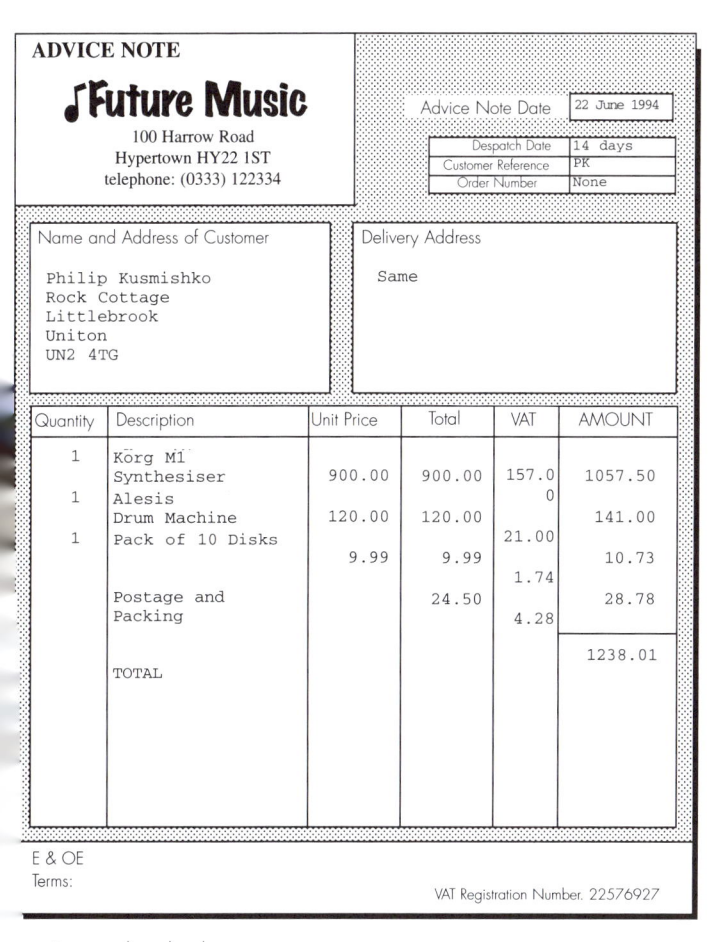

A completed advice note

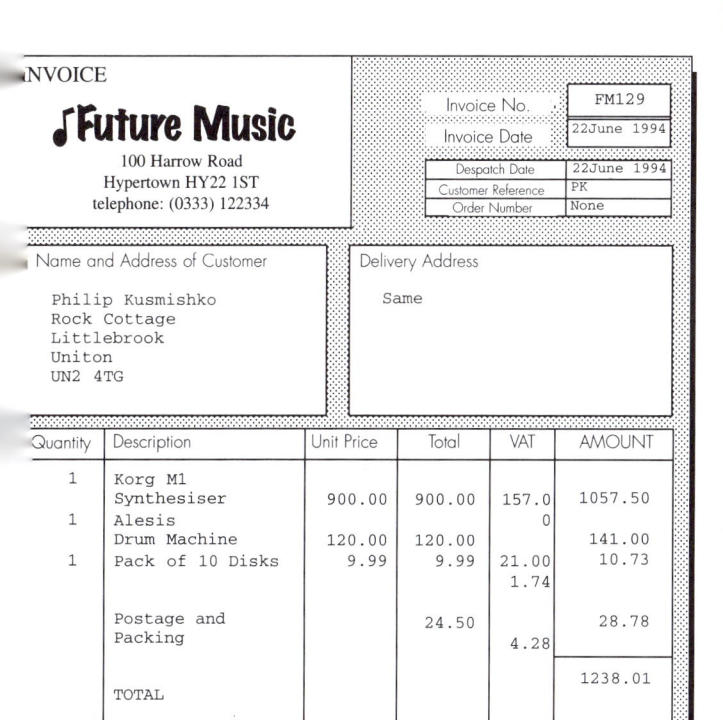

INVOICE

♪Future Music
100 Harrow Road
Hypertown HY22 1ST
telephone: (0333) 122334

Invoice No.	FM129
Invoice Date	22June 1994
Despatch Date	22June 1994
Customer Reference	PK
Order Number	None

Name and Address of Customer
Philip Kusmishko
Rock Cottage
Littlebrook
Uniton
UN2 4TG

Delivery Address
Same

Quantity	Description	Unit Price	Total	VAT	AMOUNT
1	Korg M1 Synthesiser	900.00	900.00	157.00	1057.50
1	Alesis Drum Machine	120.00	120.00	21.00	141.00
1	Pack of 10 Disks	9.99	9.99	1.74	10.73
	Postage and Packing		24.50	4.28	28.78
	TOTAL				1238.01

&OE
rms: payment must be made within 28 days of delivery

VAT Registration Number. 225768927

A completed sales invoice

DELIVERY NOTE

♪Future Music
100 Harrow Road
Hypertown HY22 1ST
telephone: (0333) 122334

Delivery Note Date	6 July
Despatch Date	6 July 1994
Customer Reference	PK
Order Number	None

Name and Address of Customer
Philip Kusmishko
Rock Cottage
Littlebrook
Uniton
UN2 4TG

Delivery Address
Same

Quantity	Description	Unit Price	Total	VAT	AMOUNT
1	Korg M1 Synthesiser	900.00	900.00	157.00	1057.50
1	Alesis Drum Machine	120.00	120.00	21.00	141.00
1	Pack of 10 Disks	9.99	9.99	1.74	10.73
	Postage and Packing		24.50	4.28	28.78
	TOTAL				1238.01

Customer's Signature _____
Date _____

VAT Registration Number. 225768927

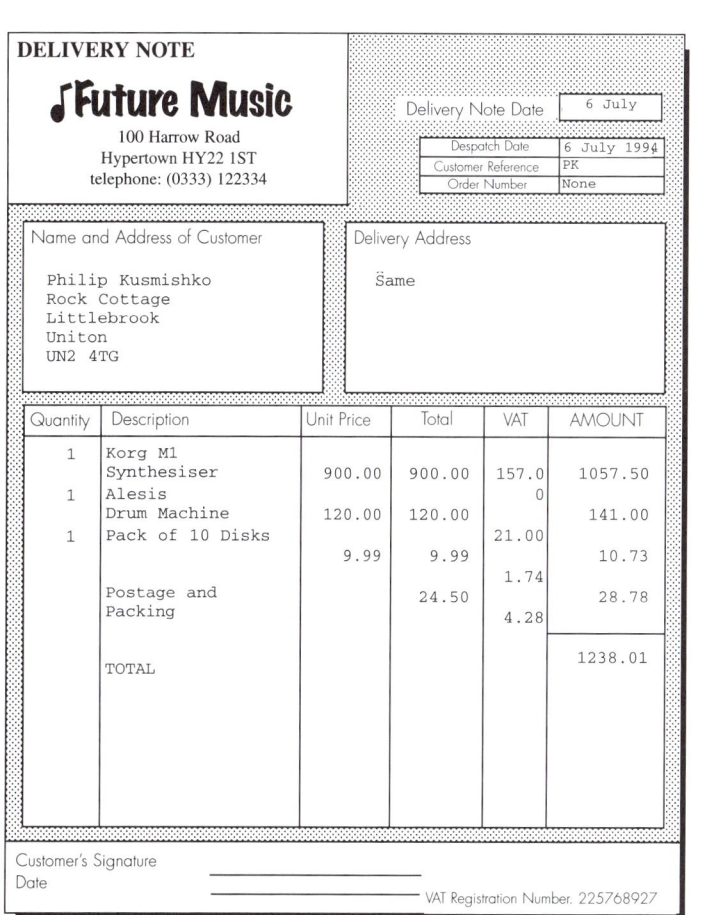

A completed delivery note

---

1 **May 5**
Mr and Mrs Tissier (2 Bond Street, London)
Stayed 2 nights in deluxe double room, having 2 dinners each, and making one telephone call for 10 minutes

2 **May 17**
Claudia Schmidt (12 Schloss Strasse, Berlin, Germany)
Stayed 5 nights in an economy single room, taking 4 dinners and using room service once

3 **May 24**
Nathan Frank (Treetops, Beverly Hills, Los Angeles, USA)
Stayed 14 nights in a deluxe single room, taking dinner each night, drinking 20 bottles from the mini bar and making a total of 50 minutes of telephone calls

(4.2.1)

Statement of account

Philip Kusmishko has bought several goods on credit. For the month ended 30 June 1994, details of his account are as follows.

At the start of the month he owed £893.26 for items purchased in May. During the month the following invoices were sent to him:

Financial and Administrative Support

6 June FM1241 £189.99
14 June FM1267 £14.20

On 25 June, Philip Kusmishko sent a cheque to Future Music to the value of £893.26.

His statement can now be prepared:
Points to note:
- The balance brought forward from the previous month is shown first.
- Any increases to the balance, in the form of invoices, are shown in the *debit* column – 'debit' is just a technical word denoting an increase in the amount owing by the customer to the business. A debit balance is in the supplier's favour.
- Any decreases to the balance, in the form of payments, are shown in the *credit* column – in this context 'credit' is just a technical word for a decrease in the amount owing by the customer to the business. A credit balance is one in the customer's favour.
- The balance is calculated by adding any debits and subtracting any credits from the previous balance.

You should check these calculations for yourself.

♪Future Music
STATEMENT

100 Harrow Road
Hypertown HY22 1ST
telephone: (0333) 122334

Customer Name	Customer Reference	Statement Date
Philip Kusmishko	VAT	6 July 1994

Date	Details	Debit	Credit	Balance
June 1	Balance brought forwards from May			893.26
6	invoice FM1241	189.99		1083.25
14	invoice FM1267	14.20		1097.45
22	invoice FM1295	1238.01		2335.46
25	cheque - thank you		893.26	1432.20
	Outstanding balance at 30 June 1994			1432.20

Name and Address of Customer

Philip Kusmishko
Rock Cottage
Littlebrook
Uniton
UN2 4TG

A completed statement

✏ ACTIVITY

Cotton King (Tower Road, Brighton, tel: 01296 80707) is a supplier of cotton and linen products. For each of the following customers you are required to prepare the statements.

1. Royal Inn (Crescent Hill, Tunbridge Wells, Kent TN12 3AB, tel: 01476 242424), customer reference RI100.

Balance on 1 May 1995		£425.20
10 May	Invoice CK909	£209.27
20 May	Invoice CK987	£24.90
27 May	Payment	£425.20

2. VB Hospital Trust (St Peter's Close, Gravesend, Berks, tel: 01917 625738), customer reference VBHT.

Balance 1 May 1995		£1,978.45
5 May	Payment	£467.09
12 May	Invoice CK926	£377.71
19 May	Invoice CK981	£209.70
23 May	Credit note CN24	£288.00
28 May	Invoice CK999	£84.40
30 May	Payment	£600.00

(4.2.1)

Payment documents

Pay slip

Pay slips vary widely from organisation to organisation. Their layout can be arranged in many different ways. Some of the calculations involved in working out tax and National Insurance can be very complicated, and many businesses have computers to do it automatically. Once the calculations are done it is a very simple matter to complete the pay slip, since it really is a question of putting information and numbers in appropriate boxes.

Example: Sophie Robinson is an employee of Brewsters International, a large brewery firm. Her annual salary is £18,600, which she receives in 12 equal monthly instalments. Her tax liability for each month (for her basic salary before any overtime, bonuses etc.) is £276.50, and her National Insurance is £112.75. Superannuation contributions (a private pension scheme) are £179.00 each month. Her National Insurance number is BB 20 19 02 A, her tax code is 340L and her payroll number is BI245. Her pay slip for August (the fifth month of the tax year, counting from April) can be drawn up as shown opposite.

This is a relatively simple example, which assumes that the employee's pay and deductions are the same every month. This is often not the case and calculations will have to be made every time the employee is paid.

The important thing to note is the cumulative figures, or the 'year to date' totals. These are running totals for the whole year so far (measured from April). In this example it is simply a matter of multiplying each monthly figure by five.

Financial and Administrative Support

BREWSTERS INTERNATIONAL		Pay statement	
Pay period	month 5	Gross Pay	1550.00
Name	Sophie Robinson	Deductions	568.25
NI No.	BB 20 19 02 A	Net Pay	981.75
Tax Code	340L		
Payroll No.	B1245		

Gross Pay in Period

Pay	1550.00
Overtime	0.00
Expenses	0.00
Other	0.00
TOTAL GROSS PAY	1550.00

Deductions in Period

PAYE	276.50
NI	112.75
Superannuation	179.00
Other	0.00
TOTAL DEDUCTIONS	568.25

Gross Pay to date

Pay	7750.00
Overtime	0.00
Expenses	0.00
Other	0.00
TOTAL GROSS PAY	7750.00

Deductions to date

PAYE	1382.50
NI	563.75
Superannuation	895.00
Other	0.00
TOTAL DEDUCTIONS	2841.25

Net Pay to date	4908.75

ACTIVITY

You are employed in the personnel department of Estuary Mainland, a high street clothes retailer. Your duties include preparing the pay slips for employees.

Gordon Kelly works in the shop. He receives a basic salary of £12,000 a year (or £1,000 a month). He also has the option of working overtime at the weekends at a rate of £7.00 an hour. He contributes £15.00 a month to a union fund.

His payroll reference number is 88. His National Insurance Number is TT 29 75 10 B, and his tax code is 340L.

From the details given below, prepare each of Gordon's pay slips for the first four months of the tax year. In the first month the cumulative totals will be the same as the month's figures. Subsequent cumulative totals must be computed by adding each month's figures together. Unless otherwise stated Gordon's details are the same for each month. (Note: the figures for National Insurance and PAYE are fictional and are not based on proper calculations.)

	Month 1	Month 2	Month 3	Month 4
Overtime	6 hours	10 hours	0 hours	20 hours
National Insurance	£104.00	£123.00	£82.00	£136.00
PAYE	£160.75	£174.25	£130.00	£198.50

(4.2.2)

Cheque

To illustrate the correct completion of a cheque the details from the earlier example have been used. Future Music, who have ordered goods from Sonic Boom Ltd, have received all the items and an invoice for £15,729.26. They decide to send a cheque in the post for the full amount. Francis Young, a senior member of management, is an authorised signatory.

Note that the counterfoil (the section on the left – also known as the cheque stub) is completed and kept as a record of:

- Date of payment
- Name of payee
- Amount of payment
- Cheque number (pre-printed – in this case 001114)

The cheque itself also shows the date. This is significant for two reasons:

- The cheque is not valid before the date shown – hence it is possible to post-date a cheque by

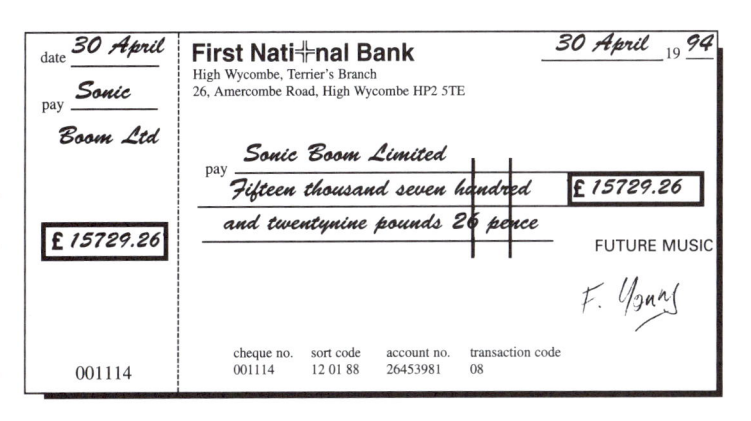

A completed cheque

Financial and Administrative Support

writing a future date on it. However, most businesses will not accept post-dated cheques, since they want the money straightaway.
- The cheque is not valid six months after the date shown – hence it is important for payees to pay them into their accounts before six months pass. Businesses are not normally slow in paying in customers' cheques.

The amount to be paid is written in words and numbers – and these must show the same amount, otherwise the cheque is not valid.

Since this cheque is being posted the drawer will not have the chance to present a cheque guarantee card. Furthermore the amount to be paid would be in excess of most guarantee cards! A lot of business is carried out on the basis of trust. If a cheque bounces (that is, it is not honoured by the drawer's bank) the supplier will expect the customer to make amends.

ACTIVITY

As an accounts assistant for Universal Goods Ltd your job includes preparing cheques for the directors to sign. The following invoices are ready for payment. Using copies of the cheques below you must draw up the cheques ready for signature, remembering to complete the cheque stub:

Supplier	Amount
British Gas	£188.27
Big Budget plc	£897.21
Timothy Cootes	£12.98
Chemical Conglomerates	£1,286.01

(4.2.2)

Petty cash voucher

A petty cash voucher is used to record payments for such things as milk, cleaning, travel and accommodation.

For example, Samina Siddiq spends £11.75 (including £1.75 VAT) on petrol while undertaking a business trip. She shows the receipt to John Walker, the petty cashier, who pays her the money and completes a petty cash voucher on 28 July 1994:

PETTY CASH VOUCHER	folio 1 15
	date 28 July 94

for what required	amount £	p
Petrol	10	00
VAT	1	75
	11	75

Signature *Samina Siddiq*
Passed by *John Walker*

A completed petty cash voucher

Note that the folio number of 115 should follow a logical sequence so that vouchers can be checked and referred to if necessary.

ACTIVITY

You are the petty cashier in a business organisation, authorised to make payments to employees for proper business expenses. You have been instructed only to pay expenses that are supported by proof of payment. You should not pay any amounts above £50 or any private costs.

From the details of the expenses given below draw up suitable petty cash vouchers. If there are

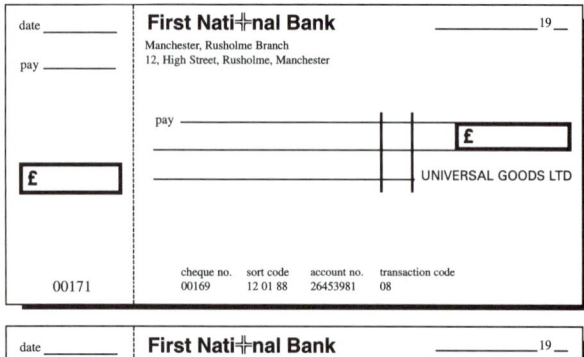

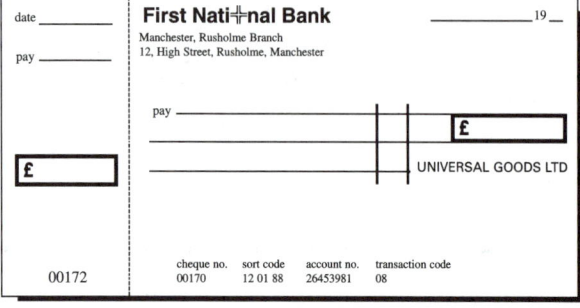

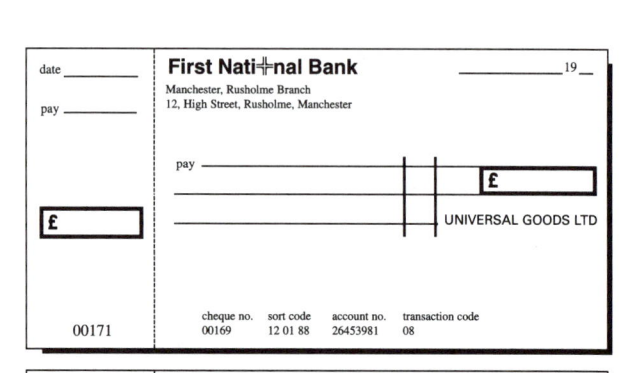

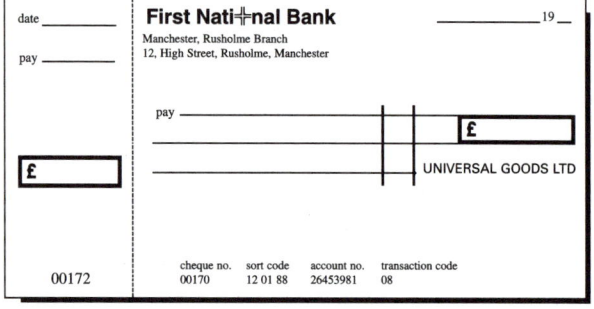

Financial and Administrative Support

any problems prepare the voucher but do not authorise it. Make a note of your concerns for the senior accountant, who will have to decide whether to make payment.

Your first voucher folio number is 27. The rest should follow in sequence.

Name of employee	Nature of expense	Supporting evidence	Gross amount (£)	VAT (£)
A. Ali	Taxi for a bsuiness trip	Receipt from taxi driver	15.00	2.23
L. Jenkins	3 pints of milk for tea breaks	Till receipt from shop	0.75	nil
M. Smith	Cleaner's wages	Cleaner's invoice	25.00	nil
P. Sefer	Cost of hotel for business conference	Hotel bill	240.00	35.74
B. McEwen	10 packets of paper for the photocopier	Receipt from stationer	70.50	10.50
Y. Gul	Drycleaning of suits	Receipt from dry cleaner	27.14	4.04
J. Peters	Rail fare for business trip	Train ticket	49.55	7.38
H. Turner	Stamps for business post	None	1.80	0.26

(4.2.2)

Receipt documents

Receipt
A receipt is a very simple document, and could be drawn up on any piece of paper, provided that it contained the appropriate information. However, businesses often have their own pre-printed receipts with their name on. Businesses with cash tills can take advantage of receipts printed automatically. Alternatively, it is possible to buy blank receipts from stationery shops.

Example: V. G. Patel is a seller of stationery. His VAT registration number is 386 2102 86. On 29 April 1994 he sells the following goods to Jayne Mason, who pays for them in full immediately:
10 packs of writing paper £0.99 plus £0.17 VAT each
1 large stapler £1.27 plus £0.22 VAT
2 packets of pencils £0.49 plus £0.08 VAT each
8 perspex rulers £0.30 plus £0.05 VAT each

Jayne asks for a receipt because she is going to claim the money back from petty cash.

Jayne Mason can now use the receipt as proof of payment for the items listed. Since the VAT and the VAT registration number have been included, this can be called a *VAT receipt*. The importance of a VAT receipt is that it can used as a legal document of VAT paid, which is necessary for any business that is going to submit a VAT return at the end of the quarter.

```
VG PATEL                          1029
Stationers
CASH RECEIPT
         Customer  Jayne Mason
         Date      29 April 1994

                          net    VAT    gross
10 packs of writing paper 9.90   1.70   11.60
    @ 0.99
1 large stapler           1.27   0.22    1.49
2 packets of pencils      0.98   0.16    1.14
    @ 0.49
8 perspex rulers          2.40   0.40    2.80
    @ 0.30
TOTAL                    14.55   2.48   17.03
signed  D. Patel
VAT registration number 386 2102 86
```

ACTIVITY

You work on the sales desk for Harun & Sons (15 Micklefield Street, Basgrove, Oxford OX25 7TH, telephone 01865 202090), a partnership selling motor spares. Today's sales include the following customers, all of whom request a receipt:

Customer: **Jerry McGuire**
Items purchased: 5 litres of oil £4.99 (including £0.74 VAT)
Pack of spark plugs £3.45 (including £0.51 VAT)
Air filter £1.99 (including £0.30 VAT)

Customer: **Sally Burgess**
Items purchased: Plastic bucket £0.99 (including £0.14 VAT)
Sponge, brush and cloth set £3.75 (including £0.55 VAT)
Plastic hose £12.99 (including £1.93 VAT)

Customer: **George Macintosh**
Items purchased: Set of 4 hub-caps £63.20 (including £9.41 VAT)
Fluffy dice £2.99 (including £0.44 VAT)
Furry seat covers £19.49 (including £2.23 VAT)
Car air freshener £2.50 (including £0.37 VAT)

Financial and Administrative Support

All these customers have paid in full for the items purchased. You are to prepare the VAT receipts (VAT registration number 299 9911 10).
(4.2.2)

Cheque

A cheque, strictly speaking, is not a receipt document. The drawer will have a cheque stub recording the amount and date paid, and the name of the payee. This, however, does not prove that the supplier ever received payment, and so cannot be counted as a document of receipt. However, as already mentioned, a record of the cheque clearing can be counted as proof of payment. Therefore, the drawer may look to evidence on the statement that the cheque has been presented for payment as proof of payment. If needs be the bank may be contacted in order to provide the original cheque and further evidence that the amount was paid into the account of the supplier.

Paying-in slip

A paying-in slip serves the purpose of detailing the monies being paid in to the bank for the bank's own records. The counterfoil also serves as a record for the person or business paying the money in.

The slips are so designed as to make them easy to complete, as the following example should illustrate.

Example: Nancy Jackson is the chief cashier for Northern Enterprise Ltd. On 14 January 1995 she has the following amounts to pay into the bank account:

Cash	2 × £50 notes
	1 × £5 note
	11 × £1 coins
	£4.78 in other coins
Cheques	£14.89 from J. T. Clarke
	£156.99 from Jyoti & Co.
	£50.00 from Alice McGrath
Credit slips	total £146.92

She then completes the paying-in slip as follows:

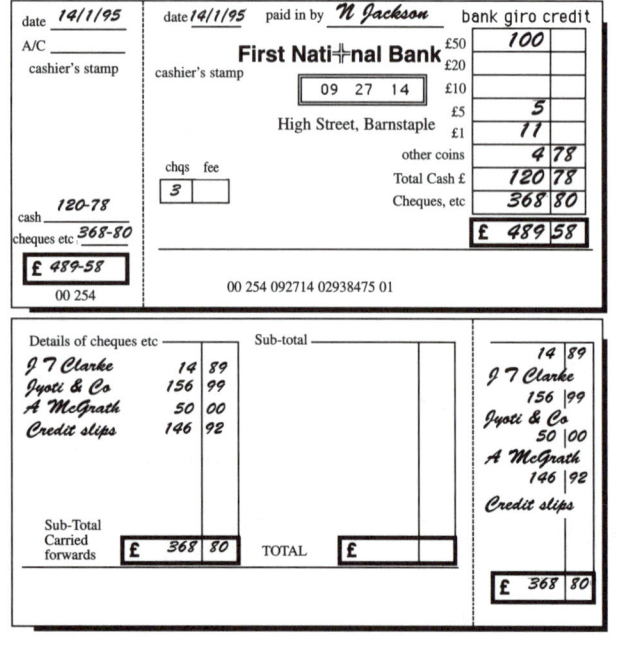

Details are simply entered into the relevant section. Details of 'cheques, etc.' refers to cheques, credit slips, postal orders and any other non-cash items.

ACTIVITY

As a cashier for Northern Enterprise Ltd you are requested to complete copies of paying-in slips for the following deposits:

Date	Cash	Cheques etc
31/1/95	3 × £50 notes	Cheques:
	1 × £10 note	A. Smith £29.90
	1 × £5 note	Z. Khan £105.99
	6 × £1 coins	C. Chang £99.50
	£8.26 in other coins	Postal orders:
		£77.20
28/2/95	4 × £50 notes	Cheques:
	3 × £5 note	Ace Games Ltd
		£148.23
	6 × £5 note	Zeta Games £154.81
	12 × £1 coins	Credit slips: £466.89
	£18.55 in other coins	Postal orders:
		£77.20

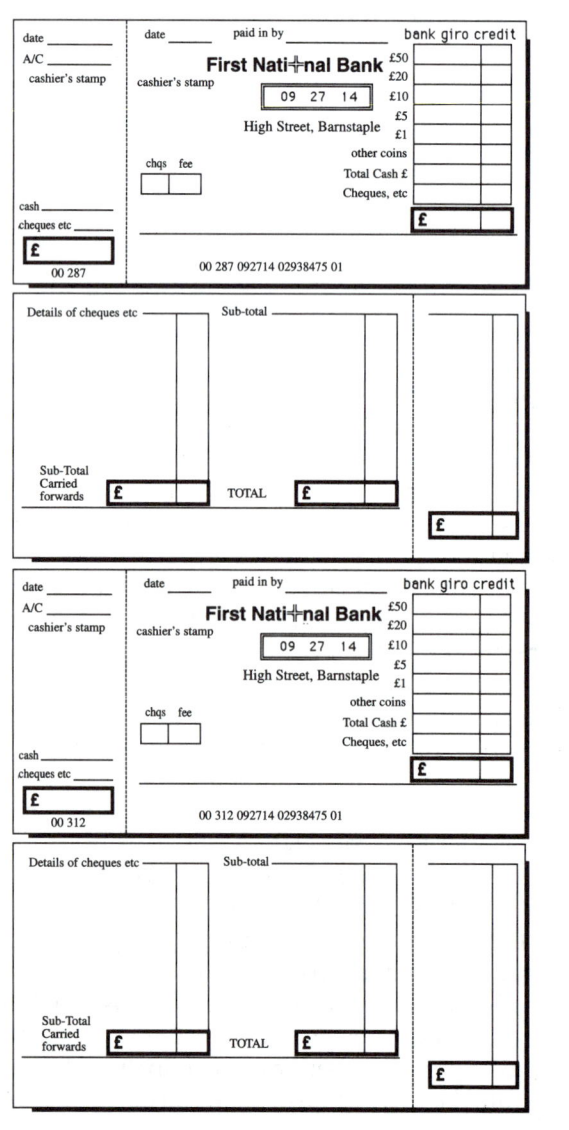

(4.2.2)

Financial and Administrative Support

Reasons for the correct completion of documents

It should be very clear by now that it is vital for a business to complete documents correctly. To put it simply, if documents are going to be used at all then they should be accurate, otherwise they are as good as useless. Therefore all the reasons previously discussed for using documents in the first place apply here. These can be summarised under two main headings: (a) accuracy and (b) reliability of data.

Accuracy is of key importance. As stated above, incorrect documents may be worse than no documents at all. If documents are not accurate then they are unreliable. Incorrect documents may lead to:

- Ordering wrong goods or services
- Paying for goods that have not been received
- Paying too much for goods or services
- Sending customers wrong goods
- Charging customers too much or too little
- Not chasing up late payers
- 'Losing' money from petty cash
- Legal prosecution
- Losing customers and suppliers

This may seem like an exaggeration, but ultimately if documents are not accurate customers and suppliers will lose confidence in the business and cease trading with it. Tax authorities may have to take criminal proceedings against the business for failing to provide accurate details of VAT, income tax, national insurance and so on.

ACTIVITY

When applying for a job as an accounting assistant you are asked about the importance of accounting information.

Make notes to prepare your answer. Referring to the range statements of the performance criteria will help you.

In an informal interview with your tutor or another person answer the following questions:
1. What are the main reasons for keeping financial records? *(4.1.1)*
2. What reasons are there for making sure that documents are completed correctly? *(4.2.3)*
3. What security checks should be made for payment documents? *(4.1.5)*

ACTIVITY

Business Furniture Stores I: Purchasing

Business Furniture Stores (BFS) is a large warehouse on the edge of a prosperous town selling a wide selection of office furniture to businesses in the area. Their address is:

Highwater Development Site
Springfield
Kent
TB87 2EE
Telephone number (01872) 562562

You are employed in their accounts department.

BFS has one major supplier, United Furnishing Ltd. You receive a copy of their latest catalogue, which includes this price list:

```
UNITED FURNISHINGS LTD
Lot 27
Broadacre Industrial Estate
Birmingham
B56 TTT
tel: 0121 678 2222
```

Catalogue Number	Description	Unit Price
0011897	2-drawer filing cabinet	79.00
0011932	small desk	37.50
0011933	large desk	45.50
0012014	office chair	12.50
0012015	office chair with arms	14.50
0012078	hat stand	28.65
0012879	conference table	127.80
0013010	coffee table	24.50

Postage and packing is charged at 1% of the catalogue price

VAT is charged on all items at 17.5%
(VAT registration number 254 0192 23)

Trade discount is offered to registered dealers at 10%

Cash discount is offered at 3% for payment within 30 days

BFS is a regular customer. Their reference number for United Furnishings Ltd is UFL4. Similarly, United Furnishings Ltd have a reference number for BFS, namely B106.

Tasks

1. You are instructed to order the following items from United Furnishings Ltd:
   10 two-drawer filing cabinets
   5 small desks
   5 large desks
   20 office chairs (no arms)
   1 hat stand
   1 conference table
   5 coffee tables

   You are therefore required to complete an appropriate Purchase Order to be sent to United Furnishings Ltd. It must be passed to your boss, Toni Pears, for authorisation.

   You should assume that BFS is entitled to the trade discount and your order form should reflect this. It is not normal to include cash discount on a purchase order.

   Your purchase order number is N882A. Use today's date. *(4.2.1)*

2. Assume that all the goods arrive two weeks after the date of your order. You must complete a goods received note. *(4.2.1)*

3. Accompanying the goods is the purchase invoice (number ABC555). You must complete this document, ensuring that all apropriate details are included. Assume that the invoice date is three days after your order. *(4.2.1)*

Financial and Administrative Support

4 Finally, within the 30 days BFS is to make payment in full. You must prepare the cheque ready for a director's signature. *(4.2.2)*

ACTIVITY

Business Furniture Stores II: Selling

Jones & Hussain are a local firm of solicitors who are refurbishing their premises. Over the last few months they have purchased several items from BFS. Today you receive the following order:

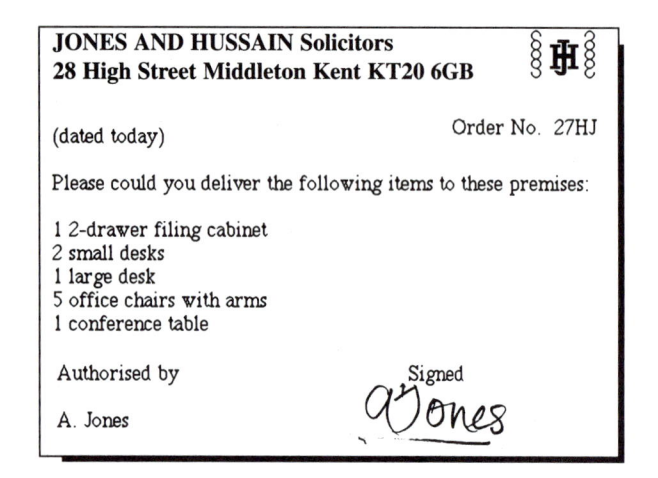

```
JONES AND HUSSAIN Solicitors         [JH logo]
28 High Street Middleton Kent KT20 6GB

(dated today)                    Order No. 27HJ

Please could you deliver the following items to these premises:

1 2-drawer filing cabinet
2 small desks
1 large desk
5 office chairs with arms
1 conference table

Authorised by           Signed
A. Jones                A. Jones
```

BFS selling prices for these items are:
two-drawer filing cabinet	£99.00
small desk	£45.00
large desk	£60.00
office chair with arms	£19.00
conference table	£150.00

1 Prepare an advice note to be sent to Jones & Hussain, informing them that delivery is likely to take place within 14 days. Jones & Hussain will not be entitled to trade discount, but may take advantage of 2% cash discount for payment within 1 month of delivery. *(4.2.1)*

3 Prepare a delivery to accompany the goods which arrive ten days after the date of the advice note. *(4.2.1)*

4 Prepare the sales invoice (number M236) for the transaction. *(4.2.1)*

5 The details of Jones & Hussain's account for this month are as follows:
   Opening balance   £432.90
   10th (month)   invoice M187   £112.36
   20th (month)   invoice M214   £380.80
   25th (month)   cheque   £432.90
   Prepare the statement of account for Jones & Hussain for the month, not forgetting to include the most recent invoice, M236. *(4.2.1)*

6 Finally, within the period allowed for cash discount, Jones & Hussain make payment in full and request a receipt. Prepare a suitable receipt document. *(4.2.2)*

ELEMENT 4.3
Produce, evaluate and store business documents

Performance criteria

(PC) 4.3.1 Explain the purpose of routine business documents

(PC) 4.3.2 Produce draft and final versions of business documents

(PC) 4.3.3 Evaluate each business document produced

(PC) 4.3.4 Compare the methods of processing business documents

(PC) 4.3.5 Reference, correctly file and retrieve business documents

(PC) 4.3.6 Identify and evaluate ways to send and ways to store business documents

Business documents

Introduction

Among the vital skills that a clerical administrator must develop are the ability to handle business information and to use it and apply it in the day to day running of the organisation and also to use the information in the tasks of problem-solving and decision-making. The data may come in many forms and may be processed in different ways. It is important therefore that administrators are able to interpret, understand and apply the information to tasks appropriately.

Information within an organisation is necessary to communicate to a wide-ranging audience. This may include customers, colleagues in the organisations and other organisations. It is important therefore that the administrator is able to identify what information needs to be conveyed, who it needs to be communicated to and the most appropriate method of communication.

Obtaining the data

In an organisation data can come from many sources and in a variety of formats. These sources may be external or internal to the organisation. It may be necessary to select from a mass of information the particular data needed for a particular job, and to assemble to information in a convenient format so that it can be more easily processed, handled and understood. This involves:

1 Identifying the information
2 Processing the information
3 Presenting it in an appropriate format

Processing the information

Once the relevant data has been obtained it is usually necessary for the administrator to work on it. This may involve:
- Referring to other information
- Making notes
- Writing summaries

- Performing appropriate calculations
- Holding discussions with colleagues

Presenting the information

The data which has been obtained and the processing which has been carried out on it will need to be communicated to a range of people within the organisation, and even outside of it. This is an extremely important part of an administrator's job.

Communication is as essential a skill as the ability to handle figures and data. There are in fact many different ways in which data and conclusions can be communicated. Examples may include the following:

- A *report* is a detailed written account of a particular investigation or issue. Reports are highly structured, and are used less frequently than letters or memos. They are very often word-processed, since precise layout is very important. They may be printed or photocopied for wider circulation.
- *Letters* have a formal structure and are used to communicate between organisations or for external communication with customers, shareholders and so on. It is usual these days to use the 'blocked' format, where all information is left-justified, with no paragraphs or other information indented. It is very important to use the correct terms. For example, a letter commencing 'Dear Sir' or 'Dear Madam' must end 'Yours faithfully'. In comparison, a letter which addresses a person by name – 'Dear Mr Taylor', for example – should be signed 'Yours sincerely'.
- *Memos* (or Memoranda) are used internally to communicate short messages to colleagues, team members or managers. They should be clearly labelled 'Memo' and include the date of the message, the name of the person sending it and the person or persons to whom they are to be sent.
- *Invitations* can be used for internal or external purposes, and should include the name and address of the person sending the information and a short message.
- *Notices* are a very useful way of communicating with a large number of people. They are ideal for short, simple messages. They are most effective when the style is brief and clear and when displayed in a convenient place.
- *Messages* may be an instruction or convey brief, factual information. The most common example is a telephone message, stating the name of the caller, a brief message, the time and date of the call and a contact phone number.
- *Graphs*, *charts*, *tables* and *diagrams* are the most useful way to communicate large volumes of numerical and analytical data quickly and visually. A wide range of methods may be used, including bar charts, line graphs, pie charts and pictograms.
- There are very strict guidelines as to how financial information should be presented, and *financial documents* must be prepared accurately and precisely.

Where information is confidential the documents should be marked 'confidential'.

ACTIVITY

Task 1
Explain the purpose to an organisation of business documents.

Task 2
Referring to Unit 3 and other sections of this book, in addition to your own research, briefly describe when you should use the following documents:
- Memorandum
- Notice
- Letter
- Invitation
- Telephone message

Task 3
What would be the most appropriate form of presenting information in the following situations?
1. Informing a customer of the outstanding balance on their account
2. Notifying a colleague of the name and address of a new customer
3. Complaining to a supplier about the quality of goods supplied
4. Informing all the members within your team of the next team meeting
5. Placing an order for raw materials with a new supplier
6. Inviting existing customers to the opening of a new store or launch of a new product
7. Summarising profit figures for a presentation to shareholders
8. Informing staff of a forthcoming social event
9. Dealing with a customer complaint
10. Informing a colleague that someone telephoned for them when they were out
11. Seeking information from a supplier about new prices
12. Congratulating staff on meeting production targets

(4.3.1)

Evaluating business documents

It is important that all business documents convey accurate and clear information to the reader. To achieve this it is necessary to ensure that the *appearance* of the document is appropriate in terms of style and format. Some documents have a very strict form of appearance. For example, formal business reports must conform to the rules of layout and content. This is to ensure that the reader knows what to expect, where to find appropriate pieces of information and is fully informed about the nature of the findings.

In addition the *language used* must be of a professional standard. This means that the document should be free from spelling and grammatical errors and use technical terms and jargon only where

Financial and Administrative Support

necessary. Most word processing packages include a spell checker and even grammatical checks. It is important to use this facility where available.

ACTIVITY

For each of the business documents listed below:
1 Identify the appropriate style and format that should be used
2 Produce an example of each, demonstrating good practice

Business documents:
Memos
Letters
Invitations
Notices
Messages
Enquiries
(4.3.1) (4.3.2)

Methods of processing documents

There are different ways of processing these documents. Generally they may be handwritten, typed or word-processed. Copies may be made by photocopying or printing methods. All these methods are commonly used by organisations. However, different methods are more suited to different situations. For example, a formal business report should always be word-processed. It is necessary to consider the cost, time taken, legibility, audience needs and quantities needed before deciding which method to use.

ACTIVITY

Copy out and complete the following table, comparing the methods of processing business documents according to legibility, cost, time taken to produce, the ability to make amendments to the document and ease of storage:

Processing method	Legibility	Cost	Time to produce	Ability to correct	Storage
Handwritten					
Typed					
Word-processed					
Printed					
Photocopied					

(4.3.3)

Referencing, filing and retrieving

Organisations need to keep a large amount of business documents. It is necessary that they are carefully filed away with suitable referencing so that they can be found quickly again if needed. Consider your local library, for example. If the books were unorganised and not arranged according to any procedure, it would be almost impossible for anyone to find a book that they wanted. Similarly, the evidence in your portfolio must be suitably referenced and ordered. This is to enable any interested parties, such as yourself, your tutors, the internal verifier or the external verifier, employers or higher education admissions tutors to readily understand the contents and access information as they choose.

Filing is often a full-time job. There are three key stages in the handling of business documents:
1 Firstly, all documents received or produced by an organisation should be *referenced*. This involves assigning a unique code to the document. Codes should be given according to a logical sequence – alphabetically, by subject, by number, by region or by date.
   - *Alphabetically*: filed according to surnames followed by initials
   - *Subject*: classified under subject headings in alphabetical order
   - *Numerically*: arranged in numerical sequence, smallest number first
   - *Date*: organised in order of dates and times, the nearest documents being the most recent date
   - *Region*: filed according to town, county or even country in alphabetical sequence

   The coding system should be as simple as possible. This enables the document to be referred to and filed accurately.
2 Secondly, the document should be *filed* for future reference. The filing should follow a simple system reflecting the code given to each document. Filing might be in filing cabinets, concertina folders, lever arch files or hanging files. The files themselves must be clearly labelled and organised and it may be necessary to produce an index for quick reference.
3 Finally, it should be possible to *retrieve* the document again at a future date if necessary. Provided the referencing and filing is maintained correctly, the retrieval should be straightforward.

ACTIVITY

Look at the following information relating to recent sales invoices from a car showroom:

Customer	Address	Date of sale	Invoice no.	Goods bought
Tony Brown	Liverpool	1/6/95	10021	sports car
Helen Humphries	Leeds	12/6/95	10049	van
Frederick Potter	Liverpool	20/6/95	10097	truck
Saffron Verdey	Manchester	5/6/95	10036	van
Kwai Chan	Selby	30/5/95	09987	sports car
Kevin Hancock	Leeds	11/6/95	10039	saloon
Sophia Robins	Selby	28/5/95	09970	saloon
Antonio Marchant	Manchester	11/6/95	10040	truck
Brenda Nylon	Leeds	3/6/95	10029	sports car
Gloria Bee	Bradford	18/6/95	10090	van
Chuck Spencer	Selby	22/6/95	10101	saloon
Gretl Zuckerman	Manchester	24/5/95	09984	saloon
Bob Hayloft	Selby	29/5/95	09999	van
Ade Pixie	Bradford	6/6/95	10037	truck
Rachel Nichols	Leeds	1/7/95	10099	saloon
Rosie Pears	Bradford	27/6/95	10088	sports car
Tyrone Caesar	Leeds	29/5/95	10000	van
Roger Hopkirk	Selby	15/6/95	10094	truck
Victor Flannery	Bradford	30/5/95	10017	truck
Moshe Solomon	Selby	6/6/95	10038	saloon

Task 1
Produce a record card for each of the above items. Each card should be of the same size and the information should be clearly and accurately presented.

Task 2
You are required to file the information according to the following criteria:
- by region
- by product
- by date
- alphabetically according to customer name
- numerically according to invoice number

For each of these you must produce an indexing system which can be cross-referenced with the files. Your tutor will be able to assess the accuracy of your filing for each stage.
(4.3.4)

Sending information
It is important for an organisation to be able to send and receive information quickly and reliably. There are a range of methods which may be used to achieve this. These include:
- Special delivery (such as courier service, Datapost, recorded delivery)
- Post
- Electronic transmission (fax, electronic mail)

The choice of method will depend upon:
- The volume of information
- The type of information (numerical, graphical, textual)
- The confidentiality of the information
- The urgency with which the information is needed
- The cost of sending the information
- The distance covered
- Whether the sender or the receiver has the appropriate equipment

Financial and Administrative Support

ACTIVITY

1 Produce a table listing the advantages and disadvantages of the following methods of sending information:
- Post
- Courier delivery
- Recorded delivery
- Datapost
- Fax
- Email

2 In each of the following circumstances decide which is the most appropriate means of sending information:
(a) A detailed, 100 page report which must arrive the following morning at an organisation 50 miles away
(b) A copy of a map to be sent to a supplier visiting the organisation tomorrow
(c) A letter confirming a meeting to be held next month
(d) A confidential bank reference to be sent to an organisation urgently
(e) A copy of the agenda for a meeting to be held tomorrow to be sent internally and externally
(f) An invoice to a customer in Hong Kong to be paid in two weeks

(4.3.5)

Storing information
Business information can be stored using a variety of methods. These include:
- Paper filing
- Computer files
- Computer backup files

Paper filing of all these methods is the most commonly used. This is because the majority of organisations record information on paper documents (invoices, letters, statements etc.)

Paper documents require storage facilities in order to file them. The records tend to be bulky, and their storage can occupy space which could be used for other purposes. As a result many organisations have introduced a system of storing information on *computer files* instead. Computer software is commonly organised around the notion of a desk with 'documents', 'files', 'folders' and even a 'waste basket'. These are in fact just ideas which make it easy for the user to have a mental picture of how the information is arranged. The data is stored in electronic form. This may be on the hard disk of the computer or on a separate floppy disk. Floppy disks can be stored in drawers and boxes.

Anyone who has had some experience using a computer will quickly learn the advantages of keeping *backup files*. Files on disk can become corrupted. This may be caused by (among other things) a virus (a program which attacks the data), a disk error arising during data input, or physical

Financial and Administrative Support

damage to a floppy disk (we recommend that you do not keep them in your pocket). There is nothing more frustrating than discovering that one's hard work is lost forever. Therefore it is common practice in business organisations to make copies of all essential computer files on a regular basis. In this way, if files are lost the user can return to the most recent copy. A common procedure is referred to as 'grandfather–father–son'. In this case three copies are kept of all relevant files at any one time:

COPY 1   oldest copy   'grandfather'
COPY 2   second oldest copy   'father'
COPY 3   most recent copy   'son'

When a backup copy is made the oldest copy (the grandfather) is deleted and replaced by the most up to date copy (now the new son). This is a double precaution. If there is a fault the user would return to the most recent copy (the son). If there is a fault with these there are still two other copies to fall back on (although more out of date).

ACTIVITY

1 Produce a table showing the advantages and disadvantages of the following methods of filing information:
   - Paper filing
   - Computer files
   - Back-up files
2 Describe the kinds of information which are most suitably stored in each of these ways.

(4.3.5) (4.3.6)

MULTIPLE CHOICE

1 The most effective way of showing sales trends over a period of 20 years would be by:
   A Graph, histogram or bar chart
   B Written report or statement
   C Numerical table
   D Verbal description

2 A memorandum (memo) is:
   A An aid to memory
   B A short informal communication used within an organisation
   C A formal statement kept as a permanent record
   D A detailed report concerning a specific issue

3 After the salutation Dear Mr Peters, it is conventional to close with the expression:
   A Yours truly
   C Yours faithfully
   C Your obedient servant
   D Yours sincerely

4 Files no longer in use which are placed in storage are known as:
   A Stored files
   B Dead files
   C Reserve files
   D Archive files

5 Chronological filing consists of filing in order of:
   A Subject
   B Name
   C Place
   D Date

6 In an alphabetical filing system, correspondence from Carton Food Products Ltd, should be filed under:
   A C
   B F
   C P
   D L

7 A system in which files are kept in pockets hanging from a supporting bar is known as:
   A Lateral filing
   B Suspension filing
   C Horizontal filing
   D Vertical filing

8 Filing consists of arranging and storing records so that they can be:
   A Easily disposed of
   B Re-routed to who requires them
   C Quickly retrieved when needed
   D Retained permanently

9 A system in which documents are filed under the name of customers is known as:
   A Sales filing
   B Purchases filing
   C Alphabetic filing
   D Subject filing

10 In subject filing, documents are arranged:
   A Numerically within date order
   B Alphabetically within topic heading
   C Alphabetically under names
   D Sequentially in numerical order

11 Filing documents according to country or area concerned is known as:
   A Map filing
   B Country filing
   C Geographic filing
   D National filing

12 After the salutation 'Dear Sir' it is permissible to close with the expression(s):
   A Yours sincerely
   B Yours truly
   C Yours faithfully
   D Yours respectively

13 Six copies of an important sales contract are best made by:
A Photo copying
B Ink duplicating
C Spirit duplicating
D Carbon paper

14 A curriculum vitae is a/an:
A Detailed list of the more important subjects studied at school
B Detailed personal record used for job applications used only when formal application forms are not available
C Outline of the pattern of life of a particular individual with detailed reference to leisure pursuits and hobbies
D Formal record including personal details, qualifications, achievements and references

15 The process to be followed in dealing with important documents is that they should be:
A Received, identified, scrutinised, sorted, processed, filed
B Received, sorted, scrutinised, identified, filed, processed
C Received, filed, sorted, scrutinised, identified, filed, destroyed
D Received, scrutinised, sorted, identified, processed, filed

UNIT ACTIVITY

National Financial Advice Services
The National Financial Advice Services (NFAS) provide financial advice and information to small businesses – how to start up a business, where to borrow money, how to cut costs, and so on.

You are employed by the NFAS to design useful leaflets and brochures to help small businesses. There is one area that you realise has not been covered by any existing materials. The business receives lots of enquiries from worried entrepreneurs who have successfully launched their businesses, but have no idea how to record transactions. They say things like: 'I am very good at having great business ideas. But I've got no time for documentation'. Or: 'My accountant flipped her lid when I gave her the shoebox that I use as my finance system'.

What would be extremely useful for all these people would be an information pack that explains how and why business documentation should be maintained. This would need to be user-friendly, easy to read, attractive to look at, informative and well organised.

You decide that you are just the right person to produce a really excellent information pack to fulfil all these requirements. You should remember to include:
- An explanation of the reasons for financial recording *(4.1.1)*
- An explanation of purchase transactions and documents *(4.1.2)*
- An explantion of sales transactions and documents *(4.1.3)*
- An explanation of payments transactions and documents *(4.1.4)*
- An explanation of receipts transactions and documents *(4.1.4)*
- An explanation of the security checks for payment documents *(4.1.5)*
- An explanation of the reasons for the correct completion of documents *(4.2.3)*
- An explanation of the software which may be used to record and monitor financial information *(4.2.4)*
- An explanation of the purpose of routine business documents *(4.3.1)*, including an evaluation of each of these *(4.3.3)*
- A comparison of the methods of processing business documents *(4.3.4)*
- An evaluation of the ways to send and store business information *(4.3.6)*

To be effective the pack must contain completed documents as examples. These should be fully described and explained. You can make up your own examples, or you may choose to use the documents that you completed as part of the Business Furniture Stores (BFS) activity. These should be fully integrated into your information pack and referred to in all the explanations. You will also need other examples to cover documents not included in the BFS activity. *(4.2.1) (4.2.2) (4.3.2)*

Directed study
This requires very carefully planning. You should avoid simply writing a report or long, wordy explanations. Remember that it is an information pack, which may be better as a collection of looseleaf pages. There should be plenty of visual appeal, so that the text is broken up into manageable chunks with diagrams, examples, arrows, colour, pictures etc.

It is important that the examples you use are fully and clearly explained at each stage. It would be no help to a business to find a collection of completed documents with no explanations.

As usual, it is essential that you refer to the original range statements of the performance criteria being assessed. This is vital to ensure that you include all the necessary documents in your information pack.

Guidance to Students on Portfolios

The requirement of the GNVQ programme is that you produce a *portfolio of evidence*. This really only means that you keep all of your assessed course work in one large file (or possibly two).

The portfolio is important because it is on this that you will be assessed. Your portfolio must show evidence of competence for each performance criterion for all:
- Mandatory units
- Option units
- Additional units (if you do any)
- Three core skills units of:
    - communication
    - application of number
    - information technology

Therefore all of your work must be clearly related to the performance criteria. Your tutors will help you with this when they set pieces of work and when the work is assessed.

The evidence may take a number of different forms, including:
- Written reports
- Case studies
- Written records of presentations, role plays, interviews or class discussions
- Photos, video or audio recordings of work produced or activities undertaken

It is also important that all the evidence is carefully indexed.

Guidance to Students on Portfolios

Tracking document for portfolio

		Evidence of competence	*Reference*

Unit 1

1.1	PC1
	PC2
	PC3
1.2	PC1
	PC2
	PC3
	PC4
	PC5
1.3	PC1
	PC2
	PC3
	PC4
	PC5

Unit 2

2.1	PC1
	PC2
	PC3
	PC4
2.2	PC1
	PC2
	PC3
2.3	PC1
	PC2
	PC3

Unit 3

3.1	PC1
	PC2
	PC3
	PC4
	PC5
	PC6
3.2	PC1
	PC2
	PC3
	PC4
	PC5

Guidance to Students on Portfolios

Unit 4

4.1	PC1		
	PC2		
	PC3		
	PC4		
4.2	PC1		
	PC2		
	PC3		
	PC4		
	PC5		
	PC6		
4.3	PC1		
	PC2		
	PC3		
	PC4		
	PC5		
	PC6		
	PC7		
4.4	PC1		
	PC2		
	PC3		
	PC4		
	PC5		

Communication

C2.1	PC1		
	PC2		
	PC3		
	PC4		
C2.2	PC1		
	PC2		
	PC3		
	PC4		
C2.3	PC1		
	PC2		
	PC3		
C2.4	PC1		
	PC2		

ion technology

I2.1	PC1		
	PC2		
	PC3		
	PC4		
	PC5		
I2.2	PC1		
	PC2		
	PC3		
	PC4		
	PC5		
	PC6		
	PC7		
I2.3	PC1		
	PC2		
	PC3		
	PC4		
I2.4	PC1		
	PC2		
	PC3		
	PC4		
	PC5		
I2.5	PC1		
	PC2		
	PC3		
	PC4		

Application of number

N2.1	PC1		
	PC2		
	PC3		
	PC4		
	PC5		
	PC6		
N2.2	PC1		
	PC2		
	PC3		
	PC4		
	PC5		
	PC6		
	PC7		
	PC8		
N2.3	PC1		
	PC2		
	PC3		
	PC4		
	PC5		
	PC6		

Integrated activities

Integrated activity 1: Focus on Business

GNVQ INTERMEDIATE BUSINESS

STUDENT NAME

ACTIVITY TITLE

FOCUS ON BUSINESS
Date Set	
Date Due	
Date Received	

Reference

Tutor

VOCATIONAL UNITS

UNIT 1

	.1	.2	.3	.4	.5	.6	.7	.8
1	O	O	O					
2	O							
3	O							

UNIT 2

	.1	.2	.3	.4	.5	.6	.7	.8
1	O							
2								
3								
4	O	O	O	O				

UNIT 3

	.1	.2	.3	.4	.5	.6	.7	.8
1								
2	O	O	O					
3								
4								

UNIT 4

	.1	.2	.3	.4	.5	.6	.7	.8
1								
2								
3								

OPTION/ADDITIONAL UNIT:

	.1	.2	.3	.4	.5	.6	.7	.8
1								
2								
3								
4								
5								

CORE SKILLS UNITS

COMMUNICATION

	.1	.2	.3	.4	.5	.6	.7	.8
1								
2								
3								
4								

INFORMATION TECHNOLOGY

	.1	.2	.3	.4	.5	.6	.7	.8
1								
2								
3								
4								
5								

APPLICATION OF NUMBER

	.1	.2	.3	.4	.5	.6	.7	.8
1								
2								
3								

O   Assessed

✔   Achieved

✘   Not yet achieved

GRADING   M   D
Theme
1
2
3
4

Background Information

People face major decisions in their lives when looking for work and deciding upon career plans. The purpose of this assessment is to give you an opportunity to review different organisations in your area and at the same time to help you decide which job or career you would like to work towards.

As part of the assessment your tutor will provide you with basic data relating to business organisations. This will include facts, figures, leaflets and company reports on business organisations that are located nearby. Visits and speakers will be arranged and you can supplement this information with your own experience. This may include your experience of working part-time in different organisations or work experience that you have undertaken. You will be expected to collect together the information in order to tackle the tasks listed below.

Scenario

You are employed as a clerical assistant for the Economic Development Unit for the local authority.

Integrated activities

As part of your duties you are taking part in a working party looking at promoting the local area to attract business organisations. The working party has decided to produce a range of promotional materials in order to attract new organisations and employees to the region. The promotional materials may include:
- posters
- leaflets
- handouts
- videos
- information packs
- other appropriate methods and materials

The objective is to raise public awareness for the area and to help develop the economic activity within it. The promotion material should be appealing and interesting, aiming to attract new organisations and employees. It should be professionally produced and the data should be easy to understand.

Task 1

Undertake the necessary research and choose which promotional method you wish to use. Your action plan should include the different types of promotional methods, with associated advantages and disadvantages. It should also state the reasons for choosing a particular method.
(3.2.1, 3.2.2, 3.2.3)

Self-directed study
Produce an action plan outlining what you are going to do. You should include details of which organisations you are going to include in your report, how you are going to contact them and when you expect to receive your replies. It is important to monitor that you are receiving information from sources contacted and that you have a backup plan if the organisations do not reply. Without the information it will prove impossible to complete the tasks.

Your action plan should also include details of information to be researched from the school or college resource centre, the local library and the local authority. The library will have useful publications that you can use. These include:
- *Social Trends*
- *Economic Trends*
- *Annual Abstract of Statistics*

The local authority will also produce useful publications which you can refer to. It is recommended that you write to the local authority for information. In your letter you should explain the purpose of your assignment as the local authority will probably be very interested in your project.

Referring to your action plan make a note of how you are going to proceed with the assignment. Remember to note the resources required and the order of tasks to be tackled.

Task 2

Produce the promotional material, including
- A brief history of the area
- Main characteristics of existing business organisations
- Factors affecting choice of location
- The benefits of moving to the area

The pack should refer to public and private sector organisations including sole traders, partnerships, companies, nationalised industries, and local and national government institutions.
(1.1.2, 1.1.3, 1.2.1)

Task 3

Produce a map of the area illustrating where existing organisations are based and outlining areas where new organisations may locate.
(1.1.3, 1.2.1)

Task 4

Having undertaken your research choose *four* organisations that you would like to research in further detail. Using the organisations as case studies produce a report which outlines:
(i) The classification for each organisation, e.g. sole trader, partnership, company
(ii) Whether each organisation comes under the private or private sector
(iii) The industrial sectors, e.g. primary, secondary, tertiary
(iv) Types of business activity for each organisation
(v) Organisational structures
(vi) Market share

Present the information in written form using suitable visual and written illustrations.
(1.1.1, 1.1.2, 1.1.3, 2.1.1)

Self-directed study
Write to and if possible arrange a visit to your chosen organisations. Make notes before the visits of the things you want to ask and the questions you need answering. Remember to write and thank the organisations for their time.

Task 5

Having researched the four organisations, decide which one you would most like to work for, with reasons. What type of job would you want to do? What qualifications do you need in order to undertake the post? What promotional opportunities are available within that career?
(2.4.1, 2.4.2, 2.4.3, 2.4.4)

Integrated activities

Self-directed study
Remember to include in the evaluation of your action plan a personal career plan for yourself, outlining what you have to do to prepare yourself for your possible future job and in what order.

Your action plan should refer to the fact that you have checked your work with the performance criteria and range statements to ensure that the work fully demonstrates the competencies tested. The work should also be checked for spelling and punctuation errors and reference should be made to this in the action plan too.

Core skills assessed in this activity

Communication level 2

Prepare written material on routine matters
Ensure that all material produced conforms to the necessary standards:
- All the necessary information is included and is wholly accurate
- All documents are legible
- Spelling, grammar and punctuation follow normal conventions
- The format used maximises audience understanding

Use images to illustrate points made in writing and in discussions with a range of people on routine matters
Ensure that all images used:
- Support the main points made
- Provide clear illustration of the points to which they refer
- Are used in the appropriate places

Read and respond to written material and images on routine matters
When using information sources make sure that you:
- Accurately identify the main points being made
- Check the meaning of unfamiliar words, phrases and images

If you use information technology to produce materials and reports you may also use it as evidence for:

Information technology level 2

Select and use formats for presenting information
Ensure that:
- Final version of information is legible, accurate and complete
- Output/final presentation corresponds with requirements
- Waste is minimised during production of hard copy
- Format options are used to create a format which displays the information effectively

Tutor guidance
Students will need to be provided with basic data relating to local business organisations. This may be best organised in conjunction with local career and library services. Visiting speakers from these and other local organisations may be best placed to provide additional help and support.

The activity may be scheduled over a six-week period. Students typically need help throughout the activity, and tutors may wish to request that key sections are reviewed or submitted in stages.

The self-directed study gives some advice on action planning. The importance of action planning cannot be over-stressed and students require constant encouragement and guidance on this.

Integrated activities

Integrated activity 2: Caring for the customer

GNVQ INTERMEDIATE BUSINESS

STUDENT NAME

ACTIVITY TITLE

CARING FOR THE CUSTOMER

Date Set	
Date Due	
Date Received	

Reference

Tutor

VOCATIONAL UNITS

UNIT 1

	.1	.2	.3	.4	.5	.6	.7	.8
1	O	O						
2			O	O				
3								

UNIT 2

	.1	.2	.3	.4	.5	.6	.7	.8
1	O	O	O	O				
2								
3								
4								

UNIT 3

	.1	.2	.3	.4	.5	.6	.7	.8
1			O					
2								
3	O	O			O	O		
4		O		O				

UNIT 4

	.1	.2	.3	.4	.5	.6	.7	.8
1								
2								
3								

OPTION/ADDITIONAL UNIT:

	.1	.2	.3	.4	.5	.6	.7	.8
1								
2								
3								
4								
5								

CORE SKILLS UNITS

COMMUNICATION

	.1	.2	.3	.4	.5	.6	.7	.8
1								
2								
3								
4								

INFORMATION TECHNOLOGY

	.1	.2	.3	.4	.5	.6	.7	.8
1								
2								
3								
4								
5								

APPLICATION OF NUMBER

	.1	.2	.3	.4	.5	.6	.7	.8
1								
2								
3								

O   Assessed

✔   Achieved

✘   Not yet achieved

GRADING   M   D
Theme
1
2
3
4

Background

Customer service is the key to a successful business, and employers are becoming increasingly aware of this. In particular employers realise the need to:
(i) Identify the needs of customers
(ii) Provide a quality service promptly and efficiently
(iii) Deal with customer queries and complaints
(iv) Communicate customer protection using appropriate methods

Organisations are recognising that customers have rights and employers have obligations to fulfil those rights. Citizens' and customers' charters aim to promote the interests of the consumer by outlining what their rights are.

The purpose of this assignment is to look at the privatisation of British Rail and to identify whether privatisation will improve the quality of services.

Scenario

You are employed by British Rail and have been given the responsibility of researching proposed changes to the railway industry following the plans for privatisation.

Integrated activities

Self-directed study

Produce an action plan detailing the process that you are going to follow in order to tackle the assignment.

Visit your resource centre and local library in order to find as many different articles relating to the planned privatisation of the railway industry. In addition, try to obtain a copy of *The Citizen's Charter* (published by HMSO, PO Box 276, London SW8 5DT, Tel. 0171 873 9090).

Task 1

In a discussion document (a structured written account) compare and contrast the roles and objectives of British Rail as it has been in the public sector, and as it will be (or is) in the private sector.
(1.1.2, 1.1.3)

Task 2

Produce a table listing the arguments for and against nationalisation.
(1.1.2, 1.1.3)

Task 3

Produce a table listing the arguments for and against privatisation.
(1.1.2, 1.1.3)

Task 4

Identify an organisational chart for a nationalised industry and a privatised organisation, showing the structure and functions for the two business organisations. How does the process of decision-making differ for the two examples?
(2.1.1, 2.1.2, 2.1.3, 2.1.4)

Task 5

Using a copy of the Citizen's Charter summarise the main features of the:
- Passenger's charter
- Compensation schemes
- Published standards

```
Keybrook
4 French Tabard Way
Wallington
Sussex

28 July

Dear Sir,

I am writing to complain about a recent train journey which I undertook between
London and Carlisle on 12 July.

I was attending an interview in Carlisle and therefore decided to take the night
sleeper in order that I could arrive in good time. The cost of the ticket was
£80, which I booked by credit card. The train left on time and I went to sleep at
about 22.00. Throughout the night I kept waking up because the train appeared to
be making funny noises and did not appear to be moving. The guard continued to
reassure me that all was all right.

The following morning I arose and got dressed ready for the interview. Imagine my
shock when I pulled open the curtains to find that the train was in Milton Keynes
station. The time was 9.00, and my interview was planned for 10.00 in Carlisle!
No mention had been made during the night or in the morning about the problems
which had resulted in this situation. Nor did I get an apology from the guard.

Needless to say I was very late for my appointment and I didn't get the job. I
therefore feel most strongly that I am entitled to a refund plus compensation for
loss of earnings from the job I didn't get. I also want an apology in writing and
a reassurance that the situation will not happen again.

I look forward to your reply.

Yours faithfully,

Christina Andrew (Ms)
```

- Performance incentives for staff

Analyse how effective the organisation is in meeting these standards now.

What effect does privatisation have on these features, and why?

(3.3.1, 3.3.2, 3.3.5)

Task 6

Identify the level of demand for the service and try to analyse whether demand increases or falls following privatisation. Give reasons for your decision.
(1.2.3, 1.2.4, 3.1.3)

Task 7

Produce a customer questionnaire which can be used to monitor customer satisfaction and identify what improvements can be implemented
(3.4.2, 3.4.4)

Task 8

The letter on the previous page has been received by your regional office of British Rail. You are required to explain in a memo the action you would take and draft a reply to the customer.
(3.3.4)

Self-directed study

The questionnaire needs careful thought. It is not good enough to simply write down questions as they occur to you. Ask yourself:
- What am I trying to find out?
- What do I need to know?
- Is this question too technical, too personal, pointless, ambiguous?
- Is the sequence of questions logical?

Try your questionnaire out on your colleagues as a pilot run. Record your findings in the action plan and amend the questionnaire if necessary.

Make sure that you constantly check with the performance criteria and range statements to ensure that your work fully demonstrates the competencies tested. Where appropriate indicate in your work the number of the performance criteria you are attempting to meet.

Revise and amend your action plan as you progress.

Core skills assessed in this activity

Communication level 2

Prepare written material on routine matters
Ensure that all material produced conforms to the necessary standards:
- All the necessary information is included and is wholly accurate
- All documents are legible
- Spelling, grammar and punctuation follow normal conventions
- The format used maximises audience understanding

Use images to illustrate points made in writing and in discussions with a range of people on routine matters
Ensure that all images used:
- Support the main points made
- Provide clear illustration of the points to which they refer
- Are used in the appropriate places

Read and respond to written material and images on routine matters
When using information sources make sure that you:
- Accurately identify the main points being made
- Check the meaning of unfamiliar words, phrases and images

If you use information technology to produce materials and reports you may also use it as evidence for:

Information technology level 2

Select and use formats for presenting information
Ensure that:
- Final version of information is legible, accurate and complete
- Output/final presentation corresponds with requirements
- Waste is minimised during production of hard copy
- Format options are used to create a format which displays the information effectively (I 2.3.4)

Tutor Guidance
At the time of writing the privatisation of British Rail existed only as a proposal. This activity will still be appropriate following actual privatisation.

Integrated activities

Integrated activity 3: Willing workers

Background

As part of your programme you will be expected to complete work experience within a local organisation. Having returned from your placement you will be asked to produce an information pack, which should include:
- Background to the organisation
- Information about employers and employees
- An organisation chart
- The type of industry/sector which the organisation operates within
- Your experiences of the placement

Task 1

Produce a variety of information sheets which describe the organisation's business activities. You will be expected to show that you have a clear understanding of how the organisation has developed and the type of market within which it operates. In particular your pack should include:
- The purpose of the business organisation *(1.1.2)*
- The industrial sector within which it operates *(1.1.1)*
- Size of the market, i.e. local, national or international *(1.2.3)*
- The type of business organisation, i.e. sole trader, partnership, company etc. *(1.1.3)*
- Whether it comes under the private or public sector *(1.1.2)*

Integrated activities

Self-directed study
Produce an action plan identifying how you are going to tackle the assessment. Remember to list the jobs to be done, research to be undertaken, resources needed and your time-scales. Make sure you constantly check with the performance criteria and range statements to ensure that your work fully demonstrates the competencies tested. Where appropriate indicate where you feel each performance criterion has been covered. Revise your action plan as you progress through your work.

Task 2

When you attend your placement, identify as many different examples as you can that illustrate that the organisation cares about its customers. You should also identify how the organisation monitors customer satisfaction. *(3.4.2)*

Can you suggest ways in which the company can improve its customer service? *(3.4.3, 3.4.4)*

Undertake some research and try to identify the different types of legal protection that exist to protect customers. Produce a table that summarises the results of your research. Produce a leaflet that could be given to customers to inform them of their rights as a consumer. *(3.3.4, 3.3.6)*

Self-directed study
You need to include in your action plan the sources you are going to use to collect the relevant information. You may also find it useful to keep a diary when on work experience, which you can refer to when completing the assignment.

Task 3

Include in your information pack different examples of how the organisation markets and advertises its product or service. Write a short summary saying whether you think the methods they use are effective and why. Remember the four Ps and the marketing mix when completing this task. *(3.2.1)*

Self-directed study
When on placement try to interview the member of staff who is responsible for marketing. Leaflets, brochures and advertisements can also be collected to help you with the work.

Task 4

During your placement try to interview a number of different staff who have key roles to play within the organisation. For each person interviewed, produce a job description and job specification based upon their job and responsibilities. *(2.3.1, 2.3.3, 2.3.4, 2.3.5)*

Self-directed study
Make notes of the questions which you want to ask before you interview the staff and write up your results as soon after the interview as is possible so that the ideas are still fresh in your mind.

Task 5

Draw a floor plan of the department in which you were working and indicate the layout of furniture, people, windows and doors. To what extent did the layout of the department meet with health and safety requirements? Produce a leaflet which can be given to all staff outlining the man features of relevant employment legislation, e.g. Health and Safety at Work Act, Equal Pay Act, Sex Discrimination Act. *(2.2.3, 2.2.4)*

Self-directed study
You may find it easier to draw a rough sketch of the floor plan when you are on placement, as you may find it difficult to remember the layout when you return to college or school. You can always produce a neater copy at a later date. Remember to refer to textbooks, leaflets and relevant journals to find the up-to-date employment legislation.

Task 6

Identify the different types of technological systems used within the organisation. Remember to distinguish between hardware and software. To what extent does the new technology improve the efficiency of the organisation?

Core skills assessed in this activity

Communication level 2

Prepare written material on routine matters
Ensure that all material produced conforms to the necessary standards:
- All the necessary information is included and is wholly accurate
- All documents are legible
- Spelling, grammar and punctuation follow normal conventions
- The format used maximises audience understanding

Use images to illustrate points made in writing and in discussions with a range of people on routine matters
Ensure that all images used:
- Support the main points made
- Provide clear illustration of the points to which they refer
- Are used in the appropriate places

Integrated activities

Read and respond to written material and images on routine matters
When using information sources make sure that you:
- Accurately identify the main points being made
- Check the meaning of unfamiliar words, phrases and images

If you use information technology to produce materials and reports you may also use it as evidence for:

Information technology level 2

Select and use formats for presenting information
Ensure that:
- Final version of information is legible, accurate and complete
- Output/final presentation corresponds with requirements
- Waste is minimised during production of hard copy
- Format options are used to create a format which displays the information effectively

Integrated activities

Integrated activity 4: Background to business

GNVQ INTERMEDIATE BUSINESS

STUDENT NAME

ACTIVITY TITLE: *BACKGROUND TO BUSINESS*

Date Set	
Date Due	
Date Received	

Reference

Tutor

VOCATIONAL UNITS

UNIT 1

	.1	.2	.3	.4	.5	.6	.7	.8
1	O		O					
2	O		O	O				
3	O	O						

UNIT 2

	.1	.2	.3	.4	.5	.6	.7	.8
1	O	O						
2								
3								
4								

UNIT 3

	.1	.2	.3	.4	.5	.6	.7	.8
1		O						
2	O		O	O				
3								
4								

UNIT 4

	.1	.2	.3	.4	.5	.6	.7	.8
1								
2								
3								

OPTION/ADDITIONAL UNIT:

	.1	.2	.3	.4	.5	.6	.7	.8
1								
2								
3								
4								
5								

CORE SKILLS UNITS

COMMUNICATION

	.1	.2	.3	.4	.5	.6	.7	.8
1								
2								
3								
4								

INFORMATION TECHNOLOGY

	.1	.2	.3	.4	.5	.6	.7	.8
1								
2								
3								
4								
5								

APPLICATION OF NUMBER

	.1	.2	.3	.4	.5	.6	.7	.8
1								
2								
3								

O Assessed

✔ Achieved

✘ Not yet achieved

GRADING M D
Theme
1
2
3
4

Introduction

The purpose of this assignment is to give you an opportunity to research local business organisations and to prepare an exhibition based upon your results. The exhibition will be for interested parents and business employers from the local community, and will reflect the quality of work students at school or college are capable of producing.

Task 1

In a group of three or four, undertake the necessary research to find out about local business organisations. You are expected to identify:

- The different types of business in the area *(1.1.3)*
- The products produced and services provided by local business *(1.2.4)*
- The types of markets which the organisations serve *(1.2.3)*
- The industrial sectors which the organisations represent *(1.1.1)*
- The scope of the markets in terms of local, national or international *(1.2.3)*
- The reasons for the location of the organisations *(1.2.1)*

Divide the tasks between your group for the most effective completion of the task. As you gather together your information, remember to arrange and index it in a file. Your tutor will check your progress each week.

Integrated activities

Task 2

Having undertaken your group research it is now important for each group member to select an organisation which is locally based or has a branch in the locality. Write a letter to the organisation requesting information on all aspects of the business. This should include:
- When they started trading
- The goods or services produced *(1.2.4)*
- Where they are located
- How the organisation is structured *(2.1.1, 2.1.2)*
- Characteristics of the customers *(3.1.2)*
- How the organisation markets its products or services *(3.2.1)*

Task 3

Undertake research into government assistance which is available to local businesses in the UK, the kind of aid available, how businesses qualify for it and whether businesses in your local area receive it. Include this information in your file. *(1.2.1)*

Task 4

Produce a map which shows the transport and communication links for the local area. How does the area link with the rest of the UK, Europe and the world? *(1.2.1)*

Task 5

The characteristics of the local working population are an important part of business activity and the location of organisations. Undertake the necessary research to identify:
- The level of unemployment for the area *(1.3.1)*
- The types of skills available *(1.3.1)*
- The main features of the workforce *(1.3.2)*

Task 6

Having completed all of your research, both individually and as part of a team, it is now important to prepare the material ready for the formal exhibition. Produce a checklist of materials and methods which could be used and give reason for choosing the methods used. *(3.2.3, 3.2.4)*

Having decided the methods to be used, prepare the materials. *(3.2.3, 3.2.4)*

Task 7

Write to local employers, parents and guardians and invite them to the exhibition. Remember to thank the employers for their help too.

Self-directed study

It is important to have a clear action plan in order to prioritise the tasks that need to be undertaken. This means that you should:
- Read through the assignment to determine exactly what you need to do in order to satisfy the requirements.
- Check with the performance criteria and range statements for further guidance on what you must do.
- Break the tasks down into manageable targets;
- Order the targets in the most logical sequence, putting any first which must be completed as soon as possible (sending for information, for example).
- Set yourself realistic dates and deadlines for each target.

The need to make an action plan becomes even more obvious when you are working in a group.

Core skills assessed in this activity

Communication level 2

Prepare written material on routine matters
Ensure that all material produced conforms to the necessary standards:
- All the necessary information is included and is wholly accurate
- All documents are legible
- Spelling, grammar and punctuation follow normal conventions
- The format used maximises audience understanding

Use images to illustrate points made in writing and in discussions with a range of people on routine matters
Ensure that all images used:
- Support the main points made
- Provide clear illustration of the points to which they refer
- Are used in the appropriate places

Read and respond to written material and images on routine matters
When using information sources make sure that you:
- Accurately identify the main points being made
- Check the meaning of unfamiliar words, phrases and images

If you use information technology to produce materials and reports you may also use it as evidence for:

Information technology level 2

Select and use formats for presenting information
Ensure that:
- Final version of information is legible, accurate and complete
- Output/final presentation corresponds with requirements
- Waste is minimised during production of hard copy
- Format options are used to create a format which displays the information effectively

Integrated activities

Integrated activity 5: People and places

Background

The aim of this activity is to undertake research into business organisations and examine and compare organisational structures and functions. The assignment will focus on your educational institution, as this will enable you to get a detailed insight into how the organisation operates and the roles and responsibilties of the people in it.

Task 1

Identify the main aims of your school or college, and the type of service offered. *(1.1.2)*

Task 2

On a map, identify where the institution is located and the catchment area from which students and pupils come to school or college. *(1.2.1, 1.2.2, 1.2.3)*

Task 3

Looking at the range of courses, programmes and training offered, identify examples where the organisation is introducing new courses as a result of changes in the market. Make a note of types of customers for which these new courses are aimed. *(3.3.1)*

Integrated activities

Task 4

Research the organisational structures for the institution and present the information using an appropriate format. *(2.1.2)*

Task 5

Analyse the relationships within the organisational chart, illustrating the different chains of command, functions and spans of control that exist. *(2.1.3, 2.1.4)*

Task 6

Choose a particular department or section of the school or college, and research the job roles within that section in detail. Produce a brief description of the main job roles. *(2.3.2)*

Task 7

Interview an employee working within that department to find out the roles and responsibilities associated with that position. In particular, you are interested in:
- Job title
- Main duties and responsibilities
- Span of control
- Typical working hours
- The name and job title of the person's line manager

From the information, produce the job description/specification for that particular role, and present your findings in an oral presentation to other members of your group. *(2.3.3, 2.3.4)*

Task 8

Evaluate the level of customer service offered to the customers of the institution (who are the customers?). In particular, identify:
- Customer needs *(3.3.1)*
- The procedure for dealing with customer queries and complaints *(3.3.3)*
- The process for monitoring customer satisfaction *(3.4.2)*
- How the service might be improved (in line with the provisions of the Student Charter, where appropriate) *(3.4.3, 3.4.4)*

Task 9

Produce promotional materials which can be used to promote your educational institution to the community. Give reasons for your choice of methods and materials used. *(3.2.3, 3.2.4, 3.2.5)*

Core skills assessed in this activity

Communication level 2

Take part in discussions with a range of people on routine matters
Ensure that in discussions and oral presentations that your contributions:
- Clear and appropriate to the subject matter
- Made in a tone and manner suited to the audience

Ensure that contributions made by others are:
- Listened to attentively
- Checked and confirmed for understanding

Prepare written material on routine matters
Ensure that all material produced conforms to the necessary standards:
- All the necessary information is included and is wholly accurate
- All documents are legible
- Spelling, grammar and punctuation follow normal conventions
- The format used maximises audience understanding

Use images to illustrate points made in writing and in discussions with a range of people on routine matters
Ensure that all images used:
- Support the main points made
- Provide clear illustration of the points to which they refer
- Are used in the appropriate places

Read and respond to written material and images on routine matters
When using information sources make sure that you:
- Accurately identify the main points being made
- Check the meaning of unfamiliar words, phrases and images

If you use information technology to produce materials and reports you may also use it as evidence for:

Information technology level 2

Select and use formats for presenting information
Ensure that:
- Final version of information is legible, accurate and complete
- Output/final presentation corresponds with requirements
- Waste is minimised during production of hard copy
- Format options are used to create a format which displays the information effectively

Integrated activities

Integrated activity 6: Entering employment

GNVQ INTERMEDIATE BUSINESS

STUDENT NAME

ACTIVITY TITLE

ENTERING EMPLOYMENT	
Date Set	
Date Due	
Date Received	

Reference

Tutor

VOCATIONAL UNITS

UNIT 1

	.1	.2	.3	.4	.5	.6	.7	.8
1								
2								
3	O	O		O				

UNIT 2

	.1	.2	.3	.4	.5	.6	.7	.8
1					O			
2			O	O				
3			O	O				
4	O	O	O	O	O			

UNIT 3

	.1	.2	.3	.4	.5	.6	.7	.8
1								
2								
3								
4								

UNIT 4

	.1	.2	.3	.4	.5	.6	.7	.8
1								
2								
3								

OPTION/ADDITIONAL UNIT:

	.1	.2	.3	.4	.5	.6	.7	.8
1								
2								
3								
4								
5								

CORE SKILLS UNITS

COMMUNICATION

	.1	.2	.3	.4	.5	.6	.7	.8
1								
2								
3								
4								

INFORMATION TECHNOLOGY

	.1	.2	.3	.4	.5	.6	.7	.8
1								
2								
3								
4								
5								

APPLICATION OF NUMBER

	.1	.2	.3	.4	.5	.6	.7	.8
1								
2								
3								

O Assessed

✔ Achieved

✗ Not yet achieved

GRADING   M   D
Theme
1
2
3
4

Background

The purpose of this activity is to investigate different *(4.2.2)* types of jobs from the local papers, and to develop within you the necessary skills for seeking employment. It is important to remember when seeking work that an employer will always recognise the importance of qualifications. This activity will enable you to identify the different types of jobs and their corresponding roles, responsibilities and salary appropriate for an employee with a business qualification at different levels.

Task 1

Look in your local and national newspapers and cut out job advertisements which a student could apply for having successfully completed:
(i) A Business GNVQ at Intermediate level
(ii) A Business GNVQ at Advanced level
(iii) A Business HND
You should aim to collect at least *four* adverts for *each* of the above.

The jobs selected should include different functions and job roles in both the private and public sectors. *(2.4.1, 2.4.2, 2.4.3)*

Integrated activities

Task 2

From the information identify how the tasks undertaken by each of the job-holders differ. What important conclusions can you draw? *(2.3.3, 2.3.4)*

Task 3

For each of the jobs for which an Intermediate student might apply, write a short job description and personnel specification based upon the advertisement and further research of your own. Choose one of the jobs and write a letter of application for the vacancy, enclosing a CV. A mock interview will be arranged for you by your tutors in order to establish the nature of the job and the skills and expertise which you could offer. *(2.3.3, 2.3.4, 2.4.4, 2.4.5)*

Background

When looking for employment it is important to be aware of the types of jobs within your area locally and nationally.

Task 4

Referring to *Economic and Social Trends*, undertake detailed investigation into the UK employment market comparing *three* regions or areas. In particular, for each region you should look for:
- Types and features of employment *(1.3.1, 1.3.2)*
- The levels of employment *(1.3.2)*

This information should be presented using appropriate diagrammatical methods. *(1.3.4)*

Background

An important influence on the UK employment market is the effect of new technology. Many employees have found their jobs have changed considerably, or even disappeared altogether, as a result of automation. Another major influence on business practice is legislation, which seeks to protect both the employee and the employer within the changing work environment.

Task 5

Identify an industry where new technology has been introduced, and explain how the jobs have changed as a result. *(2.1.5)*

Task 6

Identify relevant employment legislation which aims to protect the rights of employees, as well as placing responsibilities on them. Present this information in the form of an employee handbook. *(2.2.3, 2.2.4)*

Core skills assessed in this activity

Communication level 2

Take part in discussions with a range of people on routine matters
Ensure that in discussions and oral presentations that your contributions:
- Clear and appropriate to the subject matter
- Made in a tone and manner suited to the audience

Ensure that contributions made by others are:
- Listened to attentively
- Checked and confirmed for understanding

Prepare written material on routine matters
Ensure that all material produced conforms to the necessary standards:
- All the necessary information is included and is wholly accurate
- All documents are legible
- Spelling, grammar and punctuation follow normal conventions
- The format used maximises audience understanding

Use images to illustrate points made in writing and in discussions with a range of people on routine matters
Ensure that all images used:
- Support the main points made
- Provide clear illustration of the points to which they refer
- Are used in the appropriate places

Read and respond to written material and images on routine matters
When using information sources make sure that you:
- Accurately identify the main points being made
- Check the meaning of unfamiliar words, phrases and images

If you use information technology to produce materials and reports you may also use it as evidence for:

Information technology level 2

Select and use formats for presenting information
Ensure that:
- Final version of information is legible, accurate and complete
- Output/final presentation corresponds with requirements
- Waste is minimised during production of hard copy
- Format options are used to create a format which displays the information effectively

Integrated activities

Integrated activity 7: Geared up for sport

Background

The leisure industry is one of the fastest growing in the world economy. Many famous organisations, such as Reebok, Nike, Adidas and Umbro, have established themselves to meet the needs of customers seeking sports gear. The purpose of this assignment is to research a number of the leading organisations in the leisure industry in detail and to produce a written report and a marketing display. Focus is given to customer care, which is an area that is causing problems for Proactive Sports.

Scenario

You have been hired as a consultant by Proactive Sports, a medium-sized producer of sports gear. They are keen to found out about their main competitors and ask you to investigate the market.

Task 1

You are required to carry out research into the main organisations in the leisure industry and produce a formal report which takes into account the following requirements:
- Name the organisations that you chose to research and identify the products which the business produces. *(1.2.4)*

Integrated activities

- Identify the characteristics of the consumers who purchase the products. *(3.1.2)*
- Identify the recent trends in consumer demand for sportswear, quoting examples. *(3.1.3)*
- Identify the factors which influence the demand for sports gear. *(3.1.2, 3.1.5)*
- Identify how new products have been introduced to meet changing demand. *(3.1.5)*
- Make recommendations to the managers of Proactive Sports as to the best way they might respond to future changes in the leisure market

Task 2

Proactive Sports have asked you to produce a display promoting a range of sports gear available to customers *(3.2.3, 3.2.5)*. You should assume that Proactive Sports produce a wide range of sportswear and equipment. Your action plan prior to producing the display should identify:

- The types of promotional materials which could be used, and their associated advantages and disadvantages *(3.2.1, 3.2.2)*
- The type of promotion chosen, giving reasons *(3.2.4)*
- Resources required to produce the promotion *(3.2.3)*
- The different forms of media which could be used to help promote the products *(3.2.3)*

You should make recommendations as to where the display could be located for maximum effect.

Task 3

The finance department of Proactive Sports has received a number of complaints from customers. When you investigate the situation you discover that the financial records are badly disorganised. Customers are complaining because they are being billed too much or for the wrong goods. Frequently orders are not processed, or the wrong goods are delivered, or the wrong prices charged.

Your job as the consultant is to make suggestions as to how the finance department can be reorganised to reduce the chance of these mistakes, and thereby improve customer service. In a short formal report:

- Explain the reasons for financial recording in business organisations *(4.1.1, 4.3.1)*
- Explain purchase transactions and documents, sales transactions and documents, payment transactions and documents *(4.4.1)*, and receipt transactions and documents *(4.1.2, 4.1.3, 4.1.4)*
- Explain the security checks for payment documents *(4.1.5)*

Task 4

Working within Proactive Sports you have been asked to put together a training programme which can be used with new and existing employees to improve the quality of the customer service provided. The training programme can take any format. It may be an informative video, a booklet, a range of posters, or a staff training session. You should ensure that the training programme incorporates the following aspects:

- Reasons to meet customer needs *(3.1.1, 3.4.1)*
- How to identify customer needs *(3.4.2)*
- How to communicate effectively with customers *(3.3.3)*
- The importance of high-quality service, including the relevant legal requirements *(3.3.6)*
- The process for dealing with customer queries and complaints *(3.3.2)*

Core skills assessed in this activity

Communication level 2

Prepare written material on routine matters
Ensure that all material produced conforms to the necessary standards:
- All the necessary information is included and is wholly accurate
- All documents are legible
- Spelling, grammar and punctuation follow normal conventions
- The format used maximises audience understanding

Use images to illustrate points made in writing and in discussions with a range of people on routine matters
Ensure that all images used:
- Support the main points made
- Provide clear illustration of the points to which they refer
- Are used in the appropriate places

Read and respond to written material and images on routine matters
When using information sources make sure that you:
- Accurately identify the main points being made
- Check the meaning of unfamiliar words, phrases and images

If your training programme is presented as a training session it may be used as evidence for:

Take part in discussions with a range of people on routine matters
Ensure that in discussions and oral presentations that your contributions:
- Clear and appropriate to the subject matter
- Made in a tone and manner suited to the audience

Ensure that contributions made by others are:
- Listened to attentively
- Checked and confirmed for understanding

If you use information technology to produce materials and reports you may also use it as evidence for:

Integrated activities

Information technology level 2

Select and use formats for presenting information
Ensure that:
- Final version of information is legible, accurate and complete
- Output/final presentation corresponds with requirements
- Waste is minimised during production of hard copy
- Format options are used to create a format which displays the information effectively

Glossary of Terms

Action planning
The process of breaking tasks down into manageable targets, prioritising these targets in order of importance, and the setting of clearly defined deadlines for each target. Evidence of action planning is required to achieve grades of Merit or Distinction.

Additional units
Extra units which may be taken in addition to the minimum required number of units, which for Intermediate level is as follows:
4 Mandatory units
2 Optional units
3 Core skills of:
   Application of number
   Communication
   Information technology
Additional units allow students to study areas of particular interest and increase the value of their GNVQ. *Note*: Additional units do not contribute to the final grade.

Awarding body
Those organisations which are approved by the National Council for Vocational Qualifications (NCVQ) to award GNVQs. At present there are three such bodies:
BTEC
RSA
City and Guilds
All awarding bodies offer the same Core skills and Mandatory units. However, they offer different Optional and Additional units, and set their own external tests.

Core skills
Units of competence which relate to key areas of expertise. There are three mandatory (i.e. compulsory) core skill units:
Application of number
Communication
Information technology
There are three additional core skill units:
Working with others
Improve own learning and performance
Problem solving
Evidence for Core Skill Units should be collected in the Portfolio of Evidence and mapped against the unit specifications.

Elements
The main subheadings of a GNVQ unit. For example, Unit 1: Business Organisations and Employment, is broken down into three elements:
1.1 Explain the purposes and types of private and public sector business organisations
1.2 Investigate business organisations and products
1.3 Investigate the UK employment market

External tests
One-hour multiple choice tests set by the awarding body, to assess understanding of the underpinning knowledge of Mandatory units. Opportunities to sit these tests occur several times each year, and students may repeat tests if necessary until they are successful. *Note*: only 3 Mandatory units at Intermediate level are tested, namely Unit 1, Unit 2 and Unit 4.

Grading criteria
The standards against which student work is assessed at Merit or Distinction grades. In order to achieve these grades, evidence against the following grading themes is required:
- Drawing up plans of action
- Monitoring courses of action
- Identifying information needs
- Identifying and using sources to obtain information
- Evaluating outcomes and justifying approaches
- Synthesis
- Command of 'language'

Not all work needs to be graded. Smaller, in-class activities do not lend themselves to action planning and review, and therefore it would be difficult to attribute any grades. Evidence which is simply judged to show competence against a performance criterion may be included in the portfolio of evidence. In order to achieve a Merit grade for the award, at least one third of the portfolio of evidence must contain work of a Merit standard. In order to achieve a Distinction grade for the award, at least one third of the portfolio of evidence must contain work of a Distinction standard. Additional units do not count towards final grades.

Mandatory units
The compulsory vocational units of competence. For Intermediate Business these are:
Unit 1   Business organisations and employment
Unit 2   People in business organisations
Unit 3   Consumers and customers
Unit 4   Financial and administrative support for business

Glossary of terms

Optional units
The vocational units from which students must select at least two at Intermediate level. The Optional units available varies between different awarding bodies.

Performance criteria (or PCs)
Statements of competence which the student must demonstrate in order to achieve the award. Each unit is broken down into a number of elements, which are in turn broken down into performance criteria. They are written in such a way that they can be evidenced by student work. For example, Element 1.1 from Unit 1 is broken down into three performance criteria, as follows:
1.1.1 Describe developments in industrial sectors
1.1.2 Explain the purposes of business organisations
1.1.3 Explain the differences between different types of business ownership
1.1.4 Explain the operation of one business organisation

Portfolio of evidence
The total evidence of a student's work submitted for the GNVQ award. The portfolio must satisfy a number of requirements:
(i) It must be *complete* – there must be evidence for every performance criterion for every element for each unit across the entire range
(ii) It must be *referenced* – evidence must be matched against the unit specifications and clearly indexed
(iii) It must be *authentic* – the evidence must be the work of the student and no one else
(iv) It must be *assessed* – all work submitted must be assessed by a tutor to determine whether it meets the performance criteria and whether it should be graded at a Merit or a Distinction level, where appropriate.

Evidence may include:
- Written reports
- Records of oral presentations and interviews
- Photographs of work produced
- Video tapes and audio recordings
- Computer-generated work
- Case studies
- Short answer exercises

Range statements
Statements which define the breadth of evidence required for the porfolio of evidence. For example, the range statements for performance criterion 1.1.1, *purposes of different types of business organisation are explained*, are as follows:

Purposes: profit-making, public service, charitable
Types of business organisation: sole trader, partnership, private limited company, public limited company, cooperative, franchise, charitable, state-owned industry or service, local government

The evidence for the student portfolio must cover the entire range, although it may well be provided by several different pieces of work.

Unit specifications
A complete description of the content of a unit, broken down into elements and performance criteria with precise statements of range.

Vocational units
The general name given to units with a knowledge content. This refers to all units apart from the core skills, i.e. Mandatory, Optional and Additional units.

Solutions

Unit test answers

Unit 1
1 B
2 C
3 C
4 B
5 A
6 C
7 A
8 D
9 C
10 A
11 A
12 B
13 B
14 D
15 A
16 A
17 C
18 D
19 B
20 B
21 D
22 B
23 B
24 D
25 C
26 D
27 C
28 A
29 A
30 A

Unit 2
1 B
2 D
3 B
4 A
5 C
6 A
7 B
8 A
9 C
10 A
11 C
12 B
13 D
14 C
15 C
16 D
17 C
18 B
19 C
20 C
21 D
22 D
23 D
24 B
25 A
26 A
27 B
28 C
29 C
30 D
31 C
32 D
33 B
34 A
35 B
36 D
37 C

Unit 3
1 B
2 A
3 C
4 D
5 A
6 A
7 C
8 B
9 A
10 A
11 B
12 C
13 A
14 C
15 B
16 D
17 D
18 B
19 A
20 D
21 C
22 B
23 A
24 A
25 D
26 A
27 C
28 A
29 B
30 C
31 D
32 C
33 A

Unit 4
No unit test

Index

ACAS Advisory, Conciliation and Arbitration Service   108
Achieving targets   125–6
Administration function   90–1
  job roles   120–1
Advice note   232, 250–1
Appraisal of staff   88
Authorisation of orders   245
Autocratic leadership style   79

Bank statement   244
Bar charts   60–1
Batch production   84
Budgeting   89
Bulk increasing   26
Bulk-reducing   26
Business, definition   1–2

Careers office   127
Cash discount   230
Cash payments   236
Centralised working arrangements   75–6
  compared with decentralised arrangements   76
Chain of command   78
Charities   5, 12–14, 128
Cheque guarantee card   235
Cheques   234–6, 243, 253–4, 256
  crossings   235
Circular organisation structure   74
Citizen's Charter   198
Collective bargaining   103
Companies Act   8
Computer-based media   167
Consumables   34
Consumer protection legislation   154, 196
Consumers, definition   138
Contract of employment   43, 47, 77, 88, 101–2, 106
Contract of Sale   193–4
Cooperatives   9–10
Credit cards   236–8
Credit transactions   225, 239–40
Curriculum Vitae CV   86
Customer care   175–6
Customer needs   172–80
Customer queries and complaints   190–1
Customer service   206–15
Customers, definition   138

Data Protection Act   196–7
Debit cards   238–9
Decentralised working arrangements   76
  compared with centralised arrangements   76
Decision-making (see also Leadership styles)   123
Deductions from pay   240–1
Delegation   124
Delivery note   232–3, 250–1
Demand for goods and services   138–47
  changes in demand   147–9
Democratic leadership style   79
Departments in organisations   81–94
  summary of main responsibilities   94
Design and production function   81–4
  job roles   117–18
Despatch note   232
Directors   114–15
Disabled Persons (Employment) Act   108
Disciplinary procedures   88, 103–4, 105
Discount:
  Cash   230
  Trade   230
Distribution function   93
  job roles   122–3
Division of labour   43–4
Drawer, definition   234
Durables   34

E-mail   56
Employee and employer rights and responsibilities   99–111
Employment   39–63
  and self-employment   126–30
Employment Protection Act   88
Endorsements   235
Equal opportunities   108, 110–1
Equal Pay Act   110
Exclusion clauses   194–5

Fax   55
Filing data   260–2
Finance function   89–90
  job roles   119–20
Flat organisation structure   73–4

compared with hierarchical structures   74
Flexi-time   76
Flow production   84
Footloose organisations   27
Franchise   10–12
Fringe benefits   100
Functional relationships   114

Goods and services   224
Goods received note   229, 249
Grievance procedures   88
Gross domestic product   19–20
Guarantees and warrantees   197–8

Health and Safety   101, 104, 107, 109–10, 193
Hierarchical organisation structure   73
  compared with flat structures   74
Home-working   77

Income Tax   48, 240
Industrial sectors   18–20
Industrial tribunal   99–100
Internal customers   170
Interviewing   86–7
Invoice
  Purchase   229, 249–50
  Sales   233, 250–1

Job centres   127
Job description   86
Job production   84
Job roles   114–26
Job sharing   42
Just-in-time purchasing   84

Leadership styles   78–9
Lens-based media   166
Letter of application   86
Letters   186–7, 259
Limited liability company   8–9
Line charts   60
Line relationships   113–14
Local government   15–16
Location or organisations   26–8

Managers   115–16
Manufactured goods   33
Market research   92, 213–14

Index

Marketing function 92
   job roles 121–2
Marketing mix 36
Markets 35–8
Materials 227
Maternity pay 101
Matrix organisation
   structure 74–5
Memos 186, 259
Modem 56
Multinationals 31–2

National insurance 48, 240
Niche marketing 37
Notice 102

Ombudsman 199
Operators 116
Organisation, definition 2
Organisational structures 71–6

Pager 55
Paper-based media 165–6
Participative leadership style 79
Partnership 7
Partnership agreement 7
Payee, definition 234
Paying-in slip 243–4, 256
Payslips 100–1, 240–1, 252
Personnel function 86
   job roles 118
Petty cash voucher 241–2, 254
Pictograms 61
Pie charts 59–60
Planning 123
Positive discrimination 110
Primary sector 18
Private limited company (Ltd) 8
Private sector organisations 5–12

Private sector, definition 3
   and customer services 207
Privatisation 16–17
Problem solving 124
Product life cycle 37
Production function, Design
   and 91–4
   job roles 117–18
Profit, definition 3
Promotional techniques 156–61
Proprietors 114
Public limited company (plc) 9
Public sector organisations 14–18
Public sector, definition 4
   and customer services 207
Purchase invoice 229, 249–50
Purchase orders 228, 247–8

Quality control 84
Quality review system 210

Race Relations Act 110–11
Receipt 242–3, 255
Recruitment of staff 86–7
Redundancy 88
   pay 101
Remuneration 100–1
Reports 187–8, 259

Salaries 100, 126–7
Sale of Goods Act 195–6
Sales and marketing function 92
   job roles 121–2
Sales invoice 233, 250–1
Scale and scope of
   organisations 29–32
Secondary sector 19
Self-employment 40, 126–30
Services 34, 227

Setting targets 124–5
Sex Discrimination Act 110–11
Shareholders 8
Socio-economic groups 140–1
Sole trader 5–6
Span of control 72–3
Staff development 88
Staff relationships 113–14
Statement of account 233, 251–2
Supervisors 116
Support and service staff 116

Tables 58–9
Targets 124–6
Taxation – see Income tax
Team members 116
Team working 78
Technology, effect on
   employment 53–6
Telephone technique 185–6
Tertiary sector 19
Trade Associations 200
Trade Description Act 154
Trade discount 230
Trade unions 103
Trading standards 200
Training 48–9
Training Enterprise Council
   (TEC) 128

Unemployment 51
Unfair dismissal 102

Value Added Tax (VAT) 226
Video conferencing 55
Voluntary work 127

Wages 47–8, 100, 126–7, 227–8
Wages Act 111